Dmitri G. Safronov
Nietzsche's Political Economy

Monographien und Texte zur Nietzsche-Forschung

Herausgegeben von
Christian J. Emden
Helmut Heit
Vanessa Lemm
Claus Zittel

Begründet von
Mazzino Montinari, Wolfgang Müller-Lauter, Heinz Wenzel

Advisory Board:
Günter Abel, R. Lanier Anderson, Keith Ansell-Pearson, Sarah Rebecca Bamford, Christian Benne, Jessica Berry, Marco Brusotti, João Constâncio, Daniel Conway, Carlo Gentili, Oswaldo Giacoia Junior, Wolfram Groddeck, Anthony Jensen, Scarlett Marton, John Richardson, Martin Saar, Herman Siemens, Andreas Urs Sommer, Werner Stegmaier, Sigridur Thorgeirsdottir, Paul van Tongeren, Aldo Venturelli, Isabelle Wienand, Patrick Wotling

Band 79

Dmitri G. Safronov

Nietzsche's Political Economy

DE GRUYTER

ISBN 978-3-11-221391-9
e-ISBN (PDF) 978-3-11-075261-8
e-ISBN (EPUB) 978-3-11-075264-9
ISSN 1862-1260

Library of Congress Control Number: 2023935318

Bibliographic information published by the Deutsche Nationalbibliothek
The Deutsche Nationalbibliothek lists this publication in the Deutsche Nationalbibliografie;
detailed bibliographic data are available on the internet at http://dnb.dnb.de.

© 2025 Walter de Gruyter GmbH, Berlin/Boston
This volume is text- and page-identical with the hardback published in 2023.
Printing and binding: CPI books GmbH, Leck

www.degruyter.com

For Michael and Luka

In some remote corner of the universe poured out into countless flickering solar systems there was once a star on which some clever animals invented knowledge. It was the most arrogant and most untruthful minute of world history, but still only a minute. When nature had drawn a few breaths the star solidified, and the clever animals died. It was time, too: for although they prided themselves on knowing a lot, they had finally discovered, to their great annoyance, that they knew everything wrongly. They died and as they died they cursed truth. That was the way of those desperate animals that had invented knowledge. This would be the fate of man if he were in fact nothing but a knowing animal.

             Nietzsche ~ On the Pathos of Truth ~ 1872

Acknowledgements

Writing on Nietzsche is never easy or pleasant. Doing so in isolation—without critical support, encouragement, and regular reality-checks—can be dangerous and is not advisable.

Enveloping this project from the outset has been a truly agonistic milieu which, akin to a supportive environment, enabled it to develop beyond the author's original intuitions. This creative agon has constantly challenged without once repressing, contested without disparaging, and helped to reach higher, especially when criticising. Such an experience is a rare spiritual privilege these days, and I am incredibly grateful to the many people who, in different ways, made it possible.

This book has been in the making considerably longer than the time it took to write it, and I have accumulated many debts along the way. These are debts of tremendous gratitude which I am more than happy to acknowledge but may only hope to be able to repay one day.

First and foremost, I would like to thank Harald Wydra, who, as the supervisor of the doctoral thesis on which this book is based, gave me the intellectual freedom to explore the subject which did not strike many as having an obvious denouement. I am grateful to Harald for his unwavering support throughout the years, inspiring guidance and for the most incredible gift of unhurried reflection, which helped me to discern much of what would otherwise remain hidden. I am thankful to Helen Thompson, my second supervisor, for her encouragement as well as for challenging me to cerebrate earnestly on the manner in which Nietzsche and political economy—not the most obvious of bedfellows—could and ought to be connected.

My sincere thanks to Martin Ruehl and Hugo Drochon for their thorough and critical examination of the doctoral thesis that prompted its transformation into this book as well as for their continued support and regular injections of intellectual rigour into the project.

I would also like to thank all those who commented on individual chapters and/or otherwise generously shared their time, energy, and knowledge with me, especially Raymond Geuss, Markus Granziol, Allen W. Wood, Thomas Brobjer, Brendon Simms, Duncan Kelly, Gabriele Klunkert, Keith Ansell-Pearson, Jimena Hurtado, Robert Holub, and Dotan Leshem.

At De Gruyter, I would like to thank Christoph Schirmer for having confidence in this project from the start and for guiding me through the various stages of the editorial process. I am also grateful to the Monographien und Texte zur Nietzsche-Forschung (MTNF) Series editors—Christian J. Emden, Helmut Heit, Vanessa Lemm, and Claus Zittel—not only for giving the manuscript a chance but for their incisive comments and helpful advice which allowed me to develop and contextualise the inquiry well beyond the originally envisaged remit. My special thanks go to Vanessa Lemm, whose own work on Nietzsche and political philosophy was an important source of inspiration and whose encouragement gave me the proverbial extra push to explore the unchartered terrain. I also wish to thank the two anonymous reviewers for De Gruyter, whose valuable and stimulating suggestions helped improve critical parts of the inquiry. In revising my manuscript I was aided by an excellent young editor, Jack Graveney. My big thanks also to Anne Hiller and Adriana Stroe for their expert guidance and editing of the text for publication.

Finally, I wish to thank my family, without whose unfailing support, unimaginable patience, and encouragement this book would not have been possible.

Following the original presentation at the 'Nietzsches Perspektiven Des Politischen Internationaler Kongress' in Naumburg in October 2019, a shorter version of Chapter 5 of this thesis (Nietzsche on Slavery: Overcome or Simply Abolished?) has been published in the International Political Anthropology journal under the title 'Nietzsche on Slavery: Exploring the Meaning and Relevance of Nietzsche's Perspective' (2019; International Political Anthology 12, No. 2; DOI: 10.5281/zenodo.3555282).

Contents

Acknowledgements —— IX

Editions, Translations, and Abbreviations —— XV

Introduction —— 1

1 Approaching Nietzsche —— 10
    Reading Nietzsche —— 10
    The Gravity of Nietzsche's Concern —— 11
    No Special Licence —— 12
    'It All Hangs Together' —— 13
    Thematic Topology of Nietzsche's Texts —— 14
    Literature Review —— 20

2 Nietzsche's Political Economy: Conceptual Framework —— 27
    Preamble —— 27
    Why Political Economy —— 27
    Why Nietzsche's Political Economy —— 29
    Time Horizons, Scope, and Substance of Social Change —— 33
    Challenging Discourse —— 37
    Thinking 'Outside of All Social Orders' —— 39
    Slave Morality and Political Economy —— 42
    Silver Lining of the Coming Storm —— 50
    Concluding Remarks —— 53

3 Nietzsche and Smith on the Division of Labour —— 56
    Introduction —— 56
    Das Adam Smith Problem —— 60
    Concerning 'the Poor Man's Son' —— 63
    Nietzsche on Sympathy and Industriousness —— 64
    Aetiology of the Division of Labour —— 66
    Needs of Slave Morality —— 69
    On Becoming a Science —— 74
    Natural Law, the Final State, and the Felicity of Equilibrium —— 76
    Sympathy of the Division of Labour —— 82
    Nietzsche on the Division of Labour —— 86
    'What and Wither' of Man —— 90
    State and the Division of Labour —— 91
    Concluding Remarks —— 95

4 Nietzsche and Marx: Political Economy of the 'Upside-Down World' — 99
Introduction — 99
A Word of Caution — 102
Nietzsche and Marx at a Glance — 105
An Outline of Overlapping Political Economies — 106
Political Economy of Revolution — 113
Bruno Bauer and the Essenes' Conundrum — 117
Marx's Real 'Atomic Swerve' — 123
Religion and Revolution — 126
Changing Revolution's Pivot — 130
The Chimera of Private Property — 135
The Power of Exchange — 138
The Dark Side of Equality — 142
Lenin on Class Consciousness — 144
Silenus of Modernity: Weber's 'Terrible Wisdom' — 146
Concluding Remarks — 149

5 Nietzsche on Slavery: Overcome or Simply Abolished? — 153
Introduction — 153
Semiotic Roots of Slavery — 154
Nietzsche's Definition of Slavery — 155
Slavery, Oikonomia, and the Oikodespotes — 157
'Higher Men' and 'Rank-Ordering' — 161
Physiology and Psychology of Slavery — 166
Abolition of Slavery — 173
Capitalism and Modern Slavery — 180
Concluding Remarks — 186

6 Nietzsche on the Perils of Debt — 190
Introduction — 190
Scope of Critique — 191
Debts 'to the Ancients' — 193
Conceptual Framework — 196
Genealogy of Debt and Freedom — 197
Debt's Past, Present, and Future — 200
Communal Origins of Debt — 203
Debt Forgiveness — 205
Debt and Capital — 207
'Psychological Trappings' of Debt — 209
Concluding Remarks: Debt and Subjectivity — 214

7 Nietzsche's Critique of Debt Economy —— 220
Introduction: *'Seven Skins'* of Debt —— 220
Writings during the Founders' Crash and the Long Depression —— 222
Agency and Corruption —— 226
Democracy's Debts —— 231
Money and Banking —— 242
Psychology of Banking —— 247
Debt and Growth —— 248
Physiology and Psychology of Growth —— 250
Economic Growth and Human Development —— 252
Modern Narrative of Growth —— 254
Entropy of Growth —— 257
Geopolitics of Slave Morality —— 259
Precarious Traverse to a Less Industrious World —— 266

8 Closing Reflections on NPE: In Search of Direction —— 271
Assessing the Findings —— 271
Slavery —— 272
Debt —— 273
The Division of Labour —— 276
The Question of Agency —— 280
Nietzsche's 'Positive Project' —— 282
In the Direction of an Aesthetic Political Economy —— 284
Parting Thoughts —— 295

Bibliography —— 299

Index —— 331

Editions, Translations, and Abbreviations

The reference critical edition is the Friedrich Nietzsche Digitale Kritische Gesamtausgabe Werke und Briefe (eKGWB), which is the digital version of the critical German reference edition of Nietzsche's works, posthumous fragments, and correspondence edited by Giorgio Colli and Mazzino Montinari (Nietzsche, Friedrich (1967–): *Werke. Kritische Gesamtausgabe*, Berlin and New York: De Gruyter and Nietzsche, Friedrich (1975–): *Nietzsche Briefwechsel. Kritische Gesamtausgabe*, Berlin and New York, De Gruyter). The eKGWB is edited by Paolo D'Iorio and published by Nietzsche Source (http://www.nietzschesource.org, last accessed Feb. 27, 2023). For the majority of translations of Nietzsche's published works, the Cambridge University Press ('*CUP*') editions have been used (see the bibliography). Walter Kaufmann's classic translations of *The Birth of Tragedy* (1872), *The Gay Science* (1882), *Thus Spoke Zarathustra* (1883–1885), as well as the works collected in *The Portable Nietzsche* (Penguin Books, 1976) have also been consulted. The remainder of the translations are my own.

In particular, Nietzsche's Digital Archive, eKGWB, is the primary source for the unpublished material from Nietzsche's notebooks assembled in the *Nachlass*. Nietzsche's notes are organised according to the year, number of the notebook, and number of the notebook entry, e.g., NF-1887(year): 9 (notebook number) [185] (note number). I have relied on the published translations where possible, including *Writings from Early Notebooks* ('EN'), ed. Raymond Geuss and Alexander Nehamas, CUP, 2015, and *Writings from the Late Notebooks* ('LN'), trans. Kate Sturge, ed. Rüdiger Bittner, CUP, 2003. All other translations are my own. On two occasions, Nietzsche's quotations are referenced using 'GOA' (Nietzsches Werke, Grossoktavausgabe, Vols. XV and XVI). Nietzsche's private correspondence, which is contained in the Digital Archive, is referenced as 'BVN' ('Briefe von Nietzsche'), and each particular entry is numbered and linked to the year of correspondence, e.g., Nietzsche's final letter would be referenced as BVN-1889 [year of writing]:1256 [number of entry].

Abbreviations of Nietzsche's Titles (in alphabetical order)

AC: The Antichrist
AOM: Assorted Opinions and Maxims (HH: II, WS)
BGE: Beyond Good and Evil
BT: The Birth of Tragedy
TCW: The Case of Wagner
D: Daybreak
DD: Dithyrambs of Dionysus
DS: David Strauss, the Confessor and the Writer (UM: I, DS)
DWV: The Dionysiac World View
EH: Ecce Homo (sections abbreviated as e.g., 'Clever', 'Destiny', 'Books', etc)

EN:	Writings from Early Notebooks
FEI:	On the Future of Our Educational Institutions
GM:	On the Genealogy of Morality
GS:	The Gay Science
GSt:	The Greek State
HH:	Human, All Too Human (Vols. I and II)
HC:	Homer on Competition
HMS:	On the History of Moral Sentiments (HH, Vol. I)
KSA:	Sämtliche Werke: Kritische Studienausgabe
LN:	Writings from the Late Notebooks
NCW:	Nietzsche contra Wagner
PN:	Portable Nietzsche
PT:	On the Pathos of Truth
PTAG:	Philosophy in the Tragic Age of the Greeks
RWB:	Richard Wagner in Bayreuth (UM: IV, RWB)
SE:	Schopenhauer as Educator (UM: III, SE)
TI:	Twilight of the Idols (sections abbreviated as e.g., 'Skirmishes', 'Errors', 'Ancients', etc)
TLEMS:	On Truth and Lies in an Extra-Moral Sense
UHDL:	On the Uses and Disadvantages of History for Life (UM: II, *UHDL*)
UM:	Untimely Meditations
WS:	The Wanderer and His Shadow (HH: II, WS)
Z:	Thus Spoke Zarathustra (quotes list the part number and an abbreviated chapter title)
WP:	The Will to Power

Introduction

Nietzsche has been largely absent from conversation on political economy, past or present. The extent of his interest in the issues of political economy, either contemporaneous or more generally, has been questioned. Estimates have varied from there being 'none', to 'a passing interest', to occupying a more 'prominent place' within the context of Nietzsche's reflections on the 'general economy' of life, and even as representing an 'extensive' intellectual engagement.[1]

Interest in Nietzsche's views on the questions of economy has been growing (as well as growing in boldness) over recent years. Ascertaining a possible degree of Nietzsche's interest in, or his understanding of, political economy, however, is a different proposition to developing an appreciation for what Nietzsche's political economy ('NPE') 'would entail' or could look like. 'Would entail'—since Nietzsche's *oeuvre* is interspersed with themes of political economy from beginning to end. 'Could look like'—since Nietzsche, not unlike Plato or Aristotle, never penned a treatise on political economy.

The principal objective of the present inquiry is to introduce Nietzsche as a critical thinker on the matters of political economy, whose varied and complex insight resonates with pertinence today. Nietzsche completed most of his writing against the backdrop of the *Long Depression* (1873–1896)—the first 'truly international' crisis of the political economy of industrial capitalism—which helped pave the way to the tragedy of the Great War and was clearly anticipated in Nietzsche's writings.[2] Nietzsche's experience of the crisis, both directly and a result of unrelenting reflection on the dilemmas it highlighted, has had a profound impact on the manner and substance of his work. The Long Depression, not unlike the Great Recession of 2008, raised challenging questions and inaugurated great intellectual debates concerning the then prevailing predicament of Western civilisation and its future direction.

Present-day society has emerged from the 'Great Recession' of 2008 less assured of its ways and more aware of the fragility of its political economy. The pervasive crisis of leadership and governance in the world's leading powers in the aftermath of the crisis is manifest in the widespread sense of unease concerning the lack of clear direction and the systemic deficit of credibility. Largely unaddressed—let alone resolved—these issues have been amplified further during the Covid pandemic and in the context of the geopolitical tensions that have erupted in its aftermath, leaving us more circumspect about the *values* that continue to underpin our way of life and societal arrangements—values that we are still reluctant to confront even as their macabre consequences are becoming more evident.

---

[1] See, respectively: 'none' (Leiter 2015:237–238; Senn 2006:32); 'passing interest' (Holub 2018:136; Detwiler 1990:193); 'prominent concern' (Dombowsky 2004:1–32; Drochon 2018:246–249; Babich 2020:226–279; Merrick 2020:135–147); 'extensive engagement' (Waite 1996:33; Brobjer 1999:56; Sedgwick 2007: x–xi).
[2] See Glasner 1997:132; Davies 2018:80–83; Beaud 1981:117; Tooze 2018:473; and Babich 2020:227.

Once again, not unlike in Nietzsche's time, we find ourselves standing at the precarious cross-roads of history and peeking into the ever more volatile and uncertain future. This book argues that we would benefit from Nietzsche's critical review of the causes of the pervasive crisis of modernity, which he conceptualises in terms of the crisis of 'the modern worldview' ('*moderne Weltanschauung*') and of the 'catechism of modern ideas' ('*Katechismus der modernen Ideen*'; see NF-1873:27[44]; NF-1884:25[211]).

Set against these considerations, this book explores a twofold conjecture. In the first place, it considers whether political economy in Nietzsche's corpus can be regarded as his persistent intellectual concern. Secondly, it probes today's purchasing power of Nietzsche's thinking on the pressing issues of political economy. Nietzsche's inquiry is situated as a relentless critique of the political economy of the industrial culture of his time. Comparing and contrasting Nietzsche and Marx reveals the surprising extent to which their respective political economies overlap, as well as highlighting the radically different philosophical projects that emerge from them. Nietzsche's experience of 'Gründerkrach' of 1873 and his reflections on the *Long Depression* that ensued in its wake further help to contextualise Nietzsche's political economy.

Nietzsche's reflections on the enduring crisis of the capitalist political economy are examined in the context of three key and interrelated themes within his *oeuvre*. Namely, those of the division of labour, slavery, and debt. This book contends that examining Nietzsche's thinking on these issues, which are central to any conversation on political economy—past or present—makes it possible to establish clear and pertinent connections to our present reality. The concluding chapter approaches *NPE* as Nietzsche's attempt, through the revaluation of values to intuit the contours of the aesthetic political economy of the future.

Debt, slavery, and the division of labour are rightfully mammoth subjects. Each in its own right commands a considerable amount of literature and scholarship both within the Nietzsche tradition and in the discourse on political economy. Nevertheless, limiting the remit of this book to just one or two of these topics would fail in at least three important respects. It would fail to disclose the interconnectedness of Nietzsche's thinking on political economy, i.e., the principal quality that makes the latter both complex and pertinent. It would fail to underscore the interconnectedness of the phenomena of debt, slavery, and the division of labour, which is paramount for Nietzsche. Last but not least, it would fall short, perhaps not so much in establishing a veritable connection hitherto missing, between Nietzsche and political economy, but in testing such connection in a manner that, should it be validated, would grant Nietzsche a voice in the conversation on some of political economy's most compelling issues.

Nietzsche does not engage with any of these three subjects on a standalone basis. In his assessment, these phenomena represent the intertwined *aporias of modern industrial culture*, the tributaries of the same river, which converge in his reflection on the deployment and development of human capital. They are as integral an element of the complex social fabric of modern society as they are facets of Nietzsche's thinking. Nietzsche does not consider them unique to a particular type of the social order of modernity. By examining modern political economy's examples of 'good' (i.e., the division of labour) and 'evil' (i.e., slavery and, sometimes, debt) Nietzsche draws attention to the profound condition of *value inversions* under which modernity labours and to the precarious existential consequences that result from striving for equality at the expense of erasing difference and depreciating quality.

Nietzsche does not object to there being too much debt and too little slavery, nor does he argue that the division of labour *per se* has become exceedingly reductivistic. He does not analyse these phenomena as the specific attributes of capitalism, as opposed to socialism, or vice-versa. Rather, Nietzsche's 'strange and insane undertaking' (BGE: §230) challenges the entire discourse of the political economy of modernity, on account that the latter fails to disclose, let alone to examine, the *value of its values*, which underpin the proliferation of debt, preside over the pervasive spread of meaningless slavery, and foster the division of labour which inhibits the development of humankind instead of promoting it. Nietzsche original contribution to the conversation on political economy is to problematise the *consequences of these values*, should they be allowed to draw the full force of their conclusions. He sees his task in terms of questioning 'what results from their [i.e., values—DS] rule? For whom? With regard to what?' (NF-1885:2[190]).

In a related sense, this book argues that Nietzsche's views on slavery, debt and the division of labour provide a powerful illustration of a subject matter that makes conversation on his political economy an uncomfortable one. It helps to explain why inquiries into Nietzsche's political and economic thinking continue to develop largely separately and at a different pace to one another. Notwithstanding the consistently growing academic and popular interest in Nietzsche's political thought over the past two decades, his thinking on political economy remains rather unexplored and overlooked.

In view of Ansell-Pearson's influential assertion concerning 'a refusal in Nietzsche … to see economic issues as part of politics' (Ansell-Pearson 1994:44), this book contends that a more thorough understanding of Nietzsche's political and economic thinking would be achieved by considering these two strands jointly within the fold of political economy. I argue that *Nietzsche's economy is thoroughly political, and his politics is permeated by economic insights*. Although their synthesis appears to amplify and compound, rather than resolve or diminish, the multitude of apparent contradictions and unpalatable conjectures within Nietzsche's work, this idiosyncrasy of 'philosophising with the hammer' is something that has to be faced and can prove instructive.[3] This approach may also shed light on some of the reasons why Nietzsche—other than by association, or a shared intellectual, or spiritual affinity—is largely absent from the wider conversation on political economy.

---

[3] Furthermore, in agreement with Detwiler's suggestion, this book contends that the overall interpretation and assessment of Nietzsche's politics, inclusive of his views on economy, is directly related to Nietzsche's other philosophical concerns (Detwiler 1990:5–7).

In part, through the themes of *debt, slavery, and the division of labour*, this book explores the arduous reasons why Nietzsche, contrary even to his own predictions, is likely to remain outside of our grasp and beyond the future's horizon the boldest of us may dare imagine today. Nietzsche sensed that the *Aristotelean kyklos*, unlike Plato's, was more equivocal when it came to asserting automaticity in terms of reproducing the seasons and the patterns of political life without the loss of quality in either the constituent parts of the *polis* or in the resulting social whole.[4] Reflecting on the cycle of the types of government, first discussed by Plato in *The Statesman* (see S:302[c]-303[a]), Aristotle introduced nuanced conceptual distinctions between their 'true' and 'perverted' forms (see P:1278[b]-1279[a]). These elucidations did not, however, make it easier to ascertain how *political decay*, once it took hold, could be overcome instead of inaugurating the downward spiral. Aristotle's apprehension has—furtively—found its way into Nietzsche's political and economic thinking.[5] Analysing this quandary within the context of modernity, Nietzsche queried whether the political decay—a consequence of the levelling-out masked by the tales of economic progress—as well as possibly representing the protracted birthing of a *revitalised future* could, in fact, be the *endgame* for the generations stranded on this side of the escalating crisis of modern political economy.

Caught in the midst of civilisational malaise—breathing 'the atmosphere of this theoretical world' (BT: §17)—we remain, for a time, protected inside the thick walls of the citadel of sensibility painstakingly erected by *slave morality*—the 'most mendacious device of interpretation, with which the natural concepts of cause and effect are turned upside down once and for all' (AC: §25). These fortifications—as filters of understanding and mechanisms of meaning-making—prevent us from being able to access, let alone soberly assess, the merit of Nietzsche's argument. The 'Nietzsche discussion' to this day remains largely circumscribed by modern sensibility—the progeny of *slave morality*—the stranglehold of which he was so intent on overcoming (see HH: I, *HMS*, §107).

The load-bearing walls of *slave morality* might be crumbling but their demise, Nietzsche tells us, will be no controlled demolition. Instead, akin to a sinking Titanic, slave morality—in the final rite of exaltation—will do what it can to pull its passengers down to the ocean floor (see GM: III, §11, §15). Cruel or not, as part of the collateral damage in the developing storm, we are unable to do more than push 'further into the crisis' for the yet unknowable benefit of the yet indiscernible future of which we may never be part except, perhaps, in a metahistorical sense (see TI: *Skirmishes*,

---

[4] Plato's *kyklos* is recurring, in large part, because the concept is based on the assumption of *unchanged quality* of the reproduced parts of the social whole. In other words, through the change of the governments from aristocracy to tyranny and back, aristocracy, when at the top of the social hierarchy, would be fit for its purpose. Aristotle's 'perverted' forms of government convey the sense that once the quality of the political order drops down a level, the cycle of its changes may itself slow down or be impeded altogether.

[5] See, for example, Nietzsche's discussion in NF-1888:14[182].

§44). Nietzsche hopes to have caught a glimpse of it through the spyglass of the *eternal return of the same* (NF-1883:24[7]) and by virtue of Zarathustra's professed *amor fati* (GS: §276). But how are we to trust him and why should we? Neither to entice, nor to dissuade a potential reader, and at the risk of undoing my own undertaking, Nietzsche's angst—the essential features of his critique of the *political economy of slave morality* that permeates his entire *oeuvre* as much as he claims it saturates the world we inhabit—can be highlighted with the help of the following three propositions.

Nietzsche's *central concern* is that when 'commercial culture' takes hold in every sphere of human activity and penetrates every area of human life, metamorphosing along the way into the 'industrial culture' of modernity, the general *development of humankind comes to a halt.*[6] When the commercial logic becomes society's standard bearer, goal setter and the embodiment of its ethos—when 'value judgements become irreversibly mercantilized' and, in such form, held up as 'moral judgements' (see Klossowski 1997:150)—'the development of reason is mightily hindered' (D: §173), putting humankind's future in clear peril.[7] When the *entire political economy* of modernity becomes structured in the way that 'all you want from people is their money' (NF-1882:3[1]), humankind's development is not simply disrupted, diverted or delayed—it *stops*, and humankind gradually starts to regress, albeit under the auspices of increasingly elaborate and mendacious appearances—'the counterfeit of a phenomenon' (BT: §17).[8]

The more elaborate this fictitious reality becomes, before it also inevitably succumbs to the law of [its own] diminishing returns, the more pronounced is the humankind's regression into barbarism.[9] The retardation remains difficult to gauge since the work of 'false values and delusive words' is slow and 'long does calamity sleep and wait in them' (Z: II, *Priests*; see NF-1885:1[4]). The real degeneration occurs and is kept outside the carefully guarded contours of the 'mendaciously fabricated world', which remains 'honoured as reality' (AC: §10). This *simultaneous movement in opposite directions* continues until such time when the spreading decay becomes no longer containable and floods the perimeter of the *simulacra*, making the 'climbing around on mendacious word bridges ... between false heavens and false earths' increasingly impossible (Z: IV, *Melancholy*, §3).[10]

The appearance of *moving forward*—epitomised by the narratives of economic growth and progress (where economic growth is equated with progress and progress with the future; NF-1887:9[130]; HH: I, §25)—is concurrent with humankind's slide

---

6 See Nietzsche's discussion in D: §173, §179, §204–206 and GM: III, §17.
7 See PT, *Preface*, 248; HH: II, *WS*, §286; NF-1886:7[2] and NF-1888:15[106].
8 Baudrillard would later problematise this predicament as 'simulacra', i.e., the copy without the original (Baudrillard 1991).
9 See NF-1886:7[2]; NF-1888:12[1]).
10 See Nietzsche's 'second question of conscience' (TI: *Maxims*, §38).

into spiritual barbarism (see NF-1888:15[8]).[11] Incongruously it seems, as though caught up in the *vicious circle* dynamic, humankind is *going back* as it imagines itself to be moving forward, and by moving forward, it is relapsing further into barbarism. This two-tiered movement occurs compretently on two *interconnected* planes—spiritual and material—and critically, the forward movement, i.e., through economic progress, is a *movement into spiritual slavery* (see NF-1881:11[294]). Nietzsche insists that our *moving forward*—under the *aegis* of liberty, equality and democracy—means *more slavery*, not less, and the notion that slavery was something dark and abhorrent that humankind left behind a long time ago is nothing more than part of the dream world fabricated by slave morality 'out of psychological needs' to assuage our deep-seated fears concerning the real world, to which, in our hypnotic state, we can claim 'no right and no access'.[12]

Secondly, Nietzsche concludes that any societal architecture that aspires to reach a *higher plateau than the stomach* (i.e., material well-being), to set loftier *cultural goals* that stretch into the distant horizons (GS: §356), and to embrace 'cyclopean building' (HH: II, *WS*, §275, §283)—becomes either critically *agency dependent and unavoidably hierarchical*, and/or it has to rely on the persistent application of force to stem its own decline—i.e., to become in some form repressive and exploitative of the majority, including the tyranny of that very majority exercised mainly against itself. The truth that evades us, courtesy of *slave morality*, is, for Nietzsche, demonstrated only by 'the extent to which we permit ourselves to understand this fact' (NF-1887:10[154]). The 'production of a *spiritual-physical aristocracy*' that Nietzsche's social architecture calls for becomes impeded in the levelled-out phase of modern existence, which may turn out to be *terminal* (HH: I, *Tokens*, §243). Nietzsche's question, formulated in *Human, All Too Human* (1878) and resonating throughout his corpus, remains without an answer:

> [H]ow can the individual be set in place within the counterpoint of private and public culture, how can he play the main theme and at the same time the subordinate theme as well? (HH: I, *Tokens*, §242)

Last but not least, it is not clear whether we have truly grasped Nietzsche's meaning of 'Geisterkrieg'. It would appear *naïve* to consider it as an abstract exercise where the clashing worldviews, as though the disembodied spirits, would hover across to a deserted valley, or a clearing in the woods, to battle it out Harry Potter vs. Voldemort style—in front of the frenzied global audience glued to their iPad screens—with the dazzling

---

11 Unlike Marx, whose periodic episodes of 'momentary barbarism' are linked to capitalism's 'commercial crises' that inevitably occur along the progressive trajectory of history's unfolding (CW 6:490), Nietzsche distinguishes between a 'temporary relapse into barbarism', i.e., war (HH: *State*, §477), and a protracted 'sinking back into barbarism' (HH: I, *Tokens*, §251, §286; see UM: III, SE, §§4–6), which is interrupted by the rare instances of remission (e.g., the Renaissance).
12 See NF-1885:36[23]; NF-1885:36[48] and NF-1887:11[99].

panoply of the magic wands that project force fields in the streams of antagonistic concepts until the weaker side either yields or succumbs and vanishes in a spray of fine particles.

When *values do battle*—real people die, real towns and villages burn, real blood is spilt (see HH: I, *State*, §477). Just as, for Hesiod, there is 'good Eris'—the 'goddess of peaceable competition' and 'terrible Eris'—the bringer of war and strife (HH: I, §170; D: §38)—there is *subterranean war* and there is *physical war*. Today, both dwell under the same roof of 'Geisterkrieg', albeit the one appropriated and distorted by slave morality, from the midst of which many 'surrogates of war' intermittently emerge (HH: I, *State*, §477). Our misunderstanding of the real [causes of] enmity conjured up and falsified by slave morality has persistently impaired our ability to prevent their paths from converging (see BVN-1888:1171). The recurring *point of convergence* of 'all the easiest and best roads to wealth' (FEI: I, 18) is—in reality—the polar opposite of the *felicitous singularity* we have been repeatedly promised by the 'sirens who in the marketplace sing of the future' (GS: §377).[13]

Modernity's most grievous conflicts, one after another, continue to take place *within* the perimeter of slave morality, not without.[14] These *wars of slave morality* form an integral part of the deepening crisis of its political economy wrought by its ouroboric predicament. This tendency will eventually spell 'wars the like of which have never yet been seen on earth' unless the trajectory can be radically altered (EH: *Destiny*, §2).[15] In contrast, Nietzsche's 'Geisterkrieg' wages war on slave morality—against the 'lies of the millennia'—from beyond the grasp of its mendacious valuations (EH: *Destiny*, §1). Nietzsche sees himself as the 'dynamite' that is required to 'explode' slave morality's 'power structures' so that the revaluation of values may take place (EH: *Destiny*, §1) following the abolition of the 'old god':

> If we could avoid wars, so much the better. I could make a more useful use of the twelve billion which the *armed peace* costs Europe each year; there are *other means of bringing honour to physiology* than through lazarette. (NF-1888:25[19]; my emphasis)[16]

In the end, 'Geisterkrieg' can do no more than wind down the clock of history and clear the ground upon which the two *interminable forces*—of good and evil—can start their Penelopean metahistorical work afresh (HH: I, §251), for a time cleansed of enmity and

---

13 See, for an illustration, the argument advanced in Ray Kurweil's *The Singularity Is Near* (2005).
14 It is important to remember, and I explore this in more detail in the chapter on *Slavery*, that the physical wars and the ideational conflicts conjured up by *slave morality* represent, in substance, the same conflict, Nietzsche tells us, that is 'fought most bitterly within the single individual' (HH: I, *Tokens*, §268).
15 Nietzsche's frequently alleged advocacy of war should not be confused with his attempt to relay to us the 'the history of the next two centuries' that, on his view, 'can no longer come otherwise' (NF-1887:11[411]).
16 See Tracy B. Strong's excellent discussion in the Introduction 'Wars the like of which one has never seen' to *Nietzsche and Politics*, Ashgate, 2009, 1–29.

blissfully unaware of their embedded antagonism or the struggles that lie in wait (see BGE: §260).

As Stiegler observes, Nietzsche's 'most powerful thought is that a tendency only exists as that which constitutes the condition of its counter-tendency, which it cannot therefore be a matter of eliminating' and, in consequence, we would only be deluding ourselves if we believed that we can 'leap across two centuries' simply 'by failing to see that an historic struggle is underway and in full swing' (Stiegler 2011:55). In other words, 'Geisterkrieg' may be the necessary but not sufficient condition for enabling the *revaluation of values*, that Nietzsche calls for, but it commands an immense—hitherto *unthinkable*—price (see TI: *Preface*). The question for us is whether such an extortionate price is worth paying or whether it is best to continue tinkering around the edges—on the margins of the present oblivious to the lessons of the past and blind to the challenges of the future, sheepishly hoping that the *ouroboros of slave morality* might spare us.

The above are but a few examples of the issues that Nietzsche invites us to consider 'without melancholy' (NF-1871:10[1]). Do we feel ready to assimilate Nietzsche's meaning? Will we ever be? And, if his meaning is lost on us, does it render Nietzsche's message *meaningless*, or do we continue to plough through regardless? Should we persevere, even though it may not be within our gift either to comprehend or to witness how the law of conservation of energy and that of entropy—in the collision of circular and linear time and the cataclysmic confrontation between '*phusis*' (nature) and '*nomos*' (law)—reconcile their seemingly irreconcilable differences as they inevitably must, so that something new may emerge from the ashes of the old (Z: I, *Creator*)? Nietzsche's audacious undertaking is to think beyond the 'wreckage of stars', from which he wished to 'build the world afresh' (P&B: §12). To write to those beyond the wreckage, to those whose minds—exculpated in the anguish of the ages—would be attuned to his message, to those who might not even exist is daring, no matter what judgement we may pass on the content of Nietzsche's message. Why is it worth doing if we—the vast majority of us—are destined to perish in this wreckage?

It is worth doing, Nietzsche tells us, because all things recur eternally: history does not abolish meta-history, and it barely assails pre-history. The distant future demands that we pass on our *tragic wisdom*—the hard knowledge rather than the guilt of our mistakes—in the unremittingly Hesiodic sense of hope (D: §38) that it may influence the trajectory of the future generations—i.e., our own trajectory for *only by seeking to impact on the future can we hope to change the present* (see HH: I, *State*, §443). Nietzsche warns, however, that attempting to do so we shall encounter and will have to overcome 'tremendous forces' for 'the more a present-day individual determines the future, the more he will suffer' (NF-1884:26[231]).

In full awareness that 'the most wretched animal can prevent the mightiest oak from growing by swallowing the acorn' (UM: II, *UDHL*, §7), Nietzsche feels compelled to plant an acorn of his thoughts in the ground crawling with the 'eternally hungry' last men, 'scraping and digging in a search for roots' (BT: §23). Nietzsche's task—'this tyrant in us [who] takes a terrible retribution for every attempt we make to avoid or elude it'—dictates that it be so (HH: II, *WS*, Preface, §4). Nietzsche's worry is *not* simply that humankind should finally find its 'equilibrium' in the world of 'the inevitable dominion of the average' where nothing happens—in the lackadaisical bliss of Adam Smith's 'nation of shopkeepers' that, although it is devoid of greatness, may still have room for 'the small everyday deeds of ordinary folk ... the small acts of kindness and love', in the Tolkienian sense.[17]

Nietzsche distinctly senses something calamitous in the *obsequious indifference* of the last man: 'a kind of abyss of the future, something horrible, especially in its bliss' (BVN-1884:490). Nietzsche's critique of the *political economy of slave morality* conveys an urgent awareness that contrary to our belief that, all the storms of life and history notwithstanding, we would eventually 'land on an island', we ended up building our world on top of 'a sleeping monster', and the race for who will wake from the slumber first has entered the home straight (Z: II, *Priests*).[18] Nietzsche's *task* is to wake us before it is too late. If you believe that our *task* is *not* to abdicate in the face of the turmoil that is encircling us, not to succumb in the face of ubiquitous *nihilism* but to overcome it—I invite you to read on:

> Finally our reward is the greatest of life's gifts, perhaps the greatest thing it is able to give of any kind—we are given our *task* back (HH: II, *WS*, Preface, §5)

If nothing else, Nietzsche gives us plenty of nourishment for thought. Some thoughts may reach beyond themselves and—by informing *praxis*—become deeds.

---

17 See Nietzsche's discussion in NF-1888:14[123], NF-1887:10[17], and NF-1887:11[140].
18 See Nietzsche's important discussion of 'Public and private morality', HH: I, §25 and NF-1872:19[28].

1 Approaching Nietzsche

Reading Nietzsche

The approach to reading Nietzsche adopted in this book prioritises the transdisciplinary aspect of his thought. Bringing together Nietzsche and political economy undoubtedly poses the challenge of balance between interpretation and relevance. This is particularly important in view of Colli's injunction not to 'give weight to your own words' by 'cleverly arranging' Nietzsche's 'authentic expressions and sentences at will' in order to generate the desired meaning (Colli 1980:209).[18] Three suggestions in particular have shaped the interpretive context of the present inquiry, starting with Foucault's observation that Nietzsche's value derives primarily from 'the quality of the challenge' he poses (Foucault 1989:249). Foucault proposes to interrogate Nietzsche's thoughts in order to establish their validity as though from within: 'the only valid tribute to thought such as Nietzsche's is precisely to use it, to deform it, to make it groan and protest' (Foucault 1980:53–54).[19] Building on Foucault's suggestion, Raymond Geuss stresses the value of experimental readings of Nietzsche, which 'try out different approaches, hypotheses, valuations and forms of life', over those playing the role 'of the Consistency Police'.[20] Last but not least, the book pays heed to Babette Babich's assertion that 'the greater part of Nietzsche's potential for philosophy is still unplumbed' (Babich 2018:403).

What Nietzsche wrote and what his writings help us to understand, while not identical, particularly when placed within the historical context, are at the same time *not as different* as they may appear, in lieu of the pre-contextual continuity of meaning expressed in Nietzsche's writings to which we are able to establish cognitive connection today. The interpretive claim pursued throughout this study is that the value of Nietzsche's critique and insights results primarily from what they enable—by helping, pushing and, on occasion, forcing—us to understand about our own present reality and the possible outlines of the future. Such value, burdensome and often unwanted though it may be, is nevertheless undeniable. It synthesises the multitude of nuanced contextual influences that form part of the intellectual patchwork that is Nietzsche and, akin to a flying carpet, it inevitably delivers us to the viewing point—'6000 feet above all human haze' (NF-1881:11[141])—from which we may examine our tomorrow by probing our today illuminated by the light of yesterday and of the day before.

---

18 Colli's caution echoes the earlier famous claim by Kurt Tucholsky (Jurist 2000:211). See also Schrift's discussion of the inescapable tension between 'getting Nietzsche right' and 'demonstrating his continuing pertinence', in *Why Nietzsche Still?* (Schrift 2000:4).
19 See Westfall, 2018:24–40.
20 See Geuss' interview: https://newleftreview.org/issues/II86/articles/raymond-geuss-systems-values-and-egalitarianism, last accessed Feb. 27, 2023.

Prior to approaching the subject of Nietzsche's political economy, it is helpful to identify the broad terms of his undertaking that form the conceptual framework within which the present inquiry is undertaken. I regard the following three characteristics of his approach as imminently relevant: gravity of concern, lack of special licence, and the assertion that 'everything hangs together'.

The Gravity of Nietzsche's Concern

Nietzsche insists that we inhabit the 'world invented by a lie [that—DS] has hitherto been called the "real world"' (NF-1888:14[109]). The gravity of his concern regarding the perilous condition of humankind leaves little room for doubt:

> [M]ankind ... has become mendacious and false down to its most fundamental instincts—to the point of worshipping the *opposite* values to those which alone would guarantee its health, its future, the lofty *right* to future (EH: *Preface*, §2; my emphasis)

Nietzsche insists that humanity endorses values that firmly set it on course to self-destruction (see EN: PT, 248; BGE: §262). He identifies the prevailing values as those of *slave morality*. These values facilitate the ruination of humankind's physiological and spiritual health and, in so doing, they rob humankind of its future or, more precisely, of the right to it:

> *The root of all evil:* that the *slavish morality* of meekness, chastity, selflessness, absolute obedience *has triumphed*—ruling natures were thus condemned 1) to hypocrisy, 2) to torments of conscience —creative natures felt like rebels against God, uncertain and inhibited by eternal values. In summa: the *best things have been slandered* because the weak or the immoderate swine have cast a bad light on them—and the best men have remained hidden and have often misjudged themselves (NF-1884:25[348]; my emphasis).

Nietzsche's diagnosis is not limited to any particular area of human life and activity. He finds signs of deterioration 'hidden in every order, institution, reality' (NF-1887:10[109]), in all of 'the problems of politics, of social organisation, and of education' (EH: *Clever*, §10), as well as in 'a total extermination and uprooting of culture' (UM: III, *SE*, §4). These multiple symptoms of the 'universal sickness' of humanity, which stubbornly 'obstructs the physicians' (UM: III, *SE*, §4), are proof, on Nietzsche's view, that 'humanity has so far been in the worst of hands' of the 'slanderers of the world and violators of man' (EH: *D*, §2). The gravity of Nietzsche's concern is frequently diluted down to a reaction against his own socio-economic context. One objective of this inquiry is to demonstrate that the plangency of his critique, although it is rooted in his time, extends considerably further than the 19th century, resonating with undiminished clarity and greater urgency today.

No Special Licence

In *The Birth of Tragedy* (1872), Nietzsche tells us that even 'the sphere of poetry does not lie outside the world' and that any honest and profound poetry 'desires the unvarnished expression of the truth', on account of which it fights to 'cast off the mendacious finery of the supposed reality' (BT: §8). This book argues that one of Nietzsche's key points in approaching the subject of political economy is to dispel the 'dishonest lie' (GM: III, §19) that it should be impossible to speak intelligently about the heart of economic matters in any tongue other than that of economics. After all, the principal concern of political economy, as well as of economics, is with life and with the conditions of human existence ('Existenzbedingungen des Menschen; see NF-1880:6[421]; NF-1881:11[59]). Stiegler's point on positioning Nietzsche's critique is relevant in this context:

> Nietzsche's thought is not the delirium of a philologist lost in his books and becoming mad, isolated in his visions: it is the interpretation of a world undergoing complete transformation, that of its industrialization, which will soon lead to the First World War, and it is an interpretation that calls for the fulfilment of this transformation, that is, a call to a combat of life against its nihilistic mortification. (Stiegler 2011:56)

Nietzsche considers the economic voice to represent but one of many competing voices that can expertly speak about the subject of 'Existenzbedingungen'. Some of these voices are concerned with the means of preserving life. Others speak to life's objectives and express their concern with its enhancement. As such, the rank ordering of these voices is of critical importance in terms of determining the trajectory of life's development. Nietzsche warns that privileging economistic conceptualisations of life, as though they were endowed with special insight into the management of 'the total households of life' (NF-1879:44[6]), is a perilous path that leads, through the 'victory of scientific method over science' (NF-1888:15[51]), inevitably towards the 'nihilistic consequences of a political and economic way of thinking' (NF-1885:2[127]).

In order to avoid this, Nietzsche insists on a synthetic and integrated approach to political economy, akin to that of a *double-brain* powered with 'two [...] ventricles, one for the perceptions of science, the other for those of non-science' (HH: I, *Tokens*, §251). He envisages 'the artist enclosed in the politician' (NF-1886:5[91]) and tells us that the poet, 'like a fabulous economist' using the 'poetic power available to men but not used up in the depiction of life', could 'anticipate the kind of conditions nations and societies would prosper better under and how they could be brought about without any artificial withdrawal from or warding off of this world' (HH: II, *AOM*, §99).[21]

---

[21] Unlike Plato, who insisted on banishing poets from the *polis* because they are prone to tell lies (see R:382[a-e]), Nietzsche insists that 'the poet who can willingly and knowingly lie, can *alone* tell the truth' ('The Peacock and the Buffalo', §103, Luchte 2010:369).

'It All Hangs Together'

The overwhelming topological feature—the load-bearing wall of Nietzsche's philosophical edifice—is his assertion that 'it all hangs together' (NF-1882:4[179]). In light of this, the present inquiry highlights the following intimately connected premises as significant signposts: the 'aesthetic justification of life'[22] and 'the absolute homogeneity in all that happens', which translate into an understanding of 'truth' to the 'degree to which we *permit* ourselves to understand that fact'.[23] Glancing back at his work in a letter to Georg Brandes, penned in May 1888, Nietzsche observes:

> It all hangs together, everything has been going on well for years ... but one must see all this, as I have now seen, to believe it. (BVN-1888:1030)

This book considers Nietzsche as a meticulous aggregator, who builds from the ground up (HH: II, *AOM*, §201). He approaches the subjects of his inquiry with the 'seriousness of the efficient workman which first learns to construct the parts properly before it ventures to fashion a great whole' (HH: I, §163).[24] This approach of '*a minori ad majus, a parte ad totum*'[25] is central to Nietzsche's thought and he adheres to it steadfastly throughout (HH: II, *WS*, §2).

Nietzsche's stated objective is to learn the language of 'total accounting' (HH: I, *State*, §475) in order to understand its intricate workings within the confines of 'the total balance sheet of life' (NF-1875:5[188]). This particular 'linguistic' capability', requiring 'the highest intellect and the warmest heart', becomes a prerequisite for synthesising 'the value of life' (NF-1875:5[188]). Years of reflection and careful aggregation of the seemingly disparate elements translate into a political economy that provides a critical insight into 'the economy of human evolution' (*Ökonomie der Menschen-Entwicklung*; NF-1887:10[111]) and into the resultant 'economy of mankind' (*Oekonomie der Menschheit*; HH: II, *WS*, §197). Nietzsche's message concerning 'the great economy of the whole' (*der grossen Ökonomie des Ganzen*; EH: *Destiny*, §4) is intended for no less than the *Gesammt-Haushalte des Lebens*—the 'total households of life' (BGE: §23) and *gesammten Haushalte der Menschheit*—'all the households of humankind' (BGE: §62).[26] Nietzsche's attempt to speak on behalf of 'humanity as a whole' (HH: II, *AOM*, § 185–186) embodies the 'communal soul' (NF-1874:37[6]) as he intuits towards the end of his active life: 'one is necessary and does not know it' (BNV-1888:1030). As Lou Salomé aptly noted, it is as though, through his works, Nietzsche attempts to dissolve 'his soul into the soul of the world' (Salomé 1894:23).

---

22 See *BT*: §5, §15, §24; NF-1872:19[123]; NF-1881:11[162]; NF-1885–1886:2[106]; NF-1885:2[110]; and NF-1887–1888:11[138].
23 NF-1887:10[154]. See also NF-1888:12[1] and NF-1888:14[81].
24 'One builds one's philosophy like a beaver' (BVN-1888:1030).
25 'From the less to the greater, from the part to the whole'.
26 See Staten's discussion in *Nietzsche's Voice*, 1990:10–14.

Thematic Topology of Nietzsche's Texts

My research into Nietzsche's political economy draws on two of his own investigative techniques, both deriving from the method of perspectival seeing and knowing (GM: III, §12). The first is the technique of *triangulation*, which Nietzsche uses extensively in evaluating social phenomena. Triangulation involves placing an issue under consideration inside a conceptual triangle the vertices of which denote the lines of scrutiny with respect to the chosen subject.[27] This approach combines 'inferring from the opposite', as a way of reversing concept and value inversions (NF-1887:10[111]), with assessing any 'one thing with different eyes' (GM: III, §12). Nietzsche links the commencement of his own philosophising to having examined the nature of faith inside the 'strange triad: namely, God-Father, God-Son and God-Devil' (NF-1884:26[390]). Plato's concept of 'tri-partite soul' in examining the wide-ranging social, political, and economic phenomena becomes an important conceptual importation into Nietzsche's own thinking on similar matters, as does the symbolism of the Holy Trinity in his critique of religion. The present study contends that using triangulation to examine the highly contentious subjects of slavery, debt and the division of labour allows us to bring into focus the fuller range of Nietzsche's meaning, making it less susceptible to ideological interpretative biases.

In conjunction with the triangulation technique, Nietzsche's ideas are examined topologically, rather than chronologically, or by distinguishing between his published works and private notes (the *Nachlass*). The concept of topology derives from Greek roots and emphasises the manner of interrelation and arrangement of the constituent and continually changing parts of the whole.[28] Topology as a method of interpretation helps to develop a perspectival technique and critical framework to examine Nietzsche's thinking concerning the persistent concepts and properties of the 'general economy of life' (BGE: §23). The topological approach treats Nietzsche's corpus as a body of thought which is *continuous* in time and across his published and private material, as well as exhibiting clear circular propensities in relation to the development of its key conceptual categories.[29] My approach emphasises how different parts of Nietzsche's *oeuvre* are connected, how they interact and enable the transmission of coherent meaning within the evolving stylistic, temporal, and contextual configuration.

---

27 Nietzsche frequently engages in the analysis of the 'three assertions' (NF-1887:8[4]) in relation to a particular issue. See, for example, Nietzsche on the 'three basic forms of Socratic optimism' (BT: §14), 'three stages of illusion' (BT: §18), the 'three signs of a degenerate culture' (BT: §17), the third re-birth of Dionysus (BT: §10) and the 'three metamorphoses of the spirit' (Z: I, Three Metamorphoses). See also Geuss on 'Nietzsche's theory of the three factors' (Introduction to *The Birth Of Tragedy and Other Writings* ('BTOW'), 1999: xxvii.

28 'τόπος' ('place') and 'λόγος' ('study').

29 As expressed in this famous passage from the *Nachlass:* '... out of the simplest forms striving towards the most complex, out of the stillest, most rigid, coldest forms toward the hottest, most turbulent, most self-contradictory, and then again returning home to the simple out of this abundance, out of the play of contradictions back to the joy of concord ... the joy of the circle ...' (NF-1885:38[12]).

Deploying the topological approach in relation to Nietzsche's ideas on political economy helps to overcome a number of significant limitations of perspectives based on the periodisation of Nietzsche's works.[30] The present inquiry resists the well-established assertions that disregarding 'periods' in Nietzsche's work risks constructing a 'single, unchanging Nietzsche', which often involves 'exaggeration and misrepresentation' (Abbey 2000: xiii), or that 'Nietzsche truly becomes Nietzsche' only after having emerged from his middle-period (Franco 2011: xiv). Although 'periodising' Nietzsche may be seen as a helpful heuristic framework for studying his texts, as Lou Salomé once suggested, pronounced emphasis on the substantively different Nietzsche periods is problematic for a number of reasons (Salomé 1894:45-47).

Most importantly, fragmenting Nietzsche's work in any manner—thematically, temporally or technically—inevitably fragments Nietzsche's meaning as well.[31] Suggesting visible 'epistemological breaks' between the three periods (Abbey 2000: xii) may give the impression of making Nietzsche's apparent contradictoriness more manageable, but it also undermines the dynamic fluidity and synthetic nature of his thought.[32] Furthermore, to assume that Nietzsche differs substantively as a thinker and/or a person across the three so-called periods of his writing life contradicts his idea of 'becoming who we are' (GS: §335; cf. Ansell-Pearson 1994:26). According to Nietzsche, one is not free to change, one must strive to *become who one is*, to draw the furthest consequences from oneself (GS §270; Z: IV, *Honey*). No camel would ever become a lion, let alone a child, were these not the hypostases of one spirit (Z: I, *Metamorphoses*).

Reading of Nietzsche based on a clear demarcation between the early, middle and mature periods, inevitably yields to the suggestion of distinguishing the more from the less attractive aspects of his overall project.[33] It introduces an additional level of arbitrariness, privileging specific aspects of Nietzsche's thought that are assumed to exhibit continuity and underemphasising those that are rendered discontinuous.[34] An inadvertent consequence of insisting on the periodisation of Nietzsche's corpus is that while it could make him more 'tolerable to look at', by imputing our own 'indignations and enthusiasms' into Nietzsche's work for a 'long time and with passion', we also run the risk of his texts and their meaning 'disappearing under the interpretation' (BGE: §38).

Specifically in connection with Nietzsche's thinking on the questions of political economy, my research does not support the view that the so-called 'middle period' is

---

[30] For 'early' Nietzsche vs. the Nietzsche of the 'middle period' vs. the 'mature' Nietzsche of the 'late period', see Ansell-Pearson 1994:85–95 and 2018:2–7; Abbey 2000: xi–xiii; Sedgwick 2007:1–27; Landa 2007:16–40; Franco 2011: x–xiii; and Drochon 2016:72–79.
[31] I.e., Nietzsche's published vs. unpublished content.
[32] See Ansell-Pearson 1994:55; Drochon 2016:9,143. On a technical level, any periodisation of Nietzsche's works consistent with his own views on the matter, would likely exhibit far greater granularity and discreteness, as Nietzsche suggests in *Ecce Homo* (1888), e.g., the 'Turin period', the 'period of decadence', the 'period of severe sickness', etc.
[33] Drochon argues that the chronological reading of 'Nietzsche's middle period' is an attempt to keep open the possibility of a 'more positive democratic' reading of Nietzsche (Drochon 2016:79).
[34] See Ansell-Pearson 1994:74 and Drochon 2016:8–19, 51–52, and 59.

when Nietzsche could be seen as 'prepared to concede a great deal to the tide of modern politics' (Ansell-Pearson 1994:85).³⁵ Instead, examination of Nietzsche's private notebooks alongside his published content suggests the consistent continuity of his views in relation to the chosen themes. Some of Nietzsche's more radical formulations can already be found in *The Greek State*, which was 'composed early in 1871' (Ruehl 2004:80), while some of his final *Nachlass* notes contain perhaps some of his more conciliatory ideas on political economy (e.g., NF:1888:14[182]). The ideas expressed during Nietzsche's 'middle period' represent prototypes of the formulations he would advance in his later works, rather than concessions to the social questions of the time, while their nuclei can often be traced to the early *Nachlass* entries.³⁶

In more general terms, my examination of Nietzsche's political economy echoes the approach of Babette Babich in her extensive study of Nietzsche's philosophy of science, which squarely rejects 'the description of Nietzsche's philosophic work as something that underwent three or more stages of metamorphosis, with the so called positivistic period occupying the central position' (Babich 1994:64).³⁷ It is also consistent with Megill (1985:35–36), Yack (1986:314) and Drochon (2016:79), who point to the deeper underlying continuity of Nietzsche's philosophical corpus.

Complementing the topological reading of Nietzsche, the present study draws on some of the earlier Nietzsche commentators, who emphasised the circular propensities of Nietzsche's thought. It would be problematic to argue that Nietzsche's critique of *slave morality*, crystalised in *On the Genealogy of Morality* (1887) did not start to take shape in the two notable passages contained in *Human, All Too Human* (1878– 1880) and that, in turn, the kernels of these reflections were not already discernible in his critical sketch of the psychological underpinnings of modern 'theories of the state, of the nation, of the economy, trade and justice' (UM: IV, *RWB*, §6), as well as in some of his earliest *Nachlass* notes and unpublished essays, including *The Greek State*.³⁸ This is noted by Vaihinger in particular, who comments that Nietzsche's

---

35 See also Landa 2007:30; Holub 2018:151; Sedgwick 2007:13; and Yack 1986:341.
36 See, for example, Nietzsche's discussion in HH: I, *Tokens*, §283; II, WS, §§9–11; D: §§204–206 and 534 and GS: §21, 80, 98, 174, and –352. Cf. Kuehne 2018:89.
37 It is worth noting that the 'periodised' readings of Nietzsche consistently miss the important connection between the development of Nietzsche's thinking on political economy and his engagement with the natural sciences from which he draws some of his most critical conjectures, especially with respect to the entropic propensities of capitalism (e.g., Ansell-Pearson 1994; Landa 2007; Sedgwick 2007; and Franco 2011).
38 See Nietzsche's discussion in §45 of 'On the History of Moral Sensations' (HH, I) and §45 of 'The Wanderer and His Shadow' (HH, II). Both passages unmistakeably form a skeletal argument, which Nietzsche develops (at the right time) in BGE (1886) and GM (1887). Similar observation can be made in relation to Nietzsche's views on 'progress', which is one of the central issues discussed throughout the present inquiry (see, in particular, the formation of the *typically Nietzschean circle* by tracing the development of the concept of progress from HH: I, *FLT*, §24 through BGE: §230 to TI: *Skirmishes*, §48, where Nietzsche inevitably links 'progress' with his undertaking for 'translating man back into nature' (NF-1881:11[211]).

ideas, 'despite their aphoristic and unsystematic sequence, form a strictly coherent, logically satisfactory whole; they flow with immanent necessity from a single basic principle and combine into a seamless circle' (Müller-Lauter 1999:2).[39] Nietzsche's late ideas, already discernible in his earliest works, represent the product of the maturation of his thought process. This process, owing to its circular propensities, as well as to the topological manner of developing the key concepts has, over the course of Nietzsche's writing career, compounded the power of his insight.[40] The topological approach equally resists Heidegger's influential suggestion that 'Nietzsche's philosophy proper' is to be sought in his unpublished material.[41]

In view of the above, an acknowledgment is made that no part of Nietzsche's interactive and interacting corpus represents a self-contained, self-sufficient, or privileged repository of his ideas. Approached in this manner, Nietzsche's works require constant and extensive cross-referencing, which renders their individual boundaries —temporal as well as contextual—largely obsolete. Nietzsche speaks of his works as 'having stuck together increasingly firmly, even growing into one another and growing into one ... from the first'. His ideas did not arise in him 'individually, randomly or sporadically but as stemming from a single root' (GM: *Preface*, §2).[42] Near the end of his productive years, Nietzsche acknowledges that all of his works are held together and connected through the axis of his project for the revaluation of all values. Viewed in this context, his first published book, *The Birth of Tragedy* (1872), represented his first attempt:

> *The Birth of Tragedy* was my first revaluation of all values. Herewith I again stand on the soil out of which my intention, my ability grows. (TI: *Ancients*, §5)

---

39 See also Simmel (1978: xxiii, 40 and 76) and Jaspers (1997:210–211). Simmel notes that the peculiar circularity of Nietzsche's thinking is a result of 'trying to think without presuppositions' (Simmel 1978: xxiii, 40, 76) and Jaspers emphasises that 'the circle receives substance through a circular movement ... or a transcending breakthrough reveals something further at this boundary of thought (Jaspers 1997:210–211).

40 As Megill notes in the *Prophets of Extremity* (1985), important aspects of Nietzsche's 'mature' position are already in place in the early writings' (Megill 1985:35). Löwith comments that 'Nietzsche both ended and began his intellectual life with the recollection of the ancient world' (Löwith 1997:115). See also Kuehne 2018:78–101.

41 See Heidegger, *Nietzsche*, Vol. I, 1961:9, as well as J. Glenn Gray, 'Heidegger "Evaluates" Nietzsche', 1953:304–309 *and* Lampert's 'Heidegger's Nietzsche Interpretation', 1974:353, both of which refute Heidegger's approach. See also the excellent discussion of this issue by Julian Young, 2010:535–536. My own research has not identified any substantial epistemological inconsistency between the published and private material, no 'hidden gems' or 'smoking guns' that would override or compromise the published content.

42 As an illustration, consider Nietzsche's definition of the world as 'uncreated, eternal, indestructible, without increase or decrease' (*PTAG*: §13) and the famous *Nachlass* passage NF-1885:38[12] describing the world as being 'without beginning, without end', a force that 'does not grow bigger or smaller'. The same world, which is Nietzsche's 'Dionysian world eternally creating itself', is a topology present from some of Nietzsche's earliest notes, which by 1885 he conceptualises in terms of 'the will to power' (NF-1885:38[12]).

In this respect, the topological approach allows us to engage with the more 'untimely' quality of Nietzsche's writings—his vexatious gift of seeing the world without time (NF1887:10[3])—which tends to get overlooked when his corpus is fragmented, and discussion is focused primarily on 'the local and temporary values' (Spengler 1918:24). It is Nietzsche's untimeliness, his ability to step outside the constraints of any particular and narrowly conceived historical context, when analysing critical concepts genealogically and reconstructively, that adds to the pertinence of his critique (see Lemm 2013:179–183). As Spengler points out, Nietzsche's questions belong to the truly 'great questions of any period': they 'are fluid beyond all conception' and 'lie outside "modern" interests' (Spengler 1918:24–25). It is not, therefore, surprising that *The Birth of Tragedy*, imbued with 'hostile silence about Christianity' (EH: *BT*, §1), contains ample implications for Nietzsche's subsequent thinking on politics and economy (Ansell-Pearson 1994:63).

Topology is critical to Nietzsche's investigations because Nietzsche concerns himself with the re-occurring patterns of social phenomena, particularly with respect to 'certain features, which recurred regularly together and were closely associated' (BGE: §260). Tracing these with his reconstructive genealogy, Nietzsche insists that a conceptual 'prehistory exists at all times' and is prone to recurring (GM: II, §9) because 'the past continues to flow within us in a hundred waves' (HH: II, *AOM*, §223). This topological stance enables Nietzsche to connect such seemingly distant and disparate phenomena as 'Socratic optimism' with *slave morality* and the reign of Judeo-Christianity and further with secular modernity, as manifest in *'industrial culture'*,[43] as representing stages in the evolution of a particular cluster of values. Kellner explains that 'Nietzsche ... saw the origins of modernity in the Socratic cultural complex that worked itself through Judeo-Christianity, the Enlightenment, and modern mass societies and cultures':

> Nietzsche saw the origins of modernity much earlier in the constellation of Socratic culture and privileged cultural forms over economics in his historical narratives. On Nietzsche's view, the Socratic cultural complex generated a repressive rationalism that became the central principle of modern culture, dominating philosophy, the economy, the state, and everyday life.[44]

Positioned within this conceptual framework, the themes of slavery, debt, and the division of labour represent three central topological threads that run through Nietzsch-

---

[43] Research carried out in the context of the present inquiry suggests that Nietzsche coined the expression *'industriellen Cultur'*, using it first in *The Gay Science* (Book I, §40), as a juxtaposition to Spencer's 'industrial society'. Equally, Nietzsche appears to have inaugurated the use of 'commercial culture' (*'Cultur der Handeltreibenden'*) in *Daybreak*, §175, and in NF-1881:11[246], in contrast to Smith's 'commercial society' (last accessed Feb. 27, 2023), which appears in *The Wealth of Nations* (1776; WN1:49; WN2:269). Curiously, both Smith and Nietzsche use their respective terminology only twice in their *corpora*.

[44] See Kellner's engaging discussion of the eventual transformation of the 'Socratic Man' into the 'Last Man' in Kellner (1998): *Modernity and Its Discontents: Nietzsche's Critique*, https://pages.gseis.ucla.edu/faculty/kellner/papers/FNmod.htm, last accessed Feb. 27, 2023.

e's work from beginning to end. In relation to slavery, Ishay Landa and Andrew Huddleston, among many other commentators, concur that the topology of slavery 'cuts across the entirety of Nietzsche's corpus' (Landa 2007:27), starting with 'his early essay *The Greek State* and reverberating 'all the way through to his final works of 1888' (Huddleston 2014:142, 146). Similarly, sustained reflections on debt form a topological axis around which much of Nietzsche's thinking on a wide range of issues pertaining to political economy developed consistently from his early years.[45] The division of labour is another example of a topological lynchpin that holds together some of Nietzsche's most pertinent and prescient reflections on this central concern of political economy.

Connecting Nietzsche's critique of slavery to present-day slavery, applying his reflections on the economic crises of his time to evaluating the 2008 financial crisis, and engaging with his critical discussion of the division of labour as the supposed means of fostering progress and social cohesion in the context of today's AI-led technological revolution, provide valuable and urgently needed insights into our present condition with a specific focus on the pivotal issues of political economy such as development and growth, class and inequality, leadership and governance, the structure of society and the management of the public household. The above referenced issues are particularly pertinent in view of the mounting hidden costs of the modern way of life, including its mental, spiritual and environmental impacts.[46] At the same time, these three themes triangulate and highlight the same key problem which, on Nietzsche's view, plagues modernity, as well as threatening the future of humankind, unless the latter can achieve a critical revaluation of the *values* that govern and direct human affairs in the world we inhabit today:

> It is my contention that *all the values* in which mankind now sums up its supreme desiderata are decadence values. It is my contention that *all the supreme values* of mankind [...] are symptomatic of decline, nihilistic values that are lording it under the holiest names. (AC: §6; my emphasis)

As such, the triangulation of slavery, debt and the division of labour should help to underscore the precariousness of humankind's present predicament and, hence, the urgency of Nietzsche's call for the revaluation of all values (NF-1887:11[411]), so as to make them commensurate with the objective of the 'preservation of life and the enhancement of its value' (AC: §7) in a manner that would promise 'life a future' (AC: §58).[47]

---

45 See Dodd 2012; Goodchild 2017; Deleuze and Guattari 1975, 2003, and 2013; and Lazzarato 2012.
46 See illuminating discussion by Del Caro, 2004:352–355.
47 See Nietzsche's further thoughts on the 'elevation' and 'enhancement of the species "man"' in GS: IV, §318; BGE: §44 and §257; NF-1885:37[8]; NF-1887:10[3]; and NF-1888:16[32].

Literature Review

A relatively small yet growing contingent of historians of economic thought, economists, political theorists and Nietzsche scholars acknowledge that Nietzsche's economic thinking merits more detailed study.[48] A number of thought-provoking studies in this area of Nietzsche scholarship seek to re-examine the hitherto widely accepted view, which can be traced to Georg Simmel's insistence that Nietzsche was 'most strongly and fiercely opposed to the economic interpretation of human affairs' (Simmel 1978:483).[49] In a recent book, *Nietzsche in the Nineteenth Century* (2018), Robert Holub observes, to the contrary, that not only Nietzsche's encounters with political economy were practically unavoidable, but that Nietzsche devoted considerable time and energy to reflecting on the implications of modern political economy (Holub 2018:129–136). The present inquiry acknowledges the valuable contributions and attempts to build on the pathbreaking work of such authors as Thomas Brobjer (1999, 2013), Backhaus and Drechsler (eds., 2006), Don Dombowsky (2004), Peter Sedgwick (2005, 2007), Nigel Dodd (2012, 2014), Hugo Drochon (2016), Robert Holub (2018), and Ishay Landa (2007, 2020).

Brobjer was one of the first to demonstrate that 'Nietzsche's knowledge of political economy was much more extensive than has been realized' and that Nietzsche—throughout his writing years—read political economy widely, across different schools of thought, and engaged with both domestic and international authors (Brobjer 1999:56).[50] Brobjer's contribution lent important, empirically grounded support to the claim that Nietzsche's economic commentary was neither accidental, nor baseless. Furthermore, Brobjer critical insight, pursued in this book, is that Nietzsche's 'interest in political economy' should be more accurately understood in terms of his objection to political economy's 'manner of viewing the world', which was based on the kind of 'opposition between money and spirituality' that turned 'economic thinking' into 'the main threat to culture' (Brobjer 1999: 62–63).[51]

In 'History as a Dual Process' (2002), Derek Hillard, developing on the illuminating, albeit relatively sparse insights, highlighting the importance of economic themes in

---

[48] See Linarelli 2008:134 and Drechsler 2006:5.
[49] This view was later expounded upon by Lukács (1980:318–341) and by Karl Löwith, who found Nietzsche's corpus to exhibit a clear 'lack of concern for social and economic questions' (Löwith 1991:176). More recently, this assessment that Nietzsche was not 'interested in the workings of contemporary economy'—in view of which his emphasis on economic factors was 'surely too weak'– has been periodically restated by a number of Nietzsche scholars, including Warren (1988:223), Detwiler (1990:44, 193), Leiter (2015:237–238), and Katsafanas (2016:208).
[50] Brobjer's original 1999 article was revised in 2013 as 'Nietzsche and Economics'. Both Sedgwick (2007: x–xii) and Landa (2020:160) concur with Brobjer's view.
[51] Cf. Dombowsky 2004:29–32. Disagreeing with Brobjer, Don Dombowsky pointed out the limitations he saw to the scope of Nietzsche's political economy: 'His concept of political economy ... does not repudiate property rights, exploitation, competition, production, expenditure, surplus value or waste, which are all essential to his 'general economy'.

Nietzsche by Deleuze (1983), Connolly (1988), Staten (1989), Andrew (1995), and Schrift (1996), argued that Nietzsche deserved to be considered as 'an economic thinker', who uniquely articulated economy not only as a discourse but equally 'as a structure that is used by discourses' (Hillard 2002:40).[52]

A critical volume on *Friedrich Nietzsche (1844–1900): Economy and Society* (2006), co-edited by Backhaus and Drechsler, provided a further representative sample of the wide-ranging economic themes picked out from Nietzsche's *oeuvre* by a group of 'historically informed economists' (Linarelli 2008:134). Whilst inevitably limited in scope to examining either a particular theme within Nietzsche's *oeuvre*,[53] focusing on a specific text and period in Nietzsche's writings,[54] or highlighting Nietzschean motifs in the work of the latter-day economists,[55] this compilation laid important conceptual groundwork for further research, which informs the present study. It raised pertinent questions in relation to whether separate economic themes within Nietzsche could amount to a more comprehensive conception of economy, as well as, whether it was beneficial to continue examining Nietzsche's economic insights in isolation from his views on politics.[56] It further inspired the question of whether Nietzsche's views retained pertinence exclusively for the archives of the history of economic thought, or whether the relevance of his critique extended beyond 'the social, cultural, and economic problems of his time' (Reinert and Reinert 2006:129).[57]

Addressing the issues highlighted above, Peter Sedgwick's *Nietzsche's Economy* (2007) is an ambitious attempt to develop a more consistent and holistic interpretation of Nietzsche's economic thinking across his corpus, which 'circumvents the artificial inter-disciplinary boundaries in the discourse on economy' (Sedgwick 2007:187).[58] Sedgwick's twofold insight, critical for the argument developed in this book, consists of his intuition that Nietzsche's concern was to follow the long-term crisis of the industrial culture (Sedgwick 2007:26–34, 184) and a recognition that as 'neither socialist revolutionary, nor exponent of industrial scale liberal capitalism', Nietzsche sought 'an alter-

---

[52] Hillard's contribution is particularly relevant to this book in relation to his discussion of the inflationary propensities of the modern debt economy, which is developed in Chapter 7.
[53] Otto Kaiser's excellent article explores the theme of democracy in Nietzsche's writings (2006:229–253), Jürgen Backhaus focuses on Nietzsche's concept of responsibility (2006:87–111), while Hugo and Erik Reinert lay out Nietzsche's vision of 'creative destruction', which would become a prominent conceptual category in Schumpeter's subsequent work on economic theory (2006:55–87). Last but not least, Marcel van Meerhaeghe's analysis teases out Nietzsche's insights applicable to the understanding of 'business ethics' (2006:137–145).
[54] The emphasis of Kaiser's analysis of Nietzsche's critique of liberalism and socialism is on Nietzsche's late writings (2006:229–253), whereas Kattel's inquiry into the issues of justice and economy focuses predominantly on Nietzsche's middle period writings (2006:209–229).
[55] Hugo and Erik Reinert highlight Nietzschean influences in the work of Sombart and Schumpeter (2006:55–87).
[56] With a possible exception of Kaiser's discussion of 'Democracy and Aristocracy' (2006:229–253).
[57] See Kaiser 2006:236–240, Meerhaeghe 2006:39–49, and Reinert and Reinert 2006:74.
[58] Which expanded on an earlier article on 'Violence, Economy and Temporality' (Sedgwick 2005:163–185).

native way' (Sedgwick 2007:24). In this context, Sedgwick's nuanced, and largely chronological reading of Nietzsche's corpus, provides insightful forays into the controversial topics of the division of labour, debt, and value. His discussions of the relationship between 'nature and modernity' (Sedgwick 2007:3–6) as well as between past, present and future (Sedgwick 2007:116–130, 189) tackle important issues highlighted by Nietzsche's critique concerning the alienating potential of rationality. The latter, unleashed on modernity by the greed of the money-makers in the form of science and technology on an industrial footing, contributes to the growing and increasingly irreversible chasm between 'culture and nature' (Sedgwick 2007:32, 185–186).

However, Sedgwick's assertion that Nietzsche's 'own thinking is invaded by the language of economy to such a degree that it becomes constitutive of his philosophy as such' (Sedgwick 2007:108) results in a tendency for economic determinism that runs contrary to Nietzsche's stated preference for agonal perspectivism. Reversing the relationship between Nietzsche's economy and his philosophical project has the effect of making the latter a function and a subset of the overriding economic logic (Sedgwick 2007:187), which inadvertently diminishes the critical reach of Nietzsche's critique.[59] The present study challenges Sedgwick's conclusion that 'economy bestows upon humankind the gift of being able to become more than it is' (Sedgwick 2007:183). Furthermore, it contends that an overly economistic reading of Nietzsche risks misinterpreting a number of critical relationships within his thought. Most importantly, these include Nietzsche's 'economy of the preservation of the species' (GS: §1) and culture,[60] exchange and debt,[61] as well as the challenges of transitioning from the financial economics of industrial culture towards the 'spiritual economics' of the future (Sedgwick 2007:147–153). Sedgwick's scant engagement with Nietzsche's genealogy of values and his cursory analysis of the concept of 'industrial culture' (Sedgwick 2007: x) prevent the author from placing Nietzsche's economy into the context of his revaluational project and understate the importance Nietzsche attached to the intricate connection between the money-economy and democratic politics. Sedgwick's analysis misses out on appreciating Nietzsche as someone, who was 'able to see with uncommon clarity what happens

---

[59] In this regard, Staten highlighted the ambiguity between 'the economy of Nietzsche' and that of 'Nietzsche's text' (Staten 1989:68). More recently, Merrick pointed out potential for confusion concerning what is really at stake: Nietzsche's economy or his use of economic language? (Merrick 2020:137).

[60] Sedgwick consistently argues that 'the economic model becomes ... Nietzsche's chosen paradigm for articulating the emergence of civilisation and the meaning of culture alike' (2007:183). See also 2007:96, 110. For Nietzsche's discussion of role of culture within the context of humankind's enhancement, see HC; UM: II, *UDHL*, §2–3; GS: §109; NF-1885:2[188]; BGE: §188; and TI: *Germans*, §4.

[61] Sedgwick holds that, on Nietzsche's view, 'the world is endowed with meaning through economy' and it is 'the economic exchange principle that underlies human relations', which entails 'the possibility of enhanced human achievement' (Sedgwick 2007:102, 183). See also 2007:6–20. These propositions run contrary to Nietzsche's focus on the 'aesthetic justification of the world' *BT* (§5, §15, and §24), and the manner in which the creditor-debtor relation subdues the exchange (which is discussed in detail in Chapters 5–7 of this book).

when you try to imagine the world in commercial terms' (Graeber 2011:76). This leaves Nietzsche vulnerable to an ideological reading as a celebrant of unbridled capitalism.

Ishay Landa's thought-provoking work in *The Overman In The Market Place* (2007) as well as his more recent article on 'Marx, Nietzsche and the Contradictions of Capitalism' (2020)[62] demonstrate the extent of susceptibility of Nietzsche's writings to ideological interpretations that, quite literally, take Nietzsche at his word. Landa acknowledges that 'the validity' of his 'entire argument hinges on this reading of Nietzsche as a formulator of a new, bourgeois ethos' (Landa 2007:25). What follows is a direct intellectual confrontation with Nietzsche's political economy which, Landa insists, has been purposefully shrouded 'in hazy and lyrical veils' by scholars and researchers wishing to appropriate Nietzsche into their liberal frameworks (Landa: 38–40). Acknowledging, along with Brobjer and Sedgwick 'Nietzsche's [...] keen appreciation of the indispensable role of economic arrangements' (Landa 2020:147), Landa too focuses on the seeming contradiction between Nietzsche's unequivocal rejection of the money-economy on the one hand, and his employment of an overtly capitalistic vernacular when discussing the enhancement of life and humankind's excellence, on the other (Landa 2007:27–30).

However, unlike Brobjer or Sedgwick, Landa finds Nietzsche's motives to be not only inadvertently sinister, but deliberately so. The thrust of Landa's argument is that 'Nietzsche's apology for capitalism' underpinned 'the entirety of his project' so profoundly that when Nietzsche became aware of the shortcomings in his conception, he resorted to erecting 'a metaphysical construction in support of the market economy' (Landa 2007:36). As part of this exercise 'Nietzsche [...] specifically theologised about the vital role of money-making [...] in forming the basis for a cultural revitalisation' (Landa 2007:29). Nietzsche's other alleged wilful acts of compensating for the shortcomings of his system included the invention of the Overman, as the guardian of capitalism (Landa 2020:157), as well as the dystopianisation of 'the social individual by rewriting him disparagingly as "the Last Human"' (Landa 2020:163). Nietzsche's steadfast intention was to ensure that political liberalism (i.e., democracy) would not come to threaten capitalism by developing a radical alternative to it (Landa 2007:27). To complete the exercise, Landa suggests, Nietzsche invented 'the eternal recurrence' with the clearly stated goal of ensuring the fixity and permanence of capitalism, including its exploitative class structure (Landa 2020:148–158). The end result of Nietzsche's 'noisy quietism' is that it leaves him irredeemably stranded between 'making capitalism interchangeable with life' and, at the same time, being terrified of it (Landa 2007:157).

Landa's constructive contribution to the discussion concerning Nietzsche's political economy can be regarded as a caution as to what happens, when interpretation of Nietzsche is processed through a pre-conceived ideological interpretive filter. Whilst Landa rightly forces the reader to think more diligently about the controversial turns of Nietzsche's thought, his totalisation of capitalism in Nietzsche's thought,

---

[62] An earlier (2016) version of this article was titled 'The Social Individual and The Last Human: Marx and Nietzsche Agree To Disagree', *Critical Sociology* 45, No. 2: 253–265.

which is a step up on Sedgwick's totalisation of economy, emerges as the main limiting factor of Landa's undertaking, challenged in this book. An approach such as that adopted by Landa curtails the scope of engagement with the highly nuanced nature of Nietzsche's thinking and writing. It disregards the need to deal with the material, which runs contrary to the adopted ideological thrust. It becomes liable to producing binary and non-critical interpretations, which lose the depth and dynamism of Nietzsche's analysis. With echoes of Benjamin and Lukács resounding in Landa's work, a more detailed discussion of the risks entailed in impregnating Nietzsche's writings with an ideological bias is undertaken in the subsequent chapters.

Landa's work echoes some of the themes raised in two notable earlier surveys of Nietzsche's political economy undertaken, respectively, by Don Dombowsky (2004) and Geoff Waite (1996). In his incisive analysis of *Nietzsche's Machiavellian Politics* (2004), Dombowsky characterises Nietzsche's political economy as an 'immoralistic economy' of 'exploitation' (Dombowsky 2004:1–12). He views it as deriving from the 'doctrine of agonism' conceived in terms of a 'regulated factionalism' and 'a controlled violence', which rules out the possibility of overcoming inequality, and run contrary to the notion of 'model citizenry' (Dombowsky 2004:66). Echoing Ansell-Pearson's earlier argument, Dombowsky suggests that part of Nietzsche's undoing stems from his inability to provide 'operational detail' for his agonistic vision of political economy (Dombowsky 2004:66). Dombowsky concludes that 'Nietzsche does not, ultimately, object to capitalism' and that 'if this relation were further explored it would likely be shown that Nietzsche is a supporter of *laissez-faire* capitalism (Dombowsky 2004:29–30). Although Nietzsche makes no secret of his intention and, in fact, obligation to 'make use of existing political and economic conditions' (BGE: §61), a closer examination of Nietzsche's political economy undertaken in this study does not lend textual support to Dombowsky's conjectures. His contention that Nietzsche's engagement in 'class warfare' and his aversion and, in places, open enmity towards the revolutions of 1789, 1848 and 1871 as well as the Paris Commune follow from 'his concept of political economy' (Dombowsky 2004:66) reveals his reluctance to examine Nietzsche's views beyond the mere politics of events, transcending which Nietzsche insists upon in outlining his vision of the 'große Politik' of the future. Overall, Dombowsky's excellent and thought-provoking inquiry, nevertheless, appears to curtail its critical reach by evaluating Nietzsche's political economy against the liberal democratic criteria which Nietzsche never intended to satisfy.

A far sterner characterisation of Nietzsche's political economy can be gleaned from Geoff Waite's *Nietzsche's Corps/e* (1996). Acknowledging that Nietzsche's political economy runs deep through his corpus, Waite discovers its 'concealed root' to be 'ruthlessly antidemocratic' and 'distinctly fascoid—not fascist or national socialist—or, better, "fascoid-liberal" (Waite 1996:294). At the same time, he considers 'Nietzsche's "rhetorical play"' to be particularly effective in illuminating the 'world imagined to be definitively postcommunist' (Waite 1996:294). Waite advances familiar criticisms for the lack of empathy for the 'lives or deaths' of the workers on whose 'willing wage labour' Nietzsche erects his political economy and extends these to suggest that Nietzsche's political economy intends to put 'eugenics and euthanasia' in the service the new 'aristocracy of merit' (Waite 295, 317). Waite's account stands out from the diverse assessments of Nietzsche's political economy as, perhaps, the most politicised in the recent scholarship. Brave and abrasive, it ends us criticising a version of Nietzsche's political economy conjured up in 'its own image', which becomes a substitute for examining Nietzsche's texts with the view to ascertaining and evaluating his meanings, rather than ascribing them. Notwithstanding, the value of Waite's reading of Nietzsche is to confirm not only the importance of political economy to Nietzsche but to highlight the complex and challenging nature of Nietzsche's offering.

An example of a considerably more nuanced navigation between different ideological interpretations of Nietzsche without having to label him, which provides a useful methodological cue for the present inquiry, is found in 'Nietzsche's Money' (2012) by Nigel Dodd. The author persuasively argues that although Nietzsche was no 'monetary theorist' (Dodd 2012:48), it would be a mistake to dismiss his views on the subject 'as expressions of naïvety and romanticism' (Dodd 2012:65). By analysing the impact of Nietzsche's views on value, money, and debt on the work of Georg Simmel, Walter Benjamin, and Norman Brown, the author highlights the critical importance of Nietzsche's insight that the pivotal institutions of secular modern society—money, debt, and private property—are economic expressions of deeply ingrained moral views and values, which in turn derive from 'psycho-religious feelings' (Dodd 2012:64). Furthermore, by exploring the connection between Nietzsche's key concepts of the eternal return and the *Übermensch*, Dodd is able to demonstrate 'a complex interrelationship of religious, aesthetic, economic and monetary registers of value', which continue to shape modernity and mould subjectivity. Arguably, none of these is more important than 'guilt's manifestation as financial debt' (Dodd 2012:62). Dodd's insightful commentary on the inflationary propensities of debt, as the latter transitions from the 'barren' capital of the past into the 'interest-bearing capital' of industrial capitalism (Dodd 2012:61–62), the psychological underpinnings of industriousness (Dodd 2012:61), and the 'false nature' of equality that 'money encourages' (Dodd 2012:64)—form important vectors, pursued by the present inquiry, for exploring the role of slave morality as a powerful economic force, which 'lies just beneath money's surface' (Dodd 2012:64).

By way of concluding this brief overview of the literature, which is developing in depth and in diversity of perspectives, I would venture the following observations. The field of inquiry into Nietzsche's political economy is still relatively new and, as Drochon rightly notes in 'Nietzsche Between History, Economics and Politics' (2018), the 'lens of political economy' offers many exciting opportunities in terms of approaching and interpreting Nietzsche's work (Drochon 2018:246). The present study attempts to develop this line of inquiry by emphasising the importance of *values* to Nietzsche's political economy—a focus that is currently missing from the conversation. Related to this is my attempt to examine Nietzsche's political economy in the context of the *Long Depression* of the late 19th century. This book contends that Nietzsche's experience of the first significant economic crisis of industrial capitalism informed not only his views on political economy but influenced his philosophy more broadly. This too remains an under-researched aspect of Nietzsche's work. Textual discoveries made in the course of researching this book, many of them unexpected and some surprising, convinced me that considerably more relevant material can be gleaned from attending to Nietzsche's texts, including his still unpublished notebooks. Last but not least, developing inquiry into NPE would benefit considerably from cross-pollination among the different strands of Nietzsche scholarship.

The work of contemporary German scholars, although it is still less known and receives less attention in the Anglophone Nietzsche scholarship, supports the growing interest in Nietzsche's political economy and boasts a variety of insightful contributions. The volume, entitled *Nietzsche als Kritiker und Denker der Transformation* (2016), edited by Helmut Heit and Sigridur Thorgeirsdottir, offers wide-ranging assessments of Nietzsche as a critic, both destructive and constructive, of transformation. Critical attention is drawn to Nietzsche's thinking on the crises of humanity, past and present, as inevitably entailing the transformative aspect which stresses the interconnectedness of any 'transformation of social structures' with the 'change in individuals' (2016:3). Thorgeirsdottir's discussion of Nietzsche's 'Debt Economy' (2016:189–206) and Martin Saar's discussion of Nietzsche as 'critic of social transformation' (2016:93–112) resonate with the themes explored in the present study. In an earlier publication, Hendrik Wallat's thought-provoking '*Das Bewusstsein der Krise* (2009) examines Marx's and Nietzsche's discussion of the developing 'consciousness of the crisis' [of modern political economy] within the context of the project of 'human emancipation' (2009:519–520). Wallat's analysis problematises the propensity of critical theories, such as Marx's and Nietzsche's, to be weaponised in times of social and political strife. Drawing attention to 'Nietzsche's dangerous aesthetics' in particular, Wallat stresses that, perversely, 'Nietzsche's anti-capitalism' became ideologised by the Germany's National Socialist movement of the 1930s (2009:228, 248). In a more recent contribution, Niels Fiebig's *Nietzsche und das Geld* (2019) explores Nietzsche's frequently troubled and conflicting relationship with money. The book adds an original perspective on Nietzsche's personal circumstances and investment activities in the context of Gründerkrach as informing his views on the wider themes of political economy of the late 19th century. In an attempt to overcome the 'silo effect', which still creates inefficiencies in advancing scholarly investigations, the present inquiry aims to incorporate these and other perspectives from outside of the Anglophone Nietzsche tradition.

2 Nietzsche's Political Economy: Conceptual Framework

> I bring the war. Not between people and people [...] not between classes [...] I bring the war that goes through all absurd circumstance of people, class, race, occupation, upbringing, education: a war like that between rise and decline, between will to live and vengefulness against life, between righteousness and vicious mendacity.
> (Nietzsche, NF-1888:25[1])

Preamble

Nietzsche's thinking on the questions of politics and, on occasion, of the economy, has been contextualised in a number of ways. It has been explored as deriving from the Ancient Greeks, Plato and Aristotle in particular, or as located in contemporary political thought, encompassing the German, more broadly European, and Anglo-Saxon influences.[64] More recent studies offer a broader appreciation of Nietzsche's political thinking and its continued relevance by scrutinising his views about the 'politics of his time' (Drochon 2016) as well as by interrogating Nietzsche against the backdrop of the 'topical discourses' of the 19th century (Holub 2018:454). No comparable attempts, however, have been made to situate Nietzsche's probing examination of modernity within the wider conversation on political economy. This chapter explores some of the reasons why such connection adds a warranted angle to the discussion and highlights Nietzsche's examination of slave morality as one of the most powerful forces in structuring and directing modern political economy.

Why Political Economy

Why political economy rather than, say, economics? The choice of political economy as Nietzsche's critical lens, through which he scrutinises modernity, is predicated on the following considerations. In the first instance, it provides useful historical context to Nietzsche's thinking on the questions of economy and politics. Nietzsche writes during the time when the emerging discipline of economics, armed with new theoretical prop-

---

[64] Regarding Plato and Aristotle, see Lampert 2001, Wilkerson 2006, and Meyer 2014; regarding German political thought, see Ansell-Pearson (Ed.) 1991 and Holub 2018; regarding European political thought, see Williams 1952, Schrift 1995, and Young 2010; and regarding Anglo-Saxon political thought, see Brobjer 2007, Mikics 2003, Mabille 2009, and Ratner-Rosenhagen 2012.

ositions and the 'algebraic formulae' to prove them, vies to supersede political economy as the main vernacular of economic thinking (Roscher 1878:103). The ethical underpinnings of political economy, itself a progeny of moral philosophy, come to be regarded as somewhat anachronistic, and mathematics is called upon to revitalise the discourse on economy.[65] In addition, political economy becomes increasingly divided by heated interdisciplinary debates which concern the scope and the method of social inquiry, the universal or contingent nature of its propositions and the meaning of culture and sociality.[66]

Known as 'Methodenstreit', these disputes can be traced to the critique by the [old] German Historical School of the *abstract* mode of deductive reasoning adopted by the British classical political economists (e.g., Smith) and, in particular, of its liberal implications, including individualism and 'free trade'.[67] The [old] German historical school, formed under the influence of Wilhelm Roscher, developed as a reaction to the Classical school of political economy's tendency to axiomatise the laws of economic life. Roscher, along with Karl Knies, Bruno Hildebrand, and, later, Gustav Schmoller, sought to give prominence to the historical, ethical, cultural, and political realities in its own analyses of the economy:

> Most assuredly [...] our science has to do with men, it must take them and treat them as they actually are, moved at once by very different and non-economic motives, belonging to an entirely definite people, state, age etc. (Roscher 1878:104)

Historical school asserts the 'centrality of the 'social question' (Grimmer-Solem 2003:34) and recognises the need to adjust economic thinking and practice to its changing realities with the view to 'neutralizing its most destructive political effects' (McDaniel 2018:112). In this respect, Historical school is equally critical of the excesses of liberalism, which it sees as embedding polarising inequality, and of Marx's 'historical materialism' for its overly deterministic take on history which underwrites the theory of class struggle.[68] In addition, Roscher's comparative political economy, aiming to be conservative and pragmatic rather than decidedly antiliberal, also asserts a clear priority of *non-material wealth* as key to the overall development of society (Roscher 1878:21; see Giouras 1995:123). Political economy, viewed in this context, appears as a broad comparative study of the interaction and mutual shaping that takes place between the economic systems, political forces, and agency—contextualised historically as well as culturally. Framing the conversation on political economy in this manner entails concern with ascertaining particular conditions of existence yet avoids being pre-

---

[65] See Barkai's illuminating discussion of 'The Methodenstreit and the Emergence of Mathematical Economics', 1996:1–19.
[66] See Smith 1991:217.
[67] See Reinert and Reinert 2006:111–137 and McDaniel 2018:94–95.
[68] See McDaniel 2018:103–109 and Holub 2018:126–131.

scriptive and deterministic about it.[69] This heterogenous approach is consistent with Nietzsche's own enduring concern with 'Existenzbedingungen' encapsulated in the intellectual debates in Germany in the second half of the 19th century. Although Nietzsche does not fully embrace the German historical school and remains critical of Roscher (BVN-1868:562), his intellectual misgivings about the liberal tradition of economic and political thought as well as concerning socialism are undoubtedly informed by the German historical tradition.[70]

Where Nietzsche's approach differs drastically from the 'classics of the 19th-century political economy' (Smith 1991:21) as well as from the 'cultural scientists' of his time, who attempted to 'construct alternatives to the liberal theoretical pattern' (Smith 1991:98), is his unremitting focus on value. Reflecting on the transition from Plato's' and Aristotle's considerations of 'Ökonomie im Großen' (NF-1887:10[168]) to the political economy of commercial society, inaugurated by Smith, and the subsequent emergence of economics as an autonomous discipline with scientific aspirations under the aegis of the fledgling industrial culture of modernity, Nietzsche remains circumspect about the general direction and substance of this change (NF:1869:3[10]). In this dynamic he discerns the inevitable signs that 'philosophy [is] gradually losing the reins of science' and questions whether this process also attests to our losing sight of 'the *value* of existence' (NF-1872:19[28]; my emphasis).

Why Nietzsche's Political Economy

It has been argued that in the absence of a treatise on the subject, it is difficult to speak about *Nietzsche's Political Economy* as a formal body of thought.[71] Although Nietzsche's plans to write specifically on political economy remained unfulfilled (NF-1885:2[131]), considerable textual evidence points to his sustained interest in political economy throughout his writing years (Brobjer 1999:56–64). It would be remiss to conclude that Nietzsche falters before the challenges posed by political economy. On the contra-

---

69 Lee Levin's informed discussion of the issue of determinism in the debates between the Historical School and Historical Materialism, 1987:431–451.
70 See Brobjer 1999:56–57 on Nietzsche's engagement with Roscher. See McDaniel's discussion of Aristotelian influences in Roscher and his discussion of *oikonomia* (2018:97), which become formative influences on Nietzsche. More generally, Roscher's cyclical theory of *kyklos*, including the Platonic themes that 'military tyranny is a product of the intense social antagonisms between "money-oligarchy" ("Geldoligarchie") and proletariat that characterized degenerate, or "extreme", democracies' (McDaniel 2017:108) were equally important in shaping Nietzsche's politico-economic outlook.
71 See Merrick 2020:135–136. Robin claims that 'for all his reading in political economy, Nietzsche never wrote a treatise on politics or economics', which disqualifies him as a thinker on the issues of political economy, even if his work may have yielded 'marginal children' such as Hayek (https://www.thenation.com/article/archive/nietzsches-marginal-children-friedrich-hayek/, last accessed Feb. 27, 2023). Hendrik Wallat reminds us that notwithstanding the 'decades of work on his gigantic project', Marx also never completed his critique of the political economy of capitalism (Wallat 2009:259).

ry, as a discerning student of political and economic thought, Nietzsche actively uses the critical lens of political economy to reflect on the changing configuration of modern society, on the issue of development, as well as on the *time horizons, scope, and substance* of social change.

Nietzsche first engages with the 'dogmas of modern political economy' in his inaugural lecture 'On the Future of Our Financial Institutions' (1872). In this lecture, Nietzsche sets out his wide-ranging criticisms of the effects of money-economy, which he explores in his later works, and which comprise an important component of his critique of modernity. In particular, he chastises the narrow conceptualisation of 'utility' in terms of 'the greatest possible pecuniary gain' and highlights the repressive propensities of the money-economy, which thirsts to 'control all the means of communication between men and nations' in order to rear obsequious 'money-making creatures' at speed (FEI: I, 18–19).

The present inquiry contends that Nietzsche not only uses political economy but that it forms an integral part of his critique of modernity. Nietzsche's primary contribution is neither to identify *morality* as a potent economic force (this has been done before), nor simply to seek reinstatement of its critique into the discourse of political economy. Instead, Nietzsche problematises the profound, on his view, moralisation of the economic discourse of his time (NF-1887:9[173]). More precisely, his own project becomes to ascertain the origins and the value of the valuations of slave morality which he charges with distorting the 'grand economy' of life.[72] Nietzsche's assertion that the discipline of political economy is not in the slightest value-neutral resolutely echoes that of Marx, who maintains that:

> Political economy, this science of wealth, is […] simultaneously the science of renunciation, of want, of saving […] this science of *marvellous industry* is simultaneously the science of *asceticism*, and its true ideal is the *ascetic* but extortionate miser and the *ascetic* but productive slave (Marx, CW 3:310; my emphasis)

Nietzsche's political economy scrutinises the intricate workings of *slave morality* in the economic and political spheres of modernity. He sees the latter as having succumbed to the enchanting, yet mendacious, utterances of 'economic optimism' (NF-1887:10[17]) and the endless '*bric-a-brac*' of positivistic concepts with which *slave morality* saturates 'the market' (BGE: §10). Don Dombowsky observes that the 'conversion of Nietzschean "general economy" into "political economy" helps to sharpen his critique of the valuations underpinning modernity, which finds expression in his 'antidemocratic polemics' (Dombowsky 2004:1, 188).

---

72 See EH: *Destiny*, §4; NF-1888:14[185].

Nietzsche's political economy begins by identifying the *psychic disorder* at the core of the modern soul (GS: §120).[73] In the final essay of *Untimely Meditations* (1876), Nietzsche advances this disconcerting proposition:

> *Theories of the state*, of the nation, of the *economy*, trade, justice—they all now have the character of a *preparatory apologia* ('vorbereitend apologetischen Charakter'); it seems, indeed, as though the only task of all active spirit not used up in propelling the great economy—and power machine ('Erwerb-und Machtmechanismus') is the defence and *exculpation* of the present. (UM: IV, *RWB*, §6; my emphasis)

The implication of Nietzsche's hypothesis is twofold. The still active part of human spirit is invested in preparing the defence of the present from the criticisms that are certain to come from the future. The economic theories, which form part of this defensive armour, embody the character of an *apology*—with the connotations of excuse rather than of vindication—i.e., a tacit acknowledgement that they (at least) intuit that what they profess does *not* benefit the 'great economy' of humankind.[74] By performing the function of exonerating the present—from a charge of fault, guilt, or crime—economic theories, by implication, conceal something important about it (HH: II, *AOM*, §226). This discernment informs Nietzsche's intellectual unease:

> Could it perhaps be the case, despite all 'modern ideas' and the prejudices of democratic taste, that the victory of optimism, the predominance of reasonableness, practical and theoretical utilitarianism, like its contemporary, democracy, that all this is symptomatic of a decline in strength, of approaching old age, of physiological exhaustion? (BT: *ASC*, §4)

Nietzsche problematises the meaning of contemporary economic theories in terms of helping 'the modern soul to *forget* its feeling of guilt, rather than helping it to *return* to innocence' (UM: IV, *RWB*, §6; my emphasis). Realising, deep down, that what we *do* is damaging—that it pushes us further adrift from the goals we declare—we, nevertheless, expend considerable energy on creating the *narratives* to misrepresent reality only so that we could continue along the path we realise to be detrimental (UM: III, *SE*, §4). One may feel deeply remorseful over one's actions but, when all the words have been spoken—as though compelled by some tenebrous force of inertia—one can *do nothing different* and for that reason one has no choice but to try 'to silence the conscience', to 'put it to sleep or to intoxicate it' (UM: IV, *RWB*, §6). Nietzsche sees this tendency at work in the 'perverse sensibilities of the modern age', which seek to 'to employ the moment so as to *profit* from it, to *assess its value* as quickly as possible' only to discard it just as quickly, all the while remaining oblivious to the darkening skies overhead (UM: IV, *RWB*, §6; my emphasis). He problematises the social

---

[73] For an illustration, see Nietzsche's discussion of the psyche of the farmer 'eaten up by the big cities' (NF-1888:15[40]) and the longer-term consequences of this trend on the 'solidarity in a society' (NF-1888:15[41]).
[74] From the Greek *'apologia'* ('ἀπολογία'), meaning 'a speech in defence'.

conditions under which 'putting to sleep' becomes preferable to 'revitalising' and where the amplification of virtue signalling becomes the conduit for the modern soul to communicate its growing distress.[75]

If Nietzsche's misgivings be granted the benefit of the doubt, engaging the 'active spirit' to develop such economic theories would amount to exacerbating the aforementioned predicament, because they would help to 'conserve what degenerates' as well as ruining 'society's most gifted spirits' in the process (D: §179; EH: D, §2). When Nietzsche queries before 'what accuser' the modern spirit seeks apology, his conclusion is that the accuser is none other than this spirit's 'own bad conscience' (UM: IV, RWB, §6). In other words, the modern subject is self-surveying, cognizant of his predicament and unable to overcome it, appears predestined to slide ever deeper into the abyss of nihilism.[76] Developing an appreciation for the means and the process by which the 'active spirit' comes to preside over self-harm by perpetrating untruths to its own detriment, how it ends up so enslaved that it resorts to the desperate means of communicating its distress in the coded vernacular of liberty and equality lays the early foundations of Nietzsche's political-economic thinking.

From this heterodox groundwork rises the underestimated *importance of values* that fashion the modern spirit. From the importance of values emerges the exigency of agency. 'Who' does the doing and the talking (i.e., 'creates values') establishes an indispensable, in Nietzsche's estimation, anteriority of the actor understood in terms of the ability to own, or the will to disown responsibility for the consequences of his actions. As we shall see in the discussion that follows, Nietzsche explores this vital connection between agency and values throughout his works, including in terms of a powerful metaphor of the 'metaphysics of the hangman', as someone who takes [control of] life not by hanging bodies from the gallows but by claiming minds through the intricate and pervasive theological manipulation (TI: *Errors*, §7).[77] The mammoth task of Nietzsche's political economy—a countermovement to the 'congenital defect of all philosophers' (HH: I, FLT, §2)—becomes to trace the sickness of 'the modern spirit' back to its origins in an attempt to establish its causes rather than to focus on seeking out remedies capable of no more than alleviating its current symptoms. Nietzsche's early goal, one that—in due course—would crystalise in the call for the *revaluation of all values*, becomes to liberate humankind from its 'modern soul' (UM: IV, RWB, §6).

---

[75] The themes of hystericising modernism were masterfully explored by Joyce in the deeply Nietzschean *Ulysses* (1922), including through the iconic example of the 'lemon soap' fittingly purchased from the 'Lotus Eaters' pharmacy (i.e., an unmistakable allusion to Homer's *Odyssey*).

[76] In *Twilight of the Idols* (1888), Nietzsche conceptualises this trauma of the modern spirit in terms of 'a rape of the conscience' (TI: *Skirmishes*, 36). See also Nietzsche's discussion in AC: §43.

[77] In these terms Nietzsche discusses 'the theologians, who continue with the concept of a "moral world-order" to infect the innocence of becoming by means of "punishment" and "guilt"' (TI: *Errors*, §7). See also Nietzsche's discussion in Z: II, *Tarantulas*, and in TI: *Skirmishes*, §36.

Time Horizons, Scope, and Substance of Social Change

Modern practitioners of economic science, as though to prove right Nietzsche's assertion that the modern age—consumed by profit-making—has become incurably myopic (UM: IV *RWB*, §6), prefer to steer clear of long-term forecasting. Mathematics, which emerged victorious from the 'method wars' of the second half of the 19th century, when it was drafted into the discourse on economy as the answer to the long-term challenges of managing modern political economy, appeared rather powerless to rise to them. The difficulties of accurately forecasting the future, let alone predicting a crisis—'ubiquitous in all areas of economics and finance'—were most recently highlighted by the financial crisis of 2008 and etched in public memory by the Queen of England's famous question addressed to the bewildered audience of the world's preeminent economists: 'Why did no one see it coming?'[78] These problems have only become amplified in the wake of 2008 by the continued onset of disruptive technological change, global health emergencies, and the escalation of geopolitical tensions, which have tended to invalidate the forward-looking statements almost as soon as they were put together.[79]

The only mechanism of modern political economy that has defied this economic upheaval, just at it has survived every previous crisis of confidence in the future, has been and remains—*debt*. Just as the tales of *Gargantua and Pantagruel* (1653– 1693) once told us, it remains better to 'be still indebted to somebody or other, that there may be somebody always to pray for you' (Rabelais 1892:159). Debt appears to harbour no existential qualms concerning its continued role in our socio-economic architecture in a hundred years-time and, even, in perpetuity. The mainstream economics has 'long ago convinced itself that money, banks and [...] debt' do not merit including in the economic forecasts (Keen 2022:5), while the prominent advocates of 'infinite' debt call to abandon the clumsy orthodoxy of debt's history altogether as it is no longer relevant in today's politico-economic context.[80]

Nietzsche's analysis, which traces the *genealogy of debt* back to pre-history—in order to develop an appreciation for debt's significance as modernity's preeminent value—would suggest otherwise. Nietzsche asserts that debt in its multiple guises— as religion, morality, slavery, the division of labour and, most importantly, as *value* —has many stories to tell us. For this reason alone, it would be ill-suited to being circumscribed by the confines of economic short-termism. Nietzsche is a philosopher of

---

[78] See Steve Keen 2022:3, Geoffrey M. Hodgson (https://www.geoffreymhodgson.uk/letter-to-the-queen, last accessed Feb. 27, 2023), and *The Economist* (2009), 'What went wrong with economics', July 18, 2009, print edition.
[79] See Elliott and Timmermann 2008:3–5 as well as Mokyr 2018:32–35.
[80] See Furman and Summers (2020), who urge us to embrace the new approach to *growing debt infinitely and in perpetuity*. In the corporate world, *non-perishable loans* with interminable commitments have claimed their place a long time ago. It is worth noting that Marx predicted such 'infinity loans' thinking (CW 37:394).

recurring themes for whom 'prehistory' ('Vorgeschichte')—a term that populates his writing from the early *Nachlass* entries (1869) to *The Antichrist* (1888)—is a formative fabric of human experience:[81]

> [E]verything essential in the development of mankind took place in primeval times, long before the four thousand years we more or less know about; during these years mankind may well not have altered very much. (HH: I, *FLT*, §2; my emphasis)

Nietzsche's methodological point, although it is customarily dismissed as speculative, is nonetheless worth pondering. He tells us that *history* is a manner of containing *prehistory* rather than a matter of simply interpreting away from it, having agreed on some arbitrary starting point. The prehistoric echoes of the 'savage, primeval and wholly merciless' forces (UM: III, *SE*, §4) lie dormant deep within our psyche and we commit a great fallacy by mistaking the un-ascertainability of prehistory for its insignificance which happens within the shallow precepts of economistic reason (HH: I, *HMS*, §43).[82]

Nietzsche argues that the weaker we grow, the less able we are to resist prehistory, the stronger we will feel its gravitational force. The less subtle, irrespective of how 'clever' and 'sophisticated', our methods and tools for intuiting prehistory become (e. g., mathematics in place of ethics and aesthetics), the more frenzied our curiosity to understand it will grow, opening up an unfathomable psychological chasm of incommensurability between the means at the disposal of modern sensibility and the ends which drive it (see HH: I, §217). We are inevitably pulled back into the vortex of prehistory just as we imagine ourselves pedalling away from it at an increasingly maddening pace (BT: §15).

History and prehistory morph into the metahistorical circle where the point of origin—discernible only as Nietzsche's will to power, i.e., 'the origin of the movement' (NF-1888:14[98])—breaks up into the multiplicity of origins, each weaving its own trajectory leading simultaneously away from the breaking point and inexorably towards it. This is important for understanding Nietzsche's enduring position that more civilisation, progress and science may lead us towards and back to barbarism just as [we think] they lead us away from it into the yet non-existent but undoubtedly bright future.[83] Our ability (or lack thereof) to discern the direction of travel depends, on Nietzsche's view, on the valuations that guide our journey and on those who hold the lantern of these valuations, illuminating the path.

---

[81] See NF-1869:3[11]; HH: I, §§1–2; GS: §116; and BGE: §31.
[82] Adorno picks up on this point in *Minima Moralia* (1951), arguing that the 'persistence of pre-history', which is 'realised as constantly different, unforeseen, exceeding all expectation, the faithful shadow of developing productive forces' is gruesomely mistaken for the task of 'holding the ultimate calamity in check' (Adorno 2005:233–236).
[83] NF-1872:19[28]; HH: I, *HMS*, §40 and §42; *Tokens*, §251 and §285; and State, §477.

The particular significance of *prehistory*, on Nietzsche's view, is that it sets in motion the recurring patterns of human endeavour.[84] The cycles and the crises they generate are of *considerably longer duration* than those that have become the main preoccupation of economics and of the economists. Nietzsche would likely disagree with Marx's assertion that 'the economists know more about society as it will be' (Tribe 2015:171). Nietzsche's overarching concern is with the unfolding crisis of political economy reflected in the 'catastrophe of a *two-thousand-year* discipline in truth-telling', of which we may be witnessing the final act, itself two centuries in the making (GM: III, §27). Nietzsche tells us that we are observing and participating in the accelerating unravelling of slave morality's world order—the approaching end of its global empire. The political economy of slave morality is increasingly turning on itself in the struggle for [the remaining] resources, maintaining its influence and enslaving parts of the world that have not yet been enslaved. Behind the increasingly open confrontations, ranging from protracted trade wars to the imposition of crippling economic sanctions, and from the orchestrated regime changes to open military conflicts of our time, stands the escalating global crisis of slave morality's political economy. Having flared up, according to Nietzsche, in the second half of the 19th century—a resounding tremor in the wake of the 'death of God'—it would continue to develop as the 'great drama in a hundred acts', taking us towards the close of the 21st century.[85]

Nietzsche's timeframe fuses *repetition* and *duration* of the mini-crises of political economy, which helps to explain the assertion that his *story* is 'the *history* ('Geschichte') of the next two centuries', as though the future's narrative has already been scripted and speaks 'in a hundred signs' that have been seen before (NF-1887:11[411]).[86] Nietzsche's stance is unique even *vis-à-vis* the thinkers who rightly draw attention to the longer-term, structural changes in modern political economy.[87]

The crises of political economy Nietzsche is interested in are neither local, nor discrete, and nor short-term. In lieu of this, no framework of economic analysis—either from his time or presently available—that assumes crises to represent temporary deviations from the otherwise steady course of affairs would be sufficient in terms accommodating his concerns. As Stiegler poignantly surmises:

> [W]hat characterizes the two centuries that for Nietzsche remained still entirely to come, that he sees coming in his present, from his epoch, is the fact that the second industrial revolution takes place, and that it does so as, precisely, the intensification of industrial becoming. Industrial becom-

---

[84] No one explains the significance of 'pre-history' and the pitfalls of looking for 'the origin' better than Thomas Mann in the distinctly Nietzschean *Prelude* to *Joseph and His Brothers* (1933–1948) and Michel Foucault in 'Nietzsche, Genealogy, History' (1977).
[85] Nietzsche makes these comments in the *Genealogy*, written in 1887. Adding 200 years would take us to 2087. Nietzsche's choice of the timing points is warranted in the context of the *Long Depression*, 'the first truly international crisis', estimated to have lasted between 1873–1899 (see Glasner and Cooley, 1997).
[86] See Heller's insightful commentary (1988:5–7) for further context.
[87] E.g., Wolfgang Streeck, Andrew Gamble, and Robert Dyson among contemporary scholars.

ing is what at once brings a new force, the promise of a future that, after the death of God, will break with two thousand years of Pauline Platonism and badly digested Christianity, but that for now takes the form of a becoming-herdish, that will be for a long time, for two centuries, the exhausting of this reign, the reign of exhaustion even, that is, of discredit—which means in the first place the death of God: a becoming-old, a decadence. (Stiegler 2011:56)

Closely related to the issue of time horizons are the questions concerning the scope and substance of social change. Early on, Nietzsche tells us that economics is 'not yet a science' (NF-1869:3[10]). This comment enunciates his enduring concern with the *hierarchical position* of strictly economic knowledge in the 'the great economy of the whole', as it relates to the authentic capacity of economics to tell us something valuable not simply about a specific segment of human life, but about human life in general (EH: *Destiny*, §4; see D: §179).

Nietzsche has no quarrel with economics being one of the multitude of voices speaking about life. What he objects to most sternly is economics becoming the dominant voice in that conversation in a manner reminiscent of the ideological tyranny of Christianity over life. He would be happy to pack economics into [the grand economy of] life but remains firmly opposed to life being crammed into economics. This is why Nietzsche questions whether the valuations underwriting the discourse on political economy (and economics), irrespective of whether they are expressed in the language of morality or via the mathematical formulae, exhibit certain underlying continuity and, furthermore, whether the language of mathematics, under the guise of scientific appearance, becomes a better hiding place for such valuations, i.e., whether the science of economics remains thoroughly moralised and becomes a more effective tool of the same oppressive ideology which Nietzsche discerns in Christianity. Nietzsche's comment concerning the scientific aspirations of economics needs to be situated within the call for the transition 'from the moral to the knowing humankind' (HH: I, *HMS*, §107) as part of 'translating man back into nature' (NF-1881:11[211]; BGE: §230). It does not merely express the view that economics of his time is not yet sufficiently de-theologised and de-moralised to become a science. Rather, it contains an important premonition that economics, as an instrument of slave morality used to subjugate humankind, would get further detached from life in the future, unless the valuations underwriting it were to change drastically.

Nietzsche, likely under the influence of Lange, harbours doubt regarding whether economics was not invented as a 'science' for strictly political reasons by the particular 'kinds of servants of truth' (NF-1873:29[26]).[88] In this context, divorcing the 'science' of economics from the wider normative claims that formed part of political economy would, for Nietzsche, remain a significant issue haunting modernity. The entanglement of politics and economics, which draw from the shared pool of [reactive] valuations,

---

[88] Adorno was more scathing in this respect: '[P]olitical economy, the conception of which theory grimly gave to liberalism, is proving to be ephemeral. Economics is a special case of economizing, *lack prepared for domination*' (Adorno 2003:100; my emphasis).

would be liable to produce the systematic and pervasive debasement of the political, as it would be called upon to legitimise the perverse strutcture and functioning of the economic, whose [fully complicit] abductee it is bound to remain.[89] In order to avoid this 'democratic atomic tangle' (NF-1873:29[52]), which could become the medium for turning 'nature, life and humanity' into the 'mere addenda to the logic of the market' (Ek, Mekonnen 2014:5), Nietzsche is firmly of the view that the 'elements [...] suitable for mastering science' must include 'the deepest basic problems of ethics and [...] the question of the value of existence' (NF-1872:19[28]). To borrow from Karl Löwith, for Nietzsche, as it was for Marx, 'even the criticism of "political economy" is and remains oriented toward the totality of the historical world and the related form of human existence' (Löwith 1991:152).

Challenging Discourse

Thomas Brobjer notes that Nietzsche's refusal to pay homage to the 'professional' conversation on political economy was predicated on his objection to the very constitution of this discourse rather than the lack of knowledge and understanding of political and economic questions (Brobjer 2002:312). This book explores some of the reasons behind Nietzsche's intellectual stance. I argue that Nietzsche's refusal to incorporate himself into the conventional disciplinary discourse is, in substance, consistent with his position on the critique of Christianity and the modern social orders. He sees these phenomena as pervasively tainted by the reactive valuations of *slave morality*, born from the pathos of *ressentiment* (GM: I, §10).

Speaking the language of slave morality makes it impossible to disentangle oneself from the fetters of its reactive valuations. In considering how to overcome the 'nihilistic consequences of the political and economic way of thinking' (NF-1885:2[127]), Nietzsche does not wish to be bound by any of the conventions of the existing social orders—normative, institutional, moral, past, or present—responsible for its onset and universal spread (NF-1888:25[1]). Nietzsche wishes, for that reason, to step outside of such constructs in order to preserve a degree of intellectual distance in dealing with them. His is an audacious and highly controversial attempt to loosen, if not to break, the chains of time which inexorably confine us to the present and in so doing skew our vision. As Althusser points out, 'what classical political economy does not see is not what it does not see, it is what it sees; the oversight is not to see what one sees,

---

[89] This can be seen as a variation of 'Gresham's Law', which is an observation stating that 'bad money drives out good'. 'Gresham's Law' was recognised by the ancient Greeks, including the playwright, Aristophanes, in *The Frogs* (c. 405 B.C.) and the first *'revaluer of values'*—Diogenes of Sinope (c. 412/403—c. 324/321 B.C.) who, having allegedly misunderstood an oracle of Apollo, debased the *financial currency* instead of re-stamping *city's custom*—i.e., its *political currency* and *values* (see Diogenes Laertius, *Lives of Eminent Philosophers*, Book VI, Chapter 20).

the oversight no longer concerns the object, but the *sight itself* (Althusser 2015:22; my emphasis).[90]

Nietzsche's assertion is that the political economy of his day represents one of the primary tongues utilised by *slave morality* in secular modernity for the perpetuation of its profoundly nihilistic valuations (NF-1885:2[127]). Nietzsche views the prevailing discourse on political economy as, at the same time, disabling and disaggregating the social fabric of modernity. Political economy's development traces the transition from the Christian theology to the secular ideologies of the money-economy, including economics. This transition conceals rather than revealing, let alone resolving, the underlying tensions or overcoming the value propositions of *slave morality*, which continue to plague human affairs. In its unabating, yet disembodied quest for power over every one of life's domains, *slave morality* uses political economy to disguise the increasingly dystopian character of modernity with the tales of economic growth and progress while effectively obscuring its own *ouroboric predicament*.[91]

In order to get at the dis-embedding and disabling propensities of political economy—to expose its metaphysics of concealing own valuations—Nietzsche seeks an entry point into the conversation that would allow him to get under the carapace of the discourse on political economy. To illustrate the subtlety of Nietzsche's undertaking, it may be helpful, by way of an analogy, to engage with Nietzsche's mention of the Russian folk tale about 'Kashchey the Deathless':

> The power which resides in a certain object, is bound to a particular location. Only if the object is destroyed, the power and possibly the life contained in it would also be destroyed. The object itself is named 'death' or 'life'— 'in the egg is hidden my death' ... so goes the Russian [tale -DS] ... reminiscent of the metaphysicians who also separate the 'power' from the will. (NF-1877:22[117])

As the tale goes, so preoccupied was Kashchey with his own death that he even cast a spell on himself that would prevent him from dying or being killed. Still uncertain whether the spell made him truly invulnerable, the fearsome villain decided to remove his own soul from his body. Kashchey hid his soul in a needle, which was concealed inside an egg. The egg was placed inside a duck and the duck nested inside a hare. The hare was a locked inside an iron box, which was buried deep under the roots of a mighty oak tree, where no one was meant to find it. Having done this, Kashchey made himself better protected and more vulnerable at the same time. The principal difficulty lay in finding the well-hidden needle, while snapping it, if and once found, was easy and would spell the end of Kashchey the Deathless. Nietzsche's audacious undertaking, the objective of his political economy, is to find the proverbial needle of *slave morality*, which has become well disguised and guarded by the multiple layers of modern sensibility. In order to approach this daunting task, to start unpicking slave mor-

---

[90] Althusser echoes Nietzsche's insight concerning 'wishing not to see something that one does see; wishing not to see something as one sees it' (AC: §55).
[91] See NF-1885:2[127] and GM: I, §§10–11, and III, §§11–15.

ality's many coats, Nietzsche argues it is necessary, for him, to step outside of all existing social orders.

Thinking 'Outside of All Social Orders'

Different Nietzsche scholars and critics rightfully question the value and pertinence of Nietzsche's dis-embedded critique of modernity.[92] Adorno, among others, insisted that Nietzsche's call for the revaluation of all values would end up with no conceptual anchor in reality and no plausible foundation in society, 'as though his critique of bourgeois civilisation did not bear within itself the violence of its own historical and social facticity' (Gadamer 2000:56).[93] Still, Nietzsche's insistence that he is thinking 'outside of all social orders' (NF-1886:5[71], §14) and 'at the other end from all modern ideology' (BGE: *Free Spirit*, §44) merits careful consideration, as well as requiring contextualisation.

Nietzsche is acutely aware that it would be 'a piece of self-deception' to suppose that one may 'extricate oneself from degeneration merely by waging war upon it' (TI: *Socrates*, §11). He attempts to gain the maximum *pathos of distance* from the existing social orders and their ideologies, in order to reflect on their values in a 'moraline-free' language (AC: §6). He wishes to overcome the inverted causality of decadence, embedded in its discourses, by lifting the 'veil of corruption' from the 'ideals of humanity', beneath which hide values of decline and decadence that, in his assessment, reinforce conditions of existence detrimental for humankind (AC: §6). To overcome this constraint, he develops a radical and comprehensive critique of modern industrial culture, which he sees as a synthetic medium within which the crisis of modern values becomes disclosable (GS: §40).

Staten rightly insists on the importance of properly ascertaining 'Nietzsche's location within the conundrum' in order to accurately infer 'his implication in the terms he is manipulating' (Staten 1989:82). This study contends that part of the solution when it

---

[92] See Adorno 2002:173–217; Habermas 1990:185–187; Ansell-Pearson 1994:41; and Drolet 2013:46.
[93] It is important to consider the famous charge of 'performative contradiction' levied against Nietzsche by Adorno (2002) and his student (and stern critic), Jürgen Habermas (1990). Nietzsche's attempt to get 'outside of the social orders' is not the same as him wanting to get off of this planet in a theological sense. Rather, he attempts to *see past the thick fog of slave morality* that envelops this planet. It is important to appreciate that Nietzsche *does not object to reason* as such but to the 'false and unjustified application of the principle of sufficient reason' (*TLEMS*, 255). His war is not with *reason* in general, such but with the reason corrupted by the valuations of *slave morality*. Nietzsche's ambitious undertaking is to conceive of the transformation of [the profoundly 'instrumentalised'] reason into intellect by overcoming slave morality's distorting influence, rather than attempting to pole vault above and past reason while using the latter as his pole. Philosopher's duty is to use all resources at his disposal regardless of how critical of them he might be (BGE: §61). Nietzsche attempts to rise above the bar placed on the development of reason by slave morality, which, akin to a toxic atmosphere, envelops and saturates reason, disabling it.

comes to developing a balanced inquiry into Nietzsche's political economy lies in respecting his claim that his undertaking is an attempt to think 'outside of the existing social orders' (NF-1886:5[71]). Nietzsche's insistence on 'untimeliness' contains an important message and forms an important element of his undertaking. He sees it as his duty to 'overcome his time in himself, to become "timeless"' (TCW: *Preface*).[94] This aspect of his project remains underemphasised in the current scholarship. I argue, to the contrary, that Nietzsche's effort to extricate himself from such socio-temporal constraints is vital to his ability to problematise the political economy of slave morality.

A critique of the political economy of a specific social order—of a particular 'ism'—is not Nietzsche's intention. Instead, his critique problematises the core values shared, on his view, by capitalism and socialism, commonly regarded as the antagonistic social orders of modernity. As a result, Nietzsche's consideration on the themes of political economy involves distinct categories and unorthodox conceptualisations—his distinctive conceptual coinage—compared to those used in the conventional discourse. His stated objective is twofold. Nietzsche wishes to examine the 'physiology of values and ideals', including the 'political ideals' of modernity (NF-1887:11[143]) and to combine this analysis with an 'economic valuation' of previous ideals (NF-1887:10[10]) in order to arrive at an 'economic justification of virtue' (NF-1887:10[11]).

At first glance, Nietzsche's propositions appear counterintuitive. This seems to be the case when, for example, he suggests that we should be concerned with an 'economic valuation of morality', rather than with a moral evaluation of economy (NF-1887:10 [8]). Here, however, lies the first clue. Nietzsche hypothesises that even if there were no discernible inception point in sight as to which came first, the economic or the moral, the two realms are inextricably connected. The economy may not, in the first instance, rise from morality, but morality, as economy's mental projection, may have at some point assimilated an economic way of interpreting reality which enabled it to imprint upon the economy and, possibly, come to dominate it.

Nietzsche's approach highlights the tangled and circular relationship between the moral and the economic. His intention is to alter our frame of reference. The difficult question, on his view, is not to trace the movement from economy to morality or vice-versa, but to discern the economy in the valuations of morality which structure the economy. In particular, he wishes us to focus on the 'Circe of humanity'—*slave morality*—which, having once derived from the 'breeding ground' of economy (GM: II, §6), has since falsified 'all psychologica in the ground' (EH: *Books*, §5). On Nietzsche's view, this is certainly true in relation to debt, slavery, and the division of labour, all of which have been thoroughly distorted by the valuations of slave morality. More generally, Nietzsche maintains that what we take to be 'economic' today is not at all economic in the original sense of the 'general economy of life' (BGE: §23). All economic valuations

---

94 In this context, it is useful to recall Nietzsche's earlier discussion in *The Birth of Tragedy* concerning 'the timeless servants of their god who lives outside the spheres of society' (BT: §8).

have been thoroughly invested with *slave morality*, which, in an effort to subjugate them to its reactive power-will, sought to distance itself from life so as to establish for itself a higher provenance (GM: II, §20–21). This alone would render any moral evaluation of economy a futile exercise as morality would be called upon to evaluate itself.[95]

The task Nietzsche sets for himself is not as simple as establishing whether the economic or the moral method of evaluation came first. Nietzsche questions the origins of values rather than the origin of existence. His project does not end with an attempt to simply de-moralise economic categories and valuations, as he ventures to de-leverage our morals. Nietzsche does not draw an equivalence between life and economy in the sense of the latter designating life's furthermost frontier. Life must be continually pointing beyond itself in order to remain life which means life's true economy cannot be compressed into formulas:

> [L]ife must overcome itself again and again! Life itself wants to build itself into the heights with pillars and steps; it wants to gaze into vast distances and out upon halcyon beauties—therefore it needs height! And because it needs height, it needs steps and contradiction between steps and climbers! Life wants to climb and to overcome itself by climbing. (Z: II, *Tarantulas*)

The great economy of life is its engine, enabling life's continual overcoming of itself, but it is not life's final destination. Nietzsche considers it a perilous error to confuse life's means for its ends, because doing so invariably corrupts both the ends and the means.[96] He argues that the 'great economy' of life, having been saturated with the valuations of slave morality, ceased being 'great' and, like the politics of slave morality, has become petty and noxious (GS: §1 and NCW, *Epilogue*, §1). Deprived of its scope, depth, and subtlety and in this deformed shape forced into the cage of reductive economic abstractions, economy has been designated as life's end, causing its decline, which is nevertheless hailed as progress.

Nietzsche makes untangling these distortions his task. His project cannot be likened or limited to thoroughly polishing the darkened silver of economic values, oxidised by *slave morality*, so that their original glitter is restored. Nietzsche invites us on an arduous intellectual journey to a point where the goals that would transcend the economy as we understand it today may become discernible and 'new and more robust ideals' can be posited.[97] Nietzsche asserts that one inevitably 'digs up morality when one digs up boundary-stones' (HH: II, WS, §285) from which he infers 'the de-

---

[95] It is worth remembering that *Circe* was a sorceress, who transformed Odysseus' men into swine but was then forced by Odysseus to change them back. Nietzsche's project, however, is different. It is not about simply reversing valuations to what they were once before. Nietzsche rejects any possibility of going back in time (see GS: §377; BGE: §32). Instead, his undertaking to change men (now swine) back to being men is to build them from the beginning and thus it is a question of 'creating a foundation' for the 'world-economic point of view' (NF-1887:9[1/4]).
[96] See NF-1887:10[137] and NF-1888:14[158].
[97] See NF-1887:10[117] and UM, III, SE, §6.

pendence of all values on the morality of the religious, aesthetic, economic, political, scientific' components of the social (NF-1886:7[8]).[98] As such, Nietzsche approaches slave morality not as a mere artefact, but as a pervasive and enduring 'condition of existence' (NF-1882:6[4]). There is not, on his view, a single facet of Western civilisation—political, economic, educational, or cultural—that is not saturated by its valuations. These are 'thought through in the minutest and subtlest detail and imprinted in every will and every faculty' (D: §175). This is how *slave morality* becomes installed as 'a law, as a categorical imperative, over humanity'.[99]

Slave Morality and Political Economy

Nietzsche's critique of *slave morality* is one of the most written about as well as being one of the most contested subjects within Nietzsche scholarship. The meaning of *slave morality* within the context of *political economy*, however, represents a largely uncharted terrain. The questions of the *political and economic significance of slave morality* as well as Nietzsche's insistence on its overriding importance in shaping the social fabric of modernity (NF-1886:7[8]), remain underexplored and constitute the focus of the present inquiry. I do not propose an elaborate expedition into 'the enormous, distant, and so well-hidden land' of *slave morality* (GM: *Preface*, §7), having traversed which many a diligent reader would likely emerge no less confused as to what the big deal about it really is.

Slave morality is skilled at interpreting away from itself an interpreting itself away from reality to the point where it appears as no more than a stillborn brainchild of a few eclectic minds, a paranoid conjuration that has no bearing either on the proceedings of the real world, or on the state of human affairs. To circumvent this possible *impasse* at the hands of the beast adept at lying 'in all the tongues of good and evil' (Z: I, *New Idol*) and intent on luring one into its mind-bending labyrinths, I venture a brief sketch on which this inquiry relies in an attempt to better understand not only what *slave morality* is but *what it does* and *how it operates* in the sphere of political economy. After all, Nietzsche's important philosophical intuition suggests that it should be possible to develop an understanding of a phenomenon without having to force it into the vice of definition.

Nietzsche's concept of *slave morality* is indebted to the psychic determinism emanating from Plato's 'tripartite soul':[100]

---

98 See also NF-1887:10[8].
99 See EH: *Destiny*, §7, and NF-1888:14[105].
100 See Nietzsche's discussion in UM: II, *UDHL*, §10; HH: II, *WS*, §183; D: §76; TI: *Socrates*, §9; TI: *Ancients*, §4; TI: *Skirmishes*, §47, TI: Errors, §8, and TI: *Reason*, §4: 'the higher may not grow out of the lower, may not have grown at all'. See also Nietzsche's early 'Fragment of a Critique of Schopenhauer' (1868): '[T]here is an ethical aristocracy just as there is a spiritual one: one cannot enter it by receiving a title or by marriage. The unchangeable character is influenced in its expressions by its environment and education

> [N]o one gives man his qualities—neither God, nor society, nor his parents and ancestors, nor he himself. One is necessary, one is a piece of fatefulness. (TI: *Errors*, §8)

Within this context, slave morality denotes the system of valuations that, in a latent form, can be found in the physiological predicament characterised by the condition of the mind (*Logos*) partitioned from the spirit (*Thumos*) and nurtured predominantly by the (insatiable appetites of the) stomach (*Eros*).[101] When this disrupted configuration of the human *psyche* is immersed in the solvent of 'bad conscience' (GM: II, §14–16), where *Eros* is denounced as morally culpable, the consciousness of *being in debt*, in consequence of own deficiency, becomes inaugurated.[102] *Eros* unreflectively desires what it lacks but this desire lacks its object—that intangible ingredient, attaining which would bring about the feeling of completeness and fulfilment.

This psychological vulnerability is etched into the designation of *Eros* as the source of its continued *moral indebtedness* and a corrosive influence on *Logos*. It embeds the 'incarnate wish for being otherwise' (GM: III, §13) without supplying the means for overcoming the entanglement it accentuates. This predicament locks in the inability of *Eros* for being otherwise and constitutes the psychic feedback loop without the safety valves. Uncurbed by the 'forbidding principle' of *Thumos* (R:439[c]), it lacks the ability to sublimate its condition by generating affirmative valuations that would allow to assimilate unabridged reality (GM: II, §16).[103]

Having so suppressed 'the active and interpretative powers' of the 'value-positing eye', which is now 'turned in no direction at all', which Nietzsche likens to the disabling of reason, this volatile formation is brought into motion—*awakened*—by an injection of *ressentiment* from without which, by inducing displacement, exteriorises the causality of internal strife (see GM: I, §10, II, §12). This, in turn, gives rise to the *reactive* value-creating drives that flow within the closed circle of *slave morality*—'as the only scheme of interpretation by which man can endure himself' (NF-1887:10[121])—which is now ripe for exploitation by the forces that can draw strength from its valuations.

—not in its essence' (Kaufmann 1994:31). It is worth bearing in mind that Nietzsche conceptualises the hierarchy of the Platonic soul in terms of the 'quanta of power': 'rank is determined by the amount of power you are' (NF-1887:11[36]). Nietzsche further asserts that underwriting 'every thought, every feeling and every will' is not any 'one particular drive, but an *overall* [physiological] condition' (NF-1885:1[61]). See also Salter's excellent discussion 'Nietzsche and The War', 1917:363–364, and Safronov 2022:14–16.

101 Plato's 'tripartite soul', which Nietzsche builds on directly, is later re-conceptualised by Freud in terms of the *id* (a.k.a. Eros), the *ego* (a.k.a. Thumos) and the *superego* (a.k.a. Logos). Compare Plato's *Phaedrus*, 246[a-e] and *Republic*, 434[a]-442[d] with Freud's analysis in 'The Anatomy of Mental Personality', Lecture XXXI, 1933:107–109.

102 See Nietzsche's discussion of the 'drives transformed by moral judgement': 'the same drive evolves into the painful feeling of cowardice under the impress of the reproach custom has imposed upon this drive (D: §38).

103 See NF-1887:10[111]. This psychic dislocation, among other effects (e. g., amplifying anxiety, mental health concerns), germinates the hostile disposition *vis-a-vis* the external world. See Leonard 2012:159.

This is an important thing to highlight: political economy of *slave morality* thrives on embellishing and promoting the very phenomena it construes as morally objectionable (with good reason), the consequences of which it seeks to punish and the causes of which it conceals underneath mendacious valuations.[104]

Slave morality, Nietzsche tells us, has always existed as a configuration of the reactive power-will (BGE: §260).[105] He finds traces of slave morality as far back as 'ten thousand years', when the point has been reached 'step by step, in a few large regions on the earth, where it is no longer the consequences but the origin of an action that one allows to decide its value' (BGE: §32). It was, however, the advent of Christianity —the rise of the carefully cultivated 'metaphysics of the hangman' based on a profound revaluation of values (i.e., 'the rape of the conscience') required to conceal its predatory essence—that inaugurated *slave morality's* emergence as the most powerful worldview to have steered the proceedings of Western civilisation well into the present day.[106]

Slave morality, as a ubiquitous and subtle layer of *valuations*, represents, nevertheless, an implacable harness strapped firmly around a meagre domain of *consciousness* from which it becomes indistinguishable. This harness offers a degree protection against the harshness of reality and, at the same time, akin to the ancient practices of foot-binding, it precludes the development of the mind beyond its clearly sign-posted perimeter, as a result of which the latter remains irredeemably narrow and superficial —i.e., engineered to suit particular purposes:[107]

> [T]he thinking that rises to consciousness is only the smallest part of all [thinking; DS]—the most superficial and the worst part—for only this *conscious thinking* takes the form of words, which is to say signs of communication, and this fact uncovers the origin of consciousness (GS: §354; my emphasis)

Nietzsche tells us that values, or valuing drives, rise from deep inside (physiology, hardware) of human nature. They represent forces and a kind of psychic energy that, having risen to the surface of consciousness (software), become articulated in terms of the valuations of slave or master morality (response anchors) as the scale points or units of measurement, etched into graduated scale (ladder) of human sensibility and aptitude. Nietzsche views consciousness, the perimeter of which is demarcated by the valuations of *slave morality*, as representing 'only a net of communication between human beings' which grows under the pressure of the *need* for communication in order to reach an

---

104 Systematic distortion and demonisation of *human sensuality* represent the collateral damage of this process (see TI: *Morality*, §§1–3), and underwrite Nietzsche's undertaking for 'translating man back to nature' (NF-1881:11[211] and BGE: §230).
105 It is a critical and frequently overlooked point that 'slave morality' as an embodiment of the 'priestly spirit' pre-exists or exists outside of history, which it seeks to write and re-write (see NF-1888:14[204]).
106 See, respectively, BGE: §52; TI: *Errors*, §7; TI: *Skirmishes*, §36; AC: §27; TI: *Improvers*, §4, and AC: §21. See Nietzsche's further elucidations in NF-1875:5[91] and TI: *Morality*, §1.
107 See NF-1883:7[6]/E-3; NF-1886:5[71]; GS: §354; NF-1885:37[4]; NF-1887:9[144]; and BGE: §286.

agreement.¹⁰⁸ *Slave morality* becomes a form of crippling control over the consciousness as a result of which thinking that occurs within its boundaries is damaged through pervasive moralisation.¹⁰⁹ Nietzsche conceptualises *slave morality* in terms of the 'corruption' and 'paralysis' of reason (AC: §5, §10) and 'castration of the intellect' (GM: II, §10).

The real power of *slave morality* is that, within the framework of disrupted psychic arrangement, it does not simply influence *what* we think but also organises and structures *thinking* itself by re-directing its flow along the viaduct of its valuations (escape from which, other than an occasional accidental splash, is impossible; see D: §117; NF-1881:11[287]) such that an outcome of thinking—*what* we think—appears as a *fait accompli*. Slave morality becomes 'a kind of training in looking in a certain *definite* direction, the will to a perspective that seeks to make it impossible to see oneself' (NF-1883:7[6]), while, at the same time, pleading 'not to think too meanly of that which two thousand years of morality have bred in our spirit' (NF-1885:2[178]). In other words, *slave morality* supplies not just the projector but also the screen onto which its images are transmitted.

Slave morality delights in the aura of its ever-increasing complexity, accompanied by the unending drive to formularise reality, which it passes off as profundity and calls 'truth' (NF-1888:18[13]). However, as a product of disrupted psychic unity of the organism, slave morality is *intrinsically incapable* of operating in any other than the domain of abstract notions, i.e., represented reality.¹¹⁰ Its interaction with the real world, with the natural world, is inevitably antagonistic because *slave morality* projects a 'mendaciously fabricated world' onto the reality it seeks to subjugate.¹¹¹

Slave morality represents a *closed system of valuations* (D: §117; TI: *Skirmishes*, §5) that would rather see the natural world and human life destroyed than admit to its life-negating instincts and risk losing the stranglehold it has established over life (GM: III, §11; TI: *Ancients*, §4).¹¹² *Slave morality* becomes a particular manner of processing and receiving the world, of interpreting and interacting with it on the basis of being *unable assimilate its fullness* within itself and the corresponding inability (frequently disguised as unwillingness) to assimilate itself into the world's fullness. For

---

108 Nietzsche's views on the nature and origins of consciousness can be seen as envisaging the internet (i.e., www.)—as a network and medium of communication, which activates individual users and links them into one extensive network, which is circumscribed by specific programming rules. In like manner, consciousness is an *environment* within which individual minds are at once awakened and connected with one another. Control over the environment guarantees control over the mind. Implementation of this control is, in simplified terms, slave morality's *raison d'etre* and its chief function.
109 See Nietzsche's discussion in GS: §354; NF-1884:30[10] and AC: §14. See also NF-1885:2[203] and NF-1887:9[95] on 'enchanted and subdued' reason placed under the rule of distorted 'value judgements'.
110 Nietzsche tells us that the 'moral values as illusory values compared with physiological values' (NF-1888:14[104]). This illusoriness is also exemplified, among other things, by 'the victory of scientific method over science' (NF-1888:15[51]). See also Nietzsche's discussion in TI: *Reason*, §3, and AC: §10 and §25.
111 See NF-1870:3[11]; NF-1888:14[109]; and AC: §10.
112 See Stiegler 2011:55–57 and Safronov 2022:25–26.

this reason, before slave morality can authoritatively label some things 'good' and others—'evil', it must engage in a profound inversion of phenomenal (both, natural and social) *causes* and *effects* (AC: §25).

Throughout his writing career, Nietzsche too wrestles with the difficulties entailed in articulating the chasmic propensity of slave morality's value inversions. The key thing that he wishes to relay about slave morality's value inversions is their non-linearity. The axes of 'good-bad' and 'good-evil' are not commensurate with each other. A debt that has gone 'bad' does not [automatically] become 'evil'. The old, noble range of valuations designated by 'good' and 'bad' is a horizontal, physiological, and agonistic spectrum.[113] The revalued (by the ascetic priest) scale of 'good' and 'evil' is a psychological (i.e., conscious—imagined but lacking reality), vertical and antagonistic register. In the former case, it is a 'spontaneous' scale that extends in the direction of either of its extreme points without causing a 'contradiction'.[114] In the latter case, the scale is 'an afterthought', and 'evil' becomes something to be fought and eradicated.[115] The former represents a psychic hierarchy which requires the 'pathos of distance' in order to remain active (GM: III, §14). The latter is intrinsically reactive and inevitably succumbs to the tyranny of equalisation (HH: II, *AOM*, §89). The revaluation of 'good-bad' into 'good-evil' is not symmetrical in the sense that what was formerly 'good' is not simply renamed into 'bad'. Instead, what was formerly 'good' is demoted and refashioned as 'evil', while that which was a lowly 'bad' is upgraded and crawls up to take the seat vacated by the former 'good'. Nietzsche asserts that 'when something is designated as *evil*, it gives expression to a relation of *fear* and, accordingly, to *weakness*' (NF-1887:9[138]; my emphasis). Following this logic, he contends that as a result of 'good' being recast as 'evil', a certain alchemic 'transformation of the drives by moral judgement' takes place which allows to regard 'evil' as something objectionable, rather than representing a possibly unattractive but necessary part of human life, and just another designation of 'bad' (D: §38; GM: I, §11).

Nietzsche suggests that in order to understand the 'strange madness of moral judgements' (D: §189), it might be helpful to visualise *slave morality* as a story that needs narrating twice, from two different perspectives. He alludes to Hesiod's famous discussion of the 'five ages' in *Works and Days*. Nietzsche suggests that the author had to tell the story of the same age twice. Once, as that of the 'age of Homeric heroes' and

---

113 Nietzsche associates the original, 'noble', meaning of 'good' as signifying health, happy disposition, strength and power (of spirit), while 'bad' designates weakness, poverty (of spirit), sickness, powerlessness and wretchedness (see GM: I, §7).

114 Nietzsche readers and commentators, who pick up on his distinction between 'Schuld' (guilt) and 'Schulden' (debts), frequently overlook an equally telling distinction between 'schlecht' (bad) and 'schlicht' (simple). The original designation of 'bad', Nietzsche argues, harboured no enmity. Instead, it 'referred to the simple, the common man with *no derogatory implication*, but simply in contrast to the nobility' (GM: I, 4–5). See GM: I, §§4–5 (regarding 'schlecht' and 'schlicht') and II, §4 (regarding 'Schuld' and 'Schulden').

115 See GM: I, §11.

the second time as of the story of the 'iron age' of humanity.[116] This was done in order to accommodate two *irreconcilable* perspectives—that of the 'knightly generation' of heroes revered as 'the good old times' and its opposite—the view of those who suffered 'the terrible iron oppression of adventurous 'Gewaltmensch' ('violent men') and to whom they appeared evil' (D: §189; GM: I, §11). Unlike Hesiod, Nietzsche attempts to unwind the value inversions of *slave morality* in a single narrative where the two perspectives are forced to collide with one another in order to expose its alchemy:

> If one asks oneself what in the whole phenomenon of the sacred has been so immensely interesting to people of all kinds and times ... it is without a doubt the *appearance of the miracle* that is inherent in it, namely the *immediate succession of opposites*, of morally opposed states of the soul: it was *believed* to be tangible that a 'bad person' would suddenly become a 'saint', a good person. (BGE: §47; my emphasis)

Nietzsche argues that in reality, which has become irretrievably distorted by slave morality, 'the more terrible and greater the passions are that a time, a people, an individual can allow themselves' without being consumed by them (i.e., using them only 'as a means' and sublimating them so that 'every past evil may be put into service'), the smaller 'the kingdom of evil' will develop around them. The reverse is that 'the more mediocre, weaker and cowardly a person is, the greater the kingdom of evil' that grows around him will become until, finally, 'the lowest man will see the kingdom of evil everywhere' (NF-1887:9[138]. The inversion of values is so embedded in the human consciousness that it becomes impossible to reverse these changes by simply re-tracing one's steps using logic. The non-linear nature of inversions, highlighted by Nietzsche, underscores the difficulty entailed in conceptualising, let alone achieving, the revaluation of values, because it enslaves us so profoundly that no less than a step-change in sensibility is required in order to overturn slavish valuations.

He maintains that 'to prepare an inversion of value for a certain strong type of people of the highest spirituality and willpower' (NF-1885:3[8]) would represent a painstakingly slow process during which the ideas, which are destined one day to become 'the most powerful', must 'remain small and powerless' (NF-1881:11[158]; see GM: I, §11). A distinct impression is created that one would either have to be born with, or become open to assimilating Nietzsche's values of strength, health and power rather than trying to derive the 'right values' by deduction. The latter, Nietzsche warns, is precisely the track that slave morality wishes us to follow—as a path of piecemeal improvement and slowly becoming better (TI: *Improvers*, §1–5)—though following it would invariably impede any and every attempt at a genuine revaluation of values.

The politico-economic meaning of *slave morality* that can be gleaned from Nietzsche's writings is that of a mandate granted by the obsequious multitude for its own continued *enslavement* at the hands of the 'levellers'—i.e., the agents of reactive power who, in modernity, are exemplified by the wide array of money-interests and

---

[116] See Hesiod's discussion of the 'age of happy heroes' and of the 'iron age' (2006:101–103).

their political *attachés*, jointly—the secular priests of slave morality.[117] The essence of their craft is to make their subject, the modern slave, not only unaware of but increasingly oblivious to the gradual transformation of his condition from that of a benign 'commodity' habitually traded in the global marketplace on par with others, as Marx would have it, into that of an unreflective—abundant and greatly debased—*renewable resource*.[118] The political economy of slave morality oversees the relentless pursuit, commonly known by the name of *economic progress*, of the most efficient and economical way of utilising this resource. Under the auspices of industrial culture this is achieved by continually amplifying the innermost but unrealisable longing of the enslaved for *freedom and equality*[119] through embellishing their sense of material well-being, security and alleviation of suffering within the tightly controlled perimeter of political accommodation, commonly known as *democracy:*

> What they would like to strive for with all their powers is the universal green-pasture happiness of the herd, with security, lack of danger, comfort, and an easier life for everyone; the two songs and doctrines which they repeat most often are 'equality of rights' and 'sympathy for all that suffers'—and suffering itself they take for something that must be abolished. (BGE: §44).

Nietzsche problematises the process that gets underway with the advent of industrial capitalism as one where continued *spiritual disarmament* would eventually pave the way to tyranny and slavery. It is no accident, on Nietzsche's view, that the industrial culture of modernity 'wants everyone to crawl on their stomachs with the deepest submission to the greatest of all lies—this lie is called "equality of men"—as it honours exclusively the levelling and equalizing virtues' (NF-1885:37[14]; see TI: *Skirmishes*, §43). Mollycoddled by slave morality's mendacious narratives, individual's spirit and ability for critical thinking become gradually eroded and replaced, in the course of the formally *fair economic exchange*, with material well-being, profit-seeking, [financial] wealth creation and capitalistic trinketry.[120]

Nietzsche contends that the enslaved beckon their transformation into a consumable resource; they are fully compliant with and desirous of this 'sublime slavery' rather than rising against it (see NF-1885:2[179]). The tragedy of this predicament, according to Nietzsche, is that the modern societal architecture leaves no room for the protective *dams of agency* that would be capable of containing, let alone reversing, social decay (see NF-1888:25[1]; EH: *D*, §2). Lacking in mechanisms that would transform the *detritus* it generates into a cultural surplus, capitalism is doomed not because of its internal structural contradictions but rather due to its inherent inability to birth an

---

117 In BGE §44, Nietzsche aptly describes them as the 'falsely so-called "free spirits"' who, in reality, are 'the eloquent and prolifically scribbling slaves of the democratic taste and its "modern ideas"'.
118 See FEI: Lecture I; UM: III, *SE*, §6; HH: I, §585; HH: II, *WS*, §10; D: §175; and NF-1887:11[341].
119 See Nietzsche's discussion in BGE: §260 concerning 'the longing for freedom, the instinct for happiness and the subtleties of the feeling of freedom' as *necessarily* belonging to slave morality.
120 Nietzsche observes that wherever slave morality becomes preponderant, language tends to bring the words 'good' and 'stupid' closer together (BGE: §260).

alternative vision. All of capitalism's conceptual contrivances—growth, profit, progress, wealth—are self-referencing and incapable of pointing, let alone reaching, beyond themselves. Critically, from Nietzsche's perspective, they are culturally infertile and incapable of endowing human existence with a purpose, let alone a meaning. The nature of valuations that envelop the capitalist social order forms an impenetrable *closed system* that makes it subject to the full consequences of the *law of entropy* (aka the second law of thermodynamics).[121] The highly economic, interconnected and technological world we inhabit today is incapable of generating from within itself a non-economic surplus; material prosperity falls short of producing cultural re-birth because it has been *dishonest* about its own true cost, namely that of 'spiritual slavery', which makes a profound psychic breakdown on a global scale unavoidable (NF-1881:11[294]).

The problem Nietzsche identifies is not so much that with *slave morality* the near-perfect formula for enslavement and exploitation—eminently malleable and not explicitly dependent on overt violence—has been discovered. The real issue, on his view, is that this formula conceals a time bomb—an *infernal machine*—encoded into the consciousness of the slave by making him aware of the inescapability of his psychological predicament. This, Nietzsche tells us, makes it unavoidable that *slave morality* would eventually turn against itself just like the slave, raging against the helplessness to alter his reality, ends up 'battering himself raw on the bars of his cage'.[122] Once the collective modern slave—previously identified by Hobbes with the 'Behemoth' of the Old Testament[123] and exemplified by 'the multitude of ignorant men' (Hobbes 1990:41)—is made aware of his existential predicament, the only thing that can be done is for his brittle psychological condition to be managed until the bitter end.

The process of curtailing the symptoms comes in the form of 'universal deception and cheating', which is better known to us as the 'betterment' and 'improvement' of humankind.[124] It is implemented by applying different kinds of 'balms and ointments' designed to prevent the flare-ups of the 'popular instincts of ressentiment' (GM: I, §16, and III, §15). The bandages supplied are intended for the existential wound that, although it has been exposed (deliberately in order to profit from it), would never heal and cannot be healed. The prescribed medicines change in appearance over time from the theological to the democratic (e.g., freedom, equality, dignity, universal suffrage and education) and the liberal economic (e.g., material well-being). The so-called 'healers', whose appearance, attire and discourses also change, nevertheless, retain an element of continuity.[125] Much as they may protest to the contrary, they have no cure and can only 'help' by making the wound worse.[126]

---

121 See D: §117; GM: II, §20; TI: *Errors*, 5; and AC: §§25–26.
122 GM: II, §16; see Z: I, *Passions*; BGE: §229; and AC: §21.
123 In the *Old Testament*, Behemoth is referred to as a powerful, grass-eating animal whose 'bones are tubes of bronze, his limbs like bars of iron' (Job 40:18).
124 See TI: *Skirmishes*, §33; AC: §1, §51; and NF-1888:14[151].
125 See Klossowski 1997:4–9.
126 See GM: III, §15, §20; NF-1887:9[159].

The price to be paid for this 'theological gamble' with the fate and fortunes of humanity, cooked up in the *'witch's kitchen'* of *slave morality* (UM: III, *SE*, §4), is the highest possible, according to Nietzsche.[127] The process by which *slave morality* presides over its 'moral world order' is far from inexhaustible. It is predicated on sapping humankind's life energies and devouring the natural habitat within which humankind dwells. The more enervated the subjects become, the less energy they can spare on resistance, the more oppressive the power structures squeezing them will become. Sensing the growing weakness and apathy of the masses, these power structures will spawn the oligarchies and breed the tyrants, who will 'augment the universal insecurity and atmosphere of menace' to the point at which 'sparks and flashes may herald dreadful apparitions' (UM: III, *SE*, §4).

Neither the slave made aware of his slavery, nor *slave morality* as the organising principle of modernity (ruling principle of social organisation) can cope with their own consequences—they both end up trampled by the forces they help to unleash.[128] This is the ticking bomb of *slave morality* that Nietzsche's warning is about, the real 'Christian dynamite' (AC: §62). Nietzsche's worry, growing in intensity from the early writings to the last, when it may have finally consumed him, is that—under the spell of *slave morality*—we may, until it is too late, remain heedless of the risk that we could be, quite literally, burning the very end of the wick (hoping, subconsciously, that God will put it out at the very last moment with divinely targeted rainfall), and when the rope inevitably burns out, this social dynamite we have been diligently stockpiling would detonate causing fundamental convulsions, tremors, wars, and earthquakes, the foreboding of which haunts Nietzsche's writings.[129]

This, Nietzsche would tell us, is the *crux of the question of values* and of their importance within the context of political economy. It raises the all-important, on his view, question of whether humankind may be doomed along with capitalism or 'whether we [may] still want to live: and how' (NF-1881:11[141]). It also helps to contextualise the politico-economic dimension of Nietzsche's undertaking to ascertain the values that would 'transcend money and money-making' (UM: III, *SE*, §6), powered by his uncompromising reflections on what the 'revaluation of all values' (*Umwerthung aller Werthe*) would entail and, more importantly, what it would demands of us.

Silver Lining of the Coming Storm

Even the more incisive interpretations of Nietzsche's 'vision of the future' do not place sufficient emphasis upon Nietzsche's doubts and misgivings concerning the 'transition period' to any future state of society (Drochon 2016:176). Although the question of 'how

---

127 See HH: I, *State*, §481; HH: II, *AOM*, §186; NF-1880:6[242].
128 BT: §18; TI: *Skirmishes*, §§38–39; and Connolly 2008:51.
129 See UM: III, *SE*, §4; NF-1881:11[272–274]; NF-1884:26[282]; BGE, §242; GM: III, §18; and EH: *Destiny*, §2.

we move from his contemporary situation' to the future is widely acknowledged and some important conceptual elements of 'his political strategy for getting from A to B' are enunciated (Drochon 2016:156), less consideration is given to the nature, severity, duration, and risks that Nietzsche associates with the crisis, which must be undergone and withstood for such a transition to succeed. This clouds the possibility of even 'guessing the conditions under which future people shall live' and reinforces Nietzsche's insistence on adopting a 'non-moral perspective', which would allow his consideration to proceed 'from a distance' (NF-1883:7[6]).

This inquiry contends that one of Nietzsche's grave doubts concerns the possibility of a 'smooth transition' (Stegmaier 2016:398), i.e., whether the 'war of spirits' could play itself out decisively within the confines of the existing social order and whether the new constellation of the social and, indeed, new values could evolve organically from the crisis of industrial culture of modernity (NF-1883:7[21]). In a *Nachlass* note from 1884, Nietzsche suggested that our valuations change following the change in our 'perceived conditions of existence' (NF-1884:26[45]). Later on, however, he adds that the existing valuations would first need to draw their final consequence in order to open up the possibility for the new ones to rise to prominence (see NF-1887:11[119];[411]).[130]

We would 'first have to experience profound nihilism in order to find out what the value of our modern "values" really was' (NF-1887:11[119]). Viewed in this light, even if 'the aim of Nietzsche's war of spirits is to reignite the *struggle between slave and master morality*' (Drochon 2016:173; my emphasis), the conflict may well unfold against the backdrop of 'a material or moral catastrophe' (Klossowski 1997:152).[131] The 'catastrophe', of which Nietzsche is wary, is not likely to dissipate suddenly, and 'force majeure' may be necessary for the restoration of virtue (NF-1887:11[375]). The emergence of new values cannot happen without the crisis, but the crisis alone is not a sufficient condition for forging these new values. It is neither the purpose nor the function of the crisis to bring about a new arrangement of human affairs. Nietzsche concedes, that since the 'true for us' has been mistaken for the 'truth in itself' for such a long time, 'rethinking it may well turn out to be impossible' (NF-1881:11[286]). Rethinking becomes the task of the forces and agency that emerge from the crisis and are shaped by it in a sense of the profound 'countermovement' (NF-1888:7[114]).

---

130 Zarathustra insists that 'new values' can only be written on 'new tables' (Z: *Prologue*, §8) and that their change is always a 'change of creators', who are also annihilators (Z: *1001 Goals*).
131 Klossowski assesses this trajectory, correctly on my view, as reaching the point when 'the doctrine of the Vicious Circle', having exhausted itself, would become disclosed in terms of its bare essence and, as such, this kind of de-assimilation could be accompanied by 'a material or moral catastrophe' (Klossowski 1997:152). I would respectfully disagree with Kojève's (much as with Fukuyama's) compelling, yet placating fusion of Hegel's history with Nietzsche's excoriating critique of the world populated with the last men. See, in particular, Kojève's engaging discussion in the *Introduction to the Reading of Hegel*, 1980:159-160.

A genuine tension detectable in Nietzsche's writings could, therefore, be interpreted as follows. The crisis of modern values is further exacerbated by the potentially limited time left for any fundamental social transformation to occur and by the depleted human capital and exhausted natural resources with which to accomplish any revaluation of values before the social version of 'heat death'—viz. nihilism (or worse)—takes final hold and becomes irreversible.[132] The transition period is fraught with peril, including the unpredictable and unmitigable risk of, for example, a random asteroid wiping out human life.[133] Nietzsche's concern, however, lies squarely with the long-term consequences of modern industrial culture that, on his view, amplify the overall threat to humankind.

In his darker moments, realising, perhaps, that 'the methods by which his aim was to be accomplished had no fixed assurance' (Salter 1917a:372), Nietzsche concedes that 'ruin is preferable' (NF-1885:2[131]) to the future of 'irreversible *mediocritization*' (NF-1885:2[13]) permeated by 'the melancholy of everything finished' (BGE: §277), where '*experimentation* ceases' and a certain entropic 'stasis is achieved' (NF-1887:11[157]). It is important to appreciate Nietzsche's meaning of 'the end' in this context: 'these acute observers and loiterers discover that *the end* is approaching fast, that everything around them is corrupted and corrupts, that nothing will stand the day after tomorrow, except one type of man, the incurably mediocre' (BGE: §262; my emphasis). Nietzsche is acutely aware that 'nothing is more expensive than the new beginnings' (NF-1887:11[15–16]), and yet 'the snake which cannot shed its skin will perish' (D: §573). His hope, however, is that a window of opportunity to 'fix the animal called "man", who until now has existed and developed as 'the 'unfixed' animal' (NF-1885:2[13]) is still open and that 'the unwise, unjust, guilt-conscious man' is 'not the *antithesis*' of what is to come (and what we must become) but rather the 'necessary preliminary' (HH: I, *HMS*, §107):

> Precisely because we are able to visualize this prospect we are perhaps in a position to prevent it from occurring. (HH: I, *Tokens*, §247)

Nietzsche realises that even tinkering with the 'circular orbit of humanity' (HH: I, *Tokens*, §247) would require summoning 'not an inconsiderable mental power', one which is still on hand in the present age and may be engaged constructively in aiding such a transition (NF-1881:11[27]).

In this regard, the developing crisis of the political economy of modernity may also represent a movement in the right direction. Precarious though it may be, it proceeds in accordance with the first (conservation of energy) and second (entropy) laws of ther-

---

132 See NF-1885:2[13]; NF-1887:11[157]; and NF-1888:14[192].
133 See NF-1873:29[52] and NF-1881:11[228].

modynamics, which Nietzsche intuits from pre-Platonic mythology.[134] This injects a measure of confidence into Nietzsche's undertaking to push further into the crisis (TI: *Skirmishes*, §44), past the end of industrial culture, and, if necessary, through its collapse: 'you must wish to consume yourself in your own flame: how could you wish to become new, unless you had first become ashes?' (Z: I, *Creator*). The challenge of circumnavigating the proverbial Strait of Messina—between Scylla and Charybdis— also adds urgency to his revaluational undertaking to capitalise on the opportunity that 'even now, man and man's earth remain unexhausted and undiscovered' (Z: I, *Virtue*, §2).[135]

As the deepening crisis of modernity occurs under the thickening veil of nihilism endorsed by slave morality, it becomes of the utmost importance to Nietzsche to blow its paralysing cobwebs away with the revaluation of values, so that at least *some* might be able to recognise in time what kind of valuations are in play (NF-1888:14[123]) before modern industrial culture draws its 'strongest conclusion', not unlike in the case of Christianity, 'against itself' (GM: III, §27). Nietzsche's undertaking concerns laying the strategic groundwork for the revaluation of values and, more tactically—'for as long as we live a provisional existence'—it includes 'being our own rulers and setting up small experimental states' (D: §453) as a way of deepening the crisis of the political economy of modernity through relentless genealogical critique: 'one must go forward-step by step further into decadence' (TI: *Skirmishes*, §44).[136] It is also important to keep hold of Nietzsche's own insistence that one can only desire 'the melting away of our social order' if one 'harbours hope' (HH: I, *State*, §443) that:

> [M]en are capable of consciously resolving to evolve themselves to a new culture, they can create better conditions for the propagation of men and for their nutrition, education and instruction, manage the earth as a whole economically, balance and employ the powers of men in general. (HH: I, §24)

Concluding Remarks

Nietzsche's political economy, as is his revaluational project, are firmly anchored in this world (NF-1884:25[438]/2). Understanding them, however, requires a different intellectual space—stepping outside of the existing social orders. These two propositions are neither incompatible nor contradictory. Nietzsche's thinking about the 'economic future of humanity' (NF-1875:9[1]), as well as his conceptions of 'a world economy', entail an element of a distant prospect (NF-1887:10[134]). In order to properly evaluate these

---

134 See Nietzsche's discussion in NF-1870:7[123]; BVN-1870:76; NF-1876:15[27]; HH: I, §170; HH: II, WS, §223; D: §189 and §568; NF-1884:28[42]; and NF-1888:16[32], as well as Raymond Geuss' enlightening commentary in Geuss 2009:81–87 and Geuss 2014:9.
135 See discussion by Del Caro, 2004:101–102.
136 See Conway's compelling discussion of this in *Nietzsche's Dangerous Game*, 2002:82 and 90–91.

concepts a 'greater complexity of effects' and a 'supra-moral attitude would be required' (NF-1887:10[134]). We can discern, however, that the state of affairs Nietzsche envisages is one where 'the last man' and the 'overman' may stand 'side by side', where 'the latter are not regarded as the masters of the former' but rather as pursuing qualitatively different yet interconnected existential objectives (NF-1883:7[21]) in the spirit, which would ensure that 'everyone can carry out their work satisfactorily (NF-1881:11[176]).[137] Nietzsche's vision is radically and substantively different from anything in existence either in his time or, indeed ours. Equally, the tentative outlines of the 'political and economic unity for the sake of a world government' (EH: *TCW*, §2) in the world that 'does not form a unity either as a sensorium or as "spirit"' (TI: *Errors*, §8) appear to be more than modern sensibility, afflicted with slave morality, can adequately grasp:

> Inexorably, hesitantly, terrible as fate, the great task and question is approaching: how shall the earth as a whole be governed? And to what end shall 'man' as a whole—and no longer as a people, a race—be raised and trained? (NF-1885:37[8])

Trying to embed Nietzsche's project in either a pro-capitalistic or anti-capitalistic pathos effectively discounts the possibility that Nietzsche 'worked towards the authentic Third Way' (Hugo and Erik Reinert 2006:76) and attempted to envisage 'entirely new conditions for human development' (Salter 1917:145–146; Sedgwick 2007:24). Klossowski notably comments that in drawing up his philosophical projects Nietzsche strove above all to achieve 'the greatest contrast with our own economic organization' (Klossowski 1997:149). He goes on to point out that if Nietzsche's alternative comes across as 'aggressive', this is due to 'his apprehension of everything' the 'industrializing spirit would go on to develop in the name of an extravagant gregariousness' (Klossowski 1997:150). Considered in this light:

> Nietzsche's 'aristocratism' has nothing to do with a nostalgia for past hierarchies, nor, in order to realize this aristocratism, does he appeal to retrograde economic conditions [...] convinced that the economy has an irreversible hold over the affects—and that the affects are exploited totally for economic ends—Nietzsche constantly interprets socialist systems as pessimistic negations of life's strongest impulses. [He] describes the 'aristocracy of the future' in terms of a behaviour that is at once aggressive with regard to the so-called ends pursued by economic (Anglo-Saxon) optimism, and complicit with every phase of the process that would lead to a generalized (and hence planetary) levelling. (Klossowski 1997:150–152).

---

137 See insightful interpretations by Drochon (2016:4–20) and Franco (2014:461–463) concerning the coming about of the 'two separate spheres—a high cultural one, and a lower democratic one' (Drochon 2016:4) or 'an aristocracy within democracy' (Franco 2014:463) may be attained. My argument departs from these perspectives to the extent that understanding the severity of the crisis that may bring about such existential conditions requires further elucidation, and its outcome is far from certain, on Nietzsche's view.

The present inquiry contends that a more nuanced understanding of Nietzsche's political economy becomes possible if his undertaking is considered to represent a genuine search for the 'third way'. Before Nietzsche's 'future masters of the earth' (NF-1887:37[8]) are ideologised in terms of today's moral prejudices or summarily dismissed, we ought to allow for the possibility that Nietzsche is trying to communicate something *distinctly different*, something our modern ear may not yet be ready to receive, let alone understand. He warns that 'four or five generations' may be required for the kind of changes he has in mind to start materialising (NF-1888:15[78–79]):

> The dissolution of the custom, society, is a state in which the *new egg* (or more eggs) emerge—*eggs (individuals)* as the seeds of new societies and entities. The appearance of individuals is a sign of the attained reproductive capacity of society: as soon as it appears, the old society dies. (NF-1881:11[287]; my emphasis)

Nietzsche's analysis calls for and requires additional intellectual space, where—free from the moral prejudices he criticises—the conceptual architecture of his political economy can start to take shape and become intelligible for the 'new eggs' of the future. This primarily concerns overcoming the limitations of the existing interpretations of Nietzsche's undertaking informed by the valuations of slave morality which he attempts to overcome.

3 Nietzsche and Smith on the Division of Labour

> Where the whole man is involved, there is no work. Work begins with the division of labour.
> (Marshall McLuhan 1964:138)

Introduction

This chapter brings two seemingly unlikely interlocuters—Adam Smith and Friedrich Nietzsche—into dialogue on one of political economy's central and enduring concerns: the division of labour.[138] The two thinkers, separated by well over a century, reflected on this issue thoroughly. Smith did so in Books I and V of *The Wealth of Nations* (WN, 1776) and in the context of *The Theory of Moral Sentiments* (TMS, 1759), which 'form parts of a single' project Smith intended to 'complete in his lifetime' (Luna 1996:149).[139] Nietzsche's thoughts on the subject are interspersed throughout his corpus, including a number of *Nachlass* entries between 1869 and 1888.[140] For both, the division of labour became a central axis of reflection on political economy, as well as featuring more generally within their philosophical views. Smith's *Wealth of Nations* placed the division of labour at the fore of the conversation on political economy of his day. In Nietzsche's time, the division of labour re-emerged as 'the tip of the iceberg of a profound philosophical debate as to the very nature of human beings' (Reinert and Daastøl 1997:234).

Although there is no direct evidence that Nietzsche read Smith's work or owned a copy of *The Wealth of Nations*, substantial indirect evidence points to Nietzsche's not inconsiderable knowledge of and interest in Smith's ideas.[141] Nietzsche's motives for

---

138 I would like to express my gratitude to Professor Thomas Brobjer for encouraging me to examine the possibility of this unexplored connection between Nietzsche and Smith as well as to Professor Jimena Hurtado and an anonymous reviewer for their detailed and helpful comments on an early draft of this chapter and on Adam Smith in particular.
139 Smith's works are referenced by abbreviated titles. 'WN' stands for *An Inquiry into the Nature and Causes of the Wealth of Nations* (ed. Edwin Cannan, London: Methuen, 1904), Vols. I and II; 'WN1' stands for Volume I, and 'WN2' stands for Volume 2. Pagination follows the electronic versions: http://oll-resources.s3.amazonaws.com/titles/237/Smith_0206-01_EBk_v6.0.pdf and https://oll.libertyfund.org/titles/smith-an-inquiry-into-the-nature-and-causes-of-the-wealth-of-nations-cannan-ed-vol-2, both last accessed Feb. 27, 2023. *The Theory of Moral Sentiments*, 1759, is abbreviated as '*TMS*'. Pagination follows the Glasgow Edition (eds. David D. Raphael and Alexander L. Macfie, Oxford: Oxford University Press, 1976). *Essays on Philosophical Subjects* (1795) is referenced as 'EPS'. Pagination follows the Glasgow Edition, Vol. III (ed. William P. D. Wightman, John C. Bryce, and Ian S. Ross, Oxford: Oxford University Press, 1980).
140 Nietzsche's first *Nachlass* note on the subject is NF-1869:3[44]), and his final is NF-1888:14[221].
141 Professor Brobjer suggested a number of indirect links by which Nietzsche could have been acquainted with the work of Adam Smith. See Brobjer's discussion in *Nietzsche and the English* (2007,

not referencing Smith by name may not have been that different from those which precluded Smith from referring to the intellectual interlocutor, James Steuart, in opposition to whose mercantilist doctrines he wrote *The Wealth of Nations*.[142] Nietzsche's lack of name-dropping may also have had something to do with John Stuart Mill's characterisation of Smith's economic theories as somewhat 'obsolete'.[143] This injunction, however, would not dim Nietzsche's interest in the more timeless philosophical aspects of the question of the division of labour and, therefore, in Smith's views on the subject. After all, 'it was Nietzsche himself who once suggested that great minds are able to speak to one another across the generations' (Talay 2011:378).

Smith and Nietzsche express similar views on a wide range of issues which are pertinent to the division of labour, starting with characterising the latter as an involuntary *'propensity in human nature'* (WN1:42)[144] and a *'natural* tendency' (NF-1881:11[145]). Both distinguish between the social or, in Nietzsche's case, 'organic'/'physiological' (Moore 2003:38; NF-1888:14[174]) and the technical or, in Nietzsche's case, 'mechanistic', division of labour (see NF-1869:3[44]; NF-1871:9[64]; GM: III, §18; Müller-Lauter 1999:179), where the former represents the distribution of trades in relation to society as a whole and the latter denotes its subdivision into simple functions per-

---

JHP Books). Brobjer notes that Nietzsche read about Adam Smith, apart from in Lange, also in Lecky: *'Die Naturgeschichte der Sitten'* (1–144), in *Sittengeschichte Europas von Augustus bis auf Karl den Grossen* (1879), which contains detailed information about British moral philosophy and thinking and is extremely heavily annotated by Nietzsche with extensive comments on almost every page'. This work contains information about Adam Smith. Friedrich Lange discussed the work of Adam Smith in the *History of Materialism and Critique of Its Present Importance* (1866), which Nietzsche read carefully and commented on in his private correspondence, referencing *'Manchester Theory'* (BVN-1868:562), which alludes to the *Manchester School* of political economy, which based itself on many of Smith's ideas (see Stack 1983:276). In addition, Nietzsche likely came across the 'unbiased Englishman' (UM: III; SE, §8; and BVN-1879:921) Bagehot's discussion of Adam Smith's work (e.g., 'Adam Smith As A Person', Fortnightly Review 20, New Series, 1876, 18–42). It is equally likely that, having read Wilhelm's Roscher's *Principles of Political Economy* (1878), Nietzsche would have built a reasonable impression of Smith's ideas. Finally, Nietzsche could know of Adam Smith from his extensive polemic with (a) Herbert Spencer, whose social Darwinism owes a direct debt to Smith and whose work (both *TMS* and *WN*) and particularly Smith's 'doctrine of sympathy', Spencer explicitly revives in his own *Social Statics* (1851), and (b) Charles Darwin, who borrowed Smith's concept of the division of labour to develop the evolutionary theory.

142 In a letter to Sir William Pulteney (5th Baronet, reputedly one of the wealthiest people in Britain of his day, who built his fortune from *slave plantations* in North America and sat in the House of Commons between 1768–1805), from September 3rd, 1772, Smith wrote: 'I have the same opinion of Sir James Stewarts Book that you have. Without once mentioning it, I flatter myself, that every false principle in it, will meet with a clear and distinct confutation in mine' (Smith 1987:230).

143 See Jensen 2001:491–507.

144 Smith expresses a similar view in his *Lectures on Jurisprudence*: 'If we should enquire into the principle in the human mind on which this *disposition of trucking* is founded, it is clearly the natural inclination everyone has to persuade' (LJ(A), 352).

formed by separate workers.¹⁴⁵ Smith and Nietzsche concur about the deleterious effects of the technical division of labour, to be found in Smith's famed 'pin factory' (WN1:37), and acknowledge that, although machines may be regarded 'a product of the highest intellectual energies' (HH: II, WS, §220), they are by no means 'the inventions of those who had occasion to use' them (WN1:40).¹⁴⁶ Smith and Nietzsche are not too far apart on the 'great, original and constituent orders of every civilized society' (WN1:219), consisting of three or four classes or castes (AC: §57), where the higher ranks should be 'thoroughly insulated from the ravages of the division of labour' (Rosenberg 1965:138).¹⁴⁷

Both thinkers are acutely aware of the dangers posed by the unrestrained pursuit of profit and agree that merchants, traders and money-makers should be no more allowed to become the leaders of humankind than to extract unseemly gains from exploiting the monopolistic and oligarchic propensities of their drives tending to oppress the rest of society and arrest its development.¹⁴⁸ Smith and Nietzsche are equally wary of 'political arithmetic' (WN1:89) seeking to manipulate the inevitable ambiguity and imprecision of economic variables, as well as the corrupting influence of the 'clamour and sophistry' of merchants (WN1:129) and the money-makers (UM: IV, RWB, §6) on the political establishment. Mindful of the state's tendency to develop a 'fat stomach' (NF-1887:9[141]), Smith and Nietzsche concur on 'as little State as possible' (HH: I, State, §473) in regulating the political economy of human affairs (see Reisman 1998:365; Danford 1980:674). These and other considerations attest to the significance both Smith (see TMS:160; Montes 2003a:86) and Nietzsche ascribed to the complex interconnectedness of political economy and moral valuations (see NF-1880:7[279]; NF-1886:7[8]), originating quite possibly from the recognition of the mutual vulnerability to loss and injury, as one of the original structuring axes of human sociability (see NF-1872:19[93]; TMS:85–86). In relation to Smith, this is further supported by the well-founded insistence by the Smith scholars to consider *The Wealth of Nations* and the earlier (but reg-

---

145 For Smith, see WN1: 36–37; for Nietzsche, see NF-1869:3[44], NF-1871:9[64], D: §206, NF-1883:8[9], and NF-1887:10[8].
146 The second of Nietzsche's *Untimely Meditations* (UM: II, *UDHL*, §7), contains an almost identical sequential tracking of Smith's argument in *The Wealth of Nations* (1776, WN2:267–268).
147 For Smith, see WN1:219 and TMS:225–226 (see also Hill 2007:345); for Nietzsche, see TI: *Improvers*, §3, NF-1881: 11[145], and NF-1888:14[201] and 14[221]. Marx also comments on this issue in *The German Ideology*, arguing that an 'inversion of history' is necessary to give rise to this conception of an 'ideal "man"' by making a very Nietzschean point that 'the average individual of the later stage was always foisted on to the earlier stage, and the consciousness of a later age on to the individuals of an earlier' (CW 5:88–89; see Nietzsche on '"man" as an *aeterna veritas*', HH: I, §2).
148 For Smith, see WN1:103 (monopolies, profit), 126–129 (corrupting influence), 221 ('deceive and oppress'), and 394 ('monopolizing spirit of the merchants', 'rulers of humankind'). For Nietzsche, see UM: III, SE, §4 (corrupting influence; monopolising spirit); HH: I, State, §472 ('private companies'); II, WS, §22 ('pirates' mentality'); UM: III, SE §6, IV, RWB §6, Z: IV, Kings, and NF-1888:23[3], 25[1], and 25[344] ('leaders of humankind').

ularly revised since its original publication) *The Theory of Moral Sentiments*, as 'two parts' of one whole (Luna 1996:132–133, 149).

A more detailed look at Smith's and Nietzsche's respective arguments, however, would reveal a fundamental disagreement, the above considerations notwithstanding. For Smith, the division of labour is the principal means to 'the progress of society towards real wealth and greatness' (WN1:307), whereas for Nietzsche it represents the opposite—'the principle of barbarism' (NF-1869:3[44]), which pulls society back and contributes to the total 'depreciation of the value of human existence and human goals' (NF-1888:11[74]). Smith insists that only 'when the division of labour has been ... thoroughly established' and 'every man ... becomes a merchant', that 'properly a commercial society' can be established (WN1:49). Nietzsche warns that all commerce 'is by its very nature satanic' and that for any merchant 'the honesty itself is a speculation on profit', which leaves 'the spirit of every trader ... completely vitiated' ('*vicié*'; NF-1887:11[215]).

At the root of the disagreement sits the question of valuations and their causality. The conceptualisation of value, which emanates from the natural law doctrine, allows Smith to combine the economic valuation with 'sympathy' and 'imagination' as the key ingredients of 'human sociability' (Hont 2015:18) on the basis that all three represent integral parts of God's law. In addition, he is able to privilege the effects of the division of labour in terms of sequencing the stages of 'bettering the human condition' (TMS:50–51). Smith's economic argument allows him to posit the division of labour as the principal lever in the attainment of commercial society, which, as 'the economic norm of modernity, represents human nature's fulfilment rather than corruption' (Duncan 2006:74). Smith's ideal society, first and foremost, is 'the prosperous, materially abundant society' (Hill 2007:346).

For Nietzsche, who argues that 'valuations belong to our basic constitution' (NF-1887:[7/2]), the division of labour, which has become the 'modern cry to battle and sacrifice' (UM: II, *UDHL*, §7), is an expression of the ruling ideas of slave morality (NF-1884:25[211]), which interpret 'the feeling of value backwards' (NF-1887:10[23]). As such, instead of signifying the progress and strengthening of humankind, the division of labour, informed by the valuations of slave morality, denotes the 'withering and weakening of its parts' (NF-1887:[7/2]). Nietzsche insists that already 'in morality man treats himself not as *individuum* but as *dividuum*' (HH: I, *HMS*, §57). He challenges Smith's assertion that 'consumption is the sole end and purpose of all production' (WN1:287) and problematises this 'fundamental idea' of commercial society, which 'in regard to everything that is made [...] inquires only after supply and demand' and seeks 'to appraise it according to the needs of the consumer' (D: §175). Where Smith and Nietzsche differ, therefore, is in relation to whether the key to humankind's enhancement lies in prioritising economic growth and increasing material welfare.[149]

---

[149] See also Rosenberg 1965:128 and Danford 1980:674.

Ultimately, this boils down to the importance of economy within the structure of society and within the context of humankind's development. In this regard, Smith holds that the notions of 'civilized society' and 'commercial society' are inseparable, such that attaining the former is impossible without the emergence of the latter (WN2:269), as only economic growth can and will help bring about humankind's moral transformation (Noble 2005: loc. 1108–1118). Nietzsche stipulates that the needs of humankind's development are more comprehensively addressed in the pursuit of cultural and intellectual advancement, which itself indicate and entail the necessary degree of economic growth and the structure of society conducive to achieving such goals.[150] To Smith's conception of 'commercial society' (see WN1:49 and WN2:269), the development of which is propelled by the division of labour, Nietzsche juxtaposes his concept of 'commercial culture' (D: §175),[151] which allows him to approach the division of labour—a critical element of humankind's 'conditions of existence' (NF-1884:26[75])—using a distinctly different frame of reference.

Placing Nietzsche in a hypothetical conversation with Smith, who 'comprehended and analysed the deepest levels of the newly developing industrial market economy' (Samuels 1977:189), allows us to examine both the structural parallels and the conceptual differences, between the two great thinkers who, in their distinctive ways, expressed a clear sense of a legislative mission for the future of humanity.[152] Furthermore, this discussion enables us to examine the underpinnings Smith's and Nietzsche's respective worldviews and to better understand the nature of Nietzsche's objection 'to the whole manner of thinking which characterizes political economy' since the time of Adam Smith (Brobjer 1999:62). In Nietzsche's reckoning, political economy, imbued with the valuations of slave morality, has developed as a nihilistic discourse (NF-1885:2[127]) dominated by those who are 'transfixed by hope of eternal salvation' at the expense of those who 'invest themselves entirely in this world' (Connolly 2008:138).

Das Adam Smith Problem

It is widely considered that the origins of some important aspects of '*das Adam Smith Problem*', which remains 'still relevant' today, can be traced back to 'German' discus-

---

[150] See HH: I, *State*, §464.
[151] Cf. Ansell-Pearson and Bamford, who suggest that 'Nietzsche appears to have been exposed to the term "commercial society" from his reading of Taine's history of English literature' (2020:168). The line of argument developed in this chapter builds on the earlier findings by Thomas Brobjer (see fn. 113), which allow for the possibility that Nietzsche was at least as likely to have come across this concept indirectly in relation to the work of Adam Smith.
[152] For Nietzsche, see NF-1881:11[141]; NF-1885:35[9]; Löwith 1997:94; and Ansell-Pearson 2011:51–52. For Smith, see WN1:345; Haakonssen 1981:92; and Smith 2020:128–135.

sions' found near the 'end of the 1890s'.[153] The problem concerns a perceived inconsistency between the 'sympathetic' conception of human behaviour in Smith's 1759 'Theory' (i.e., TMS) and the subsequently 'selfish' conception of human conduct in his 1776 'Inquiry' (i.e., WN).[154] Nietzsche's analysis of the division of labour can be said to have anticipated this debate. He scrutinises the underlying tension, unresolved by Smith, between the objective of spiritual heightening, on the one hand, and the pursuit of material wealth, on the other.[155]

Smith was undoubtedly aware of this issue, which was highlighted in discussions of the Athenian school of Greek antiquity.[156] Furthermore, in his highly nuanced analysis across TMS and WN, Smith conceded that commercial society, by opening up—at least in principle—the pursuit of material wealth to 'the great mob of mankind' (TMS:62), would risk succumbing to inferior valuations:

> In the middling and inferior stations of life, the road to virtue and that to fortune, to such fortune, at least, as *men in such stations* can reasonably expect to acquire, are, happily in most cases, very nearly the same. (TMS:63; my emphasis)[157]

This 'conflicting picture of human motivation' (Otteson 2000:70) would present a potential problem for the 'benevolent wisdom, which governs the universe' (TMS:277) and 'directs all the events of human life' (TMS:292). Smith, nonetheless, gravitated to the conclusion that 'the plan ... is all that depends upon the architect' (TMS:99), and while 'humanity, or human nature, is always existent and is always the same' with respect to 'the governing principles', which accord with 'the will of the great Director of the universe', the individual human natures remain highly 'irregular' and extremely diversified (see EPS:121; TMS:108, 177, 236). Although, within such a conception of providence, normativity and agency, social perfection may prove difficult to achieve (Evensky 2005:118), 'social harmony' remains well justified as an aspirational goal, progress towards which is well within mankind's inherent desire and capacity for bettering its condition, so as to 'imitate the work of a divine artist' (see TMS: 8, 183, 247–248).

Smith's overriding objective of bettering humankind's condition would thus be best served by the establishment and observance of such 'systems of behaviour' for promoting individual and collective happiness (TMS:326), which are based on 'the general rules' of justice and morality 'by which sympathies act' and which agree with 'the

---

[153] See Otteson 2000:69, 2002:168; Montes 2003a:63; Wilson and Dixon 2006:251; Tribe 2008:518, 2015:4–5.
[154] See Tribe 2008:519.
[155] Otteson formulates this tension as 'between moral injunctions to beneficence and other virtues, on the one hand, and the apparent amorality of economic markets on the other (Otteson 2000:69).
[156] See WN1:288; TMS:167, 226; Evensky 2005:118; Wells and Graafland 2012; Griswold 1999:7–21; Hanley 2009:86–91.
[157] Smith expressed similar concern in *WN:* 'An augmentation of fortune is the means by which the greater part of men propose and wish to better their condition. It is the means the most vulgar and the most obvious' (WN1:288).

governing principles of human nature' (TMS: 165, 319–320). This would reflect the propitious balance in the distribution of 'prosperity and adversity', as well as of collective happiness and individual liberty, which would promote 'the real improvement of the world we live in' from which the 'mankind are benefited' and 'human nature is ennobled' (TMS: 167, 184–185, 229). This logic allows Smith to transition between 'sympathy' and 'the division of labour' without putting these two notions into an insoluble conflict with one another and instead to focus his analysis in *The Wealth of Nations* on the synergistic permutations of the two natural propensities of human nature.[158]

Nietzsche's approach is distinctly different to that of Smith. The initial antinomy to Smith's *Theory of Moral Sentiments* is to be found in *On the History of the Moral Sensations* (1873),[159] which contests the seemingly generic nature of sentiment by emphasising the physical origin of sensation (NF-1888:14[119]).[160] Nietzsche argues that 'sympathy' is 'a prelude with a dreadful termination' and an expression of 'refined wickedness', which could end up being 'more painful than suffering' (HH: I, HMS, §§45–50). Subsequently and more substantively, Nietzsche engages with the subject in *On The Genealogy of Morality* (1887),[161] where he explores the 'actual physiological causation of *res-sentiment*' (GM: III, §15) and confronts the pervasive rise of the 'reactive sentiment' in modern society (GM: II, §11).

Nietzsche calls into question a 'certain blind faith in the goodness of human nature' (HH: I, HMS, §36), which underpins Smith's *Theory of Moral Sentiments*. Later, in *The Antichrist* (1888), Nietzsche discusses it in terms of 'a distorted and dishonest perspective' which invariably gives rise to 'the pathos […] that calls itself faith' (AC: §9). He suggests that the standard of proof for the belief in the goodness of human nature is 'at bottom merely another faith, namely, that the effect one expects from faith will not fail to appear' (AC: §50). Nietzsche maintains that such conceptions exhibit strong 'aversion to the dissection of human actions' honestly enough so as to reveal 'the nakedness of the soul' (AC: §37). His view is that, absent such an exercise, theoris-

---

158 In this context, it is worth taking note of Marx's criticism of Smith as moving 'in a perpetual contradiction' between his attempt to 'penetrate the inner physiology of bourgeois society' (i.e., TMS –DS) and merely describing 'its externally apparent form' (i.e., WN –DS), thus succeeding only in expressing 'the apparent connections without any internal relation' (CW 31:391; see also CW 33:345–345). Marx's criticism resonates discernibly in Nietzsche's own reflections on the subject.

159 Although HMS (1873) and GM (1887) were directed specifically towards *On the Origin of Moral Sensations* ('OMS', 1877) by Paul Rée as well as towards Schopenhauer, the principal argument developed by Rée in OMS, bears remarkable affinity with Smith's TMS, save for the replacement of the metaphysical influences with naturalistic claims, and could be regarded as a recurrence of 'the Adam Smith problem'. In addition, HMS contains some of Nietzsche's most important insights on political economy (e.g., exchange and the division of labour) which are pertinent for the discussion undertaken vis-à-vis Smith, as well as vis-à-vis Marx. See Janaway 2007:75 and Robin Small, who links the argumentation of Smith, Rée, Spencer, and Nietzsche in *Nietzsche and Rée: A Star Friendship*, 2007:144 as well as Small on Rée in *Basic Writings*, 2003:77–89.

160 See Titchener 1914:301–307.

161 Further referred to as *the Genealogy*.

ing about human nature would lead to erecting 'a false ethics', where religion would be inevitably called upon 'to buttress it' (AC: §37). In consequence, 'the shadow of these dismal spirits' would end up clouding not only ethical reflection; such obscurity would inevitably fall 'across even physics and the entire perception of life' (AC: §37).

Nietzsche further problematises a 'certain superficiality in psychological observation', which is liable to set 'the most dangerous traps for human judgement' (AC: §37) on the basis that one tends to forget 'the origin of designations and believes them to be inherent irrespective of consequences' (AC: §39). Nietzsche's psychological scrutiny of the 'faith in the goodness of human nature' (HH: I, *HMS*, §37) and the "laissez-faire" dogmas of political economy espousing belief in an 'unconditionally salutary success' (NF-1872:19[28]) highlights, therefore, the real possibility that the consequences of Smith's system which advocates the 'perseverance in labour' and praises the 'courage not to be ashamed of modest labour' (HH: I, *HMS*, §37) might diverge substantially from the imagined intentions of the 'system-builder' (UM: III, *SE*, §8) in case the real 'driving forces and valuations' behind these consequences were not necessarily in accordance with God's will (NF-1885:35[31]). It is, therefore, likely that Nietzsche would at best see Smith's 'economy of goodness' as 'the dream of the boldest utopians' (HH: I, *HMS*, §48).

Concerning 'the Poor Man's Son'

The difference between Smith's and Nietzsche's views concerning both psychology and causality, which inform their respective analyses of the division of labour is perhaps best exemplified by the allegory Smith offers in *TMS* of 'the poor man's son, whom heaven in its anger has visited with ambition' (TMS:181–191).[162] This individual, 'enchanted with the distant idea of felicity' which would have him adjoin to the 'superior rank of beings', exerts himself with dedication and 'unrelenting industry' to the 'toilsome pursuit' of this felicity symbolised by 'wealth and greatness':

> Through the whole of his life he pursues the idea of a certain artificial and elegant repose which he may never arrive at, for which he sacrifices a real tranquillity that is at all times in his power, and which, if in the extremity of old age he should at last attain to it, he will find to be in no respect preferable to that humble security and contentment which he had abandoned for it. (TMS: 181)

It is only 'in the last dregs of life', when his body is 'wasted' and his mind is 'galled', that he develops an appreciation for what 'wealth and greatness' really are: the 'mere trinkets of frivolous utility'. Alas, much as he may lament the 'ambition, vanity and indolence of youth', which enticed him into spending his life trying to please the sensibility of an 'impartial spectator' by emulating the rich and the powerful, the deed is done, and he has participated to the full extent of his talents in churning the wheels

---

[162] §§ IV.i.8–IV.2.11 of *TMS*. Unless referenced otherwise, all further citations in '...' pertaining to Smith's allegory are sourced from this passage.

of the illusory 'oeconomy of greatness'. Smith, however, discerns a silver lining in this unfolding of 'the secret wheels and springs' of human nature. Such individuals, who are driven by the desire for recognition, enter into the pursuit of material gain, made possible under the auspices of commercial society, 'of their own accord'. They are moved by no other than sympathy, when they invite 'the impartial spectator enter into the principles' of their conduct. And even though sympathy operates by 'deception', it is this 'deception which rouses and keeps in continual motion the industry of mankind' (TMS:183). In this context, the individuals, without either 'knowing it' or 'intending it' appear—as though 'led by the invisible hand'—to advance the 'interest of society' (TMS:183). As the material welfare increases, facilitated by the division of labour, individuals and societies would reach a point in their development when, no longer constrained by material need, they would be in a position to allocate a greater share of energy and resources towards spiritual and intellectual development, thus reclaiming the original and felicitous provenance of sympathy (TMS:25).

Nietzsche on Sympathy and Industriousness

Smith's analysis allows for fairly harmonious conceptual transitions between sympathy and self-interest, moral improvement and the division of labour, the maximisation of individual utility and promotion of the collective good. Nietzsche, by querying the psychology of sympathy that underlies the logic of Smith's argument, arrives at diametrically opposed conclusions. For him, 'sympathy and industriousness'—both attributes of *slave morality* (BGE: §260)—belong squarely to 'modern vices' (NF-1887:9[141]). Unlike Smith, Nietzsche considers sympathy to be a passive and derivative sentiment (NF-1888:14[119]), which is subject to manipulation as a 'current feeling' that allows 'to count oneself the same as others' in some respect (NF-1886:7[6]).[163] Under the guise of 'impartiality ('*Uneigennützigkeit*') and universal validity' (NF-1886:7[4]) 'hard industriousness' is promoted and endorsed as a virtue, albeit a 'herd virtue' of the 'industrial masses' (NF-1887:9[44]). At the same time, no disclosure is made about the 'extreme dangerousness' of such industriousness (GS: §21). Nietzsche highlights at least three aspects in which industriousness, as a secular offshoot of sympathy (BGE: §58), signifies danger.

Nietzsche argues that by representing industriousness as 'the way to wealth an honour', the individual is conditioned to 'adopt a way of thinking and behaving that once it has become a habit … will dominate him to his own ultimate disadvantage' (GS: §21; see NF-1881:11[180]). 'Glorification of work' would lead the individual not only to consume 'an extraordinary amount of nervous energy', but also to effectively

---

163 See the section titled *Towards the Critique of the Herd Virtues*, as well as NF-1885:37[8], where Nietzsche argues that sympathy is usually 'with all that suffers', which is why it is intimately connected to the doctrine of equality.

appoint his industriousness 'the best policeman', thus making himself the prime suspect and his own worst fear (D: §173). In other words, Nietzsche suggests that individuals set free to look for paid work only become instrumentalised and enslaved by this chimera of freedom (HH: II, WS, §288) for the benefit of 'those who commend work' (D: §173). The latter, fully aware of the psychological deception taking place—not entirely unlike Smith's 'impartial spectator' (TMS:183)—amplify and exploit this deception to their advantage under the slogans of promoting 'the general good' (GS: §21). The end result is that individuals, who end up living 'in continual pretense and … anticipating others', expend their spirits 'to the point of exhaustion' (GS: §329).

Once 'blindly raging industriousness' (GS: §21) is incorporated into the modern psyche, it does not simply plateau, let alone diminish, after society and its members reach a certain threshold of material comfort. Quite the opposite, 'noisy, time-consuming industriousness' (BGE: §58) exhibits inflationary propensities as the '"herd" "mass" "society" expands its needs into the cosmic and metaphysical values' as the only venue available to it, the substitute for fulfilment and contentment or, in other words, sympathy for itself turned inward (NF-1887:9[44/2]). Nietzsche argues that sympathy, as a form of awareness of the 'mass society's' predicament, ends up being weaponised by those who shepherd the 'weak and the sick', who are united by it, as the means by which they would conquer and win (NF-1888:14[182]). Contrary to Smith's assertion that the 'industry of mankind […] ennobles and embellishes human life' and obliges the earth to 'redouble her natural fertility' (TMS:183–184), Nietzsche argues that industriousness fundamentally disrupts modernity's relationship with culture and art by turning the latter into mere entertainment, 'recreation and distraction' for 'weary and exhausted' spirits (HH: II, WS, §170, §280). Humankind's relationship with the earth, 'exemplified by 'our rape of nature with the help of machines', becomes equally damaged with the advent of industrial civilisation (GM: III, §9)

Where Smith conceives of progress and the gradual improvement of mankind, Nietzsche intuits a systematic debasement of the underlying quality of existence (NF-1888:15[8]). In view of these considerations, Nietzsche, unlike Smith, does not believe that sympathy can either reconstitute itself or emerge in a new light at the far end of the development of commercial society. In Nietzsche's reckoning, sympathy, having 'covertly' nurtured the 'rudimentary psychology' of 'bad conscience' (see D:§173–174; NF-1888:14[125])—including by 'awakening the industry of man' (TMS:186), promoting the division of labour and conjuring up the *fata morgana* of economic growth—ends up being one of the primary causes of nihilism, through which 'the whole of existence is vulgarized' (GS: §40; see NF-1887:9[44/2]), rather than just the existence of the lower ranks, as Smith argued (WN1:288).

One of the challenges Nietzsche's critique poses for Smith's political economy would concern the manner in which humankind, individually and collectively, would be able to transform itself from a 'moral to a knowing mankind' (HH: I, HMS, §107). The path that leads to the creation of civilised society envisaged by Smith could be, in Nietzsche's assessment, likened to a butterfly that wishes but is unable to break free from the cocoon of commercial society because it cannot overcome the gravity and inertia of commercial culture's valuations. The metaphorical butterfly ends up, therefore, confined in the building whose foundation is bound to become increasingly decayed, yet 'incapable of repair'.[164] Problematising the consequences of commercial society in light of the 'inertia' of its moral feelings and valuations (NF-1886:7[6]) provides the initial outlines for the kind of jeopardous 'interregnum', which Nietzsche suspects might be 'reserved for Europe in the next two centuries' (GM: III, §27).

Aetiology of the Division of Labour

Two aspects of the conversation on the division of labour are of particular relevance in relation to Smith and Nietzsche. The first concerns the *causality* of the division of labour. The second, flowing from the first, is the extent to which the division of labour can be regarded as a 'social bond', or a key ingredient of the 'social cement' (see Samuels 1977:199–200; Danford 1980:695) which binds the members of society into a whole, as opposed to being the means by which society is segregated into atomistic and isolated agents who busy themselves with maximising marginal utility (Hill 2007:346). In this respect, the question of achieving the 'collective good' justifiably arises, setting the scene for a broader discussion about humankind's developmental paths and priorities.[165]

Nietzsche's thinking on the subject develops under the influence of the Athenian school, which included Plato and Aristotle (Drochon 2016:29), in whose company Xenophon merits inclusion. All three shared the view that the division of labour arose from the innate 'diversity of human natures' (Trever 1916:34–35, 71, 96).[166] Plato in particular maintained that that 'to begin with, our several natures are not all alike but different', and that whereas 'one man is naturally fitted for one task' another's aptitude is 'for another' (R:370[a-b]).[167] In other words, the division of labour is the consequence of the diversity of human natures, rather than being its cause. The division of labour is seen as arising from 'the necessary dependence' of these diverse natures upon each other (Trever 1916:34): the 'marketplace', where 'buying and selling' takes place and money acts as 'a token for the purpose of exchange', is merely a medium in which this interdependence manifests itself (R:371[b]). In this respect, it may be viewed as an enduring basis of human sociability, the vitality of which is dependent on the preservation of its diversity. Importantly in this context, Plato along with Aristotle and Xenophon, held that 'one function of the division of labor should be to limit the industry

---

164 See D: §453; HH: I, *HMS*, §107; and HH: I, *State*, §466.
165 See Myers 1967:432; Martin 1990:282; Mosini 2009:1–3; and Montes 2003:68, 743.
166 See Trever's *History of Greek Economic Thought* (1916) for a detailed comparative discussion of Plato, Aristotle, and Xenophon vis-à-vis some of Smith's key theses (Trever 1916:34–97).
167 Sections from Plato's *Republic* can be accessed at http://www.perseus.tufts.edu (last accessed Feb. 27, 2023) and are referenced as they appear (e.g., 'R:575[a]'). All cited passages are cross-referenced against Henry Desmond Pritchard Lee's translation of *The Republic* (Penguin Books, 1905).

and commerce to the 'performance of their proper tasks' and to 'keep them from degenerating into mere money-making devices' (Trever 1916:36). This becomes a critical consideration for Nietzsche also, as he distinguishes between the work which is directed towards satisfying a specific *need* and *'neediness'*—i.e., 'working for the universal possibility of satisfaction in general' (Löwith 1991:267; see EN: *TLEMS*, §2). The former makes one an *expert* who is able to invest herself fully into her work and expects as much of others (see NF-1879:40[3]). The latter produces a twofold requirement for (a) a mediator wedged between the buyer and the seller, the producer and the consumer, and (b) an alienated wage earner, a powerless cog in the industrial machine spawning an ever-widening array of fictitious needs and desires:

> All the manifestations of such a life are accompanied by dissimulation, the *denial of neediness*, the splendour of metaphorical intuitions and, in particular, the immediacy of illusion. Neither their house, nor their gait, nor their clothing, nor their clay jug betrays the fact that it was invented by a need; it seems as if all these things were meant to express a *sublime happiness ... a play with seriousness*. While man guided by *concepts and abstractions* can only ward off unhappiness and strive for the greatest possible freedom from pain without wresting any happiness for himself from these abstractions.[168] (EN: TLEMS, §2; my emphasis)

Working for the satisfaction of needs that are endowed with human significance rather than being subjugated to the logic of mechanical utility, places certain organic limits on the amount of growth, understood in economic terms. It also reflects a certain *hierarchy of aptitudes* and consequently a spectrum of 'fractioning of human faculty'. The division of labour was seen as establishing a certain *directional linkage*, whereby it remained an implied responsibility of guardians, who would be released from the traffic of industry and commerce so that they could become pure 'expert craftsmen of civic duty' (R:395[b-c]), shielding the weaker and less capable members of the *polis* by curbing the exploitative excesses of commerce and money-making.

Smith views the causality of the division of labour very differently. Developing on Hutcheson's logic, elaborated by Hume, Smith maintains that 'the difference of natural talents in different men is, in reality, much less than we are aware of' and what apparent difference there is, it is 'not ... so much the cause' but 'the effect of the division of labour' (WN1:43).[169] The 'natural tendency' that Smith identifies is not for human natures to differ. Rather, it is 'the general disposition to truck, barter, and exchange being brought, as it were, into a common stock' that allows individuals to emerge from the undifferentiated state where each one is burdened with having to perform all tasks

---

[168] Nietzsche echoes Marx, who also laments the mechanical division of labour which 'destroys every *remnant of charm* in [the wage labourer's –DS] work and turns it into a hated toil' (CW 35:639; my emphasis). See also an excellent discussion of this point in Vasquez 1973:205–206.

[169] In the *Lectures on Justice* (1763; abbreviated as 'LJ'), Smith makes the same point more forcefully: 'Disposition to barter is by no means founded upon different genius and talents. It is doubtful if there be any such difference at all. Genius is more the effect of the division of labour than the latter is of it' (LJ 1896: Part II, *Police*, §5, 170).

for themselves and, by dividing labour, to become differentiated. In other words, the division of labour does not arise because individuals are innately different but because, guided by the natural disposition to barter, they may so become (LJ:170). As Trever concludes, 'Smith considers the diversities in human nature to be the effect rather than the cause of the division of labor' (Trever 1916:35). It is important to note here that, from the outset, underpinning Smith's argument and powering the logic of the division of labour is an assumption of innate *equality* between individuals—the uniform ground bass of human nature.

Smith consequently argues that the division of labour is limited by the extent of the market (WN1:45), rather than that the market should be limited by such division of labour as reflects the pre-ordained diversity of human natures. Smith infers a degree of objectivity in respect of both, the division of labour and the market in order to distance them from the pitfalls of human nature. He identifies both, conceptualised in terms of the natural, general and universal disposition, as the engines of growth, capable of leading all human beings to greater overall prosperity (WN1:45).[170] Inverting the causality of the division of labour allows Smith to construe value in economic terms. However, such a recasting away from the orthodoxy of the qualitative, the given and from the unknowable towards the tangible, quantifiable and more knowable—becomes increasingly dependent on the notion of *equivalence* by means of which exchange can be facilitated and the conceptual obstacles to the proliferation of the division of labour, growth of the market and economic progress can be removed. As Nietzsche aptly puts it, the logic informing Smith's arguments would lead 'to interpret the difference in power as a difference in value: so that the relationship no longer revolts' (NF-1886:7[6/2]).

A further consequence of Smith's argument is that it effectively blurs the boundary between the notion of the social division of labour, which produces craftsmen, philosophers and artists, and the technical division of labour, which produces de-specialised workers and dulled atomistic individuals (Vincent-Lancrin 2003:222). One illustration of their different approaches to causality is found in Smith and Nietzsche's discussion of the relationship between the pursuit of luxury and the decline of society. Whereas Smith 'accepted that it was luxury that destroyed the ancient republics' (Hont 2015:89), Nietzsche argues that 'when a people approaches destruction, when it degenerates physiologically, then licence and luxury follow from this', as a manner of 'craving for ever stronger and more frequent stimulation' (TI: *Errors*, §2).[171] Nietzsche further asserts that 'confusing cause and effect' is far from accidental and that it represents a particular method of valuation which, although it may appear to promote

---

170 In *The Human Condition* (1958), Arendt speaks of the *division of labour* in terms of 'an unnatural growth ... of the natural' against which 'the political' world of the *oikos* proved 'incapable of defending' itself and which has been 'the *greatest single factor* in this constant increase since its inception' gradually paving the way for 'the industrial revolution' (Arendt 1998:47).

171 The notion of 'licence', informed by Plato's discussion in *Politeia* becomes important to Nietzsche's critique of the money-maker's ascent in modern society.

'all the supreme values of mankind', is fundamentally 'symptomatic of decline' and 'nihilistic' (AC: §6).

Nietzsche links the 'resolve to be so scientific about everything' (BT: *ASC*, §1) with the 'inversion of the value-positing eye' (GM: I, §10) from 'one does what one is' to 'one is what one does'. This becomes pivotal for Nietzsche's inquiry, including in the context of the division of labour. In the first instance, the logic of Smith's argument can be said to exhibit the same 'will to the inversion of truth' (BGE: §59), which Nietzsche first identifies in *The Birth of Tragedy* (1872) in relation to Socrates. He argues that Socrates' 'unshakeable faith that thought—using the thread of causality—could penetrate the deepest abysses of being and prove capable not only of knowing being but of *correcting* it', also concealed a 'sublime metaphysical illusion' (BT: §15; my emphasis) from which the 'beautifully seductive and tranquillising utterances about the 'dignity of man' and the 'dignity of labour' (BT: §18) would inevitably ensue until such time that the teleological optimism, concealed in the essence of scientific logic would suffer shipwreck and 'bite its own tail' (BT: §15). Becker's observation in 'Adam Smith's Theory of Social Science' (1961) adequately enunciates Nietzsche's concern:

> Exhibiting the common trend of *men of the Enlightenment*, classical economists afflicted with a didactic impulse to set things right ... they were, more often than not, ideological innovators, conceiving of themselves as *secular priests*, shouldering the responsibility for advancing the cause of humanity abandoned by a deistic God (Becker 1961:13; my emphasis).

This allows Nietzsche to approach the question about the division of labour in a different way to Smith, i.e., do individuals divide up labour and if so, on what basis, or does labour divide individuals as well as dividing up each one of them and, if so, on what basis? Although Nietzsche's 'inverted Platonism' (NF-1870:7[156]) by no means returns him squarely to the original positions of the 'Athenian School' (Schrift 1991:43–46), drawing on their insights enables him to posit the division of labour as at once 'an unfinished problem' and as a 'problem of civilisation', which includes the question of progress (NF-1887:9[185]), and by so doing to challenge the logic of the Smithian argument. In search of the answers and in order to start unmasking the harmful illusions of modern political economy, Nietzsche travels back to the uncomfortable 'questions of origin and beginnings', which modern sensibility prefers 'to put out of its mind' (HH: I, §1). His investigation proceeds by triangulating the notions of the division of labour, equivalencies (i.e., equality) and exchange, aiming to understand wherefrom the insistence on 'sameness of character and sameness of value concepts' (NF-1887:9[173]), which is particularly critical to Smith's political economy, derives.

Needs of Slave Morality

Smith ostensibly maintains that the satisfaction of *material needs* is the gateway to attending to the higher—spiritual, as well as intellectual (i.e., non-material) pursuits. The division of labour is central to the problem of the satisfaction of needs of both kinds. In Smith's assessment, an opulent commercial society, attained at the advanced stages of the division of labour, enjoys a greater ability for the satisfaction of individual as well as collective needs, notwithstanding that its 'relations of benevolence' would be significantly weaker (Hont and Ignatieff 1983:3–5):

> In an uncivilized nation, and where labour is undivided, every thing is provided for that the natural wants of mankind require; yet when the nation is cultivated and labour divided, a more liberal provision is allotted them; and it is on this account that a common day labourer in Britain has more luxury in his way of living than an Indian sovereign. (LJB: 161)

Smith suggests that the division of labour is, in fact, not only the answer to the question of needs but also instrumental to inducing the kind of progress, i.e., economic growth, absent which the more 'primitive' societies with limited 'opportunities for material accumulation' would remain incapable of 'freeing their populations from the grip of natural scarcity', curtailing the development of the individual as well as of the society in general (Hont and Ignatieff 1983:3–9, 44). Within the commercial setting even the individuals, who may be 'motivated by unlimited desire', are also tricked—by either Providence or by Nature, which, by making them industrious 'furthers the progress of economies' and thereby promotes the satisfaction of needs, including those of the poorest members of society (Yamamori 2017: 343). In this manner 'the road to fortune' and 'the road to virtue' are bound to converge at which point the members of 'the superior stations of life' would be joined by those in 'the middle and inferior ranks of life' on their shared journey of progress (TMS:56, 62–64; see Hont and Ignatieff 1983:12).

Nietzsche, in contrast, attempts to explain why Smith's vision cannot come to pass on account of being based on flawed assumptions concerning the causality of human needs and, consequently, the role of the division of labour in satisfying them. One area that Smith does not scrutinise sufficiently, and which becomes pivotal to Nietzsche's inquiry, concerns the inter-relation and, indeed, the *balance* between the satisfaction of the material and the spiritual needs in individuals and societies. Nietzsche devotes considerable attention to the question of needs from his earliest written notes to the very final. In addressing the issue, he follows the same logic that he applies in relation to the division of labour. His starting point is the *irrepressible diversity* of human needs (NF-1876:23[48]) of the 'natural' (NF-1887:10[156]) and 'social' (NF-1872:19[175]) varieties:

> We have different needs, a different growth, a different digestion: we need more, we also need less. There is no formula for how much a spirit needs for its sustenance; but if his taste is for independence, for coming and going quickly, for wandering, perhaps for adventures that only the quickest can cope with, he would rather live freely on narrow fare than be unfree and stuffed. (GS: §381)

Even if our basic needs were the substantively the same, they would be communicated in 'different languages' (NF-1873:29[88]) and just as we may all 'need food, the needs of our taste are different' (NF-1879:42[15]). As such, the division of labour is neither a catch-all for the satisfaction of undifferentiated needs, nor should it designate the process by which the qualitative differences between the labourers can be gradually levelled out. On the contrary, Nietzsche argues that the function of the division of labour is to preserve this difference, meaning it should be viewed as the end of the satisfaction of needs rather than merely its means. The division of labour in industrial society, which is predominantly mechanistic, misconstrues this fundamental relationship and, by reversing its ends and means, profoundly distorts the conceptualisation of needs and their satisfaction.

Nietzsche's emphasis throughout is placed on the 'social needs'—of immaterial kind and capable of birthing values—which, he argues, 'bind men together most firmly' and act as the real foundation of society in the absence of which 'man lives in eternal obfuscations'.[172] He continues by suggesting that the *needs* and *valuations* are inseparable, such that the latter are the 'result of our innermost needs' (NF-1885:34[86]), even if the 'original causes of each need are forgotten' (NF-1879:42[15]):

> [I]t is our needs that interpret the world: our instincts and their pros and cons. Every drive is a kind of lust for power, everyone has their perspective, which they would like to impose as a norm on all other drives. (NF-1886:7[60])

The problem with Smith's argument, highlighted by Nietzsche, is twofold. In the first place, the 'civilisation of commerce', advocated by Smith, is inevitably based on the 'intention for equal needs' (NF-1887:11[157]) and the division of labour, powered by this logic, works to achieve it. In this context Nietzsche problematises the critical role played by *slave morality* in reconfiguring the realm of human needs by infusing it with valuations which translate into the 'needs and the level of understanding of the religious masses' (NF-1887:11[294], [295]). In this manner, slave morality invariably informs the conceptual schema of the division of labour in Smith's political economy. Nietzsche points out that *slave morality*, working initially through the Christianit doctrine and subsequently through the secular 'commercial society', recognises the 'easy communicability of need' as the 'the mightiest of all the powers that have hitherto ruled over man' (BGE: §286; NF-1884:30[10]). Seizing upon the fact that deep down 'man is a worshipping animal' (GS: §32), it privileges 'only average experiences and common experiences' as the basis for its valuations (BGE: §286). From this viewpoint, the conceptualisation of 'similar needs and similar experiences with similar signs' proceeds to train our senses so that 'the "same world of appearances" which returns again and again may ultimately acquire the appearance of reality'.[173] In the communication of needs 'quickly and clearly' and in their very communicability, Nietzsche locates a hidden 'surplus of power' which, he argues, slave morality discovers and perfects into an art form (GS: §354).

---

172 See NF-1872:19[175]; NF-1885:34[86]; and AC: §31.
173 See NF-1887:9[144]; BGE: §286; and GS: §149.

This circumstance makes the issue of *whose* needs prevail in the drive for uniformity—or could instead emerge as a *countermovement* to their increasing standardisation—all the more important:

> The 'ascending' life and the descending life: both formulate their *highest needs into tables of values*. (NF-1888:15[2]; my emphasis)

When the needs that require satisfying are 'sick, base, and vulgar', *any political economy* built upon them and used for their satisfaction is bound to acquire the same attributes as the needs 'which it is to gratify' (AC: §37). Nietzsche cautions that when the 'herd animal needs' ascend to become society's 'ideal' (NF-1887:11[137]) they bring along an 'utter lack of psychological integrity', which infiltrates all branches of the social world and crowds out other valuations by 'tyrannizing exceptions' (NF-1887:9[44]). Echoing the insights of the Stoics, the Athenian school, as well as Goethe's premonitions, Nietzsche warns that 'when the boundary of needs ceases to be narrow', it spells trouble (NF-1869:3[44]). Society's subsequent developmental trajectory becomes hostage to the never-ending process of satisfying the same needs and the sameness of these needs dressed up as infinite desires:

> [T]he lower species 'herd' 'mass' 'society' unlearns modesty and exaggerates its needs to *cosmic and metaphysical values*. This vulgarizes the whole existence: insofar as the masses rule, they tyrannize the exceptions, so that they lose faith in themselves and become nihilists. (NF-1887:9[44]; my emphasis)

The division of labour is an important method for the satisfaction of needs and for the perpetuation of the monotony of these needs under the growing myriad of guises. However, the needs it is purposed to satisfy are formulated on the basis of the valuations of *slave morality*. This, in Nietzsche's reckoning, makes the division of labour into both an engine of economic progress and an instrument of *slave morality*, a medium for the propagation of its valuations and for the satisfaction of the needs it formulates and communicates in order to preserve these valuations and safeguard the power conferred by them. The division of labour, informed by the valuations of slave morality, privileges, proliferates, and aids in the satisfaction of a certain kind of needs as well as insisting on their endless repetition (not to be confused with Nietzsche's eternal return, as Landa does, 2020:148-158). While it promotes the satisfaction of material needs, it devalues their spiritual equivalent (see NF-1875:11[59]). The system of valuations of *slave morality*—akin to an algorithm that feeds the logic of the machine known to us as 'the division of labour'—represents, on Nietzsche's view, a closed system of inputs which do not and cannot reproduce anything beyond themselves. In effect, Nietzsche suggests that the fundamental premise of commercial society is based on the interpretation of needs which arises from the closed system of valuations of slave morality. The range of needs inevitably becomes constricted by these valuations, while the amplitude of needs within the permitted range is allowed to expand infinitely.

In Smith's commercial society the division of labour becomes the chief method of economic appropriation of the world based predominantly on the satisfaction of economic needs, the proliferation of which crowds out other human requirements, including the spiritual and aesthetic. Economic conceptualisation of needs, reflected in the division of labour which prioritises economic appropriation of the world, finds its ultimate expression in creating and universalising the *need for money* as an objective (i.e., natural) need within the money-economy, where every pursuit ends up aimed at 'earning a great deal of money' (UM: III, *SE*, §6). The economic categories reproduced through the division of labour within the commercial society are incapable of pointing beyond themselves. In the similar fashion, money as the ultimate mechanism for the mediation of human needs becomes the end which does not allow to see beyond itself. Having reduced and subjugated human experience to its own abstract form, money as a value filters out those human needs which it cannot quantify and find appropriate means for satisfying — i.e., those needs that money cannot adequately value on its own terms cease being recognised as needs. In other words, money dispossesses the individual of her spiritual and aesthetic needs. As a result, Nietzsche argues that no cultural rebirth is possible at the far end of the path to material prosperity. Nietzsche draws our attention to the fact that the key consequences of political economy, let alone of economics, are not economic. Political economy imbued with the valuations of slave morality and promoting material welfare as a gateway to the spiritual enhancement of humankind achieves only spiritual degradation. The outcome of pursuing material prosperity while forgetting to 'take care of our future needs' (NF-1883:7[238]; 16[57]) is the pervasive nihilism of political economy:

> We notice needs in ourselves, planted there by the *prolonged moral interpretation*, which now appear to us as needs for the untrue; on the other hand, it is these needs on which the value seems to depend for the sake of which we endure living. This *antagonism*—not esteeming what we know and no longer being permitted to esteem what we would like to pretend to ourselves—results in a process of dissolution. (NF-1886:5[71/2]; my emphasis)

Nietzsche draws an unequivocal connection between the proliferation of 'atomistic needs' within commercial civilisation and the 'famous "metaphysical needs"' that 'Christianity has taught best and for the longest time' (BGE: §12). Without first overcoming the 'atomism of the soul' embedded in the valuations of slave morality, which dominate every branch of commercial society, it would not be possible to counteract its harmful effects. Nietzsche identifies the task to 'demoralise the world' as our *critical need* without satisfying which 'one could no longer live' (NF-1883:24[7]). He compares the difficulty and the jeopardy of such an undertaking to 'a merciless *war* on the knife' (BGE: §12). Overcoming the 'atomism of the soul' would require, on Nietzsche's view, a careful investigation into the genealogy of values which underpin Smith's political economy.

On Becoming a Science

Smith is widely credited with transforming the discourse on political economy from a leisurely pursuit of the *'natürlicher Philosoph'* into a science (see WN1:345; Worland 1976:248; Montes 2003:723; and Mosini 2009:2–3). Tracing this transformation, in the course of which political economy and subsequently economics align themselves, for a time, more closely with classical physics—primarily with Newton's mechanics—forms an important aspect of Nietzsche's early thinking on political economy and informs his critique of the 'mechanistic interpretations of the world' (NF-1885:34[204]).

Nietzsche problematises the importation into the discourse on political economy of metaphysical assumptions, which he also detects in contemporary physics 'because one hoped with it and through it to best understand God's goodness and wisdom' (GS: §37; §344). Nietzsche considers that 'mechanistic physics' is 'still not naturalistic enough' in its efforts to overcome 'the shadows of God' (Cox 1999:216), which continue reproducing as the 'Christian conscience translates and sublimates into scientific conscience, into intellectual purity at any price' (GM: III, §27). With this, Nietzsche senses a clear possibility of political economy becoming another 'modern-scientific side piece to the belief in God' (NF-1881:11[201]; see HH: I, *HMS*, §37).

Few 'carefully placed' metaphors (see Minowitz 2004:404, fn. 30; Klein and Lucas 2011) have inspired as much academic debate as Smith's 'invisible hand'.[174] Notwithstanding a plethora of interpretations, it has so far proved impossible to dismiss the possibility that the 'invisible hand' denotes 'the doctrine of providence'.[175] Nietzsche would concede that nature, which 'knows no regard for the final objective', occasionally brings into existence 'things of the greatest appropriateness without having willed them' (HH: I, *HMS*, §38). However, the 'concept of nature' is missing from natural law thinking, such as Smith's, where 'everything is moral' (NF-1887:11[394]). As long as this remains the case, an interpretation of 'this world as "necessary" and "predictable" not because there are laws in it, but because there are absolutely no laws' (BGE: §22), conceals theological premises. In this respect, Nietzsche's criticism of 'the Christian', who lives in the promise of '"inexpressible glories" in that he accepts gifts and expects and receives the best he knows at the *hands of divine love* and grace and *not at his own hands*' (D: §546), is not entirely misplaced. Some years later, Zarathustra would add that it is always 'the invisible hands that torment and bend us the worst' (Z: I, *Tree*).[176] In other words, Nietzsche problematises the continued subliminal influence —on the level of 'an unconscious imperative' (GM: III, §24)—of metaphysical assump-

---

[174] See Hont, 2015:91–92; Oslington, 2012:433–435; and Martin, 1990:273–284.
[175] See Oslington 2012:433; Luna 1996:141–142; Mosini 2011:11; and Hont 2015:91–92. Concerning alternative interpretations, see Kennedy 2009:240 (a 'casual metaphor'), Arrow and Han 1971:1 ('a poetic expression of the most fundamental of economic balance relations'), and Friedman 1980:1, 27, 93 (the 'key insight' into the cooperative, self-regulating "power of the market" to produce our food, our clothing, our housing [...] without central direction').
[176] See Martin 1990:271.

tions in the increasingly secular and pragmatic considerations of human affairs, including Smith's conceptions of political economy.[177] When Smith compares the universe to a 'complete machine' (EPS:113) 'endowed with secret wheels and springs' (TMS:19) and to a 'coherent system, governed by general laws and directed to general ends', such as 'its own preservation and prosperity' (EPS:113), Nietzsche would recall the *'deus ex machina'*, which 'translates the metaphysical solution into the earthly one' (NF-1871:14[2]) and retort that:

> [A]s soon as god appears in the machine, we realize that behind the mask is Socrates, trying to balance happiness and virtue on his scales. (NF-1870: *Sokrates*, §1)

From this starting position, Nietzsche views the transition of political economy from the domain of *phronesis* to that of *epistêmê*[178] as being a precarious journey, which since the days of Socrates remains underwritten by a 'sublime metaphysical illusion', which 'accompanies science as an instinct' (BT: §15).[179] For Nietzsche, as for Aristotle, economic questions remain a matter of 'practical significance' and 'not yet a science' (NF:1869:3[10]).[180] As *phronesis* (φρόνησῐς), political economy belongs in the domain of *praxis:* it is concerned with 'where something must be done' (NF-1879:44[6]). Its objective, as expressed by Aristotle, is to develop an understanding of what it means to 'act well', and what acts would promote 'good life in general' (NE: VI, §5). In line with this, Nietzsche notes that any discourse on economy must be 'judged by its consequences on life' (NF-1888:15[42]) and argues against 'the so-called laws of nature and especially the economic laws of nature' (NF-1879:44[6]).

Under the influence of Friedrich Lange (1828–1875), Nietzsche becomes concerned with political economy's susceptibility to ideological manipulation. Particularly as a new science, political economy is 'not nearly independent [...] in every respect it first needs a value-ideal, a value-creating power, serving which it would be allowed to believe in itself' (GM: III, §25). Nietzsche problematises the lack of spiritual defences 'against the sirens who in the marketplace sing of the future' (GS: §377) and seek to make 'science ever more profitable in economic sense' (UM: II, *UDHL*, §7). In his semi-

---

177 See NF-1888:14[105]: 'A morality ... at length enters consciousness as a law, as dominating—And therewith the entire group of related values and states enters into it: it becomes venerable, unassailable, holy, true'.
178 From the Greek 'φρόνησῐς' (phronesis), meaning prudence, practical virtue, and practical wisdom, to 'ἐπιστήμη' (episteme), meaning scientific knowledge or understanding.
179 See Kellner's engaging discussion of the eventual transformation of the 'Socratic Man' into the 'Last Man' in 'Modernity and Its Discontents: Nietzsche's Critique' (1998): https://pages.gseis.ucla.edu/faculty/kellner/papers, last accessed Feb. 27, 2023.
180 Developing Socratic ideas, Aristotle considers five virtues of thought: phronesis (practical wisdom), epistêmê (scientific knowledge), technê (craft and art), nous (intuitive and inward reason, intelligence, the 'eye of the soul' or the 'third eye'), and sophia (philosophic wisdom) (See NE: VI, §§3–11). Aristotle and Plato share a common meaning of 'phronesis' as 'intelligent awareness in general' and 'practical prudence' (See Aristotle 1999: NE, 345). Aristotle's discussion preserves the Socratic connection between phronesis and virtue (See Engberg-Pedersen 1983:236).

nal work on the *History of Materialism and Critique of Its Present Importance* (1866), Lange too comments on the correlation between the moments when the discourse on political economy starts to acquire a scientific veneer and when economics starts to become the preferred discourse of 'capital accumulation' (see Lange 1877:423– 425). As a science, economics acquires the power to transform its appearance as the phenomenon of questionable provenance into an object of modern virtue (see Lazzarato 2012:44). Pondering a possible connection, Lange gravitates towards the view that the fledgling discipline of economics, with its excessive propensity for abstraction and reductivism, would likely fall prey to specific power interests within the 'economy of the bourgeois life' (see Lange 1877:124, 423–424).

Nietzsche, who read Lange extensively and with considerable enthusiasm, evidenced in his correspondence from this period (BVN-1868:562), shares his concern that precisely by claiming 'cold impersonality, value-neutrality', scientific precision and empiricism as its criteria and standard of proof, political economy, infused with this new air of scientific respectability (NF-1885:35[31–32]), would be made to work ever harder on behalf of the money-makers as the legitimating narrative of the 'contemptible money-economy' (UM: III, *SE*, §4).[181] He argues that this vulnerability of the new modern science can be traced back to the metaphysical assumptions that more generally underpinned the mechanistic worldview and underwrote the pursuit of the natural sciences of the time (GS: §344).

Natural Law, the Final State, and the Felicity of Equilibrium

Nietzsche reckons that the 'mechanistic way of thinking'—an outgrowth of the natural law doctrines ('*Naturgesetz*')—is bound to remain 'a philosophy of the foreground (NF-1885:34[247]). Mechanistic conception provides no instigation for developing an understanding of the world that would be commensurate with its unabbreviated nature. Instead, it creates a fragmented view of the world suited to itself while at the same time 'concealing the real motives' for doing so (NF-1884:25[314]; NF-1888:15[42]). The inherent 'simplification of the external world' (NF-1885:35[247]), which Nietzsche sees natural law doctrines as promoting, inevitably harbours 'the claims of the creator' (NF-1885:34[204]). The 'creative mechanic' (HH: II, *AOM*, §9) behind such doctrines is required as their 'moving force' (NF-1885:1[30]) in at least two capacities: as the balancing item for the reductivism of theoretical abstractions, and as a repository of the unintended consequences of mechanistic interpretations of the world (UM: II, *UDHL*, §6).[182] In other words, this third actor is required to ensure smooth operation of this particular worldview:

---

[181] See the excellent investigation into the formative influence of Lange on Nietzsche, including his 'earliest and last writings', in Stack's *Lange and Nietzsche*, 1983:6.
[182] See also NF-1884:25[423], where Nietzsche equates the idea of the '*trust* world order' with the notion of God ('*das Vertrauen in die Weltordnung ("in Gott")*') and GS: §357.

> So that something can be known in a mechanical world order ('*mechanische Weltordnung*'), there must be a *perspective apparatus*, which 1) allows a certain standstill 2) simplifies 3) makes it possible to select and omit. (NF-1884:25[336])

Deriving from such premises, the mechanistic interpretation and valuation of the world entails the precarious potential to develop into 'the most negative of all possible modes of thinking' (NF-1885:34[204]), particularly as it permeates 'the politics of nations' (NF-1875:9[2]).

For Smith, however, it is 'the very suspicion of a fatherless world' that would be 'the most melancholy of all reflections', capable of infusing human understanding 'with nothing but endless misery and wretchedness' (TMS:235). His epistemological platform derives from the premise 'that material phenomena display an underlying order, which is the result of universal laws', which further demonstrates 'the principle of design' (Clark 1989:52) put in place by the 'all-wise Architect and Conductor' (TMS:289):

> [A]ll the inhabitants of the universe, the meanest as well as the greatest, are under the immediate care and protection of that great, benevolent, and all-wise Being, who directs all the movements of nature; and who is determined, by his own unalterable perfections, to maintain in it, at all times, the greatest possible quantity of happiness' (TMS:235).

As Viner argued, 'Adam Smith's system of thought, including his economics, is not intelligible if one disregards the role he assigns in it to the theological elements' (Viner 1972:82). Natural law can be shown to posit the aim and to indicate the means by which this aim may, at the very least, be navigated towards. Arguing that 'the social and the physical universes are merely different aspects of one reality', Smith—a keen student of physics (see Hetherington 1983:498–500; Martin 1990:275)—devises the 'research program to find the natural laws of the social universe much like Newton had for the natural universe' (Clark 1989:54). Smith traces the origins of the division of labour, responsible for the 'great improvement in the productive powers of modern man' back to the fundamental and felicitous propensity in human nature 'to truck, barter and exchange' (WN1:36).[183] The division of labour, Smith argues, by liberating the individual from having to 'procure every necessity and convenience of life' for himself (WN1:44), helps to mitigate the natural 'hatred of labour' (WN2:203), delivers greater security for all and becomes the principal source of innovation, improving productivity, facilitating the process of exchange, expanding the scope of the market and instigating economic growth (Hill 2007:346) towards an 'opulent', 'thriving and civilized society'.[184]

---

[183] See Martin's discussion of the discovery of the division of labour as the key law governing human behaviour (Martin 1990:276). See also *General Introduction* to *An Inquiry Into The Nature and Causes Of The Wealth Of Nations* (eds. Roy H. Campbell and Andrew S. Skinner, Oxford: Oxford University Press, 1976, particularly 20).

[184] See WN1:40–44; Aspromourgos 2013:267; and Berry 2018:65.

As Schumpeter aptly surmised, in positing the division of labour as 'practically the only factor in economic progress', 'nobody, either before or after A. Smith, ever thought of putting such a burden upon the division of labour' (Schumpeter 2006:182).[185] An important point that Smith's argumentation highlights is that, although the division of labour is naturally present within the human constitution, it lies as though dormant, and our ability to take advantage of it grows only gradually, in line with the increase of our appreciation of God's intent upon discovering the further reaches of the pre-ordained natural order. For the majority of human history, the division of labour remains limited, in particular, by the extent of the market (WN1:45). It develops only incrementally, albeit in a progressive direction, through the multiple stages of humankind's development from 'hunting' to 'pasturage' to 'agriculture', and only starts to approach its 'compleat' [sic.] potential with the advent of commercial society (Meek, Skinner 1973:1103–1109).

As part of his argument, Smith aims to demonstrate that the division of labour is not the only phenomenon that follows natural law; rather, the entire economic process exhibits similar directionality. Smith maintains that, considered dynamically rather than statically (Luna 1996; Blaug 1997), such components of the economic process as wages, costs, the rate of profit, demand, supply the 'prices of commodities', along with debts and credits would be 'continually tending to equality', which represents their 'natural state':[186]

> The whole of the advantages and disadvantages of the different employments of labour and stock must, in the same neighbourhood, be either *perfectly equal* or continually *tending to equality* ... this equality ... can take place only in the ... natural state of those employments. (WN1:106–118)

Just as with the division of labour, it is less relevant whether the 'natural state' can be achieved, let alone maintained (Myers 1976:569). Its primary significance, as with sympathy, stems from it becoming a directional signpost for progress (WN1:118).[187] Viewed in this light, Smith's political economy has been interpreted as a system that remains imbued with the spirit of natural law, where God not only 'coordinates the economic mechanism', but also 'ordains a benevolent outcome' (Martin 1990:274). In other words, Smith's 'general faith that the universe is a generally self-correcting and equilibrating natural order' (Hill 2007:348) emanates from a very specific theological premise of the benevolent system design put in place by a like-minded Architect.[188]

---

[185] Cf. Arendt 1998:47.
[186] See Smith's discussion in particular in WN1: Chapters 7 and 10.
[187] See Smith's discussion in TMS, which invokes the Hesiodic metaphor of the 'Fortunate Islands, a life of friendship, liberty, and repose; free from labour, and from care, and from all the turbulent passions which attend them' (TMS:32).
[188] See Hont 2015:91; Myers 1976:560; Arrow, Hahn 1971:2; Hahn 1973:1–2; Heilbroner 1979; Clark 1989:49; Hetherington 1983; Mosini 2009:2–15; and Diemer and Guillemin 2011. See also Montes 2003:723–724. Although Montes argues that 'the popular view of Smith as a forerunner or founder of

Nietzsche would question the provenance of the Smithian 'natural state' in the same manner that he would problematise any conception of 'the final state' (NF-1888:14[188/4]). His concern is whether interpretations and valuations, such as those proposed by Smith, develop 'with respect to the intention and conformity of this intention with the "law"', where 'conformity with the law is already posited as the ultimate goal' and the rest is therefore 'reduced to mere mechanics', intimating that 'life has no more problems' (NF-1888:15[42]). Nietzsche would question whether the natural law thinking is correct in relation to positing 'cause and effect' (NF-1888:15[42]). If it could be shown that natural law misinterprets causality, it would call into question any notion of equality or equilibrium flowing from its analysis as singularly felicitous in origin, and therefore, truly capable of guiding humankind in the direction of the 'civilized and thriving nations' (WN1:36), rather than towards some shipwreck scenario, in which humankind could perish.[189]

Nietzsche's genealogy, which 'works its way backward in time [...] thereby disentangling the separate strands of meaning that have come together in a (contingent) unity in the present' (Geuss 1999:14) forces him to focus on discovering the possible 'difference at the origin, of the kind' that may surprise and disturb us.[190] What if, Nietzsche conjectures, *systems of belief*—such as the natural law doctrine—are, in fact, 'false coasts' that mistake cause for effect (Z: III, *Tablets*, §28)?[191] What if we are building our understanding of how best to manage the political economy of human affairs back-to-front (TI: *Errors*, §2)? Among other things, such possible 'difference at the origin' may result in consequences opposite to the ones intended, and 'our progress' may amount to a regressive movement (NF-1881:11[331]).[192] Nietzsche would take the opposite side of the argument to Smith in order to explore the possible undertones of infelicity implied by Smith's conception of political economy and by the role of the division of labour in this context.

In what could easily be considered a direct comment on Smith, Nietzsche asserts that 'a theory like that of free trade, presupposing that universal harmony must result of itself in accordance with innate laws of progress' is riddled with 'ecumenical goals' which become projected on 'the whole earth' and continues to be guided by the notion of 'a God' who 'broadly directs the destinies of the world and [...] all the apparent twists and turns in its path notwithstanding, is leading mankind gloriously upward' (HH: I, *FLT*, §25). In contrast, Nietzsche's thinking on political economy takes root in the second

---

general economic equilibrium theory must be laid to rest' (Montes 2003:723), he lists a significant number of academic accounts that do not share his assessment.
189 See Z: III, *Gravity*, §2; and Conway 2002:16–18, 107–111, and 236.
190 See Ansell-Pearson's *Introduction* to the revised edition of *On The Genealogy of Morality* (2007: xx).
191 Nietzsche's discussion in Z: III, *Gravity* and *Tables* lends itself to being read as a direct critique of Smith's notions of the 'people of customers' and 'nation of shopkeepers' (WN2:114).
192 In a later note from the *Nachlass*, Nietzsche elaborates on this point by suggesting that 'Faith in "progress"—in the lower spheres of intelligence it appears as ascending life; but this is self-deception; in the higher spheres of intelligence as descending life' (NF-1886:7[8/B]).

law of thermodynamics, known as the Law of Entropy. Although this law is still trapped in the 'nets of the metaphysical bird-catchers' (BGE: §230), it pushes right up against these nets by considering the more problematic aspects of the 'final state' of equality, represented by the concept of the thermodynamic equilibrium.[193] In thermodynamics, equilibrium represents the maximum entropy and minimum energy of the system, branded by Thomson as 'a state of universal rest and death',[194] otherwise known as 'heat death'—i. e., the condition in which transformations of energy and matter have ceased and the atrophy of the system becomes complete.[195] In a manner resembling Smith's adaptation of the logic of Newtonian mechanics to the dynamics of political economy (TMS:183), Nietzsche explores the expository range of the concept of entropy applied to the social sphere, albeit with greater awareness of the 'nets of alternative metaphysical schemata' inevitably stalking such inquiries (Stack 2005:188).[196] In view of the ambiguity of the terminology—not unlike Smith, who never uses the term 'equilibrium' directly[197]—Nietzsche never resorts to the use of 'entropy', when examining its underlying reality.[198] He 'translates' the thermodynamic equilibrium (i.e., entropy),

---

[193] As elucidated by Rudolf Clausius and William Thomson (aka Lord Kelvin), who built on the earlier work by Sadi Carnot and Julius Mayer from the 1850s. Clausius formulates the second law of thermodynamics in his original article *'On the Motive Power of Heat, and on the Laws which can be Deduced from it for the Theory of Heat'* (1850). Less than a year later, working independently of Clausius (Sharlin 1979:114), Thomson arrives at another formulation of the *Second Law* (https://zapatopi.net/kelvin/papers, last accessed March 12, 2023), which states that 'it is impossible, by means of inanimate material agency, to derive mechanical effect from any portion of matter by cooling it below the temperature of the coldest of the surrounding objects'. It is worth noting that Mayer (NF-1881:11[24 – 25]: 25[136]) and Thomson (BVN-1881:139; NF-1888:14[188]) feature in Nietzsche's reflections on entropy directly and Clausius indirectly through the notion of 'disgregation' (NF-1885:43[2]).

[194] To quote from Thomson's *On The Age of The Sun's Heat* (1862): 'The result [of the law of entropy – DS] would inevitably be a state of universal rest and death if the universe were finite and left to obey existing laws. But it is impossible to conceive a limit to the extent of matter in the universe; and therefore science points rather to an endless progress, through an endless space, of action involving the transformation of potential energy into palpable motion and thence into heat, than to a single finite mechanism, running down like a clock, and stopping for ever. It is also impossible to conceive either the beginning or the continuance of life, without an overruling creative power; and, therefore, no conclusions of dynamical science regarding the future condition of the earth can be held to give dispiriting views as to the destiny of the race of intelligent beings by which it is at present inhabited (Thomson 1862: *On the Age of the Sun's Heat*).

[195] It is important to keep in mind that Nietzsche considered the law of entropy as elucidated by Mayer, Clausius and Thompson as a variant of mechanistic thinking. All three scientists in considering the possibility of reversing the effects of entropy inevitably appeal to divine providence. See the quotation from William Thomson in the preceding footnote.

[196] For an excellent discussion of Nietzsche's engagement with thermodynamics, see Holub 2018:360 – 407.

[197] Two reference editions of *The Wealth of Nations* (The Glasgow Edition, Oxford University Press, 1976, and Cannan's classic edition from 1904) were cross-checked for this purpose.

[198] Instead, Nietzsche makes use of the specific terminology of disgregation, which was coined by Robert Clausius in 1862. Clausius, who formulated the concept of disgregation in the process of studying en-

considered as both a tendency and 'the final state' (NF-1888:14[188/4]), to denote the gradual loss of difference and erasure of quality. The loss of quality results from 'stagnation of the forces' (NF-1881:11[245]) which expresses itself in the growing 'anarchy of the atoms and disgregation of the will' (TCW: §7) until the 'stationary level of mankind' (NF-1887:10[17])—the 'great adiaphoria' ('*große Adiaphorie*'; NF-1888:14[83])—is threatened, making earth not 'worth living' on (NF-1886:4[7]).

The 'end state', as conceptualised by Nietzsche, does not simply problematise prevalence of decline over progress as a possible consequence of industrial society (NF-1881:11[340]).[199] Nietzsche's engagement with the theme of entropy is a starker way of highlighting the problem contained in mechanistic thinking. Entropy, both physical and social, raises the stakes and creates a sense of urgency around the intervention of the 'creator *spiritus*' (NF-1888:14[188]) in order to either reverse the effects or slow the onset of entropy. That is, unless the heat death was always 'part of God's plan for the history of the universe' (Tattersall 2014:20).[200] Assuming that it is not, Nietzsche's point is that, regardless of the existence and the possible benevolence of God, entropy is a constitutive feature of the physical world and, he argues, of human experience. Since entropy is not an otherworldly phenomenon, dealing with it, as a condition of humankind's continued existence on earth, is at least as much a question of human agency as it could be God's problem to solve. Nietzsche would contend that Smith's political economy is not well equipped to deal with such challenge. Due to the theological assumptions behind it, Smith's division of labour would be a contributor to the rising entropy, dependent on the 'invisible hand' for the alleviation of its detrimental effects (see TMS: 184, 234). Although Smith was not directly aware of the law of entropy, given that *The Wealth of Nations* was written almost a century prior to its formulation in the 1850s, valuations embedded in Smith's argument would resist the concerns raised by the notion of entropy as a possible outcome of his 'thriving and civilized society'.

As far as Nietzsche is concerned, neither the concept of the conservation of energy nor that of entropy is new. Rather, it is possible to develop a plausible appreciation of their likely repercussions from the Greek mythical tradition.[201] Hesiod's famous didactic poem *The Works and Days* (Ἔργα καὶ Ἡμέραι), which was composed around 700 B.C. (BVN-1870:76), contains two critical aetiologies that convey the notion of entropy: the myth of *Prometheus and Pandora* and the *Myth of the Five Ages*. Smith, however,

---

tropic transformations, considered it as a 'more fundamental concept' than the 'summarising concept of entropy' (Klein 1969:140).

199 See Spengler's relevant discussion of entropy as 'the most conspicuous symbol of decline', which employs Faustian imagery reminiscent of Nietzsche's The Birth of Tragedy, Spengler 1918: Vol. I, Chapter 11, § 14, 420–422.

200 See also Thomson's *Mathematical and Physical Papers*, Vol. V, Cambridge University Press, 1911: 1898:88[27].

201 See Nietzsche's discussion in *Untimely Meditations*, which reference the Hesiodic 'iron age' as the 'fifth act' of humankind's passage on earth, with clear resonances to the entropic tendencies of modernity, the limitations of the mechanistic interpretations, including of history, and their infelicitous consequences (UM: II, *UDHL*, §2, §8). See Kragh 2016 for further context.

works within a conceptual framework that shields him from recognising the more troubling side of the equilibrium until the very end, when it is too late to do anything about it (NF-1887:11[411], §2). Like Nietzsche, Smith draws on Hesiod's *The Works and Days* but with reference to 'The Fortunate Islands' (TMS:32), as though confirming Nietzsche's observation in *The Antichrist*:

> [S]uch a doctrine is [...] incapable of contradicting: it does not even comprehend that there are, that there can be other doctrines; it cannot imagine a contradictory judgement. Where it encounters one, from innermost sympathy it will mourn over 'blindness'—for it sees the 'light'—but it will offer no objection. (AC: §32)

Already in *Untimely Meditations* (1873–1876), Nietzsche sounds the alarm against any form of 'belief that mankind will at any future time attain to a final ideal order of things, and that happiness will then shine upon it with an unwavering ray like the sun of the tropics' (UM: IV, *RWB*, §11):

> If the world process were directed towards a final state, the state would have been reached by now. The sole fundamental fact is, however, that it is not directed towards a final state. (NF-1887:11[71])

Nietzsche contends that, if on the scales of probability, the 'end state' would sooner resemble infelicity (i.e., entropy and heat death) than felicity (i.e., harmony and the Promised Land), striving towards it would be reminiscent of the fate of 'those desperate clever animals', who 'to their great annoyance' laboured under the misapprehension which, contrary to their expectation, led them to extinction (EN: *PT*, 252). Nietzsche does not rule out the possibility that, absent a thorough revaluation of values, humankind may well follow the same path. He insists, therefore, that the 'state of equilibrium' should not be mistaken for having reached 'the summit' (NF-1887:10[138]). This could prove a particularly regrettable error if the 'final state' turned out to be 'a part of the more general enterprise of denying life, depreciating existence, and promising it a death ('heat' or otherwise)' (Deleuze 1983:42, 46).

Sympathy of the Division of Labour

In light of the above considerations, Nietzsche would argue that the assumptions which inform the discussion concerning the division of labour are of critical importance: none of them are 'impartial and general reflections' (HH: II, *WS*, §5), free from the 'schemata of values' which designate the 'dominant cognitive paradigms' (Stack 2005:151) of commercial culture. As he suggests in *Daybreak*, these schemata form the 'basis of all our judgements and "knowledge"' and represent a closed system from which there can be 'no escape and no backway … into the real world' (D: §117). Such system, Nietzsche argues, resists valuations that do not conform to its master logic: it is not possible to catch anything in its nets 'except that which allows itself to be caught in precisely these nets' (D: §117). Nietzsche identifies Christianity as an example of such a closed system of valuations, which continually generates new iterations of itself while preserving continuity of its underlying valuations which safeguard it against dissent and repel heterodox valuations. He would draw a direct parallel between Christianity and the way in which commercial society, as envisaged by Smith, is fundamentally constituted with respect to its methods of valuation. The division of labour, as the central concept around which Smith's political economy develops, cannot, on Nietzsche's view, be immune from these valuations. On the contrary, it should fully incorporate (inwardly) and project (outwardly) such valuations, which underwrite Smith's worldview. More than that, Smith's theory acts as a conduit through which these specific valuations become mediated, imprinting on the general discourse of political economy. Nietzsche insists therefore on the importance of uncovering these valuations and developing an appreciation of their implications.

Both Smith and Nietzsche characterise the division of labour as being somewhat involuntary. Smith traces its origins to 'a certain propensity in human nature' (WN1:42),[202] and Nietzsche argues that it is a phenomenon that is rooted deeply in human physiology and psychology (see NF-1888:14[201], [221]). In a note from 1881, Nietzsche references the 'natural tendency for the division of labour' (NF-1881:11[145]). Both thinkers suggest that some *a-priori* notion of exchange is imprinted in the human psyche as 'the' or 'a' beginning to which we can trace both language and thought' (Graeber 2011:76):

> Fixing prices, setting values, working out equivalents, exchanging—this preoccupied man's first thoughts to such a degree that in a certain sense it constitutes thought. (GM: II, §8)

However, a critical ontological distinction has to be made from the outset. Smith starts with the 'sympathetic exchange', where the utterance of 'mutual wants' (LRBL:203) is anchored in the underlying parity of contracting parties 'in the sense of similar aspirations and the awareness of men's similar abilities' (Danford 1980:694–695; Hill 2018:3).[203] Where Smith assumes an underlying equality as the structuring axis of human affairs, Nietzsche insists on physiological inequality (i.e., difference), which leads him to conceptualise the asymmetry of credit, rather than the symmetry of exchange, as 'the archetype of social organisation' (Deleuze 1983:135).

Smith's approach to the division of labour entails an increasingly quantitative, albeit not yet fully mathematical conceptualisation of value, notwithstanding 'his admission that a quantity of labor is an "abstract notion"' (Myers 1976:565–666). Although Smith recognises that economic variables, such as the division of labour, do not lend themselves fully or exclusively to mathematical precision and the completeness of em-

---

[202] Smith expresses a similar view in his *Lectures on Justice (1763)*: 'If we should enquire into the principle in the human mind on which this *disposition of trucking* is founded, it is clearly the natural inclination everyone has to persuade' (LJ:171).
[203] Adam Smith, *Lectures on Rhetoric and Belles Lettres* ('*LRBL*'), ed. J. C. Bryce, Oxford University Press, 1983.

pirical proof, his discussion of the division of labour is primarily concerned with cost reductions, productivity improvements, profit maximisation, and market expansion (WN1:45–48; see Myers 1967:432–438; Aspromourgos 2013:268). Throughout *The Wealth of Nations*, Smith maintains that the division of labour increases the productivity of 'useful labour' (WN1:101, 218–219). He argues that 'the whole *quantity* of industry annually employed ... naturally aims at always bringing the precise *quantity* ... of supply' to the market (WN1:75; my emphasis) while admitting that finding the market clearing price is not always possible. Importantly, 'the value of any commodity ... is equal to the *quantity of labour*' (WN1:54; my emphasis). The 'great increase of the *quantity of work*', which is the direct consequence of the division of labour, also becomes the source of value creation (WN1:38; my emphasis).

Smith's well-known example of the *pin factory* (WN1:37,81) elaborates on the benefits that the technical division of labour can bring (Vincent-Lancrin 2003:210) and helps connect the division of labour with economic growth (Schmeder and Boyer 1990). Smith's further reaching point, however, is to suggest that 'the effects of the division of labour, in the general business of society' and 'in particular of manufacturers', including the 'very trifling ones', such as the 'trade of the pin-maker', are essentially the same (WN1:36). In other words, by thinking of value-creation in economic terms, it becomes possible not only to blur the boundaries between the social and the technical division of labour by positing that they are regulated by the same principles (Vincent-Lancrin 2003:210–212) but also to render the social division of labour, as deriving from an anachronistic class system (Hont 2015:93) without a basis in 'what constitutes the real happiness of life' (TMS:185). Once the notion of equality (in exchange and in the relative position of the contracting parties) underwrites the logic of the division of labour, there should be no reason, other than social inertia and resistance to change, why—with the adequate education and training—the difference between 'a philosopher and a common street porter' could not be completely overcome (WN1:43). This line of thought would prove of considerable consequence in terms of re-shaping politics with the advent of modernity in a manner which becomes of key importance for Nietzsche (NF-1887:9[44/2]).

Smith effectively argues that the division of labour, as the harbinger of technological advancement and economic growth, can take society part of the way towards 'the social good of a prosperous promised land' (Noble 2005: loc. 1116)—i.e., the 'improved and civilized society' (WN1:33; WN2:268). However, on its own, the division of labour 'does not quite deliver us to the other side', for there is 'no economically necessary reason why advanced industrialization should produce political liberty' (Fukuyama 1992: xv and 143). In other words, another powerful force and stimulant is required to assist the division of labour in fostering humankind's development past the largely economic benefits which commercial society can provide (see TMS:116–117 and 137). For Smith, this is the notion of sympathy, which 'runs through all ranks of men', as the 'fellow-feeling with the misery and distress' of the poor as well as with the wealth which 'the rich man glories in' (see TMS:50–51 and WN1:42). It constitutes mankind's 'most agreeable emotion', the necessary and equally universal corollary of the propensity to 'truck, barter and exchange' (WN1:42) in 'bettering' the human condition:

> To be observed, to be attended to, to be taken notice of with sympathy, complacency, and approbation, are all the advantages which we can propose to derive from it. (TMS:50)

The equality of all 'ranks of men' in relation to sympathy, which binds them with the same logic of 'the great purpose of life' (TMS:50), is more palpable than in the case of the division of labour, which on its own, as a purely economic instinct, is prone to exaggeration and excess: it exhibits a certain propensity to erase its own benefits when pursued without restraint.[204] The need for 'social recognition' (Hurtado 2016:299) and 'status seeking' (Hont 2015:92), as an expression of universal 'fellow-feeling' (TMS:13), leads Smith to develop 'an ethically capacitated' view of the 'natural concord that ensures equilibrium in economic transactions' which would transcend the basic 'mechanical equilibrium of a particle' (Dixon and Wilson 2009: 85 and 90). At a certain threshold, which may well embody the meaning of Smith's 'invisible hand', the merely economic growth in 'productivity' outstrips 'the growth of selfish acquisitiveness' (Hont 2015:93),[205] thus enabling the moral transformation, where sympathy would regain an upper hand in charting the further course of human development, not so much by displacing the division of labour as by complementing it in a more assertive manner.

This becomes a leitmotif of the secular liberal eschatology, narrated among others by Keynes (Markwell 2006:7) and, more recently, Fukuyama.[206] In other words, Smith sees the division of labour and sympathy as the integral parts of the same providential design' (Noble 2005: loc. 1008), which combine into the 'seamlessly unified discourse' (Hont 2015:18–19) of the 'divine economy of creation and salvation' (Noble 2005: loc. 1108). The mechanism by means of which commercial society, brought about by the division of labour, also becomes enabled as 'the source of morality' (Hont 2015:18–19), would derive from the 'sameness of character and sameness of value concepts' (NF-1887:9[173]), which Nietzsche problematises as the objectionable core of 'ethical materialism' (BVN:1887:9[173]). Nietzsche's critique links the Smithian variety of 'sympathy' to the origins of the political and 'the division of labour' to the origins of the economic components of the capitalist social order. Nietzsche traces their shared origin back to an underlying concept of theological equality, the principal tenet of slave morality, which renders Smith's argument inescapably teleological.

---

[204] See Hurtado 2016:298–305; Vergara 2001:93; Coase 1976:529; Macfie and Raphael 1976:20–22; and Myers 1976:570 on the notion of *sympathy* as subtly directing the conduct of human affairs and moderates the excesses of 'self-love'.
[205] See Smith's discussion in TMS:184.
[206] See Fukuyama's *The End of History and The Last Man* (1992), which echoes Smith's argument.

Nietzsche on the Division of Labour

Nietzsche, in contrast to Smith, claims that all great things happen 'far away from the market place' (Z: I, *Flies*). Like Aristotle before him, Nietzsche distinguishes between 'praxis' and 'poesis'.[207] Making that which sells is fundamentally different from making something out of 'sublime happiness' (EN: *TLEMS*, §2), such that only the latter bestows 'distinction upon individuals' (HH: II, *WS*, §280). From his earliest writings, Nietzsche's focus in relation to the division of labour is on its *quality* and social content rather than on quantity:

> 'Mechanistic conception' wants nothing but quantities: but the power is in the quality. (NF-1885:2[76])

Nietzsche insists on distinguishing between the two primary connotations of the division of labour, the *organic and the mechanistic*, and resists any encroachment upon the former by the latter, which becomes an increasingly prominent feature of commercial society. The organic division of labour is rooted in his concept of becoming 'what one is' (EH: *Clever*, §9): 'in spite of everything, you only become what you are (despite everything: want to say education, teaching, milieu, coincidences and accidents)' (NF-1888:14[113]).[208]

Nietzsche takes the division of labour ('*Arbeitstheilung*') to convey a sense of 'work sharing' in respect of one (singular) quantum of labour, which society faces as a *social whole* and attending to which holds it together and gives it purpose. Performing this labour helps achieve two cultural objectives, (1) preservation and (2) enhancement of society, which for Nietzsche, are synonymous with raising humankind higher (NF-1881: 11[176]).[209] Nietzsche insists that within the community 'all work together and enjoy the spoils of their work together (NF-1883:8[9]).[210] The division of labour, as such, denotes the 'separation of the affects within society' (NF-1887:10[8]) in the context of apportioning social responsibility between its different segments, which are seen by him as (a) qualitatively different in terms of their aptitude, understood in terms of the

---

207 *Praxis* derives value of action from the process of acting, it is not driven by considerations of time or as being a means to another end. *Poesis*, which is much closer to Smith's usage, treats work as a means to an end and is concerned with the efficiency of production, like in the example of Smith's pin factory. Nietzsche equates *praxis* with work from which one derives genuine pleasure, and critiques *poesis* as the vulgar means of 'warding off boredom at any cost'. He is highly critical of the modern virtue 'consisting of doing something in less time than someone else' (GS: §329), which is the central premise of Smith's division of labour (see HH: I, §611 on *Boredom and Play* and GS: §42 on *Work and Boredom*). See informative discussion of praxis and poesis in Balaban 1990:185–198.

208 See NF-1888:14[113]: 'You become a decent person, because you are a decent person: that is, because you are born a capitalist of good instincts and prosperous relationships' ('*Capitalist guter Instinkte und gedeihlicher Verhältnisse*').

209 Once again, Nietzsche's reflections echo those of Aristotle; see *Politics*, 1253[a]19.

210 This part of Nietzsche's discussion bears direct resemblance to the accounts of the Essenes by Josephus (1956:369–383) and Philo of Alexandria (1993:905–907; #12.75–13.91).

underlying physiology and psychology, which—combined—give rise to distinct sensibilities; and (b) hierarchically arranged (HH: I, *State*, §441). In *Daybreak*, Nietzsche argues against the injustice of the mechanistic division of labour, which seeks to reduce an individual to 'a part of a machine' and to use him up in that manner (D: §206). This becomes pivotal in terms of conceptualising value:

> [M]an has value and meaning only insofar as he is a stone in a great edifice; and to that end he must be solid first of all, a 'stone'—and above all not an actor! (GS: §356)

The distinction between being a 'part of a machine' and a 'stone in the great edifice' is critical for Nietzsche. The former is expendable and replaceable (individually insignificant), the latter is enduring and essential to upholding the 'great edifice', which extends beyond the individual. The former supports an anonymous process directed to uncertain ends, while the latter is part of the canvas of life. The former is merely an impersonal means, deprived of the possibility of finding fulfilment. The latter is an end and able to achieve completion. The 'edifice' confers meaning on each of its 'stones'; the machine does not. Some great machine may well generate an attractive image projected onto the wall of a building, but it would be disassociated from and leave no trace of the of the character of those used up in this endeavour. Nietzsche's 'edifice', representing the great canvas of life, captures the character of each individual stone used in its creation.

Nietzsche insists on the importance of 'the surplus of the advantages of uninterrupted labour', which lead to the creation of 'complex organisms', and outweigh even their 'considerably increased maintenance and production costs' (NF-1887: [15–16]). Such labour cannot be performed by 'an actor', meaning an individual attempting to play a social role they are 'not qualified' for in terms of aptitude.[211] The division of labour also features in Nietzsche's discussion on the ordering of rank, which 'sanctions a natural distance between several physiological types (characters, temperaments, etc.)', as well as expressing his ideas on the subordination within society 'based on the observation that there are three or four kinds of man, each destined for different types of activity, and each best developed, as this activity through division of labour also belongs to all of them'.[212]

Nietzsche's hypothesis is that the division of labour is primarily organic and only epiphenomenally mechanistic. The optimal division of labour would make organic and mechanistic division of labour commensurate with each other, so that each individual is placed 'according to his nature, in such a position where he can achieve the highest that lies within his realm' and which is in no way correlated to the wages the worker is paid (NF-1887:9[34]). This does not, on Nietzsche's view, interfere with the growing com-

---

[211] Nietzsche's discussion in Part IV of *Thus Spoke Zarathustra* is instructive here. See, in particular, the sections entitled 'On the Higher Man' and 'Conversations with the Kings'.
[212] NF-1888: 14[201] and 14[221]. See also NF-1887:11[36]: 'What decides rank is the quantum of power that you are [critically, not the power that you have–DS]; the rest is cowardice'.

plexity of the technical division of labour but, unlike Smith, Nietzsche would insist that technical division of labour can neither supersede nor substitute the organic, if preserving and enhancing the quality of any kind of output is prioritised (EN: *TLEMS*, §2). Nietzsche's envisaged social structure also entails a degree of fluidity necessary to calibrate the effects of the organic division of labour, whereby 'an exchange' between the different ranks would demote the 'more obtuse and less spiritual' and promote 'the more liberated' in their place, thereby maintaining 'the open sea of indeterminate desires' (HH: I, *State*, §439).

Nietzsche's aspirational aim is that 'the pillars of the social order rest on this foundation: that everyone cheerfully regards that which he is, does and strives after [...] and feels as he does so *'I would not change places with anyone'* (HH: II, *AOM*, §396; my emphasis). His thinking therefore highlights the importance of conceiving such conditions of existence whereby each individual, no matter where they may end up on 'the long ladder of an order of rank and differences in value between man and man' (BGE: §257; NF-1885:34[199]), can remain a *whole individual*, who represents the maximal potency of capability and attainment circumscribed by their endowment. While it is perfectly acceptable, on Nietzsche's view, that one may represent a *lesser force*, being *less of a force* than one is capable of becoming, is objectionable.[213] Nietzsche's intellectual challenge to the mechanistic division of labour, normalised by Smith's political economy, is that it advocates turning each individual into less of a force.

Nietzsche's logic suggests that the division of labour *by itself* should not psychically fragment an individual further. He argues that, although 'in as highly developed a humanity as ours now is, everyone acquires [...] access to many talents' (HH: I, §263), the critical objective of matching one's aptitude to appropriate pursuits becomes jeopardised when the division of labour is approached mechanistically, i.e., strictly with the view to costs and profits.[214] As Nancy Love points out, work, for Nietzsche, 'should express, as it did in ancient times, the worker's whole personality' (Love 1986:184). Nietzsche's overarching concern is that when the reverse becomes reality, the division of labour would inevitably produce 'a very isolated man', who 'is too weak and falls into enslavement' (NF-1869:3[44]):

> [T]he division of labour by organisms brings with it at the same time a degeneration and weakening of the parts, and finally death for the whole. The downfall of organic life in its highest form must be as much the result as the destruction of the individual. (NF-1886:7[2])

---

213 Nietzsche thinks of the 'underprivileged' in the context of the distinction between the more '*whole* human beings' and the 'ordinary people'. In *BGE*, when discussing the 'multitude', he refers to them as '*unvollständige Menschen*' in the sense of physiological as well as psychological incompleteness (BGE: §257–268; GM: I, §17). The 'lower ranks' cannot, on Nietzsche's view, compensate for their incompleteness and rely squarely on the 'higher individuals', who supply meaning, values, and direction to them (HH: I, *MAH*, §521). Underlying incompleteness, however, does not disappear altogether and through the division of labour incomplete souls can also made more useful (NF-1887:10[8]), but only as long as they serve a worthwhile goal posited by the worthy leaders (NF-1887:10[17]).
214 See D: §179 and AC: §57.

Although Nietzsche concedes that the 'mechanical operation of society' (D: §206) 'releases a vast quantity of energy that would otherwise lie dormant' (HH: II, WS, §220), he argues that when, through the division of labour, the senses become 'detached from thinking and judging', a permanent loss of quality results and individuals' developmental potential is inevitably impaired. In contrast, in the past, certain capabilities merely 'lay in them, undistinguished and even earlier, these must have been one' (NF-1885:1[91]). Nietzsche suggests that the problem with the mechanical division of labour is not simply that 'man becomes a screw where the factory rules' (NF-1871:9[64]) but that, by disengaging senses from thinking, it disrupts the pivotal underlying *psychic unity*, which can 'mightily hinder' an individual's ability to develop (D: §173).

Nietzsche suggests that the economic categories, unable to capture the entire range of value capable of being reflected in the products of one's work rather than in one's [wage] labour, lead to the situation where, through its incessant division regulated predominantly by the considerations of supply and demand (i.e., profit), labour gradually becomes reduced to such a level that its individual functions can be adequately measured and expressed through the economic categories, such as 'price'. The 'automaton-like "detail" workers at the expense of skilled, aestheticized artisans' (King 1991:331), become equated to such functions, while that part of labour which cannot be reflected in the profit and loss statements, is eliminated from the production process and becomes, to borrow Marx's terminology, part of man's 'alienated essence'. Nietzsche's views on this aspect resonate strongly with Marx, who laments the 'mutilation of the labourer into a fragment of a man' precisely by 'estranging him in the intellectual potentialities of the labour process' (CW 35:639).

Nietzsche associates one clear manifestation of the psychic unity, which is disrupted by the mechanistic division of labour, with the individual's sense of 'complete responsibility'. The latter, Nietzsche maintains, is purposefully destroyed by the mechanical division of labour so that no one remains a complete individual (NF-1887:11[252]; 10[8]). This has the effect of reducing the existence of the working majority to a state of 'hibernation' in which 'life can just about be maintained without actually entering consciousness' (GM: III, §17).[215]

In other words, economic growth, as a function of the division of labour, inhibits the holistic development of individuals and societies instead of promoting it. While the exchange and the division of labour may facilitate the process of economic growth, they do so by fragmenting the individual in a more profound sense than Smith would have it. As a result, economic growth cannot be posited as representing the development of the whole individual, or of the whole society, which is 'a body on which

---

215 Adorno develops this line of thought in 'Sociology and Psychology' (1967), arguing that individual's efforts to *preserve* themselves under capitalism end up 'surrendered to irrationality' since these are subordinated to economic goals of economic agents which has the effect of splitting of the ego 'off from that of consciousness and thus lost to rationality'. By inhibiting any mediation between the ego and consciousness capitalism can effectively exploit 'the primitive core of the unconscious' in the weakened individuals who can no longer resist such exploitation (see Adorno 1967, Part II:16–20).

no limb is allowed to be sick' (NF-1888:15[1]). At best, economic growth is the development of a fragment and cannot represent a worthwhile goal of human development any more than the division of labour can be the intrinsic source of value creation. Where Smith considers such a trade-off to be inevitable (TMS:184),[216] and believes the problem of de-personalisation to be remediable (Hill 2007:348), on Nietzsche's view, the *damage cannot be undone.*

'What and Wither' of Man

The difference between Smith's and Nietzsche's treatment of the division of labour is further highlighted in their discussion concerning its long-term effects on the overall well-being of individuals and societies. Both thinkers are conscious of the fact that under the auspices of commercial society, its individual members and society as a whole become increasingly divided by labour. They recognise similar dangers implicit in the technical or mechanistic division of labour. Once again, their approaches and the conclusions flowing from their respective analyses differ considerably. Nietzsche argues that the division of labour expedites the transition from *'individuals'* to *'private persons'* (HH: I, *State*, §472) who lack the sense of community that was integral to 'society [Gesellschaft] in the old sense of that word' (GS: §356).[217] The 'atomistic chaos' of commercial society lacks the ethos and the material necessary for building 'the new form of community' ('Gemeinschaft'; NF-1883:16[50]) of 'free individuals' (NF-1880:8[61]), which would be a 'fellowship rather than the flock' (NF-1882:4[48]).[218]

Nietzsche concedes that the eventual mechanisation of the worker, who would come to 'resemble an infallible machine endowed with machine-like virtues', may be inevitable under capitalism (NF-1887:10[11]). He insists, however, that such an 'existence requires philosophical justification and transfiguration', which stretch well beyond the worker's immediate utility and considerations of expediency' (NF-1887:10[11]). Absent such justification and in view of the lack of the 'redeeming class', Nietzsche considers turning an individual into an appendix of a machine to be 'a piece of stupidity' and squandering of human capital.[219] He further asserts that mindless and mind-numbing exploitation, which disregards the vital importance of 'the wellbeing of the worker', necessarily accounting for contentment of both body and soul, would amount in the long run to 'an exhausting of the soil at the expense of the future and an imperilling of society' (HH: II, *WS*, §286). In Nietzsche's mind, the mechanism for the division of labour is inextricably connected to the aims it pursues and to the meaning it confers onto individuals throughout the process. Unlike Smith,

---

216 See Hill 2007:343–348; Rosenberg 1965:135; and Coase 1976:543–546.
217 Nietzsche draws a purposeful distinction between the notions of society and community. See Kaufmann's fn. 61 of GS: §§356 and 304.
218 See the excellent discussion of this point by Vanessa Lemm in *Homo Natura*, 2020:176–177.
219 See NF-1885:2[131]; NF-1887:9[35]; and HH: II, *WS*, §286.

Nietzsche does not believe that such goals and meaning can derive from or be navigated towards the economic domain. The latter has an important role to play, but one which must remain auxiliary. This reinforces Nietzsche's question concerning the means and agency that could create and supply such meaning as would keep the individual and society whole.

Smith addresses the issue of the deleterious effects of the division of labour in the final book of *The Wealth of Nations* He acknowledges that, over the horizon of a lifetime, any individual divided by labour 'generally becomes as stupid and ignorant as it is possible for a human creature to become' (WN2:267). The mechanistic division of labour 'corrupts the courage of his mind […] it corrupts even the activity of his body' and proliferates 'at the expense of his intellectual, social, and martial virtues' (WN2:267). Like Nietzsche in *Human, All Too Human* (see HH: I, §140; II, WS, §220), Smith recognises that performing specialised labour brings with it the 'uniformity of stationary life', which manifests itself in the 'torpor of the mind' and gradually renders an individual incapable of judging not only 'the great and extensive interests of his country' and of public life, but also 'of forming any just judgment concerning many even of the ordinary duties of private life' (WN2:267). Notwithstanding such risks, Smith believes that the proliferation of specialisation through the division of labour is worthwhile because of the benefits economic growth will in due course accrue to all individuals, including 'the lowest ranks of people', to whom 'universal opulence will extend' (WN1:40), helping them translate material welfare into spiritual and intellectual advancement (Rosenberg 1965:139). As Muller argues in *The Mind and the Market* (2003), Smith valued the market because the economic transformation of life entailed the notion that, in the end, it would 'make men better, not just better off' (Muller 2003:52). In order to reach the point of felicitous singularity where economic progress instigates cultural rebirth, according to Smith, there is no better lever than the:

> [N]atural effort of every individual to better his own condition […] it is so powerful a principle, that it alone […] is capable of carrying on the society to wealth and prosperity. (WN1:31)

State and the Division of Labour

Smith's proposal for remedying the 'pernicious effects' of the division of labour on the human faculties, and for revitalising their 'strength and agility' with 'the new vigour' (WN2:194, 267), largely relates to the corrective actions by the government. Within the scope of its narrow political mandate, the government must nonetheless take particular *pains* to render individuals 'otherwise' (WN2:268) by fulfilling its 'third and last duty', which concerns the 'expense of public works and public institutions' that are not in their conception economical (i.e., 'the profit could never repay the expense') but are 'in the highest degree advantageous to a great society' (WN2:214). One example of this is the establishment of a 'compulsory and publicly funded education' (Hill 2007:347):

> For a very small expence [sic.] the public can facilitate, can encourage, and can even impose upon almost the whole body of the people, the necessity of acquiring those most essential parts of education. (WN2:270)

In other words, not only can the deleterious effects of the division of labour be remedied within the safety of the 'existing social and political arrangements' (Hill 2007:345), but remedying them can achieve the quadruple objective of (1) improving individuals' ability, irrespective of rank, to self-direct and maximise utility, (2) preserving 'public tranquillity' and improving social cohesion (see WN2:43, 272, 278–284), (3) promoting greater respect among the lower ranks 'of their lawful superiors' (WN2:273), and (4) strengthening 'public spirit' and furthering the 'happiness of society' (TMS:186).[220]

One issue that Smith does not sufficiently scrutinise, which Nietzsche explores at length, is the ability of the government to effectively remedy the deleterious effects of the division of labour under the auspices of commercial society (NF-1887:9[173]).[221] Neither does Smith engage critically with what would become of the 'lawful superiors' in commercial society, and whether, in the Platonic sense of society's guardians, these 'lawful superiors' and the government could operate with sufficient immunity from the pervasiveness of the 'money trade' (HH: II, WS, §285) and the 'greed of the money makers' (UM: III, SE, §4–7), which infiltrates every segment of life and every area of human activity (see D: §175; NF-1887:9[44]). Although Nietzsche can be said to share Smith's misgivings about any institution that would attempt to 'organise everything anew out of itself' (UM: III, SE, §4), he would question the ability of the modern state, let alone the government, not to be 'swept away by a hugely contemptible money-economy' (UM: III, SE, §4).

As Lester Hunt rightly points out, Nietzsche's critique of the state is not primarily concerned with how much power it possesses or what its policies should be (Hunt 1985:462–463). Rather, Nietzsche scrutinises these aspects of the state against the backdrop of the prevailing valuations. This leads him to question, unlike Smith, the ability of the modern state not to become captive to the (largely theological) valuations from which it grows (i.e., religion and slave morality) and which it works to safeguard, albeit with superficially different—secular—means (BGE: §58). Nietzsche links the corrupting influences of economic logic with the interests of 'tutelary government', acting as 'a pa-

---

[220] Smith discusses his approach to and the benefits of education in a consistent fashion between *TMS* and *WN*.

[221] It is worth keeping in mind that both Smith and Nietzsche frequently use the terms 'state', 'government', 'commonwealth' and, in Smith's case, 'sovereign', interchangeably.

tron of all the prudent egoisms' (UM: II, *UDHL*, §9),[222] by tracing the origins of both phenomena back to religion:

> The *interests* of tutelary government and the interests of religion go hand in hand …the belief in a divine order in the realm of politics, in a sacred mystery in the existence of the state, is of *religious origin*. (HH: I, *State*, §472)

In its secularised form, the modern state, in Nietzsche's assessment, is as much a product of commercial culture as are its individual members. Positioned within the system, the modern state is a purveyor of commercial culture as well as being its product. On Nietzsche's view, this compromises the ability of the government, as well as of the state behind it, to remedy the damaging effects of the division of labour on individuals. Where Smith sees a limited yet valuable role for the state en route to attaining civilised society, Nietzsche envisages quite different long-term consequences of the process. As Sedgwick points out, 'for Nietzsche, the public realm is held in thrall to the power of money' (Sedgwick 2007:6), which renders it unable to resist, let alone control the spread of 'private interests' that seek to usurp every segment of the public domain, gradually breaking it down and carving it up using the logic of business efficiency, productivity gains and the division of labour (HH: I, *State*, §472). While Smith's hope for achieving complete individuals and thriving societies ultimately defers to the 'invisible hand', working through a felicitous interaction of sympathy with the division of labour, Nietzsche argues in favour of cultural rebirth through the revaluation of all values and calls on the great individuals—'masters and experts'—capable of creating new meaning and values.[223]

The principle that best supports the division of labour, on Nietzsche's view, is not the idea of increasing productivity, achieving economic growth or securing profit. Nietzsche contends that to want 'to buy as cheap as possible—where possible for no more than the operational costs—[and] to sell as dear as possible' represents the merchant's morality, which is 'really only a more prudent form of the pirate's morality' and has nothing to do with creating value (HH: II, *WS*, §22). He further argues that, guided by the logic of 'the harmonious endurance of all that is human' (HH: II, *AOM*, §186), the utility of the division of labour should be judged by whether it aids in the creation of values of sufficient magnetism to render every function required for powering the 'great economy of life' necessary. Serving the higher purpose of life's enhancement would incorporate all required functions by bestowing upon them meaning and justification, which is a reward and payment for their sacrifices and effort, as well as pointing the way forward (EH: *D*, §§4–8). The division of labour,

---

[222] This runs close to Smith's own conception, as discussed in Book V (Chapter 1, Part III) of the *Wealth of Nations* with regard to the first and the second duties of the government, being, respectively, protection from 'violence and invasion' and from 'injustice and oppression'. See also Nietzsche's discussion in HH: I, §235; *State*, §472; and II, *WS*, §22, §284.
[223] See UM: II, *UDHL*, §2; and HH: I, §251 and §318.

for Nietzsche, is a manner of staying connected with reality—expressed through the 'reverential attitude to nature' (Leonard 2012:164)—and transmitting this connection into the objects of one's labour, rather than producing saleable commodities. Nietzsche would attribute very different value to the pins produced in the factory, after it has implemented the productivity improvements envisaged by Smith, as compared to the ones created by the community of expert craftsmen.[224]

Furthermore, while Nietzsche would share Smith's assertion that the wage labourer is incapable of 'comprehending his interest' (WN1:220), he would argue, contrary to Smith, that the individual liberty of the wage-labourer does not automatically enhance his ability for self-direction. In the absence of a worthy meaning given to his endeavour, the wage-labourer, reduced to a mere function, is bound to become less valuable as an individual the less 'costly' he becomes as a labourer (WN1:250). This process of devaluation continues until he gradually becomes a fully disposable commodity at the mercy of the profit-logic (Drochon 2016:93).[225] Nietzsche insists:

> At bottom, man loses his belief in his own value if he ceases to be the vehicle for an infinitely valuable whole: i.e., he conceives of such a whole in order to believe in his own value (NF-1887:11[99], §1)

The great mass of individuals divided by labour, Nietzsche tells us, are transformed into 'private persons', who are incapable of the kind of reconfigurative transcendence that would be required of them in order to ascend to the liberal Promised Land of social harmony. Lowering 'the level of human pain and displeasure' inadvertently lowers 'the level of capacity' for spiritual growth and joy (GS: §12), which eventually amounts to 'turning humanity into sand'—into an infinite number of grains of sand, lacking in purpose, direction and meaning (D: §174):

> There is an extraordinary danger in believing that humanity as a whole would grow and become stronger when individuals become flabby, equal, average. (NF-1888:15[65])

As Conway comments, the challenge of 'the cultural production of sovereign individuals' becomes 'incompatible with the diminished resources at the disposal' of the modern age at the end of 'the somnambulant reign of the nodding, blinking "last man"', beyond which looms an even 'more ominous peril: the advent of the will to nothingness, whereby humanity orchestrates its own annihilation' (Conway 1997:17–19).

In his final work, *Ecce Homo*, in the section on *Untimely Meditations* (1873–1876), Nietzsche speaks 'of the false economy of the "division of labour"'. This *'false economy'* privileges superficial gains, such as an improvement in economic welfare, at the price of losing something far more valuable, which Nietzsche associates with the 'loss of pur-

---

[224] See HH: I, §585, and D: §206. See also, concerning Nietzsche's approach to *value*, HH: I, §533; II, WS: §25 and §283; and TI: *Skirmishes*, §38.
[225] See Nietzsche's discussion in UM: III; *SE*, §6; GS: §40 and §356; NF-1884:25[344]; and GM: III, §28.

pose' (EH: *Untimely*, §1). The question he reflects on is: what kind of agency can provide meaning, and by what means can it be created, transmitted and maintained? For Nietzsche, a task of such magnitude befits only 'the guardians and custodians of humankind' (NF-1887:10[39]). These exceptional human beings—by virtue of their character and synthesising sensibility, which demonstrates a profound appreciation of the interconnectedness of everything existent and manifests itself in an unrelenting sense of responsibility for the entirety of society—are uniquely constituted, on his view, in a manner commensurate with the 'hardest challenge' of leading and ruling over others.[226]

Importantly, these 'world rulers' (NF-1884:26[32]) and 'the lords of the Earth' (NF-1885:39[3]) should be capable not only of justifying the past and procuring meaning in the present but also of guaranteeing the future by setting developmental trajectories that would both entail the preservation ('*Erhaltung*') of life and enable its enhancement ('*Steigerung*'/'*Erhöhung*'; NF-1885:2[179]), conceived in terms of intellectual refinement and cultural achievement. In the words of Myers, such individuals would represent 'the principle' as well as 'the force carrying society towards a high level of cultural, artistic, and intellectual achievement' (Myers 1967:432). As Nietzsche stresses:

> [T]he levelled species requires justification: that justification is the service of a higher, sovereign type who stands upon it and can only rise to his own task from that position. (NF-1887:9[153])

Nietzsche's argument amounts to asserting that commercial culture, which denotes particular conditions of existence, is constrained by its prevailing valuations in a manner that inhibits production of the leaders of the requisite calibre.[227] They too become the enslaved products of commercial culture, rendering them unfit to act as the 'redeeming and justifying' class capable of leading humankind (NF-1885:2[127/6]).[228]

Concluding Remarks

Smith's aspiration was for 'political oeconomy' to be 'considered as a branch of science' (WN1:345). Scrutinising this proposition as 'a purely scientific problem', Nietzsche would query whether it is sufficiently 'free of metaphysical interference' (HH: I, §10) and independent of 'a metaphysical mode of explanation' (HH: I, §17). Using the thread of Nietzsche's argument allows us to problematise 'the uncanny force of metaphysical conceptions' (HH: I, §237) that permeate Smith's political economy. These conceptions

---

226 See HH: I, §521; Z: II, *Self-Overcoming*; AC: §57; NF-1887:10[111]; and NF-1887:11[286], #B-D. This line of Nietzsche's argument bears close echoes of Plato's and Aristotle's ideas expressed respectively in *The Republic* (Book IX, 590c-590d) and in *Politics* (Book I, 1254a [1]), last accessed Feb.27, 2023.
227 See Andrew's pertinent discussion, 1995:33.
228 See Drochon's insightful discussion, 2016:91–97.

may 'have dispersed ... in social discourse' under the guise of 'completely disinterested contemplation' (HH: I, §2) but they still denote particular 'type of valuations' that 'lie behind' Smith's 'logical procedures' (BGE: §2).

Nietzsche contends that 'it always remains a metaphysical faith upon which our faith in science rests' (GS: §345) and a 'mistake in reasoning'—namely, beginning from 'the everlasting, the hidden God' (BGE: §2) as the foundational assumption— still 'lies at the bottom', becoming discernible only through the scrutiny of 'the most painstaking observation' (HH: I, §1). On this basis and in view of Smith's ambition to act as a legislator of humankind's future,[229] Nietzsche urges his readers to recognise the risks of positing a 'metaphysical outlook', however well disguised, as the 'ultimate foundation upon which the whole future of mankind is ... invited to establish and construct itself' (HH: I, §22). He argues that 'all that has hitherto made metaphysical assumptions valuable ... is the worst of all methods of acquiring knowledge, not the best of all' (HH: I, §9).

Nietzsche would challenge Smith's 'economic optimism' (NF-1887:10[17]), arguing that it would produce the opposite of its intended effects: 'the entire system of commercialism (of which the division of labour is an integral part)', under the guise of generating 'great levels of liberty' (Hill 2007:346) and curbing the excesses of 'self-love' (WN1:42), would only exacerbate these excesses and lead to further 'metamorphoses of slavery' (NF-1886:7[61]).[230] It is possible that Smith may have already harboured doubt in relation to whether the conceptual premises of his system would deliver the goods it promised and whether it would not, instead, come under increasing pressure from, if not be undone by, the very means (e.g., the division of labour) he proposed to direct humankind's development towards a civilised and thriving society.[231] In particular, as Stephen Miller observes, 'even in Smith himself there is a certain amount of scorn for commercial man, a scorn that is evident when he speaks of "a nation of shopkeepers". Though Smith defended commerce, he often found himself exasperated by commercial man' (Miller 1980:120).

Nietzsche would agree with Smith that it is possible to imagine such 'conditions of society ... in which there will be no selling and buying, and in which the necessity for this will become quite lost' (GS: §31). He would insist, however, that the path to such conditions of existence would have to prioritise cultural and spiritual advancement over economic growth. Only those strong enough in spirit can develop economically without being corrupted by the 'psychological trappings' of 'buying and selling' (GM: II, §8). Only under such premises can commerce, as well as politics, entail a different meaning, 'acquire nobility' and attract 'individuals who are less subject to the prevailing conditions of things' to pursue them (GS: §31). For this to happen, we need to rec-

---

[229] See WN1:345; Haakonssen 1981:92; and Smith 2020:128–135.
[230] Nietzsche's assessment echoes that of Engels: 'Modern economics—the system of free trade based on Adam Smith's Wealth of Nations—reveals itself to be that same hypocrisy, inconsistency and immorality which now confront free humanity in every sphere' (CW 37:801).
[231] See Myer's discussion in 1976:572, as well as Wells and Graafland 2012.

ognise the harm resulting from the inversion of value concepts, which at present mask the retrograde movement of humankind under the pretense of progress (NF-1881:11[331]; [340]):

> A kind of means has been misunderstood as an end: conversely, life and the enhancement of its power have been demoted to a means. (NF-1887:10[137], Nietzsche's emphasis)

Nietzsche argues that when the political economy of human affairs is based on 'conformity with the law', which is already posited as the 'ultimate goal' (NF-1888:15[42]), it can only develop as a closed system from which 'there is absolutely no escape, no backway, or bypath into the real world' (D: §117).[232] In this respect, Nietzsche's intellectual challenge to Smith is whether his political economy would survive the death of 'the old God' (GS: §343),[233] and whether from within itself, it could generate alternative valuations:

> Can we remove the idea of purpose from the process and then affirm the process in spite of this? (NF-1887:5[71])

This is particularly relevant, on Nietzsche's view, because anchoring the political economy of human affairs *vis-à-vis* an external reference point (e.g., the benevolent Architect) would eventually undermine the validity of the latter but without fostering an alternative value-generating capacity, which Nietzsche likens to realising 'that you are being fooled and yet without power to not be fooled' (NF-1886:5[71]).[234] In *the Genealogy*, Nietzsche argues that this almost physiological need for 'external stimuli' is an 'essential feature' of slave morality and ressentiment (GM: I, §10). Combining non-commensurability to the old standards with the inability to generate any replacement would, on Nietzsche's view, develop into the 'nihilistic consequences' of any theory, including the 'political and economic way of thinking' (NF-1885:2[127]).

As such, Nietzsche would see the real task of political economy in generating new valuations. This would be impossible, Nietzsche insists, without changing the frame of reference, i.e., until such time that we can 'dispatch all metaphysical comforts to the devil' (BT: *ASC*, §7) and start evaluating political economy by 'its consequences on life' (NF-1888:15[42]).[235] Nietzsche aims to set his own thinking on the matters of political economy squarely against such 'metaphysical plausibilities' (HH: I, §109) and to anchor his analysis in 'this ephemeral, seductive, deceptive, lowly world' (BGE: §2).

---

[232] See also BT: §15 for Nietzsche's elucidation of this dynamic.
[233] See Wydra's illuminating discussion of this point, 2015:37.
[234] See also NF-1888:15[42].
[235] Nietzsche is careful to differentiate his argument away from the utilitarian variety, which also stipulates the importance of considering the consequences. Nietzsche argues that the utilitarian approach does not add up to considering 'the great economy', as it projects the 'biological value' of 'an inhibited life' onto its analysis of the consequences of action, rendering such analysis fragmented (NF-1888:14[185]).

Nietzsche's hypothetical polemic with Smith allows us to follow some of the political-economic consequences of a worldview permeated by the valuations of slave morality. It also provides a glimpse into the crisis of modern political economy highlighted by Nietzsche's critique and the need for revaluation that Nietzsche attempts by thinking 'outside of all social orders' (NF-1886:5[71], §14) that are saturated with precepts of slave morality.

4 Nietzsche and Marx: Political Economy of the 'Upside-Down World'

> The honesty of a contemporary scholar ... is to be decided on the basis of his attitude to Nietzsche and Marx. Those who do not acknowledge that they could not carry out considerable parts of their work without the work done by these two are cheating themselves and others. The world in which we ourselves exist intellectually is a world largely moulded by Marx and Nietzsche. (Max Weber[237])

Introduction

Weber's observation, widely echoed to this day, intimates a difference between Nietzsche and Marx. At the same time, it suggests that the intellectual milieu we inherited from modernity was *not* predominantly shaped by either one of them but by both.[238] Amalgamating Nietzschean influences with an intellectual indebtedness to Marx in his 'sociocultural critique' (Solms-Laubach 2012:77), Weber may also have put forth a prediction of sorts: that, while the future world may still be the world Marx and Nietzsche remonstrated against, it would not be the world of which either of them had dreamt. In other words, Weber may have highlighted our implicit inability—a certain existential constraint—to move beyond Nietzsche and Marx, a failure to overcome their critique. If we are still *trapped* in the world Nietzsche and Marx rebuked and tried to find the way out of, pondering over their reflections on the *human condition* in the context of political economy ought to have continued pertinence. This is particularly true in a world 'by many measures even more unequal than the capitalist order against which Karl Marx wrote in revolutionary protest' (Wood 2014:252), the inequality of the kind which Nietzsche would by *no means* endorse.

Today, when it seems easier for us to envisage 'the thoroughgoing deterioration of the earth and of nature than the breakdown of late capitalism' (Jameson 1994: xii),

---

Note: I am grateful to Professor Allen W. Wood and to Dr. Markus Granziol for commenting on the early drafts of this chapter and for their generous, probing, and insightful criticism of my work.

237 Baumgarten, Eduard (Ed.) (1964): *Max Weber: Werk und Person*, 1ˢᵗ edition, Tübingen: J.C.B. Mohr, 554–555.

238 Most recently, Cristaudo asserts that 'among the moderns, two men—Nietzsche and Marx—tower above all others as prophets calling for the fashioning of new types of human beings' (Cristaudo 2017:370).

some may argue that our real-time experience of the world is more Nietzschean than Marxian. Still, in terms of its underlying *economic processes* we may recognise many of capitalism's features highlighted in Marx's critique.[239] Today, as it was in Marx's time, the 'price of capital (i.e., interest rate)' is determined by the incessant struggle between capitalists 'over the division of the profit' (CW 32:509; 3:435). The accumulation of capital still lends a veil of anonymity to its proprietors making it just as 'impossible to tell from the money itself, how it got into the hands of its possessor, or what article has been changed into it' (CW 35:120; CW 29:462). In other words, capital continues its apparently dis-embodied existence. Up until now, no amount of 'compulsion from society' has made capital any less reckless (CW 35:275), nor has it reined in the 'capitalist's boundless greed for riches' (CW 35:164). This greed continues to generate 'excess capital' which seeks to offset the secular decline in its rate of profitability by stagnating the real wages of the working people, the 'pauperisation of the great mass of producers' and by the continuous creation of *'relative overpopulation* of labourers'—a 'mass of human material always ready for exploitation' (CW 35:624–626; CW 37:249–255; my emphasis).[240]

In order to understand capitalism's 'secrets of profit-making'—i.e., the 'conversion of money into capital' (CW 35:176)—we still need to 'desert the sphere of circulation and commodity exchange', which Marx likens to the 'very Eden of the innate rights of man where alone rule Freedom, Equality, Property and Bentham' (CW 35:186) and to follow him on his descent into capitalism's dungeons—reminiscent of Danto's *Inferno*—where the prosaic 'C-M-C' is transmuted into the spellbinding 'M-C-M'.[241] The 'alchemistical retort of circulation', continually reaching new dizzying heights, has only tightened its iron grip on the hearts and minds of capitalistic subjects (CW 35:123). Just as in Marx's time, the 'metamorphosis of a commodity' continues to 'assert itself' periodically 'by producing a crisis' which lays bare the contradiction between 'the personification of objects and the representation of persons by things' (CW 35:123–124; 148–149). The connection Marx asserted between the 'accumulation of capital and wealth at one pole' and 'the accumulation of misery, agony of toil, slavery, ignorance, brutality, mental degradation, at the opposite pole' remains intact (CW 35:640; CW

---

239 See Werner Bonefeld's insightful discussion of 'primitive accumulation' as remaining central to the social constitution of modern capitalism and its mechanisms of expropriation (Bonefeld 2011:379–399).
240 A considerable body of academic literature is devoted to the analysis of *'excess capital'* in the global economy, the multi-decade stagnation of *'real wages'* in the global economy and the *'pauperisation of great mass of producers'* (e.g., Amazon vs. small retailers, supermarkets vs. farmers). The most troubling inference, however, at which both Marx and Nietzsche arrive is that capital (or debt, in Nietzsche's case) seeks to dampen the consequences of its own seemingly limitless expansion by dissolving the effects of financial inflation in accelerating *human inflation*, understood in terms of the increase in human capital and the corresponding disinvestment in social and human capital.
241 'C-M-C' stands for 'commodity-money-commodity' and 'M-C-M' denotes 'money-commodity-money', i.e., the formulas of capital's creation. See Roberts 2017:24–56 and 244–256 for an enlightening interpretation of Marx's *Capital* against the conceptual backdrop of Dante's *Inferno*.

37:249). All the while, the 'antagonistic character of capitalistic accumulation' (CW 35:640) shows no signs of abating:

> One capitalist always kills many others. Hand in hand with this [...] expropriation of many capitalists by few, develop, on an ever-extending scale [...] the conscious technical application of science, [...] the entanglement of all peoples in the net of the world market, and with this, the growth of the international character of the capitalistic regime. Along with the constantly diminishing number of the magnates of capital, who usurp and monopolise all advantages of this process of transformation, grows the mass of misery, oppression, slavery, degradation, exploitation. (CW 35:750)

Marx maintained, however, that the developing crisis of capitalism's political economy would *inevitably* culminate in 'the revolt of the working class' in which the 'capitalist integument shall burst asunder', private property would be abolished and the 'expropriators shall be expropriated' (CW 35:750).[242] Yet Marx's expectation that the 'centralisation of the means of production and socialisation of labour' would eventually reach a point where they 'become incompatible with their capitalist integument' (CW 35:750) has not (yet) materialised, or something else might be amiss in his calculations. Partly as a result of this, Nietzsche's analysis of the *spiritual consequences* of the economic processes problematised by Marx—i.e., the pervasive and increasingly militant nihilism that engulfs modernity, crystalising in the 'nihilistic consequences of political and economic way of thinking' (NF-1885:2[127]) and inhibiting the possibility of transformative *praxis*—appears as a compelling supplement to and an extension of Marx's theories.[243]

We still grapple with the apparent dichotomy between Marx's economic and Nietzsche's spiritual diagnoses of modernity. Henrdik Wallat's nuanced study of Marx and Nietzsche, 'Das Bewusstsein der Krise' (2009), links the two critiques into the singular and enduring 'consciousness of the crisis' which enunciates the work of both thinkers (Wallat 2009:12–15). This may, in turn, accentuate Weber's prescient wisdom, namely, that we continue to need both Marx and Nietzsche to make sense of our predicament as the search for a different future (in which their critiques would be overcome) goes on without an end in sight and increasingly resembling a race against the clock. Where Marx charges ahead above ground, Nietzsche distinctly appears to be speeding along, in a broadly similar direction through an underground tunnel. Both

---

[242] Marx argues that 'proletariat and wealth are opposites' created by 'the world of private property' such that the 'private property, as wealth, is compelled to maintain itself' it will insist on perpetuating proletariat as the necessary condition for maintaining itself. For this reason, the proletariat is '*compelled* as proletariat to abolish itself and thereby its opposite, private property' (CW 4:35–36). Aware of the antithetical basis of its existence private property is forever 'restless'—i.e., it senses the inevitability of its fate (CW 4:36).

[243] Wilhelm Roscher, whose work on political economy Nietzsche read, noted that 'how detrimental it is to ignore the *psychological nature of Political Economy* is evident from the errors of Karl Marx, who personifies things in a manner almost mythological' (Roscher 1878:104; fn. 6). See also Stiegler's illuminating discussion in *The Decadence of Industrial Democracies*, 2011:36–93, and Solms-Laubach 2007:304–305.

Marx and Nietzsche use the analogy of the 'upside-down world' to convey the quintessence of the object of their investigation. However, where Marx conceptualises the 'upside-down world' of capitalism (CW 3:326), Nietzsche goes right into the middle of it, quite possibly through the door opened by Marx and, dwelling inside this 'inverted, upside-down, empty world of phantoms in which we live' (D: §118), he finds the values of slave morality.[244] As Deleuze remarked, if Marx was 'the dawn of our culture', Nietzsche was 'the dawn of a counterculture'— they were both parts of the advent of our present (Deleuze 1973:160).

The trouble with Marx is that he has written too much (and co-authored more) to remain clear, consistent, and easy to grasp, even for the majority of those 'whose class interest is in agreement' with his argument (Russell 1946:818). The trouble with Nietzsche is that, having written considerably less, he never intended to be clear or easy to understand, especially for the majority. Nevertheless, buried under these idiosyncrasies lie hidden both strong congruencies and great disparities between their views. Notwithstanding a great body of excellent academic work penned around Nietzsche and Marx, no comparative study of their political-economic projects has been undertaken. This under-explored terrain, if diligently mined, will undoubtedly unearth much that would illuminate our understanding not only of the world we inhabit today, but of *what* needs to change and the *true cost* of bringing about such change. This chapter does not attempt to deliver conclusive comparative justice to these great thinkers. Rather, by examining Marx's and Nietzsche's views about the trajectory of humankind's development, my intent is to illuminate certain aspects useful for understanding Nietzsche's approach to political economy against the backdrop of Marx's towering theoretical edifice.[245]

A Word of Caution

When comparing and contrasting Nietzsche and Marx, one ought to proceed in awareness of the two *biases* that inadvertently penetrate any discussion of the two great German thinkers of the late 19th century. In the first instance, a distinction needs to be

---

[244] See further Nietzsche's discussion in GM: Preface, §4; AC: §25 and NF-1887:11[3]. Conceptual affinity with Marx's concept of the 'upside-down' world equally extends to Nietzsche's critique of religion, which he extends beyond Marx.

[245] My view, having read, re-read, and compared many a passage in Nietzsche and Marx, is that Nietzsche's knowledge and understanding of Marx's (and Engels') work extends *considerably further* than Brobjer was able to substantiate in his piece on 'Nietzsche's knowledge of Marx and Marxism' (2002). See, for instance, Nietzsche's address to the 'philosophers of the present and the future, not in theory but in *praxis*, in practice' (GS: §372); Marx and Nietzsche on using '"man" as an *aeterna veritas*' (CW 5:88–89 and HH: I, §2); Nietzsche's discussion in D: §206 and Marx in CW 28:410–412 concerning the 'external goal' and the 'Asiatic forms' of modern sociality. Compare Engels' critique of Carlyle (CW 3:451–456) with Nietzsche's discussion in UM: III, *SE*, §4 ('the waters of religion are ebbing away') and, later, in GS: §40.

made between 'Marx and the Marxists' (see Wood 2014:267–268, 301; Stedman-Jones 2018:188) in much the same way as Goethe once drew sharp contrast between Newton and the multiple cults of the self-appointed Newtonians[246] or, indeed, as Nietzsche highlighted the difference between Christ—the 'noblest human being' (HH: I, *State*, §475)—and Christianity in terms of the latter being the deeply ideological enterprise, which ends up usurping its 'founder', inevitably 'mutilating' and loading him 'with alien features' suited to its own political agenda (see AC: §24, §29, §40).[247] A discerning reader needs to distinguish between Marx's meaning and the interpretation of that meaning by those who claim to follow his teachings, whether in theory or in practice. The few who come up with theories that illuminate important aspects of our existential reality are *not* the same kind of people as those many who use these influential theories, invariably for very different purposes.[248] For this reason, Nietzsche reminds us, 'virtue' must be defended 'against the preachers of virtue' as the latter tend to become 'its worst enemies' (NF-1887:10[109]).[249] Nietzsche's particular caution, which resonates in this context, is that when it comes to a truly revelational teaching, such as that of Marx, one ought to beware of a *triumvirate* that might preside over such intellectual venture, as often 'three thinkers' may end up 'equaling a spider':

> In every philosophical sect *three thinkers* follow one after the other in the following way: the first produces out of himself the seed and sap, the second draws it out into threads and spins an artificial web, the third lurks in this web for victims who get caught in it—and tries to live off philosophy. (HH: II, *AOM*, §194; my emphasis)[250]

A further distinction to be drawn is that between Marx and Marxist theory and the Soviet experience. The latter is often held up as 'evidence' of both the successes and the pitfalls of Marx's theories and of the subsequent Marxist interpolations.[251] This confusion often comes to bear on the Nietzsche-Marx/Marxism polemic (Eagleton 2011:109–111; Kline 1969:166–167), especially when it is suggested that Marx's dream

---

246 See Iliffe 2016:93–131 and Jackson 1994:682–683.
247 See, for example, Misrahi's suggestion that Marx's apparent anti-Semitism in the notorious 'On the Jewish Question' (1845) is 'non-Marxist (1972:136). A deeper and more delicate layer still, that merits exploring in this context, is the relationship between Marx, as the 'ideas man', and Engels as the more skilled writer and revolutioniser. Cf. Löwith on 'Marx becoming Marxism' (1993:44).
248 Einstein's famous $E=mc^2$ and the infamous Manhattan Project, culminating in the horrors of Hiroshima and Nagasaki in August of 1945, represent, possibly, the most striking illustration of Nietzsche's concern, which applies fully to Christ and to Marx.
249 See Rockmore's insightful discussion of Lenin's alleged misappropriation of Marx's economic theories for revolutionary purposes (Rockmore 2018:192).
250 This observation certainly rings true if we consider either Jesus, Peter and Paul or Marx, Engels, and Lenin. See Heilbroner 1999:86.
251 See Fromm 2004:34 and Wood 2014:314. For illustrations of approaches which tend to fuse Marx with Marxism, see Terry Eagleton 1990 and 2011. See also Wood's comment in 2014:270–271.

descends into the nightmare of Stalin's Russia as inevitably as Nietzsche's dream materialises in the horrors of Hitler's Germany.[252]

In particular, it is a facet of the liberal tradition which, in bending Nietzsche and Marx to its interpretive will, frequently attempts to play Marx/Marxism and Nietzsche off against one another—so as to weaken and discredit them both. Marxism, as a potent intellectual current, responds in kind. As there is no Nietzsche-ism to speak of, such surreptitious liberal attempts of incorporation remain sheepishly unaddressed in Nietzsche scholarship.[253] Marx and Nietzsche are different and may disagree profoundly on some critical points, but they are *not enemies* or, rather, they are not the kind of enemies they are often portrayed to be. Marx is no more an alternative to Nietzsche than Nietzsche is a substitute for Marx. As Henri Lefèbvre—echoing Weber—famously asserted, the modern world is both 'Marxist' and 'Nietzschean' at the same time (Lefèbvre 2020:28). A common fallacy to avoid is the assumption that, while Marx belongs to the subject matter of political economy, Nietzsche does not. The focus of Nietzsche's critique is expressly the *upside-down world of capitalism*, the political and economic manifestations of which Marx chastises in his work (CW 3:326). Where Marx's economic critique does not reach, Nietzsche's psychological examination of economic categories—*as values*—helps to extend the reach of the critique of modern political economy:

> [T]he critique he has provided has been far more subtle and specific than, for example, Marxist theory, which has condemned ideologies en bloc, but has never succeeded in *entering into their inner workings*, their lies, as deeply as Nietzsche. (Adorno 2000:172; my emphasis)

Nietzsche cautions against excessive attempts to 'mediate' between any 'two resolute thinkers'—to make them sound 'the same'—as such approach betrays only 'weak eyes' (GS: §228). Still, there is considerably more *agon* between the two thinkers than there is *antagonism* and, as Nancy Love argues, bringing 'two of the greatest critics of modern society' together produces a more powerful critique of modernity than 'either critique does alone', precisely because they question similar issues from different perspectives without, however, being complementary or attempting to resolve each other's contradictions (Love 1986:2–17).[254]

---

252 As a representative example of these *recurring* liberal misconstruals, see Russell 1946:642 and 719.
253 Cf. Waite 1996:20.
254 See also the notable discussion by Tracy Strong in *Friedrich Nietzsche and the Politics of Transfiguration* (1992) on the structural convergence of Marx's and Nietzsche's critiques of capitalism.

Nietzsche and Marx at a Glance

The genesis of Marx and Nietzsche's respective worldviews can be traced to the thinkers of Greek antiquity.[255] Both excelled at classics and wrote their doctoral dissertations on pre-Socratics. In their theses, Marx and Nietzsche grappled, albeit indirectly, with the issues of *truth*, the *role of human agency* and the *praxis of philosophy* or, in Nietzsche's case, philology.[256] Skidelsky reminisces that when 'Marx was twenty-four, a contemporary wrote of him: "Imagine Rousseau, Voltaire, Holbach, Lessing, Heine and Hegel fused into one person...and you have Dr. Marx"' (Skidelsky 2000:1). The endorsement of young Nietzsche by 'Friedrich Ritschl, a generally conservative professor at Leipzig'—as someone who would one day grace 'the front rank of German philology'– was every bit as emphatic (Kaufmann 1994:7–8). Marx's intellectual path led him through the dense forest of Hegel's phenomenology, while Nietzsche's beckoned him to navigate the thick mists of Schopenhauer's pessimism. Both accepted their respective intellectual challenges and sought to overcome their teachers. Outside of academic pursuits, Marx and Nietzsche's personal journeys, not unlike their work, share many a similarity as well as taking many a different turn, leading them towards contrasting conclusions. At the end of their respective intellectual pilgrimages neither Marx nor Nietzsche bequeathed to us a detailed vision of what their 'ideal society' might look like. Marx's communism, in the final reckoning, does not reveal itself as either a 'state of affairs to be established' or as an 'ideal' to which reality would have to be moulded (CW 5:49). Nietzsche leaves us with an apocalyptic vision of the crises, wars and earthquakes that will plague our present and our children's future as humankind convulses with the birthing pains of '*great politics*' (EH: *Destiny*, §1).

Bertrand Russell, who found Nietzsche impossible to coalesce into the liberal worldview, had nonetheless conceded that 'Nietzsche's prophesies as to the future', although they were no more than the 'power fantasies of an invalid', had nonetheless 'proved more right than those of liberals' (Russell 1946:794). Russell had no such praise to give to Marx, whom he found 'difficult to classify' but much easier to integrate as 'an outcome of British classical economics' and a successor to the liberal revolutionary movement of the 'time of Milton' (Russell 1946: 811).[257] Russell's divergent assessments of Nietzsche and Marx contain important clues for developing a better understanding

---

[255] See Love's review of the 'overlapping intellectual origins' of Nietzsche and Marx, 1986:20–29.

[256] Marx, unlike Nietzsche, received his PhD on *The Difference between the Democritean and Epicurean Philosophy of Nature*, albeit 'in absentia', from the University of Jena in 1841. Nietzsche was awarded an 'honorary doctorate' by the University of Leipzig in 1869 on the merit of his other published work. Concerning Marx, see *The First Writings of Karl Marx*, 2006:20–41, and in relation to Nietzsche, see Jensen's 'Nietzsche's Valediction and First Article', 2014:99–115, and Jonathan Barnes' 'Nietzsche and Diogenes Laertius', 2014:115–139.

[257] Russell, like many liberal thinkers to write after him, considers that liberalism and Marxism 'are philosophically *not very widely separated*, both are rationalistic, and both, in intention, are scientific and empirical' (Russell 1946:817; my emphasis). See also the excellent discussion of the manner of Marx's incorporation by 'travesty' in Eagleton 2011:238–239.

of the scope and the substance of Nietzsche's undertaking as well as for situating it within the context of the liberal and Marxist critiques.

An Outline of Overlapping Political Economies

The political economies of Marx and Nietzsche can be conceptualised as an undertaking to enable the process of fundamental social change with the view to attaining such 'Existenzbedingungen' ('conditions of existence') that would enable realisation of the full scope of the individual's abilities, while contributing to a flourishing human community.[258] Conditions of existence conducive to such transformation of *human potentiality* are synonymous with the notion of *wealth* beyond material abundance, which Marx and Nietzsche—in contrast to the classical political economists[259]—would endorse:

> What is *wealth* if not the absolute unfolding of man's *creative abilities*, without any precondition other than the preceding historical development, which makes the totality of this development— i.e., the *development of all human powers* as such, not measured by any previously given yardstick —an end-in-itself, through which he does not reproduce himself in any specific character, but produces his totality, and *does not seek to remain something he has already become, but is in the absolute movement of becoming?* (CW 28:411–412; my emphasis)

This approach can be traced back to Aristotle's reflection concerning the kind of life that would be 'most desirable for almost all men, and ... whether the same life is most desirable both for the *community* and for the *individual*, or a different one' (P:1323[a]). Both thinkers analyse the conditions of existence which hinder the free and comprehensive development of human potential and aim to identify the chief causes of such hindrances. As Love aptly surmises, 'to show man that the conditions which frustrate his creative powers are his own creations, Marx and Nietzsche question the premises of modern society' (Love 1986:5). Conceptually, both projects entail a notion of *positive transcendence* of modernity's socio-economic conditions which reaches further than the economic *praxis*. In their distinctive ways, Nietzsche and Marx attempt to answer the questions which Nietzsche raises in *The Case of Wagner*, namely, 'where does all the *mischief* in the world come from?', and how does one 'get

---

[258] For Marx, see CW 5:78 ('Only within the community has each individual ...'); CW 5:38–63 (the discussion of 'Communism and Private Property'); CW 28:419–420; and Megill 1970:382–386. For Nietzsche, see Clark and Wonderly, 2015:118–122 as well as Young 2015:1–4.

[259] The founding authors of political economy, including James Steuart (1712–1780), Adam Smith (1723–1790), Jean Baptiste Say (1767–1832), and John Stuart Mill (1806–1873), did not have to go to great lengths to define the object of their inquiry. 'Wealth' seemed obvious enough to form part of the titles of their respective treatises. Wealth has also been conceptualised by them as representing the *material wealth*, criticising which differentiates Marx and Nietzsche from the conventional discourse on political economy.

rid of the disaster' and 'of the old society' (TCW: §4)? [260] Moved by the desire to understand 'the whole highly complicated system of antagonisms that constitute the 'modern world' (BVN-1874:398) sets Nietzsche and Marx apart from the political economists of their time philosophically as well as methodologically.[261] Marx asserts this clearly in *The Economic and Philosophic Manuscripts of 1844*:

> [W]e have to grasp the *intrinsic connection* between private property, avarice, the separation of labour, capital and landed property; the connection of exchange and competition, of *value and the devaluation of men*, of monopoly and competition, etc.—we have to *grasp this whole estrangement* connected with the money system. (CW 3:271; my emphasis)

Without once using the term 'capitalism' ('Kapitalismus'), Nietzsche and Marx advance multi-pronged critiques of the 'industrial world' (HH: I, *State*, §440) and of the 'money-economy' (UM: III, *SE*, §4) as capitalism's essential features. They scorn the pervasive culture of greed underwriting these constructs, which they see as bending modernity—politically and economically—to its reactive will and reactionary valuations at the expense of cultural rebirth (Miller 1980:120). Echoing Nietzsche and Marx, Thomas Mann captures this predicament poignantly in *Reflections of a Nonpolitical Man* (1918):

> What is science today? Narrow and hard specialization for profit, exploitation, and control. What is culture? Humanity perhaps? Breadth and goodness? No, nothing more than a means for earning money and for dominance. What is philosophy? Perhaps still not a way of earning money, but also very narrow specialization in the style and spirit of the times. Just look at him, your 'German burgher' of today, this imperialistic mine owner who would not hesitate to sacrifice five hundred thousand human beings and twice as many more to annex Briey and to be lord of the world! (Mann 1987:98)

Marx points out that 'the only wheels' which the capitalist political economy 'sets in motion are greed and the war amongst the greedy' (CW 3:271).[262] Both thinkers recognise unequivocally that within this architecture of political economy 'money has become a world power' and 'the very principle of life' of modern society:[263]

> Money is the universal *self-established value of all things*. It has robbed the whole world—both the world of men and nature—of its specific value. Money is the *estranged essence of man's work* and man's existence, and this alien essence dominates him, and he worships it. (CW 3:172; my emphasis)

---

260 In *The German Ideology* Marx also uses 'mischief' to describe the conditions when 'machinery and money' act upon the social relations in society as 'destructive forces' (CW 5:52), aided by the 'mischief' of the bourgeois misconstrual of 'the conception of right' (CW 5:362).
261 See King's' insightful discussion of this in relation to Marx, 1991:328–329.
262 See also Marx's (and Engels') discussion of greed in CW 3:237, 309, and 533 as well as CW 35:400.
263 See CW 3: 173–174; CW 35:143; GSt, 171; and UM: IV, *RWB*, §5.

Deeper than that, Marx and Nietzsche draw a direct connection between religion (or, God) and money as the key causes of *objectification* and *alienation*. In secular capitalist modernity, God, although he may well be dead (according to Nietzsche), does not disappear.[264] Rather, he dissolves into debt, or into capital, just as 'guilt' becomes superseded by 'nihilism' and the moneymaker—or 'Mr. Moneybags', as Marx would have it—replaces the 'ascetic priest', ensuring the unbroken line of succession of the 'alien', in substance, *reactive power:*[265]

> Selling is the practical aspect of alienation. Just as man, as long as he is in the *grip of religion*, is able to objectify his essential nature only by turning it into something *alien*, something fantastic, so under the domination of *egoistic need* he can be active practically, and produce objects in practice, only by putting his products, and his activity, under the domination of an *alien being*, and bestowing the significance of an *alien entity*—money—on them. (CW 3:174; my emphasis)[266]

Both Marx and Nietzsche, in their own ways, take to the 'mist-enveloped regions of the religious world' (CW 35:83) and 'the vast, distant and hidden land of morality' (GM: *Preface*, §7) in order to explain, respectively, the 'whole mystery of commodities, all the magic and necromancy that surrounds the products of labour as long as they take the form of commodities' (CW 35:87) and the descent of the principal tenets of slave morality from the economic categories (GM, II, §4–6).

Nietzsche and Marx problematise the rapid and inevitable diminution of the meaning and value of human existence under the auspices of capitalism (see BGE:§203; NF-1888:14[9]; CW 28:412), while acknowledging the need to 'make use of the existing political and economic conditions' (BGE:§61) in order the inaugurate the process of transformation. They do so, in part, by emphasising the 'social character of production' which they regard as having retained 'the possibility of the universal development of the individual' (CW 28:94, 439, 465; NF-1887:9[60]) once the 'common economic management of the earth' has been achieved (WP: §866). Both highlight the alienating propensities and nihilistic consequences of the capitalist political economy (see Löwith 1991:152–155), including its highly instrumental and destructive relationship with the natural world.[267] Marx and Nietzsche are among

---

[264] See GS: §§108–109, §125 and §343. In *The German Ideology*, Marx makes a similar point, arguing that 'the absurdity of merging all the manifold relationships of people in the one relation of usefulness, this *apparently* metaphysical abstraction arises from the fact that in modern bourgeois society all relations are subordinated in practice to the one abstract monetary-commercial relation' (CW 5:409; my emphasis).

[265] This insight becomes the leitmotif of Nietzsche's *Zur Genealogie der Moral* (1887): the world governed by religious guilt is the exact same world that is governed by the 'brutal greed for money'—i.e., debt (UM: IV, *RWB*, §4).

[266] Nietzsche makes an almost identical claim in D: §204 ('what one formerly did 'for the sake of God' one now does for the sake of money'). Nietzsche and Marx highlight the element of a 'satanic loan' as a feature of capitalistic exchange (Nietzsche; NF-1887:11[215]) and that in his profit, which in essence is theft, the capitalist suffers 'on his dead mammon' (CW 3:237).

[267] See CW 28:337; BGE: §62; GM: III, §9; Sedgwick 2007:185; and Eagleton 2011:233.

the first to contend that man's alienation from his essence grows in proportion to the increase of his illusory control over nature and urge, in their distinctive ways, a return to nature.[268] Both protest the usurpation of science—'the *theoretical progress* of humanity'—by the capitalist economy.[269] Marx, in particular, emphasises that 'capital does not create science, but exploits it' (CW 34:33), which 'leads to separation of science from labour and at the same time to the application of science to material production' (CW 33:364), amplifying the character of this production in the distinctive manner of the Faustian bargain.

Marx and Nietzsche inveigh against the deleterious and disenfranchising characteristics of the division of labour and problematise the long-term dangers of modern age's unbridled *industriousness*.[270] They measure individual freedom by the *amount of leisure*—emphasising 'free time—which is both *idle time* and *time for higher activity*'—that would 'naturally transform its possessor into a different subject', who would then be able to 'enter into the direct production process as this different subject'.[271] Both entertain the notion of a 'sovereign individual' (GM: II, §§1–3)[272]—the spirited beneficiary of comprehensive development rather than the devitalised recipient of narrowly defined vocational training for the sole benefit of the capitalistic mode of production (see D:§455; BGE:§201):

> [F]ree time, i.e., time for the *full development* of the individual, which itself, as the greatest productive force, in turn reacts upon the productive power of labour. From the standpoint of the immediate production process, it can be considered as the production of fixed capital, this fixed capital BEING MAN HIMSELF (CW 29:97)

Arguing that the development of an individual as 'fixed capital' is in direct contradiction with the objectives of the 'bourgeois political economy' (CW 28:412, CW 29:97; UM: III, *SE*, §6; HH: I, §585), Marx and Nietzsche problematise the overtly hypocritical and limited nature of any form of 'political emancipation', which is used to conceal the reality of economic and spiritual enslavement.[273] As Miriam Leonard eloquently puts it, Marx intuits that 'not only could political emancipation exist side by side with economic enslavement, but also that the political emancipation afforded by the capitalist state

---

[268] Not to be confused with Rousseau's nostalgia for the return to the 'state of nature'. For Marx, see Forster and Burkett 2016:9, Burkett 1999:223–257, Stanley 1997:449–473. Cf. McLaughlin 1990:95; and Benton 1989:74–77. For Nietzsche, see NF-1881:11[211] and BGE: §230.

[269] See CW 34:33; and UM: III, *SE*, §§4–6.

[270] See CW 29:22–24 and Love 1986:174–187.

[271] See CW 29:97; see HH I: *Tokens*, §283; my emphasis. Cf. Arendt on 'productive slavery and unproductive freedom' (1998:90–91).

[272] See the excellent discussion of Nietzsche's 'sovereign individual' by Lanier Anderson (2021:1–24). Cf. Leiter 2011:101–119.

[273] For Nietzsche, see TI: *Skirmishes*, §37, starting with '"Equality", as a certain factual increase in similarity, which merely finds expression in the theory of "equal rights", is an essential feature of decline'. For Marx, see Bottomore's insightful discussion in *Karl Marx: Early Writings*, 1963:11–25.

actually requires economic enslavement' (Leonard 2012:153). Nietzsche would add that the individuals who are politically and formally free—i.e., dispersed and atomised—become essential in creating more sublime forms of oppression.[274]

Nietzsche, like Marx, foresees the inevitable structural decline of the capitalistic State at the hands of 'private contractors' but not before the State cannibalises 'the public space' (or 'civil society', as Marx would have it), systematically shrinking and devitalising it before 'privatising' it completely (HH: I, *State*, §472).[275] Both foresee that the more the modern capitalist state swells in terms of size, the more it would lack in terms of substance and resources to tackle the real problems affecting its subjects, shifting the social burden off of its own balance sheet into the hands of unscrupulous 'private contractors', whom it will continue to finance by going further into debt until it can do so no more. Marx and Nietzsche scorn bourgeois 'political democracy' (CW 3:159) and envisage a 'democracy of the future' (HH: II, *WS*, 293) that would encapsulate the 'true unity of the general and of the particular' (CW 3:30) thus enabling the 'genuinely human' rather than merely 'political' emancipation (CW 3:160; NF-1887:11[226/1]). Both thinkers emphasise the sense of our collective responsibility—in our role as the 'usufructuaries' of the earth—to 'hand it down to succeeding generations in an *improved condition*' (CW 37:763).

Without providing any detailed blueprints, Nietzsche and Marx both write with a view to a future that should reach 'higher than the present' (BT: §11), culturally as well as by representing 'a higher economic form of society' (CW 37:763). Their respective visions are informed by a shared recognition that the genuine emancipation of the individual invariably entails aesthetic connotations.[276] Marx and Nietzsche would agree that the 'capitalist production is hostile to certain branches of *spiritual production*, for example art and poetry' (CW 31:182) and that the division of labour under capitalism suppresses the free development of 'artistic talent' (CW 5:394). Even in the abolition of private property, Marx's objective is to achieve 'the complete emancipation of all human senses and qualities' (CW 30:300) so that in a communist society, there would be 'no painters but only people who engage in painting among other activities' (CW 5:394). Nietzsche designates 'physiology of aesthetics' as one of the 'delicate problems hitherto untouched' (GM: III, §8). He links the very 'thinkability of freedom' to the considerations of 'transcendental aesthetics', which demarcate the outer boundary of his emancipatory project:

---

274 Adorno would echo this thought in *Negative Dialectics* (1967), arguing that 'freedom can come to be real only through coercive civilisation' (Adorno 2007:147).
275 For an informed discussion of Marx, see CW 3, Preface, XIII–XV as well as CW 3:6–10 and 40–45. The inevitable decline of the State under capitalism is something that, in Marx's thinking, is cured by the proletarian revolution that would abolish its exploitative premises.
276 See King's excellent 'aesthetic interpretation of Marx's materialism' in 'Political Economy and "The Laws of Beauty"', 1991:323–335.

We don't get beyond the aesthetics—I used to think a god takes pleasure in looking at the world: but we have the essence of a world that humans have gradually created: its aesthetics. (NF-1881:12[29])

On the more philosophical plane, both thinkers wrestle with the timeless questions at the intersection of necessity, freedom, and human agency. Tackling the issues of how to achieve human self-realisation and what architecture of society would best promote it, the 'study of the historical origins of society' becomes an important building block for Nietzsche and Marx alike (see Love 1986:5). In search for answers, both deal with the Daedalean inversions ('Umschlag') of concepts and meanings. Marx uncoils the 'antithetical transmutations' of commodities into capital, while Nietzsche unravels a myriad of theological value inversions.[277] In both instances, these *non-linear inversions*—i.e., inversions, having stepped into which makes it neigh impossible to back out of them by simply retracing one's steps—create a pervasive *false layer of consciousness* that, acting as the comprehensive filter for processing reality, invariably misconstrues its perception, contributing to alienation (Marx) and nihilism (Nietzsche).

Both Nietzsche and Marx resort to the highly metaphorical use of language in order to extend the critical reach of their analyses by operating at 'the very threshold of what could be communicated' (BT: *ASC*, §2). The sense of inextinguishable tension between 'production and exchange' as highlighted in Marx is no less palpable in Nietzsche's discussion of the 'economic origins of moral concepts' (Cooper 2008:622–623). It is no coincidence that the death of God should be announced in the Temple of Exchange—in the 'market place' (Z: *Prologue*, §2–3). To Marx's three 'metamorphoses of capital' (CW 28:330–331) Nietzsche juxtaposes the 'three metamorphoses of the spirit' (Z: I, *Metamorphoses*), arguing that it is not the metamorphoses of appearances that would free humankind but the transformations of its spirit, which is 'the life that itself cuts into life' (Z: IV, Leech).

Marx's work, not unlike that of Nietzsche, lends itself to a wide range of contrasting interpretations. As we shall see, Marx and Nietzsche frequently employ similar arguments to express their views but for different underlying reasons.[278] Marx, who writes a great deal about the creation of value (e.g., 'surplus-value') and extensively criticises the immorality of capitalism (see CW 3:309–341), says conspicuously little about values, other than those of capital and conceived in the predominantly economic sense.[279] One key line of differentiation between Marx's and Nietzsche's political economies is the difference between 'capital' and 'debt'. Marx scrutinises *capital* as one of the custodians of capitalism's temporal essence, whereas Nietzsche casts his cri-

---

[277] For Marx, see CW 35:120; CW 28:330–331; and CW 29:64. For Nietzsche, some pertinent illustrations can be found in BGE: §59 and §195; GM I, §7 and GM II, §20–21; TI: *Skirmishes*, §41; as well as NF-1888:15[44] and 15[90].
[278] See Landa's informed discussion in 2016:253–254.
[279] See Bonefeld and O'Kane 2022:5. Cf. Meszaros' excellent discussion of Marx's conception of 'positive transcendence' (1970:127–129).

tique of modernity in terms of *debt* which, he insists, is a dimensional time-traveller inhabiting the worlds of religion, morality, economy and politics simultaneously, as though to demonstrate that all these different realms are the constituent parts of the universe of modern values.

Although Marx acknowledges capital's provenance in debt (CW 28:428), his critique of it relies, in significant part, on the underlying notion of *reciprocal exchange* (CW 29:64; CW 35:157), whereas Nietzsche's starting point is the ingrained *asymmetry of power* between creditor and debtor. As we shall see from the discussion that follows, Nietzsche's debt is *not* a direct antithesis of Marx's capital. Nietzsche conceives of debt as capital's *alter ego*, or as *negative capital*, in order to extend the analysis of its repercussions beyond the economic sphere, i.e., to expose the deep roots of capitalism's *arbor vitae* as originating from within the human psyche. Marx also acknowledges that while capital is not 'a very mystic being' as an economic category, it invariably becomes such where its role in forging social relations is concerned (CW37:814).[280] Still, where Marx's critique focuses on capital's perverse workings in the political and economic spheres, Nietzsche traces the subversive conditions and valuations under which capital becomes transformed into debt, which becomes both structural and superstructural—i.e., *'Schulden'* and *'Schuld'*.

This becomes particularly relevant in the context of their insistence on the *radical restructuring* of society. Where Marx's political economy identifies private property as the primary target of its critique, Nietzsche's political economy targets the theologically constituted notion of equality. Marx envisages a *worldwide proletarian revolution* that would upend the capitalist social order and, by abolishing capital's hatchery—*private property*—make it possible to bring the class struggle to an end (see CW 20:149, 441). Nietzsche calls for a comprehensive *revaluation of all values* that would overturn the 'traditional social structures' (BGE: §44). These two proposals are as radical as they are radically different. Marx appeals to the oppressed *majority* to alter the course of history by heeding the call of historical destiny (see CW 42:96). Nietzsche's plea—also made on humankind's behalf—could only be heard by the smallest of minorities in a distant future that would be capable of transcending the encumbrances of *slave morality* which, on Nietzsche's view, permeates not just some of the modern social orders but modernity itself.[281] Although refraining from 'writing recipes for the cook-shops of the future' (CW 35:17), both authors unequivocally wish to arm their respective constituencies with their theories.[282] Marx acknowledges that 'the appreciation which *Das Kapital* rapidly gained in wide circles of the German working class is the best reward of my labours' (CW 35:13). Nietzsche

---

[280] See also Bonefeld 2022b:105.
[281] See Nietzsche on the 'tremendous self-examination: *becoming conscious of oneself, not as individuals but as mankind*' (NF-1887:9[60]; my emphasis).
[282] For Nietzsche, see GS: §377; NF-84:25[227]; NF-1885:35[9]; TI: *Ancients*, §5; Löwith 1978:94; and Lampert 1986:81.

attaches high hopes to his 'greatest doctrine': he intends to 'teach us something' important by means of it (NF-1884:25[227]).[283]

Political Economy of Revolution

From the critique of their socio-political present, Nietzsche and Marx draw strikingly different conclusions. This difference reveals, in particular, sharply contrasting *conceptions of history*. Marx's history is an epic, quasi-Hegelian canvas depicting the inexorable and homogenising forward march of the social orders propelled by the development of humankind's productive forces, which manifests itself in the conflict of antagonistic classes, gearing up for the decisive battle between the oppressed proletariat and the ruling bourgeoisie.[284] Nietzsche's history also engenders a conflict at its core, albeit one with starkly divergent contours. It is embodied in the incessant struggle between the forces representing master and slave morality—the ascending and descending life tendencies—which, akin to the tidal waves, ebb and flow overseeing the succession of the stronger ages by the weaker epochs and vice-versa.[285] Marx may well have considered capitalism a 'transitory form of social organisation' that would 'elevate the productive powers of humanity—albeit at terrible human cost—to the point where they would offer abundance to all in a higher and freer society' (Wood 2014:270). Nietzsche's prognosis is not as optimistic. He argues that as the 'the age of harmless false-coinage draws to an end' (D: §551), capitalism left to its own devices—i.e., absent the *revaluation of values* and allowed to draw the full consequences of the *valuations of slave morality* that underwrite it—could spell the end of world.

In contrast to Marx, Nietzsche draws an important distinction between 'conditions of existence' representing 'the whole content' (NF-1875:9[1]) and the 'perceived conditions of existence', which comprise 'the sum total of opinions incorporated into humankind' for the purpose of ensuring durability of a particular type of social organisation (NF-1884:26[45]; NF-1881:11[262]). These 'perceived conditions of life', which inform and are, in turn, informed by our valuations, are not quite the same as Marx's superstructure (NF-1884:25[397]). Instead, they are more akin to an adhesive wedged between the economic basis and the political superstructure that holds them

---

[283] TI: Ancients, §5. See further Löwith 1978:94 and Lampert 1986:81.
[284] Quasi-Hegelian since Marx does not view history's totality as the dialectic movement of reason. The difference comes with the replacement of the *States* with *class struggle* as the locomotive of history. Quasi-Hegelian also since Marx's view draws also from Adam Smith's conception of 'the four stages of society', which are inextricably linked with the evolution of property (see LJ: 107–153). See CW 25:10, 25–28, and 254 as well as CW 26:361–365 for the relevant elaborations on the materialist conception of history by Engels. See also Lee 1975:47–53; Blanchette 1983:114–120; Cohen 2000:1–28; and Murzban 2010:22–34.
[285] See BGE: §260; NF-1887:11[133]; and NF-1888:14[182].

together. Nietzsche argues that our valuations 'must stand in some relation' to these perceived conditions of existence—'a kind of simplification of the external world'—and will 'change if our conditions of existence or our belief in them change', inaugurating the more profound transformation of the social organism (NF-1884:25[397];NF-1885:34[247]). The question remains in relation to the nature of the precipitant of the change in valuations.

Courtesy of contemporary economists who, by and large, discount the labour theory of value and discard Marx's hypothesis that the rate of profit tends to fall, it has become customary to shrink Marx's political economy to 'commodity fetishism', which inspired a plethora of theories developed under the notion of *reification*, and to theories of 'alienation'. These two conceptual categories, in and of themselves entirely ineffectual, are considered as relevant in explaining modern society. Reducing Marx's emancipatory project to the mere 'politics of redistributive justice and social equality' (Bonefeld and O'Kane 2022:5), these bourgeois ideologues neglect the key precept of Marx's undertaking—to change the world rather than merely interpret it (CW 5:5, Thesis 11). Marx's political economy cannot be properly understood in separation from his revolutionary theory, with which it is *inextricably linked*.[286]

> It is easy to see that the *entire revolutionary movement* necessarily finds both its empirical and its *theoretical basis* in the movement of private property—more precisely, in that of the economy. (CW 3:297; my emphasis)

Marx's political economy is a 'positive science' (CW 5:37) that seeks to provide a scientific rationale for the necessity of the proletarian revolution as arising from within the contradictions of the capitalist mode of production.[287] As Korsch points out, 'the cri-

---

[286] This connection is downplayed in the *current* Marxist scholarship, which prefers to consider Marx's *political economy* and his *revolutionary theory* as separate issues. This approach turns Marx into a critic of capitalism, incorporated to the left of the conventional bourgeois discourse, rather than into capitalism's revolutionary transformer. Nietzsche would view this in terms of 'taming of the human animal' (NF-1888: 16[10]) in an effort to 'discharge explosives' contained in his work 'harmlessly' and 'if at all possible to prevent their formation and accumulation: this is the instinct of every civilised society' (NF-1888:16[9]). Being a socialist political economist does not necessarily make one a revolutionary thinker, let alone a practitioner of revolutionary *praxis*, e.g., Marx's contemporary and a notable socialist economist, Léon Walras (1834–1910). Marx, however, does not come to embrace the revolution from his study of political economy. Marx was a revolutionary long before he became a political economist. Löwith masterfully captured this intellectual evolution of Marx: 'at first he criticized religion philosophically, then he criticized religion and philosophy politically, and at last he criticized religion, philosophy, politics, and all other ideologies economically' (Löwith 1954:204). Marx's entire philosophy (*fully inclusive of his political economy*) is *predicated* on transforming and being transformed into *revolutionary praxis* (see Blackburn 1976:3–35). As he states in the 'Introduction' to the 'Contribution to the Critique of Hegel's Philosophy of Law' (1843), 'philosophy cannot be made a reality without the abolition of the proletariat, the proletariat cannot be abolished without philosophy being made a reality' (CW 3:187; see CW 4:258). The 'reality' implied by Marx's argument is none other than the reality of the proletarian revolution.
[287] See Rothbart's illuminating discussion in 1981:41–55 as well as Laibman 2019:541.

tique of political economy, which Marx began in *Capital*, can only be completed by the proletarian revolution, i.e., by a real change of the present bourgeois mode of production and of the forms of consciousness pertaining to it' (Korsch 2016:112–113). Throughout his *oeuvre*, Marx argues that 'the emancipation of the working classes must be *conquered* by the working classes themselves' in order to bring about the universal '*economical emancipation*' as 'the *great end*' of their struggle 'to which every *political movement* ought to be subordinate as a means' (CW 20:14, 441; my emphasis). The cause of occasional disagreement in the academic literature is whether the revolution advocated by Marx is meant to be *violent*.[288] Marx and Nietzsche would concur that *real revolutions*—the ones that bring about fundamental and lasting changes—need not be bloody.[289] Nietzsche would hasten to add that the 'seductive spectacles' we have come to mistake for revolutions often entail a sense of 'homesickness' for blood and violence, which accompany the flare-ups of the 'popular instincts of resentment' exploited for 'idealistic purposes'.[290]

To de-revolutionise Marx's political economy would be comparable to detaching Nietzsche's critique of modernity from his call for the revaluation of values. Nevertheless, an explicit connection between a political economy and a revolutionary theory would raise a red flag in Nietzsche's mind. How and why should a revolution flow from the theory of political economy, no matter how critical that theory may be of the existing social order? How does even the most sophisticated (for its time) labour theory of value, which exposes the exploitation of the worker, chastises the misappropriation of surplus-value by the capitalist and problematises the bourgeois system of juridic right that legitimises them, conjure up a revolutionary force? These questions would undoubtedly rise to the front of Nietzsche's mind, and it is unlikely that Marx's answer below would satisfy him:

> The weapon of criticism cannot, of course, replace criticism by weapons, material force must be overthrown by material force; but *theory also becomes a material force* as soon as it has *gripped the masses*. (CW 3:182; my emphasis)

At the end of his critique of capitalism's political economy, Marx places proletarian revolution. Conceptually and sequentially, the 'revolution' would come in at about the same place where Nietzsche would say 'revaluation'. Nietzsche is firmly of the view that 'if a change is to be as profound as it can be, the means to it must be given in the smallest doses but unremittingly over long periods of time' (D: §534). Any significant re-formatting of collective consciousness in order to endure needs to be adminis-

---

[288] See Singh's informed discussion in 1989:PE9–PE20.
[289] See Schaff 1973:263–270 and Hook 1973:271–280 concerning the often 'politically motivated' importation of violence into Marx's theory of revolution. See Stedman-Jones on revolution as process rather than event (2018:201–202). In relation to Nietzsche, see the excellent discussion in Montinari and Large 1997:23–29.
[290] See Nietzsche's discussion in D: §534; GS: §5; BGE: §38 and §229; and TI: *Skirmishes*, §48.

tered in a manner that does not annihilate the host from the outset (HH: I, *Tokens*, §224).

A revolution may trigger the process of re-engineering collective consciousness, but it can by no means be all that is required to achieve lasting results. At the same time, for any theory or teaching to culminate in and incite a revolution something else needs to be added into the mix. This 'something' that Nietzsche has in mind cannot be backward-looking, it cannot be about that which is the object of critique, it cannot be about the 'past-present' which is to be rebelled against. The real appeal of a revolution is not in what it aims to destroy but in that which it aspires to put in its place.

Nietzsche would argue that in every 'theory of revolution', one inevitably finds a great 'dose of delusion' (HH: I, *State*, §463). Marx's case is no exception, in that a powerful delusional ingredient—a particular aspirational vision of the 'final destination'—would be required to animate the 'theory' in such a way that it could provide the 'spiritual weapons' to the masses, just as the proletariat would become transformed into the 'material weapons' of such philosophy (CW 3:187). Nietzsche considers it of paramount importance to understand where the aspirational vision of the future draws its power from: what values underwrite it and supply intellectual and spiritual oxygen for its theories as well as animating its battle-cries. Furthermore, he argues that the ability to 'grip the masses' with any particular teaching presupposes 'knowledge of a certain average type of souls who have not yet recognised that they belong together'—i.e., knowledge with certain theological characteristics (GS: §353).

The kind of proletarian revolution Marx prophesised has not (yet) occurred (see Debord 2005: §87–88). He warned that 'if we did not find latent in society as it is, the material conditions of production and the corresponding relationships of exchange for a classless society, all attempts to explode it would be quixotic' (CW 28:97). It is possible that such conditions and the necessary relationships have not yet matured sufficiently within the framework of the capitalist social order. Viewed historically, attempts to forcibly change the system of property ownership failed to deliver on the promise of overcoming exploitation, oppression, and enslavement, at least for any historically meaningful periods of time or on the scale sufficient for Marx's vision to materialise and to take hold.[291]

Nietzsche's political economy helps explain how the longer-term aspirations of one revolution can become diminished and hijacked by the successful development of another to the point where 'the most necessary revolution' would also 'appear the most unlikely' (Marcuse 1972:7). In contrast to Marx, Nietzsche's critique draws our attention to the stealth revolution—the 'invisible' slaves' revolt in morality—that unfurls in broad daylight. Nietzsche's critique highlights the diffusive propensities of the slave revolt which aims at and achieves systemic domination within the fabric of capitalist society, spreading from the economic and material to the spiritual and cultural as well as to the intellectual and psychological spheres of life. This process not only captures the

---

[291] See the excellent discussion of this in Wood 2014:270–273.

vast majority of free and equal subjects in its nets but it does so in such a manner that the individuals, by virtue of constituting this silent and fragmented majority, gradually lose the ability to experience themselves as [an oppressed] class. Such a predicament, if it came to pass, would nullify Marx's aspirations for the critical role of class consciousness and substitute it for the ineffectual and highly individualistic anti-class consciousness. Although we may no longer 'perceive the weight of our chains' (HH: II, WS, §10), which has shifted decidedly from our arms and feet into our *psyche*, devitalising it, the real 'moral revolution', subterranean though it may appear, continues unabated, 'directed against the enervated, devastated and aged peoples' (NF-1884:25[286]). Developing on Nietzsche's analysis, Adorno would later note:

> The omnipotence of repression and its invisibility are the same thing. The immeasurable pressure of domination has so fragmented the masses that it has even dissipated the negative unity of being oppressed that forged them into a class in the nineteenth century. In exchange, they find they have been directly absorbed into the unity of the system that is oppressing them. (Adorno 2003:97–110)

Nietzsche's critique, in contrast to Marx, does not problematise the demise of a particular type of social order as much as it highlights the decline of the social order as such under the auspices of *slave morality*. Just as Marx's political economy and his revolutionary theory can sometimes be viewed as separate intellectual undertakings, there is a tendency in Nietzsche scholarship to consider Nietzsche's critique of 'the slave rebellion in morals' (BGE: §195) as separate from his critique of capitalism, exemplified by the 'contemptible money-economy' (UM: III, *SE*, §4). In both cases, such approach loses sight of one simple but important fact, namely, that behind both elements of Marx's and Nietzsche's respective critiques stands *exactly the same world*, the world we inhabit, the world beyond the boundaries of which neither Nietzsche, nor Marx wish to venture in their respective analyses (see Bonefeld 2022a:18). Nietzsche's ascetic priest, standing at the pinnacle of the slaves' revolt, is just as intricately related to modernity's ascendent money-maker as Marx's political economy is bonded with his revolutionary theory. Nietzsche, contrary to Marx, argues that this connection is enabled by the valuations of *slave morality*. The same 'missing link'—that stands behind Marx's political economy and revolutionary theory, and Nietzsche's critique of slave morality and the money-economy—is the unvanquished shadow of the dead God (GS: §109).

Bruno Bauer and the Essenes' Conundrum

One underappreciated intellectual thread connecting Nietzsche and Marx runs through the work of Bruno Bauer.[292] A certain degree of cross-pollination between the three

---

[292] Brobjer makes this connection, albeit indirectly, via Heine (see Brobjer 2008:300; fn. 7). Löwith dis-

thinkers, although scarcely acknowledged, cannot be ruled out. In particular, Bauer's study of early Christianity and its historical origins represents an important intellectual archway through which both Nietzsche and Marx have undoubtedly walked.[293] Nietzsche considered Bauer a 'Nietzschean' and one of his 'most attentive readers', who even borrowed Nietzsche's ideas.[294] Nietzsche's critique of David Strauss in *Untimely Meditations* (1873), bears uncanny structural similarities to Bauer's own criticism of Strauss.[295] Some consider Bauer's critique of early Christianity to be more insightful and penetrating than Nietzsche's (Rosen 1977:9) or, at the very least, anticipating Nietzsche's *Zur Genealogie der Moral* (Löwith 1991:349). At the other end of the spectrum, an argument is made that Bauer's influence on Marx's political and economic thinking remains underestimated (see Rosen 1977; Rockmore 2018:192). Bauer, Marx's one-time fellow Young Hegelian, went from being a close associate and mentor to becoming the target of Marx's stinging criticism in 'On the Jewish Question' (1843).[296]

Bauer published his seminal and final monograph, entitled *Christ and Caesars* ('Christus und die Caesaren'), in 1877, a decade prior to Nietzsche's *Zur Genealogie der Moral* (1887) but some years after Nietzsche's 'David Strauss, the Confessor' (1873). One significant yet underexamined aspect of Bauer's work for Marx's and Nietzsche's thinking on the questions of political economy lies in his extensive discussion of the writings of Philo of Alexandria (c. 25 B.C.—50 A.D.), a prolific author, who penned 'Every Good Man is Free', and of Josephus Flavius (c. 30 A.D.—100 A.D.), the author of *The Jewish War* ('Bellum Judaicum', 75–79 A.D.).[297] Both works contain an important examination of the 'three forms of Jewish philosophy' within the Judaean society, with a particular emphasis on the social and politico-economic architecture of the Essenes' sect, who separated from the rest of the Jewish community around the 2nd century B.C. (see Feldman 1989:390–422). They did so, it is maintained, in opposition to the usurpation of the office of high priest by 'Jonathan Maccabeus, and, later,

---

cusses Bauer, Marx, and Nietzsche brilliantly, albeit without connecting them, see Löwith 1991:343–350 and 368–373.

293 See a tribute penned by Engels on Bauer's death in April 1882, 'Bruno Bauer and Early Christianity', CW 24:427–436. Earlier, Engels alluded to this knowledge in Part I: Philosophy of Anti-Dühring (1877).

294 See, respectively, BVN 1888: §1071, letter to Varl Spitteler, dated July 25, 1888; EH: *UM*, §2; and BVN 1882: 286, letter to Theodor Curti, dated July–Aug. 1882.

295 See Bauer's influential 'Kritik der Evangelischen Geschichte der Synoptiker und des Johannes', 1841 (Rosen 1977:35–37), 'Entdecktes Christentum, Eine Erinnerung an das achtzehnte Jahrbundert und ein Beitrag zur Krise des neunzehnten' (1843), and 'Philo, Strauss, Renan und das Urchristentum' (1874). Importantly, the first two essays contributed to Bauer's intellectual rift with Marx on the question of 'political emancipation', which Marx wrestled with in 'On the Jewish Question' (1843).

296 It is worth keeping in mind that Marx was intimately familiar with Bauer's work. See McCarthy 1984:47 and Wood 2014:260–261.

297 Coincidentally, *Flavius* is also the name of one of Timon's servants in Shakespeare's play *Timon of Athens* (1623), used by Marx in the *Economic and Philosophic Manuscripts of 1844* (last accessed Feb. 27, 2023) to examine the role of money.

Simon Maccabeus', on account of which the Essenes shunned Temple worship and all but withdrew from the townships in order to pursue their own—unique and highly orthodox—manner of communal life, which allowed them to flourish for over a century:[298]

> The Essenes have a reputation for cultivating peculiar sanctity. Of Jewish birth, they show a *greater attachment to each other* than do the other sects. They shun pleasures as a vice and regard *temperance and the control of the passions as a special virtue*. ... Riches they despise, and their *communal possession of property* is truly admirable; you will not find one among them distinguished by greater opulence than another. They have a *law* that new members on admission to the sect shall *surrender their property to the community*, with the result that you will *nowhere see either abject poverty or inordinate wealth*; instead, everyone, like brothers, shares in one *common fortune*, formed from the combination into one whole of the individual property of each of them. They select individuals to attend to the interests of the community as one whole, the special services of each officer being determined by the whole body. There is *no buying or selling* among themselves, but each gives what he has to any in need and receives from him in exchange something useful to himself; and even in the absence of reciprocal exchange, one may ask for what is necessary from whomever he wishes. ... They display an extraordinary interest in the writings of their ancestors, singling out in particular those which make for the *welfare of soul and body.* ... It is a *point of honour with them to obey their elders and a majority.* (Josephus 1956:369–383)[299]

The paradox of which Nietzsche and Marx would likely have become aware in their intellectual travails through Bauer's work, as well as by studying the original writings of Philo and Josephus, is that the Essenes—who did not 'engage in commerce', did not permit 'hoarding of money', 'renting or selling of land', who 'had no slaves and condemned slavery', kept 'one purse and one budget' and cared for 'the sick, the young, and the aged'—existed as a highly nuanced *social hierarchy* based on the strict 'order of rank' that was neither exclusively religious, nor was it based solely on seniority.[300] The order of rank embedded in the Essenes' community also had clear military connotations.[301] These lines of subordination, however, existed alongside 'the principle of equality ... beyond all power of description'.[302] Instructive parallels can be drawn with the composition and functioning of the *oikos* of the Greek antiquity. Indeed, Josephus himself acknowledges strong affinity to 'the sons of Greece' and the Pythagoreans

---

298 See Wacholder 1989:159 concerning the 'communal life of the Essenes' as well as Meeks 1983: 32 and 105. Some authors argue that Essenes were barred from the Temple worship rather than separating themselves (see Feldman 1989:31–35). Cf. Timothy H. Lim, 'Essenes in Judean Society' (https://blog.oup.com/2021/01/essenes-in-judaean-society-the-sectarians-of-the-dead-sea-scrolls/, last accessed Feb. 27, 2023).
299 Josephus' notes directly echo the writings of Philo of Alexandria on the Essenes in *Quod Omnis Probus Liber Sit* ('Every Good Man is Free'); see Philo 1993:905–907 (#12.75–13.91).
300 See Nietzsche's *Nachlass* entries referencing the *Essenes*, where Bauerian allusions are clearly discernible: NF-1880:4[160] and [164] as well as NF-1887:11[383]. Regarding *Philo*, see NF-1880:4[157], [163], and [164].
301 See Philo (1993), *Quod Omnis Probus Liber Sit*, #12.82 (906).
302 See Philo (1993), *Quod Omnis Probus Liber Sit*, #12.79–85 (905–906).

(Josephus 1956:383), whom Nietzsche describes as the 'finest statesmen of their day' (D: §347).[303]

The Essenes' conundrum is pertinent because it illuminates the political-economic dilemmas which Nietzsche and Marx reflected on extensively in their work.[304] It also helps to highlight the different lines along which Nietzsche's and Marx's political-economic thinking developed, as well as delineating the significant degree to which the two political economies would overlap. This conundrum centres on the factors that determine community's enduring social architecture. An overriding inference, where Nietzsche and Marx are concerned, is whether *economic relations*, comprised of property, commerce and money should be regarded as the *consequence* of the social relations and structure of society, or as their *source and motive force*. Neither Marx nor Nietzsche approach this intersection of economy and sociability as an 'either/or' situation. Both develop an intricate appreciation of the *circular* manner in which social relations constitute economic reality while the economic categories inform and reinforce a certain kind of social reality that embeds a particular type of economic relations. Marx attempts to disable the exploitative circle, where conceptualisation of reality reduces experience of it to conceptualised reality. Nietzsche searches for ways to move beyond this circle altogether. In this respect, the *question of value* becomes an important differentiator. Should value, including the value of money (see HH: II, *WS*, §25), be determined by and originate from the *social relations* between its participants, or should money determine the value of social relations and, by extension of its participants? Marx famously states that by conflating the *relation* between the private labour of individual producers and the collective labour of society in the same absurd form—

> [T]his ultimate *money* form of the world of commodities [...] actually *conceals*, instead of disclosing, the social character of private labour, and the *social relations* between the individual producers. (CW 35:86; my emphasis)

Reflecting on the social consequences of the gradual subjugation of life's various domains to the logic of money-making, Nietzsche identifies the risk, if not the inevitability, that the erstwhile value-setters would end up being swept up into the whirlwind of commodities on par with them and no longer able to control their own value (see Geuss 2014:103).

---

[303] See Baumbach 1989:174–175. The *oikos* is discussed in detail in the chapter on slavery. In BGE, Nietzsche also speaks of 'an ancient Greek polis' as an example of the 'aristocratic commonwealth' (BGE: §262).
[304] In the *Economic and Philosophic Manuscripts of 1844*, Marx alludes to the 'still immature communism that seeks an historical proof for itself—a proof in the realm of what already exists—among disconnected historical phenomena opposed to private property, tearing single phases from the historical process and focusing attention on them as proofs of its historical pedigree' (CW 3:297). See also his extensive discussion of 'propertyless tribes' in the *Outlines of the Critique of Political Economy* (aka *Grundrisse*), Vol. I (CW 27:410–420).

In the case of the Essenes, these riddles are demonstrated by the compresence of *communal property* and *strict hierarchy*, albeit not extending to slavery. If the Essenes' community was based on the principle of *communal property*, how could there have been a strict order of rank and what could it have been based upon? If the Essenes' sect was built around the *order of rank*, how could there have been economic equality, i.e., no slavery and no private possessions? What can be made of their *politics*—the domain lifted out of the mundane, concerned with justice and ethics, designated as a concern of the very few, and yet—deriving legitimacy from the broadest possible participation? In which direction did the arrow of causality point: from agency (i.e., the 'superstructural') to economy (i.e., the 'basis'), or *vice-versa?* Could the delicately balanced social equation have been more nuanced and complicated still, as the economic relations and the model of agency embedded in the Essenes' communal life seemed to co-exist without seemingly determining one another? Could their *religious beliefs* (law and morality in one) have represented the overarching and anchoring consideration, steadfast adherence to which sustained both the economic basis and the social structure of the Essenes' society as well as nurturing its agonistic politics?[305]

This may sound like a modern restatement of the ancient debate between the proponents of 'man's relation to matter' (i.e., the materialists) and the advocates of man's attachment to spirit (i.e., the idealists)—both vying for recognition as the driving force of history and holding the key to the fulfilment of humankind's destiny.[306] Nevertheless, the tension between the superstructural, the economy and agency, which straddles them, becomes the *critical juncture* where Marx's and Nietzsche's politico-economic thinking would diverge. Nowhere is this difference more pronounced than in Nietzsche's and Marx's respective positions on the causality linking capitalism and religion. For Marx, religion is *not* the central problem. Almost to the contrary, in the 'heartless' and alienating world of capitalism, religion is required as a palliative:

> Religion is the *sigh of the oppressed creature*, the *heart of a heartless world*, and the *soul of soulless conditions*. It is the opium of the people. (CW 3:175)

Marx considers Christianity a 'fitting form of religion' for capitalism in view of both sharing the homogenising and commodifying propensities which reduce the traffic of human affairs to trading in abstractions (CW 35:90).[307] In the spirit that mankind 'sets itself only such tasks as it is able to solve' (CW 29:263), the real battle, as far as Marx is concerned, is socio-economic, i.e., changing the conditions that give rise to religion as an imaginary antidote to themselves. Only by prevailing in this battle would the eventual disappearance of the need for religion be made possible. Consequently,

---

305 Could their God also have been different then, could he have demanded different things of his followers, could he have been someone to wrestle with rather than to obey?
306 See Russell 1946:812.
307 Both Nietzsche and Marx point specifically to *Protestantism* as the religious seabed of capitalism (CW 3:309; HH: II, *AOM*, §97; and NF-1887:10[54]).

Marx argues that only when the 'transparent and rational' representation of reality of everyday life between individuals, as well as between humankind and nature prevails over the 'religious reflections', religion will vanish, and the individual shall be free (CW 35:90). Unlike Weber, who follows the logic of Nietzsche's critique of religion more closely, Marx does not anticipate the possibility that the *veil* of that very rational representation of society, which Marx hopes to provide by means of his political economy (CW 35:91–92), would become its *iron cage* (Weber 1992:123).

Marx treats religion as an 'analogy'—i.e., the *master abstraction*—by means of which to explain the workings of the capitalist economy as 'the fantastic form of a relation between things' (CW 35:83).[308] Although Nietzsche would agree that 'religion quietens the heart of the individual' in times of distress (HH: I, *State*, §472), he maintains that religious ideas, which express the valuations of *slave morality*, are not simply analogous to capitalism, they make capitalism possible. For Nietzsche, as it would be for Weber later, capitalism—understood both politically and economically—grows directly out of Christianity. This is why Nietzsche makes his *apparent* agreement with Marx that 'religion can even be used as a means for obtaining peace from the noise and exertion of cruder forms of government, and purity from the necessary dirt of all politics' strictly *conditional* on the possibility of 'the most subtle type of rule'—i.e., something that neither Christianity, nor capitalism are capable of cultivating (BGE: §61). Nietzsche would assert that in fighting and even in defeating capitalism Marx would not be squaring off against the real enemy but only against its most powerful known manifestation, its five-star general. Defeating such powerful but ultimately false adversary would not spell the end to the ills of society Marx wishes to cure. More likely, it would only force the spirit of religion—slave morality—to seek other manifestations, embedding itself deeper in the process.

Conceptually, from this point onwards, the pivotal axis of Marx's political economy crystallises in the *question of property* relations, which he comes to regard as the essential gateway to forging emancipated agency, capable of achieving new values.[309] For Nietzsche, property relations (economy in general), although seen as secondary in terms of importance, nevertheless reflect the dominant values, themselves a product of agency. The economy, Nietzsche argues, has basis in [slave] morality rather than, as Marx maintains, morality reflecting the prevailing mode of production as part of the social relations that grow out of and around private property (CW 3:279).[310] This becomes a key distinction in the approach Nietzsche and Marx take concerning the *role of values*. The anchor for Nietzsche's project becomes the question of *values* and, therefore, of *agency* with which the quality of values is inextricably connected:

---

[308] See also Stedman-Jones 2018:192.
[309] See Levine's excellent, historically informed discussion of the intellectual influences informing Marx's outlook on property, 1987:431–451. Cf. Eagleton 2011:119–120.
[310] Cf. Wood 2014:263.

'the question concerning the origin of moral values is a question of the very first rank because it is *crucial for the future of humanity*'. (EH: *D*, §2; my emphasis)[311]

Marx's Real 'Atomic Swerve'

Nietzsche, like Plato and Aristotle, considers that human nature is ruled by the fundamentally unchangeable physiological determinism, notwithstanding how much we may protest to the contrary.[312] For Marx, like for Hume and Smith, human nature is anything but 'fixed':

> Today [the proletariat] are the slaves of the bourgeois, and in them he sees nothing but the instruments (the bearers) of his dirty (selfish) lust for profit; tomorrow they will break their chains and reveal themselves as the *bearers of human development* which will blow him sky-high together with his industry. (CW 4:282; my emphasis)[313]

Marx is 'no longer prepared to embrace the idea of some sort of timeless, Platonic "human essence" as a blueprint somehow fixed beyond all nature and history' (Schacht 1991:125). He insists that all 'essential relation must first be discovered by science' (CW 35:542). This would necessitate stepping away from the unyielding canon of the 'childish world of antiquity' (CW 28:412) in an effort to incorporate the 'intellectual achievements of the Enlightenment' (Avineri 1968:4) represented, in the field of political economy, by the ground-breaking work of Adam Smith and David Riccardo. Marx's epistemological leap in their direction involves a dramatic change in the direction of the arrow of causality. Marx comes to the view that the only premise upon which it would be possible to construe the connection between political economy and ethics as 'scientific' would be to allow political economy to 'express moral laws in its own way', accepting that allowing political economy to 'speak its own language' would be no guarantee that it would 'speak ethically' (CW 3:311). In other words, ethics can neither guide nor govern political economy but the objective laws of political economy, derived scientifically, can help inform and guide ethical norms of society. (CW 25:138). The far-reaching importance of Marx's intellectual stance is at least twofold. Admitting that

---

311 See NF-1883:14[29]; 24[33]; and AC: §8 concerning the connection between agency and values.
312 See UM: II, *UDHL*, §10 and NF-1885:41[6–7]. Nietzsche believes that although we never cease *becoming what we are*, we *do not change* fundamentally. One of the key deceptions of *slave morality*, he tells us, is to make people believe that they can change, become better, act differently, etc. (see NF-1888:14[30]). This, however, should not be confused with Nietzsche's view that the degrees in which the *three basic ingredients of the Platonic soul* structure, the complex webs and the innumerable modalities of their interactions make up the irreducible 'complexity and multiplicity of the subject' (see BGE: §12 and NF-1885:40[42]) and 'an inextricable multiplicity of ascending and descending life-processes' (NF-1887:11[226]), which render man and humankind 'unfixed'.
313 In *The German Ideology*, Marx insists that *'for the production of* [...] *communist consciousness* [...] the *alteration of men* on a mass scale is *necessary'* (CW 5:52–53; my emphasis).

the conclusions drawn by the theories of political economy may not always be ethical helps to embolden revolutionary intuitions by providing them with a theoretical (i.e., as though 'disinterested') backing. Secondly, the role of values becomes downplayed—i.e., values are designated as something that could wait and would follow where political economy would lead once it is on the right track. Conceptually, this makes the task of resolving the problems of political economy a matter of utmost priority in the wider context of advancing the revolutionary cause.

Since the days of his doctoral dissertation, Marx was taken by the idea that the declination, or the *swerve* of the atom—lifting the curse of destiny from its path—would be necessary to alter the predetermined course of history. For Marx, the swerve illuminates the contours of an 'overarching framework of liberating humans from the oppression of the gods' (Asmis 2020:241). In terms of his political economy Marx's undertaking becomes synonymous with liberating humankind from the oppression of the God of all class-based societies—private property. Changing the economic basis of society, the nexus of which he traces to *property ownership*, would become Marx's enduring *punctum Archimedes*.[314] Developing an awareness of the necessity to alter the economic basis of society, which distorts and enslaves consciousness (private and public alike), in order to set in motion the process of human emancipation would become Marx's *atomic swerve* that, once transformed into the revolutionary *praxis*, would allow one to 'snap the *fati doedra* ('bonds of fate')' that he saw engendered in the class struggle (CW 1:49).

Nietzsche, equally 'a modern man', in developing his critique of modernity, including its political economy, retains steadfast affinity to the philosophical intuitions of antiquity.[315] To Marx's *'fati doedra'* Nietzsche juxtaposes the notion of 'amor fati' as an expression of the 'ultimate liberator' from the chains of the 'world of historical values and counterfeit rules' (NCW: *Psychologist*, §3). Only this kind of transcendence Nietzsche considers as commensurate with restoring the proper functioning of the 'great economy' of life (NCW: *Epilogue*, §1). The question Nietzsche may well have addressed directly to Marx is this: 'Let's assume *someone* is occupied with *Democritus*, the question is always on my lips: why not *Heraclitus*? Or *Philo?*' (UM: II, *UDHL*, §5; my emphasis). Marx, in order to subvert the Democritean determinism, opts in favour of the Epicurean *atomic swerve*—quite possibly for political rather than philosophical reasons.[316] Nietzsche, who takes the opposite side of the argument, would contend that Marx's reasoning fails to overcome the essential determinism of the ancients.

---

314 Cf. Stedman-Jones argues that Marx's vision for the 'supersession of private property' was 'shattered by the disenchanting failure of the 1848 revolutions', after which Marx moved on to the critique of capital (2018:189). See Wood's important elucidation of Marx's position, 2014:301–316.
315 Cf. Löwith 1945:283.
316 See Peter Fenves' insightful discussion (1986:433–452), starting with a quotation from Marx's letter to Ferdinand Lassalle (1825–1864) dated December 21, 1857: 'I have a great tenderness for the latter philosopher [*Heraclitus*], and of the ancients I only prefer Aristotle more. The later philosophers—Epicurus (*especially this one*), Stoic, and Skeptic, I've made an object of special study more out of [political -DS]

Nietzsche's challenge to Marx can be understood in the following terms. Nietzsche suggests that the possibility or, rather, the impossibility of doing things differently does not pertain specifically to capitalism. This possibility/impossibility must have always existed. If this were true, then only *wishing* this deterministic constraint away could give rise to theories such as those of Marx. These theories, however, would be destined to remain utopian because they are ultimately based on effacing something fundamental that cannot be changed. Nietzsche, in his stead, acknowledges this constraint (GS: §276). He argues, however, that recognising the reality of fundamental constraints (e.g., inequality, exploitation) also yields the possibility of doing things differently compared to how things have been done so far. Hence, Heraclitus, or Philo (UM: II, *UDHL*, §5).

Attempting to 'break the bonds of fate' Marx alters the lines of causality by switching around two of the hypostases within the hierarchy of the trichotomous Platonic soul—spiritual and material—that are bound by the underlying physiological determinism which, in the final reckoning, translates into specific valuations that either support ascending life or promote descending life and preside over its 'chronic degeneration' (TI: *Skirmishes*, §33). Subverting and simplifying the intricate architecture of the Platonic soul, Marx privileges the material (structural) element over the spiritual (superstructural) one.[317] In consequence, individual and 'public consciousness' become answerable, as though to the *new master*, to the material imperative which, not unlike in the case of Adam Smith, is said to hold the keys to spiritual emancipation (CW 20:441). This reinterpreted line of causation, in a marked departure from Smith, also connects Marx's aspirations for genuine emancipation at the very 'end of pre-history of human society' ('Entstehungsgeschichte', CW 29:264) to the inevitable and victorious *proletarian revolution*, i.e., the modern re-enactment of the revolt of the enslaved, this time from the chains of capitalistic oppression (CW 5:53).[318] Nietzsche would see no accident in the parallel being drawn between the *proletarian revolution* and *early Christianity* which, 'like every great revolutionary movement, was made by the masses'.[319] Nietzsche would contend that the emancipatory pathos of the revolt against the oppres-

---

than philosophical interest' (CW 40:226; my emphasis). Fenves notes that one ineligible word in the letter is the one I populated with 'political' in square brackets to mirror the editors of the *Marx-Engels Werke* (Berlin, 1960–1883, XXI, 547). This is potentially significant if the nature of the Nietzsche-Marx divide, explored here, is more political than philosophical, particularly in light of Marx's own assertion that '*political emancipation is not the final and absolute form of human emancipation*' (see Bottomore 1963:10; my emphasis).

317 Nietzsche considers that the '*socialists' conception of the highest society*' represents '*the lowest in the order of rank*' (NF-1888:14[6]; my emphasis).

318 Marx designates capitalism as 'the last antagonistic form of the social process of production' and stipulates that 'No social formation is ever destroyed before all the productive forces for which it is sufficient have been developed, and new superior relations of production never replace older ones before the material conditions for their existence have matured within the framework of the old society' (CW 29:263–264). See Tabak 2012:51–79 for an engaging discussion of Marx's 'structuralism'.

319 *Marx and Engels on Religion*, 1957:184, as well as CW 25:96, 603, and 682.

sors—having lost none of its potency—proves, in Marx's case, still capable of 'seducing even the most noble spirits' (TI: *Skirmishes*, §48).[320]

Religion and Revolution

Nietzsche and Marx would share the path to positing that 'man makes religion, religion does not make man', and that simply uncovering the 'origins of religion' is not sufficient for overcoming it (CW 3:175). At this point in the conversation Marx stipulates that the underlying economic structure of society gives rise to religious belief which, as 'an inverted world-consciousness', serves to legitimise and to protect the economic structure of 'an inverted world' (CW 3:175). Marx posits the case of *double inversion* that translates into a socially engineered phenomenon known to the majority of us as 'reality'.[321] State and society—the outward expressions of this 'inverted world'—use religion as their 'general theory', which precludes the individual from developing self-awareness of his predicament and consequently stops the 'human essence' from 'acquiring any true reality' (CW 3:81, 143, 175).

The individual, in Marx's assessment, 'is no abstract being squatting outside the world'; rather, he is someone who 'makes his life-activity the object of his will and of his consciousness', being able to distinguish between himself and his life-activity (CW 3:175).[322] At the same time, the individual inevitably ends up constituted as an 'the ensemble of the social relations' of his creation (CW 5:4; Thesis 6) forming a self-reinforcing loop. In the *Grundrisse* (1857–1861) Marx adds that 'society does not consist of individuals, but expresses the *sum of the relationships and conditions* in which these individuals stand to one another' (CW 28:195; my emphasis).[323] Phrased differently, upon the [distorted] economic basis—represented by private property—the individual creates an 'inverted world' in the pervasive unfairness of which he ends up trapped with no more than religion (i.e., 'the fantastic realisation of the human essence'—i.e., ideology) to guide him through its elaborate labyrinths.[324] Capital, as a

---

320 Nietzsche explains how this deception works in NF-1877:25[1]. For further context, see also Nietzsche's discussion in BGE: §202; TI: *Skirmishes*, §34 and §48, as well as AC: §62.
321 Marx discusses a similar mechanism of *double inversion* in relation to the process by which commodities are converted into money and money into capital, i.e., where C-M is also, concurrently, M-C and the outward appearance of exchange conceals the substance of the metamorphosis by means of which surplus-value is covertly created and extracted, leaving in its wake alienated and deceived labour (see CW 35:118).
322 Marx would later add that what turns individual into an 'abstract being' and 'transforms him into a spiritual and physical monster' is the increase in the 'division of labour' as a result of increase in 'civilisation' (CW 3:220–221). Nietzsche echoes this thought in HH: I, §57 and NF-1884:25[189]).
323 Later, in *Capital*, Vol. I, Marx also notes that 'capital is not a thing, but a social relation between persons, established by the instrumentality of things' (CW 35:753).
324 CW 3:175, 298, and 316. See in particular Marx's discussion of the 'transformation of all private property into industrial capital' as representing 'the total victory of private property' (CW 3:316).

'form of property' (CW 28:412), is also an integral part of this inverted economic reality, albeit with one distinction. Marx views capital as a *time-specific* phenomenon—a form of private property—pertaining to the emergence of capitalism. Private property can be regarded as capital's progenitor—its historical 'premiss'—which, by controlling the 'mode of distribution' within society and enabling the circulation of commodities, creates the socio-economic framework within which capital can proliferate.[325]

The inverted social world, in the form of the state and society, protects the lie—the 'original sin' of private property—as it enlists all individual members of society in hiding private property's infelicitous origins in plain sight by normalising it as the bedrock of [the class-divided] social organisation.[326] The state and society enforce the economic basis, while ideology serves to legitimise both the structure and the superstructure:

> The *categories of bourgeois economy* ... are *forms of thought* expressing with social validity the conditions and *relations* of a definite, historically determined mode of production, viz., the production of commodities. (CW 35:87; my emphasis)

To a certain extent, Marx's critique of economic categories—e.g., private property, wage labour, capital, surplus value, the division of labour, and 'the general law of capitalistic accumulation' (CW 35:634)—can be understood as an attempt to tease out from the otherwise spectral economic forms the social relations that breathe life into them and give reality to these economic abstractions to the point of being overwhelmed (i.e., *inverted*) and subjugated by them.[327] In other words, private property does not possess any (independent) significance other than that mediated by the social relations that inform it. The same social relations embed private property as an unquestionable economic institution of capitalist economy, making it appear an outcome of 'a pretended law of Nature' (CW 35:616). Marx argues that, just like in the case of religion, the economic assumptions thought unquestionable remain simply unquestioned. Interrogating them leads Marx to the necessity of dismantling the economic forms of capitalist economy in order to allow the qualitatively different social relations to germinate within the transformed economic receptacles, rather than trying to revitalise (i.e., to 'un-

---

325 See CW 28:170 and 209; CW 29:462–463; and CW 35:89. Engels described money capital as 'the alienated abstraction of property' (CW 3:476).
326 See Bonefeld 2022:192. Echoing Marx, Adorno problematises private property as 'the old form of rule' that comes to bear on the development of the 'economic apparatus' as a 'modifying factor' that, to some extent, lies outside 'the system of political economy' but remains 'central to the history of domination' (Adorno 2003:100–104).
327 This line of analysis becomes important in the works of the leading figures of Critical Theory, Horkheimer, Adorno and Marcuse, in particular. See Bonefeld 2022a:16–18 and Bobka and Braunstein 2022:37.

invert') the social relations within the prevailing economic and political institutions of capitalism.[328]

The economic basis—the real locus of unfreedom, exploitation and injustice, according to Marx—ends up buried under these two layers of inversion which divert critical attention away from it. Ideology, as *false consciousness*, protects 'the inverted world' and ensures individual's *alienation* from his essence (i.e., from the real world). False consciousness and alienation, which encode subjectivity, feed directly into and sustain the algorithm of capitalism's political economy, within which the individual ends up twice deceived.[329] Once, concerning the nature of the superstructure (e.g., the state and the society) she creates. Twice, because to interpret the substance of her creations and to make existence in this habitat palatable she is only allowed recourse to ideology as the 'general theory'. For as long as these conditions persist, the individual is precluded from understanding something important about the real state of affairs. Namely, that she is the chief instrument of her own enslavement who, by virtue of the subtle and pervasive indoctrination, lacks awareness of her predicament (CW 35:85).[330] Even if such individual should get an occasional inkling that she is 'being fooled', the system—which she has been instrumental in setting up—is meticulously constructed in such a way that inside it this individual lacks any 'power not to be fooled' because surrendering this power was an essential building block in erecting that very system (NF-1886:5[71]). The Babylonian cacophony of its hoots, cackles and wails notwithstanding, the only way in which meaning-making is mediated in the world so constructed—to enable her to make sense of the social universe she inhabits—is provided by the means the primary function of which is to protect its premises from disclosing their essence by continually robbing her of hers. Marx concludes that 'the most extreme forms of estrangement' (CW 28:439) proliferate under the auspices of capitalism:

> In the bourgeois economy—and in the epoch of production to which it corresponds—this complete unfolding of man's inner potentiality turns into his total emptying-out. His universal *objectification*

---

[328] Nietzsche problematises the periodic 'destruction of the phenomenal world' as resulting from the conflict where 'the cultural *lie, which pretends to be the only reality*' attempts to subjugate 'the genuine truth of nature' (see BT: §8, §17; my emphasis).

[329] Nietzsche makes a similar point stating that 'in the great world of money [...] the poor and the industrious', used in a purely instrumental fashion (i.e., as a means) get taken advantage of at least twice (HH: II, *WS*, §25).

[330] See Lowith's poignant observation, shared by Adorno, that Marx's critical insight is not, strictly speaking economic but, rather, concerns deciphering the workings of the social system the necessary condition of the existence of which is that its inhabitants should remain alienated from themselves and from each other and the systemic prerogative of which is, therefore, to generate precisely such subjects *ad infinitum* (Löwith 1991:152–155). This concern, whether it be originally Marx's or not—a parallel can be drawn to Luke 23:34 ('Father forgive them for they do not know what they are doing')—resonates audibly throughout Nietzsche's *oeuvre*. Adorno would later explain that once 'reified consciousness' becomes total, it is no longer possible to escape it (see Adorno 2003:109–110 and 2007:346).

becomes his total *alienation*, and the demolition of all determined *one-sided aims* becomes the sacrifice of the [human] end-in-itself to a wholly *external goal*. (CW 28:412; my emphasis)[331]

So profound is the individual's self-estrangement, which protects the genesis of private property and of every class-based society, on Marx's view, that only a radical solution, i.e., *revolution*, would suffice to extract the individual out of this comatose existence, to wake her up to the gruesome reality of her enslavement (CW 5:52–53). It would take no less than upending of the *economic basis* of this 'inverted' society in order to overcome religion and the predicament of human 'self-estrangement' once and for all. The revolution has to come first because consciousness can only be liberated once the economic conditions which enslaved it in the first place have been fundamentally—i.e., at the level of property ownership—altered:

> Socialism is the declaration of the *permanence of the revolution*, the class dictatorship of the proletariat as the necessary transit point to the abolition of class distinctions generally, to the *abolition of all the relations of production* on which they rest, to the *abolition of all the social relations* that correspond to these relations. (CW 10:127)

Against the backdrop of the inexorable succession of historical epochs, Marx does not scrutinise the ruling values that stand behind the inversion of the world, focusing instead on the 'ruling ideas' of a specific period.[332] Where ideas symbolise change, valuations provide continuity that allows a worldview, such as *slave morality*, to endure as the host and under the guise of new ideas. A degree of conceptual inconsistency is discernible in Marx's position on ideas *vis-à-vis* values, on the one hand, and in his treatment of capital *vis-à-vis* private property, on the other. The latter comes across as the repository of values that underwrite the history of class domination, whereas capital, as a more historically-specific phenomenon, pertains to the realm of ideas. Marx scrutinises capital, as expressing the quintessence of the time-specific social relations, but he calls for the abolition of private property, acknowledging, albeit indirectly, the ontological relationship between these two economic categories. He does not, however, analyse private property from the viewpoint of values that it helps to eternalise and

---

[331] Compare this to Nietzsche's discussion in the famous aphorism 'The Impossible Class' in *Daybreak* (§206) *and* to HH: II, *AOM*, §186. The structural and phraseological parallels to Marx are striking, including the true cost of the 'one-sided preferences' (HH: II, *AOM*, §186), the logic of the argument concerning the sacrifice of spirituality and individuality to an 'external goal' and the discussion of the 'Asiatic form' of communal organisation (Marx, CW 28:410) and the 'Asiatic perseverance' (Nietzsche, D: §206) in the context of the growth of population and the resulting pressures on the traditional property and communal relations.

[332] CW 5:59. See Wood 2014:270. Russell suggests that Marx's conviction in the progressive unfolding of history allows Marx to side-step values and ethics more generally (see Russell 1946:788). Nietzsche argues that we all need to be deceived. It is our way of normalizing reality and making human life bearable. The crucial difference, however, is who deceives us (or, who do we allow and empower to deceive us) and to what ends?

which, in turn, enable private property to become less tractable by transforming into capital. This is particularly evident from Marx's discussion on the nature of money which, as is in Nietzsche's case, is substantively informed by Goethe's insights (CW 3:324). Marx maintains that

> Since money, as the existing and *active concept of value*, confounds and confuses all things, it is the general confounding and confusing of all things—the *world upside-down*—the confounding and confusing of all natural and human qualities (CW 3:326)

Unlike Nietzsche, however, Marx does not inquire after the values that enable money's ascent to the pinnacle of value and endow it with the seemingly otherworldly power to turn the human world upside down. For this reason, Nietzsche would suggest that in his quest to establish '*the truth* of the world', and precisely by wishing to do away with 'the world beyond *the truth*' (CW 3:176, 463), Marx becomes beholden to the very call of the 'metaphysical bird-catchers' (BGE: §230) he is attempting to overcome. To borrow from Foucault, Marx ends up looking for '"that which was already there"— the image of a primordial truth fully adequate to its nature'—even if his search 'necessitates the removal of every mask to ultimately disclose an original identity' (Foucault 1977:142).[333] Paradoxical though it may sound, Marx circumnavigates the conscious realm that connects capitalism, socialism (and, indeed, communism) and Christianity by the unbreakable bond of the valuations of *slave morality* that persist in the very '*permanence of the revolution*'.

Changing Revolution's Pivot

Nietzsche would argue that an important 'blind spot' remains in Marx's theories as they fail to deliver the 'finishing stroke' to decisively expel the 'celebrated "metaphysical need"' (NF-1884:26[220]). God, who is adept at 'making himself small' (NF-1884:26[220]), can thus 'continue to lead a dangerous afterlife in places where no one suspects it' (BGE: §12).[334]

Marx's disdain for the hypocritical employment of the hollow and inverted concept of 'equality' in bourgeois politics and in jurisprudence (i.e., the 'procedural equality' before the law; CW 6:228) is well documented.[335] Neither was Marx deaf to the facts that 'one man is superior to another physically, or mentally' and that 'unequal individuals (and they would not be different individuals if they were not unequal) are measurable only by an equal standard insofar as they are brought under an equal point of

---

[333] See also Nietzsche's discussion in NF-1885:2[189] on the need to go beyond the criticism of values to examining their origins.
[334] See also Nietzsche's discussion of 'God [who] makes himself small and pushes his way through the whole world ... also as a demon of annihilation' (NF-1884:26[220]).
[335] See Wood 2014:253–273 and Eagleton 2011:102–105.

view' (CW 24:86–87).³³⁶ In fact, the early phases of the communist society would represent a clear *hierarchy*:

> [In] a communist society [...] as it emerges from capitalist society [...] the individual producer receives back from society—after the deductions have been made—exactly what he gives to it. [...] He receives a certificate from society that he has furnished such-and-such an amount of labor [...] and with this certificate, he draws from the social stock of means of consumption as much as the same amount of labor cost. The *same amount of labor* which he has *given to society* in one form, *he receives back* in another. (CW 24:86; my emphasis)

Putting aside the obvious difficulties of overseeing such an enterprise in practice, the equal right in the above social setting does not transcend 'the narrow horizon of bourgeois right in its entirety'. It is still a 'right of *inequality* in its content, like every right' (CW 24:87).³³⁷ For Marx, however, this inequality is ultimately temporary because it rests upon a different economic foundation—that of communal property. This factor, on Marx's view, would help to dramatically change the social landscape, overcoming, in the process, the religious bias of the revolution. But does it?

Marx's frequently cited opposition to the 'barrack-room communism' ('Kasernenkommunismus')³³⁸ notwithstanding, it is difficult to overlook conceptual affinity between the logic of his argument laid out in his *Critique of the Gotha Programme* (1875) and the *Book of Acts* in the *New Testament*, attributed to St. Luke the Evangelist. In particular, the second chapter (Acts 2) speaks of the 'the day of the Pentecost', which did not 'fully come at once', and of Peter who, speaking on behalf of the risen Christ to the devout men 'out of every nation under heaven', laid out a powerful vision of a different future and of a different way of communal living and baptised them into *his* 'doctrine and fellowship':

> And all that *believed* were together, and had *all things common*; and sold their possessions and goods, and parted them to all men, as every man had need. And they, continuing daily with one accord in the temple, and breaking bread from house to house, did eat their meat with gladness and singleness of heart (Acts 2:44–46)

Luke's narrative invokes the *proto-communist* philosophy of the Essenes, as outlined by Philo and Josephus, as well as resonating with Marx's own view which, in a secularised form, would not only become the cornerstone of his political economy, but also underwrite the Marxist method of historical materialism, including the conceptualisation of the progressive unfolding of history propelled by the forces of class struggle.³³⁹ Marx's

---

336 Nietzsche makes a virtually identical point in NF-1887:9[173]. See also Wood on Marx's 'radical rejection of all universal moral standards' (Wood 2014:268).
337 See Nietzsche's discussion in AC: §57 on inequality of rights and in HH: I, *HMS*, §93.
338 This has to be contextualised within Marx's and Engels' polemic with Bakunin and Nechayev; see Marx 1988a: Vol. XXIII, 542–543.
339 See Engels 1970:57–58.

revolutionary theory that informs his political economy, starting most poignantly with *The German Ideology* (1846) and *The Communist Manifesto* (1848), singles out the question of *property ownership* as the conceptual seabed upon which the complex network of social relations and social consciousness grow.

Marx identifies *property* as the receptacle invested of social relations, the depository from which social relations, constitutive of social reality at large, develop through the course of historical epochs, as one mode of production is superseded by another (see Mayer 1975:704–705). The other side of this *same process* is that the social relations that spring from property also work to embed themselves deeper into the institutional framework of society, into its laws and customs as well as into the human *psyche*, endowing a certain form of property with a sense of permanency. Property not only pulls together the different ages into the prevailing narrative of history in the service of the ruling classes; it also gives history a direction and class struggle a purpose. The unifying force of the logic of private property and contrived sociability, becoming indistinguishable from one another, morph into the homogenous ideological narrative of capitalism which in modernity can be communicated through the inverted lens of capital 'that attributes social power to things' (Prusik 2022:154). Viewed in this manner, Marx undoubtedly sees economic reality as ultimately socially constituted. In the end, an individual, a commodity, an exchange, capital and private property are nothing more than the respective sums of social relations that constitute them (CW 35:92). The tricky thing Marx asks his readers is to get their minds around is the fact that 'without knowing it' (CW 35:84–85), individuals working through the array of economic categories constitute and perpetuate the social relations that, in turn, constitute them (see Marcuse 1988:151). It is a feedback loop wherein the 'material forces acquire spiritual life, and human existence becomes a dumb, material force' (Löwith 1991:154). The radical transformation of the *institution of property* and the drastic transformation of *human nature* thus present themselves as inseparable tasks. Both are equally required in order to disable capitalism's vicious circle that normalises the extreme degrees of human alienation.[340]

Convinced that 'right can never be higher than the economic structure of society and its cultural development conditioned thereby', Marx consistently argues that consciousness, the highest development of which would be required to reach communism (see Debord 2005: §88), could only follow where the economic structure of society would lead:

> The mode of production in material life determines the general character of the social, political, and spiritual processes of life. It is *not the consciousness* of men that determines their existence, but, on the contrary, their *social existence* determines their consciousness. (CW 29:263)

In order to achieve the emancipation of individual and collective consciousness, it becomes imperative first to alter the economic basis of society. In Marx's thinking, *eco-*

---

340 See CW 28439. See also Löwith 1991:156 and Adorno 2003:109–110.

nomic equality—as perceived through the prism of communal property ownership—represents the necessary, if not sufficient, condition for emancipating individual's consciousness and for moulding autonomous agency.[341] Echoing the attitude of the Essenes towards property, the issue of its *ownership* becomes the unambiguous kernel of Marx's political economy that underpins his call for its abolition:[342]

> [T]he *laws of private property*—liberty, equality, property—property in one's own labour and the ability to freely dispose of it—are *inverted* into the propertylessness of the worker and the alienation of his labour, his relation to it as alien property and vice versa (CW 29:64; my emphasis)

Marx equates the overturning of private property with the 'revolution in the whole social order' as denoting the essence of the 'theory of the Communists' (CW 6:498).[343] His later discussion in the *Critique of the Gotha Programme* (1875) can also be seen as drawing on the spirit of the Essenes' worldview in at least two critical respects. Marx recognises the 'inevitable defects' of *organic inequality* between the individual members of society. He argues that inequality only becomes exacerbated by the division of labour which reflects the ownership of the means of production in the hands of the few and is additionally distorted by the 'the narrow horizon of bourgeois right' (CW 24:87). Marx contends that 'only in a higher phase of *communist society*', where the enslaving propensities of the division of labour and the 'antithesis between mental and physical labour' are fully overcome,[344] thus freeing up 'all the springs of co-operative wealth flow', would it become possible to realise the aspiration of receiving contributions 'from each according to his ability' whilst providing to 'each according to his needs' (CW 24:87).[345] Doing so would approximate the ideal of the Essenes' community that operates outside of the capitalistic constraints of 'reciprocal exchange', enabling it to '*treat all men with equal kindness and live together in a communal way*'.[346] The road leading to such state of social affairs is a long and arduous one. Marx acknowledges

---

[341] Economic equality is not to be confused with 'distributive equality/justice', see Wood 2014:253. See also Engels' letter to Joseph Bloch (September 21–22, 1890) for an important elucidation on *historical materialism*; CW 49:34–36.
[342] See CW 29:261 and the *Manifesto of the Communist Party*, Chapter 2, 'Proletarians and Communists' (CW 6:497–507). See also Petrucciani's insightful discussion in 'Adorno's Criticism of Marx's Social Theory' (2015:21–22). Cf. Postone 1994:52–58.
[343] This call is initially sounded in *The German Ideology* (1846, see 'Private Property and Communism'; CW 5:48–53), *The Communist Manifesto* (1848, Chapter 2, 'Proletarians and Communists', CW 6:497–507) and repeated in the later writings, including the *Capital*, Vol. I (CW 35:750–751).
[344] See Philo's discussion concerning 'an equality of labour with a natural good condition of body, and an equality of art with self-instructed nature, so that both of them are able to carry off equal prizes of virtue' ('On the Migration of Abraham': XXX.167 in *The Works of Philo* 1993:362).
[345] Marx borrowed the famous slogan '*De chacun selon ses moyens, à chacun selon ses besoins*' from Louis Blanc's (1811–1882), Plus de Girondins (1851). See also, Lefèbvre 1972:113–114.
[346] See Philo (1993), *Quod Omnis Probus Liber Sit* ('Every Good Man is Free'), 12.75–13.88. Eagleton's formulation of Marx's take on equality echoes Philo; see Eagleton 2011:105.

that the offer of 'abundance to all in a higher and freer society' would only be achieved at 'terrible human cost' (Wood 2014:270):

> [A]t *first* the development of the capacities of the human species takes place at the cost of the majority of human individuals and even classes, *in the end* it breaks through this contradiction and coincides with the development of the individual; the higher development of individuality is thus only achieved by a historical process during which individuals are sacrificed for the interests of the species in the human kingdom, as in the animal and plant kingdoms, always assert themselves at the cost of the interest of individuals. (CW 31:348)

The *first part* of the cited passage resonates with Nietzsche's view that 'every enhancement of the type "man" has so far been the work of an aristocratic society … that accepts with a good conscience the sacrifice of untold human beings who, for its sake, must be reduced and lowered to incomplete human beings, to slaves, to instruments' (BGE: §257). Then, however, comes Marx's all-important *atomic swerve* away from the punitive determinism of the ancients and towards the promising economic liberalism of Smith and Riccardo. In agreement with his notable predecessors, Marx hypothesises that '"*in the end*" all will be well and the interests of the human species and those of the individual—i.e., of all the individuals then alive—will coincide' (McCarthy 1984:58). Unlike Smith and Riccardo, Marx maintains that in order for such convergence to take place, the vampirical nature of capitalism (CW 35:241) manifested in the systematic misappropriation of *surplus-value* generated by the propertyless labour must be categorically overcome.[347] Marx's call for the abolition of private property, although undoubtedly substantiated by his elucidation of the *labour theory of value*, does not directly follow from that theory. Connecting property and revolution—as though expressing a wish to speed up the procession of history—is something else, something that could balance the scales of historical justice:

> The *revolution is necessary* […] not only because the ruling class cannot be overthrown in any other way, but *also* because the class overthrowing it can only in a revolution succeed in ridding itself of all the *muck of ages* and become fitted to found society anew. (CW 5:53; my emphasis)

The 'muck of ages' metaphor in this context merits some attention. The 'positive transcendence of private property' goes to the heart of Marx's concern with reclaiming the 'estranged human essence' (CW 3:296–297). Marx maintains that even if determinism and the drive for domination were lodged in the fabric of existence, humankind is *not compelled* to it as destiny: both can be overcome by the power of reason. Marx's revolution, in part, appears as a recognition of the impossibility of breaking free from the mental constructions of the inverted world of capitalism, the impossibility of overcoming the exploitative ethos of economic categories by merely political and economic means. Such is the power of inverted reason (or, unreason) that it would require no less than the 'social revolution' to undo this inversion and re-awaken reason. No

---

[347] See Marx, CW 4:35–35; 35:214, 263–264, and 306.

other form of political action—'limited and dichotomous' by definition—would be powerful enough to blow away the cobwebs of inverted reason (CW 3:205). Only

> A social revolution is found to have the point of view of the whole because it represents man's protest against a dehumanised life, because it starts out from the point of view of a separate real individual, because the community, against the separation of which from himself the individual reacts, is man's true community, human nature. (CW 3:205)

Although the 'social revolution' is not a shortcut to emancipation, it acts as a one-time trigger for altering the direction of the humankind's trajectory that would hand over the reins of human destiny into the hands of reason. In this context, 'the muck of the ages' refers to the cumulative historical baggage of valuations that conceal 'the vileness of private property, which wants to set itself up as the positive *community system*' (CW 3:296).[348] Revolution is necessary in order to overcome the *inertia of history* presented by the ruling classes as inevitability and normalised through inverted sociability. Marx, not unlike Nietzsche, intuits the danger that this inertia, spawned by the inversion of reason, would produce the 'great adiaphoria' (NF-1888:14[83]). Unless its spread is forestalled, it could thwart the project of emancipation leaving in its wake 'swamps and stagnant pools' (UM: III, *SE*, §4) that would only magnify alienation, turning it eventually into a self-fulfilling prophecy, i.e., unable to birth a different future.[349] Nietzsche would add, however, that even 'liberated' reason could play part in leading us to new and more pervasive forms of domination just as we come consider dismantling them.

The Chimera of Private Property

The question of human essence is an equally important concern for Nietzsche, although viewing property through the lens of values provides him with a very different perspective. Nietzsche contends that 'possession of property is the only thing that distinguishes' the 'wealthy liberal bourgeois' from the 'socialist revolutionaries' (HH: II, *AOM*, §304). He argues that taking property out of the equation would expose the uncomfortable *likeness of valuations* that empower the presumed ideological adversaries. This is why Nietzsche's own critique neither focuses on nor objects to private property as the primary cause of society's politico-economic woes (see HH: II, WS, §285). Posses-

---

[348] This is consistent with Marx's view that 'the tradition of all the dead generations weighs like a nightmare on the brain of the living' (CW 11:103). In *The German Ideology*, Marx specifically derides liberalism for endowing private property with the sense of the right: liberal private property-owners, at the beginning of the French Revolution gave *private property* a liberal appearance by declaring it *one of the rights of man*' CW 5:208).

[349] Echoing Marx, Nietzsche argues that the promise of a 'new beginning' required *not only* to 'redeem all that is past' (Z: III, *Tablets*, §12) but to overcome the 'thick melancholy' of the 'preachers of death' which threatens humankind's future (Z: I, *Preachers*).

sions, for Nietzsche, are a matter of spirit and temperament: 'only he who has *spirit* ought to have possessions' (HH: II, *AOM*, §310). In every other scenario, 'possessions are a public danger' (HH: II, *AOM*, §310). Under capitalism—because private possessions encourage every form of excess. Under socialism—communal possessions breed envy, stifle initiative and normalise complacency. Both, therefore, feed psychology of *ressentiment*.

The question of property, for Nietzsche, like many other pivotal concerns of political economy is ultimately a matter of agency. In this respect, Nietzsche closely follows the logic of Plato's argument that society's guardians *should not possess private property* in order to maintain single-minded commitment to their political role in maintaining the just state (see Plato, *Republic*, 464[a-e]).[350] The abolition of private property is a one-sided misconstrual of the problem, in aid of specific revolutionary agendas since 'we, the heirs and inheritors of the entire past of the old culture', are by no means free to 'decree our own abolition and may not wish away a single part of it' (HH: I, *State*, §452). Instead of resorting to any form of 'forcible redistribution' of property Nietzsche urges to carefully examine the values that would demand such a course of action. He insists that 'one must want more than one has in order to become more' (NF-1885:37[11])—but 'more of what?' becomes the key question. If the answer to it is money, property, material wealth, or power deriving from these things, one would never become 'more' as a result of the growth in their possessions. One would never be able to 'live through life itself' but only through its external (i.e., incomplete or, worse, inadequate) representations, invariably lacking the very 'thing' one covets the most. Property that *gives power* and property that merely *illustrates power* while emphasising its own non-essential relationship to it are two radically different propositions, on Nietzsche's view.[351]

He contends that only when one loses worldly possessions can one can know 'what is truly his' and may yet 'discover that he is richer than before' (HH: II, *AOM*, §343).[352]

---

[350] The question of property is by no means a vacuous issue for Nietzsche. His views on the subject are informed by Plato and Epictetus in particular. Nietzsche closely follows the logic of Plato's argument that society's guardians should not possess private property in order to maintain unwavering commitment to their critical political function in upholding the just state (see Plato, *Republic*, 464[a-e]). Echoing Plato, Epictetus maintains that 'the theatre [is] the common property of all the citizens', i.e., explicating the notion of the state as a 'common good' intended to be shared by everyone and which does not engender hostile opposition to private property (see Epictetus, *Discourses*, Book II, Chapter 4). Equally, this consideration establishes a legitimate connection to the *Essenes conundrum*, outlined earlier, concerning the relationship between societal hierarchy and property ownership.

[351] This distinction also encapsulates the critical difference between *being* and *becoming*. See NF-1885:37[11] and TI: *Skirmishes*, §38, with an emphasis on the difference, respectively, between wanting to 'be something' and 'to become strong'.

[352] Nietzsche's view exhibits considerable affinity with the insights of Epictetus throughout both, *Discourses* and *Enchiridion*. For instance, in relation to losing 'external' possessions: 'I have lost nothing that belongs to me; it was not something of mine that was torn from me, but something that was not in my power has left me' (see Ritter 1846:206). This aphorism could also relate to Nietzsche's own experience in the wake of Gründerkrach of 1873 (see Chapter 7 for further details).

In light of this, any form of power which derives from and is granted on the basis of abstract representations would incurably lack authentic authority and would end up endorsing reactive valuations in its bid to hold on to its position at any cost.[353] Although economic pursuits are worthwhile and necessary, they are, ultimately, the rightful mainstay of the mediocre (D: §179; BGE: §253; and TI: *Germans*, §4), and it is only if the world should fall into their hands entirely that the level of existential threat to humanity would increase disproportionately (NF-1884:25[523]).[354]

Nietzsche does not prioritise either property, or wealth as posing an imminent threat. Instead, he focuses on their *excess*, particularly when property and wealth are allowed to concentrate in 'private hands' (HH: II, *WS*, §285). Echoing Marx, Nietzsche argues that curbing such excesses by regulation and legislation is ineffective, because bourgeois law inadvertently protects and encourages the excessive propensities of capitalist society. Unlike Marx, Nietzsche insists that in order to regulate excess effectively the complete revaluation of the values which underwrite and maintain the capitalist system would be required. What is necessary, on Nietzsche's view, is '*a gradual transformation of mind:* the sense of justice must grow greater in everyone, the instinct for violence weaker' (HH: I, *State*, §452). For these reasons Nietzsche regards the question of property ownership as a *red herring* and warns against excessive focus on this issue. Targeting the problem of excess, however, as the one of the great unsolved riddles of political economy, becomes the critical line of investigation within NPE.

In the absence of a drastic change in the evaluating perspective, Nietzsche would find a critical element to be missing in Marx's political-economic architecture, namely *agency* capable of embodying the kind of values that would not only hold together its various pieces but would guarantee its health and longevity (EH: *Preface*, §2). This happens because Marx avoids dealing with 'that most difficult and captious form of backward inference in which the most mistakes are made: the backward inference from the work to the maker, from the deed to the doer, from the ideal to those who need it, from every way of thinking and valuing to the commanding need behind it' (GS: §370). Nietzsche would argue that Marx's call for the abolition of private property becomes not only the nexus of the qualitatively different economic and social relations, but also the portal through which *slave morality* successfully smuggles its valuations. The abolition of private property becomes the *trojan horse* inside which *slave morality* would successfully pass between the fledgling social order of capitalism and the, then theoretical, world of socialism. Property becomes the nesting place from which these valuations would propagate until they eventually undermine the aspirational appeal engendered in its communal ownership.

---

353 See Weber's discussion of 'economically conditioned power', which substantively corroborates Nietzsche's views (1946:180–181).
354 The 'mediocre', for Nietzsche, is far from being a derogatory term. In many places, he speaks of the 'mediocre' as society's 'center of gravity'. The problem occurs, on Nietzsche's view when they start to 'accommodate themselves to the mob and flatter the instincts of the "disinherited"' (NF-1888:14[182]). See also Nietzsche's discussion in NF-1885:36[3]; NF-1887:10[84]; and NF-1887:10[109].

The Power of Exchange

Exchange sits at the very heart of the money-economy. It is the latter's enabling process which, at the same time, presides over the creation of *surplus value* and conceals its misappropriation, thus appearing to embed inequality. Viewed in this light, exchange acts as a configurator of social relations and supports the social structure—it is an important 'substratum that underlies all of social life and history' (Cook and Whitmeyer 1992:110). For Marx, as for Nietzsche, the concept of exchange carries important information not only about the functioning of the money-economy but, more importantly, about the underlying structures of power and domination that exchange helps to perpetuate.

Marx and Nietzsche would agree that any exchange (of commodities) can only have the formal appearance of a free, fair, and equal transaction (CW 28:386). As Weber would later clarify, 'the emergence of economic power' is frequently the 'consequence of power existing on other grounds' (Weber 1946:180).[355] In a passage in *The Wonderer and His Shadow*, entitled 'A Fair Exchange', Nietzsche writes:

> If money is the *exchange object* it must be considered that a shilling in the hand of a rich heir, a day-labourer, a shop-keeper, a student are quite different things: according to whether he did almost nothing or a great deal to get it, each ought to receive little or a great deal in exchange for it: in reality it is, of course the other way around. In the *great world of money* the shilling of the laziest rich man is more lucrative than that of the poor and industrious. (HH, II, *WS*, §25; my emphasis)

Nietzsche's aphorism highlights not only familiarity with Marx's views on *exchange values* (vis-à-vis *use values*) as merely a social construct that comes to dominate reality.[356] Importantly, this passage communicates Nietzsche's substantive agreement with Marx that the appearance of a formally unencumbered exchange cloaks the embedded inequality of power positions.[357] Economic exchange is a *hoax* that merely places inequality on a formally equal footing.[358] Money, in this context, absorbs the underlying inequality and becomes its expression, albeit, having been *alchemically* converted into an as though value-neutral and universal medium for the exchange of equivalents,

---

[355] See also Weber 1978:334. The subject matter of *societal architecture* resulting from economic exchange becomes one of the central threads of Critical Theory. Adorno famously questions whether society, which is *actually* propagated by capitalism corresponds to its concept: 'Is there really a free and just society that corresponds to [the] world of free and just exchange? (Adorno 2016: 616–617).

[356] See Marx's discussion in *Das Kapital*, Vol. I (CW 35:46–48). Marx's analysis of exchange values and the role of money was later also picked up by Roscher (see Roscher 1878:342). Nietzsche's comments, however, resonate with Marx's meaning more strongly than with Roscher's.

[357] See Marx's discussion in CW 28:428 and CW 29:64 and 462.

[358] Adorno's verdict is more scathing: 'free and honest exchange is itself a lie' (Adorno 2005:43). See also Bobka and Braunstein on the 'equality in the process of exchange' as reproducing 'the inequality of classes and individuals' (2022:37).

which obscures the original disparities.[359] This spectrality allows money to ascend from being the humble means of exchange to the towering heights of becoming the ultimate value of capitalist society. Working as it does in the context of the money-economy, exchange normalises the underlying inequality by making it invisible, implicitly highlighting that the money-economy simply *cannot function* in the absence of such inequality: its nefarious magic would quickly dissipate.

Highlighting, as Marx does, the disparity between *price* and *value* which is camouflaged by the commercial exchange, Nietzsche effectively sides with the labour theory of value arguing that any form of exchange can be 'honest and just' *only* when each of the participants in it 'demands as much as his own object seems *worth to him*, including the *effort* it cost to acquire it, its rarity, the *time expended*, etc., together with its sentimental value' (HH: II, *WS*, §25).[360] Elsewhere, Nietzsche asserts that fair exchange presupposes 'approximately equal power positions' between the parties (HH: I, *HMS*, §92). Only this position would result in an exchange by means of which 'each acquires what he values more than the other does', having priced his own 'commodity' at full cost—i.e., 'one gives to the other what he (i.e., the other –DS) wants to have and in return receives what one oneself desires'(HH: I, *HMS*, §92). This, according to Nietzsche, is a *genuine satisfaction of needs*, as no inequality changes hands in the course of this exchange. Nietzsche's use of 'wants' and 'desires' draws an *intentional contrast* with the accepted economic vernacular of 'supply' and 'demand' (D: §175), which he sees as a distorted scale for determining our needs. Nietzsche's 'wants' and 'desires' derive from what one *actually 'demands'* as necessary for the purposes of 'enlightened self-preservation' rather than what the money-maker stipulates one 'needs' on the basis of his own profit-calculations.[361]

Furthermore, Nietzsche's conception of *fair exchange* entails economic as well as non-economic (i.e., gifting, sacrifice, forgiveness) elements. These non- or supra-economic components are required in order to periodically re-balance the scales of justice (HH: I, *HMS*, 92), which become skewed in the course of commercial exchange. He contends that the 'competitive market' operating via the commercial exchange, where 'we buy from strangers and work for strangers', distorts the relationship between the buyer and the seller as it does between *value* and *price*, leading to the eventual erosion of value (HH: II, *WS*, §283). He argues that in a fair exchange, when an 'artisan, does or makes something for us, we are happy to pay him [...] *beyond the price*' in order to re-

---

[359] See also Marx's important comment that money (aka capital) does not and cannot 'alter the inner conditions of valorisation' already entailed in the exchange and only 'projects them outward', albeit under the aura of 'independence' (CW 28:376). See also Lenin's poignant commentary on Marx's theory of money as 'the highest product of the development of exchange', which 'masks and conceals the social character of all individual labour, the social link between individual producers united by the market' (LCW: 21:61).
[360] See Marx's discussion in CW 28:75–76.
[361] Marx stipulates that 'capital only undertakes projects which are profitable, profitable, that is, *from its own point of view*' (CW 28:455).

flect the value entailed in the product of his work (HH: II, *WS*, §283). Nietzsche compares paying 'beyond the price' to a 'kind of sacrifice on our part' and names it the 'respect tax'. This notion, he argues, is an expression of our fundamental 'sensibility' and the real 'standard of measurement of the degree of commerce between human souls' (HH: II, *WS*, §283). For these reasons Nietzsche concludes that 'the characteristic of *exchange* is the original characteristic of justice (HH: I, *HMS*, 92)

Where Marx and Nietzsche would disagree is on the question of whether exchange gives rise to inequality (Marx), or merely reflects and codifies it (Nietzsche), in both cases inevitably distorting reality. Once again, Nietzsche takes the logic of Marx's argument to a deeper level by reflecting on 'the great economy of the whole' (EH: *Destiny*, §4), where inequality reveals itself as one of its organic features (NF-1886:7[2]; BGE: §259). As such, it precedes any form of economic inequality, which is only an expression of the underlying structure of the economy of life. While Nietzsche agrees that inequality can and should be moderated, he cannot accept, as Marx does, that it can be decisively overcome. Moreover, attempts to do away with this critical function of life—for either utopian or dystopian reasons—may distort the fabric of existence, upsetting delicate balances we may not (yet) fully comprehend, creating perverse long-term consequences and making worse, i.e., sicker, that which—with the best of intentions—was intended to be improved, i.e., made healthier and stronger.

Nietzsche's own argument, however, would run into an unsurprising problem. While he would advocate abandoning attempts to cure inequality with and through economy, the reverse of this proposition—i.e., to *cure economy with inequality* would be entirely unintelligible to the modern ear. It would necessarily be so, Nietzsche would tell us, because neither 'economy', nor 'inequality' can any longer be understood appropriately, i.e., in their *pre-inverted,* pre-moralised meanings. This is the sublime power of *slave morality* Nietzsche wants us to become cognizant of in order to be able to resist it. Slave morality's meaning and value inversions are designed to 'obstruct the physicians' (UM: III, *SE*, §4) by forming a closed circle without an exit point, which makes it *impossible* to retrace and restore the original meanings by simply reversing *slave morality's* propositions—they would invariably translate into 'non-sense'. Yet, paradoxical though it may sound, curing economy with inequality is precisely what Nietzsche argues is necessary in order to restore life's vitality and to build genuine communities.

Nietzsche does not advocate the moneyless economy (BVN-1888:1070). However, he envisages such economic structures where money is not allowed to usurp social relations and to become their source and the key determining factor (HH: I, *HMS*, §92). He argues that the workings of the money-economy, enabled by exchange, sway the focus away from the satisfaction of needs in the direction of the wasteful satisfaction of desires.[362] In this process, exchange becomes contaminated by the valuations of *slave*

---

362 Weber would later elaborate on this point by arguing that the inexorable *instrumentalization of reason* which accompanies the evolution of the spirit of 'economic acquisition' eventually leads to

morality and loses sight of its 'original purpose' and the authentic function of promoting *'enlightened self-preservation'* (HH: I, *HMS*, §92; my emphasis).[363] Informing Nietzsche's views on the non-monetary aspects of exchange is the notion of 'little economic communalities' (D: §132), the members of which can 'live and act as a collective individual' (HH: I, *HMS*, §92). This line of thought exhibits conceptual affinity with the community of the Essenes and the Greek *oikos*. Here the transactional commodity exchange, which ends up becoming an unbridled chase after profit when fuelled by money, also encompasses the moderating influence of 'gift-giving', i.e., non-selfish (possibly non-monetary) economic practices which, in turn, arise from the considerations of communitarianism expressed by the long-term investment horizons required for building a stronger and sustainable future.

Nietzsche suggests that life's primordial conflict and the basic inequality resulting from it becomes distorted (perverted even) when it is re-domiciled into the realm of economy and becomes expressed through the economic categories, which are wholly inadequate to reflect the fulness of the economy of life because they invariably seek to 'obliterate all the sharp edges of life' (D: §174). Reconfigured through the conceptuality of economic abstractions this conflict becomes transformed into the structure of the pointless reactive domination of the material forces over nature and humankind: 'as soon as any kind of merchant sets the price with *reference to the need* of the other, he effectively becomes a brigand and extortioner' (HH: II, *WS*, §25).

As we shall see later, the distortion Nietzsche problematises in the case of 'exchange' is substantively similar to when *pre-moralised* debt is (metaphorically) transported from the realm of life's economy to the realm of theology and morality where it undergoes a profound re-programming at 'the freezing point of the will' (HH: II, *AOM*, §349) and is subsequently reinstated in the domain of political economy, now imbued to the point of non-recognisability with the valuations of *slave morality*. Working in this altered hypostasis, debt—as much as exchange, private property, and money—weaves the thick webs of social relations, which inform Marx's 'inverted world of capital' (Prusik 2022:149). This logic will form the crux of Nietzsche's argument that the money-economy represents the pinnacle of the Procrustean economisation of life and a precarious *dead-end* because *economy is incapable of pointing beyond itself.* It intrinsically lacks not only the means for doing so but also the capacity to generate or to aid in generating such means, only to turn the limited means that it does have into humankind's ends and, possibly, its end.[364]

---

the latter ceasing to be the means 'for the satisfaction of material needs' and becoming, instead, 'the state of mind' itself (Weber 1992:18).
363 'Enlightened self-reservation' is a key leitmotif of Nietzsche's political economy. It denotes the means by which *knowledge* is acquired (and often manufactured) within the constraints of the money-making mentality, which side-steps and suppresses the [possibility of the] development of genuine understanding in order to enhance its power position, which invariably happens to the detriment of life and nature.
364 See AC: §25 and NF:1888:14[158].

The Dark Side of Equality

The key consideration that allows Marx to posit not simply the primacy of the economic over the superstructural but also to postulate the necessity of the *abolition of private property* by means of proletarian revolution is the underlying notion of *equality*.[365] Exploring the intricacies of the 'twofold social character of labour', Marx asserts that the 'equality of every kind of labour' that becomes attributed to commodities in an exchange is only possible, in the first instance, by 'virtue of its being *human labour*, which character, therefore, assumes in the product the form of *value*' (CW 35:85; my emphasis). Nietzsche would argue that in making this connection to the underlying plateau of human equality, Marx inadvertently re-domiciles the fundamental proposition of Christianity, its theological nexus—the 'lie of the equality of souls'—into his political economy and revolutionary theory:[366]

> [I]f faith in the 'prerogative of the majority' makes and will make revolutions—it is Christianity beyond a doubt, it is *Christian value judgments*, that every revolution simply translates into *blood and crime*. The 'equality of souls before God' this falsehood, this pretext for the rancor of all the base-minded, this explosive of a concept which eventually became revolution, modern idea, and the principle of decline of the whole order of society is *Christian dynamite*. (AC: §43; my emphasis)

Nietzsche argues that it is secondary under which guise the 'prerogative of the majority' enters the conversation, i.e., whether it is ascertained *vis-à-vis* the God of Christianity (BGE: §219), asserted *vis-à-vis* the 'community of property' (CW 29:21) or whether, as Eagleton surmises, equality should come to denote 'attending equally to everyone's different needs' (Eagleton 2011:104).[367]

Nietzsche problematises *any* such 'earthly solutions' on the grounds that these simultaneously encompass 'faith in the eventual triumph of truth, love, justice, i.e., socialism: "*equality of persons*"' (NF-1887:11[148/4a]).[368] This notion of equality, Nietzsche argues, does not derive from either nature or physiology (BGE: §22) but from [slave] morality (NF-1888:15[41]), which informs religion (NF-1888:15[30]) before becoming the mantra of modern democratic politics:

---

[365] Cf. Eagleton 2011:238–239 and Wood 2014:252–274.
[366] Nietzsche insists that 'the entire socialist ideal' is 'nothing but a clumsy misunderstanding of that Christian moral ideal' (NF-1887:10[170]). See also Nietzsche's discussion in NF-1887:11[148/4a-d].
[367] See Engels, 'Draft of a Communist Confession of Faith' (1847), CM:60–65. For Nietzsche's position, see HH: II, *AOM*, §304.
[368] See also Nietzsche's discussion in NF-1876:23[25]: 'Socialism is accused of overlooking the actual inequality of human beings; but that is not a reproach, but a characteristic, for socialism decides to overlook this inequality and to treat people as equal, that is, to allow the relationship of justice to occur between all, which is based on the assumption that all are equally powerful, equally valuable; just as Christianity treated men as equal in regard to sinful depravity and the need for salvation'.

> Another Christian concept, no less crazy, has passed even more deeply into the tissue of modernity: the concept of the 'equality of souls before God'. This concept furnishes the *prototype of all theories of equal rights:* mankind was first taught to stammer the proposition of equality in a religious context, and only later was it made into morality: no wonder that man ended by taking it seriously, taking it practically!—that is to say, politically, democratically, socialistically, in the spirit of the pessimism of indignation. (NF-1888:15[30]; my emphasis)

Although the miraculous transition of 'equality' from the lofty heights of theological speculation to the earthly domain of political economy conjures up the benign outward appearance of delaying 'the arrival of the "kingdom of God" into the future, on earth, in human form', substantively it signifies that 'fundamentally one has held fast to the belief in the old ideal' (NF-1887:11[226]). Under the auspices of industrial culture, the explicit belief in God may have vanished (NF-1886:7[6]), but the narrative of equality does not diminish, let alone disappear (NF-1886:7[6]). The conduit for this 'dream of conditions in which this perfect man will be in the vast majority' (NF-1887:11[226/3]) changes so as to appropriately encapsulate the 'turmoil of secularisation'—the 'instinct of the herd' does not simply acquire a voice but gains sovereignty, i.e., it becomes the chief purveyor of the narrative of equality (NF-1886:7[6]; NF-1888:14[40]). Marx too openly acknowledges the religious underpinnings of 'political democracy', which continues the enslavement of individual rather than her emancipation:

> Political democracy is Christian since in it man, not merely one man but every man, ranks as sovereign, as the highest being, but it is man in his *uncivilised, unsocial form, man in his fortuitous existence, man just as he is, man as he has been corrupted by the whole organisation of our society, who has lost himself, been alienated, and handed over to the rule of inhuman conditions and elements—in short, man who is not yet a real species-being.* That which is a creation of fantasy, a dream, a postulate of Christianity, i.e., the sovereignty of man—but man as an alien being different from the real man—becomes in democracy tangible reality, present existence, and secular principle. (CW 3:159)

Marx thinks that in order remove inequality from the system completely, cure politics, overcome religion and reclaim the estranged human essence, it is necessary to inject, by means of a worldwide proletarian revolution, equality into the economy by abolishing private property. This will not only expose the hypocrisy of the bourgeois politics but will make it impossible, thereby bringing many centuries of class struggle to the end.[369]

Nietzsche sees this dynamic unfolding in a different way. The transition from the theological to the secular represents the continuation of 'the weakening of man' (NF-1884:26[99]). The secular phase of this process is bound to be marked by the gradual weaponisation of the concept of 'equality' because democracy can no longer appeal to Providence. This circumstance makes democracy 'more natural and less mendacious' but at the same time more vulnerable and volatile because it is still charged with protecting the unchanged set of valuations only with less armour and weaponry

---

[369] See the excellent discussion of this in Nitzan and Bichler 2009:27–33.

at its disposal (NF-1887:10[77]). This combination, in Nietzsche's assessment, represents one of the most calamitous developments of modernity in the wake of the 'death of God'. Democracy does not provide the means to unlocking, let alone realising, the 'sovereignty of man'. Quite to the contrary, Nietzsche argues, democratisation is more akin to the proverbial opening of the floodgates which, by unleashing 'the herd instinct', shatters the bond of religion that hitherto kept 'the hostile forces in check' and transforms 'equality' into the 'Christian dynamite' (AC: §43). Since Marx does not explicitly consider the role of values, he overlooks a critical, on Nietzsche's view, circumstance, namely that 'the *will to equality*' is none other than a form of 'the *will to power*—the belief that something is thus and thus—the essence of judgment—is the consequence of a will that as much as possible shall be equal' (NF-1885:2[90]; my emphasis).[370]

Lenin on Class Consciousness

Marx sees the proletariat as 'a class [...] from which *emanates the consciousness* of the necessity of a fundamental revolution, the communist consciousness' (CW 5:52). Nietzsche would question the means by which 'the alteration of men on a mass scale', required to launch the revolution, and which can only actualise itself in 'a practical movement, a revolution' (CW 5:52–53) would be achieved and, more importantly, by whom.[371]

To better understand the consequences of Marx's oversight with regards to the import of the valuations of *slave morality* into his revolutionary theory, it is helpful to refer to Lenin's rather Nietzschean insight into the psychology of the proletariat.[372] In one of his important early works, entitled 'What Is To Be Done?' (1902), he argues that 'the spontaneous development of the working class movement' can achieve no more than a 'trade-unionist consciousness' (LCW 5:384). This falls short of the revolutionary 'socialist consciousness' and represents a yet another form of 'the ideological enslavement of the workers by the bourgeoisie' (LCW 5:384). The problem Lenin identifies is that the 'economic struggle of the workers is very often connected with the bourgeois politics' (LCW 5:387).[373] In other words, the working masses are *incapable* of working out the politics appropriate to their aims:

---

370 See also Nietzsche's discussion of socialism as a 'question of power not justice', and a 'great lever in the play of political forces' in HH: I, *State*, §446 and §473.
371 I am not engaging here with the intricacies and controversies of Lukacs' account in *History and Class Consciousness* (1923) concerning how 'false consciousness' grows in place of the revolutionary class consciousness.
372 See Debord's illuminating commentary, 2005: §§98–105.
373 The Frankfurt School, Adorno in particular, elaborate on the point that the economic and ideological enslavement of the masses under capitalism does not enable them to mature politically.

> Class political consciousness can be brought to the workers only from without, that is, only *from outside the economic struggle*, from outside the sphere of relations between workers and employers. (LCW 5:422)

In order for the proletariat to take its historic struggle to the decisive heights theorised by Marx, it would require having its class conscience 'awakened' by the small party of dedicated professional revolutionaries who 'subordinate the economic struggle' for reforms to the 'revolutionary struggle for freedom and socialism' (LCW 5:406) or, as Nietzsche would have it, the 'ideologues of revolution' (BGE: §202). By fulfilling the role of 'propagandists' and 'political agitators' (LCW 5:410)—who must 'saturate the proletariat with the consciousness of its position and the consciousness of its task' (LCW 5:384)—the revolutionary party would aid in the comprehensive development of proletariat's political consciousness, making it more organised and less spontaneous, i.e., ready to embrace the battles ahead (LCW 5:418–422).

Lenin's analysis bears an uncanny resemblance to Nietzsche's discussion, in the *Genealogy*, on the beginnings of the slave revolt in morality, which equally required an impetus, provided in that case by the ascetic priest—representative of a small and well-organised minority of strategic thinkers—who crops up 'regularly and universally, in almost every age' but does not 'belong to any one race' and can 'emerge from every class of society' (GM: III, 11). The ascetic priest, an 'expert in self-discipline' and adept at interpreting suffering of all kinds (GM: III, 7, 15), makes himself indispensable by engineering 'such state of affairs' (A: §26) in which he 'compels acceptance of his evaluation of existence' (GM: III, 11). As a shepherd entrusted by the multitude with 'value-conferring power' (A: §26), he works tirelessly to prevent 'anarchy and the ever-present threat of the inner disintegration of the herd' (GM III, 15) by providing the direction and the outlet for their ressentiment and distress (GM: III, 15). Akin to Lenin's professional revolutionisers, the ascetic priest is the master 'direction-changer', who achieves his feat by infusing the consciousness of the masses with a critical element they are incapable of generating from within themselves. By doing so, the multitude becomes beholden to the ascetic priest, so that even when the time comes to 'detonate this explosive material' this is done 'without blowing up either the herd or the shepherd' (GM: III, 15):

> [The] ascetic priest has indeed pressed into his service indiscriminately the whole *pack of savage hounds in man* and let loose now this one and now that, always with the same end in view: to *awaken* men from their slow *melancholy*, to hunt away, if only for a time, their dull pain and lingering misery (GM: III, 20; my emphasis)

Incidentally, Nietzsche argues that moving the notion of equality from the metaphysical domain to the heart of political economy and revolutionary theory would have the inevitable effect of making socialism, should it ever take shape of a social order of modernity, forbiddingly expensive and, in consequence, excessively tyrannical and short-lived (HH: I, *State*, §473).[374] Even though Nietzsche considers experiments in socialism to be unavoidable and, to some extent, desirable (see NF-1881:11[222]; NF-1885:35[9]; NF-1885:37[11]), he urges to 'never make equal what is unequal' and to beware of the 'poisonous poison' of 'the doctrine of equality' that is doomed to 'remain surrounded by such *gruesome and bloody* events, which infuse it with 'a kind of glory and fiery aura' capable of invoking the idea of the Revolution' as the only suitable means to emancipation and equality (TI: *Skirmishes*, §48; my emphasis).[375]

Silenus of Modernity: Weber's 'Terrible Wisdom'

To return briefly to Weber, with whom we started this chapter, one critical issue stands out from his extensive transdisciplinary endeavour pursued in the fields of interpretive sociology (Solms-Laubach 2012), political theory (Anter 2014; Shaw 2014; and Cherniss 2021), political economy (Binns 1977 and Adair-Toteff 2021), jurisprudence (Feldman 1991 and Deflem 2008) and cultural criticism (Stauth 1992). It is Weber's inability to find an exit from capitalism's self-consuming predicament. In an effort to establish the genesis of capitalism, he goes to considerable lengths and ponders the conceptual depths of its heterogeneous theoretical groundwork. Weber carefully differentiates capitalism away from greed, arguing that the 'unlimited greed for gain is *not in the least identical* with capitalism, and is still less its spirit' (Weber 1992: xxxi). Capitalism does not create greed any more than greed creates capitalism. Both can be seen re-appearing throughout history in different forms.[376] Not unlike Nietzsche, Weber approaches greed as a particular *disposition* and a kind of *energy* that finds in capitalism favourable conditions for self-propagation and, therefore, fosters the development of capitalism by installing itself as one of capitalism's cardinal values (Weber 1978:1295):

> *Capitalism* living from loan usury, or from the state, its credit and supply needs, and from colonial exploitation, *is nothing specifically modern* ... the *mentality* of the unscrupulous big financier and speculator can he found at the time of the prophets no less than during Antiquity and the Middle Ages. (Weber 1978:1203).

To some extent, Weber's unfinished magnum opus, *Economy and Society*, which he began in 1914, lends itself to being read as a meticulous elaboration of Nietzsche's

---

[374] Nietzsche supports this inference by highlighting the following three contributing factors, each pertinent to the present inquiry: (1) 'abundance of state power'; (2) 'annihilation of the individual'; (3) turning nature into a 'useful organ of the community' (HH: I, *State*, §473).
[375] In this context, the liberal-democratic version of equality which both Marx and Nietzsche consider purely notional and hollow, represents a less virulent form of the 'doctrine of equality'—just strong enough to deceive people into thinking they might be equal, it is far less likely to result in bloodshed. The socialist doctrine of equality, which links politics and the economy (i.e., property) is, by comparison, a more potent threat to the capitalist social order.
[376] See John Love's erudite discussion of Weber and 'ancient capitalism' (1986a:152–172).

On the Genealogy of Morality (1887), enabled also by the skilful application of Marx's historical method and the clarification of economic terminology. In a consistent and systematic manner, Weber traces the transformation of some ancient, if not pre-historic, economic categories, such as debt, money, and exchange, into the legal norms, regulatory practices, socio-political institutions, and moral values of the modern money-economy and capitalistic society at large. Building on Nietzsche's intimation that the Germans are 'the bearers of the Protestant spirit' (NF-1880:3[137]), Weber develops a theory of capitalism as an economic system that represents the direct 'product of the Reformation' (Weber 1992:49). He recognises the importance of the *cultural critique of economy* and religion in order to elucidate capitalism's workings in a holistic manner.[377] In particular, Weber seeks to develop an 'understanding of the manner in which *ideas* become effective forces in history' (Weber 1992:48), which leads him in the direction of sociology as the analytic method capable of problematising 'the cultural significance of money-economy' (Weber 1994:124) as, at the same time, necessary for the 'emergence of capitalism' and 'a presupposition of modern bureaucracy'.[378] He sums up his approach as 'the scientific investigation of the general cultural meaning of the socio-economic structure of human communal life'.[379]

In particular, Weber focuses on the *closed* socio-economic architecture of capitalism characterised by the pervasive spread of 'instrumental rationality', which becomes regarded 'as the necessary condition for economic and political progress, whatever the human cost' (Clarke 1991:313). His analysis points to an increasingly fragmented society and fractured sociability overwhelmed by 'bureaucratic domination' (Royce 2015:276–278). Weber comes to regard the 'tremendous cosmos of the modern economic order', brought into life by ascetic morality, as a merciless machine, which dominates absolutely and determines 'the lives of *all the individuals* who are born into this mechanism, not only those directly concerned with economic acquisition, with irresistible force' (Weber 1992:123). Almost directly paraphrasing Nietzsche's passage from *Human, All Too Human* (HH: II, *MAH*, §585), Weber predicts that capitalism will continue to do so 'until the last ton of fossilized coal is burnt' (Weber 1992:123).

The tendencies that Weber identifies—whether it be the unremitting *drive for rationalisation* that beckons into existence the leviathan of bureaucratisation, the inexorable *instrumentalisation of reason* that accompanies the evolution of the spirit of 'economic acquisition' which, through a long period of indoctrination, becomes 'the state of mind' (Weber 1992:18), or the gradual *transformation of work* from the spiritual vocation into the 'vocation of making money in order to facilitate the development of business to the point of extending its imperatives to every dimension of existence: to the

---

[377] See, in particular, Weber's exemplary discussion of 'The Economy and the Arena of Normative and De Facto Powers' in *Society and Economy* with an emphasis on the evolution of the ethos of the 'disprivileged strata' of society (1978: Vol. I, Part II, 311–635) and on 'The Social Psychology of the World Religions' and 'The Protestant Sects and the Spirit of Capitalism' (1946: Part III: Religion, 267–323).
[378] Weber 1946:66 and 204 as well as 1978:963–964.
[379] David Frisby, 'Introduction' to *The Positivist Dispute in German Sociology*, 1976: xxiii.

point of annulling this existence itself' (Stiegler 2011:65–66)—do not allow him to move past the gateposts of modern nihilism problematised by Nietzsche as the crowning achievement of *slave morality*. For all the clarity and definition Weber introduces into his comprehensive sociological survey of capitalism, his emphasis on *value neutrality* (Weber 1946:243–250, 267) leaves him trapped in it. Unable to resolve the dichotomy that simultaneously promotes 'the rational, specialised division of labour and fragmentation of the soul', Weber cannot steer clear of envisaging the social process that promises much freedom and yet, inexorably, delivers greater enslavement (Löwith 1993:123).

The felicitous point at which the division of labour might induce spiritual rebirth eludes Weber. Although he may concur with Nietzsche's intuition that neither capitalism nor any of its discourses, including political economy, are capable of incorporating the 'judgements of the highest spiritual and cultural values' (Weber 1992:124), Weber stops short of joining Nietzsche's call for the *revaluation of all values*. At the same time, having exposed the unsavoury anatomy of the 'spirit of capitalism', Weber is unwilling to endorse Marx's suggestion concerning its violent uprooting.[380] This leaves him lamenting the 'progress' of secularisation as a universalising dynamic by means of which, as though decreed by fate, 'the cloak of rationality becomes humankind's iron cage (Weber 1992:123). Inside it spirituality is eroded and replaced with 'pure utilitarianism' heralding the era of the 'specialists without spirit, sensualists without heart'—i.e., Nietzsche's spectral 'last men'. All that remains is the 'nullity' that imagines itself to have 'attained a level of civilization never before achieved' (Weber 1992:124–125).[381]

Weber's placid apprehension concerning the practical impossibility of a 'positive project' for the humankind caught in the clutches of instrumental reason made manifest in modernity's unfolding leaves the argument between Nietzsche's revaluation and Marx's revolution unresolved. The further Weber moves away from necessity to contingency and discards the future-orientated teleology, the more he is faced with the prospect of humankind's negative progress and no means to forestall it. The ultimate challenge Weber's own analysis poses, having effectively become 'the "missing link" between Marx and Nietzsche' (Emden 2008a:609), is whether we are destined to continue to use Nietzsche and Marx as a pair of ontological crutches as we limp towards the future of the obsequious 'last man' and risk to 'perish miserably' in capitalism's quicksand (Wood 2014:271) or whether we, at some point, will be able to harness the Promethean strength required to turn their theories into 'a material force' (CW 3:182) to be wielded as the proverbial Nietzschean hammer. It is, therefore, not entirely surprising that in times of crises and social strife Marx and Nietzsche come to designate the extreme points on the spectrum of the possible, if not the achievable. Not en-

---

[380] Weber draws strong parallel between 'transvaluation' and 'revolution' (Weber 1946:250). See Löwith's masterful analysis of the differences and similarities between Marx and Weber (Löwith 1993:42–51).
[381] Weber's conclusions echo Nietzsche's discussion of the 'poor wretches' in UM: III, *SE*, §4. See also Shaw 2014:345–350; Clarke 1991:313; and Mommsen 1977:374–375.

tirely unlike the mythical Scylla and Charybdis they stand guard either side of the narrow water in the strait of Messina, waiting for someone brave enough to dare to navigate the treacherous passage.

Concluding Remarks

Nietzsche argues that *slave morality*, having claimed undivided ownership of the notion of equality—a distant echo of our indiscernible origins—exploits its unusual hold over the human psyche. This involves manipulating individuals and societies into believing that formalistic *equality* represents the answer to society's gravest ills while systematically undermining the underlying quality of life at the behest of reactive power interests. The drive for 'human equality' does not make individuals more equal. The systematic dismantling of the autonomous subject exhibits 'the tendency to make men more and more *alike*' which, on Nietzsche's view, is equivalent to making them worth less, more susceptible to tyranny and more unequal to the task of building a worthwhile future or a strong community (NF-1887:9[173]).[382] Perhaps one of the most disquieting inferences that Nietzsche's *critique of equality* prompts is that, in the end, equality [of souls] before God *achievable in this world* is destined to become synonymous with *numeric equality*, which would irreversibly drive the unquantifiable 'soul' from the equation. Numeric equality, as the *only possible 'unprejudiced' form of equality*—of digits, as digits and between digits—is precisely that, into which modern society, hurriedly digitizing all areas of human endeavour, is transforming its individual members by obliterating the remaining traces of individuality while eulogizing the ever new horizons of 'freedom' and 'human happiness' (NF-1887:10[17]; NF-1887:11[111]).

Marx, like other great humanist thinkers to come before and after him, finds the notion of equality *irresistible*, to the point of allowing it to permeate his theories. Nietzsche would conclude that the apparent short-comings of Marx's revolutionary theory and the incompleteness of his political economy stem from the fact that neither makes *slave morality* its target: neither formulates values that would overcome it. If they did, it would be discovered that property, private or otherwise, was not the source from which social relations and societal architecture ensued. Nietzsche would contend that inequality is ineradicable and even if we were all equal in property, within such artificially created equality we would still strive for some form of 'accommodation' (NF-1878:30[162]). Our task, properly understood, is not to try to overcome inequality in all of its manifestations but to learn from it. We need to learn to discern the inequality which is conducive to the heightening of humankind from the inequality which under the slogans of equality promotes the erasure of life's quality so that it could ex-

---

[382] Losing sight of the subject, whom Marx wishes to see emancipated and made sovereign, inadvertently leaves his argumentation susceptible to the Althusserian criticism of the 'process without subject' (Althusser 1971:120–121). Cf. Tabak 2012:1–26.

tend its reactive power over humankind. To recognise different types of inequality, it is important, on Nietzsche's view, to inquire into the genealogy of values that underpin them.

For this reason, where Marx insists that the unequivocal abolition of private property is the essential condition for the emancipation of the individual, Nietzsche would argue that 'one must destroy morality if one is to liberate life' (NF-1886:7[6]; see NF-1884:25[211]). Nietzsche's revolution, if we were able to conceive of his undertaking in such terms, would represent the opposite of Marx's idea. It would resemble 'a declaration of war on the masses by higher men' (NF-1884:25[174], [243]) as the only course of action that could ultimately benefit these masses and humankind in general by engendering difference, the principle of agon, and structures of subordination rather than sacrificing life's quality on the Procrustean bed of [artificial] equality.[383]

Marx may, indeed, succeed in defeating *capitalism* on the conceptual battlefield. His political economy, however, would inevitably fall prey to *slave morality* and therefore fail to overcome it decisively. Capitalism—just like any other social order of modernity (on Nietzsche's view)—is the embodiment of slave morality except that slave morality is bigger, more powerful, and more robust than capitalism. Valuations of slave morality are neither broken nor overcome by means of a revolution that abolishes private property. They are adept at surviving all revolutionary upheavals and finding new ways to incorporate themselves into the changed socio-economic arrangement. The conceptual keyhole through which these valuations transition from the reality of capitalism, chastised by Marx, into his vision of communism is invariably provided by the notion of equality. In Marx's case, equality attaches itself to the perceived necessity of changing the property ownership. In the end, Marx, who insists that it would not be possible to '*arrive at communism or socialism by way of metaphysics or politics*' (CW 5:468; my emphasis), does not appear to have found another way. The Essenes' conundrum still stands before Marx as an unyielding Sphinx. Nietzsche would insist that in order to slay the proverbial dragon, it would be necessary to dismantle the still metaphysical notion of equality rather than trying to abolish private property.

For Nietzsche, *slave morality* is the single most powerful force that moulds and directs modern political economy. In contrast to Marx, Nietzsche sets out to demonstrate that the capitalist social order is, at the very least, as much inwardly (or substantively) sustained by *slave morality* as it is outwardly (or epiphenomenally) dependent on private property, capital, and commodity exchange. Nietzsche would argue that, since the advent of Christianity, the valuations of slave morality have *actively informed the economic bases* of the successive modes of production, rather than passively flowing from them. These valuations act as clay for the social relations that make private property into the bedrock of the capitalist social order, not the other way around.

---

[383] See Nietzsche's discussion in NF-1872:19[41]; Z: I, *Virtue*, §2; NF-1885:1[122]; and NF-1885:37[11].

Nietzsche's *critical point*, however, is this: the valuations of *slave morality* not only enable Marx (and others) to see private property as he does—as the Achilles' heel of capitalism, abolishing which would cause the entire edifice of capitalism to unravel thus enabling its positive transcendence. Nietzsche argues that these valuations also anticipate and invite such critical perceptions of themselves. The real danger Nietzsche sees is that *slave morality* helps to inform the most radical repudiations of its own chimerical manifestations by creating false trails. Private property, in and of itself, is not the eye of the monster as it appears to Marx. It is, on Nietzsche's view, a false clue and a deliberate distraction (HH: I, *State*, §452). However, when property, irrespective of whether its basis is private or communal, becomes infused with the valuations of slave morality, it may well spell the end of humankind should these valuations be allowed to draw the full strength of their life-consuming logic. Akin to the shapeshifting Empusa, *slave morality* propagates by repeatedly conjuring up such images of itself that would become targets of indignation and critique.[384] While this may give 'the boldest of utopians' (HH: I, *HMS*, §48) something to fight against, Nietzsche's fear is that they will be invariably chasing the shadows of *slave morality* and battling spurious adversaries long after the real enemy has 'left the building' and may well have switched sides. Slave morality is entirely unscrupulous when it comes to who (or what) it chooses to weaponize—Jews, debt, private property, equality or crises—only to throw its discarded 'means' under the proverbial bus of history when it serves the purpose of preserving and extending its reactive power over humankind (HH: I, *State*, §472; D: §204).

For these reasons, Nietzsche would find Marx's intellectual assault on capitalism misdirected. He would, instead, urge to 'bring this *whole economy* (which begins in Europe with Christianity)' of slave morality 'to light and to court' (NF-1884:25[174]). This would be necessary if achieving genuine emancipation of the individual and promoting humankind's advancement were authentic goals, neither of which would be obtainable solely by revolutionary means of the kind Marx envisioned. The revolution of the upside-down world—tasked with placing it back into the upright position—is not sufficient if the pervasive cloak of value inversions continues to firmly cover it, still distorting reality. Revolution, no matter how radical, is no guarantee that the logic of the system which is brought down will be overhauled. The latter, Nietzsche tells us, is a discrete undertaking. In order to understand what it would take, it is important to inquire into the valuations that underpin the system marked for deposition. Revaluation of values—of the broken-down economic categories and of the social relations temporarily vacated by the revolution—would be necessary in order to create the possibility of genuinely altering humankind's developmental trajectory.[385]

---

384 This is the meaning Nietzsche conveys in his discussion of the *ressentiment* (= *slave morality*) 'becoming creative', of the lengths it goes to and the metamorphoses undergoes in order to create 'evil' from the 'not-evil' (GM: I, §10). Marx comes close expressing the same when he describes capital as 'dead labour, that, *vampire-like*, only lives by sucking living labour, and lives the more, the more labour it sucks' (CW 35:241).

385 See Nietzsche's discussion in D: §453 and HH: I, *HMS*, §107; see also HH: I, *State*, §466.

Nietzsche's project entails supplanting the layer of instrumental rationality with which slave morality keeps weaving its impermeable webs of anti-life valuations and building the iron cages from which human consciousness is unable to escape. This is why, as shall be discussed in subsequent chapters, Nietzsche insists upon the fusion of the mythical with the scientific, on the cross-pollination of the economic and the aesthetic in order to fundamentally alter the manner in which humankind acquires knowledge as understanding rather than creating ever more sophisticated conceptual devices with which to dig its own premature grave (see HH: II, WS, §189). The rather different contours of Nietzsche's project of human emancipation start to become discernible. Whether Nietzsche's undertaking succeeds in taking him further than Marx in resolving the Essenes' conundrum remains the subject of the present inquiry.

5 Nietzsche on Slavery: Overcome or Simply Abolished?

> Whatever forms of state and society may arise,
> all will forever be only forms of slavery. (Nietzsche,
> NF-1881:16[23])

Introduction

Nietzsche's analysis of slavery, although increasingly explored within Nietzsche scholarship, remains virtually untapped within the context of the broader and growing debate on the issue, both as a legacy of the past and as the present-day reality.[387] This chapter explores his controversial views on the subject, understood both historically and in the context of modern society. Nietzsche's discussion of slavery adds a pertinent, if challenging, dimension to examining such central concerns of political economy as the nature and role of leadership, subordination, hierarchy and the questions of development and inequality.[388] The key focus of Nietzsche's inquiry is on slavery as an enduring facet of human existence. His genealogical inquiry leads him to explore the psychological aspects of slavery and to conceptualise it in terms of human vulnerability, which increases susceptibility to exploitation. Nietzsche contends that as a barometer of modern society's *physiological well-being*, as well as a repository of its externalities, slavery is an integral element of modern industrial culture.

Nietzsche's more audacious claims—pronouncing exploitation 'a basic organic function of life' (BGE: §259) and slavery as belonging to the 'essence of culture' (GSt, §6, 178) and necessary 'for the formation of a higher organism' (see NF-1881:11[134]; NF-1887:10[111]), in the service of which 'the vast majority of ordinary human beings' must toil (BGE: §61)—are well known and, in some cases, regarded as sufficient reasons to discourage further inquiry into his thoughts on the subject.[389]

In a *Nachlass* note from 1885, Nietzsche explicitly links the subject of political economy ('*Volkswirthschaft*') with the question of slavery (NF-1885:2[131], §7). Huddleston notes that slavery remains a constant aspect of 'Nietzsche's thinking from his early essays (*The Greek State*) to his final works of 1888' (Huddleston 2014:146). It is as difficult

---

[387] For the probing and insightful examination of Nietzsche's views on slavery, see Ruehl (2003, 2004, and 2018), Huddleston (2012 and 2014), Church (2015), and Drochon (2016).
[388] Nietzsche's views on the 'division of labour and slavery' (NF-1885:2[76]) are often treated as inseparable.
[389] See Ruehl 2003 ('Politeia 1871'); Sedgwick 2007:150–155; Landa 2007:27; Drochon 2016:52–55 and 93–98; Ansell-Pearson 1994:40–45 and 66–73; and Holub 2018:145–147 for further context regarding the discussion of Nietzsche's justification of for exploitation and slavery.

to separate Nietzsche's discussion of slavery from his critique of slave morality as it is to disconnect the latter from his analysis of modern industrial culture. Nietzsche asserts that 'in some form and under some name' exploitation will always exist (NF-1885:2[13]). Whether this exploitation is called slavery, wage labour, or comes under the guise of a respectable professional occupation such as those of a 'statesman, businessman, official, or a scholar' is secondary (HH: I, *Tokens*, §283). Reflecting on the issue within the context of modernity, Nietzsche contends that capitalism's relationship with slavery does not come to an end with the abolition of slavery and that modern society, under the auspices of industrial culture, engages in the 'sublime development of slavery' (NF-1885:2[179]).[390] Meanwhile, slavery, its formal abolition notwithstanding, continues to weigh heavily on modern consciousness as an unpaid and possibly unrepayable debt. By engaging with the subject of slavery, Nietzsche develops a wide-ranging discussion about the 'conditions of existence'—how we organise our lives and the ways in which we provide for our basic as well as more complex needs, including the issues of psychological well-being and mental health, as well as the question of spiritual versus material welfare.

Semiotic Roots of Slavery

Nietzsche's discussion of the semiotic roots of slavery enables him to draw a critical distinction between exploitation, as a more fundamental aspect of existence, and slavery as more epiphenomenal. On Nietzsche's view, 'life itself is, at its mildest, exploitation' (BGE: §259). The primary aspect of exploitation, which Nietzsche gleans from Ancient philosophers, is not the unfair appropriation of the results of another's labour and even less so an outright ownership of one human being by another.[391] Rather, Nietzsche thinks of it is a modality of interaction between the qualitatively different and hierarchically ordered parts of society, which allows not only for its preservation but also entails the potential for individual as well as collective enhancement (GM: II, §17). In *The Antichrist*, Nietzsche speaks of 'slavery in a higher sense', as the sole and ultimate condition under which 'the more weak-willed human being can prosper' (AC: §54).

---

390 See NF-1885:2[13] and [179].
391 Nietzsche's understanding of exploitation is informed by the thinkers of antiquity, including Xenophon, Plato, Aristotle, and Cicero, who did not regard exploitation as objectionable. Cicero in particular, whose work including the political dimensions of 'the Roman concept of culture' Nietzsche knew in detail and lectured on (BVN-1874:345/CvG), had distinguished between the exploitation of human and natural resources and linked both to the origins of property and wealth (*De Officiis*, um.44.v.u.Z; last accessed March 4, 2023).

Slavery, to borrow from Galbraith, becomes a 'socially-modifying reference', which grants a degree of 'functional anonymity' to exploitation (Galbraith 2004:15).[392] Nietzsche speaks of the 'metamorphoses of slavery', which at one time 'disguises itself under the cloak of religion' and later 'transfigures itself through slave morality' (WP: §357).[393] At a linguistic level, Nietzsche concedes a fairly straightforward solution to the unsavoury sound of slavery. He is aware that the modern world 'anxiously' avoids 'the word "slave"' (GSt., 164), and suggests that slavery can be discussed 'under a more moderate name' in a manner similar to the times when the word slavery 'in no way seemed repugnant, let alone reprehensible' (NF-1871:10[1]).[394] Nietzsche's own use of *'Sklaverei'* to discuss the slavery of Greek antiquity as well as the New World slavery is both technically Platonic (i.e., the 'one to speak of the many') and poses an etymological challenge to modern sensibility. Nietzsche is well aware that ancient Greek slavery did not exist as a unitary phenomenon (GS: §18). In this respect, use of the term *'Sklaverei'* to discuss the phenomenon of slavery stretching across different times and cultures, as if slavery remained somehow static, can also be exploited. Nietzsche contends that 'not even metaphorically does the word "slave" possess its full power for us' (GS: §18). Slavery needs to be understood as a link in the semiotic process by means of which the phraseology employed to denote exploitation continually interprets away from its substance.

Nietzsche's Definition of Slavery

In *Ancient Greek and Roman Slavery* (2017), Peter Hunt argues that the definition of slavery has historically suffered from the same 'imprecision and complexity' that 'affects many other key concepts and crafts that historians rightly consider crucial to their craft: capitalism, industrialism, the market economy, democracy, imperialism, law and others' (Hunt 2017:20). Nietzsche's own definition of slavery is of that variety and as such, it is an important entry point into the wider discussion of the subject. In *Human, All Too Human*, he provides the following criteria:

> [H]e who does not have two-thirds of his day to himself is a slave, let him be what he may otherwise: statesman, businessman, official, scholar. (HH: I, *Tokens*, §283)[395]

---

392 See Galbraith's discussion in *The Economics of Innocent Fraud* (2004), where he refers to it as a 'socially modifying reference' (Galbraith 2004:15), which grants capitalism 'functional anonymity': 'When capitalism, the historic reference, ceased to be acceptable, the system was renamed. The new term was benign but without meaning. ... The word capitalism is still heard but not often from acute and articulate defenders of the system. ... In the reputable expression of economists, business spokesmen, careful political orators and some journalists, it is now 'the Market System' (Galbraith 2004:5–8).
393 See also NF-1886:7(1).
394 See an engaging discussion of this point in Huddleston, 2014:147 and in Church 2015:253–254.
395 See Paul Franco's engaging discussion in *Tocqueville and Nietzsche*, 2014:460–463.

Nietzsche goes on to suggest that 'true humanity demands that everyone be evaluated only in light of the condition' in which one 'discovers one's higher self' and not in that of 'his working-day unfreedom and servitude' (HH: I, §624). In *The Gay Science* (1882), he adds that 'even the most powerful men on earth' may be slaves if they are 'not at their own disposal' (GS: §18). As such, Nietzsche's definition is only superficially about time. In substance, Nietzsche's position is not that different from Marx's view in terms of considering 'all free time' at the disposal of the individual, including 'leisure and time for higher activity', as time available 'for the full development of individual' that should be invested accordingly (see CW 29:22–24; 97).

Although, as Huddleston notes, Nietzsche construes slavery 'very broadly indeed', his formulation is not intended to be of the 'catch-all' variety (Huddleston 2014:146). Rather, Nietzsche suggests an inverse relationship between value-creation and the modern 'way of always keeping busy' (D: §203), which forms part of his diagnosis of the modern condition. Amplified by the division of labour, modern busyness also represents Nietzsche's concern that not only 'the division between labour and leisure disappeared' but that labour itself becomes increasingly specialised and meaningless (Love 1986:181). It is reflected in the 'conscience of an industrious age' that does not permit us to 'bestow our best hours on art', which counts only as 'a recreational activity' to which we devote the 'remnants of our energy' (HH: II, WS, §170).

Our 'busyness' ('*Geschäftigkeit*'), which Nietzsche identifies with slavery, is symptomatic of a deeper pathology. It is, in a manner of speaking, a 'law of diminishing returns' in that today it takes many more busy individuals, who are busier than ever before as well as from a much younger age than before, to create less and less of that which is valuable. One of the concerns Nietzsche's definition points towards is that this inverse relationship is not indefinite in duration. It would expire having reached a point where individual is fully divorced from and is no longer required for the creation of that which would be deemed valuable. Behind the universal haste of modern life and our urge to 'labour at our daily work more ardently and thoughtlessly than is necessary to sustain life', Nietzsche detects a certain 'feeling of wretchedness' one would experience should one 'stop and think' (UM: III, *SE*, §5). He contends that one prefers to be 'in flight from himself' and to lie about it, so as to project the appearance of contentment and 'an air of noisy festivity' than to confront the source of 'the wretchedness he feels' (UM: III, *SE*, §5).

Nietzsche's scrutiny of 'industriousness' as a psychological predicament is inseparable from his critique of *slave morality* (BGE: §260). His argument problematises industriousness as a form of self-inflicted punishment and reparation for sin, albeit without the redemptive attributes of atonement and penance. Instead, industriousness is an externalisation of the deeply embedded sense of guilt for causing the death of God. Critically, as Löwith notes, 'work has lost its curse ever since the bourgeois-Christian world began to do "work" in order to avoid "desperation" and to speak of the "blessing of work"' (Löwith 1991:288). The murder of God rendered the debt owed to him *unrepayable but not cancelled* and, as a result, it amplified the urge to at least pay the interest on this debt (GM: II, §§21–22). The darker side of industriousness—a 'modern vice' in

Nietzsche's assessment (NF-1887:9[141])—is that it makes individual 'ruthless against himself' and yet it keeps silent about its 'extreme dangerousness' (GS: §21). In this respect, industriousness is intimately related to religion—Christianity in particular—which, although it is 'privately harmful' is nonetheless endorsed as societal norm (GS: §21). Since its objective is to prevent individuals from ever 'thinking otherwise' and considering their 'preservation and development more important' (GS: §21), Nietzsche also argues that the instrumentalising and enslaving propensities of industriousness (HH: II, WS, §288) conceal those who benefit from this organised collective endeavour (NF-1887:9[44]), i.e., 'those who commend work' (D: §173). Paradoxically, industriousness is the price the modern individual pays for his notional freedom. It is, therefore, hardly surprising that we do not customarily associate 'being busy' with being enslaved. Nietzsche tells us that we should and that the reason why we do not has to do with the real hardship which freedom represents. He contends that a telltale of whether one is a slave or free is what one does, when one does not have anything that he 'must' do—something our industriousness helps to conceal. In other words, for the majority, slavery offers a more comfortable and manageable form of existence—particularly if one does not associate oneself with being a slave.

There is, however, a high price to pay for any kind of ignorance that presents itself as bliss. In this respect, the flip side of 'busyness' appears no less problematic and forms an important axis of Nietzsche's inquiry. He warns us that 'the blindly raging industriousness ... keeps silent about its extreme dangerousness' (GS: §21) and posits 'laboriousness' as objectionable (TI: *Errors*, §4). He ponders the reasons for which the slave might be—or should be—kept busy in the first instance, as well as what happens to the slave should he be 'liberated' and cease to be busy. Is there a felicitous exit from the state of the 'universal haste', in which modern society immerses itself (UM: III, SE, §§4–5), for 'the "productive"' but also the deeply deficient man it has created (HH: I, §210)? This line of inquiry entails a prescient warning concerning the longer-term consequences of 'keeping busy' on the individual and collective well-being, understood in terms of spiritual and mental health (NF-1873:32[44]).

Slavery, Oikonomia, and the Oikodespotes

The Ancient Greek discourse on '*οἰκονομία*'[396] is scarcely referenced as a formative influence on Nietzsche's views on political economy in general and on slavery more specifically.[397] Throughout his *oeuvre*, Nietzsche's use of '*Oekonomie*' (NF-1888:14[182]) and *Ökonomie* is distinctly different from the meaning he conveys by using '*Nationalökonomie*' (NF-1869:3[10]), '*Wirtschaft*' (NF-1881:11[249]) and '*Ökonomik*' (TCW: §9; NF-

---
[396] See Leshem 2016:225–231.
[397] In a recent article, Merrick distinguishes the '*oikos*', along with the '*debtor-creditor*' relations, as the formative element of Nietzsche's thinking on economy (Merrick 2020:139).

1888:25[7]). Both *Oekonomie* and *Ökonomie* retain clear connotations of the Greek 'οἰκονομία' as denoting a deeper rooted 'economy in the law of life' (TI: *Morality*, §6), which is concerned with the fundamental aspects of existence. The proper business of *Oekonomie* is to reflect the 'total balance sheet of life' (NF-1875:5[188]), which requires seeing 'past the immediate factual data' (HH: II, *WS*, §287) in order to adequately capture the 'innermost nature' of the great economy of life (NCW, *Epilogue*, §1). Nietzsche's use of *oikonomia* further stresses the interconnectedness of the 'economy of the whole' (EH: *Destiny*, §4) with the 'economy of the earth' (NF-1876:19[79]). Οἰκονομία's most direct meaning pertains to the management of the household (Aristotle, *Politics*, 259a) and Nietzsche too directs his message towards the 'total households of the world' (NF-1885:43[1]) and 'of humankind' (BGE: §23 and §62).[398] Nietzsche's linguistic lament concerning the modern day misuse of *Ökonomie* conveys a clear sense that the composition of *Oikonomia* he envisages is not exclusively material (D: §179).[399]

In order to appreciate the conceptual anchoring of Nietzsche's thinking on slavery, it is important to consider the spirit of the passages from Xenophon's *Oeconomicus*, as one of the earliest treatises on economics, which to this day remains 'one of the richest primary sources for the social, economic and intellectual history of classical Athens' (Pomeroy 1994: viii).[400] In particular, Nietzsche's thinking on social hierarchy, governance and development exhibits a strong affinity with Xenophon's key insights.[401] A central theme of Xenophon's wide-ranging discussion is a sense of the intricate interconnectedness of all parts of the *oikos*, a primary constitutive unit of *oikonomia*.[402] Neither the preservation nor the enhancement of the *oikos* could be sustainably achieved either at the expense of some of its parts, or by employing dishonourable means of securing an advantage by those at the top of the *oikos* pyramid for themselves and to the detriment of their subordinates. *Oikos* is set up in a way that it can only develop and prosper as a whole and while its success remains transparent (Xenophon 1994:141). As Nietzsche puts it in *Human, All Too Human*, the work of ants, cyclops, and geniuses is equally necessary, for without it 'melody could not be melody' (HH: II, *AOM*, §186).

---

398 See Staten's illuminating commentary on Nietzsche's use of this terminology in 1989:68.
399 As Leshem points out, within the context of *Oikonomia*, ethics and economics are inseparable in so far as the main task of economic rationality is to advance the good and wholesome life (Leshem 2016:226). See Mark Golden, 'Slavery and The Greek Family', in *The Cambridge World History of Slavery: The Ancient Mediterranean World*, Vol. I, 2011:135.
400 *Xenophon's Oeconomicus*, translated by Sarah B. Pomeroy and published by Oxford University Press in 1994, is used. Further quotations referencing Pomeroy's analysis are referenced as ('Pomeroy 1994: '...'). Quotations directly from *Oeconomicus* are cited as ('Xenophon 1994: ...').
401 Nietzsche owned a copy of Xenophon's *Oeconomicus*. Aside from his direct reading of Xenophon, including *Oeconomicus*, Nietzsche may have also come across Walter Bagehot's reference to Xenophon's thoughts in *Physics and Politics* (Bagehot 2010:25).
402 See Peter Hunt's discussion in 'Slaves in Greek Literary Culture' (2011:28) and Mark Golden on 'Slavery and the Greek Family, (2011:135) in *The Cambridge World History of Slavery: The Ancient Mediterranean World*, Vol. I, 2011.

Employing the beehive and the queen bee as symbols, Xenophon highlights the pivotal role of leadership in governing the *oikos*. He ponders how one best achieves the objective that the members of the household should follow the 'master of a household' (*'oikodespotes'*)[403] in a manner similar to that in which bees tend to submit to the queen bee (Xenophon 1994:141).[404] What is it about the queen bee that establishes her position, legitimises her leadership and inspires lasting loyalty, when she is not the most useful member of the hive in the strictly productive sense? In dialogue with his wife, *Ischomachus*, a knowledgeable head of a 'flourishing Athenian *oikos*' (Pomeroy 1994:31), identifies the following key functions and characteristics of the *oikodespotes*: these (a) do not allow members of the *oikos* to remain idle; (b) receive what each brings in and distribute a fair share to each; (c) supervise construction and long-range plans; (d) ensure that the young are reared to maturity, to be fit to lead the next generation;[405] (e) nurse 'any of the slaves' who fall ill; (f) consider it an 'honour to be the guardian of the estate for the children; (g) remain humble (Xenophon 1994:145–147). Fulfilment of these duties ensures the preservation and enhancement of the *oikos* in a manner that binds its different parts by empathy rather than coercion or punishment (Xenophon 1994:141–147).[406]

There is an equally clear sense in Xenophon that neither can leadership be achieved, nor a sense of responsibility properly discharged by means other than one's own effort, example and transcendence, as may be required (Xenophon 1994:147). Critically, one does not become a great leader either by violence or by the cynical exploitation of resources at one's disposal to secure one's own benefit. In Nietzsche's words, true leadership cannot be 'improvised' and the 'exceptional human beings', much like the Athenian *oikodespotes*, have to 'constantly legitimise themselves as higher—as born to command' (GS, §40; see also GM: III, §28).[407] The *oikodespotes* achieve this by making their subordinates more valuable by investing in their development. Nietzsche acknowledges this in his discussion of 'Nero's paradox', stating that at the end of the process where the oikodespotes have properly discharged their responsibilities, the slave ends up being worth more than his superior (NF-1884:25[344]).

Other distinctive features of the *oikos* follow from the structure and manner in which *oikodespotes* discharge their duties. No part of the *oikos* is explicitly set up

---

403 Leshem 2013:51.
404 See also Plato's corresponding discussion of this issue in *The Republic*, 253b-254a, for relevant background.
405 Compare this with Nietzsche's comment in *Untimely Meditations*: 'if men are to labour and be useful in the factory of science before they are mature science will soon be ruined just as effectively as the slaves thus employed too early (UM: II, *UDHL*, §7).
406 In *Human, All Too Human* (1878), Nietzsche expresses an almost identical thought concerning 'the enduring advantage of all conditions and classes' and 'the wellbeing of the worker, his contentment of body and soul—so that he and his posterity shall work well for our posterity too and be relied on for a longer span of time than a single human life' (HH: II, *WS*, §286). See Trever's relevant discussion of Xenophon in *A History of Greek Economic Thought*, 1916:71.
407 Nietzsche's views in this regard resonate with Aristotle, see *Politics* 1254[a]21–22.

for the purpose of generating financial gain.[408] One significant implication of the beehive analogy is a natural limit to the growth of the *oikos* and the resulting circular propensities in relation to its management. Although the *oikos* is not intended to be entirely self-sufficient, it is far from being a unit aimed at consumption alone. A considerable proportion of its requirements are sourced and produced from internal means. The surplus generated by the collective effort of the *oikos* is not primarily material or financial. Rather, it is a particular kind of 'luxurious surplus' (NF-1887:10[17]), expressed in terms of time freed up for the pursuit of philosophy, art and politics.[409] Generation of the surplus in the *oikos* is either the result of the abundance of means or, more frequently, of the moderation in the needs and wants of its members precisely to make available space and time for pursuits outside of the economic sphere—i.e., for spiritual development.

This manner of setting priorities deriving from the rational economisation of needs also finds reflection in the form and structure of subordination of the kind found in the *oikos*, which has not yet been embedded as an antagonistic social relation, and therefore has not become a psychological burden (NF-1871:10[1]).[410] The hierarchical structure of the *oikos* does not become an obstacle to apportioning a sense of dignity and value to all of its members (Huddleston 2014:149–150). In other words, the rigid structural antagonism of the *oikos* is tempered by the agonistic dynamic required for its proper functioning so as to enable all 'to live and act as a collective individual' (HH: I, *HMS*, §94) and to provide a proxy for a social context where the 'inequality of rights' may become 'the condition for the existence of any rights at all' (AC: §57).[411] Nietzsche stresses that rights arise only when there is a mutual recognition that 'the other', whatever his respective capacity, is 'valuable, essential, irreplaceable' (HH: I, *HMS*, §93).

In the prevailing ethos of the Ancient Greek *oikos*, which is synthetic rather than atomistic and communitarian rather than individualistic (HH: I, §111), slavery was *not* regarded as a moral question.[412] Wilhelm Roscher—'an important and highly productive political economist', author of the influential *Principles of Political Economy* (1877), whose work Nietzsche read (Brobjer 1999:56)—observed that 'the feeling of *moral deg-*

---

408 See important discussion by John S. McClelland on the meaning of slavery as it appeared in the political thought of Greeks up to and including Aristotle in *A History of Western Political Thought*, 1996: 57–60.
409 See Xenophon: *Oeconomicus*; Leshem, 2016a; and Booth, 1993. Cf. Marx, CW 35:243.
410 McClelland notes that 'it is by no means clear that the ancient Greeks had a 'bad conscience' about slavery' (McClelland 1996:72). Leshem refers to an 'unthinking' and 'uncritical' acceptance of slavery (Leshem 2016:226–228) and Drochon points out that 'a degree of slavery, understood in the Nietzschean sense' was a feature of society based on the distinction of the order of rank (Drochon 2016:95–97).
411 Nietzsche intuits this possibility already in *Human, All Too Human*, published a decade prior to *The Antichrist*, in a notable passage *Of the Rights of the Weaker* (HH: I, *HMS*, §93). Nietzsche's view on the agonistic features of the oikos run contrary to Marx's conception of the antagonistic class struggle.
412 See Williams in *Shame and Necessity*, 1993:125. See also Arendt on the 'pre-political' nature of the oikos in Arendt 1994:265 and 1998:146.

radation which slavery, abstraction even made of its abuses, awakens in us' is entirely unknown in antiquity and, paradoxically, 'it is not to be supposed that slavery, at this stage, is so oppressive even to those who have been deprived of their freedom' (Roscher 1878:212–213). The Athenian slaves were considered an integral part of the *oikos* (Wiedemann 1980:1).[413] Importantly, this meant that the Ancient slave, unlike the modern wage-labourer, was less disposable and that the logic of the *oikos*, enacted through the responsibility of the *oikodespotes*, called for the maintenance of the slave beyond any narrowly defined 'economic utility' (HH: II, *WS:* §286).

Nietzsche's line of argument suggests that slavery, as a form of subordination, could only make *oikonomic*—i.e., not economic—sense. When considered in that light, it ceases to be the kind of slavery which understandably raises the 'red flag' in modern sensibility. A twofold inference from Nietzsche's discussion is that (a) slavery could never make purely economic sense, and (b) slavery starts to become barbaric with the development of commercial society. The latter (i.e., the rise of money and commercial intercourse) is, in turn, intimately and troublingly related to the advances in rationality (e.g., economics) and its associated emancipatory pathos.[414] When slavery becomes reduced to the narrow formula of utility (i.e., cost and profit) and exchange values, it becomes embedded as a reactive power relationship based on the cynical exploitation deriving from the disinvestment of the individual. Nietzsche urges us to think about these factors as some of the reasons why slavery becomes brutal and barbaric, no matter what liberatory terminology veils it. He draws a causal link between Western civilisation's celebration of becoming cleverer and more progressive, on the one hand, and slavery's becoming uglier and more pervasive, on the other.

'Higher Men' and 'Rank-Ordering'

In order to understand Nietzsche's 'slave', it is helpful to try and understand Nietzsche's 'higher man'. The 'higher man' and the 'slave' appear similar in at least two respects. Most importantly, neither is 'defined by origins of any kind' (Klossowski 1997:158). Nietzsche suggests that the 'primal source is the same in all men' (NF-1871:12[1]) and that even 'the highest human being must be conceived as an image of nature' (NF-1884:25[140]). Nietzsche's distinction does not depend on (a) *race* (see NF-

---

[413] In *Greek and Roman Slavery*, Thomas Wiedemann notes that 'slavery was an essential division of the household (*oikos, domus*), and that other bonds of dependence and economic exploitation were comparatively insignificant ... in the classical period' (Wiedemann 1980:1). Bertrand Russell concurs that 'in antiquity the slaves were always part of the family' (Russell 1946:186).

[414] Nietzsche observes that 'it is possible for the sciences to flourish in a barbarised culture' (NF-1872:19[171]).

1885:2[57]),[415] (b) *citizenship, nationality or statehood* (see NF-1885:37[8]), (c) *heredity* (see NF-1887:9[45]) or *'birth-right'*,[416] (d) *social status or class*, (e) *wealth*, (f) *gender*,[417] or (g) *physical strength*.[418] Instead, Nietzsche has in mind a certain *physiological disposition* that is pre-political, in the sense of being rooted in the pre-moralised economy of life (BGE: §231; AC: §57).[419] This temperament is incorporated into the higher man's 'origins' and codified by them but it does not derive from them alone and nor can it be sustained by them entirely (HH: I, *State*, §479).[420] In *The Gay Science*, Nietzsche emphasises that formal distinctions, such as those of class and heredity, do *not* serve as the decisive criteria of differentiation: 'a Greek of noble descent found such tremendous intermediary stages [...] between his own height and ultimate baseness that he could scarcely see the slave clearly' (GS: §18).

The figure of Epictetus, whose work Nietzsche 'read with some care' (Elveton 2004:192) and to whom he owes much in terms of his own thinking on 'slavery and freedom' (Epictetus 1865:255) is pertinent in this context. Epictetus—one of the most important proponents of Stoicism, was 'born into slavery' (Ritter 1846:196). His most penetrating claim, which resonates throughout Nietzsche's corpus and becomes the conceptual *anchor of his political economy*, defines the situatedness of human existence:

> Fortune is an evil chain to the body, and vice to the soul. For he whose body is unbound, and whose soul is chained, is a slave. On the contrary, he whose body is chained, and his soul unbound, is free (Epictetus 1865: *Fragments*, VII, 404)

The real face of slavery, in Nietzsche's reckoning, is spiritual slavery. Nietzsche praises Epictetus as a 'silent, self-sufficient man within a universal enslavement' who is not subjugated by this predicament and is thus able to able to transcend it (D: §546). Nietzsche draws Epictetus and a Christian slave as the polar opposites. The Christian slave represents someone 'weak in will and in mind'—representative of the enslaved majority which has bowed to its enslavement. The means by which personal slavery

---

[415] We should recognise the racial aspect of Nietzsche's polemic as important and meriting a separate examination. However, consideration of race was not the driving or the determining factor of Nietzsche's views on exploitation and slavery (see GS: §377).
[416] Nietzsche's 'noble man' is 'der vornehme Mensch' (BGE: §260), i.e., someone who 'stands in front', rather than 'der Edelmann' (EH: *Wise*, §3), who is simply a 'nobleman' by birth. Also see Nietzsche's discussion in HH: I, §456.
[417] 'The perfect woman is a higher type of human that the perfect man, and also something much rarer (HH: I, §377). 'Nietzsche considers genius to be a feminine genius' (Biddy 1991:98). In a note from the early *Nachlass*, Nietzsche says that 'the woman as mother prevails and determines the degree and the phenomena of culture: in the same way as the woman is destined to supplement the disordered state' (NF-1870: 7[122]). In *The Gay Science*, Nietzsche submits that 'life is a woman' (GS: §339).
[418] See BGE: §257.
[419] Once again, Nietzsche develops his position from a deeply Aristotelian premise, see Politics 1255[a] 21–[b]9 and 1254[b]16. See also Lemm's insightful discussion, 2013:182.
[420] See the excellent discussion by William Salter, 1917:405–406.

becomes fused with and made indistinguishable from 'universal enslavement', first under the auspices of Christianity and subsequently under capitalism, becomes a critical thread of Nietzsche's inquiry into the genealogy of modern values. Importantly, Nietzsche would build on Epictetus' idea that 'the chain of the body' is unbound most effectively by 'the baseness of money', i.e., exactly the same means by which the spirit is enslaved (Epictetus 1865:404).

Nietzsche's second important point is that the 'higher and the lower spheres of life' are inextricably connected and necessary for each other: 'every atom affects the whole being' (NF-1888:14[79]). On multiple occasions, Nietzsche asserts that 'the ruler and his subjects are of the same kind' (NF-1885:40[21]) and the noble and the less noble 'belong together and are of one species' (HH: I, §111).[421] The 'pathos of distance' that separates and has to separate them should not be taken to mean the absence of an inseverable connection between them (BGE: §257). This cannot be overstated, as the manner of their connection and the mode of their interactions reveal a great deal about the 'conditions of existence' and the prevailing values within any given social arrangement. Building on Aristotle's distinction between the 'non-slave' and the 'slave',[422] Nietzsche extrapolates a more nuanced relationship between the 'master' and the 'slave'. For him, these signifiers denote the farthest points on a broad spectrum of sensibility and aptitudinal hierarchy.[423] Each is, at least partly, shaped by that in opposition to which it is defined as well as exerting a similarly defining influence upon its opposite (NF-1886:5[61]).[424] In *Ecce Homo*, Nietzsche suggests that 'the word "*Übermensch*" designates a type of supreme well-being, in contrast to "modern" people, to "good" people, to Christians and other nihilists' (EH: *Books*, §1). Klossowski points out that Nietzsche's 'great human being' lives within the 'unexchangeable' and resists incorporation (Klossowski 1997:158), while Sloterdijk reminds us of Nietzsche's position that 'the history of humanity is yet to know real nobility' (Sloterdijk 2013:57–58).

It is important to note that Nietzsche's 'order of rank' is equally posited as a system of multiple '*natural degrees*', as opposed to consisting merely of the unitary 'opposites' that become prevalent in modernity on the basis that the 'opposites' are 'easier to comprehend' (NF-1887:9[107]). Already in the lecture cycle *On the Future of Our Educational Institutions* (1872), Nietzsche insists that 'countless intermediate degrees are necessary from the broad, heavily burdened foundations to the free-rising summits, and that precisely here the saying must apply: *natura non facit saltus*' (NF-1872: *FEI*, IV). In one of his final letters to Georg Brandes, written in December 1888, Nietzsche talks about the

---

421 Nietzsche's insights in this regard can be viewed as building on Aristotle's *Politics*, where Aristotle insists that 'if the slave deteriorates the position of the master cannot be saved (*Politics*, 1278[b]).
422 See Aristotle, *Politics*, 1254[b].
423 See Aristotle, Politics, 1254[b]16.
424 Cf. Hegel's 'master-slave' dialectic, discussed by him in the section of *Phenomenology of Spirit* (1807) entitled 'Lordship and Bondage', where Hegel describes the development of self-consciousness through the meeting of two beings.

'tremendously long ladder of ranking', which alone can serve as the basis of natural 'hierarchy between man and man' (BVN-1888:1170).

In *Human, All Too Human*, Nietzsche suggests a detailed outline of the spectrum of qualitative individual differences, which he uses to articulate the subtle degrees separating the ordinary from the great:

> We can distinguish *five grades* of traveller: those of the *first* and lowest grade are those who travel and, instead of seeing, are themselves seen—they are as though blind; next come those who actually see the world; the *third* experience something as a consequence of what they have seen; the *fourth* absorb into themselves what they have experienced and bear it away with them; lastly there are a few men of the highest energy who, after they have experienced and absorbed all they have seen, necessarily have to body it forth again out of themselves in works and actions as soon as they have returned home. It is like these five species of traveller that all men travel through the whole journey of life, the lowest purely passive, the highest those who transform into action and exhaust everything they experience. (HH: II, *AOM*, §228; my emphasis)[425]

Using the analogy of 'five grades' Nietzsche describes an intricate physiological mechanism for transmitting meaning and values, any disruptions, let alone artificial breaks, in which are to the detriment of every single link as they are to the whole and its future prospects. All 'five grades' of passengers travel on exactly the same train through the journey of life. It is primarily, albeit not exclusively, in this sense, Nietzsche tells us, that all the passengers are precisely equal and necessary for one another: they share in the mutual vulnerability (NF-1872:19[93]; HH: I, *HMS*, §92).[426]

In a *Nachlass* note from 1887 entitled '*On Ranking*', Nietzsche argues that the 'higher man' possesses a different, more acute and synthesising sensibility, when compared to the 'typical man'. The latter is able to process a 'small corner' of reality but cannot cope well when 'the multiplicity of elements and the tension of opposites grows' (NF-1887:10[111]). To the 'calm of the strong soul, which moves slowly and displays an aversion to anything that is too lively' (NF-1887:7[7]), Nietzsche juxtaposes the anxiety of the 'poor in spirit' (NF-1884:26[75]), who are unable to deal with 'an overwhelming abundance of what lives' (NF-1886:7[7]). Equally, Nietzsche stresses the enormity of personal responsibility that lies on the shoulders of the 'higher men' in respect of their subjects: 'he, who commands must carry the burden of all who obey' accepting the risk that the burden involved in commanding is always 'an experiment and a hazard' (Z: II, *Self-Overcoming*). In *Human, All Too Human*, he argues that the task of producing 'supreme

---

[425] Nietzsche's classification of the spectrum of sensibility displays a notable connection to Aristotle's distinction concerning the 'five virtues of thought'. Developing on Socratic ideas, Aristotle considers five virtues of thought: phronesis, epistêmê (scientific knowledge), technê (craft and art), nous (intuitive and inward reason, intelligence, the 'eye of the soul' or the 'third eye') and sophia (philosophical wisdom) (NE: VI, §3; last accessed March 4, 2023). Nietzsche discusses this in relation to 'the ancient Greeks' in HH: I, *HMS*, §96).

[426] Nietzsche's insight resonates with Aristotle's allegory of the 'sailors' as 'partners in the community' of life, see P:1276[b]; see also P:1252[a]31–1–32 concerning the nature of the union of master and slave so that 'both may be preserved'.

cultural values' at the same time means that 'the inner life' of the leaders is 'so much harder and more painful' (HH: I, *State*, §480).

Nietzsche sees this aptitude for responsibility as an irrefutable consequence of the fact that '*die grossen Menschen*' are who they are. Greatness, first and foremost, 'means giving direction' (HH:I, §521). Nietzsche's conjecture is that these individuals do not have a choice in the matter: they are 'compelled' to it (NF-1887:11[286]). As such, 'the higher man' represents 'the height of collective self-esteem':

> [I]t compels the individual to represent the pride of the whole ... he must speak and act with extreme respect for himself as he represents the community in person ... the responsibility for the whole draws and allows the individual a broad look, a stern and dreadful hand, a modesty and coldness and greatness of bearing, which he would not concede for his own sake. (NF-1887:11[286], #B-D)

Nietzsche's analysis underscores the intricacy and the vital importance of the connection, albeit not the full interchangeability, between the 'higher and the lower spheres of life', the noble and the slave, the great and the ordinary, the genius and the mediocre. He insists that the nature of this connection is neither economic, nor political in the first instance. This is critical for understanding of Nietzsche's conception of *community as a fellowship*. The latter is not the result of an abstract spirit that permeates every member of the human collective who become taken by some compelling idea and a vision of the future associated with it. The communitarian spirit, Nietzsche tells us, is a physiological disposition of a small group of individuals—very few in number—who work to make their vision a reality, including by forcing it upon the amorphous majority (GM: I, §4–5). However, the *agonistic* axis is prevalent in the creation of a community.

'The obeyer', Nietzsche writes in a *Nachlass* entry from 1885, 'by no means gives up his own power' and equally, 'in commanding there is a concession that the opposite's power has not been vanquished' (NF-1885:36[22]). Instead, this manner of connecting acts as a conduit for creating meaning and values, as well as a complex network of affects and relations via which meaning and values are communicated throughout society and can be jointly owned, while the responsibilities can be apportioned according to aptitude (NF-1884:26[173]). Developing his analysis further, Nietzsche argues that the connection between the 'spheres of nobility and the slaves' (GM: *Preface*, §4)—becomes irreparably distorted under the auspices of modern industrial culture to a large extent because this relation becomes usurped by 'those who commend work' (D: §173) and reconfigured in essentially reductionist economic and financial terms.

Nietzsche's extensive discussion of 'rank-ordering' provides an important entry point into his consideration of slavery as a psychological predicament. He maintains that the underlying source of inequality is neither economic, nor political (NF-1888:[134]). Inequality is not an entirely manufactured outcome or a socially imposed constraint. Nor is it a consequence of specific institutional arrangements: 'to be a public utility, a wheel, a function, for that one must be *destined by nature:* it is not society' (AC: §57; my emphasis). In *Beyond Good and Evil*, Nietzsche contends that 'at the bottom of us, really "deep down", there is, of course, something *unteachable*, some granite of spiritual *fatum*, of predetermined decision and answer to pre-determined selected questions. Whenever a cardinal problem is at stake, there speaks an unchangeable "this is I'" (BGE: §231; my emphasis).

Consequently, Nietzsche's 'underprivileged' are not just the politically or economically underprivileged. (NF-1886:5[71], §8, §14). Instead, Nietzsche thinks of the 'underprivileged' in the context of the distinction between the more '*whole* human beings' and the 'ordinary people'.[427] In *Beyond Good and Evil*, when discussing the 'multitude', he refers to them as 'unvollständige Menschen' ('incomplete individuals') in the sense of their physiological flaws resulting in psychological frailty (see BGE: §§257–258). His argument problematises none other than the manner in which such underlying— psychological and physiological—differences between individuals become embedded in the social fabric of society and reinterpreted by slave morality using the terminology of economic and political inequality.[428] Nietzsche's discussion of slavery challenges 'the opposite instincts' of the modern age, which he sees as growing from 'the deepest subservience to the greatest of all lies—called "equality of men"' (NF-1885:37[14]). His contention is that inequality too becomes utilised as a 'battle cry' by those wishing to advance specific agendas of reactive power, as though in the name of equality (NF-1885:37[14]; see NF-1887:11[135]).

Physiology and Psychology of Slavery

Developing the argument that, although inequality is made manifest within the social context, it does not arise exclusively from this context, Nietzsche's examination of slavery problematises the latter in terms of human vulnerability. He argues that when slavery (as a form of subordination) is taken out of the *oikonomic* context of 'mutual recognition of not causing harm' (NF-1872:19[93]), which safeguards individuality, and exposed in a de-personalised manner (e.g., a wage labourer exposed to the full force of commercial setting), it results in greater susceptibility to exploitation (GS: §117). Nietzsche's polemic in *The Wanderer and His Shadow* allows to consider slavery as a form of 'reflection over the other's vulnerability and capacity for suffering' by those who wish to inflict the hurt (HH: II, *WS*, §33).[429] As Zarathustra would point out, 'he who cannot obey himself, will be commanded' as such is 'the nature of living creatures' but the nature of commanding differs greatly depending on who commands (Z: II, *Self-Overcoming*).

---

[427] See also NF-1887:10[111].
[428] This position differentiates Nietzsche's analysis from both the Marxist and the liberal democratic traditions and presents a point of great angst for them both as it allows neither for Nietzsche's incorporation nor for his conclusive dismissal.
[429] See Nietzsche's discussion in HH: I, *HMS*, §93.

Nietzsche's inquiry into the root causes of slavery conceptualises the latter as a particular physiological disposition, which becomes translated into the predicament of 'psychic suffering' (GM: III, §16). Nietzsche emphasises the importance of getting the causation between physiology and psychology right:

> If someone cannot cope with his 'psychic suffering', this does not stem from his psyche, to speak crudely; more probably from his stomach (GM: III, §16)

Nietzsche's assertion is that beneath the 'psychic suffering', a 'certain weariness and heaviness' and a 'certain exhaustion' are usually found, and that 'the deep depression, the leaden fatigue and the black melancholy' are rooted in a 'physiological feeling of obstruction and inhibition' (GM: III, §16). This physiological condition can be translated into psychological distress: psychology is none other than physiology that happens in one's head. Psychology is a manner of normalising one's physiological condition. The 'true reason' why the slave 'feels ill' is inevitably physiological in Nietzsche's assessment (GM: III, §15). The predicament, however, 'through lack of physiological knowledge' is dealt with in a way that its 'cause and its cure can be sought and tested only on the psychological-moral level', which Nietzsche posits as his 'most general formula for what is usually called a "religion"' (GM: III, §16). For this reason, he considers it critical to understand *who* articulates physiology using the vernacular of psychology.

Our understanding of the psychology of slavery, as that which 'happens in the head', requires 'a physiological elucidation and interpretation, rather than a psychological one' (GM: I, §17). Our error is to interpret the underlying physiological deficiency as a psychological one, thereby inverting cause and effect and creating the framework where physiological incompleteness can be exploited by slave morality as psychological vulnerability. Nietzsche's important point is that an individual's valuations reveal something vital 'about the structure of his soul' (BGE: §268), and that these valuations can never have consciousness, i.e., psychology, as their 'starting point' (NF-1887:9[13]).

In his assessment, modes of valuation represent the furthermost—pre-linguistic—boundary of human awareness which forms the underbelly of our conscious experience. Values lurk beneath all contemplation and underwrite intentionality. They derive from the unspoken depths of human psyche before it is filtered through the strainer of consciousness and becomes structured in accordance with the rules of grammar. Values communicate, but not in words. Akin to gravity, they represent specific fault lines in agency's curvature which determine the path of becoming 'what one is' (EH: *Clever*, §9). When analysing a moral dilemma, investigating an intellectual conundrum, or unfurling the springs of action, values will be found at the farthest ends of the chains of reasoning—no matter how resolute, courageous, and conscientious—used to dissect them (HH: I, *MAH*, §614; BGE: §289). Nietzsche argues that slave morality, by psychologising certain aspects of the human physiological constitution, disassembles the human psyche and hollows it out so that it can prey upon as well as weaponise it to establish the power of reactive valuations over the fragmented and directionless individual. For this reason, Nietzsche insists on the importance of digging deep: breaking through the multiple semiotic coats that obscure the phenomenal down to its valuational foundations, and sometimes needing a hammer to do so (TI: Preface). To reach the threshold of incommunicable is the prime objective of Nietzsche's genealogical critique (BT: ASC, §2).

Nietzsche's hypothesis is that the values of slave morality (e. g., humility, charity, pity, sympathy, kindness, equality) are not 'good in themselves', as much as they are 'good for something' (GM: *Supplementary*, I/96)—e. g., as 'useful' balms and psychological ointments for a particular pathology (GM: III, §14). In this respect, the essence of *slave morality* is thoroughly practical—it is to be found in its *utility* (BGE: §260). This utility and the value of this utility become the subject of Nietzsche's genealogical scrutiny. Nietzsche acknowledges that the slave undoubtedly possesses psychological complexity (GM: I, §§6 – 7). However, these qualities remain unfulfilled and incomplete as they cannot be synthesised physiologically (see NF-1887:10[111]; GM: III, §§13 – 18). Ken Gemes notes that the slave's immediate problem is the inability 'to integrate that complexity into an active whole' (Gemes 2001:358). This inability to make sense of either his volatile psychological predicament or the *ressentiment*, which stems from it, forms the nexus of the slave's vulnerability (Wallace 2007:112 – 119). Nietzsche suggests that the slave's discontent with his lot 'was not invented entirely by the priests', or by his masters (GM: III, §18), and that at some level it represents the physiological 'essence' of his miserable condition' (D: §206).

In *the Genealogy*, Nietzsche invokes the ancient Greek meaning of nobility deriving from the 'word ἐσθλος ... the root of the one who ... has reality, who is real, who is true ... to distinguish it from the lying common man' (GM: I, §5). Positing 'truthfulness' as a 'character trait', Nietzsche points out that *deceitfulness* of the weak correlates to a certain cowardice (or fearfulness) resulting from the insufficient sense of worth or incompleteness.[430] He suggests that 'the higher man is distinguished from the lower by his fearlessness' (NF-1887:11[112]) and that fear felt by the 'weak' only dissipates 'in the middle' where he is 'no longer alone' and surrounded by his like he 'feels no reproach' as to his 'form of being' (NF1887:10[39]). Whereas 'the noble man is frank with himself', deceitfulness serves to compensate for the incompleteness of the slave's reality (GM: I, §10). In other words, the slave's happiness needs to be 'constructed artificially', they have to 'lie themselves into it' (GM: I, §10). As such, this artificial happiness manifests itself in 'wishing not to see something that one does see; wishing not to see something as one sees it' (AC: §55). The lie helps to complete the fragmentary nature of the slave's sensibility: he has to *borrow* from the abstract in order to make his incomplete reality appear whole (GM: III, §18).[431] In order to better understand the psychology of the

---

[430] 'In the word κακός as in δειλός (the plebeian as opposed to the ἀγαθός) cowardice is underlined: this perhaps gives a hint in which direction one has to seek the etymological origin of the multiply interpretable ἀγαθός' (GM: I, §5; last accessed March 4, 2023).

[431] In a *Nachlass* note from 1872, Nietzsche claims that 'the liar uses words in order to make the unreal appear as real, i.e., he misuses the firm foundation (NF-1872:19[230]). In a further note from 1884, Nietzsche suggests that 'the herding instinct comes to words in words' (NF-1884:27[15]). See also NF-

slave, Nietzsche leans on the logic of Epictetus, who considers that striving for things that are 'beyond our power' can become a stumbling block and cause harm:

> [I]f you attribute freedom to things by nature dependent, and take what belongs to others for your own, you will be hindered, you will lament, you will be disturbed, you will find fault both with gods and men. (Epictetus 1865:375)

In the first instance, Epictetus considers one's physical body, i.e., *physiology*, as largely 'outside our own affairs' (Epictetus 1865:375). Secondly, he notes the latent propensity of the slave to compensate for the things he lacks with *abstract representations*. Thirdly, doing so can only be accomplished by means that are ultimately *deceitful*. Fourthly, pursuing this path one inevitably comes to grief and is never satisfied. Last but not least, Epictetus points to who can take advantage of the slave's existential predicament, which is no one's fault, and how this takes place. Epictetus gives careful consideration to the faculty that 'judges the appearances of things' and, although Epictetus and Nietzsche may disagree on whether this should be the 'reasoning faculty', what becomes important for Nietzsche is Epictetus' observation that 'the right use of appearances' by virtue of this faculty has been placed 'in our power' (Epictetus 1865:1–5). What any *ephemeral thing* may become and especially 'the correct use of impressions (*phantasiai*)' depend on our use of the 'faculty which is capable of judging of appearances' (Epictetus 1865:5). Epictetus' deliberations provide Nietzsche with a prototype of a *proactive value-creating* capacity that comes from within rather than from any external compulsion:

> [I]f you will take care of this faculty and consider it your *only possession*, you will never be hindered ... no one will ever compel you, no one will restrict you ... no one will hurt you ... nor will you suffer any harm. (Epictetus 1865:4, 375)

The 'good' and the 'bad' of a particular tool or technology—of money, for example—or of any other object 'outside of our power', does not intrinsically derive from that object. These objects can only abide as lifeless surfaces, vacant shells, and empty vessels until they are invested with the intentionality, and endowed with the will, reason and determination of a human being, i.e., being one way or another evaluated by the faculties within our remit. This is why it becomes so important for Nietzsche to understand not just the kind of valuations that come to inhabit these objects but the value of these valuations and, consequently, from whom these valuations originate.[432]

Once again, Epictetus provides important clues when he connects *deceitfulness* and *money* by asserting that only 'the dishonest man derives advantage in money' (Epicte-

---

1884:26[75], §3, 'The world of opinions—how deep value-estimation goes into things is so far overlooked: how we are stuck in a self-created world, and in all our sensory perceptions there are still moral values', as well as NF-1887: 10[111]. See also Nietzsche's discussion in #2 of *TLEMS* concerning 'the intellect—the master of deception' as coming to the aid of a 'needy man' (EN: *TLEMS*, #2).

432 See, for example, Nietzsche's discussion in NF-1873:29[192] and NF-1879:40[3], which echo Epictetus.

tus 1865:234). Epictetus asserts that to gain power over an individual, the latter must be persuaded to enter the endless chase after things that are destined to remain outside of his power to possess completely. This reactive conceptuality reconfigures every *need* into a craving and a wanton desire, while subordinating non-material needs to material ones.[433] In the vernacular of political economy, this trajectory signifies the gradual shift away from the satisfaction of needs towards the satisfaction of wants, away from the concept embedded in the Greek *oikos* in the direction of Smith's 'commercial society', away from the 'use values' towards 'exchange values' and, inexorably, in the direction of the supreme exchange value—'a value-carrier ['Werthtrager'] in time and space'—we call money.[434]

Nietzsche would translate these developments into a tenebrous narrative of revelling in economic progress and heralding the golden age of material prosperity while sinking ever deeper in spiritual debt. He understands that the valuations propagated by the ascetic priest (in Judeo-Christianity) and by the money-maker (in secular modernity)—both of whom he considers 'a close relative of the sick and the destitute' (GM: III, §15)—which underpin their considerable power over the 'domain of suffering' derive from the same reactive ethos of *slave morality*. As such, the evolutionary directionality of these valuations, which come to dominate modernity, becomes central to his genealogical investigation and its focal point: the psychic vulnerability of the slave reconfigured by the reactive powerbrokers into susceptibility to exploitation.

Nietzsche argues that the slave's 'physiological inhibition' causes him to become *psychologically indebted*. This is of critical significance in relation to the kind of valuations such individuals are capable of since debt, in the final count, is a destructive force within the contours of such psychic constitution[435]:

> [H]e does not understand the reverse side of things as necessary: he combats the evils as if one could dispute them ... he does not want to accept that one goes hand in hand with the other and thus he wishes to *obliterate:* the typical character of a thing, a state, a time, a person, by endorsing only a part of their qualities and desiring to *abolish* all others. (NF-1887:10[111]; my emphasis)

Looking deeper still, Nietzsche discerns a certain psychological propensity in the slave, left to his own devices, to succumb to the 'dull lethargy and the feeling of weakness' growing from 'his discontent, his aversion to himself' (GM: III, §18). The 'herd instinct', as an inclination to aggregate in large numbers, is another corollary of the same 'pathological condition' (GM: III, §18; see NF-1882:3[1]). Increase in scale may represent a greater quantum of energy, with short-term destructive propensities (NF-1887:9[145,(a)]), but it does not by itself amount to a different quality of that amplified energy. Nietzsche

---

[433] See Epictetus 1865: *Fragments*, VII, 404 and X, 405.
[434] Roscher 1876:342; see also Marx, CW 35:46, 81, 97.
[435] Epictetus maintained that the 'lover of money' could never be the 'lover of humankind' (Epictetus 1865:405).

argues that in the absence of leadership the herd remains directionless—always at risk of inner disintegration (GM: III, §15)—and cannot 'endure itself' (NF-1885:2[179]).

Already in *Untimely Meditations*, Nietzsche suggests that the majority, who are 'only servants, assistants, instruments'—unable to self-direct and give themselves meaning—are 'never happy in being what they really are' (UM: III, *SE*, §6). Nietzsche conceptualises slavery in the context of the fight against 'the deep depression of the physiologically obstructed' (GM: III, §15), including with the help of 'a form of mechanical activity' (GM: III, §18–19). Mechanical activity, i.e., physical (and any kind of monotonous, repetitive, mind-numbing) work, is seen as not only providing relief but as a necessary means to lift the slave 'out of his most personal element in his discontent' by 'completely diverting the interest of the sufferer from the pain' and providing him with a sense of certainty, 'a certain encouragement, and indeed some discipline to forget himself' (GM: III, §18).

Within these parameters, it becomes possible to see that Nietzsche's discussion of slavery is an inquiry into human physiological incompleteness and psychological vulnerability, understood both individually and collectively. Nietzsche conceptualises it in terms of one's ability to self-direct, self-legislate and give oneself values, or—in other words—the ability to create. The lack of such a synthetic sensibility exposes psychological vulnerability, which is taken advantage of and becomes embedded into the social fabric. Nietzsche contends that 'the master of the weaker becomes stronger to the extent that the weaker cannot assert his degree of autonomy' (NF-1885:36[18]). In this context, the questions of *how* and by *whom* this vulnerability is taken advantage of, Nietzsche argues, illuminate critical aspects of the political economy of a particular formation, its driving forces and values, as well as indicating its future trajectory.

Nietzsche's argument suggests that the 'Circe' of slave morality—'the most vicious form of the will to lie' (NF-1888:23[3])—operates in precisely this manner. Its starting point is to give meaning to the slave's discontent with himself, of which the slave cannot make sense, by projecting it outward. The ascetic priest transforms the slave's internal predicament into an injustice perpetrated from without—i.e., by external causes: 'I suffer: someone or other must be guilty' (GM: III, §15). By conjuring up a 'hostile external world, upon whose otherness it is logically dependent' (Conway 1994:329), this false consciousness, which 'morality enters as a law, along with the entire group of related values and states' (NF-1888:14[105]), leads the slave as though away from the origin of his psychological strife (GM: III, §15).[436]

The cause-effect relationship becomes inverted, and a new lens of abstraction through which the world can be interpreted is created (NF-1872:19[204]). The slave's physiological incompleteness becomes psychologised through *slave morality*. The problem, for Nietzsche, is that slave morality, having started with false premises, ultimately falls short in delivering on its promises (GM: III, §20). It is unable to dispel, break or

---

436 I.e., the birth of *ressentiment's* 'imaginary revenge', which initially reverses 'the evaluating glance to the outside instead of back onto itself' (GM: I, 10).

overcome the original predicament it sets out by denouncing and promising to overturn.[437] The slave's psychological vulnerability, preyed upon the priest, keeps him steadfastly on the trajectory, which inexorably guides him back to the inception point: i.e., to himself, so that he can make peace with that which he cannot escape (GM: III, §20).[438] As Nancy Love points out, in the end, ascetic priests 'teach man that he is the cause of his suffering' (Love 1986:124). Having undergone this transformative journey 'at the freezing point of the will' (HH: II, *AOM*, §349), the slave now dwells in the 'self-created world of opinions' where all are 'slaves and equal in slavery' (NF-1887:11[341]), albeit with the critical difference of no longer being able to detect 'the weight of the chains' (HH: II, *WS*, §10)[439] As Zarathustra warned, 'even a prison' of slave morality would 'seem like bliss' to the 'restless people', who can 'enjoy their new security' in its inescapable nets (Z: IV, *The Shadow*):

> It will come, one day, that hour that will envelop you in a golden cloud where there is no pain: where the soul has the enjoyment of its own weariness and, happy in a patient game with its own patience ... without end, without aim, without desire ... this is how all invalids feel and speak. (HH: II, *AOM*, §349)

Nietzsche asserts that 'no one talks more passionately about his rights than he who in the depth of his soul doubts whether he has any' (HH: I, §597). The purpose of slave morality is not to transform the slave into a master (of himself), but rather to ease the pain of his discontent with himself and to make the slave embrace himself as he is—the slave: 'to help the modern soul to forget its feeling of guilt, not to help it to return to innocence' (UM: IV, *RWB*, §6). This is the curse of the 'last man', who makes the earth and everything on it small in terms of worth (Z: *Prologue*, §5). And even though the 'last man' may call himself free, he is not 'one of those who had the *right* to escape from a yoke' (Z: I, *Creator*).[440]

In *Schopenhauer as Educator*, Nietzsche asserts that 'culture is the child of each individual's ... dissatisfaction with himself', which urges creative spiritual growth (UM: III, SE, §6). Things, however, change with the ascent of the 'last man', who is 'no longer able to despise himself' and consequently no longer knows of either love or creation. (Z: *Prologue*, §5). This internalised inability to feel dissatisfaction with oneself, expressed as willingness to accept oneself as one is with all the 'limitations of the "I",

---

[437] See Raymond Geuss in *A World Without Why*, 2014:13.
[438] See HH: WS, §33: '*One needs time if one is to transfer one's thoughts from oneself to one's opponent* and to ask oneself how he (i.e., the opponent) can be hit at most grievously' (my emphasis).
[439] See Conway's insightful discussion in Conway 1994:329.
[440] This conjecture is masterfully dramatized in Bulgakov's satirical novel *Heart of a Dog* (1925; last accessed March 4, 2023), in which a distressed stray dog, named *Sharik*, miraculously transfigured into a human using the advances in medical science, remains bedevilled by the innate anxieties of his former self. Bulgakov's work, which was influenced by Nietzsche, highlights an intangible, yet no less real for that reason, issue of unbridgeable aptitudinal difference.

as though they were cause for celebration rather than capitulation', becomes the 'hallmark of industrial and utilitarian culture' (NF-1881:11[50]).

Abolition of Slavery

The abolition of slavery becomes, for Nietzsche, a critical target in terms of exposing the deep-seated hypocrisy of slave morality.[441] In *The Wanderer and His Shadow*, Nietzsche makes clear his opposition to 'physical and spiritual enslavement', as forms of pestilence and barbarism (HH: II, *WS*, §275; see NF-1883:7[167]). However, by triangulating the significance of the abolition of slavery as (1) a 'tribute to dignity' (NF-1887:9[173]), (2) the key issue of political economy (NF-1885:[100], [103]) and (3) as linked to Judeo-Christianity (NF-1887:[135]), Nietzsche challenges it on two grounds. The first is the issue of *intellectual honesty*, a charge he first levels against the Alexandrian culture's denials of the necessity of slavery:

> The Alexandrian culture, to be able to exist permanently, requires a slave class, but with its optimistic view of life it denies the necessity of such a class, and consequently, when its beautifully seductive and tranquillising utterances about the 'dignity of man' and the 'dignity of labour' are no longer effective, it gradually drifts toward a dreadful destruction. (BT: §18)

Subsequently, in *Human, All Too Human*, Nietzsche adds that 'everyone who desires the abolition of slavery and abominates the idea of reducing people to this condition … must at the same time realise that slaves live in every respect more happily and in greater security than the modern worker', while 'the work done by slaves is very little work compared with that done by the worker' (HH: I, *State*, §457).[442] Modern 'vanity', in his assessment, desires the 'abolition of slavery' in order to disguise its own obsequiousness and inability to alter the social fabric on any other level than the most superficial—that of 'small politics' (BGE: §208).[443] Nietzsche echoes Marx's argument concerning the meaninglessness of any political emancipation that only sought to replace 'the barbaric horrors of slavery' with 'the civilised horrors of over-work' (Marx 1990:345). The formal *legal freedom* of the former slave—now a free wage-labourer—is but the cynical window-dressing for the slavery of the capitalistic labour market.[444] Furthermore, Nietzsche's criticism of the vainglory of the political abolition of slavery can be said to mirror Marx's critique of the political abolition of private property:

---

441 Between 1878 and 1887, Nietzsche writes five *Nachlass* notes on the subject in addition to addressing it in his published works, including *The Case of Wagner*.
442 Nietzsche's views echo those of Roscher, who notes that 'the systematic over-working of servants or slaves, in the interest of their masters, is *scarcely thinkable* in an uncultured age … in the absence of commercial intercourse' (Roscher 1878:212–213).
443 In this context, it is worth remembering that, for Nietzsche, 'vanity is an atavism' (BGE: §261).
444 See Löwith's excellent commentary in *From Hegel to Nietzsche*, 1991:153–154.

> [T]he political annulment of private property not only fails to abolish private property but even presupposes it. The state abolishes, in its own way, distinctions of birth, social rank, education, occupation, when it declares that birth, social rank, education occupation, are *non-political distinctions*, when it proclaims, without regard to these distinctions, that every member of the nation is an equal participant in national sovereignty, when it treats all elements of the real life of the nation from the standpoint of the state. Far from abolishing these *real distinctions*, the state only exists on the presupposition of their existence. (CW 3:153; my emphasis)

To place this in the context of Nietzsche's invectives concerning the abolition of slavery, the political abolition of the latter not only presupposes slavery's continued existence, but its objectification only reinforces slavery, embedding it further in the human psyche precisely by making it invisible to the eye bewildered by its astonishing feat of disappearance, courtesy of reification by abolition. In one of his final published works, *The Case of Wagner*, Nietzsche goes further still. He speaks about the abolition of slavery in terms of 'the instinctive uncleanliness in relation to oneself', and the unwillingness 'to gain clarity in relation to oneself'. These comments form the basis upon which Nietzsche chastises the German Kaiser: 'At this very moment the German Kaiser calls it his Christian duty to liberate the slaves in Africa' (TCW: §3). To Nietzsche, the triumph of value inversion is manifest in the thought of the proponents of slave morality to use the most enslaving instrument there is, i.e., Judeo-Christianity, to liberate the already enslaved (D: §546).[445] This does not only represent the case of compounding physical slavery with spiritual enslavement, which he speaks out against (HH: II, WS, §275). Further reaching is Nietzsche's targeting of Hegel's emancipatory polemic, which Nietzsche shares with Alexander Herzen.[446] It would, he argues, be a futile and hypocritical enterprise to throw oneself into liberating others from the clutches of slave morality ahead of one's own liberation.[447] This position is consistent with Nietzsche's earlier note from the *Nachlass* in which he considers the abolition of slavery to belong in the same conceptual amalgam as Judeo-Christianity, i.e., as 'the ostentatious words for something completely different (yes, the contrary!)' (NF-1887:11[135]).

Nietzsche problematises the notion of an 'ideal' (e.g., the abolition of slavery) by suggesting that it stands for the 'slandering and re-baptising' of old values (NF-1887:9[173]).[448] In the case of Christianity, as Ronald Osborn points out in *Humanism and the Death of God* (2017), 'the fact that Christianity was deeply complicit from the beginning in the projects of European colonialism, slavery and imperialism' gives po-

---

[445] Marx too chastises the European—the English and the Dutch in particular—on similar grounds, i.e., for preaching Christianity as the tool of liberation of the slaves in Africa (see Marx 1990: 376 fn. 74, 599 and 916).
[446] Nietzsche read and 'strongly recommended' Herzen's 'Memoirs of a Russian' (BVN-1872:248, letter to Carl von Gersdorff from 02/08/1872).
[447] Concerning Herzen, see Yack's discussion in *The Longing for Total Revolution*, 1986:241. Concerning Hegel, see Williams 2012:36–38.
[448] 'It is always wrong to expect a "progress" from an ideal: the victory of the ideal has always been a retrograde movement' (NF-1887:11[135]).

tency to Nietzsche's comprehensive challenge of slave morality's value-inversion, which spearheads modernity's drive for liberation and progress (Osborn 2017:212–213). In *Daybreak*, Nietzsche goes so far as to suggest that 'Christianity was devised for another class of ancient slaves for those who had a weak will and weak reason—that is to say for the majority of slaves' (D: §546).

Nietzsche's second and related objection to the abolition of slavery comes from the viewpoint of the *total cost* that would be involved in overcoming slavery in more than just the name. Stated briefly, Nietzsche understands the total cost in the sense of 'total accounting': as expressing 'the sum total of all costs and sacrifices' of achieving a stated objective (HH: I, *State*, §475, §481).[449] Considered within the context of the debate on the abolition of slavery in America, the issue of what to do with emancipated slaves—i.e., whether to integrate or expel them—remained one of the most divisive in American history. Its clear echoes resonate to this day (Foner 2012:17–19). Viewed in light of the tremendous cost of overcoming vs. abolishing slavery, Nietzsche's question to the proponents of the abolition can be formulated in the following terms: has slavery been overcome with its abolition, or simply made more invisible and more deeply embedded into the social fabric?

Slavery, for Nietzsche, is not contemptible in and of itself, notwithstanding that it is an indelible reminder of humankind's past lowliness, from which man 'lifted himself' (HH: I, *HMS*, §40).[450] Importantly, for Nietzsche, slavery is not a static phenomenon. It is akin to a drag force (i.e., resistance) that remains interminably pointed in the direction of the 'animality of nature' (HH: I, *HMS*, §40). Humankind will never become that of which slavery is not part (NF-1881:16[23]). Slavery denotes a condition that requires continual Herculean overcoming. As far as he is concerned, the abolition of slavery is a form of psychological deception. Abolishing slavery is akin to making its outward man-

---

[449] Sedgwick appropriately suggests that Nietzsche's total cost perspective can be understood in terms of 'a general economic principle: social life is not static, it includes elements that either expand or contract, and every gain (expansion) by someone somewhere is possible only in virtue of there being an equal or greater than equal loss (contraction) on the part of someone or something somewhere else' (Sedgwick 2007:151, 107). For some of Nietzsche's own clearest formulations of the *total cost approach*, see D: §206 and the *Nachlass* note NF-1887:10[17].

[450] Much is made of Nietzsche's 'contempt' for slaves and for slavery. His terminology in this regard, however, is rather nuanced and ambivalent, which holds important interpretive keys. In *HMS*, he speaks of 'disregard' for the slave ('*Missachtung des Sclaven*', HH: I, *HMS*, §40), rather than of contempt. Discussing the origins of 'good' and 'evil' in *BGE*, Nietzsche uses '*Verachtung*' (BGE: §260) or '*Menschenverachtung*' (BGE: §93) to denote contempt and to describe the slave as 'contemptible' ('*verächtliche*'; BGE: §260). He also uses '*Geringschätzung*' as a form of disdain or contempt for the 'uncleanliness of the spirit' (BGE: §58). However, at the same time, he argues that the 'subtlety and strength of evil (i.e.,—the master morality meaning of evil, DS) block incipient contempt' (BGE: §260). Etymologically, 'contempt' can likely be traced to the Greek 'τεμνω', which means to cut and/or to intersect. This being the case, contempt might have connotations of a state or condition one wishes to be rid of or to cut from one's present condition. This might help to explain contempt as a reactive sentiment and a valuational category of slave morality (e.g., BGE: §93). See also Nietzsche's distinction between 'schlecht' (bad) and 'schlicht' (plain, simple), in GM: I, §4, as an entirely *agonistic* one.

ifestations invisible rather than making the phenomenon of slavery disappear altogether from the constellation of factors and forces (i.e., *affects*) that comprise the contradictory phenomena of life. Throwing away the mirror in which slavery is reflected achieves very little in terms of altering the underlying substance of the phenomenon. On the contrary, it has the effect of making slavery grow uglier, as is usually the case with *any* unattended social iniquity (HH: I, *HMS*, §41).

In a perhaps counterintuitive manner, the abolition of slavery is a way of objectifying it, a way of stupefying a force into an object, as though the latter could be discarded at will and as soon as its utility—as a barbaric mechanism of extracting economic benefit—has been depleted. As such, the abolition of slavery is a tacit acknowledgment that slavery has not been overcome, let alone eradicated. Abolition is a form of psychological abdication before one of the most vexatious affects of human nature. If slavery were a 'radical evil'—which is possible to stipulate under the 'higher and deeper conceptions of good and evil'—in order 'to understand *ourselves*, we must understand *it*; but if we are then ourselves to rise higher, we must rise above it' (HH: I, *HMS*, §56). None of these objectives, on Nietzsche's view, are achieved by the abolition of slavery.

Nietzsche's contention is that modern sensibility, more intolerant of the word 'slavery' than of its reality, is only informed by slavery as a recent historical phenomenon (GS: §18). The word 'slavery' is itself a relatively recent phenomenon, dating from the Middle Ages. It purports to designate every form of slavery as though it were some generic phenomenon. By blurring the boundaries between the historical forms of slavery this linguistic contrivance disguises the fact that the 'slavery' which has been abolished was, according to Nietzsche, the 'slavery of the barbarians' (NF-1869:3[44]) that had nothing in common with the *oikonomic* slavery of Antiquity. Modern slavery was, on Nietzsche's view, an example of the slavery of the slaves, by the slaves and over the slaves. As such, it could not have been anything but ugly and reprehensible because, and this is a critical distinction for Nietzsche: 'there were never slaves without masters' (NF-1881:16[23]).

In a *Nachlass* note from 1885, Nietzsche suggests that the abolition of slavery is symptomatic of the nihilism in the political economy of modernity, evidenced by 'lack of a redeeming state, of a justifier' (NF-1885:2[131]). A conclusion that can be drawn from his discussion of the abolition of slavery is that celebrating it as though it represented the great victory over a heinous evil hides the great tragedy and the direct evidence of our ethical degeneration reflected precisely in the fact that such slavery as was abolished had ever been allowed to come to pass in the first instance. The abolition of slavery, on Nietzsche's view, only removes the real causes of this barbaric slavery further from the modern mind's eye.

Beneath the surface of a rousing but inevitably self-subsuming and self-referential 'battle cry'—'the alleged tribute to human dignity' (NF-1887:9[173])—Nietzsche discerns the rise of the new forms of 'impersonal' (D: §206) and 'anonymous' (HH: II, *WS*, §288) slavery, which will no longer have a readily recognisable voice or image. Nietzsche warns us that 'these great words have value only in battle, as a standard: not as realities' (NF-1887:11[135]). The abolition of slavery, on his view, is spearheaded by the 'will to one morality', which manifests itself in the drive to increase uniformity serving the 'interest of profitability' (NF-1887:10[11]). Part of this process involves slavery being reconfigured into an economic phenomenon and found wanting on that score. Paradoxically, the abolition of slavery has made it easier to exploit the 'liberated' slaves, including by vastly increasing their numbers and thereby diluting the 'unit cost' of producing a worker. As Adam Smith pointed out already in *The Wealth of Nations*, 'the work done by freemen comes cheaper in the end than that performed by slaves' (WN1:93).[451] As a form of exploitation, slavery is eventually found to be economically unviable (see Roscher 1878:215). Hence, it is abolished but only to be re-designed by money to fit the purposes of secular industrial culture. As Charles Hall, a renowned British economist, noted in *The Effects of Civilisation* (1850; last accessed March 4, 2023), the ills of pre-modern society were more concealed than cured by transition to capitalism:

> Adam Smith thinks Mr Hume has great merit in having been the first that observed that manufacturers had abolished the servile dependence of the people on the great feudal barons; but Dr Smith was not aware of this new species of dependence of the lower orders on the rich, which is established in its stead, in most civilized states. (Hall 1850: 42; last accessed March 4, 2023)[452]

Nietzsche points out one further aspect of hypocrisy associated, on his view, with the abolition of slavery. He warns that under the cover of the 'seductive and tranquilising utterances' unavoidably hides 'a very particular kind of man', who 'tries to gain mastery—more precisely, a very particular instinct' (NF-1887:9[173]). In the previous note, Nietzsche characterises this instinct as 'the dark instincts of those men of a democratic era who are dissatisfied, ambitious, disguised from themselves' (NF-1887:9[170]). He goes on to suggest that a particular 'lust for power' urges these men on and finds reflection in the agenda of the 'equality of men':

> 'Equality of men': what is hidden behind the tendency more and more to posit men *as equal* simply because they are men. 'Interestedness' in respect to common morality (the trick: making the great desires, avarice and lust for power into patrons of virtue). (NF-1887:9[173])

---

451 It is worth noting that Smith views slavery 'as an almost natural inclination' to be found in human nature. See Bowles' discussion: 'Smith argued that 'slavery takes place in all societies at their beginning, and proceeds from that tyrannic disposition which may almost be said to be natural to mankind' (1978, LJ(B), 134). Thus, slavery (a feature also arising from man's 'natural inclinations') was a usual feature of all societies in their infancy. However, the subsequent abolition of slavery was by no means natural. Smith's argument as to the causes of emancipation underwent some change, but it is clear from all his writings that the abolition of slavery should not be expected as a general rule: 'We are apt to imagine that slavery is entirely abolished at this time, without considering that this is the case in only a small part of Europe; not remembering that all over Moscovy and all the eastern parts of Europe, and the whole of Asia, that is, from Bohemia to the Indian Ocean, all over Africa, and the greatest part of America, it is still in use. It is indeed almost impossible that it should ever be totally or generally abolished. [1978, LJ(A), iii.101]' (Bowles 1986:114).
452 https://archive.org/details/effectscivilisa00hallgoog/page/n10, last accessed Feb. 27, 2023.

Nietzsche seeks to establish a *direct link* between the economic logic of profit-making and the abolition of slavery: 'common morality is enforced only because it procures a benefit' (NF-1887:9[170]). He suggests that the former slaves, instead of reclaiming their individuality with the abolition of slavery, would only further 'cease to be differentiated … in their needs and demands' (NF-1887:9[173]). Nietzsche contends that just because the formal slavery is no more does not mean an improvement in the condition of the liberated slaves. On the contrary, the abolition makes it more certain 'that they are going to wither', albeit now as free and autonomous agents (NF-1887:9[173]). He equates this with 'the tyranny … or uniformity in favour of the rulers', which only alleges 'a tribute to "human dignity"' (NF-1887:9[173]) but never intends for it to materialise. This note from the late *Nachlass* leaves little doubt in relation to whom Nietzsche considers the prime beneficiaries of such a reconfiguration:

> How far all kinds of businessmen and the avaricious, all those who have to *grant and request credit*, need to insist on *sameness of character and sameness of value concepts:* world trade and exchange of all kinds enforces and, as it were, buys itself virtue. The same classes make use of immorality whenever that serves their purpose. (NF-1887:9[173]; my emphasis)

Beyond the echo of the 'battle cry', the abolition of slavery has little to do with moral enlightenment and more with perpetuating more subtle forms of 'impersonal and anonymous slavery' (HH: II, *WS*, §288). Through abolition, slavery transitions into a less tangible form that is 'adorned with such inoffensive names that they do not arouse the suspicion of even the most delicate hypocritical consciousness' (GM: II, §7).

On Nietzsche's view, the inability to overcome slavery as a requirement and cynically benefiting from it instead is a distinguishing feature of modernity. While 'the glitter of general disinterestedness dazzles', it also 'conceals knavery and harshness' (HH: I, *State*, §443). In other words, Nietzsche sees modern slavery as developing on the cross-roads of exploitation and profit, which become the driving forces of the capitalist political economy.[453] Klossowski as well as Deleuze and Guattari highlight this point in Nietzsche's analysis: modern slavery's forms as well as its content correspond to the 'aims and meanings in which even the most enslaved elements participate'—i.e., slavery cannot help furthering itself when it furthers the capitalist economy (Deleuze and Guattari 2013:345). As Holub aptly surmises, 'the ideology-laden platitudes of democracies only conceal the basic economic nexus of slavery' (Holub 2018:144).

In *The Half Has Never Been Told* (2014), Edward Baptist develops an empirically based argument concerning the critical role of both slave labour and the slave trade in the development of American capitalism.[454] He deconstructs the accepted wisdom,

---

[453] See an informative overview of and discussion of this issue can be found in '*Did Slavery Make Economic Sense*' (The Economist, *Economic History*, Sept. 27, 2013; last accessed March 4, 2023).

[454] Baptist's argument echoes the book advanced earlier by Eric Williams in his seminal work *Capitalism and Slavery* (1944), where he argues against the entrenched view that linked the ideas of economic and moral progress, the latter evidenced by the abolition of slavery, as the main engines of capitalistic

verified until recently by the 'stamp of academic research, of the idea that slavery was separate from the great economic and social transformations of the Western world during the nineteenth century' (Baptist 2014: xix). Baptist provides numerous examples of the unsavoury origins of modern global finance. One of them demonstrates how the 'commodified slaves', turned into widely traded international financial securities and collateral in the 1820–1830s, were the real-life prototype of the modern financial products, such as mortgages (Baptist 2014:248, 270). Elsewhere, in *Slavery's Capitalism* (2016), Beckert and Rockman find that in some of the Southern States, slave mortgages regularly 'generated more circulating capital in a given year than did the revenues from crops produced by slave labour' (Beckert and Rockman 2016:17).[455] Slave-based mortgages remained a popular and attractive long-term financial investment at the time when the concept and the practice of slavery were becoming increasingly politically and socially unacceptable either side of the Atlantic:

> In effect, even as Britain was liberating the slaves of its Empire, a British bank could ... sell an investor a completely commodified slave: not a particular individual who could die or run away, but a bond that was the right to a one-slave-sized slice of pie made from the income of thousands of slaves. (Baptist 2014:248)

Baptist argues persuasively that the capitalist economy and capitalism as the social order in America, as well as in Britain and elsewhere in Europe, rose on the back of the slave trade, slave labour and slave finance. Echoing Nietzsche's own conclusions, he also points out that slavery tends to become increasingly brutal when it is pursued for profit. Prominent American sociologist Du Bois, in his famous book *Darkwater: The Twentieth Century Completion of Uncle Tom's Cabin* (1920), which chronicles the horrors of black slavery in America in the early part of the 20th century, problematises it with the following probing question:

> We ask, and perhaps there is no answer, how far may the captain of the world's industry do his deeds despite the grinding tragedy of its doing? How far may men fight for the beginning of comfort, out beyond the horrid shadow of poverty, at the cost of starving other and what the world calls lesser men? (Du Bois 1920:91)

Nietzsche tells us that slavery has not been overcome with abolition. Rather, only its outward appearance has changed. Anti-Slavery International today echoes Nietzsche's conclusions: 'Slavery did not end with abolition in the 19th century. Instead, it changed its forms and continues to harm people in every country in the world'. Zarathustra's prescient words are worth keeping in mind: 'Do you call yourself free? I want to hear your *ruling idea* and not that you have escaped from a yoke' (Z: I, *Creator*).

---

development. Williams' work demonstrates the key impact of slave trade on economic development under the auspices of the social order, which prides itself on the abolition of slavery.

455 See Bonnie Martin's detailed examination of the slave mortgaging practices in 'Neighbor-to-Neighbor Capitalism' in *Slavery's Capitalism*, 2016:107–122.

Capitalism and Modern Slavery

Capitalism actively reconfigures the concept of slavery. As is cogently argued in *New Frontiers of Slavery* (2016), redesigning slavery has undoubtedly been 'an integral aspect of the "great transformation", modernity, and capitalist development' (Tomich 2016:2). In *Human, All Too Human*, Nietzsche notes that 'as at all times, so now too, men are divided into slaves and the free' (HH: I, *Tokens*, §283). What does Nietzsche suggest happens to slavery in modernity? Part of his concern is with the travails of an 'old foe': the *principium individuationis* (BT: §1), which he traces from the 'proto-Christian Socrates' and through its various incarnations to modernity (Leonard 2012:162–165). Nietzsche tells us: 'the very isolated individual of the modern age is made too weak and bound to fall into servitude' (NF-1869:3[44]).

Capitalism advances by teaching such an individual 'to see boredom as though lit up by a higher charm', so that the 'mechanical form of existence' would appear 'as the highest, most venerable form of existence' (NF-1887:10[11]). Nietzsche surmises that the modern individual 'regards himself as free' largely because 'he no longer *perceives* the weight of the chains' (HH: II, *WS*, §10). At the same time, however, the real motive forces, which formulate the moral imperatives of industrial culture so as to ensure self-advancement—namely those of 'profitability, amusement and expediency'—remain hidden from view (NF-1887:10[11]). In this respect, as Love notes, 'industrial culture' drifts towards 'stylized barbarity', which thrives on the 'production of parts without a whole' and 'specialisation without synthesis' (Love 1986:182).

A critical point made by Nietzsche is that industrial society engages the vocabulary of dignity, freedom, and equality precisely in order to foster the 'sublime development of slavery' (NF-1885:2[179]). Beneath the platitudes of the emancipatory vernacular (HH: I, *State*, §443), this involves taking full advantage of the slave's psychological vulnerability. Through the precepts of slave morality this vulnerability is moulded into the subjectivity of the labourer in such a way that 'labour becomes indistinguishable from "work on the self"' (Lazzarato 2012:33; see also GM: III, §18). In *the Genealogy*, Nietzsche speaks of 'a shattered nervous system added on to the sickness; and that applied on the largest and smallest scale, with individuals and with masses' (GM: III, §21). He problematises modern slavery as primarily an 'impersonal enslavement' in which individuality is dis-embedded (or precluded from developing) and the void is filled with economic affects designed to keep the economy functioning while supplying the economic subject with illusions of autonomy from it (D: §206).

Modern slavery becomes less visible at least in two respects. Slavery's physical manifestations are outsourced beyond the perimeter of the Western world where slavery continues to be the logical choice of the capitalist system in terms of providing a necessary cost-effective boost to the economy, so that it can continue to thrive.[456] With-

---

[456] See van den Anker 2004: vii–viii and Domar 1970:18–21. Marx argued that when 'capital is sent abroad, this is not done because it absolutely could not be applied at home, but because it can be em-

in this perimeter, however, slavery does not perish either: it is increasingly internalised into the multiplicity of drives, which become diffused throughout the fabric of the consumer society. Focus on the enslaving propensities of industrial culture is central to Nietzsche's critique of modernity. On the one hand, Nietzsche correctly anticipates the emergence of a consumer society that would become enslaved by the incessant 'satisfaction of its own needs' (Klossowski 1997:158). As Nietzsche's argument goes, 'the greedy exploitation of every minute brings forth ... the self-seeking drives of the soul', leaving 'all men' feeling 'in themselves only the self-seeking worm' (UM: III, SE, §4). Yet, at the same time, this 'worm'—emblematic of the 'world of commerce' (UM: III, SE, §4)—remains 'eternally hungry' and dissatisfied, 'no matter how much it devours' (BT: §23). As Nietzsche contends in *Human, All Too Human*, this predicament makes an individual 'obligated to a society, nailed to a place and incorporated into a state'—i.e., it makes him a slave (HH: II, AOM, §317).

Helping to embed this industrial culture structurally is the comprehensive political drive for 'equalization ... in the guise of democratization practiced by industrial society' (Klossowski 1997:165). One concomitant effect of the equalisation drive, which entitles everyone to 'believe they have the right to any problem' (NF-1884:25[298]), is an unavoidable increase in the levels of 'anxiety' (HH: II, WS, §170) and 'agitatedness' (HH: I, §285). The 'extreme movement' of modern civilisation 'in terms of speed and means' (NF-1888:14[182]) helps to deliver agitated and anxious individuals into the therapeutic lap of the consumerist cycle, thereby reinforcing the 'Vicious Circle', where his own industriousness, amplified by the 'guilty conscience' of the unrepayable debt and converted by his labour into commodities, is fed back to him, which 'implies, for Nietzsche, a reduction of the human being' (Klossowski 1997:165–167). The latter, as we can infer from Nietzsche's argument, occurs in parallel with the ever-expanding periphery of the self-consumptive industrial culture (GS: §21).

These two intertwined and mutually reinforcing trends—consumption and agitated anxiety—promote the 'universally enslaving economy' of industrial culture (Klossowski 1997:165). Nietzsche argues that such a social arrangement is attainable only at a very high cost. Behind the symptoms discussed above, Nietzsche hypothesises a far deeper process of 'physiological decline', the final destination of which would be to 'turn the Earth into a hospital' (NF-1886:4[7]; see HH: II, WS, §188). Nietzsche's warning concerns the impending mental health crisis (NF-1888:14[182]) when the thought of a *vita contemplativa* becomes impossible 'without self-contempt and bad conscience' (GS: §329). This aspect is aptly captured by Klossowski:

> Nietzsche has the irrefutable premonition: the total effacement of differences in the satisfaction of needs and the homogenization of the habits of feeling and thinking will have, as its effect, a moral and affective numbing ... the human being will no longer feel itself; nor its substance, nor its power—even though it will henceforth be capable of exploiting other planets (Klossowski 1997:165).

---

ployed at a higher rate of profit in a foreign country' and that the higher rate of profit reflects higher level of exploitation of labour (CW 37:255).

As a result, modern individuals become enslaved through the absence of formal slavery. They find it difficult to carry on with their daily lives, which entail an inscrutable contradiction of living enslaved—what Klossowski refers to as 'congenital servitude' (Klossowski 1997:157)—whilst believing themselves to be free.

An inference that can be drawn from Nietzsche's multifaceted analysis of modern slavery, therefore, appears to be that 'atomistic individuals' (NF-1882:4[83])—no matter how free, equal, and dignified they may feel themselves to be—should encounter increasing difficulty in regarding their existential condition as worthwhile (HH: II, WS, §209). Already in *The Greek State*, Nietzsche warned of a potentially 'enormous social problem': 'even if it were true that the Greeks were ruined because they kept slaves, the opposite is even more certain, that we will be destroyed by the lack of slavery' (GSt: §6). This, Nietzsche intimates, is liable to become a point of colossal psychological distress and a mental fracture from which tremendous anxiety of the modern age would rise to the point where 'the burden of living becomes too heavy' (HH: II, AOM, §401).

Nietzsche's analysis also suggests that secular slave morality (as industrial culture) reconfigures the slave's psychological habitat. Debt turned into guilt, which converts the 'war of force' into the 'war of cunning' (GM: III, §15)—i.e., the first and most successful experiment in making reactive power virtual and its enslaved subject self-surveying—lies at the heart of the capitalistic enterprise and prepares the ground for the mass production of the subject who is indebted both psychologically and financially. The internalised sense of indebtedness as guilt plays a critical role in vastly expanding the commercial reach of modern slavery under the auspices of capitalism. Far greater numbers—including the former masters—are swept into the fold of slave morality which, in its secularised form, operates through the discourse on democracy as well as the doctrines of economic liberalism.[457] This is partly the reason why Nietzsche insists that 'the slave-like character of morality ... continually generates new forms of similar slavery' (NF-1884:25[163]). Nietzsche's argument is aligned with Marx's view, expressed in the *Economic and Philosophic Manuscripts of 1844*, that capitalism's 'deformity and dulling of the workers and the capitalists' produces the self-conscious and self-acting human commodity'—i.e., a 'mentally and physically dehumanised being' (CW 3:284).

Perhaps the crucial reason why Nietzsche finds modern slavery as disagreeable as he does is due to the degradation it induces of the '*die grossen Menschen*' into Carlyle's 'Captains of Industry' (Carlyle 1843:333–341) and Spencer's 'regulative, ruling and employing classes' (Spencer 1873:154–157).[458] While the latter declare it their 'first ambi-

---

[457] See Nietzsche's discussion in BGE: §202; BT: ASC, §4; NF-1884:25[345]; and NF-1885:2[13].
[458] See, as an illustration, Carlyle's description: 'The Leaders of Industry, if Industry is ever to be led, are virtually the Captains of the World; if there be no nobleness in them, there will never be an Aristocracy more. ... Captains of Industry are the true Fighters, henceforth recognisable as the only true ones: Fighters against Chaos, Necessity and the Devils and Joetuns; and lead on Mankind in that

tion' to be 'a noble master, among noble Workers' and becoming 'a rich Master'—a distant second' (Carlyle 1843:333), on Nietzsche's view, they fail to meet the exacting demands of the *'die grossen Menschen'*. Nietzsche finds the 'luminaries of industry' fundamentally deficient and incapable of genuine leadership. He likens them to the 'blood sucking dogs, speculating on misery of every kind', while advancing their self-interest (GS: §40). Elsewhere, he describes them as 'only slaves, who lie ... about their slave-like nature and work' (NF-1881:16[23]). Nietzsche's criticism is by no means limited to the captains of industry: the entire 'market place' of modern society is 'full of pompous jesters' (Z, I, *Flies*). In *Zarathustra*, he likens the political leaders of modernity—'the men of the hour' (Z: I, *Flies*)—to the 'honey-mouthed importunate dogs' and the kings to the 'false showpieces for the stupidest and the craftiest and whoever today traffics with power' (Z: IV, Kings). One attribute connects these three representative elites of secular society—their profound falseness: they all know themselves to be 'not the first of men' and only having to pretend to be' (Z: IV, Kings).[459] No matter how 'tired and disgusted with this deception' they may become, they would not know how to stop lying (Z: IV, Kings).

In *Ecce Homo* (1888), Nietzsche tells us that 'the decadents need the lie as it is one of the conditions of their preservation' (EH: *BT*, §2) but with perilous consequences for the rest, as 'all the problems of politics, of social organisation, and of education become falsified through and through because one mistook the most harmful men for great men' (EH: *Clever*, §10).[460] When the 'leaders of humanity' (NF-1888:23[3]) become decadent, 'exoteric' in their outlook (BGE:§30) and 'intestinal' in their modus operandi (see UM: III, *SE*, §4; IV, *RWB*, §6), those 'in the lower spheres of the world', who are of the 'weaker soul' and 'lower life force', are left to their insufficient own devices (BGE: §30). The entire society suffers a *loss of value* and degenerates, while impersonal enslavement flourishes:

> Material prosperity, the comfort that satisfies the senses, is now desired, and all the world wants it above all else. Consequently, it will meet a *spiritual slavery that never before existed* (NF-1881:11[294]; my emphasis).[461]

---

great, and alone true, and universal warfare; the stars in their courses fighting for them, and all Heaven and all Earth saying audibly, Well done!' (Carlyle 1843:337–338).

459 In the same passage in *Zarathustra*, Nietzsche argues that, in contrast to the political and business powerbrokers of his time, 'the peasant today is the best and the most noble type' which 'should be ruler' (Z: IV, Kings). Nietzsche is commenting on the social strife in Germany during the 1870–1880s, which became manifest in the profound dislocation of the agricultural community in the wake of the financial crisis, which was one of the burning social issues in Germany of that time. See Davies' insightful commentary, 2018:75–76 and 100–103.

460 See Nietzsche's discussion of this in NF-1887:9[184]: 'for a hundred years now, a sick man has been accepted as a leader in politics'.

461 Nietzsche's view exhibits considerable affinity with the discussion of Epictetus on the 'slavery of the soul' in *Enchiridion* (see Ritter 1846:204), an insight equally shared by Marx: 'man becomes ever poorer as man, his need for money becomes ever greater' (CW: 3:302–306).

The 'conditions of existence' which embody and reflect these values make it virtually impossible for the great individuals to emerge and make a difference.[462] Today, the 'strong' no longer shape the 'weak', making them stronger. On the contrary, they are shaped by the 'weak', making themselves and everyone around them weaker. These leaders of humankind, in Nietzsche's assessment, accelerate the process of the devaluation of values instead of promoting their revaluation. This is the basis for Nietzsche's assertion that 'those who are at the top of society today are physiologically condemned' (NF-1888:25[1]). In this respect, Nietzsche notes that 'the degeneration of the rulers has created the greatest madness in history' (NF-1884:25[344]). In the words of Zarathustra:

> There is no harder misfortune in all human destiny than when the powerful of the earth are not also the first men. Then everything becomes false and awry and monstrous. ... then the value of the rabble rises higher and higher and at last the rabble-virtue says: Behold, I alone am virtue! (Z: IV, Kings)

This paves the way for the proliferation of meaningless and wasteful slavery, which engulfs all social classes and every sphere of life (see D: §175; HH: II, WS, §286).[463] Nietzsche contends that it demonstrates that slave morality is not only a potent economic force (NF-1885:2[182]) but that it is also 'the greatest danger' (GM: I, §12) because it confirms us, moderns, as 'the last men, and the slaves' (EH: *Destiny*, §5). Nietzsche's point is that unless there are those, working for whom enables access to a higher meaning and value-creation, 'this enormous mass of political and commercial forces' is wasted for nothing, and that slavery in such a context can only be barbaric (NF-1881:11[221]).

Nietzsche foresees the eventual 'mechanisation of mankind' as a function of the 'total economic administration of the earth'. He argues, however, that, absent worthy goals (NF-1885:38[13]), the 'maximum point of exploitation' will only ever correspond to the 'minimal forces', 'minimal values' and the most dwarfish of individuals. Nothing of enduring value would be created and exploitation would amount to being its own end rather than assisting in the enhancement of life's value (NF-1885:2[179]). Hence Nietzsche's stark conjecture that 'the theory of freedom of will is an invention of the ruling classes' (HH: II, WS, §9). Unable to supply value and meaning, the modern 'captains of industry' can do no more than perpetuate slavery in different forms so long as it continues to serve their greed (UM: III, SE, §4–6).[464] Such perpetuation of slavery,

---

462 See Nietzsche's point that 'the time of kings is no more' (Z: III, Old and New Tablets, §21) as well as NF-1888:14[182]; NF-1885:1[4]; and NF-1885:37[8].
463 See an insightful discussion of this point in Love 1986:180–183.
464 One of Nietzsche's most scornful inferences in this regard is found in a *Nachlass* note from 1881. Addressing it, to the 'self-owned' ('*Ihr Selbsteigenen*') autocrats ('*Ihr Selbstherrlichen*') of the future, Nietzsche characterises those men, who 'think themselves to be high above' everyone else in the modern society—'princes, merchants, officials, farmers and military men' ('*Fürsten, Kaufleute, Beamte, Ackerbauer, Soldaten*')—as 'only slaves, who do not work for themselves as eternal necessity would have it' (NF-1881:16[23]). Nietzsche contends, rather presciently, that only in 'a future age one would be able to

however, is not free of consequences. These accrue up to a point where incremental improvements in material well-being can no longer provide a *bona fide* substitute for spiritual and mental well-being squandered along the way (HH: II, *AOM*, §317). Nietzsche posits this as a central concern in relation to modern industrial culture:

> It is clear that what I am fighting is *economic optimism:* the idea that everyone's profit necessarily increases with the growing costs to everyone. It seems to me that the reverse is the case: the costs to everyone add up to a total loss: man becomes less—so that one no longer knows what this tremendous process was actually for. A 'What for', a new 'What for'—that is what mankind needs. (NF-1887:10[17])

Nietzsche's analysis of modern slavery can be read as a cautionary tale about the high price that invisible costs exact: 'we pay the highest price for any one-sided preference' (HH: II, *AOM*, §186). His reflections on slavery problematise the comprehensive hollowing out of human spirit and the diminution of the individual's worth as the true cost we incur on such developmental trajectory which, to him, represents the most regrettable squandering of energy and resources. Nietzsche warns that the energy 'by which the mills of the modern world were driven' comes first and, and only then, and a long way after, the truth' (HH: II, *AOM*, §226). As a result, we are prone to regard for a long time as 'progress' the process which, in substance, represents as the 'retrograde movement' (HH: II, *AOM*, §226: §178) and a 'secret path of decline' (BGE: §10). Furthermore, Nietzsche's scrutiny of modern slavery problematises the ouroboric propensities of modern political economy which, underwritten by slave morality's thirst for domination over life, remains predicated on continual devourement earth's resources and depletion of human capital.

As Conway points out, beyond the reign of the 'last man' looms 'a more ominous peril: the advent of the "will to nothingness", whereby humankind orchestrates its own annihilation in a final, apocalyptic frenzy of Dionysian expenditure' (Conway 1997:17). This self-destructive characteristic of the 'so-called industrial culture' makes it, on Nietzsche's view, 'the most vulgar form of existence that has yet existed' because it leaves individuals 'at the mercy of brute need ... to sell oneself' (GS: §40). Nietzsche, therefore, urges to bring back into the picture the *hidden costs and contingent liabilities* of industrial culture. He insists that they must be brought onto the *'balance sheet of life'* (NF-1875:5[188]) in order for us to be in a position to have a meaningful and honest discussion about the state of society, its developmental trajectory, and its future prospects.

---

see this presently indiscernible spectacle' for what it really is when 'the illusions' by means of which these men of the moment 'lie to themselves about their slave-like work' can no longer confer legitimacy upon the false hierarchy upon which the existing social order, including its ruling classes, is premised (NF-1881:16[23]).

Concluding Remarks

Nietzsche contends that throughout human history slavery has never disappeared. He is confident that slavery will remain rooted in existence long after 'our social order will slowly melt away' (HH: I, *State*, §443). In a *Nachlass* note from 1881, Nietzsche insists that 'slavery is universally present, although no one wishes to admit it' (NF-1881:11[221]). His challenging analysis of slavery establishes credible connections between three overlapping trends in the development of Western culture, customarily associated with humankind's *progress*, which transform the nature of slavery. Nietzsche argues that the yearning for liberty, which coincides with advances in rationality, also coincides with the development of the money-economy and that these three facets of industrial culture combined make slavery more pervasive, more sophisticated, and more deeply incorporated into the social fabric of modernity than ever before. Persistent denials and misconstruals of slavery have only had the effect of fortifying it.

This process of incorporation entails, on Nietzsche's view, a combustive danger insofar as modern slavery acts as a mirror for the modern conscience. It brings up the following acute predicament: 'the entire past of the old culture was erected upon force, slavery, deception, error; but we, the heirs and inheritors of all these past things cannot decree our own abolition and may not wish away a single part of them' (HH: I, *State*, §452). Referring to the modern secular state in *Thus Spoke Zarathustra*, Nietzsche alleges that 'whatever it has it has stolen' (Z: I, *New Idol*). According to Nietzsche, this presents a twofold issue of evaluating such history and deciding how to move on from it. In *Slavery's Capitalism* (2016), Beckert and Rockman elaborate on the problematic aspects of this dilemma:

> A scholarly revolution over the past two decades ... has recognized slavery as the foundational American institution, organizing the nation's politics, legal structures, and cultural practices with remarkable power to determine the life chances of those moving through society as black or white. An outpouring of scholarship ... leaves little doubt that the new United States was a 'slaveholding republic'. In comparison, only a small segment of recent scholarship has grappled with the economic impact of slavery. Only in the past several years has scholarship on finance, accounting, management, and technology allowed us to understand American economic development as 'slavery's capitalism'. And only now is there enough momentum to leverage some basic facts ... into a fundamental rethinking of American history itself. (Beckert and Rockman 2016:2–3)

Beckert and Rockman's assessment resonates with a number of earlier notable studies. Developing on Randall Robinson's argument put forward in *The Debt: What America Owes to Blacks* (2000), Feagin argues that in the similar fashion to the way Europe benefited from slavery, 'today ... prosperity, long life expectancies and high standard of living of white Americans are significantly rooted in centuries of exploitation and impoverishment of African Americans and other Americans of Colour' (Feagin 2004:50). Analysing various and wide-ranging estimates of the potential financial cost of nearly 250 years of institutionalised slavery and nearly 400 years of racial oppression, which he equates with 'theft and ill-gotten gains' in the US, Feagin concludes:

> [E]ven by rough calculations, the sum total of the worth of all the black labor stolen by whites through the means of legal slavery, legal segregation, and contemporary racial discrimination is truly staggering—many trillions of dollars. The worth of all that labour, taking into account lost interest over time and putting it in today's dollars, is perhaps in the range of $5 to $24 trillion. (Feagin 2004:55)

Nietzsche would argue that financial compensation alone would not extinguish the debt, which is not financial in nature and would, furthermore, represent the perpetuation of the values which once underpinned slavery. The real extent of the dependency on slavery, both present and historic, is not yet fully acknowledged. This problem might be compounded by the failure to have built anything truly worthy on its foundations, which would transcend slavery as a historical legacy, disabling its antagonistic crux and helping to craft a plausible way forward. Nietzsche's criterion for constructing the worthy future is 'to do something that would make the thought of life even a hundred times more appealing' (GS: §278). Equally, 'only he who constructs the future has a right to judge the past':

> When the past speaks it always speaks as an oracle: only if you are an architect of the future and know the present will you understand it. (UM: II, *UDHL*, §6)

Slavery reflects the deep-seated guilt associated with the brutality of early capitalism, which remains an unpaid debt. The predicament it creates is that modern society, which has come to abhor the notions of exploitation and slavery, remains deeply complicit in their continued existence. Nietzsche suggests that in such a predicament, one's enjoyment of the present would be accompanied by a 'profound weariness', as he gazes into the future for he knows 'in advance that his posterity will suffer from the past as he does' (HH: II, *WS*, §249). Such weight, which is liable to increase over time, Nietzsche warns us, is well capable of petrifying the modern conscience:

> Man ... braces himself against the great and ever greater pressure of what is past: it pushes him down or bends him sideways, it encumbers his steps as a, dark, invisible burden which he can sometimes appear to disown and which in traffic with his fellow men he is only too glad to disown. (UM: II, *UDHL*, §1)

Klossowski suggests that Nietzsche's analysis anticipated the critical juncture where 'the thought of the *Vicious Circle* will become ... intolerable' (Klossowski 1997:160). This growing invisible burden also contains a radicalising and self-destructive nexus (BGE: §242). Left to its own devices, it may lead to a scenario where the ineradicable logic of exploitation would turn against its most ardent deniers, who would become its new target: 'equality of rights could all too easily be changed into inequality and in violating rights' (BGE: §212). As Gianni Vattimo perceptively observes in *Nihilism and Emancipation*:

> If we do not want—as indeed we cannot, except at the risk of *terrible wars of extinction*—to give way to the temptation of resurgent fundamentalisms grounded in race, religion, or even the defence of individual national cultures against invasion by 'foreigners', we will have to imagine a humanity with at least some of the characteristics of Nietzsche's *Übermensch*. (Vattimo 2003:55)

Nietzsche's critical and incredibly uncomfortable insight in relation to slavery remains this: one does not belong to either a nation, a country, a state, a social class or to a particular stratum within the political and economic architecture of society as deeply and as fundamentally as one belongs to a rank—a physiological rank. For as long as we insist on breaking intellectual and political spears in the meaningless battles of nationalism, chasing the chimeras of legal emancipation and economic domination, we are doomed to continue along the path of needless and meaningless exploitation in the service of the reactive power interests. This is the reason why Nietzsche urges us to think about 'the configuration of society without melancholy' (NF-1871:10[1]). This requires reflecting on the forms of subordination that would be commensurate with the task of 'the 'preservation of life and the enhancement of its value' (AC: §7) in a manner that would promise and guarantee 'life a future' (AC: §58).[465]

At the same time, however, Nietzsche's analysis posits a significant challenge: only when 'the slave-like valuations', which over the centuries have presided over the most abhorrent forms of slavery by slaves, have been overturned, might a different meaning and understanding of slavery become possible (see NF-1884:25[174], [211]). Any constructive discussion of the new forms of subordination has to break free from the value propositions of slave morality, which place material considerations atop of the agenda in order to debilitate the spirit. Nietzsche's argument suggests that where values, wealth, achievement and progress are measured primarily in financial terms any structure of subordination will inevitably be geared to 'earning a great deal of money' (UM: III, *SE*, §6) and, as such, incompatible with fostering cultural advancement. He argues that the 'aesthetic justification of life' (BT: §5) creates different demands on individuals' aptitude and reveals a more authentic structure of rank-ordering and subordination. As Drochon notes, 'Nietzsche believes … demand for a new cultural aristocracy … arises from a universal need to have one's life (aesthetically) justified' (Drochon 2016:95). Without finding new modalities of subordination that would entail a wholesale revaluation of values, 'a host of the most astonishing operations will no longer be capable of achievement and the world will be the poorer' (HH: I, *State*, §441). Nietzsche insists that, in order to gain mastery over slavery and to exploit it, to get to a position from which exploitation, as an irreducible existential attribute, could itself be exploited, directed, and bent to one's will, it is imperative that we be inserted into the very thick of slavery (NF-1881:11[221]).

These considerations merit inviting Nietzsche into the current debate on slavery as part of the broader conversation around development and inequality. Nietzsche's discussion raises probing questions, which challenge our perceptions of slavery and urge

---

[465] See Drochon's insightful discussion of the future of slavery in Drochon 2016:90–95.

us to stop trivialising the thorny and uncomfortable issues associated with it. Nietzsche's discussion of slavery highlights such aspects of it as are not regularly considered within the prevailing discourses on political economy.[466] Nietzsche compels us not to be so *blasé* as to believe that exploitation and slavery are relics of the past, challenging us to recognise the impact which slavery in different forms—both past and present—continues to make on the world. Nietzsche's own scrutiny of slavery translates into a pressing call for reconsidering our conditions of existence with the view to finding commensurate ways of living with each other in the world we inhabit. Growing empirical evidence attests to the prescient nature of Nietzsche's analysis and justifies its closer critical consideration. Although it has been suggested that 'the arguments Nietzsche puts forward in defence of slavery seem alien […] to us […] because they run counter to our ingrained liberal and democratic sentiments' (Ansell-Pearson 1994:78), his views need examining precisely for that reason.

---

[466] Drochon highlights the tendency in the secondary literature to 'detach the physical and political' aspects of slavery 'from its more psychological or internal ones', on which Nietzsche focuses his attention (Drochon 2016:95).

6 Nietzsche on the Perils of Debt

Introduction

Conceptual scrutiny of debt represents the lynchpin of Nietzsche's political economy. As Deleuze points out, Nietzsche considered debt to be 'the archetype of social organisation' (Deleuze 1983:135). Nietzsche argues that the debtor-creditor relationship, one of the first things to be inscribed into human consciousness (see GM: II, §4, §8, §20), is galvanised by the moralisation of the concept of debt under the auspices of Judeo-Christianity (GM: II, §21), which embeds the latter as the key structuring property of the entire 'economy of human relations' (Sedgwick 2007:51). The moralised concept of debt—the ancestral capital corrupted by the valuations of slave morality—inaugurates the 'slaves' revolt in morality' (BGE: §95) and comes to denote the inverted axis of power (GM: I, §7). It transforms the intergenerational capital, represented by the pre-moralised and proactive idea of 'ancestral debt' (NF-1888:14[221]) into the 'reactive pathos' of secular debt (GM: II, §11), which encumbers modernity and drastically alters the course of humankind's development (GM: II, §20).

The *Genealogy* represents Nietzsche's critical engagement with debt as a value in an attempt to elucidate the origins of the 'contemptible money-economy' (UM: III, SE, §4), which spreads to every corner of the 'industrial world' (see HH: I, §440; D: §175) and which Nietzsche critiques extensively in his earlier work. Although *the Genealogy* can be regarded as the centrepiece of Nietzsche's discussion of debt (Cooper 2008:622), his engagement with the subject can be traced to much earlier *Nachlass* notes as well as to some of the early published work. Throughout his *oeuvre*, Nietzsche contends that it is not debt alone that emerges as an offspring of Judeo-Christianity into the 'haste and overexcitedness of secularisation' (NF-1874:35[12]) but that the entire 'great world of money' (HH: *AOM*, §25) grows on its foundation. As Lazzarato surmises in *The Making of the Indebted Man* (2012):

> Money is first of all debt-money, created ex nihilo, which has no material equivalent other than its power to destroy/create social relations and, in particular, modes of subjectivation. 'Debt-money' or 'credit money' ... is not attached to any material standard, nor does it refer to any substance except for the debt relation itself. (Lazzarato 2012:35, 97)

In *Untimely Meditations* and *Human, All Too Human*, Nietzsche critically engages with the broad range of effects of the money-economy, which proliferates through 'money-making' (UM: III, SE, §6) and the 'trade in money' (HH: II, WS, §285). These early insights are expanded upon in *Daybreak* and in *The Gay Science* prior to being subjected to Zarathustra's perspectival scrutiny. Critique of the money-economy then circles back on itself in *the Genealogy*, where 'Nietzsche *returns* to the double theme of indebtedness and redemption' (Shapiro 1994:368) and synthesises it into a comprehensive *critique of debt* as a tool of slave morality and its role in modern political economy. The *Genealogy* provides, therefore, an important interpretative key to understanding Nietzsche's critique of the money-economy, particularly where the connection between debt and the 'money-economy', as part of the same complex of power relations, is concerned (D: §204).

This chapter examines key aspects of Nietzsche's thinking on debt across his corpus. Peeling away the semiotic coats, Nietzsche's genealogical inquiry traces the concept of debt back to the point where the conceptual boundaries between debt and equity begin to blur and society appears as a communal enterprise in which all members—past, present and future—were acknowledged as stakeholders (HH: I, HMS, §41).[468] Commending us to be 'more minded of the demands of equity and more willing to lend a helping hand' (HH: II, AOM, §304), Nietzsche engages with the notion of *intergenerational capital*. His inquiry is more accurately understood in terms of tracing its transformations from expressing active power and reflecting a purposeful community bound together across its ranks, to debt as the representation of reactive power in secular modernity, which fractures the social whole, encumbers the individual and society and 'imperils the future' by perpetuating squandering and excess (HH: II, WS, §286).

Scrutinising debt as *inverted capital* provides Nietzsche with a substantively different frame of reference for developing a critique of its pivotal role within the contours of the 'industrial world' (HH: I, State, §440). The central focus of Nietzsche's examination of debt concerns the nature of its values. Shifting the focus away from the instrumental analysis of debt, as a mechanism through which commerce flows, to the examination of a broader range of its forms in modern society with a direct focus on its function as a repository of values of slave morality adds a potent analytical lens, currently missing from the prevailing perspectives.[469]

Scope of Critique

This chapter builds on the insights articulated most prominently by Derek Hillard (2002), Peter Sedgwick (2007), Ian Cooper (2008), and Nigel Dodd (2012), who emphasise Nietzsche's focus on the interchangeability between the domains of 'material debts and moral guilt' (Hillard 2002:50). In particular, Cooper and Dodd argue that one of Nietzsche's critical insights was to grasp the frequently intractable interchangeability between the 'moral economy of debt' and 'the moral economy of guilt', such that guilt may readily manifest itself in the shape of 'financial debt' (Dodd 2012:62; Cooper 2008:606).[470] As Nietzsche puts it, 'money is something that slips through everyone's

---

[468] See Hillard 2002:45–46 and Malko's discussion in *Economics and Its Discontents*, 2015:24–26.
[469] See TI: *Socrates*, §11 on the importance of the frame of reference to avoid being bound by the system one sets out to critique.
[470] Shapiro goes further by suggesting that Nietzsche draws *equivalence* 'between *Schuld* (guilt) and *Schulden* (debts)'. See Shapiro 1994:369.

fingers', and therefore, one should learn to 'handle it and the money-changers with gloves on' (NF-1883:22[1]).

The main points of reference from which Nietzsche's critique of debt develops throughout his writings can be summarised in terms of debt's thoroughly political nature, debt as power and debt as a set of valuations. His central claim is that within the precepts of industrial culture of modernity, debt—both financial and spiritual—is primarily *political*. Debt, Nietzsche tells us, is by no means a delimited economic category of purely financial magnitude. It would be incorrect to conceive of debt as merely a part of some larger economic, financial, or industrial machine. Debt is its own enterprise and its economy is comprehensive, extending to all aspects of human existence. It is the whole multifaceted and layered industry, unlike any other industry we know. Debt is a figurative *quantification of power* that not only crosses the boundary between the economic and political realms but binds these two realities together with more force and viscosity than is commonly understood (see NF-1880:6[183]). In this respect, Nietzsche's analysis of debt as straddling the economic and the political domains is distinctly different from both the liberal economic thinking that habitually construes the political sphere as lying beyond the reach of debt, as well as from the prevailing Marxist notion of capital as 'an economic magnitude', Marx's acknowledgment of the 'social relation' aspect of capital notwithstanding (Nitzan and Bichler 2009:6, 28–29).

Debt, as money, displaces God as that which is capable of conjuring up 'the highest feeling of power' (D: §204). To facilitate the spread of its influence to every sphere of life, both public and private, and to valorise the profit logic of the money-makers, debt requires 'representation' (D: §203). Nietzsche posits debt and democracy as the twin secular extensions of the Judeo-Christian slave morality, which combine into the ethos of commercial society and industrial culture: 'what one formerly did 'for the sake of God' one now does 'for the sake of money' (D: §204).[471] In the late *Nachlass*, Nietzsche suggests that the basic nature of all trade can be understood in terms of debt, i.e., as a 'loan with the implication: give me back *more* than I give you' (NF-1887:11[215]).

Nietzsche's critique of money-making exposes the *cluster of values* that legitimise the capitalist social order and empower the agents, institutional and private, who become 'the patrons' of these values (UM: IV, *RWB*, §6). Such values are embedded in the prevailing modern interpretations of what it means to live well in the world, and communicated through the narratives of economic growth, industriousness, and profit-seeking. They also inform the prevailing notions of 'progress' (NF-1885:36[48]), notwithstanding the mounting evidence of their damaging effects on the state of humankind—ranging from mental health (NF-1888:14[224]) to the environment (GM: III, §9)—which Nietzsche considers to be symptomatic of deeper 'physiological decadence' (NF-1888:14[224]) to which the growth of debt [financial and moral] is key. Nietzsche's other vital assertion is that the political economy of debt, in order to endure and to remain legitimate, must rely on a carefully crafted *subjectivity*, which is moulded

---

[471] See Dodd 2012:52–54.

from the earliest opportunity to the point of cultivating an obedient multitude of 'Lotus eaters'.[472] The modern essence of this Homeric allusion is aptly captured by Noam Chomsky in *The Common Good* (1998):

> The goal is a society in which the basic social unit is you and your television set. If the kid next door is hungry, it's not your problem. If the retired couple next door invested their assets badly and are now starving, that's not your problem either. (Chomsky 1998:29)

Triangulating the aforementioned propositions, Nietzsche demonstrates that the over-reliance of industrial society on debt is both inevitable and a clear symptom of its growing physiological exhaustion. A key manifestation of this declining trend, conjoined with the growth of debt and its enslaving propensities, is the pervasive crisis of leadership and governance of the global political economy (NF-1888:25[1]). In order to appreciate the scope and the depth of Nietzsche's critique more fully, it is important to start by considering his 'debts to the ancients' (TI: *Ancients*, §1).[473]

Debts 'to the Ancients'

Nietzsche's critique of the modern money-economy is deeply rooted in the insights of Plato and Aristotle.[474] It builds on the understanding of the complex interplay between the money-making and democratic politics, as mediated through debt, which encompasses a wide array of meanings and functions.[475] Furthermore, Plato's *Republic* and

---

472 The image of the 'Lotus eaters' is used by Plato in his discussion of the 'democratic man' in *The Republic* (561[e]-562[d]). Plato's reference is to Homer's *Odyssey*, Book IX, [80–105].
473 This chapter focuses primarily on Plato's *Republic* (Books VIII and IX) and Aristotle's *Politics*. For ease of use, citations from *Republic* can be accessed at http://www.perseus.tufts.edu (last accessed Feb. 27, 2023) and referenced by their section number, e.g., 'R:575[a]'. All cited passages are cross-referenced against Henry Desmond Pritchard Lee's (Penguin Books, 1905) and Benjamin Jowett's (CreateSpace Independent Publishing Platform, 2018) translations of Plato's *Republic*. Citations from Plato's *Laws* can also be accessed at http://www.perseus.tufts.edu and are referenced as, e.g., 'L:743[d-e]'. Similarly, citations from Aristotle's *Politics* are referenced as, e.g., 'P:1157[b]', and citations from the *Nicomachean Ethics* are referenced as e.g., 'NE:1129[a]; both texts can be accessed at http://www.perseus.tufts.edu). For a more extensive analysis, see Safronov 2022, 'Nietzsche, Plato and Aristotle on Priests and Moneymakers', *Nietzsche-Studien*.
474 See Shapiro's argument that 'Nietzsche was working under the spell of Plato and Aristotle' (Shapiro 1994:361). Aristotle's influence, although not as pervasive as Plato's, is relevant in the context of Nietzsche's treatment of money, interest and debt (Langholm 1984:128–134; Kattel 2006:217–218; Sedlacek 2013:85; and Graeber 2011:290), as well as their entanglement with democratic politics (Graeber 2011:229).
475 For '*power*', see R:555[c], 566[a], and P:1257[b]–1258[b]); regarding '*subjectivity*', see R:553[c-d], 560[b-e], 561[e], 562[a-c],572[c], 576[d]; and regarding '*enslavement*', see R:555[e]. See also Ansell-Pearson 1994:43–44 and Andrew 1995:3–4 and 30.

Laws[476] as well as Aristotle's *Politics* supply significant conceptual material on which Nietzsche relies on in mapping out the crisis of the political economy of industrial culture.[477] Last but not least, Plato's reflections on the mechanisms of value inversion and Aristotle's penetrating criticism of 'false finance' or 'chrematistik' (Trever 1916:105 – 110) resonate through Nietzsche's critique of the industrial culture and its prime agents: the moneymakers. As discussed earlier, an important distinction is that Nietzsche's principal objection to democracy and equality is not in relation to their particular political forms. He is acutely aware of the different meanings these carried in ancient Athens as opposed to industrial modernity. His opposition to 'democracy, as a principle or doctrine of government', rather stems from the characterisation of it as a form of 'physiological degeneration', expressed in the ascent of 'herd morality', including the misarchism as well as the tyrannical propensities embedded in the democratic mindset (Drochon 2016:141).

Plato contends that oligarchy and democracy are *forms of excess*, symptomatic of 'the same malady', which becomes 'more widely diffused' in the democratic setting (R:563[e]-564[a]). Nietzsche actively engages with the underlying connection and continuity between oligarchy and democracy (NF-1884:26[282]; BGE: §242). Oligarchic 'insatiate lust for wealth and neglect of everything else for the sake of money-making' (R:556[c], 562[b]) persists through the transition to democracy and finds a new form of manifestation in the 'thirst for liberty' (R:562[c-d]).[478] Advancing the cause of liberty also facilitates the ascent of the money-makers to the positions of power (R:564[d]), while liberty becomes designated as the 'criterion of good' (R:555[c],562[b]).[479] In this new guise, 'the principle of appetite and avarice', installed as 'the great king of the soul' (R:553[c-d]; 564[e]), becomes pivotal in moulding the subjectivity of the members of the polis (R:562[c].[480] It also spreads to every corner of private and public life (R:562[e]), as does the influence of the money-makers, who, as Nietzsche notes, 'become the ruling power in the soul of humanity' (UM: IV, *RWB*, §5). The privileging of material well-being and the pursuit of wealth under the political premise of democracy (R:564[e]) gradually upends the social fabric of the polis (R:563[e]-564[c]):

---

476 Plato's final dialogue, *Laws*, develops on many aspects of the economic discussion Plato brought up previously in *Republic*.
477 See Z: IV, *Kings*; BGE: §30; EH: *BT*, §2; and *Clever*, §10 as well as NF-1884:25[344], 1885:37[14], 1887:9[184], 1888:14[182], and 1888:25[1]). See also Drochon 2016:167.
478 See Aristotle's discussion in P:1157[b]-1258[b].
479 See Plato's (L:743[d-e]) and Aristotle's discussion in P:1258[b] and in *The Nicomachean Ethics*, NE: 1121[b].
480 See Raymond Geuss concerning Plato's idea of how a particular 'notion of the good' becomes a seabed of values and helps mould particular conditions of existence in *Changing the Subject*, 2017:52 – 54. In Plato's words, 'the principle of appetite and avarice', as 'the great king of the soul' enslaves 'the rational and high-spirited principles' by allowing 'to calculate and consider nothing but the ways of making more money from a little and the other to admire and honour nothing but riches and rich men, and to take pride in nothing but the possession of wealth and whatever contributes to that' (R:553[c-d]).

> These money-makers with down-bent heads, pretending not even to see … but inserting the sting of their money into any of the remainder who do not resist, and harvesting from them in interest as it were a manifold progeny of the parent sum, foster the drone and pauper element in the state. And they are not willing to quench the evil as it bursts into flame. (R:555[e]-556[a])[481]

Plato intimates that the democratic social setting is neither stable, nor durable. It becomes increasingly dependent on the 're-naming' of values in favour of the 'braggart discourses' (R:560[d]), which Nietzsche refers to as 'slandering and re-baptising' of old values (NF-1887:9[173]). When the latter 'prevail in the conflict' of ideas, they help to transform democratic subjects into the 'willing slaves and men of naught' (R:561[e], 562[a-d]). Gradually, the doses of excess in the form of 'magnificent and costly rites' (R:560[e]) and the use of debt increase to mask the deteriorating trajectory and to conceal the degeneration of the leaders (R:562[d-e]).[482] Plato associates particular danger to society with the 'rulers, who owe their offices to their wealth' (R:555[c]). Lacking in moderation, they are capable neither of fiscal prudence nor of supplying aspirational values to the members of the polis (P:1263[b]). Instead, they encourage excess and 'wasting of substance' in the young, while 'their object is, by lending money, to become still richer' and augment their power (R:555[c-e]).[483] This leads to the creation of 'the fiercest extremes of servitude' from 'the height of liberty' (R:563[a]-564[a]).

On a more practical level, Nietzsche shares Plato's and Aristotle's misgivings concerning lending at interest of any kind (L:742[c]; 743[d]; 915[d-e]). He concurs with their insistence that any commercial lending should—by law—be transacted squarely at the *risk of the lender* (R:556[a-b])[484] to prevent economic growth nourished by debt (see L:743[d-e], 744[a], 850[a]; P:1257[b]) and to preclude lending from descending into usury (see Sedlacek 2013:85–86) and becoming the 'foundation of false finance … pursued as a science of gain' (Trever 1916:101–102).[485] Furthermore, considering debt's temporalities, Nietzsche shares Plato's and Aristotle's intuition that excessive borrowing from a speculative future risks 'exhausting the soil at the expense of the future and imperilling society' (HH: II, *WS*, §286).

Nietzsche does not simply give Plato and Aristotle's concerns a modern voice. Their insights inform Nietzsche's intuition to consider debt as a *value*, in the sense of a multifaceted socio-cultural and economic phenomenon, rather than a mere instrument of

---

481 See NF-1871:10[1], GSt), UM: III, *SE*, §§6–7, and D: §175.
482 For Nietzsche's ideas, which show considerable affinity with Plato's, see HH: II, §317; WS: §209; and SZ: IV, *Kings*.
483 Plato argues that those, who rise to the top in such systems prioritise staying in power. When such leaders run out of means for placating the public, '*impeachments, litigation and lawsuits*' flow (R:565[c]), and when these run their course, these leaders will seek to make *wars* so as to divert attention and resources to an external cause exploited to their advantage (R:556[e],557[e], and 575[a]).
484 See L:742[c], 849[e]-850[a], and 915[e] as well as Aristotle's P:1263[b], which denounces the system set up in 'flattery' of the creditors.
485 See P:1258[b-c] and L:744[a]). Aristotle's views on interest and usury (see P:1258[b-c]) mirror those of Plato, as expressed in *Laws* (See L:742[c], 743[d], and 921[c]). See also Graeber 2011:194–195.

finance. Plato's dialogues connect debt and the origins of justice (R:331[c]-332[c-d]; 333[c]) and posit it as a medium of intergenerational continuity (R:330[b], 506[e]-507[a]). Importantly, Plato's deliberations on debt are couched in the proto-Christian terminology of 'good and evil' in that 'good is a debt a just man owes to his friends and evil is the debt he owes to his enemies' (R:332[d]). Plato and Aristotle also problematise the precarious nature relationship between debt and growth. Their insight that economic growth (see P:1257[b]; L:850[a]), let alone growth sustained by debt, does not provide the answer to the question of how to live well (see R:555[c]; L:744[a])[486] and their distinct sense of unease in relation to the entanglement of debt and democracy in times of economic turmoil, help Nietzsche to problematise the inverse relationship, resulting from the valuations of slave morality, between the physiological health of society (L:744[a]), on the one hand, and the level of its indebtedness or, to be more precise, the extent to which debt becomes a burden inhibiting its spiritual development, on the other (EH: *Destiny*, §5). Last but not least, Nietzsche's take on modernity's 'double movement in democratization' (Appel 1999:130) appears more perilous than Plato's and Aristotle's conceptions of *kyklos* would suggest.[487]

Conceptual Framework

The *Genealogy* (1887) is generally regarded as one of Nietzsche's 'finest books' and the most 'important and systematic' work within his *oeuvre*.[488] At the same time, it remains one of the most heavily contested of his writings (Kail 2011:214): underexplored aspects of his message continue to surface. At present, no consistent reading of the *Genealogy* through the lens of the political economy of debt exists, although a number of authors note this critical connection.[489] This chapter contends that extrapolating from Nietzsche's critique of slave morality broadens our appreciation of the workings of debt within the fabric of modern society.

In drawing on the etymological connection between the German '*Schuld*' (guilt) and '*Schulden*' (debts) (GM: II, §4), Nietzsche advances a threefold conjecture: (a) debt is not primarily or exclusively economic; (b) mediation between debt's ontological and its secular meanings through the filter of slave morality forms a critical constitutive axis of the entire 'economy of human relations' (Sedgwick 2007:51); (c) debt denotes a system of valuations which cannot be reduced to the symmetry of exchange. In par-

---

[486] See Aristotle's *The Nicomachean Ethics*, 1097[b]-1098[a].
[487] See Lampert's excellent discussion of Nietzsche's misgivings re the perils of modern democracy in *Nietzsche's Task*, 2001:176–248.
[488] See Kaufmann's *Editor's Introduction* to Ecce Homo in *On the Genealogy of Morals and Ecce Homo*, Revised Edition, Kaufmann (Ed.), Vintage 2010:201, as well as Ansell-Pearson's *Editor's Introduction* to *On The Genealogy of Morality*, CUP, 1994: ix.
[489] See Andrew 1995:3–5; Deleuze and Guattari (1975, 2013); Graeber (2011); Lazzarato (2012); and Dyson (2014:88).

ticular, 'the mediation between the ontological status of debt and the sociology of debt', as a mechanism for 'the production of truths about the history of debt and indebtedness' (Roitman 2005:75), serves to obscure debt's multiple functions and identities in modern life. A critical passage in *Daybreak* entitled 'The delusion of a moral world-order' demonstrates the effect of interchangeability of debt's meaning:

> There is no eternal necessity, which demanded that every debt ('Schuld') be repaid—it has been a dreadful and to only a minuscule extent useful delusion that such a thing existed:—just as it is a delusion that *everything is debt which is felt as such*. It is not things, but opinions about things that have absolutely no existence, which have so deranged mankind! (D: §563, my emphasis)

'Schuld' in the above passage has as clear a meaning in the sense of 'guilt' as it would in the sense of a 'debt'. This is one of the reasons, on Nietzsche's view, why debt is often misconstrued. He problematises the 'moral world-order' which grows out of the profound repositioning of concepts and meanings in the course of which not only the positions of 'things' and 'opinions' are reversed but the respective meanings and valuations associated with these 'things' and 'opinions' are inverted. As a result, disembodied 'opinions about things' become invested with meaning that confers on them the power of valuations. Nietzsche suggests that the combination of these two displacements results in a revaluation of values such as was achieved by the slave revolt in morality. Following Nietzsche's logic, it becomes possible to see how debt lends itself to 'a false and prejudiced interpretation' by those who seek to 'secure advantage by doing so' (GM: II, §11).[490]

Genealogy of Debt and Freedom

Nietzsche's discussion of debt is intricately connected to his reflections on one of philosophy's oldest conundrums—freedom. In *Human, All Too Human*, Nietzsche asserts that we 'can only *dream* ourselves free and not make ourselves free' (see HH: II, AOM, §33, §39; WS, §9).[491] He contends that in the first instance, 'we are unknown to

---

[490] See Staten's important contribution to this issue in *Nietzsche's Voice*, 1990:54.
[491] This is Nietzsche's consistent position from his earliest notes in the *Nachlass* to the final ones: 'Man has the right to nothing; he has obligations for the benefits he has received ... even if he gave his life, he would not give back everything he has received' (NF-1887:11[270]); See also NF-1870:8[57]). See also Nietzsche's discussion in BGE: §19 and §21; TI: *Skirmishes*, §38; and AC: §54. In *Surface and the Abyss* (2010), Peter Bornedal proposes an alternative interpretation and argues that Nietzsche narrates a story 'that (phylo-genetically) starts in our prehistoric past, and presupposes the existence of an original freedom, which is gradually restricted, finally resulting in the psychological crippling, the systematic destruction, of contemporary man' (Bornedal 2010:405). Whilst very helpful in terms of investigating the origins of consciousness (Bornedal's prime objective), this interpretation falls short of accounting for what Nietzsche considers to be a natural physiological hierarchy.

ourselves and with good reason' (GM: *Preface*, §1).[492] This is sufficient, on Nietzsche's view, to characterise our fundamental existential predicament: even 'a free-thinking Inca noticed that the constant wandering of the sun was a sign of bondage' (NF-1870:5[56]).[493] Nietzsche's *Nachlass* note from 1881 further suggests that 'we are all slaves, even if we wanted to be dreamers' (NF-1881:291).[494] He insists, however, on treating 'origin' and 'purpose' as 'separate problems' (GM: II, §12).[495] In consequence, the genesis of our being here is not as relevant as what we do with being here.[496] In other words, the 'origin' or origins—i.e., our being here—is a matter of pre-history which is inaccessible to our cognition:

> [N]o one is responsible for man's being there at all, for his being such-and-such, or for his being in these circumstances or in this environment. The fatality of his essence is not to be disentangled from the fatality of all that has been and will be … the mode of being may not be traced back to a *causa prima* (TI: Errors, §8)

In contrast, 'purpose' is a question of history, which we make happen. Equally, what or who may be designated as the *causa prima*—a symbolic projection of our being strangers to ourselves—is of secondary importance as opposed to the values such conception may come to embody and represent (UM: II, *UDHL*, §9).

Acknowledging that 'humanity' displays a general sense of 'being indebted towards its beginnings' (GM: II, §20),[497] Nietzsche nonetheless maintains that 'the *causa prima* of man and the beginning of the human race' could mean a number of things ranging from our ancestors, to nature, 'animals or trees' (D: §31), God or even 'existence in general' (GM: II, §20–21).[498] To whom or to what specifically the debt is owed acquires significance for structuring human experience only once 'the germinating sensation of indebtedness' (GM: II, §8) is assigned symbolic meaning (GM: II, §13). This has profound implications for Nietzsche's ideas on freedom which, much like debt, becomes a barometer of life's value, 'measured in individuals as in nations' alike (TI: *Skirmishes*, §38). Freedom, taken to mean the extent of resistance to the condition of indebtedness, which has to be 'constantly overcome' (e.g., Prometheus) amid 'the effort it costs to stay aloft' (TI: *Skirmishes*, §38), becomes a critical conceptual filter that crystallises one's

---

[492] See Gemes' instructive essay *We Remain of Necessity Strangers To Ourselves*' (2006:191–208).
[493] As Roitman surmises in *Fiscal Disobedience* (2005), 'the truth of the subject's condition is found … in this original state of dependence' (Roitman 2005:75).
[494] This echoes a letter Nietzsche penned almost fifteen years prior: 'if a slave dreams in prison that he is free and released from his bondage, who will be so hard-hearted to wake him up and tell him that it is a dream?' (BVN-1867:551).
[495] See Ansell-Pearson, *Introduction* to the revised edition of *On The Genealogy of Morality*, CUP, 2007: xx.
[496] See Poellner's influential exposition in *Nietzschean Freedom*, 2009:157.
[497] See May's discussion in *Nietzsche on Freedom and Autonomy*, Gemes and May (Eds.), 2009: xix–xx.
[498] See Dombowsky 2004:40 ('… for Nietzsche, when all is said and done, there is neither free will, nor unfree will in itself'), and Karzai 2019:99 (Nietzsche's 'interpretation of will is purely sociological').

character, determines its worth and denotes the 'pathos of distance' (see HH: I, *HMS*, §107; Z: II, *Self-Overcoming*; BGE: §19, §212).[499] Nietzsche's freedom is properly understood as an unceasing battle one must wage not to sink into debt. Following Nietzsche's method of inferring from the opposite (NF-1881:11[330]), his discussion of freedom is instructive for understanding his meaning of debt.

Nietzsche insists that if freedom remains something that one merely *desires*, one *does not and cannot* possess it: freedom can only be conquered, and it has to be wrestled from the Gods.[500] Furthermore, he argues that 'the claim for independence, for free development, for *laisser aller* is pressed most hotly by the very people for whom no reins would be too strict' (TI: *Skirmishes*, §41). Since freedom is 'a result of fitness' and a 'facility in self-direction' (WP: §705), when it concerns 'the socio-political domain', for the majority, freedom 'must be held in check the longest'.[501] This is so because under the label of 'freedom' hides 'the most terrible and thorough desire of man, his drive for power' (NF-1885:1[33]). This riotous drive, although effective when 'only getting rid seems the goal' (NF-1887:9[145a]), is incapable of building anything worthwhile in its wake: its destructive properties are not complemented by creative and moderating ones. This one-sidedness, which conceals propensity for excess (HH: II, *AOM*, §186), prepares fertile ground for the rise of 'petty politics' (Drochon 2016:156–160), on the one hand, and of the money-economy, on the other. These twin tendencies enable the 'crudest and most evil forces' (UM: III, *SE*, §4) to ascend from within the herd by exploiting its 'power instinct'—amplifying it at first and eventually turning it against the herd (GM: II, §21). This prompts Nietzsche's conjecture that 'the theory of freedom of will is an invention of ruling classes' (HH: II, *WS*, §9). Through the precepts of slave morality, they seek to *liberate the unfree* by creating a powerful impression of 'feeling no new chains' (HH: II, *WS*, §10). This, Nietzsche suggests, becomes the new manner of exploitation under the auspices of industrial culture.[502]

Nietzsche's views on freedom contain considerable information concerning the expository power of debt, which is capable of illuminating 'the whole highly complicated system of antagonisms that constitute the "modern world"' (BVN-1874:398), including its many 'hidden contradictions' (Conway 2002:234). By its presence as much as through its absence, debt—much like the notions of 'free will or unfree will' (see BGE: §21; AC: §15) —defines our world and imprints on life in a myriad of ways. Derrida, who builds on Nietzsche's approach, surmises that 'the ritual circle of debt', which 'reconstitutes itself

---

[499] See engaging discussion of the pertinent aspects of Nietzsche's concept of freedom in Pippin's 'How to Overcome Oneself', (2009:75–77) and Owen's 'Autonomy, Self-Respect and Self-Love' (2009:210–213) in *Nietzsche on Freedom and Autonomy* (2009).
[500] See BGE: §260; TI: *Skirmishes*, §38; AC: §54. Gemes and Janaway helpfully elaborate on the distinction in Nietzsche's views on freedom in relation to agency and as an existential condition, see 'Nietzsche on Free Will, Autonomy and the Sovereign Individual', 2006:321–357.
[501] See HH: II, *WS*, §9; I, *State*, §460; Z: II, *Great Events*, and Nietzsche's discussion of the 'types of the will to power in disguise' in NF-1886:7[6].
[502] See Abbey 2000:24–25, Dombowsky 2004:40, and de Almeida 2007:118.

according to the laws of the unconscious', gradually envelops ethical, legal, political and economic structures through the array of its multiple and compresent manifestations (Derrida 1991:16–26). He argues that the task of understanding the power of debt is linked to developing an understanding of its sprawling and overlapping symbolism (Derrida 1991:23). This is consistent with Nietzsche's focus on the manner of interaction between the material and non-material forms of debt in their capacity as repositories of values. By becoming normative, these expedite humankind's transition towards modern, secular industrial culture. Deleuze and Derrida argue that Nietzsche's understanding of debt as a value is particularly relevant within the context of a society that 'is not exchangist' but is rather subject to the 'regime of debt' (Deleuze and Guattari 1975:187). Nietzsche's genealogy of debt, on their view, allowed to raise the problem of debt in the most 'incisive fashion' (Deleuze and Guattari 1975:192–193).

Debt's Past, Present, and Future

Nietzsche argues that debt's tremendous power in terms of structuring human experience derives from it being one of the first notions—a 'primeval idea' (GM: II, §4)—to be inscribed in language and in human thought more generally (GM: II, §8). What makes debt so inscrutable, on Nietzsche's view, is that while 'the consciousness of being in debt' is itself prehistorical, debt is by no means an ahistorical phenomenon (GM: II, §20). Crossing the boundary between pre-history and history is one of the factors that obscures the meaning of debt. It stands in the shadows before history and at the threshold where history begins debt becomes a vital narrator of history as we know it. In the words of the British economist Alfred Mitchell-Inness, who explored the historical origins of money, debt, and credit:

> From the earliest days of which we have historical records, we are in the presence of a law of debt ... The sanctity of an obligation is, indeed, the foundation of all societies not only in all times, but at all stages of civilization; and the idea that to those whom we are accustomed to call savages, credit is unknown and only barter is used, is without foundation. From the merchant of China to the Redskin of America; from the Arab of the desert to the Hottentot of South Africa or the Maori of New Zealand, debts and credits are equally familiar to all, and the breaking of the pledged word, or the refusal to carry out an obligation is held equally disgraceful (Mitchell-Innes 1913:391).

Mitchell-Innes' theory of the credit origins of money can be juxtaposed with Mauss' investigation of *The Gift* (1925). Both theories represent a case of selective history told from a particular perspective, but both—one through the vernacular of *debt* and the other through the narrative of *gift-giving*—also speak of the critical *social relation* that underlies and enables the forms in which exchange of objects takes place. In quite a similar vein, although Nietzsche's narrative of 'Schulden' and 'Schuld' may be challenged in relation to the occasionally inconsistent historical evidence, it remains more difficult to fault his psychological intuitions about the effects of the 'moralisation of debt' (GM: II, §21) and, more importantly, the reasons why such moralisation was possible and why it prevailed over humankind's gradual march towards 'atheism' as 'a sort of second innocence' that, by breaking the shackles of debt, could have signified a return to the original, pre-debt, state (GM: II, §20). Why was the psychological image of that possibility itself indispensable to forging the 'iron impossibility' of discharging the debts (GM: II, §21)?

Nietzsche conjectures that debt is most commonly associated with debt owed to a 'primeval ancestor' (GM: II, §22).[503] The notion of the ancestor represents a critical juncture, connecting the present with both the past and the future, which is 'promised by the past' (TI: *Ancients*, §4). Nietzsche's analysis of debt can be regarded as a reflection on the paradox of the 'fall of Man' masterfully formulated by Milton in *Paradise Lost* (1667):

> The debt immense of endless gratitude,
> So burthensome still paying, still to owe;
> Forgetful what from him I still received,
> And understood not that a grateful mind
> By *owing owes not, but still pays, at once*
> *Indebted and discharged; what burden then?* (4.42–57; my emphasis)[504]

This juncture, according to Nietzsche, lays out a spectrum of possible physiological states stretching from the 'triumphal yes to life' (TI: *Ancients*, §4) to the 'most radical rejection of its value' (NF-1885:2[127/1]). Projection of ancestral connection into the future denotes the sinew of intergenerational continuity. It can signify either an abundance of strength and resources available for 'paying the ancestral debt', or the lack thereof (NF-1888:14[221]). Ancestors, 'as powerful spirits', can either continue to 'lend their power' (GM: *Preface*, §3), or withhold it, in which case ancestral debt becomes a burden (GM: III, §9).

Nietzsche emphasises that the creditor-debtor relationship undergoes a vital transformation 'through interpretation into a relationship of the present generation to their forebears', partly because 'people recognize an indebtedness', but more importantly because the state of indebtedness becomes a revealing measure of physiological health and vitality of the present *vis-à-vis* the past as well as an assessment of its fitness for the challenge of the future (GM: II, §19). The proverbial ancestor becomes a mirror in which the present sees its own reflection not only to marvel at its current condition but also in order to discern the likely outlines of its future self. The symbolic ancestor becomes a conduit for both the empirical and the metaphysical (GM: *Preface*, §3). Some of Nietzsche's latest *Nachlass* notes echo some of his earliest in this regard.[505] He argues

---

503 The concept of debt owed to ancestors, Platonic in its connotations, is something that Nietzsche has been considering long before it made its way to *The Genealogy* in 1887 and can be traced to much earlier *Nachlass* notes from 1874; see in particular NF-1874:32[64]).
504 Citation of *Paradise Lost and Paradise Regained* is from the *Riverside Milton*, ed. Roy Flannagan, Boston, 1998.
505 See Nietzsche's discussion in NF-1875:11[14] and NF-1880:7[158].

that 'the highest reverence' before life is expressed in the obligation that 'one has to pay the debts of his ancestors', which forms the 'instinct of tradition' and determines its resistance to interruption (NF-1888:14[220]). This distinction becomes critical in the context of a 'weakening, degenerating' society that faces the prospect of 'imminent disintegration' (GM: III, §9). In such a society, the debts of the past as well as debts to the past become a burden and something that it tries to extricate itself from (GM: III, §9) embarking instead on the nihilistic path of 'squandering the capital of its forebears' (NF-1888:14[226]) for the sake of gilding the present (BT: §24) at the expense of the future.[506]

Now that Nietzsche's own perspectival eye is also 'focused in this direction' (GM: II, §8), he is concerned with tracing the transformation of 'the awareness of having debts' into 'the burden of unpaid debts', which expresses itself in 'the longing to have them settled' (GM: II, §20). This examination 'of the feeling of indebtedness towards a deity', which 'continued to grow', enables Nietzsche to make inferences pertinent to understanding the levers of secular debt. Reproaching earlier generations of 'genealogists of morality' (GM: II, §4), Nietzsche highlights the Janus-faced nature of debt: it is equally economic and non-economic, material and spiritual, temporal and timeless, tangible and ethereal, enticing and entrapping.[507] He conjectures that it is not always or exclusively material or financial debt that burdens and, equally, that the repayment of economic debt does not necessarily release one from bondage in the wider existential sense. Severing this vital conceptual connection between non-material (timeless) and material (temporal) debt disperses its meaning as a value, as a result of which our understanding of the phenomenon becomes fragmented and confused.

Separating these two aspects of the meaning of debt also allows the concept of debt to be appropriated by slave morality as denoting a 'condition of existence' (NF-1882:6[1,4]). Slave morality interprets debt in order to codify and assert the normativity of such existence—i.e., life as life in debt and life of the indebted—so as to advance its power objectives (NF-1887:10[186]). Nietzsche's discussion in the *Genealogy* in particular draws our attention to the fact that material debt's equally powerful *Doppelgänger* is to be found in the realm of slave morality. His analysis of this double aspect of debt demonstrates that the power of debt stems precisely from the *indeterminacy* conferred

---

[506] See Nietzsche's discussion in UM: III, *SE*, §4; HH: II, *WS*, §286; GM: *Preface*, §6; and EH: *Destiny*, §5.
[507] In this respect, Nietzsche's analysis of debt exhibits structural similarities with Marx's characterisation of the 'credit relationship': 'within the credit relationship, it is not the case that money is transcended in man, but that man himself is turned into money, or money is incorporated in him. Human individuality, human morality itself, has become both an object of commerce and the material in which money exists. Instead of money, or paper, it is my own personal existence, my flesh and blood, my social virtue and importance, which constitutes the material, corporeal form of the spirit of money. Credit no longer resolves the value of money into money but into human flesh and the human heart. Such is the extent to which all progress and all inconsistencies within a false system are extreme retrogression and the extreme consequence of vileness' (CW 3:215).

upon it by the interchangeability of material and moral debt.[508] Concentration of control over the production and dissemination of these two varieties of debt in the same hands gives rise to a ubiquitous set of reactive power relations within a carefully crafted normative perimeter.[509] From this premise, Nietzsche traces the transformation of debt from denoting a psychological disposition to designating a social relation, which plays a critical role in the formation of subjectivity (see HH: II, WS, §186).

Communal Origins of Debt

Nietzsche's discussion of the 'pre-historic' meanings of debt draws out several of its pertinent features (GM: II, §9). Effectively, debt represents a *communal obligation* (see Dodd 2014:14–26; Karzai 2019:151). It is a *social bond* and *medium of inter-generational continuity* that bind communities together (GM: II, §19). It entails an active notion of assisting a community's *progress and development*. It designates the *basis of the relationship* between the community as a whole and its individual members as well as between different communities (GM: II, §9). Debt is something that grows overtime but without necessarily becoming an encumbrance on either the community or its individual members. It also reflects the original conception of justice, which regulates the amount and the rate of production of debt, mediated via the community's hierarchical structure. These various characteristics, informed by a pre-history that 'exists at all times or could re-occur' (GM: II, §9), form the intricate 'economy of obligation', which serves as the 'continual groundbass' of the 'social structure of trust' (Muldrew 1998:7).

Although Nietzsche proceeds 'from the individual as a multiplicity' (NF-1884:26[141]), he is a communitarian thinker, concerned with rediscovering the 'community of life' (see Lemm 2020:176–180). Julian Young argues that there is no 'incompatibility between Nietzsche's 'individualism' and his 'communitarian' outlook which holds 'the flourishing of the community as a whole' as its highest value (Young 2015:5). Nietzsche is firmly opposed to 'everyone being their own priest' (NF-1888:15[23]) as, in the final count, 'the social instincts far outweigh the individual' (NF-1883:8[9]). As Rutherford points out, 'in a world in which everything is inextricably connected to everything else, and necessarily is as it is [...] there is no fact about our existence for which we are individually accountable' (Rutherford 2011:524).[510] In the same vein, debt is conceived of as an obligation owed by the community as a whole:

---

508 This bears uncanny resonance with the *particle-wave duality* dilemma, expressed by Einstein and Infeld in *The Evolution of Physics* (1938): 'It seems as though we must use sometimes the one theory and sometimes the other, while at times we may use either. We are faced with a new kind of difficulty. We have two contradictory pictures of reality; separately neither of them fully explains the phenomena of light [replace 'light' with 'debt' –DS], but together they do' (Einstein and Infeld 1938:278).
509 See Nietzsche's discussion of the means by which power of the priest is maintained and furthered in NF-1888:14[199].
510 See TI: *Errors*, §8 ('there is nothing besides the whole').

'all debts are common debts of the cooperative' in the same sense as that 'all members work together and enjoy the spoils of their work together' (NF-1883:8[9]). This line of thought can be traced to some of the earlier notes from the *Nachlass*.[511] In particular, these emphasise the designation of debt as promoting a *social bond* within the community, as opposed to alienating and estranging its individual members:

> Even if one were not linked to another by the old debt of gratitude or by the 'federal alliance' [*Bundesgenossenschaft*], and yet desired its help—and this is precisely our case: he would have *two things* to prove: above all, that his request would benefit others, or at least that no harm to the community shall result from it. Only then can one count on community's gratitude with certainty. (NF-1874:32[64])

Nietzsche maintains that ancestral debt is never fully repaid, nor is its full repayment deemed necessary or even desirable (D: §563). On the contrary, to 'extinguish the debt of former times' is tantamount to imagining 'a banished god' (NF-1880:7[158]), which would represent a disruptive development to the 'continuity of communal life' (NF-1883:8[9]). This is a critical consideration as ancestral debt, in Nietzsche's reckoning, is akin to capital (i.e., equity) from the viewpoint of the subsequent generations. As something 'left behind', ancestral debt cannot be claimed by the original contributors, nor removed from the communal balance sheet. As capital, ancestral debt can be either squandered or augmented (and, if necessary, overcome) by the current and future stakeholders.

Nietzsche points out that this logic also applies to a 'lawbreaker who has broken his contract and his promise to the whole' (GM: II, §9) and, in consequence, is treated as though the loan extended to him from the communal capital, by means of which he could participate in the latter, is cancelled or deemed as fully repaid (NF-1887:10[50]; HH: II, *WS*, §22). In other words, community reaffirms itself as "a unit" [*als "Einheit"*]' (NF-1888:14[196]) by cancelling the debts of its transgressor. Nietzsche stresses that the notion of debt in the dealings between the members of the community remains approximate and imprecise, where the amount of debt is concerned. In this context, the settling of debt necessarily involves an element of 'equity' and 'good will' in the dealings between the creditor and the debtor, who 'come to an understanding' (GM: II, §9). Furthermore, Nietzsche highlights the critical role of *rank-ordering* in limiting the growth of debt and constraining the power of the creditor: when it comes to discharging debts —good and bad—the strong 'come to an agreement among themselves' and 'force the weak to do the same' (GM: II, §9).[512] As a result, as Shapiro observes in *Nietzsche on*

---

[511] A *Nachlass* note from 1885 emphasises this aspect: 'All unity is only unity as organisation and cooperation—just as a human community is a unity—as opposed to an atomistic anarchy, as a pattern of domination that projects an image of a unity but is not a unity' (NF-1885:2[87]).

[512] Love comments that for Nietzsche, when the original exchange 'occurs between respective debtors and creditors, domination creates a unity, which conforms to nature' (Love 1986:176). Furthermore, Nietzsche's thinking on the role of hierarchy as critical in limiting growth, particularly fuelled by such artificial means as debt, draws very clearly on Aristotle's reflections on the benefits of an econom-

Gifts (1991), debt is not seen as a steadfast obligation but rather as operating within the context of social 'relations, in which terms are capable of being determined' outside the strictly monetary sphere of equivalents (Shapiro 1991:30).

Debt Forgiveness

One of Nietzsche's concerns, which extends his reflection on the communal origins of debt, is the manner in which the creditor-debtor system operates within a social setting in terms of its ability (understood as both capacity and willingness) to protect and, if necessary, to forgive transgressors. Understanding the factors contributing to the ability to forgive informs Nietzsche's appreciation of the desire to punish. This criterion is another finely balanced indicator of a society's physiological health and strength. Nietzsche tells us that in a thriving society, where the collective creditor is strong, the individual debtor would be forgiven out of the excess of strength, which expresses itself as mercy:

> As a community grows in power, it ceases to take the offence of the individual quite so seriously, because these do not seem to be as dangerous and destabilizing for the survival of the whole ... the wrongdoer is no longer 'deprived of peace' and cast out ... instead the wrongdoer is carefully shielded by the community from this anger, especially from that of the immediate injured party, and given protection. (GM: II, §10)

Nietzsche further observes that 'as the power and self-confidence of a community grows, its penal law becomes more lenient' and 'the 'creditor' always becomes 'more humane' just as 'the amount of his wealth determines how much injury he can sustain without suffering from it' (GM: II, §10).[513] In *Beyond Good and Evil*, Nietzsche insists that 'the noble human being [...] helps the unfortunate [...] not from pity, but prompted by an urge begotten by an excess of power' (BGE: §260). Finally, he argues that a thriving society can reach a point in its development where debt forgiveness becomes a desirable form of communal therapy, renewing the social bond. Nietzsche refers to debt forgiveness as 'the noblest luxury', that of 'letting the malefactors go unpunished', which is both 'a self-sublimation of justice' and an affirmation of strength (GM: II, §10). Here, 'justice is found in the territory' of an active sentiment: 'to be just is always a positive attitude' (GM: II, §11). Alan Schrift considers this characteristic of abundant strength to be 'in the foreground' of Nietzsche's vision of the 'noble economy', understood in terms of its 'feeling of fullness, of power that seeks to overflow, the happiness of high tension, the consciousness of wealth that would give ['schenken'] and bestow ['abgeben]' (Schrift 1996:198). Nietzsche is sympathetic to the idea of limiting creditor

---

ically 'static' society for the purposes of attaining true well-being as well as the dangers that 'chrematistik' represents in this context.

513 The creditor become 'rich enough for them: he is able to squander without becoming poor' (NF-1888:14[119]). See also GM: II, §10 ('parasites') and AC: §16.

power, including through debt forgiveness, and rightly considers it an element of the 'great economy of the preservation of the species' (GS: §1).[514]

The concept of forgiveness and its application become inverted in a society ruled by the 'reactive pathos' (GM: II, §11). Nietzsche argues that such a society would be structured in a manner that prioritises creditor protection and minimises, or rules out, that of the debtor: when a society 'is weakened or endangered, harsher forms' of the penal code and of creditor protection against the debtor 'will re-emerge' (GM: II, §10).[515] In this scenario, the creditor, for all his represented power, ends up the weaker counterparty in substance and requires legal protection *vis-a-vis* the transgressing debtors. Critically, in this setting, the creditor's power is represented by the narrative of debt and the values which legitimise, protect, and reinforce it. In this case, 'justice is found in the territory of reactive sentiment', which infuses it with the 'spirit of revenge' by the weak over the strong (GM: II, §11) and grounds it in the principle that 'one has to pay one's debts' (Graeber 2011:369). The logic that dictates that 'everything can be paid off, everything must be paid off', seeks to embed this inverted creditor-debtor relationship as normative (GM: II, §11). As Schrift suggests, Nietzsche thereby distinguishes 'the slave economy' from 'the higher, or nobler economy', consequently pursuing a 'different type of justice:[516]

> The lower, baser, *slave economy is grounded on the law of equal returns:* justice demands that all debts be paid in kind; the creditor is unable to forget the debt, and the debtor is obliged to return some equivalent form of payment. This notion of justice operates in those societies whose economies depend on rules of exchange and, we might note, it serves as an axiom of capitalist economies. (Schrift 1996:198; my emphasis)

An inference that can be drawn from Nietzsche's argument, however, is that the very insistence on the principle that 'all debts must be paid' conceals a certain psychological dependence on debt as the mainstay of reactive power. Within this logic, debt, as a form of the 'endless chase after gain' (Love 1986:181), must grow to excess at the breaking point of which the real power of the creditor—'to punish'—is revealed in his being protected from the consequences of self-perpetrated excess at the expense of the debtor, who would bear the disproportionate cost of bailing out the creditor. This common feature of the financial crises of capitalism was highlighted by Graeber in relation to the 2008 crash:

---

[514] Some of the earliest references to *debt forgiveness* can be traced back to around 1750 B.C., when King Hammurabi of Babylon is believed to have authored *The Law Code of Hammurabi*, which contains a series of clauses limiting the power of the creditor (e.g., §§112–114, 116) including debt forgiveness (§48). See informative discussion in Harper 1904:27–30 and 99 as well as Hudson 2018: loc. 244.

[515] See Nietzsche's discussion in HH: I, *State*, §156 and §475; HH: II, *WS*, §229; UM: III, *SE*, §2; and NF-1888:15[23].

[516] Graeber develops a similar line of argument in relation to the underlying principles of the global financial systems and its core institutions (see Graeber 2011:369).

> [O]n a certain level, it was exactly what it seemed to be: a scam, an incredibly sophisticated Ponzi scheme designed to collapse in the full knowledge that the perpetrators would be able to force the victims to bail them out. (Graeber 2011:373)

The creditor, therefore, becomes increasingly dependent not simply on the uninterrupted continuation of the debt cycle, but on the amplification of this cycle to excess, which is periodically checked in his favour through the mechanism of creditor protection built into the system. Sedlacek's analysis expresses a similar sentiment, when he characterises the aftermath of the 2008 debt crisis as a 'reverse debt jubilee' for the creditors, no matter how much this may go 'against all principles of sound reason and of basic fairness':

> Our modern society, paradoxically, cannot function without the *institute of this unfair forgiveness of debt*. Every here and now, we ourselves practice an unfair forgiveness of debt and unfair treatment. (Sedlacek 2013:135)

Nietzsche's argument suggests that a strong and thriving political economy would deal with its debtors differently. If we were to take the defaulting mortgage holders in America in 2008 as an example, the bail-out money, in principle if not in practice, would have been directed to them to enable—and more importantly to *'force* them to reach a settlement' of their debts (GM: II, §9; my emphasis). In other words, to repay the debt owed to the banks, which would have prevented the latter's collapse that threatened the entire global financial system. The reverse of this situation exposes not only the extent of reactive power [of the creditor] in and over society, but more importantly the lack of options in addressing the debt problem.[517]

Debt and Capital

In summary, Nietzsche's genealogy blurs the conventional boundaries of understanding of debt and makes it appear equity-like. It encompasses the possibility of sustaining a loss without retribution (i.e., debt forgiveness). Debt is never fully repaid, and it can never be precisely measured. It is dealt with, including the settlement of claims, by agreement, which prioritises communal cohesion and continuity, as opposed to a full and final repayment. As Rafael Winkler aptly surmises, 'the creditor-debtor relation, in the way Nietzsche uses it, has little to do with a "contract"' (Winkler 2007:94). The notion of remuneration that Nietzsche envisages resembles receiving dividends in acknowledgment of success and honouring the obligation, rather than passively living on interest payments (NF-1880:6[183]). Nietzsche's idea of debt underscores society's identity as a 'collective individual' (HH: I, *HMS*, §94) rather than as a collection of indebted 'atomistic individuals' (NF-1882:4[83]). Debt, in Nietzsche's conception, is not an anony-

---

[517] See Dodd's discussion, 2012:58.

mous concept, which underscores its active power and resistance to being exploited as a means of reactive power. Debt is also set to grow over time but without becoming a burden that would impede the functioning and development of either the community or of its individual members.

With the view to the above, Nietzsche's debt would be more accurately characterised as a form of multifunctional *intergenerational capital*, 'which carries all the virtues and talents in the world at interest' (NF-1878:34[8]). Nietzsche frequently invokes the language of the 'capital of ancestors' and of the 'capital of the past ages', which can be 'accumulated from generation to generation' (see HH: I, §156, §475; NF-1888:15[65]), 'preserved and hidden' (HH: II, WS, §229), or 'squandered' (see UM: III, SE, §2; NF-1888:15[23]). Nietzsche thinks about the development of humankind as occurring in cycles, circumscribed by the laws of thermodynamics, where the 'ascending and descending lines' (NF-1871:7[145]), much like the oscillations between the growth of spiritual capital and its erosion, represent phases of 'expenditure of energy and its transformations into life' (NF-1887:10[138]).[518] Each historical epoch, like each social order, can be evaluated on the basis of whether it represents an accumulation of capital (HH: I, State, §475) or its depletion and a corresponding growth in debt (TI: *Skirmishes*, §37; NF-1888:24[1]). Nietzsche scrutinises this dynamic in terms of how 'acquired and stored up energy of many generations', synonymous with the significance of life (UM: III, SE, §6), can be 'least squandered and dispersed but linked together by a firm ring and by will' (NF-1884:26[409]). In this context, Nietzsche's linking of development and capital is significant:

> The doctrine of moderation derives from observing nature, what is to become high and strong, must always *increase its power like capital*, and may *itself not want to live on it*. (NF-1880:6[183], my emphasis)

Once again, Nietzsche emphasises that capital is not a purely economic magnitude. Capital, like debt, is an embodiment of power. From Nietzsche's conjecture we can infer that *all capital wishes to become debt* for it craves the certainty of debt's easy power. This is the proverbial chink in the psychological armor of the 'strong ages' that slave morality seizes upon (NF-1887:10[168]; NF-1888:14[142]). Transitioning from capital to debt signifies, most importantly, a transformation in the nature of power from active to reactive. Accumulating capital across generations is a hard task and increasing its power is a continual communal endeavour. Living off debt, which devours that which has been accumulated seems easy, except for the final repayment. In Nietzsche's interpretation, capital that crosses the threshold between active and reactive power becomes debt. In so doing, it sheds the characteristics of intergenerational continuity and this rupture with tradition imprints on the future development of the community.

---

[518] The following *Nachlass* notes summarise the aspects of Nietzsche's thinking on cyclicality of development: NF-1881:[148], [269], [308], and [312] as well as NF-1888:16[32] and 24[1].

The logic of this formulation of capital, as the engine of development and a continuous collective work-in-progress, resists the idea of living off capital's interest by treating it as primarily generating economic rents (Shapiro 1994:374). Secondly, by emphasising 'moderation' and the 'need of proportion', the notion of capital implies a natural limit to the amount and pace of growth. More precisely, it would also imply a limit on the level of indebtedness in the system: individually or collectively, it can only afford as much indebtedness as it is able to forgive without imperilling itself functionally and in terms of future prospects. Finally, Nietzsche's discussion precludes debt from being used as an instrument of reactive power (see HH: I, *State*, §451; NF-1884:26[173]). This helps to avoid 'a crisis of internalization' in which debt is no longer inscribed merely on the bodies of men and women, but in their consciousness' (Shapiro 1994:374).[519]

Nietzsche's concept of capital is critical in the context of the broader conversation on *development*. At stake, as far as Nietzsche is concerned, is whether debt and the debtor-creditor relationship are incorporated as an element of a much wider concern regarding the development of humankind, or whether development of humankind ends up placed within the normative context of the creditor-debtor relationship. The latter would, on Nietzsche's view, designate the conditions of existence where the communal spirit is broken, atomistic tendencies flourish and seek new structures and principles for organising society on the basis of 'a (contingent) unity in the present' (Geuss 1999:14). By tracing the consequences of the 'constellation of credit and debt' carried over into the moral sphere and by dissecting the 'body of belief that has grown up through the economic principles being given a moral bearing', Nietzsche reconstructs the transformation of intergenerational capital into the narrative of debt which becomes the anchor of normativity under the auspices of modern industrial culture to demonstrate it 'to be in fact the product of will to power' (Cooper 2008:622). Viewed through this prism, modernity and industrial culture are represented by political economy in a protracted downcycle, where transformations of energy have become wasteful (D:§179) and intergenerational capital is being depleted (NF-1888:14[226]), while no clear exit strategy can be formulated within the constraints of the existing system and its values.

'Psychological Trappings' of Debt

There is a particular reason why Nietzsche places 'the relationship of buyer and seller, creditor and debtor' alongside one another and, at the same time, warns that these are riddled with 'psychological trappings' (see GM: II, §8; NF-1887:11[215]). Nietzsche argues that the concept of debt, as a unifying nexus of psychic life, is seized upon by Christian (aka slave) morality. It is used to unleash the slave revolt, which becomes one of modernity's most powerful structuring forces. In a critical insight, Nietzsche links the 'in-

---

[519] See also Reginster's discussion in 'The Genealogy Of Guilt' (2011:66–67).

terest' charged on the irredeemable debt of *guilt* to 'bad conscience', which leads him to regard Christianity as a form of spiritual usury (NF-1881:11[52]). As humankind becomes inoculated with 'bad conscience', a certain 'simultaneous leap and fall into new conditions of existence' occurs and changes 'the whole character of the world in an essential way' (GM: II, §16). The whole 'moral conceptual world of "debt", "conscience", "duty" and "responsibility"' is not only carefully crafted and nurtured around it (GM: II, §6), but becomes internalised 'in the minutest and subtlest detail and imprinted in every will and every faculty', as expressing the character of an entire culture (D: §175). With this, debt ceases being purely transactional and acquires distinct moral and, therefore, political connotations. Its influence spreads by 'misemploying and appropriating' the domains of science, culture, art, and education as well as by leveraging the mechanisms of the State and the stock exchanges in order to craft legitimising narratives around the emerging conditions of existence.[520] Debt acquires the power of normativity, through which the economic realm and the money-economy rise to prominence within the social fabric. Development becomes re-interpreted in terms of economic growth and the agents of the money-economy, as 'the representatives of what at present exists' (HH: I, *State*, §443), set the agenda and tone for the conversation on political economy and legitimise themselves by valorising the profit motive, i.e., the 'greed of the moneymakers' (UM: III, *SE*, §6). Within this dynamic and with the ascent of the new type of creditor, the *money-maker*, debt comes to wield considerable power over the economic realm, while the latter comes to wield exorbitant power over all of society (HH: I, *State*, §447).

Nietzsche suggests that the range of debt's meaning and its reach varies depending on the status and relative power of contracting parties. Debt between counterparties of equal power and standing is a different proposition to debt which binds unequal counterparties. In the first scenario, debt transaction derives from and settles into the foundation of 'all "good naturedness", "equity", all "good will", all "objectivity" on earth' (GM: II, §9). In the second, it is inculcated with the 'psychological trappings' that surface when an 'economic paradigm' becomes fused with 'the moral sphere' (Cooper 2008:622). With the help of sophisticated moralistic contrivance, debt is conceptualised as a compensation for the deficit of physiological strength, a substitute for a lack of vitality. Nietzsche is unequivocal in his objection to ascribing to debt any equalising and compensating properties (TI: *Skirmishes*, §48). To do so would represent a misconception of the same order as the suggestion to use Christianity for liberating slaves (see TCW: §3; NF-1887:11[135]). As a representation of power, rather than an authentic source of authority, debt does not nullify the deficit but only reinforces it and incites its reactive and oppressive propensities (GM: II, §11). However, with the help of slave morality, debt becomes the most intoxicating illusion of power—'the demon of power'—for the physiologically powerless (see D: §202, §262; TI: *Skirmishes*, §19–20). In a note from the late *Nachlass*, Nietzsche highlights the importance of the turning point where a 'purely

---

520 See Nietzsche's discussion in UM: III, *SE*, §6; NF-1871:10[1], *GSt*; and HH: I, *State*, §447.

physiological value judgement', denoting the 'feeling of powerlessness' and lack of inner worth, 'translates itself into a moral judgement' which expresses 'the culture of the classes' and 'is always a sign of lower culture ... ruled by revenge' (NF-1888:14[29]).

For 'the disgruntled, the under-privileged, the unfortunate'—who in the first instance suffer most profoundly 'from themselves' (GM: III, §13)—debt, lending, the money trade, and money-making provide a window of opportunity and become a 'crowbar of power' (Z: I, *New Idol*) with which to claim a degree of power they did not otherwise possess, to climb the social ladder as they otherwise could not envisage doing, and to exact a measure of revenge against the otherwise unreachable individuals and segments of societal architecture:

> *Man* can endure the most terrible contempt (like the Jews), but he must have the *feeling of power* somewhere (such as money). (NF-1880:5[21]; my emphasis)[521]

Debt becomes the critical medium for inverting the axis of power: 'through the punishment of the debtor, the creditor takes part in the rights of the master' (GM: II, §5).[522] By offering the prospect of lifting the weak and sinking the powerful (GM: II, §6), debt can also channel the revenge of the weak against the strong, which is where that 'uncanny and perhaps inextricable link-up between the ideas of "debt and suffering" was first crocheted together' (GM: II, §6) and added into 'all previous estimation of value, inevitably corrupting the latter (NF-1887:10[2]).

Most importantly, debt becomes an instrument of power capable of re-configuring the social fabric of a community by splitting it into the atomistic and indebted individuals and subsequently re-aggregating such 'atrophied individuals' into the anonymous (i.e., powerless) democratic majorities (NF-1882:4[83]; NF-1885:2[100]). At the same time, the new creditor power accumulates in the hands of those who crave it for its own sake (NF-1887:9[145]), which makes them likely to misuse it. Nietzsche suggests that such agents lack the necessary physiological integrity for discharging power appropriately and without excess. For them, debt becomes power they can no longer do without: akin to having a 'gnawing worm' inside, which demands feeding (see GM: III, §8, §14, §23), it compels them to amass ever more of itself (GM: II, §11). Debt-seeking, thus perceived, becomes an expression of a reactive and self-referential 'power-lust' (see UM: *RWB*, §6; D: §204), which 'flowers like it always has done, in secret, like a violet but with a different scent'—the scent of ressentiment, which seeks to 'sanctify revenge with the terms of justice' (GM: II, §11). As Simone Weil pointed out, 'the preser-

---

[521] Nietzsche's proposition contrasts with Marx's suggestion that 'the Jew has emancipated himself in a Jewish manner, not only by acquiring financial power, but because both through him and without him, money has become a world power and the practical Jewish spirit has become the practical spirit of the Christian peoples' (CW 3:173–174).
[522] Nietzsche's earliest insight on money becoming an estimate of damage and measure of punishment can be traced to a *Nachlass* note NF-1879:42[9].

vation of power is a vital necessity for the powerful since it is their power which provides their sustenance' as well as forming a vicious circle where 'the master produces fear in the slave by the very fact that he is afraid of him' (Weil 1958:62).

One of the key issues that Nietzsche focuses on here concerns the *inflationary characteristics* debt acquires in the absence of the order of rank: it 'broadens out and grows, *like a polyp, so wide and deep* that in the end, with the impossibility of paying back the debt' the concepts of debt and punishment converge on each other (GM: II, §20; my emphasis). Debt's inflation—its ability to grow in *width* (i.e., in relative size, in the economy, for example) and in *depth* (i.e., to penetrate different spheres of society, both tangible and intangible)—appears as a *differential* rather than a *linear* phenomenon and a *relative* rather than an *absolute* magnitude. It underscores Nietzsche's point that debt is not an exclusively economic category but a quantum of power and, to be more precise, a measure of the degree to which reactive power reaches into every corner of social architecture. In order to grow stronger, debt does not need to simply grow in size or to command a higher interest rate. Instead, its relative increases in one area can coincide with relative decreases in others and this pattern of ebbing and flowing amplifies debt's overall earnings and power.

The repressive levels of highly punitive moral and political debt can co-exist with low financial indebtedness and vice-versa. The puzzling reality, not unlike our experience of the present, is possible where financial debt may continue to grow exponentially while we can imagine ourselves becoming freer and life as becoming better. Debt thrives on differential inflation because it conceals the aggregate power it exerts over society. However, as Shakespeare poignantly observed, these illusions only mask one certainty: namely, that one way or another debt always extracts its 'pound of flesh'. This dynamic reaches a climax, Nietzsche tells us, when 'the maximal god yet achieved' (GM: II, §20) sacrifices himself in 'an extremely strange and curious' (GM: II, §19) rite of debt forgiveness, which simultaneously represents 'Christianity's stroke of genius' (GM: II, §21), setting it apart from all other religions, and seals the transformation of the creditor-debtor relationship into the reactive pathos:

> [N]one other than God sacrificing himself for *man's debt*, none other than God paying himself back, God as the only one able to redeem man from what, to man himself, has become irredeemable—the *creditor sacrificing himself for his debtor*, out of love (*would you credit it?*—), out of love for his debtor! (GM: II, §22; my emphasis)

This insight Nietzsche quite possibly owes to Epictetus, who claimed that 'having borrowed just once is not enough to make somebody a debtor, but it is necessary in addition that he *continues to owe* the money and hasn't paid off the loan' (Epictetus 1904:22; my emphasis). Nietzsche elaborates on this logic by offering a profound psychological insight: it does not so much matter what one owes, as long as the consciousness of being in debt is embedded in the psyche. One important consequence of the 'moralisation of the concepts of debt/guilt and duty' is that any prospect of repaying the debt becomes 'an iron impossibility' (GM: II, §21), while at the same time the 'burden of unpaid debts and the longing for them to be settled' is transformed into the requirement for debt repayment becoming the normative pillar and a key structural feature of the debt economy and of the creditor-biased legal system that grows around it (GM: II, §20). As Simon Wortham surmises in the *Time of Debt* (2013; last accessed March 5, 2023), 'the radical asymmetry of power finds its echo and confirmation in "infinite and irredeemable" debt—one that simultaneously must and cannot be repaid—"indebted man", as both a universal and an individual figure, comes to the fore' (Wortham, 2013).[523] Reversing the concepts of debt and duty, 'initially against the debtor' but ultimately against the creditor (GM: II, §21), also reverses the 'direction of development' (GM: II, §20) in a number of important respects.

First and foremost, the relationship of the present to both past and future is altered. This is the temporal aspect of debt, which, Nietzsche stresses, modern man understands the least (GM: II, §19). The 'death of god' (see GS: §108, §125, §343) and diminishing reverence towards the past does not automatically result in 'the second innocence' (GM: II, §20).[524] Rather, it means that reality's 'faith in the future ... wanes irrevocably', bringing about a change in the valuations relating to 'the conditions of self-preservation' (AC: §16). Nietzsche's argument is that the death of god orphans the present from the past and changes its attitude to the future, which becomes sacrificed to the present as a form of compensation for the psychic rupture thus created.[525] The result is a 'nihilistic turning away from existence', which is left inherently worthless' (GM: II, §21), because its new primary measure of value is a snapshot of itself—i.e., 'entirely without value' (NF-1885:36[10]).

On top of this, the circulation of ancestral debt, as a form of intergenerational capital and guardian of communal development, is interrupted and becomes replaced with the circulation of debt as the means of maintaining reactive power interests. Although with the advent of industrial society the forms of indebtedness change from the outwardly religious to the more secular and embedded—e.g., material and financial—overall indebtedness as a form of consciousness and a measure of the overall burden upon individuals and societies living 'in the age of atomistic chaos' (UM: III, *SE*, §5) with 'the biggest, heaviest feet' (Z: IV, *The Ugliest*), continues to grow. 'The bond' holding the hostile forces in check 'broke, the pressure relaxed', releasing the psychological springs and allowing them to uncoil (UM: III, *SE*, §5)[526] This predicament, on Nietzsche's view, extends as well as exacerbates the crisis of the political economy of modernity.

---

[523] See Nietzsche in GM: II, §21. See also Wortham's discussion: https://www.radicalphilosophyarchive.com/article/time-of-debt-on-nietzschean-origins-of-lazzarato/, last accessed Feb. 27, 2023.
[524] Nietzsche argues that in a weakening and disintegrating community, the 'consciousness' of indebtedness to the past weakens (GM: II, §19).
[525] Critically, 'resentment against the future surfaces as a will to take revenge against those who support responsibility to the future' (Connolly 2008:51).
[526] This, one of Nietzsche's central insights, exhibits strong affinity with Dostoyevsky's notion developed in *Crime and Punishment* (1866), that the real nature and extent of one's indebtedness crystallise in one's consciousness most powerfully only when the creditor is slain. Nietzsche discovered Dostoyev-

Concluding Remarks: Debt and Subjectivity

A critical element of debt's power as a value is its ability to mould subjectivity. Lazzarato, whose argument exhibits structural parallels to Nietzsche's, notes that the secularisation of 'the creditor-debtor relationship entails a radical change in the measure of value' in modern society: 'it is through debt that evaluation as a technique for governing behaviour comes to takes hold […] in every economic and social sphere (Lazzarato 2012:138; my emphasis). Debt involves both the 'production and control of subjectivity' through the notions of 'guilt and responsibility' embedded in the individuals from the earliest possible time (Lazzarato 2012:42–46).

One sphere where the workings of the money-economy and of debt display a broad range of their power is that of higher education. Applying the logic of Nietzsche's analysis to the present-day phenomenon of student debt helps highlight several central aspects of his critique. Most important among these is the interplay between the material and immaterial manifestations of debt in the context of incorporation and dispossession. Student debt, as a means of promoting wider access to higher education,[527] has been steadily rising in recent years—particularly in the US[528] and in the UK—prompting concern over a potential debt crisis.[529] It has been noted that the US universities, in particular, lead the way in proactively in-debting their students by concealing from them the full cost of education.[530] This unfolding dynamic highlights the predicament of the indebted subject, who willingly incurs financial debt in order to secure the means of being duly incorporated as an indebted subject in a much broader sense.[531] Noam Chomsky, echoing Nietzsche's logic, famously observed:

---

sky, 'the only psychologist from whom' Nietzsche 'had something to learn' (TI: *Skirmishes*, §45) around the time of writing the *Genealogy*, as evidenced in his correspondence around this time (BVN 1887:800, 812 and NF-1888:15[9]). However, Nietzsche's *Zarathustra*, especially in Book IV, *The Ugliest Human Being*, also exhibits the line of psychological analysis of indebtedness which strongly echoes that of Dostoyevsky.

527 See 'Student Loan Statistics' as of December 2020: https://commonslibrary.parliament.uk/research-briefings/sn01079/, last accessed Feb. 27, 2023.

528 In the US, student debt is now the second highest consumer debt category behind mortgage debt and the number of US borrowers with student debt is now almost two and a half times higher than the entire higher education student population in the US. See the relevant debt statistics: https://www.forbes.com/sites/zackfriedman/2022/02/03/student-loan-debt-statistics/, last accessed Feb. 27, 2023.

529 See discussion by Daniel Johnson in 'What Will It Take to Solve the Student Loan Crisis?': https://hbr.org/2019/09/what-will-it-take-to-solve-the-student-loan-crisis, last accessed Feb. 27, 2023.

530 See Paulina Cachero and Francesca Maglione in 'Most Colleges Don't Tell Students the True Cost of an Education': https://www.bloomberg.com/news/articles/2023-04-27/how-much-does-college-cost-confusing-fasfa-aid-letters-hamper-families?cmpid=BBD042723_BIZ&utm_medium=email&utm_source=newsletter&utm_term=230427&utm_campaign=bloombergdaily&leadSource=uverify%20wall#xj4y7vzkg, last accessed April 27, 2023.

531 See 'The Student Debt Crisis: Could It Slow Down the US Economy?': https://knowledge.wharton.upenn.edu/article/student-loan-debt-crisis/, last accessed Feb. 27, 2023.

Well, how do you indoctrinate the young? There are a number of ways. One way is to burden them with hopelessly heavy tuition debt. Debt is a trap, especially student debt, which is enormous, far larger than credit card debt. It's a trap for the rest of your life because the laws are designed so that you can't get out of it. If a business, say, gets in too much debt it can declare bankruptcy, but individuals can almost never be relieved of student debt through bankruptcy. They can even garnish social security if you default. That's a disciplinary technique.[532]

In the olden days, Nietzsche tells us, education was a way of instilling in students a sense of indebtedness to those who taught them: 'for the ancients the goal of agonal education was the well-being of the whole, of state society' (HC: 192). In modern society, composed of increasingly atomistic individuals, the bond of spiritual indebtedness becomes less effective (HH: I, *Tokens*, §227). As such, 'debt to society' becomes replaced by financial indebtedness, which, unlike 'the debt of gratitude', burdens rather than empowers (Schiff 2012:358).[533] Peter Schiff observes that through the modern education system 'we have created this big constituency of highly indebted young people—they are like indentured servants'.[534] The incorporation of aspiring students into the debt economy as borrowers disconnects them from the wider society to which they would once have owed a debt of gratitude. Instead, the axis of responsibility and duty to keep their promise (of repayment) has shifted squarely in the direction of specific financial institutions to which the debts are owed. Nathalie Sarthou-Lajus cogently adds that debt effectively limits the horizons of self-realisation, because 'the indebted subject' ends up caught in 'the double exigency' of always being reminded of their status as a debtor, which undermines their ability to one day accomplishing that, which debt could supposedly enable them to do (Sarthou-Lajus 1997:71).

Nietzsche problematises this means of incorporating individuals, who become 'time-bound through and through' (UM: III, *SE*, §6), as the 'universal deficiency' of modern education (D: §546). Education, he tells us, is an opportune juncture in one's development to be 'inoculated with something new', albeit in a measured manner which would ensure that the recipient is able to assimilate the vaccine. Once inoculated, however, 'the task of education' becomes 'to imbue him with such firmness and certainty that he can no longer as a whole be in any way deflected from his path' (HH: I, *Tokens*, §224). In this respect, Nietzsche considers modern education to be the more effective means of 'keeping the people subject ... in fear and obedience', precisely because it 'constitutes a net of expectations within which every young man is caught' (HH: II,

---

[532] See Chomsky's commentary on 'Corporate Business Models Hurting American Universities' (2014): https://chomsky.info/20141010/, last accessed Feb. 27, 2023. See also Chomsky's commentary from 2011 on student debt as a 'disciplinary technique' for producing compliant and efficient components of the consumer economy: https://web.archive.org/web/20110412213902/http://www.ottawacitizen.com/business/Chomsky+talks+fear+western+society/4587270/story.html, last accessed Feb. 27, 2023.
[533] See also Fitzsimons 2007:3.
[534] See Schiff, Oct. 23, 2018: https://www.schiffradio.com/guns-butter-moon-ep-402/, last accessed Feb. 27, 2023.

AOM, §320). At the same time, the 'speedy education ... of youthful souls' aims to get these individuals 'ready for employment as soon as possible' and *definitely* 'before they are able to mature' (see UM: II, *UDHL*, §7; III, *SE*, §6).[535] In fact, causation becomes inverted, and one is deemed 'mature as soon as one becomes employable' (D: §455). These 'infamous means', used 'to blind the youths' (UM: II, *UDHL*, §7), help develop 'a money-earning being' who is, by design, incomplete and allowed only as much culture or education 'as it is in the interest of general money-making and world commerce' (UM: III, *SE*, §6). This, Nietzsche argues, has the effect of making individuals 'smaller and more governable', while at the same time it is 'hailed as "progress"' (NF-1885:36[48]):

> It is with men as with the charcoal-kilns in the forest. Only when the young have ceased to glow and are carbonized do they become useful ... as material for heating ... great machines (HH: I, §585)

In this respect, modern education, 'directed by the fantasies of jailers and hangmen' (D: §13), becomes an appendix of the money-economy, which is interested primarily in producing *current individuals*—quite literally 'minted like coins'—as facilitators of the great machine of exchange and commerce, albeit with the *diminishing value* of each individual coin, since the goal is to create as many of such 'current human beings as possible' (UM: III, *SE*, §6).[536] Increasingly answerable to the requirements of 'supply and demand' (D: §175), 'universal education' helps to further the reach of the money-economy, adding to the ever 'increasing velocity of life' (UM: III, *SE*, §5). The money-economy directs the immature sterling mediocracies (UM: II, *UDHL*, §7) to 'look for work in order to be paid: in civilized countries today almost all are at one in doing that ... for them work is a means and not an end in itself. Hence, they are not very refined in their choice of work, if only it pays well' (GS: §42).[537]

One of Nietzsche's most penetrating insights in this respect relates to the *raison d'être* of the secular state. Nietzsche argues that the state, like religion before, is tasked with benefiting the 'masses *not yet of age*' (HH: I, *State*, §472; my emphasis). The secret of the secular state's power, Nietzsche tells us, is that it rules over the *immature* souls and *uncritical* minds. Perpetuating this collective psychic immaturity becomes its key function and the core constitutive feature of governability. Not only can the immature souls be willingly and unreflectively exploited but, when such exploitation takes extreme forms, including 'famines, financial crises, [and] wars' (HH: I, *State*, §472), only they can be fooled into thinking that these extreme events are somehow not the integral parts of the comprehensive system of social control, which oppresses

---

[535] See Franco's discussion, 2014:458.
[536] Nietzsche first develops this idea in 'Lecture One' of the 'On the Future of Our Educational Institutions' (1872).
[537] In this respect, Nietzsche's critique reaches beyond Marx, who also remonstrated against 'the intellectual desolation artificially produced by converting immature human beings into mere machines for the fabrication of surplus value' (CW 35:403).

them by maintaining their immaturity (NF-1886:5[71]). Not allowing souls and minds to mature is the key to the continuity of exploitation within modern political economy, as well as to understanding its purpose. Keeping souls and minds immature—i.e., breeding a type of modern 'lotus eaters', who are, at best, 'generic creatures, but not distinct individual and unique human beings' (HH: I, *Tokens*, §283)—represents, counterintuitive though it may seem, an area of significant continuing investment by the state, channelled in part through the system of education. Nietzsche asserts that 'a democratic commonwealth' produces 'atrophied individuals' (NF-1885:2[100]) in accordance with the key tenet of *slave morality* that one not only pays one's debts but does so obediently, as an 'amiable and creditable payer and borrower' (NF-1881:11[73]). The drawback of this kind of exploitation is that it is incapable of 'enlightened self-preservation' in the long-run (HH: I, *HMS*, §92). Instead, just like the immature subjects it produces and governs over, such system is bound to remain immature and *unenlightened* beyond the remit granted to it by the valuations of slave morality which, Nietzsche contends, will become the main cause of its decay and eventual extinction.

When a university graduate enters the world in financial debt, the use of his income from employment would soon be earmarked for debt service. By the time student debt combines with other forms of debt (e.g., a mortgage), the former student may well become 'a man [who] is no longer a man confined, but a man in debt' (Deleuze 1995:181). Discharging one's financial debts takes priority over discharging one's debt to society: creditors prosper at society's expense. Thus, the young and immature, educated *en masse* with the logic of money-making, become the subordinated and compliant cogs in the debt machine of the industrial culture, which they inadvertently help to strengthen. As Geuss observes in *A World Without Why* (2014), the education system thus structured ends up turning out 'the pliable, efficient, self-satisfied cadres that our economic and political system uses to produce the ideological carapace that protects it against criticism and change' (Geuss 2014:231).

Nietzsche focuses, then, on a critical issue: namely, that 'the urge for the most generalization of education' entails the propensity to instrumentalise the latter largely as 'a means of acquisition' of subjects (NF-1870:8[57]). Under the veneer of social progress and greater equality projected by universal education, he detects the cynical need to fulfil the requirements and to further the enslaving propensities of the money-economy:

> [A]s much knowledge and education as possible, therefore as much demand as possible, therefore as much production as possible, therefore as much happiness and profit as possible—that is the seductive formula. (UM: III, *SE*, §6)

Nietzsche problematises the idea of universal education as 'a bogus concept' and a part of the world 'shrouded in humbug', which is erected by the money-economy seeking to advance only itself by increasingly indebting its subjects (UM: III, *SE*, §7). Furthermore, under the banner of universalisation, the expanding scope of higher education, aiming to capture ever greater constituencies, reflects the inflationary tendency of debt, which fuels the money-economy (UM: III, *SE*, §7). This inflationary dynamic is not without peril, however, and sooner or later it is liable to hit the law of diminishing returns. Although the 'sterling mediocrity', parcelled out into the money-economy, may temporarily prove 'more profitable in the economic sense' (UM: II, *UDHL*, §7), 'the fatal tendency' of fostering money-making pursuits over meaningful ones (UM: III, *SE*, §4–7) is that it becomes increasingly costly in terms of the spiritual value squandered in the process (D: §179), and is likely to backfire in the long-term by fostering the causes of its ultimate unravelling.[538]

Nietzsche argues that subjectivity, thus moulded, goes well beyond making the subject 'reliable, regular and necessary' (GM: II, §1). The identity of indebtedness, ingrained from as early an age is as possible and in as great a number as possible, creates a controlled and self-controlling society, which endorses debt the critical normative axis of its political economy. At the same time, increase in debt is also indicative of the extent of the reactive power exercised in society over the indebted. Nietzsche's critique demonstrates that in secular modern society, debt—as both a value and a conduit—plays a key role in setting implicit boundaries and defining the parameters of the conversation on development so as to make it conform to its own requirements.

Nietzsche's further penetrating point is that when money becomes all that is wanted and asked of people, when it becomes all that people ultimately desire and the worth of human pursuits is measured predominantly in its terms—individuals and societies, paradoxical though it may seem when viewed against the backdrop of improving standards of material welfare, *stop developing* and start regressing in the sense of spiritual well-being (see HH: II, *WS*, §186 and NF-1882:3[1], §405). Nietzsche urges 'the re-education of the human race' (D: §13) and argues that unless education is stipulated as a strategic *developmental priority*, conceived outside the demands of the money-economy and the logic of money-making, it too will form part of the degenerating tendencies in society, rather than contributing to its development and heightening.

To conclude, Nietzsche's critique problematises debt as an instrument of reactive power, which is economic only in its form. The substance of debt penetrates far deeper into the social fabric of modern society, structuring its normativity, directing political proceedings, and defining subjectivity. Conceiving of debt as a property of the human psyche, a pre-linguistic reflection of the hierarchical architecture of existence and life's intricate structures of subordination which organises human consciousness and informs experience, furnishes Nietzsche with a unique and unorthodox frame of reference for scrutinising the phenomenon in question. His careful genealogical reconstruction of debt into ancestral capital reveals the extent to which slave morality's reactive valuations have inverted debt's original meaning, as well as reconfiguring its functionality. Extending this analysis further leads Nietzsche to conceptualising debt in terms of the 'fundamental question of value and disvalue' (AC: §54). This allows him to follow debt's transitions between the different spheres of modern society, enabled by a cer-

---

[538] See NF-1872: *FEI*, III.

tain continuity of valuations which survives when economic debt becomes moral, political, or psychological and vice-versa. Nietzsche's insightful analysis suggests that 'moralised' debt can be used as a storm gauge of modern political economy, measuring its disquietude which rises as society's physiological vigour wanes, and it descends deeper into nihilism.

7 Nietzsche's Critique of Debt Economy

> I challenge you all; you atheists, for instance!
> How are you going to save the world? How to find a
> *straight road of progress*, you men of science, of
> industry, of cooperation, of trade unions, and all the
> rest? How are you going to save it, I say? By what?
> By debt? What is debt? To what will debt lead you?
> (Dostoyevsky, *The Idiot*, 1868)

Introduction: *'Seven Skins'* of Debt

In 'Schopenhauer as Educator', Nietzsche invokes the metaphor of a 'hare with seven skins' in order to describe human nature which, to him, remains 'a dark and veiled thing' (UM: III, *SE*, §1). By extension, this allegory is well suited for describing debt. Debt's omnipresence in today's world is more than matched by its opacity, as it 'becomes more subtle, insidious, incomprehensible' (TI: *Error*, §3).[540] As Thomas Piketty surmises in *Capital in the Twenty First Century* (2014), 'to be sure, we are in debt' (Piketty 2014:114). In many respects, debt has become the norm and modern society has become not simply accustomed to debt but increasingly predisposed towards it (Ferguson 2008:43). Standing 'at the very beginning of the philosophical tradition' (Shapiro 1994:358), debt has over the ages become widely accepted as a 'fundamental social fact' and established as a pertinent feature of the political economy of modernity (Roitman 2005:74), where 'money, debt, interest—are all things we cannot imagine being without' (Sedlacek 2013:80–81). Notwithstanding that debt is the pivotal institution of the capitalist society, no satisfactory theory exists that would provide a clear definition of what debt is, let alone of what it does.

Tracing the transformations by means of which debt develops into *'a regulative fiction'* (GS: §344) of modern political economy, Nietzsche suggests that it started when the economic mode of understanding the mundane was expanded to encompass the majority of life's proceedings. Projected onto the spiritual sphere, where this modality of interpreting reality was inscribed in language and subjected to the grammatical contrivances of *slave morality*, effectively transformed debt into the cardinal value of reactive pathos.[541] Nietzsche's critique posits debt as a highly synthetic proposition, around which a complex 'conventional lexicon' is bound to have devel-

---

[540] John Ruskin, with whom Nietzsche is familiar (NF-1884:25[139]), stated in *Unto This Last* (1860), that 'all money, properly so called, is an acknowledgment of debt; but as such, it may either be considered to represent the labour and property of the creditor, or the idleness and penury of the debtor' and that 'the intricacy of the question' of debt 'has been much increased by the (hitherto necessary) use of marketable commodities' (Ruskin 1997:185; fn. 2).
[541] See Dodd's excellent discussion in *The Social Life of Money*, 2014:89–94. See also Morrisson 2018:974–975 and Cooper 2008:605–629.

oped over time (Shapiro 1994:368). Viewed in this light, Nietzsche's critique of the money-economy is more accurately understood as forming part of his scrutiny of the ubiquitous *economy of debt*, which encompasses but is not limited to the examination of the emerging debt economy from the social and psychic fabric of industrial capitalism of the late 19th century.

Many debt analysts agree that 'debt emerges as a slippery concept with its contingent and implicit components, its secreting off-balance-sheet', which with the passage of time makes 'debt too complex and too opaque to understand' (Dyson 2014:16, 635).[542] Sigridur Thorgeirsdottir, reflecting on Iceland's experience of the 2008 crisis surmises that 'it has become increasingly clear that the financial economy is at its core a debt economy' where debt is at the very heart of the 'crisis of financial capitalism' (Thorgeirsdottir 2016:189–190). Nietzsche would add that unwinding the tangled clew of debt, one should expect that every single of debt's skins 'betrays something but conceals even more' (BGE: §32). Furthermore, as is the case with 'every abyss underneath every ground', looking under the 'groundwork' of a phenomenon such as debt, it is important to remain aware of the real 'linguistic danger' surrounding debt as a concept and a form of reactive politico-economic *praxis* corresponding to it:[543]

> [O]ur economists have not yet wearied of scenting a similar unity in the word 'value' and of searching after the original root-concept of the word. As if every word were not a pocket into which now this, now that, now several things at once have been put! (HH: II, *WS*, §33)

Looking deeper into the question of debt, one should therefore expect to uncover 'more extensive, stranger and more suspicious' things (BGE: §289). However, the leitmotif that cuts through this semiotic maze surrounding debt (GM: II, §13) is the *question of it as a value*, or, as Roitman puts it, 'the "truth" of debt' (Roitman 2005:74). In this respect Nietzsche stands out from the wide field of political economists by *directly* linking debt not only with reactive politics—liberal and illiberal, democratic and authoritarian alike—but by designating it as a *gauge* of the general decline of humankind. Analysing debt through the prism of value enables Nietzsche to access it on at least two juxtaposed planes, namely those of *material welfare* and *spiritual wellbeing*. Although debt, viewed instrumentally, may appear indispensable to improving the material welfare (e.g., stimulating economic growth and invigorating commerce), by helping to ach-

---

[542] The sense of debt's conceptual impermeability is discussed in detail in Sedlacek's *'Economics of Good and Evil'* (2013) as well as in Graeber's *'Debt: The First 5000 Years'* (2011). Christopher England argues that debt's opaqueness makes it 'easier to evade judgement and harder to assign responsibility' (England 2019:70) and Paul Krugman famously noted that 'nobody understands debt'. Thorstein Veblen (last accessed March 5, 2023) concluded in 1908, 'the failure of classical theory to give an intelligent account of credit and crises is in great part due to the habitual refusal of economists to recognise intangible assets' (Hodgson 2016:180).

[543] See HH: II, *WS*, §55; and BGE: §289. Nietzsche's discussion of the 'linguistic dangers' shares considerable affinity with Marx's views expressed in *The German Ideology* ('Language and Thought', starting with 'For philosophers, one of the most difficult tasks'; CW 5:446).

ieve this objective on borrowed terms, it also acts as a detractor from enhancing the spiritual wellbeing. Nietzsche regards debt as an artifice by means of which the one-sided transfer of value from the spiritual to the material domain is effected and, once achieved, this enterprise inevitably depreciates and squanders value.

Debt helps to define what should be regarded as 'progress' (i.e., as 'good') and the means by which such progress (i.e., 'improvement' and 'betterment of mankind') should be achieved and measured.[544] Overseeing the construction of the future of material plenty but wanting in terms of spirit, debt invariably undermines the overall vitality of its edifice. In this respect, Nietzsche can be said to echo Marx's notion of debt as Moloch, who 'claims the *ownership of all wealth which can ever be produced*, and everything it has received so far is but an instalment for its all-engrossing appetite'—i.e., set upon emptying out humankind's future potential while enslaving its present (CW 37:394; my emphasis). Nietzsche's challenging contribution to our efforts to understand debt, therefore, lies in his analysis of it as a marker of *'reactive pathos'* in society, an indicator of its [declining] physiological robustness, and a key factor in shaping [obsequious] modern subjectivity.

Writings during the Founders' Crash and the Long Depression

Four of Nietzsche's works in particular, stretching from *Untimely Meditations* (1873) to *The Gay Science* (1882), contain some of his fiercest criticisms of the *money-economy* as well as an extensive discussion of the 'cares and concerns of the social world' (Ansell-Pearson 1994:1–7). One common factor, which is referenced less frequently in contextualising these works, is that they were penned during the time when Germany was in the grip of a severe and protracted economic and financial crisis, which broke out in 1873 and reverberated through every segment of Germany's social structure and its political economy for over two decades.[545] Rather than simply belonging to the 'early-middle' periods of Nietzsche's writing, these works lend themselves to being read as his reflections on a *crisis within the crisis*—an important time when he frees himself 'from what did not belong' in his nature—when the themes percolating in his earlier essays begin to acquire the clarity of articulation that would distinguish his subsequent work (EH: *HH*, §2). Nietzsche's own, somewhat open-ended acknowledgment of this in a letter to Georg Brandes, penned in February of 1888, states that 'between the "untimely meditations" and "human, all too human" lies a crisis' (BVN 1888:997).

As we can learn from Nils Fiebig's inquiry into *Nietzsche und das Geld* (2019), Nietzsche's experience of the financial crisis was not simply confined to that of an observer. Nietzsche, who looked to supplement his 'reliable Basel pension with income

---

544 See GM: III, §17, and TI: *Improvers*, §5.
545 Many analysts agree that the Long Depression lasted well over two decades stretching from 1873 to 1896 (see Copelovitch and Singer 2020:135 as well as Rosenberg 2011:19–28).

from capital assets', was, like many of his contemporaries, no stranger to investing on the stock exchange (Fiebig 2019:72). Nietzsche's investment exploits did not go unnoticed by his many critics, who described him as the 'philosopher of the big capital' ('Großkapitals') and even 'the doorkeeper of the influential bankers like Rothschild and Bleichröder' (Fiebig 2019:15–17). In a manner characteristic of the time, his purchases included some risky bonds issued by the 'railway companies, banks and mining companies' and did not show much regard for the credit risk these investments entailed, which became apparent only when the market fell sharply in 1873 (Fiebig 2019:71–73). Nietzsche's investment ambitions, directed largely towards supporting his publishing efforts, suffered a serious setback as a result of the crisis and the losses incurred, which considerably curtailed his income, undoubtedly informed his thinking on certain aspects of the money-economy and the psychology of its functionaries (Fiebig 2019:19–23, 73–74).

Every crisis, in Nietzsche's assessment, is also an overcoming: a shedding of old skin, a cleansing of spirit and a realisation (NF-1886:5[71]). In his own case, this intellectual and spiritual reckoning is manifested in *Thus Spoke* Zarathustra (1883–1885) which is permeated with reflections on the decade of the crisis and crystallises his philosophical stance:

> When I came to mankind for the first time, I committed the hermit's folly,
> the great folly: I situated myself in the market place. (Z: IV, *Higher Man*, §1)

In *Zarathustra*, Nietzsche's incisive analysis, tracing the transformation of the 'market place' psychology into the enduring consciousness of crisis, truly takes shape, particularly so in its final—fourth—part, completed in 1885. Zarathustrian narrative pulls together many if not all of the ingredients Nietzsche would use in articulating his critique of slave morality:

> The *market place* and the people resembled the sea when a *storm charges in:* everyone *fled apart* and *into one another*, and especially in the *spot where the body had to impact* (Z: *Prologue*, §6; my emphasis)

One factor which is important to appreciate here is that 'the market place' allegory, so central to Zarathustra's travails, represents none other than the 'mishmash' of modern politics and economy—its political economy (Z: IV, *Kings*). Having thoroughly examined it, Zarathustra discovered 'no greater *market place* on earth [...] than good and evil' (Z: I, *Thousand and One Goals*; my emphasis).

Building on Zarathustra's revelations, Nietzsche's analysis of the economic, social, cultural, and psychological consequences of 'Gründerkrach' and the 'Long Depression', which ensued from it, culminates in his comprehensive critique of the slave revolt in morality across the two of his seminal works—*Beyond Good and Evil* and *The Genealogy*. The continuity of slave morality's valuations, which Nietzsche intuits already in some of his earliest writings, became powerfully exposed in the aftermath of the economic crash of 1873, helping Nietzsche to crystalise his criticisms of them in his later writings. In this respect, Nietzsche's 'search for philosophy' can and should be seen as taking place against the backdrop of the economic tremors that shook the social fabric of society in the aftermath of the 1873 crisis.

The Long Depression, which started with 'the "Founders' Crash" [Gründerkrach]' of 1873, severely dislocated the fledgling industrial society in Europe, impacting Germany and Austria most harshly, and in the United States of America (Davies 2020:291). On May 9th, 1873, which came to be known as 'Black Friday'—triggered by the sustained and largely uncontrolled speculation—the value of shares traded on the Vienna Stock Exchange collapsed, sending shock waves across the stock exchanges in Europe, most notably in Berlin, and across America, starting with New York.[546] The 1873 crisis was, in a perverse way, a *debt crisis*. As though proving right Pantagruel, who claimed it is better to 'always be indebted to somebody' (Rabelais 1892:159), the main trigger for the Founders' Crash was the repayment of the *war debts* by Germany to its domestic creditors following the war reparations from France after the latter was defeated in the 1870–1871 military campaign. In addition to Bismarck's insistence that France should pay the considerable (five billion francs) war indemnity in gold, in December of 1871 Germany unilaterally stopped minting silver coins and adopted the gold standard, to which America was forced to respond by the like measure two years later in 1873.[547]

Debt, however, did not disappear from view for long after the repayment. Accentuating the period of economic expansion, known as the 'Gründerjahre' ('Founders' Years'), it resurfaced in greater quantities in the form of the highly speculative investments in the business and banking ventures in Germany, Austria, and the US. Hundreds of these newly formed companies, many without any track-record of operation, borrowed extravagant amounts internationally using bonds secured by mortgages on the land and real estate, the value of which was vastly exaggerated in the short-lived euphoria which took hold on both sides of the Atlantic. When the inflationary growth and the associated asset bubbles burst suddenly and violently, vast sums were wiped off the valuations of stocks traded and financed internationally—in Vienna, Paris, Zurich, Berlin, London, and New York—and the long period of economic and political decline set in.

The 1873 crisis is seen as an important precedent-setting development in the international political economy. Many of its features were repeated in the subsequent politico-economic cataclysms and a growing body of academic literature draws on the comparisons between the three great crises of industrial capitalism—those of 1873, 1929 and 2008.[548] The simple point, which merits a degree of generalisation, is that

---

546 See Copelovitch and Singer for a succinct and well-informed overview, 2020:137–140.
547 The war indemnity paid by France to Prussia represented the 'largest such transfer in history, amounting to about one-quarter of the German gross domestic product' (Fohlin 2007:21).
548 Although my subsequent discussion focuses primarily on the upheavals of 1873 and 2008, most of the features these two crises apply to the Great Depression of 1929. See Kurth 2011; Lynn 2011; Goldstein 2012; Eichengreen 2014; Roberts 2016; and Copelovitch and Singer 2020:124–136.

the Long Depression of 1873 (industrial capitalism's first), the Great Depression of 1929 (capitalism's most infamous) and the Great Recession of 2008 (financial capitalism's most recent) exhibit strong structural similarities.[549] All three were debt crises preceded by significant liberalisation of regulation.[550] All three were designated as 'Great' at some point.[551] All three crises signalled the end of the highly speculative stints of economic expansion and heralded the start of protracted economic upheavals and stagnation lasting, in each case, over a decade.[552] All three crises were international in scope and each—progressively global, exposing the growing interconnectedness of the world's political economy.[553] All three crises caused considerable rift between liberal politics and liberal economics, which co-presided happily over the brief periods of the 'good times'. Tremendous political instability, social strife, and dislocation on both sides of the Atlantic ignited the radicalisation of political discourse on either end of the political spectrum. In all three instances—no one, economists least of all, saw the crashes coming. As Henry Hyndman observed in relation to the 1873 crisis:

> Suddenly, in the midst of the greatest apparent prosperity, when the promoters and contractors have their hands full of work; when merchants and traders are congratulating themselves on the extent of their turnover; when manufactures, mine-owners and shipping companies are dividing their most satisfactory profits; and when the workers are being paid a somewhat better rate of wages—at that juncture a change for the worse begins. (Hyndman 1902:1)

Damage caused by all three crises spread far beyond the economy and, unlike the 'economy proper', damage to the wider society was never properly addressed, let alone repaired. The first two Depressions—Long and Great—helped pave the way to the catastrophic world wars. It is hardly an accident that Adam Tooze should complete his incisive examination of the 2008 financial crisis with an ominous comparison:

> There is a *striking similarity* between the questions we ask about 1914 and 2008. How does a great moderation end? How do huge risks build up that are little understood and barely controllable? How do great tectonic shifts in the global order unload in sudden earthquakes? How do anachronistic and out-of-date frames of reference make it impossible for us to understand what is happening around us? Did we sleepwalk into crisis, or were there dark forces pushing? Who is to blame for the ensuing human-induced, man-made disaster? (Tooze 2018:617; my emphasis)

It appears that broadly the *same questions* haunt the great crises of modernity. This is another good reason to examine Nietzsche's experience of and his reflections on the crisis of 1873 in order to see if these may yield a relevant perspective currently missing

---

[549] See Kindleberger 1990:310–312.
[550] See Fohlin 2007:21 (concerning Germany pre-1873); Bhide 2011:87–101; and Tooze 2018:17 (on the multidecade period of deregulation prior to 2008).
[551] See Rosenberg 1943:58.
[552] In all three cases, (politicians') hopes of a quick economic recovery were dismissed by a series of continued economic setbacks and relapses into recession.
[553] See Davies (2018:146) in relation to the crisis of 1873.

from the scholarship as well as from our broader appreciation of the causality of these recurring crises of the capitalist political economy. After all, Nietzsche was held by some as personally responsible, if not for directly causing World War One, then for deliberately weakening every moral fibre of Western civilisation, which made its slide towards the war all but inevitable.[554]

Agency and Corruption

One of the notable social discourses in Germany, seeking to attribute 'personal moral responsibility for the financial crisis', problematised the pervasive spread of *corruption* in the German political establishment, as well as of *fraud* in its commercial and financial circles:[555]

> Men quickly translated the crash into a political and moral indictment of the whole society. Corruption became the charge of the day. (Stern 1970:61)

The theoretical explanations, placing the blame on the 'anonymous market forces' and seeking to compare them to natural calamities, aka earthquakes, were deemed inadequate. Furthermore, no one in the German society appeared immune from the accusatory rhetoric, which reached to the very top of political establishment, implicating even the once irreproachable Bismarck, who was accused of granting commercial privileges to private companies in 'return for cheap stocks' (Davies 2018:114–122). Nietzsche suggested that 'three-quarters of the upper classes indulged in permitted fraud and had the stock exchange and speculations on their conscience' (D: §204). It felt as though the financial crisis exposed the absurdity of the artificial distinctions in society 'based on class, race, occupation or upbringing': everyone was complicit, no one was responsible, and no one seemed able to help. Society's guardians were found wanting and leading their people into the disaster rather than keeping them out of it, prompting Nietzsche's stinging criticism that 'what is at the top of society today is physiologically condemned' (NF-1888:25[1]). Society, which in the run up to the crash took 'much delight in individuality' and celebrated itself as consisting of 'many individuals' (GS: §23) suddenly found itself desperately searching for, yet unable to find, a communal mechanism for overcoming its angst.

Nietzsche, who remained one of the 'dissonant voices' fearing the 'extirpation of the German spirit' in the aftermath of victory in the Franco-Prussian War of 1870, was 'not heard' at the time (Stern 1972:231, 699). Yet he deals substantively with this perilous, on his view, consequence of the 1873 crisis in an important passage from *The Gay Science*—one of the book's longest aphorisms—entitled 'The Signs of Corrup-

---

554 See Voegelin 1944:177 and Stewart 1915:149–188.
555 See Davis' informed discussion of this subject in *Transatlantic Speculations*, 2018:16, 99–127.

tion' (GS: §23).[556] Elaborating on the themes previously developed in *Untimely Meditations*[557] and even borrowing some of its phraseology, he offers us an incisive psychological anatomy of the economic crisis, the repercussions of which spreads well beyond the economy. Nietzsche starts by identifying four signs 'of those states of society [...] which are designated with the word "corruption"'. The first is an atmosphere of profound *irrational fear* ('Aberglaube') which, taking different forms, grips society, becomes its 'order of rank' and even 'appears as progress'. Those who decry corruption become portrayed as adherents of the old—'pre-superstition'—doctrines and advocates of the old order of things, which has been superseded and is, as though, no longer relevant.[558]

In its very rational attempts to get to the causes of the crisis, society descends to a lower *plateau* of politico-economic discourse and intellectuality, which serve to normalise the damage caused by the catastrophe. The second symptom of a 'society in which corruption spreads', highlighted by Nietzsche, is the onset of *exhaustion*, which is, perhaps, the most precarious one. He argues that the times of rapid economic expansion, such as the one Germany underwent in the run up to 'Gründerkrach', are accompanied by a transmutation of the 'ancient national energy' into the unrestrained pursuit 'of the comforts of life' which the 'countless private passions' go after with the same fervour with which they once strove for the 'warlike and athletic honors'. The underlying instincts, exhausted by the incessant hunt after material gains, become *less healthy*, and this lack of vigour lowers society's internal resistance—its psychological immunity—making it more susceptible to the inflammatory discourses which become ignited by the onset of the crisis and aim to attribute blame:

> [I]t is precisely in times of 'exhaustion' that tragedy runs through houses and streets, that great love and great hatred are born, and that the flame of knowledge flares up into the sky. (GS: §23)

Nietzsche suggests that underneath the thin veneer of civility, society does not become more peaceable, as is preached by the advocates of political and economic liberalism. Society's potential for violence and cruelty does not 'dissipate drastically' but rather, it becomes suppressed and 'becomes more refined'. One striking attribute of the 'times of corruption' is that the 'art of wounding and torturing others with words and looks reaches its supreme development' precisely because—in the aftermath of the crisis—such words fall into the fertile soil of the weakened collective and individual psyche, inaugurating 'malice and the delight in malice':

> The men of corruption are witty and slanderous; they know of types of murder that require neither daggers nor assault; they also know that whatever is said well is believed. (GS: §23)

---

[556] For the remainder of this section, unless stated otherwise, '...' denote quotations from GS: §23.
[557] See Nietzsche's discussion of the *money-economy* in UM: III, *SE*, §4.
[558] It is critical to note that in the onset of irrationality under the guise of the intellect 'demanding its rights', Nietzsche recognises a 'symptom of enlightenment' (GS: §23).

Society's irrationality, combined with the growing psychic exhaustion, grant licence to the reactive, quasi-tyrannical political and economic actors who escalate the experience of the crisis by engaging in constant 'in-fighting'. The combined result of their actions is to embed the spiral of social decay deeper into the fabric of society until gradually 'the final tyrant' would emerge and 'put an end to the weary struggle for sole rule—by putting weariness to work for himself'. As decline reaches into every part of society, corruption spreads in similar all-encompassing patterns, claiming increasingly nobler natures who, driven by desire 'to achieve some security from the terrifying ups and downs of fortune', make peace with being 'bribed only "for today"' and succumb to 'anyone who is rich and powerful' and shows that he is 'ready to pour gold' into the 'nobler hands'. Nietzsche argues that as this dynamic of decay takes hold in society, it privileges the 'self-seeking drives of the soul' which, in turn, fundamentally alters society's perspective, making it increasingly myopic and circumscribed by the 'greedy exploitation of every minute' (UM: III, *SE*, §4). Individual and collective ability to discern the future—which appears too incalculable to be grasped—becomes temporarily suspended. This, Nietzsche asserts, completes the vicious circle of social decay, turning individuals into the willing participants in and the helpless witnesses to the unfolding calamity, which presents itself as *fait accompli* and alone capable of stopping the slide into barbarism by unleashing it.

In summary, Nietzsche's analysis problematises the spiral of societal decay set off by the 1873 crisis that would eventually pave the way to the outbreak of World War One. Much as Nietzsche's 'final tyrant' can be understood in terms of an individual rising from the chaos of a protracted crisis, the notion can also be interpreted as representing the apogee of the crisis itself, i.e., as its inexorable culmination in war. The repercussions of the economic crisis, as surveyed by Nietzsche, reach far beyond the economy and reverberate through the social fabric of society considerably longer than most economic analyses would suggest. Economic crises are neither self-contained in terms of their consequences, nor do they represent the full reset of the system to its 'default settings'. The main damage caused by the economic crisis, Nietzsche argues, is not at all economic and 'the psychical sufferings of the private person' do not get adequately addressed by religion, let alone by the secular State (HH: I, *State*, §472).

Repairing the economy in the aftermath of the crisis is not only different from the task of repairing of society; the concept of economy itself becomes progressively redefined (and reduced) to fit that which can be addressed by purely economic means. The damage caused or exacerbated by the economic crisis which remains unaddressed within such framework is transferred deeper into the social fabric of society, causing its further deterioration. As Davies surmises in relation to 'Gründerkrach', the 'spiritual wounds the panic had inflicted were deep, and the prolonged economic downturn of the 1870s only intensified the experience of social strife and conflict' (Davies 2018:109).[559]

---

[559] See Hyndman's informed discussion in *Commercial Crises of the Nineteenth Century*, 1902:99–128.

One perverse consequence of striving after 'material comforts' is that it gradually conditions collective consciousness to regard the world which is becoming 'uglier than ever' as 'a more beautiful world than there has ever been' (HH: I, §217). Nietzsche intuits a certain *continuity of valuations* between those that privilege the seeking of material wellbeing (i.e., paying homage to the valuations of the moneymakers; see NF-1888:14[182]), those that lay the groundwork for the crisis by encouraging and legitimating the excesses of such pursuits, and those that embed the crisis in the collective and individual consciousness, disabling our psychic resistance to it, thus, helping to escalate the social upheaval, the unfolding of which brings to the fore agents who personify the dynamic of the crisis by ruthlessly exploiting the vulnerabilities it has exposed. Through this process which unfurls simultaneously in us, through us and without us, we temporarily become the canvas upon which the forces unleashed by the crisis depict their grim narrative with the brushes firmly in the hands of the reactive and increasingly tyrannical powerbrokers. Nietzsche's political economy of an economic crisis furnishes us with an explanation that has no requirement and, indeed, no place for any conspiratorial elements in order to disclose not just the genesis of the crisis but also its likely outcomes.

Nietzsche's analysis, which extends from *Untimely Meditations* to *The Gay Science*,[560] makes it clear that society in the form of the money-economy does not possess the necessary means to heal the social wounds inflicted by an economic crisis. The means required to repair the social fabric, Nietzsche tells us, are not exclusively or even predominantly economic and financial. They have to do with the valuations that underpin the matrix for the allocation of resources and formulating societal priorities which, in turn, depends on the agency.[561] The political economy, powered by the profit logic, would invariably find new ways of satisfying its unchanged requirements in the changed, i.e., inferior, economic circumstances. Its *modus vivendi* precludes it from healing social divisions in order that it may continue to profit from them. Such exploitation of social discrepancies can only be carried out at the expense of storing up the tensions it produces, for the peaceful release of which the money-economy possesses no agonistic transformative mechanisms.

Valuations of *slave morality* that govern the money-economy and represent the closed system of values eventually turn against themselves. Davies comments that 'the moral economy' of the 1873 crisis, which 'denounced the dishonesty, selfishness, and greed of the capitalist, nonproducing class', i.e., all those things which cooked up and precipitated the crash in the first place, reflected a growing realisation that 'the financial panic was a symptom of a wider and more profound societal decay' and the questions of 'responsibility and human agency' extended to querying 'the system of capitalism and economic liberalism itself' (Davies 2018:109, 116).

---

560 It is also important, in this context, to consider *The Greek State* (1870/1) as well as *Thus Spoke Zarathustra* (1883–1885). Nietzsche's analysis of the genesis and consequences of the 1873 crash through the lens of the prevailing valuations resonates through both these works.
561 See Drolet 2013:37 and Salter 1917a:376.

The three poignant ways in which the fledgling capitalist social order was challenged in the aftermath of 1873—the 'combination of anticapitalism, anti-Semitism, and anti-liberalism'—were neither new nor specific to a particular geography, 'national peculiarities' notwithstanding.[562] Rather, the distinguishing feature of these phenomena was their increased *relative intensity* which was reflected in the deep polarisation of the political and economic debates of the time.[563] This intensification of these outbursts of *ressentiment* continued in the aftermath of the 1929 crash on both sides of the Atlantic.[564] Fast-forwarding to the more recent, and still very much in living memory, 2008 financial crisis, similar discourses were once again visibly present in its wake and similarly paved the way for the right and left-wing populist movements around the world.[565] Nietzsche, who sees the escalating crisis of the political economy of modernity unfolding as 'the great drama in a hundred acts' across the 'two centuries' (GM: III, §27), would consider the Panic of 1873 as part of a larger social dynamic and a precursor of greater calamities to come. The repeating patterns of dislocation produced, in the wake of these recurring economic crises, and the gradual intensification of these manifestations lend further support to Nietzsche's hypothesis highlighting a certain *continuity of valuations* which direct the proceedings of modern political economy and invariably produce and amplify its crises overtime. They also attest to the money-economy's (powered by these valuations) inherent inability to transcend itself and, instead, inflicting increasingly grievous injuries on humankind and the Earth.

Nietzsche's critique of the debt economy focuses on three main issues. It scrutinises the relationship between debt and democracy. It examines the role of debt in the context and the narratives of economic growth. Last but not least, it focuses on the role of money, banking, and the financial intermediaries in fuelling economic crises, on occasion beyond the point of containment by economic means. In light of the most recent, i.e., the 2008 financial crisis, arguably none of the aforementioned pressure points appears more troubling than the emerging signs of a divergence in the developmental trajectories of the capitalist economy and the liberal democracy. This schism reaches further than simply the 'catastrophic policy failures' and denotes a 'deeper and more serious problem' afflicting 'western economies and societies built on them', likened by some to a creeping sense of a 'failing social and economic model'.[566]

---

[562] Stern 1970:51; Davies 2018:116–123; and Copelovitch and Singer 2020:136. See Brustein's enlightening discussion of the rise of Antisemitism in the context of the 1873 crisis, 2003:210–213.
[563] See Holub 2018:273–277; Brustein 2003:4–5; and Davies 2018:114–116 for pertinent contextualisation.
[564] See Brustein 2003:3; Klapsis 2014:189–192; and Greene 2016:34–37.
[565] See Stern 1972:16; Tooze 2018:22, 430; Eichengreen 2018:7–12, 52–53; and Brustein 2003:158, 188.
[566] Tooze 2018:457. Elsewhere, Tooze refers to 2008 as the 'deep crisis of modern politics' (Tooze 2018:13) where 'the financial and economic crisis of 2007–2012 morphed between 2013 and 2017 into a comprehensive political and *geopolitical crisis of the post–cold war order*', exposing the 'long-term problems of modern capitalist democracy' (Tooze 2018:20; my emphasis).

Democracy's Debts

Today, Western societies appear to stand at the fork in the road where the debt economy and democracy may be forced to part ways unless they succeed in conjuring up a version of 'socially pacified capitalism' (Streeck 2014:180) infused with 'an *illusion of equitable growth*' (Streeck 2014:186). Nietzsche would not regard this predicament as a new phenomenon. He problematises the 'democracy of concepts' as providing the fertile soil for breeding such illusions:

> Nowadays the *democracy of concepts* rules in every head—many together are master: a single concept that wanted to be master would now, as aforesaid, be called an 'idée fixe' (HH: II, WS, §230)

Nietzsche, whose ideas on democracy were undoubtedly informed by the experience of the Long Depression, would remind us that conjuring up such political illusions, which invariably mask the process of society's decay, continues to be invariably linked with the alchemy of debt.

The relationship between *debt and democracy* forms a critical axis of Nietzsche's critique of the political economy of industrial culture. He approaches democracy, much like debt, from the point of view of its value focussing on the discrepancy between its utility and the values for which democracy stands, i.e., equality, freedom, and dignity. Nietzsche's assertion is that the *value of democracy* and *democracy's values* are two distinct concerns, while the temptation to equalise them conceals something important about the nature and the genesis of democracy. This line of inquiry, unorthodox in political theory, allows Nietzsche to conceptualise democracy as a political formalisation of theological [conceptions of primordial] indebtedness and, therefore, of enslavement, based on the values of *slave morality*.

Nietzsche problematises democracy as locus of valuations, corresponding to a particular physiological disposition, from which the 'principles and doctrines of government' (Drochon 2016:101), 'institutional arrangements' and 'types of behaviour' develop (Crick 2002:5). He argues that the promise of democracy within the confines of industrial society can only be a deeply flawed one as it remains essentially undeliverable beyond the slogans 'expanded into a political theory', which seemingly underwrite the social contract of industrial culture (TCW: §7). Echoing Tocqueville, Nietzsche contends that democracy, a *secular offspring of Christianity*—'Christianity made natural' (NF-1887:10[77])—is born of a metaphysical overpromise but it remains restricted to the insufficient and strictly secular means of delivering upon it (see AC: §42).[567] Drochon points out that 'Nietzsche is quite singular in the nineteenth century in denouncing democracy and Christianity as one' (Drochon 2016(a):1067).[568]

---

[567] See Nietzsche's comments in NF-1885:34[60] and in the letter to Franz Overbeck, dated 02.23.1887 (BVN-1887:804). See also Franco 2014:450, Stewart 1915:135 and Jaspers 1997:259.
[568] In *Tocqueville and Nietzsche* (2014), Paul Franco enunciates Tocqueville's influence on Nietzsche's thinking concerning democracy. Tocqueville discussed extensively the connection between democracy

> [W]e have reached the point where we find even in political and social institutions an ever more visible expression of this morality: the democratic movement is the heir of the Christian movement. (BGE: §202)

In this respect, Nietzsche likens democracy to 'the new horses' driving the carriage on 'the same old wheels' along 'the same old streets' with the chief difference being that now it is 'the wellbeing of the nations that rides in this vehicle' (HH: II, WS, §292).[569] Nietzsche warns that the promise of future universal material plenty—'the rule of shopkeepers' (NF-1888:14[192])—is bound to remain 'incommensurable with actual wealth', which society thus structured would be able to generate from its own resources (Lazzarato 2012:46). In addition, the 'prophets of the commercial class' would never make good on their promises (D: §175). This is a further and critical distinction of Nietzsche's critique of democracy. As Franco emphasises, Nietzsche 'does not simply equate democracy with Christianity' but argues that it is a pale and impoverished version of religion of—a distant 'echo of Christianity'—stripped of 'the spiritual tension' (Franco 2014:459).

Nietzsche, however, goes further to argue that democracy is *not* an autonomous political development. His view is that both democracy and debt, i. e., political and economic liberalism, have both dwelt as *latent potentialities* within the Judeo-Christian doctrine from its inception, nourished by the valuations of slave morality and waiting patiently for their time, when Christianity would eventually relinquish its theological throne with the advent of secular society. Nietzsche maintains that the ideas of 'universal harmony' and of the 'glorious upward trajectory' in humankind's development, previously championed by Christianity, have passed *directly* into the theories of 'free trade' and democratisation (HH: I, §25). He insists on the unequivocal connection between the 'civilisation of commerce' and the 'political equality of votes'—these two phenomena contemporaneously develop alongside one another *not* by accident but because both, the money-economy and modern democracy, spring from exactly the same metaphysical—Christian—root (NF-1887:11[157]). This is why, precisely as the 'waters of religion are ebbing away', the vacant domain—as though 'intensifying Faustian bargain' (Goodchild 2020:70)—is claimed by the rising tide of the money-economy propelled along by the rolling waves of 'cross-border democratisations' (UM: III, SE, §4).[570] This allows Nietzsche to connect the rising 'demand for equal rights' with the 'emana-

---

and Christianity, but Nietzsche's hostility toward religion and democracy 'sharply divides Nietzsche from Tocqueville' (Franco 2014:456).
569 See Drochon's insightful framing of the subject, 2016(a):1055–1068.
570 Nietzsche's passage resonates strongly with Engels' critique of Carlyle: 'Since however the place of the old religion could not remain entirely vacant, we have acquired a new gospel in its stead, a gospel that accords with the hollowness and lack of substance of the age—the gospel of Mammon. The Christian heaven and the Christian hell have been abandoned, the former as doubtful, and the latter as absurd—and you have acquired a new hell; the hell of modern England is the consciousness of "not succeeding, of not making money"' (CW 3:451).

tion of greed' (HH: I, *State*, §451), and to argue that democracy possesses an accommodating predisposition, as well as a requirement, for debt.[571]

Nietzsche posits a deeper connection between debt and democracy within the context of commercial society on the basis that both democracy and 'those who have to grant and request credit' *insist* upon equality in the sense of the 'sameness of character and sameness of value concepts' (NF-1887:9[173]). Nietzsche argues that this 'sameness' becomes the universal currency for trading 'virtue' on the stock-exchanges at the crossroads of the economic and the political sphere.[572] In the political arena, in particular:

> To aim for *equal rights* and ultimately *equal needs*, an almost inevitable consequence of our kind of *civilisation of commerce* and the *equal value of votes in politics* ... in the end the experimentation ceases, as it were, and a certain standstill is reached. (NF-1887:11[157], my emphasis)

Democracy too becomes a form of exchange of votes for promises, which lends itself to being facilitated by debt (NF-1887:9[173]). Whereas in the past creditors financed warring factions or states, within a democratic setting they can advance their money-making interests by financing the rivalry of political parties in the proverbial 'war for votes'. In this respect, democracy and debt, as though two sides of the same coin, denote a particular existential condition and, by deriving from the same disposition, they represent the same values, the same ethos (NF-1888:14[210]).[573] In a *Nachlass* note from 1881, Nietzsche characterises the 'political madness' of his day as a secularisation of the 'religious madness of earlier times' (NF-1881:11[163]). As Connolly notes in *Capitalism and Christianity* (2008), 'every institutional practice—including economic practices—has an ethos of some sort embedded in its institutions', without which these institutions would collapse. This ethos, Connolly argues, is of the Christian tradition or a particular variant thereof (Connolly 2008:3–5).[574]

Nietzsche sees neither debt nor democracy (see NF-1880:3[98]; BGE: §203; NF-1887:11[157]) as expressions of physiological strength and spiritual vigour—the necessary elements underpinning creative ability of 'a strong age' (TI: *Skirmishes*, §37). With the 'healing instinct, both physiological and psychological' disabled (NF-1888:14[210]),

---

571 Lazzarato concurs that 'debt is not only an economic mechanism, it is also a technique of government' (Lazzarato 2012:33).
572 Conceptual and linguistic similarities between Nietzsche's *Nachlass* note NF-1887:9[173], referenced above, and a quotation from 'The Currency and the Panic' in the Bankers' Magazine (February 1, 1875), used by Davies in *Transatlantic Speculations* (2018:83) are revealing in this respect: "The *uniformity in value and appearance* of our paper currency", one American writer argued, "the cheapness and ease with which domestic remittances are made, the fact that it *pays debts, and, in appearance at least, discharges all the functions of money*, are considerations which foster the error, that, as a nation, we are so absolute in our independence and so peculiar in our situation, that the laws of political economy are silent and inoperative'" (my emphasis).
573 See Siemens' engaging discussion of this in 2009:30–33.
574 Connolly's insightful account acknowledges but places less emphasis on Nietzsche's view that democracy develops out of the ethos of Christianity; see 2008:59.

neither debt, nor democracy is self-sufficient when it comes to self-preservation and furtherance. Both phenomena are premised on concealing their full power and moderating their range of affects, which translates into the need to be represented (D: §§203–204, §546).[575] Democracy, on Nietzsche's view, exhibits an inbuilt predisposition for debt and the latter, in order to proliferate to every corner of society, albeit without being thrust into the spotlight, requires democratic politics as its medium (NF-1888:14[182]). In *The Greek State* (1872), Nietzsche already connects 'the massive spread of liberal optimism' with 'the fact that the modern money-economy has fallen into strange hands' (GSt, 171). As Henry Ford tellingly noted in his autobiographical book:

> The people are naturally conservative. They are more conservative than the financiers. The people are on the side of sound money. They are so unalterably on the side of sound money that it is a serious question how they would regard the system under which they live, if they once knew what the initiate can do with it'. (Ford 1922:179)

Exploring this connection further, Nietzsche tells us that democracy is also a release of the forces 'of laziness, of weariness, of weakness' (NF-1885:34[164]) and 'a symptom of failing power, approaching old age, physiological exhaustion' (BT: *ASC*, §4). He later adds that embedded in democracy is the notion of decay in a sense of 'the diminution, of man, making him mediocre and lowering his value' (BGE: §203).[576] Nietzsche even suggests that absent the threat of socialism, democracy under capitalist economy would inevitably lead to 'the total mollification of the democratic herd animal' as there is nothing within the construct of this social order—i.e., the interaction between its economic basis and political superstructure, to borrow from Marx—that forces it 'to retain spirit' (NF-1885:37[11]). When weakness and exhaustion become the standard of value in politics—i.e., 'when anemia is construed as an ideal' (EH: *D*, §2)—the democratic mandate of political parties ends up restricted in two important respects. Firstly, in terms of the extent of the political leaders' ability to mobilise an electorate's effort and to summon the strength required to build a stronger present and to guarantee the future (see HH: I, §251; EH: *D*, §4–8).[577] Secondly, Nietzsche argues, the temporal horizons of democratic politics become compressed by the very nature of the forces democracy releases and has to harness, as 'the strength to build becomes paralysed and 'the courage to make plans that encompass the distant future is discouraged' (GS: §356).[578]

---

575 E.g., a more extreme or naked form of debt, such as usury, would make it more unacceptable and, therefore, easier to confront. The same would apply to the unrestrained forms of democracy, which could threaten the rule of the mob.
576 See Nietzsche's critical discussion in TI: *Errors*, §2.
577 See Nietzsche's discussion of 'the production of the supreme cultural values', which requires that the 'inner life' be 'so much harder and painful' (HH: I, *State*, §480). See also well referenced discussion of today's take on this constraint by Martin Wolf (2010) in 'How to Walk The Fiscal Tightrope That Lies Before Us', Financial Times, London (UK), 17 Feb 2010:9.
578 In '*A Glance At The State*', Nietzsche suggests that eventually democratic state 'is no longer equal to the demands of these forces' (HH: I, *State*, §472).

Constrained by the enervation of its subjects and hemmed in by the short-term horizons, which now circumscribe the political realm, democracy's focus shifts to embellishing the present in a manner that undermines the legacy of the past and diminishes the promise of the future, although it does not diminish the incessant promising of a brighter future.[579] As Siemens points out, Nietzsche problematises the 'tension between the equal distribution of happiness or contentment advanced by democratic values, on one side, and the future of humankind, on the other (Siemens 2009:30).

This breaking up of intergenerational continuity, which leads to aimlessly squandering the accumulated 'capital of ancestors' (HH: I, §156, §475), Nietzsche would argue, represents a detrimental reversal in the conditions of existence and makes *owing debt to the ancestors* fundamentally different from *owning the debt of the ancestors:* the former speaks to the vigour and confidence 'to undertake projects that would require thousands of years for their completion' (GS: §356), the latter—to the weakening of the future generations accomplished by the 'frivolous deification of the present' (BT: §24).[580] In this vein, Nietzsche problematises democracy's ability to return fiscally prudent agents 'with a genius for organisation' (GS: §356) as its chosen leaders, who would 'promise as much displeasure as possible as the price for the growth of an abundance of subtle pleasures and joys' (GS: §12). Instead, Nietzsche tells us, all political parties 'are now obliged to flatter the "people" and to bestow upon it alleviations and liberties of every kind' (HH: II, WS, §292), which transforms democratic politics into a competition of short-term promises and likens the politicians themselves to actors (GS: §356).[581] Whereas democracy ends up being a short-term and increasingly grandiloquent exercise of promising the bright future, recycled ad infinitum, debt yearns to impose itself over the humankind's long-term horizons, encircling and enslaving that future. Debt ensures that the future, delivered by its means, never corresponds to the promised future. This 'good cop - bad cop' dynamic between debt and democracy, manifest in the discrepancy [of horizons and effects], obscures the continual reproduction of the unchanged valuations of slave morality.

It also ensures that, from the outset and by design based on the antithesis of rank ordering, democracy—like Judeo-Christianity before it—finds itself in a state of deficit *vis-à-vis* its 'promise of inexpressible glories' (D: §546). This predicament is bound to persist for as long as 'the purpose of all politics [...] is to make life endurable for as many as possible', which entitles the 'as-many-as-possible [...] to determine what they understand by an endurable life' (HH: I, *State*, §438). This double-bind of decline, resulting from the conceptualisation of a 'fulfilled life' in terms of economic wellbeing, calls for 'as little displeasure as possible, painlessness in brief' (GS: §12), and delivers the latter by means of politics that has 'swallowed up all serious concern for really spi-

---

579 See UM: III, SE, §4; HH: II, WS, §286; GM: *Preface*, §6; and EH: UM, §3.
580 For a modern take on this issue, see John Coleman, 'Democracy's Debt Dilemma', Harvard Business Review, April 24, 2012, and Richard C. Schragger, *Debt and Democracy*, 2012:864.
581 I.e., 'let the best promise win', albeit Nietzsche questions the truthfulness of such promises, see EH: BT, §2, and *Clever,* §10.

ritual matters' (TI: *Germans*, §2)—i.e., the predicament Plato warned about develops in that the 'rulers come to resemble subjects and subjects come to resemble rulers'.[582] In this context, Nietzsche problematises democracy's will and ability to exercise stringent control over fiscal behaviour, including over the incurrence of debt, by means of the 'citizens' power to elect fiscally prudent agents and to decline to elect fiscally imprudent ones' (Schragger 2012:865–866). 'Citizens' power', in Nietzsche's logic, becomes an example of a compelling aspirational slogan, which, at the same time is a misnomer, concealing and legitimising the opposite reality of squandered strength (NF-1887:11[135]).

Democracy can no more afford to deliver on its promise than to renege on it. Consequently, it faces the challenge of *covering the shortfall* between the promise and reality. This discrepancy, Nietzsche argues, creates temptation to bridge the gap by any means necessary and within the shortest time possible: 'one lives for the day, one lives very fast, one lives very irresponsibly: precisely this is called "freedom"' (TI: *Skirmishes*, §39). Nietzsche even suggests that politicians and merchants are alike, when it comes to the 'speed of mental calculation' required for seeing many things quickly, but which precludes them from being able 'to see one thing'—to synthesise an active whole from many things—as they no longer possess the 'facility in measuring according to a standard' (HH: II, *WS*, §296), other than the making of profit.[583] Echoing Plato and Aristotle, Nietzsche argues that to function, democracy has to keep 'enhancing the weakness of the will' of the electorate (NF-1885:35[9]) by progressively raising the stakes from 'making free' to 'granting equal rights' and to 'expecting privileges' (NF-1887:10[66], 10[77]) because it is the *sine qua non* of democratic governance that 'whoever wants to retain power flatters the mob … must have the mob on its side' (NF-1888:14[182]).[584]

> The demagogic character and the intention to appeal to the masses is at present *common to all political parties:* on account of this intention they are all compelled to transform their principles into great al fresco stupidities painted on the wall (HH: I, *State*, §438).

Nietzsche warns that this process of manipulation of the democratic subject, which only masks the latter's decay, will continue by producing the 'extremest forms of personalisation' that will manifest themselves in the demands for and the granting of the 'extremest form of equality of rights, tied to an optical magnification of one's own importance to the *point of insanity*' (NF-1887:11[226/2]). This is possible, Nietzsche argues, because modern society gradually becomes reconfigured into an amalgamation of disparate individuals—each of whom is a minority of some kind and with a grievance of

---

582 See Plato R:562[e]. Nietzsche's insights exhibit considerable affinity with Plato's idea, see HH: II, §317 (on how a 'possessor becomes a slave'), WS: §209, as well as Z: IV, *Kings*. See Nietzsche's representative discussion of these issues in NF-1885:10[1]; NF-1885:2[15]; NF-1887:9[153]; GM: I, §2; AC: §43; and TI: *Skirmishes*, §37.
583 Cooper notes that 'the *bourgeois calculus* equates, in Nietzsche's words, 'intelligence and property', 'wealth and culture' (Cooper 2008:611; my emphasis).
584 See Appel 1999:130–131.

some sort—believing that each one is entitled to their own tailor-made social contract (NF-1888:14[197]). Nietzsche's idea, which certainly rings true in light of the experience of the Long Depression and in the aftermath of the 2008 Great Recession, is that democracy as a concept, a kind of politics and a form of governance, lends itself to being polarised by the powerbrokers on either end of the political spectrum. Democracy can just as easily become a powerful political and an ideological tool in the hands of the far right as being employed by the far left of modern politics.

From some of his earlier *Nachlass* notes to some of the last, Nietzsche likens this reliance of democratic politics on the increasingly inflated assurances to the effects of 'narcotics' (NF-1870:3[11]; NF-1888:14[192]), 'stimulants' (NF-1888:15[37]) and 'intoxication' (GS: §86). These are symptomatic, on his view, of the 'craving for ever stronger and more frequent stimulation' the weaker the democratic agent becomes (TI: *Errors*, §2).[585] 'Narcotics', however, have to be paid for, and this is where 'the sirens who in the market place sing of the future' can and do begin making significant inroads into the social fabric of society (GS: §377) as they seek entry points into the corridors of power, since 'in all political questions—questions of power are at stake' (NF-1887:9[121]). Democracy thus seems destined to come under the influence of the 'contemptible money-economy' and the moneymakers (see NF-1871:10[1], GSt; UM: III, *SE*, §6; Z: I, *Idol*).[586] Nietzsche argues that although 'money is power' and 'no one wants to hide it under a bushel'[587] the money-makers, conscious of 'just how much power is in their hand' (NF-1888:14[182]), remain reticent 'to lay it on the table' and consequently seek 'a representative which can be laid on the table' (D: §203).[588]

Nietzsche contends that in the form of democratic politics money-makers acquire a representative, which no longer represents rank but exclusively money and consequently, the money-makers 'use their power always in one direction'—they support everything liberal (NF-1888:14[182]).[589] In light of this, Nietzsche highlights the corruption

---

[585] Pertinently, in the *Genealogy*, Nietzsche characterises slave morality in terms of a 'stimulant, an inhibitor ... and a poison' (GM: *Preface*, §6) and Christianity, as having the 'most ingenious means ... to narcotize' (GM: III, §17).

[586] See earlier discussion in 'Concerning the 'psychological trappings' of debt'. Putting this into today's context, in *The Endless Crisis* (2012), Foster and McChesney argue that in the context of the 2008 financial crisis, '*debt can be seen as a drug* that serves, under conditions of endemic stagnation, to lift the economy. Yet the use of it in ever larger doses, which such a process necessitates, does nothing to overcome the underlying disease, and serves to generate its own disastrous long-run side effects' (Foster and McChesney 2012:70; my emphasis).

[587] A likely reference to a parable of Jesus as it appears in Matthew 5:14–15, Mark 4:21–25, and Luke 8:16–18, i.e., '...for nothing is hid, that shall not be made manifest; nor [anything] secret, that shall not be known and come to light' (Luke 8:16–18).

[588] Nietzsche's argument can be summarised as follows: an elected politician would only then be a responsible fiscal agent when she is independent (i.e., a sovereign individual). She can only be independent if she is an expert. If she is not an expert, she will inevitably serve the interests of the money-makers by representing them (see NF-1879:40[3]).

[589] See Nietzsche's more extensive discussion of this in NF-1888:14[182]. See Davies' discussion in the context of the 1873 crisis, 2018:96. See also Ansell-Pearson, who argues that the development of political

of political instinct, as well as of the political actors, as the inevitable corollary of such accommodation. Nietzsche's criticisms are echoed in Davies' recent analysis of the Gründerkrach years, where she suggests that 'corruption had become so rampant that German society was now easy prey for social democracy' (Davies 2018:114). Nietzsche's argument implies, therefore, that the critical element of the social contract of modernity is that between the democratically elected politicians on the one hand and the money-makers on the other rather than the one between the democratically elected politicians and the electorate, which is simply an illusion conjured up to confer an air of legitimacy on the former. This is another reason for Nietzsche to insist that the democratic liberty is no more than an 'invention of the ruling classes' (HH: II, WS, §9), which in reality only means freedom to make money for those who can and in a manner that is no longer frowned upon as it was in the 'former times' (UM: IV, RWB, §6).

Debt presents itself as if it were 'a magic shortcut'[590] and an answer to democracy's prayers by supplying 'the principal explanation for the strange sensation of living in a society without foreseeable rupture' (Lazzarato 2012:47). Democratic politics and the debt economy develop a symbiotic, yet asymmetrical relationship where the debt economy helps to prop up the promise of democracy and in return, the latter supports the expansion of the debt economy's hold over the industrial society and its members, reproducing a kind of inflationary vicious circle, which can already be seen as forming in Plato's thinking and which Klossowski aptly describes in *Nietzsche and the Vicious Circle*.[591] Connolly eloquently expresses this using the metaphor of a hurricane produced 'out of heretofore loosely associated elements', which redefines one's 'relation to God [i. e., democratic politics –DS] and the economy, until one or the other or both are said to command you to do what you already insist upon doing (Connolly 2008:51–52). Istvan Hont also highlights the *historical connection* between debt and democracy. He points out the circular intertwining of the debt dynamic with that of the capitalist economy and the emerging democratic state en route to modernity:

> The more republican a state became, the more difficult it was to get rid of the debt because the loans to the state mostly came from its own citizens, whose interest and property the state was supposed to protect. (Hont 2015:125)[592]

---

and economic strands of liberalism is inseparable (Ansell-Pearson 1994:10). See Noreena Hertz on the democratic politicians becoming increasingly 'indebted to or enmeshed with business' (Hertz 2003:9).
590 See the discussion by Cottarelli in *What We Owe: Truths, Myths, and Lies about Public Debt*, 2017:62.
591 See Plato, R:[553c-555c; 564a] and Klossowski 1997:149 and 165–167. Marx makes a similar point more forcibly in *The German Ideology*: the modern state, which, purchased gradually by the owners of property [...] has fallen entirely into their hands through the national debt, and its existence has become wholly dependent on the *commercial credit* which the owners of property, the bourgeois, extend to it' (CW 5:90).
592 See relevant discussion by Foster and McChesney on the developing dependence of politics in America on the issuance of debt from 1970s onwards (Foster and McChesney 2012:23–24).

However, becoming thus indebted, i.e., to its creditors, whose money-making interests become embedded and prioritised, raises another pertinent concern enunciated by Sedlacek, who builds on Nietzsche's argument: 'what sense does it make to measure riches', if one had to borrow 'to acquire them?' (Sedlacek 2013:86).[593] In other words, what kind of an illusion is being supplied to the democratic subjects and what is the nature of the 'pound of flesh', which the creditors demand for services rendered?

'The masses', according to Nietzsche, neither fully understand nor are allowed to understand the means by which promises made to them by 'all political parties', locked in the 'short-winded' and 'demagogic' struggles with one another, would be delivered until such time that 'an earthquake' will have 'displaced the former boundaries and contours of the ground', i.e., result in a crisis of some sort (HH: I, *State*, §438). Henry Ford is alleged to have claimed that 'it is perhaps well enough that the people of the nation do not understand our banking and monetary system, for if they did ... there would be a revolution before tomorrow morning'.[594] Importantly, the masses do not understand that by means of democratic politics that makes them 'more governable'—which is now universally 'desired as progress' (NF-1885:36[48])—they also become increasingly enslaved (see BGE: §203, §242) by being incorporated into the debt economy. Nietzsche suggests that the democratic multitude does not fully appreciate 'the calamitous consequences of their narrow-mindedness' (HH: I, *State*, §438):

> The mild air of democratic well-being weakens the capacity to reach conclusions, or even to conclude. One follows—but one can no longer see through to what follows. (NF-1885:37[11])

He argues that 'it is easiest to maintain and develop' such a hypnotic condition of the multitude 'in a democratic society: when the cruder means of defense are no longer necessary and a certain habit, order, honesty, justice, trust is part of the average conditions' (NF-1887:10[61]).[595] In other words, Nietzsche conjectures that the democratic forms of governance become more lenient as and because their outward repressive features are replaced with debt as the new principal instrument of creating and incorporating subjectivity.[596] Nietzsche argues that this helps to create an illusion of a social construct 'in which everyone enjoys their own social "contract"' (NF-1888:14[197]), whereas in reality, a society thus constituted has ceased being one social whole, 'a

---

[593] Varoufakis puts a similar point across more forcefully: 'In market societies all wealth is nourished by debt and all of the unimaginable riches created over the past three centuries owe their existence to debt. Debt, as Doctor Faustus shows us, is to the market societies what hell is to Christianity: unpleasant yet indispensable' (Varoufakis 2013:58–59).
[594] See Social Justice, April 19th, 1938, 10.
[595] As Chomsky aptly surmises, 'In democracy you can't force people so you have to control what they think' (Chomsky 2003:397).
[596] Nietzsche's conjecture in this regard appears to be validated by the IMF's claim that 'the private sector's debt has tripled since 1950' and became 'the driving force behind global debt'. See 'New Data On Global Debt (2019): https://blogs.imf.org/2019/01/02/new-data-on-global-debt/, last accessed Feb. 27, 2023.

unit', which makes its 'naïve' members weaker and more exposed to manipulation and enslavement, including, increasingly, by means of debt (see NF-1881:11[294]; NF-1888:14[197]).[597]

In *Ecce Homo*, Nietzsche contends that the priest, who also rules by weakening rather than by strengthening individuals, has to 'conserve what degenerates' in order to maintain power except that the price for such rule, 'when seriousness is deflected from the self-preservation and the enhancement of the strength', is the pervasive spread of decadence (EH: *D*, §2). Within the modern secular society, Nietzsche would argue, democracy governs in a manner similar to that of priest, just as the debt, which also becomes adapted to being an instrument of secular governance, transitions from being a debt to God to becoming a debt to the money-makers, who now enjoy considerable power, including through the support from the democratic state, which in turn 'has in its hands the most effective instruments … not only to unchain energies, but at the right time also to yoke them' (UM, III, *SE*, §6).

The problem Nietzsche identifies is that although democracy can successfully transform its repressive functions, it does not overcome them. Instead, democracy's repressive attributes—ineradicable manifestations of its predatory core valuations—become concealed beneath the outwardly peaceable appearance. Just like in the case of Christianity, these reactive political instincts—buried under the vernacular of freedom and equality—adapt to the changed conditions but do not disappear (NF-1885:2[165]). Nietzsche argues that the process of democratisation itself becomes the modality by means of which these instincts learn to discharge themselves.[598] This has the consequence that repression is able to do its work behind the scenes where it actively moulds repressed subjectivity of democratic agents. This work, including democracy's gradual degeneration, which happens behind the decorated façade of democratic institutions, becomes more difficult to track, let alone to reverse. By targeting, initially and increasingly, the social, economic, and political excesses in society, democracy exhibits a propensity to become excessive and very passionate about its excessiveness which remains its blind spot (HH: II, *WS*, §293). As a result, we lose sight of the possibility that the tyranny to which every democracy eventually succumbs is not, as is conventionally assumed, something foreign that happens to democracy. Democracy's sliding into tyranny is not the work of external factors but rather of the tendencies that are integral to democracy itself, as a latent form of tyranny, where the tyrannical rule becomes the final form of its development that turns against the elements and the instincts which have nurtured it.[599]

Applying Nietzsche's conjecture that the democratic promise can be supplied progressively by means of debt to today's reality in some of the world's wealthiest economies, it is difficult to disagree that for the majority of democratic subjects democracy

---

[597] In this respect, analogy can be drawn to the present 'gig economy', where a growing number of workers (e.g., an estimated 5 m in the UK in 2019) are classed as independent contractors.
[598] See HH: II, *WS*, §275; NF-1885:36[48]; and NF-1887:9[8/b].
[599] See HH: II, *WS*, §281, and NF-1885:2[13].

can be experienced primarily 'on credit'.⁶⁰⁰ An ever expanding array of the forms of debt allows to extend as well as to intensify democratic experience today as well as enticing and, in some cases, compelling to it: mortgage debt, student debt, consumer debt, in-store credit, auto-credit, book now pay later holidays credit, hire purchase credit, credit card credit—to name but a few.⁶⁰¹ Price, exacted for this kind of experience, is a double bind, by means of which the individual is largely reduced to being an economic agent and by being so reduced, as this reductivism becomes constitutive of subjectivity as well as becoming normative, he is also enslaved, albeit inconspicuously. Crucially, such facets of social well-being as the living standard and a sense of entitlement cease being a function of attainment and become a function of the availability of credit.⁶⁰² This radically different incentive becomes a critical ingredient of the 'despairing boredom of the soul' and 'idleness in all its varieties' or, in other words, a fertile ground for the nihilistic attitude to life, to the world, and to the future (HH: II, *WS*, §220). Inferring from Nietzsche's argument, Lazzarato surmises that:

> The debt economy occupies the terrain of the political in order to transform each individual into an indebted economic subject (Lazzarato 2012:53)

In helping to moderate the shortcomings of democracy as a form of 'decay of political organisation' (BGE: §203) and to delay the 'death of the state' (HH: I, *State*, §472) within the setting of democratic governance, debt serves clearly political purposes, which is equally necessary for its own self-preservation. In this combination, Nietzsche notes, both debt and democracy exhibit expansionist and consolidating propensities of a 'supraterrestrial institution', requiring the same 'veneration' (HH: I, *State*, §472), 'sacrifice' (UM: III, *SE*, §6), and 'idolatry ... formerly rendered the church' (UM: III, *SE*, §4).⁶⁰³ This leads Nietzsche to problematise democracy and debt as the two elements and two manifestations of the same reactive will to power, with deep theological roots, which seeks to 'conserve what degenerates'.⁶⁰⁴

A further complication emerges from the interlocking of the politics of overpromise and debt. It becomes exposed in the aftermath of severe social dislocations, when the 'threat of systemic collapse' becomes palpable (Tooze 2018:472) and when the state appears 'no longer equal to the demands' of holding in check the 'savage forces that beat a path' through such crises (HH: I, *State*, §472; see also I, *Tokens*, §246) and the 'states of emergency' inevitably weaken the 'forces of democracy' (HH:

---

600 See Posner-Weyl 2018:30 (regarding 'saddling them with debt that they cannot pay') and Mian-Sufi 2014:178–216 (regarding systematic weakening of individual's ability to resist credit).
601 See Dowd 2000:157–159 and 204.
602 See Roche and McKee 2012:9–10.
603 This interpretation would be consistent with Nietzsche's assertion that in democracy 'everything should become politics', i.e., including debt (HH: I, *State*, §438).
604 HH: I, *State*, §472; EH: *D*, §2. See also Nietzsche's discussion in UM: III, *SE*, §6 on the expansion of the democratic state driven by the premise of 'the happiness of the greatest number and development of great communities'.

II, WS, §281). Echoing Plato, Nietzsche argues that while 'every oligarchy conceals the lust for tyranny' (GM: III, §18), it is only the eventual unravelling of democracy—as though through an 'involuntary arrangement'—that paves the way for the 'cultivation of tyrants', who are not necessarily 'the most spiritual' (BGE: §242). Much as they may preach 'making their city safe for the friend of democracy' (R:566[b]) and deny that they are tyrants (R:566[e]), unlike the doctor, who may prescribe a purgative for society's ills, the tyrants may well do the opposite (R:566–568) as their power grows the greater in proportion with the deepening decay.[605]

Nietzsche's own conception of the future democracy—'as of something yet to come' (HH: II, WS, §293)—can be discerned from his discussion in *The Wanderer and His Shadow*. Democratic governance Nietzsche envisages is steadfastly agency-dependent.[606] Foretelling the gradual fusion of foreign and domestic policy, Nietzsche invokes the image of the future *diplomats*, who are at the same time 'cultural scholars, agriculturalists and communications experts', and who do not need to 'rely on the armies' to engage in their arguments (HH: II, WS, §292). This position is consistent with Nietzsche's thoughts on the nature of political leadership where society's guardians represent it in all of its respects at once. This, for Nietzsche, is key to overcoming the antagonism embedded in the petty and fragmented democratic politics of his time, which is powered by the valuations of slave morality. Furthermore, in order to 'guarantee as much independence as possible', democracy needs to strive for the *continual overcoming* of the socio-political excesses manifested most strikingly by the 'two impermissible classes'—the super-rich and the propertyless, whom Nietzsche considers to represent great danger to society at all times (HH: II, WS, §293). Nietzsche's thought is not simply to deprive these groups of 'the right to vote' but to achieve such agonal composition of the social fabric where these excesses are continually abolished by society's very functioning (HH: II, WS, §293).

Money and Banking

The role of money (paper money, to be specific), banks and bankers in creating and fuelling debt crises in 1873 and in 2008 has been widely publicised and thoroughly examined. On both occasions, aided by the near absence (or collapse) of prudential supervision, the virtually unlimited credit creation by private institutions followed from the

---

[605] See TI: *Skirmishes*, §38–39, and EH: *D*, §2.
[606] In a note from 1881, Nietzsche notes that 'the free person is a state and a society of individuals.—The development of herd animals and social plants is very different from that of the individual.—Individuals who live alone, if they do not perish, develop into societies, a lot of work areas are developed, and also much struggle for food space time. Self-regulation is not there all at once. The freest man has the greatest sense of power over himself, the greatest knowledge about himself, the greatest order in the necessary struggle of his forces, the relatively greatest independence of his individual forces, the relatively greatest struggle within him' (NF-1881:11[130]). See also NF-1885:35[47].

significant increase in the supply of paper money.[607] This happened in America, where the gold standard was suspended during the Civil War (1861–1865), and in Austria, where paper money was not backed by specie reserves (see Davies 2018:28, 44). In Germany, following the reparations received from France, the banking industry experienced phenomenal growth as well as being one of the largest beneficiaries of the economic boom between 1870–1872.[608] Unable to utilise all of the available capital domestically, German banks invested heavily in the speculative start-up ventures in both Austria and the US. As though closely following the script of Goethe's *Faust*, this left all three countries' economic and financial systems destabilised and 'vulnerable to speculative excess' upon which the enterprising banks and bankers did not miss an opportunity to capitalise.[609] Not unlike in the build-up to the 2008 financial crash, this was achieved by converting the liquid short-term borrowings from the markets, which were assumed to always be available, into the illiquid, long-term and highly speculative debts on both sides of the Atlantic, but primarily in America (Davies 2018:62–63).

In the run-up to 1873, investment capital poured into the bonds secured by the fictitious mortgages and intended to finance the *railways*, construction of which, in many cases, had not yet commenced. In 2008 debt investments directed into the highly illiquid, long-term and speculative *residential real estate* followed the identical logic.[610] Inability to see the coming crash, particularly in Germany in 1870s, was linked also to the growing presence and influence of bankers and civil servants who sat on the corporate boards of important businesses, which they were also financing and, not infrequently 'overcapitalizing in order to award themselves handsome fees' (Davies 2018:152).[611]

On both occasions, in 1873 and in 2008, the realisation that virtually *all money was debt* because the private banks 'do not loan any existing money but instead create new money out of nothing' (Werner 2014:16–18), arrived too late to stem the onset of universal panic which beckoned the deep and protracted economic recession. Within a year of the Berlin stock exchange crash, 'over sixty banks and a hundred industrial firms failed in Germany' (Copelovitch and Singer 2020:138; Zucker 1975:135). The Panic of 1873 proved equally devastating in the US, where the collapse of Jay Cooke & Company—America's pre-eminent investment bank which epitomised Faustian alchemy on the global scale —eventually led to the bankruptcy of over 100 banks nationwide (see Davies 2018:28–44).

---

607 See Fohlin 2007:23–24.
608 Over a hundred new banks were founded in Germany between 1870–1872 (Fiebig 2019:71–72).
609 In the context of the 1873 crash, Davies notes that during the boom years for the economy, 'the speculative mindset, it seemed, was permeating every sphere of life, and the thirst for quick profit knew no limits' (Davies 2018:54).
610 Most commentators concur that the 'same runaway market-driven process of credit creation', masterminded by the unrelenting 'business logic of bankers' in the lead up to 2008 exacerbated the severity of economic dislocations on the global scale (see Tooze 2018:86, 88–89).
611 See further Davies 2018:111–113 and Brustein 2003:208.

A crucial aspect of Nietzsche's critique of the debt economy relates to the issue of money creation and financial intermediation, which highlight the propensity of modern political economy to maintain itself through the proliferation of debt. Nietzsche sees the growing concentration of money creation in private hands and on unprecedented scale as one of the main drivers of economic instability in Germany of the 1870s. Nietzsche's initial comments alluding to this issue appear in the early notes in the *Nachlass*, where he highlights propensity of the tightly-knit oligarchy of the 'truly international, homeless, money hermits' to perfect the skill of 'misusing politics as an instrument of the stock exchange and both the state and society as mechanisms for their own enrichment' (NF-1871:10[1]).[612] Nietzsche is keenly aware of the risk entailed in the globalising trends, induced and amplified by the spread of the money-economy, when it is fuelled 'by the brutal greed of money alone'.[613] This risk is particularly pertinent to the banking industry where Nietzsche correctly predicts that the 'immense conglomerates would take the place of isolated capitalists', exacerbating the speculative excesses and leading to the 'stock market falling under the curse that casinos have fallen to' (NF-1870:5[105]). In this respect and echoing Goethe, Nietzsche argues it is critical that *creation of money* be taken out of the private hands and 'forcibly', if needs be (HH: II, WS, §209):[614]

> [W]e must *remove from the hands of private individuals and companies* all those branches of trade and transportation favourable to the accumulation of great wealth, thus *especially the trade in money* ... (HH: II, WS, §285; my emphasis)[615]

He considers the private 'trade in money'—a particularly harmful variety of 'the sudden or unearned acquisition of riches' (HH: II, WS, §285)—to represent 'a great danger to society', which he likens to 'obesity ('a repulsive swelling sickness') that has become one of modernity's chief social diseases to be confronted—a call, which is widely echoed in the aftermath of both, the crash 1873 and the crisis of 2008.[616] Nietzsche tells us that many a generation are required before it is possible to develop mastery over money and as such, only 'the wise ... of the highest intelligence' can be invested with 'the monopoly of the money market' because they alone would be capable of giving it direction and goals that reach above and beyond the interests of money-making (NF-1881:11[82]).

---

612 Cf. Cooper, 'Nietzsche, Money and *Bildung*', 2008:605–629.
613 See UM: IV, *RWB*, §4; NF-1884:25[178]; NF-1885:37[9]; BGE: §61; and EH: *CW*, §2.
614 There are direct echoes of Plato in Nietzsche's thinking on this issue, see R:564[e].
615 Although there is no direct evidence that Nietzsche read Marx's arguments concerning capitalism's globalising traits and money, structural parallels between Nietzsche's thoughts and Marx's are discernible here. See Renton 2001:125–131 concerning private money creation and Marx on capitalist globalisation in *The Communist Manifesto* (CW 6:482–487).
616 See Richard A. Werner (2016), 'The Alchemy of Banking' in Binswanger, *Money and Magic*, 1994:142–157.

His concern can be understood as threefold. Firstly, Nietzsche's analysis directly challenges a widely held view that the intermediaries, including financial intermediaries, do not influence prices, or the allocation of resources' (Gorton, Winton 2002:1). Nietzsche argues to the contrary by pointing out the *structural similarity* between the secular intermediaries, who come under multiple guises, and the ascetic priest. Both, according to Nietzsche, are the agents of *slave morality*, who start from the position of craving power but lacking the means to acquire it:

> What gives authority when one does not have physical power in one's hands (no army, no weapons of any kind—)? How, in fact, does one gain authority over those who possess physical strength and authority? Only by arousing the belief that they have in their hands a higher, mightier strength. Nothing is sufficiently strong: the mediation and service of the priests is needed. They establish themselves as *indispensable intermediaries*. (NF-1888:14[189]; my emphasis).

Nietzsche argues that financial intermediaries, not unlike the ultimate intermediary—in the guise of the ascetic priest—inflate their importance by shrouding themselves in sophisticated theories on the matters of vital importance to our lives, interspersed with dizzying *formulae* and technical jargon, the meaning of which they alone understand and are capable of mediating. These intermediaries create, in effect, have their own kind of religion by means of which they make themselves indispensable, societies subjugated and which they guard with all their strength.

In a note from late *Nachlass*, Nietzsche emphasises the importance of changing the 'governing point of view' ('Hauptgesichtspunkt') precisely in order to diminish the scope and reduce the influence of the intermediate structures ('Mittelgebilde'), which deliberately create and exploit oppositions for their benefit (NF-1887:10[63]). He points out that any kind of mediator would 'almost involuntarily falsify the nourishment they mediate' and 'in addition they want too much for themselves as payment for their mediation' (HH: II, *WS*, §282). The bigger and the more powerful such mediators grow, at the expense of 'the original productive spirits' (HH: II, *WS*, §282), the more likely is society to become dependent on debt-money (HH: II, *AOM*, §310), and far in excess of what is necessary 'to sustain our life' (UM: III, *SE*, §5). As such, and as with any necessary evil, it is incumbent on society's stewards to make and keep these mediators 'as small as possible' (HH: II, *WS*, §282).

It would not be far-fetched to suggest that Nietzsche would advocate breaking up the global financial oligarchy. Taking away the power to create money from these banks would make it possible to transform them from being the profit-driven agents of fictitious economic growth and creators of debt—making 'our modern life extremely costly' (NF-1885:34[162])—into the viable intermediaries of economic activity more commensurate with serving the network of decentralised 'little economic communalities', which would make up the economic fabric of the wider society (D: §132).[617] Nietzsche's proposal is entirely consistent with his understanding that lending

---

[617] See Cameron and Dombowsky 2008:123.

must come from the calculated *ability to sustain loss*. Nietzsche considers that extending credit has to be done at creditor's risk, which would preclude bailing out over-extended lenders.

Secondly, Nietzsche links banking's casino-like proneness to generate excesses spilling over into crises to is its dangerous propensity to re-awaken base stereotypes and reignite old theological enmities of *slave morality*. Nietzsche connects the rise of Antisemitism, particularly pronounced in Germany in the aftermath of the 1873, directly to the perversions of the money-economy which, losing sight of 'total accounting', scapegoats 'the youthful stock-exchange Jew' as 'the most repulsive invention of the entire human race' in order to conceal the true causes of its failures (HH: I, *State*, §475).[618] Dismantling this pernicious stigmata attached to Jews becomes an enduring leitmotif of Nietzsche's philosophical undertaking and an integral part of the project for the revaluation of all values.

Last but not least, Nietzsche's conjecture forces us to consider the question of how debt comes to develop from being a facilitator of economic activity into the driving force of economic behaviour or, formulated differently, why the financial intermediaries have been allowed to amass such considerable power in regulating the political economy of human affairs? Nietzsche argues that under the auspices of the debt economy, 'anyone possessing money and influence can transform any opinion into public opinion' (HH: I, *State*, §447). In so doing, he calls into question ability of the modern state, much as it seeks to 'organise everything out of itself' (UM: III, *SE*, §4), to provide adequate governance of the political economy and to effectively 'bind hostile forces' contained therein (UM: III, *SE*, §4). On the one hand, the state comes under the increasing influence of 'despots and money-makers' (UM: III, *SE*, §4). On the other, it has to contend with the 'the gradual rise of the cross-border democratisation' (HH: II, *WS*, §292). The secular state's 'unconditioned urge for control' (NF-1885:37[9]) ends up wedged between placating the masses and pandering to the money-makers (HH: II, *WS*, §293). Within this context, debt invariably presents itself as 'the magic shortcut', supposedly allowing to satisfy both ends of the predicament, albeit by perpetuating the logic of unsustainable money creation.

An inference from Nietzsche's analysis is that prudent debt management, including through regulation and control of money creation, is not compatible with the premises of democratic politics, which is subjected to irreconcilable demands and, in the final instance, yields to the logic of 'money alone' (see NF-1885:37[9]; D: §175).[619] With that in mind, Nietzsche argues that 'constitution of the state' must be determined 'by the most comprehensive regard for all human actuality' (HH: II, *AOM*, §220). To achieve this, it is necessary to divorce 'the questions of utility' from all considerations of political expediency (HH: II, *WS*, §292). In other words, it would take a particular type

---

618 See Brustein's insightful discussion in *Roots of Hate*, 2003:205–224.
619 Binswanger argues that 'today and in past centuries, the creation of private paper money has been legitimised by governmental collusion' (Binswanger 2016:145).

of agency to break the vicious circle of debt. Nietzsche considers this is only possible within the framework of the council of experts—with 'the conscience for the over-all development of man' and bound by the most comprehensive personal responsibility (see BGE: §61, §212)—as the highest law-giving body charged with a small number of strategic priorities of statecraft (HH: I, §318).

Psychology of Banking

Nietzsche's argument reaches further still in terms of understanding of what it would take to inhibit the profit-logic enshrined in the debt economy. Drawing on his critique of industriousness as the modern vice, Nietzsche challenges its rationale by questioning, whether the servants of the debt economy hasten to give their 'heart to … money-making' because ultimately 'everyone is in flight from himself' (UM: III, SE, §6). He even cautions against asking 'the cash-amassing banker' about the purpose of his restless activity on account that such actors, hostages to *slave morality*, are unable to see through the fog of their unquestioned obedience to the 'stupidity of the laws of mechanics' (HH: I, *Tokens*, §283). Combined, more often than not, with a superficial 'external goal' (D: §206) of 'earning a very great deal of money' (UM: III, SE, §6), it leads to the 'greedy', yet thoughtless, 'exploitation of every minute' (UM, III, SE, §5), the end result of which is 'contemptible' personal enslavement (see NF-1876:19[21]; NF-1880:6[341]). Nietzsche argues that while the 'blindly raging industriousness creates wealth', it does so inevitably at the price of 'blunting the senses' and 'depriving the organs of the very subtlety' required to enjoy that wealth (GS: §21). One ends up caught in the self-perpetuating dynamic whereby 'one does not know how to make anything of all its industriousness and money except always still more money and still more industriousness' (GS: §21).[620] Furthermore, Nietzsche makes explicit the dangers to one's well-being and development posed by such industriousness, which, although it is 'privately harmful', continues to be endorsed as a societal norm and a virtue (GS: §21). Such society may feel 'sorry for the youth who has worked himself into the ground', but it remains programmed to regard it a far greater risk 'if the individual would think otherwise and consider his preservation and development more important' (GS: §21). As a result, even in the death of such an individual, the society would only mourn the loss of a 'devoted instrument', which (not who!) 'was ruthless against itself', while at the same time ramping up the production of countless more such instruments (GS: §21).

Nietzsche problematises this grave predicament of the industrial culture embedded in modern sensibility, which has completely lost sight of the notion that 'prosperity is physical and intellectual' rather than material (NF-1885:34[76]), and that the true 'enjoyment of culture' is only 'to some extent a matter of money' but much more critically

---

[620] See also Nietzsche's discussion in *Daybreak:* §204 and §206.

—it is 'a matter of spirit' (HH: II, *AOM*, §310), because 'the highest and the most illustrious human joys' exist outside the financial sphere and cannot be purchased (see NF-1885:41[6]; 41[7]). Nietzsche issues an urgent call for the 'moderation of industriousness' (GS: §210) which would be achieved by setting such developmental goals that 'would transcend money and money-making' (UM: III, *SE*, §6), transforming 'the most industrious of all ages' (GS: §21) by reinstating the importance of greater 'contemplativeness and simplicity' (UM: III, *SE*, §6).

The task of slowing down and disabling the debt-creating machine, obsequious appendices to which bankers have become, is no benign undertaking as it would involve changing the entire matrix for setting objectives and decision-making. Nietzsche calls on the bankers to become experts of investment rather of investing, i.e., the kind of experts who develop a painstaking understanding not [only] of what they are investing, i.e., money, but of that into which they are investing. Put slightly differently, what Nietzsche suggests is a form of the revaluation of all values. He is clear concerning the harm of not heeding the plea 'to wash one's soul ever cleaner from the market place' (NF-1885:41[7]). Namely, it is that today's money-makers, collectively represented by one of the most prestigious and sought after professions, rank as some of the main contributors to the pervasive 'impoverishment of the spirit and the senses' and as instigators of 'a premature decline' of humankind (GS: §21).[621] In order to understand the weight of Nietzsche's conjecture more clearly, it is important to follow it through to his analysis of growth.

Debt and Growth

Following the logic of Nietzsche's argument on the complex affects of debt within the context of modernity gradually brings to the fore more fundamental assertions, which underwrite its political economy and inform its governing outlook. Arguably, few of these would be more pertinent than the doctrine of growth—'the one binding measure of humanity's development' and the central tenet of industrial culture, which has gradually drawn 'all areas of life into its vortex' (Binswanger 2016:2–12).[622] Economic growth as well as the proliferation of economic thinking promoting it were the notable features of both the 1873 and the 2008 crises. Nietzsche links these types of growth to

---

[621] A powerful artistic insight into the origins and the psychology of investment banking, which echoes Nietzsche's concerns, can be found in Stefano Massini's *The Lehman Trilogy* (2013).

[622] In a recent inquiry into the origins of modern economy, *A Culture of Growth* (2017), Joel Mokyr argues that 'a critical cultural belief in the "virtuousness of growth" is a belief in progress and specifically in economic progress. Such belief has positive, normative and prescriptive components' (Mokyr 2017:19). Earlier, in *Butterfly Economics* (1998), Paul Ormerod singled out [economic] growth as by far by far 'the most striking feature, which distinguished industrial capitalism from all previous social and economic systems' (Ormerod 1998:150).

the expansion of rationality at the expense of spiritual growth, which he associates with the development of the intellect.[623]

The Long Depression of 1873 and the Great Recession of 2008 were both preceded by periods of rapid and highly inflationary economic growth. Nietzsche captures the inflationary character of growth, which preceded the Long Depression, in a note from the late Nachlass:

> We have increased the speed of all means of transport tenfold: at the same time, however, our need for speed has increased a hundredfold. (NF-1887:11[296])

Nietzsche's comment suggests that this kind of growth, in order to take place, would require an accommodating environment, one that would feed and legitimise this type of unrelenting 'chasing after one's own tail'. Earlier, in *The Gay Science*, Nietzsche problematises this predicament in terms of the pervasive corrosion of the social fabric of society (GS: §23). In both instances—1873 and 2008—economic expansion rested on questionable foundations, was surrounded by heavy promotion, shrouded in corruption and financed largely by debt. Just as the 2008 crisis began with the bursting of the *housing bubble* in the United States, which was almost universally mistaken for meritorious economic growth for some years previously, Gründerkrach of 1873 signalled the bursting of the *railroad bubble*, also mostly in the United States, which was also lauded as spectacular economic growth buoyed by the 'development of new industries', none of which could compete with the railroad construction in terms of its investment lure. Between 1868 and 1873, some 80,000 of railroad tracks were laid in the United States, Germany and Austria, with the US accounting for over 60% of the total.[624] In every aforementioned jurisdiction 'reckless gambling followed so soon as it was found that railway construction was likely to prove profitable' (Hyndman 1902:55). Tooze's analysis of the anatomy of the 2008 crisis reveals the overwhelming extent to which the global economy has come to depend on the 'growth model', notwithstanding that this dependence spawned an increasingly skewed distribution of systemic costs and benefits, produced 'contradictory geopolitical consequences' in the run up to the crisis as well as in its aftermath, notwithstanding that such growth has been and remains driven increasingly by debt.[625]

---

[623] The connotations of this differentiation are telling. Intellect rises from physiology. Rationality grows from psychology. Intellect is an open system of interpretations. Rationality is a closed system of valuations. Intellect generates synthetic proportions. Rationality functions by means of abstract categories and analysis. Intellect creates and revels in diversity. Rationality establishes tyranny of concepts. Intellect operates from the position of natural abundance and seeks to assimilate (new and different). Rationality is the product of psychic deficit and seeks to compensate. Intellect is agonistic. Rationality is antagonistic.

[624] See Davies 2018:3–4; Fohlin 2007:16; and Stern 1979:302.

[625] See Tooze 2018:17–53 and 108–152.

Physiology and Psychology of Growth

Growth is an important conceptual category within Nietzsche's thinking and his views on the physiology and the psychology of growth, in particular, offer some illuminating explanations in this context. In the first place, he contends that 'to have and to want to have more—growth, in one word—that is life itself' (NF-1885:37[11]). However, he then distinguishes between the two types of growth—active and reactive—as being distinctly different, including in respect of their consequences. The first type is creative rather than imitative, it is growth that aims to generate surplus rather than being infinitely compensatory and producing excess. Active growth comes to denote broadly conceived development, whereas reactive growth is represented development, where the growth of a particular segment of the whole is projected on to this whole, as though representing its holistic development. Starting with the premise of self-sufficiency and physiological abundance, active growth seeks to 'assimilate new' in order to 'make itself richer' rather than to make itself whole (BGE: §230). It acts from a position of excess 'digestive capacity' (BGE: §230) and abundance of 'metabolic power' (NF-1881:11[182])—it seeks to 'incorporate new experiences' in a manner of 'filing new things into old files'(BGE: §230).

Nietzsche argues that in weaker or declining organisms, growth tends to be reactive—i.e., an infinite process of compensation for the lack of intrinsic vitality (NF-1881: [316]). Powered by 'greed', this kind of growth—regardless of whether it is in relation to 'individuals, peoples, states or societies'—cannot either be moderated or accomplished—i.e., it cannot stop, as 'the apparent possession still knows how to elude us' (NF-1881:11[19]). Nietzsche argues that such growth, unless 'it can incorporate itself' by subordinating to a higher whole, in the sense of 'becoming a function' of something greater than itself, something that would allow to reach 'the out-of-itself' (NF-1881:11[19]), would remain destined to continue with the endless and yet, fruitless, dynamic of overcompensation (NF-1881:11[134]). Distinguishing between these two modes of growth, Nietzsche suggests existence of an intuitive 'reciprocal predisposition' that recognises and strives for the 'hierarchy of spirits' and an order of rank, absent which organisms and forces alike, squander themselves aimlessly.[626]

In a further *Nachlass* note from the same notebook 'M.III.1', entitled 'the basic idea of commercial culture' (NF-1881:11[246]),[627] Nietzsche contends that when 'the lower classes' are dissatisfied 'at the sight of the rich', it is not necessarily or exclusively that they covet the possessions of the rich.[628] Rather, what 'obsessively stimulates the imagination' is the 'image of happiness', albeit, as though the happy disposition itself derived from the possessions and not vice-versa (see NF-1881:11[246]; HH: I, *HMS*,

---

[626] See Nietzsche's discussion of the requirements for a great culture in NF-1872: FEI, V.
[627] Not to be confused with the passage from *Daybreak* (§175), entitled 'Fundamental Idea of Commercial Culture' ('*Grundgedanke einer Cultur der Handeltreibenden*').
[628] This is a possibly direct juxtaposition to Smith, who argued in the *Wealth of Nations* that it is 'the affluence of the rich', which excites the 'indignation of the poor' (WN2:203).

§81).⁶²⁹ In other words, the 'slave's eye' wishes to 'persuade itself' that the happiness of the strong is not genuine (BGE: §260). Such mistaking of cause and effect—i.e., thinking that 'you have to have something to be something' (NF-1885:37[11])—gives rise to the insatiate desire to compensate, which can never fulfil itself because it is pursuing something that does not exist unless it is given, something that cannot be acquired, no matter how much material wealth one may amass in the process (TI: *Reason*, §4).⁶³⁰ Nietzsche argues that neither strength, nor power can be acquired, let alone purchased (NF-1887:9[145]), unless they are already present in 'the overall condition' (NF-1885:1[61]), and furthermore, that for the unfree, 'the freest man' is equally 'the most coveted' and unreachable, since the psychic cost of his freedom is either forbidding (see HH: I, *HMS*, §107; NF-1881:11[130])⁶³¹ or simply unconscionable (BGE: §260).⁶³²

Growth conceived in economic terms reveals a disposition of incompleteness and unhappiness with one's [overall] condition. It represents a form of endless striving for the unobtainable, compensation of the deficit which can never make whole. These ingredients also form the physiological basis of *slave morality* and its valuations. In *the Genealogy*, Nietzsche links this to the self-contradictoriness of the physiologically deficient ascetic life, which plays out as 'an unfulfilled instinct and power-will' (GM: III, §11). Physiological deficit becomes articulated psychologically in the language of material possessions (e.g., property, money, debt), which come to represent that intangible element of well-being and inner harmony, which is lacking. However, when such represented happiness fails to transform into the 'feeling of overflowing power' (GM: III, §25), it is psychologised through the medium of *slave morality*, whereby fusing 'the sickness' with 'a shattered nervous system' turns it into reactive power (GM: III, §21). Driven by the 'green eye' of envy, it cannot and will not stop, until it becomes master 'not over something in life but over life itself', even if this end is achieved at the price of undermining 'physiological growth' and 'life's deepest, strongest and most profound conditions' which, among other things, lend power to the ascetic ideal (GM: III, §11).⁶³³ These insights develop on Nietzsche's earlier reflections concerning reactive

---

629 See also NF-1881:11[180] and Nietzsche's discussion in a later note: 'I am learning more and more: the difference between people is how long they can keep themselves in high spirits. Some barely an hour, and some want to doubt whether they are capable of high spirits. There is something physiological about it' (NF-1881:11[326]).

630 Earlier, in *HH*, juxtaposing 'quiet fruitfulness' to 'overeagerness', which betrays 'jealousy, envy and ambition', Nietzsche argued that 'if one is something, one does not actually need to do anything' (HH: I, *Soul of Artists*, §210)

631 In *BGE*, Nietzsche argues that 'it almost determines the order of rank how profoundly human beings can suffer ... profound suffering makes noble; it separates' (BGE: §270).

632 The strong individual's happiness is 'associated with a high state of tension, the consciousness of a wealth that wants to make gifts and give away' (BGE: §260).

633 This line of analysis is later echoed by Adorno and Horkheimer in *Dialectic of Enlightenment* (1947), where they argue that 'what counts as *progress* today is the *domination* of external and internal nature which, *impelled by the instinct for self-preservation, threatens to destroy what it is meant to preserve*' (Cook 2014:21). Simon Jarvis makes a similar point in relation to *capital's* propensity to thrive on the

growth as seeking to 'incorporate as much as possible' and being 'impelled to exploit' and 'tyrannise' the weaker (NF-1881:11[134])—i.e., to increase one's power at the expense of others—since it is incapable of self-affirmation.

Economic Growth and Human Development

Economic growth and human development are by no means one and the same for Nietzsche. Neither is necessarily synonymous with progress, which can occur 'forwards and backwards' (see UM: II, *UDHL*, §8; NF-1887:10[111]). Nietzsche problematises the modern idea of progress as a 'false one' and as representing less 'value, elevation, advance, strengthening' (AC: §4). Such a modern notion, which has become interchangeable with the notion of economic growth, takes effect in linear time and represents only a fraction of the developmental spectrum (NF-1888:15[8]).[634] Development is a comprehensive and painstakingly slow process[635] and, although it occurs within time, development is not strictly bound by the time's linearity.[636] It can curve back upon itself, and frequently it exhibits circularity.[637] As such, Nietzsche tells us that development is more akin to a growing tree, which is 'different and new in every moment' in a nonlinear fashion (NF-1881:11[293]):

> Like trees we grow—this is difficult to understand, as is all of life—not in one place only but everywhere, not in one direction but equally upward and outward and inward and downward; our energy is at work simultaneously in the trunk, branches and roots; we are no longer free to do only one particular thing, to be only one particular thing. (GS: §371)[638]

Sedgwick observes that for Nietzsche, 'every development of humankind is marked by a necessary degree of pain: for every benefit there is a corresponding cost' (Sedgwick 2007:107). When, as it happens under the auspices of industrial society, development becomes equated with and reduced to the idea of growth formulated in economic terms, which becomes 'the current folly of nations' (D: §206), the notion of develop-

---

'annihilation of individual's life', as 'individual's self-preservation is not in itself a matter of any importance' (Jarvis 1998:83).

634 Discussing the possibility of *progress* in *Human, All Too Human*, Nietzsche insists that 'progress in the sense and along the paths of the old culture is not even thinkable' (HH: I, §24). See also Nietzsche's discussion concerning the will's 'inability to go backwards', which becomes a 'curse for everything human' (Z: II, *Redemption*), and the passage from TI: *Skirmishes*, §44: 'today too there are still parties whose dream it is that all things might retreat backwards like crabs. But no one is free to be a crab'.
635 See HH: II, *WS*, §198, NF-1884:25[438], and BGE: §251.
636 See Nietzsche's reflection in NF-1881:11[184]: 'probably the real time is unspeakably much slower than we humans perceive the time ... the real world is moving much slower, but infinitely richer in movements than we suspect'. See also an earlier *Nachlass* note NF-1870:7[117].
637 See Nietzsche's discussion in HH, I, §292, and II, *AOM*, §125.
638 See also Z: I, *Tree on the Mountainside*.

ment suffers fragmentation and distortion. Throughout *Untimely Meditations* as well as in *Daybreak*, Nietzsche remains highly critical of the inflationary economic boom of the *Kaiserreich* after 1871, with a particular focus on the effects of economic growth on the state of culture and education.⁶³⁹ Nietzsche's criticism in this respect is two-fold. In the first instance, economic growth—a variant of the 'growth of'—is a zero-sum game at best by the time all the intangible costs and 'awkward fractions' (UM: II, *UDHL*, §1) of it have been brought on to 'the total balance sheet of life' (NF-1875:5[188]). Economic growth, which becomes the organising principle and the banner of humankind's development, as though representing 'the unconscious goal of all the anthills on earth' (NF-1872:19[160]), runs contrary to the ethos of the 'little economic communalities' (D: §132) and has the effect of uprooting and undermining communities, which cannot prove their viability on economic basis alone (NF-1885:37[9]).⁶⁴⁰ At the same time, economic growth for its own sake wastes 'a great sum of inner value' (D: §206) and owing to a profound misconstrual of the term 'Economy' ('*Ökonomie*'), 'the most precious thing, the spirit' (D: §179), ends up squandered.

Nietzsche's second conjecture is that a notion of growth, which would be commensurate with development, cannot be material, let alone economic. He hypothesises that only enhancements *of* culture ('*Erhöhungen der Cultur*') provide the foundations and the conditions of all growth' (NF-1885:2[128]). For this reason, when Nietzsche discusses cultural development, he does so in terms of the 'uncanny conditions for every growth *in* culture' ('*Wachsthum der Cultur*') rather than the growth '*of*' culture (see NF-1872:19[64]; BVN-1886[754]; my emphasis). In other words, for Nietzsche, growth is not a process of growing in size, in quantity, or in amount. Rather, it is a growth in depth, intricacy, multiplicity, complexity and in height (NF-1888:15[65]). As such, growth is not a quantitative but rather a highly qualitative category and the channels through which and the ends towards which growth is directed, as well as the modalities of its expression (i.e., economic vs. aesthetic) are far more critical in evaluating its worth. Nietzsche considers the utility of economic growth to derive from it being a means of 'forcing to retain spirit' (NF-1885:37[11]) and as such—distinctly auxiliary and subordinated to the task of cultural enhancement (NF-1888:14[158]). Any increase of wealth and property, unless it is primarily channelled towards spiritual and intellectual development, would be tantamount to aimless squandering.⁶⁴¹ As such, any notion of 'be-

---

639 See In particular, Nietzsche's discussion in UM: III, *SE*, §§4–7 (with an emphasis on growth pursued in the '*blind spirit of laissez-faire*') and §§179–206 in *Daybreak* with an emphasis on the modern misunderstanding of the notion of *oikonomia*. See also elucidating commentary on this in Ansell-Pearson 1994:10–26, in Rampley 2000:179, and in Reinert and Reinert 2006:111–137.

640 The logic of Nietzsche's argument is consistent with his position that slavery could never make sense on economic grounds alone and that, in fact, this form of subordination becomes the barbaric and objectionable *slavery we know* only when the oikonomic context (i.e., community) is destroyed by the advances of industrial age.

641 See also Nietzsche's discussion in NF-1881:11[82] on the need to provide direction to the money-makers concerning the transformation of wealth above their goals and way of life.

coming more', for Nietzsche, is synonymous with 'becoming stronger' (NF-1888:14[81]).[642]

Modern Narrative of Growth

What happens when development becomes construed in terms of economic growth and striving for material wealth? Nietzsche's argument suggests that when economic growth becomes a major vector of human development, it leads to the emergence of the agents, who, akin to a Faustian 'eternally hungry man' (BT: §23), signify a creeping physiological deterioration of society. Highlighting the 'physiological agreement' concerning the symptomatology of values (TI: *Socrates*, §2), Nietzsche notes that the forces likely to rise to the top in a social construct that privileges economic growth by elevating it to the rank of virtue and legitimising it as progress would, in substance, correspond to the objectives of 'descending life' (NF-1888:25[1]) and would themselves be an 'expression of … an inhibited life' (NF-1888:14[185]).

Growth, transformed into the modern virtue, would represent for Nietzsche an example of the 're-baptising of old values' (NF-1887:9[173])[643]—in this case, of the wayward humankind's journey back to the *Promised Land*, albeit in the secular setting of modernity and notwithstanding that this journey may no longer be shepherded by the priests, whose place has been taken by the modern-day democratic politicians, business leaders and bankers (i.e., the money-makers). The underlying psychological algorithm, however, directing this trajectory has remained unchanged and gives rise to the somewhat *Orwellian loop* of 'who controls the past controls the future: who controls the present—controls the past' (Orwell 2004:37).

Furthermore, such reactive forces would 'conserve what degenerates' by any means necessary, as this forms the basis of their power and represents the price that they have to pay in order to maintain their rule (EH: *D*, §2). In this context, debt fulfils a twofold function. It acts as a stimulant, in the context of an 'impoverished and degenerating life' (GM: *Preface*, §3). Nietzsche suggests that the constitution of industrial society has exhausted the 'instincts … out of which future grows' and squandered both 'all the material' (GS: §356) and the 'organising ability' necessary to draw on such resources (TI: *Skirmishes*, §39).[644] As a result, modern society has reduced itself to the 'undemanding' politics of spiritual decrepitude, which is a direct expression of the philosophy of debt: 'you cannot want less from people than if you just want their money' (NF-1882:3[1], §405).[645]

---

642 See NF-1885:41[6] and the elucidating discussion by Neal Curtis in *War and Social Theory*, 2006:8–11.
643 'It is always wrong to expect a "progress" from an ideal: the victory of the ideal has always been a retrograde movement' (NF-1887:11[135]).
644 This encapsulates the essence of the conflict at the heart of the fiscal-monetary dichotomy of modern political economy. See also Nietzsche's discussion in TI: *Skirmishes*, §38, and in NF-1887:11[375].
645 See Conway's illuminating discussion around these issues in *The Birth of the State*, 2009:39–42.

However, the growing exhaustion and dwindling resources manifested in the gradual loss of 'the building spirit' (NF-1884:25[438]) would only amplify reliance on debt, both as a form of self-fulfilling prophecy and as a means of delaying the day of reckoning. In this context it is worth noting that *debt* is a clear genealogical antecedent of the relatively recent phenomenon of economic growth.[646] Exploring the connection between debt and growth, using Nietzsche's logic, would suggest that they share a particular transmission mechanism—a 'kind of positing of causes' (i.e., causality)—with an expressed 'preference for particularly selected and preferred kind of explanations' (TI: Errors, §5). Nietzsche maintains that 'the banker almost instinctively thinking of "business" is 'no different from the Christian thinking of "sin" (TI: Errors, §5). Reflecting on the connection between debt and growth, Binswanger evokes the notion of 'an ever-improving future' as 'a vital ingredient' of the debt economy:

> Precisely through gearing the economy to money value, the world's limit ... can be pushed back further and further. It becomes lucrative to open up ever new channels. The world expands. Thus the money-economy makes possible a growth in the economy that promises ever greater prosperity. (Binswanger 2016:101)

In *Wealth, Virtual Wealth and Debt* (1926), Frederick Soddy argued that debt, which is 'subject to the laws of mathematics rather than physics' is an 'imaginary negative quantity' (Soddy 1926:78), as opposed to wealth—'a positive physical quantity' (Soddy 1926:78)—which is subject to the 'laws of thermodynamics' (Soddy 1926:79). Whilst debts grow at compound interest and 'do not rot with old age and are not consumed in the process of living', the growth of wealth sooner or later inevitably runs up against the physical constraints (Soddy 1926:79). A growing number of empirical studies in the decade since the 2008 crisis suggest that a continuously increasing number of units of debt is required to generate a unit of economic growth as well as a unit of wealth (see Kumar, Woo 2010). Foster and McChesney argue, in particular, that 'the expansion of debt', which creates the illusion of growth also conceals the reality of the 'stagnation-financialization trap', whereby continued growth of debt ultimately contributes to the corrosion of the entire economic and social order, hastening its decline' (Foster and McChesney 2012:70–71).

Notwithstanding that the rate of debt creation has long since outpaced that of wealth, there are no plausible indications that the growth of debt is about to slow down. This raises a twofold question. If it is no longer economic growth that underpins debt creation, what does? Put slightly differently, what factors (and forces) underpin continued debt creation notwithstanding the growing evidence of its diminishing productivity? This would be particularly pertinent if all wealth in market societies were 'nourished by debt and all of the unimaginable riches created over the past three centuries ultimately owed their existence to debt' (Varoufakis 2013:58–59). Nietzsche's argument suggests that the proponents of such a system would do everything in their

---

[646] See Rostow 1992:26; Trainer 2014:168; McCloskey 2006:20–25, 2016:68; and Victor 2019:4–9.

power to conceal its consequences (TI: *Skirmishes*, §39) and to obscure the means by which the growth of the weakening societies is effected (HH: II, *AOM*, §226).[647] Already in *Human, All Too Human*, Nietzsche asserts that money and riches 'only appear quite different from what their wretched origin would lead one to expect because they are able to mask themselves' (HH: II, *AOM*, §310).[648] In this respect, the causality of excess debt in the developed democratic societies, where debt has long since become a form of luxury, lends itself to being understood in terms of Nietzsche's discussion in *Twilight of the Idols*. Nietzsche maintains that 'licence and luxury follow ... when a people approaches destruction, when it degenerates physiologically', in a manner consistent with 'craving for ever stronger and more frequent stimulation' (TI: *Errors*, §2). Following on from this, in the following passage from *The Antichrist*, in the manner consistent with Nietzsche's 'thought experimentation' (BVN-1888:991), 'sin' is substituted for 'debt':[649]

> Psychologically considered, 'debts' become indispensable in any society organised by priests: they are the real handles of power. The priest lives from the 'debts', it is essential for him that people are in debt (AC: §27)

The above illustrates that Nietzsche's argument challenges both the *causality* traditionally associated with debt in relation to growth, and the *genealogy* of this relationship. Within the perimeter of industrial culture, debt and growth present themselves and operate as the mutually dependent and mutually reinforcing phenomena. The rising level of debt is not only or primarily a passive response to the otherwise objectively ascertainable requirements of the growing economy, but rather, debt compels this growth, creating a version of 'strange' self-referential loop.

Debt, according to this logic, is not an adjutant of economic growth but rather debt compels economic growth by means of which alone, in the modern secular society, it can continue to proliferate, as a reactive will to power, while concealing its growth and diffusing its affects in the web of complex interactions within the expanding perimeter of the 'strange loop' of its relationship with growth. Nietzsche would argue that '*Schulden*', much like '*Schuld*', is ultimately 'self-gratifying' and can only feed on itself.[650] Notable contemporary debt analysts concur that 'in an era of finance ... finance mostly finances finance' (Foster and McChesney 2012:70). This raises intriguing questions which, with the experience of the 1873 and 2008 crises, merit a more central place

---

647 See *Nachlass* notes NF-1886:4[7] and NF-1888:14[182]. In this context, Nietzsche's discussion in HH: I, *State*, §481 on the real costs of war is also imminently relevant. Nietzsche argues that the 'highest costs' are not incurred 'where these are usually thought to lie'.
648 Nietzsche's position exhibits affinity with Marx's view that 'if money, according to Augier, "comes into the world with a congenital blood stain on one cheek", capital comes dripping from head to foot, from every pore, with blood and dirt' (CW 35:748).
649 In the like experimental manner, 'the priest', as a progenitor of the banker and of the democratic politician, can be substituted for either or both.
650 See GM: II, §21, and III, §14.

within the discourse of political economy: would [the present day] debt economy survive if growth ceased being 'a dictator on the throne of economic policy' (Dowd 2000:200), and would growth 'dethroned' persist in the absence of the debt economy?

Entropy of Growth

In his polemic with Herbert Spencer, on the law of entropy, which Spencer associated with 'universal and infinite progress' and 'growth of heterogeneity',[651] Nietzsche observed that when slave morality (i.e., governing values) and scientific findings disagree, as they do on the question of the possibility of infinite growth in the face of rising physical entropy, science is often asked to step aside (see BVN-1886:[754]; NF-1888:23[5]; AC: §49).[652] Nietzsche problematises a clear contradiction he sees as residing at the heart of any proposition of 'an infinite progressus', which makes such concepts 'inexplicable' (NF-1888:14[188]) and akin to being 'a kind of astrology' (NF-1880:6[242]). He considers 'Spencer's picture of the future of man' to be a prime example of misrepresenting entropy to suit the 'present ideals' (NF-1881:11[98]). As Connolly aptly puts it, the 'underlying resentment against the weight of … responsibility to the future makes you eager to silence the voices of responsibility (Connolly 2008:51).

It is not a new revelation that continuous, let alone infinite, economic growth is not plausible in the world of finite resources.[653] The second law of thermodynamics, better known as the *law of entropy*, tells us so.[654] It is, however, also likely to remain subject to conjecture and fertile soil for political expediency, for as long as these resources last, or the system finds new ways to keep expanding, and/or an unexpected discovery helps to alter the entropic algorithm:

> Today's system is predicated on the progressive conversion of nature into products, people into consumers, cultures into markets and time into money. We could perhaps extend that growth for a few more years by fracking, deep-sea oil drilling, deforestation, land grabs from indigenous people and so on, but only at a higher and higher cost to future generations.[655]

This reinforces the question of why modern society should be beholden to the idea of growth, so much as to elevate it to the status of a cardinal modern virtue and an

---

[651] See Spencer (1863), *First Principles*, Chapter 3, §56, and Chapter 16, §§130–136. Last accessed March 12, 2023.
[652] Not entirely unlike seen in the disagreements between science and political expediency on climate change and, more recently, on the coronavirus pandemic.
[653] See Soddy (1926), *Wealth, Virtual Wealth and Debt*; Bataille (1967), *The Accursed Share*, Vol. I (*Consumption*); and Georgescu-Roegen, *The Entropy Law and the Economic Process* (1971) and *Energy and Economic Myths* (1976).
[654] See Binswanger 2016:101–102; Rifkin 1979:61–62; and Seaford 2009:157.
[655] Charles Eistenstein (2012), 'We Cannot Grow Ourselves Out of Debt': https://www.theguardian.com/commentisfree/2012/sep/03/debt-federal-reserve-fixation-on-growth, last accessed Feb. 27, 2023.

icon,[656] adherence to which may, at times, even assume militant forms, as Binswanger argues (Binswanger 2016:102)? What untold harm would befall humanity, if the 'world economy' stopped growing and the condition of the world ceased to be measured in terms of economic growth? What would get exposed as the frothy tide of growth recedes and who would stand to lose? Furthermore, why would infinite, or even indefinite economic growth be required, if the Promised Land were firmly within humankind's grasp?

The notion of infinite or indefinite economic growth, as measuring humankind's 'progress', illustrates Nietzsche's point: it is simultaneously imbued with a metaphysical premise that anticipates the final state (e.g., the 'great redemption from all past guilt' (BGE: §202), forgiveness of the debt, 'second innocence' (GM: II, §20), and a secular acknowledgement of the impossibility of arriving at such destination, which is embedded in the notion of infinite growth and progress (TI: *Skirmishes*, §21).[657] This predicament was subtly captured in Keynes' ironic argument concerning the *Economic Possibilities for our Grandchildren* (1930), namely that if we could just bear with 'avarice and usury and precaution' as 'our gods' for at least another hundred years, they would, and only they could, 'lead us out of the tunnel of economic necessity into daylight', upon seeing which 'great changes in the code of morals' would occur (Keynes 1930:371–372).[658] However, as Nietzsche contends, such hopeful thinking is inculcated with metaphysical traps (BGE: §230). This is how metaphysical belief helps to mould such conditions of existence within the constraints of physical entropy, which are incompatible with these constraints by gradually plotting the 'nihilistic' trajectory of 'the total depreciation of life' (TI: *Skirmishes*, §21). Nietzsche argues that if we wish to 'continue building the existing world', we cannot, at the same time, keep representing it as false because 'our valuations are an integral part of the process of building':

> How important is it when the entire religions say: 'Everything is bad and wrong and false!' This judgment of the whole process can only be a judgment of misguided men! (NF-1884:25[438])

Such 'misguided men' would, for the sake of personal gain and empowerment (i.e., to compensate for their physiological deficit), posit values that are detrimental to the development of humankind as a whole. This, according to Nietzsche, is an example of the kind of antagonistic 'opposition' and 'contradiction' (NF-1887:[63–64]) that is liable to amplification and exploitation in the hands of specific power interests and at the expense of 'the existing world, as the only foundation, upon which everything earthly-living has hitherto toiled, so that it appears as it does (durable and changing *slowly*)' (NF-

---

[656] See Dowd 2000:200; Mokyr 2017:19; and McCloskey 2010:27, 111, and 2016:168.
[657] Nietzsche's noteworthy conjecture is that 'anticipation' of redemption originates from a 'need', which is testament to a physiological condition of incompleteness and weakness (See TI: *Skirmishes*).
[658] The logic of Keynes' argument runs close to the one developed by Smith across *TMS* and *WN*, as discussed in Chapter 3, which is subsequently updated in Fukuyama's narrative on *The End Of History and The Last Man* (1992).

1884:24[438]). In Nietzsche's reckoning, it is possible to trace these power interests back to 'physiological values' (NF-1888:14[185]).

Nietzsche warns that when 'the strongest natures' are no longer commensurate with their task, the onset of turmoil becomes inevitable (HH: I, *Tokens*, §224). The erosion of agency—in modernity most pronounced at the top—is not merely an innocuous symptom of political decay but its leading indicator and guarantor that retrogression will only continue to gather pace (see TI: *Skirmishes*, §43). The loss of agency, Nietzsche argues, does not affect only to the upper echelons of society. It spreads to every part of the collective individual. One consequence of this degenerative process, absent the revaluation that Nietzsche urges, is that the forces that can be expected to come to the fore as the crisis of modern political economy escalates, driving humanity ever closer to the precipice of barbarism, would be 'savage, primal and wholly merciless' (UM: III, *SE*, §4). Nietzsche warns of 'a winter's day' that lies before us (UM: III, SE, §4). In light of Nietzsche's prediction, the growing sense of unease that comes from drawing parallels between 2008 and 1914 may not be entirely unwarranted, particularly against the backdrop of the 1873 international financial crisis, which helped pave the way to the Great War.

Geopolitics of Slave Morality

> 'Evil men have no songs'. How is it, then, that the Russians have songs? (TI: *Maxims*, §22)

Nietzsche maintains that industrial society lacks the requisite agonistic architecture to help it overcome self-induced crises of political economy by sublimating society's 'psychical sufferings' (HH: I, *State*, §472). Instead, for a long time after the economic tremors subside, society continues to oscillate between the two extremes positions which represent, on Nietzsche's view, 'the deepest of modern inclinations'—i.e., 'to collapse or to explode' (UM: III, *SE*, §4). Eric Voegelin aptly surmises that the 'consciousness of the crisis' persists long after the actual economic turmoil is over and can in of itself prove to be a destructive force capable of causing 'violent disturbances' (Voegelin 1944:181). Society's anxiety and restlessness denote the state 'of universal insecurity and an atmosphere of menace' which are prone—akin to the 'sparks and flashes' in the 'cauldron of the witch's kitchen'—to surreptitiously generate 'dreadful apparitions' (UM: III, *SE*, §4).[659] Nietzsche argues that this predicament becomes augmented further within the confines of the modern *nation-states*, which amplify rather than diffuse the building social pressures (Drolet 2013:25).

---

[659] Commenting on the build-up to World War I, Voegelin notes that 'the state of the Western World proved so chaotic that a general war could erupt without a clear political purpose on the part of any of the participating Great Powers' (1944:181).

Geopolitical tensions invariably tend to escalate in the aftermath of the deep economic crises (Tooze 2018:13–20). Numerous smaller wars and proxy conflicts between the Great powers preceded the outbreak of both world wars. This was certainly the experience in the aftermath of the Long Depression. Nietzsche's logic suggests that war becomes another manifestation and an extension of the same escalating crisis of the political economy of *slave morality*. He identifies three important markers which help to track deepening of the crisis. These are the levelling tendencies of *slave morality* which manifest themselves in the proliferation of the *religiosity of exhaustion*, for which 'God is far too extreme a hypothesis', or in its counterpart—'the most extreme forms of *nihilism*' (NF 1886, 5[71]). The onset of nihilism, in either the religious or the secular form, accompanies and is accompanied by the immense spread of the liberal-optimistic worldview' (NF-1871:10[1]) expressed in the *democratisation of politics* and the rapid development the *money-economy*.[660]

Nietzsche challenges the persistent liberal narrative that democracies and money-economies are, by virtue of their constitution, peaceable.[661] He contends that, although the instinct of the financier may be naturally conservative (NF-1888:14[182]), and the multitude might, for a time, be democratically pacified (HH: II, WS, §275; NF-1885:36[48]), both can be as easily radicalised. Cultural nationalism can easily grow out of embracing conservative values.[662] In the absence of the 'future "masters of the earth"' with the psychic aptitude to legislate on behalf of humanity, democracy —gradually, yet inescapably—ceases to be a 'pliant and subtle instrument for getting hold of destinies of the earth' (NF-1885:2[57]; NF-1887:9[119]) and becomes, instead, 'the form of decline in organising power', which makes society more volatile and 'emotionally explosive' (TI: *Skirmishes*, §39; GM: I, §6). As such, although the industrial society may temporarily dull and divert its underlying warlike instincts—convert, for a time, its 'tools of war into instruments of peace' (NF-1887:9[140])—it does not overcome them in either form of liberalism—political (i.e., democracy) or economic (i.e., the money-economy)—because the valuations of *slave morality* that underpin these social schemata remain, in substance, predatory and bloodthirsty—unable to heal the wounds they inflict and expose (GM: III, §15).[663] Industrial culture's 'assurances of peace are merely narcotics' (NF-1888:14[192]), as are those of slave morality, and all it takes to open the pandora's box wherein 'multiple surrogates for war' are confined is an economic crisis (HH: I, State, §477).

---

660 'Our modern, noisy, time-consuming industriousness, proud of itself, stupidly proud, educates and prepares people, more than anything else does, precisely for "unbelief"'. (BGE: §58). See Voegelin 1944:178 and Drolet 2013:40–41.
661 See Drolet 2013:25–28; Kaufmann 2004:5–48; Mousseau 2000:472–507; and Mintz and Geva, 1993:484–503.
662 See Emden's discussion of slide from the 'unintelligible other' to the 'political other' in the discourses of the 19th century, 2008:241–242.
663 Nietzsche's discussion in GM I, §6, and III, §10 and §20, is instructive here. See also Drolet 2013:31–33 and 42.

In this context, Nietzsche's reflections on the future role of Germany in Europe (and more broadly), as well as on the geopolitical risks Germany—a recently unified nation-state and an Empire—would face in the aftermath of 'Gründerkrach' form an integral part of his critique of the political economy of slave morality. Above all, Nietzsche highlights the precariousness of transition from the 'petty' nationalistic politics of slave morality to the 'great politics' of the future that would 'set goals beyond gold and gain', overcome the artificial and harmful division between 'domestic' and 'foreign' policy, embrace long-term perspectives, and enable decision-making with the 'consciousness of humanity' rather than for the benefit of individual states, power brokers and ideologies.[664] An important aspect of Nietzsche's concept of 'große Politik' is that, unlike 'kleine Politik', it is neither determined nor evaluated by specific events and agency. Nietzsche's approach to 'große Politik' is not strictly historical. Instead, he seeks to establish appropriate and enduring connections by examining valuations that underwrite the unfolding of that which becomes historical context (see Lemm 2013:160–162). The transition from 'kleine Politik' to 'große Politik' is an essential aspect of and an enabling mechanism for the transition from the moral to the knowing humankind (HH: I, *HMS*, §107). Importantly, Nietzsche's project for the cultural rebirth of humanity (and of Germany) cannot properly take off, let alone materialise, if *slave morality* were to gain the upper hand around the world and become its governing outlook.[665] Anticipating that 'the time is coming when the struggle for the supremacy of the earth will be waged … in the name of fundamental philosophical doctrines' (NF-1881:11[273]), Nietzsche formulates the general geopolitical challenge of modernity in the following terms:

> How is the earth to be administered as a whole? And why should 'man' as a whole—and no longer a people, a race—be raised and bred? (NF-1885:37[7])

It is important to keep in mind that the 'social wars' of modernity, the outbreak of which Nietzsche regards as inevitable, would, *in substance*, represent 'wars of concepts'. He sees the coming wars waged predominantly 'against the commercial spirit and restrictions of the national spirit'—and not as enmity between peoples and individuals (NF-1881:11[273]). However, when the conflicts of antagonistically inclined sys-

---

[664] See FEI: I; UM, III, *SE*, §6 ('beyond gold'); HH: II, WS, §292 ('domestic') and FEI: I, 18–19 ('long-term'); and NF-1887:9[60] ('consciousness'). On two occasions, Nietzsche even expresses the idea of 'withdrawing' culture to the new geographies (Mexico, in particular) in order to preserve the possibility of rejuvenating it (NF-1881:11[273]; NF-1884:25[112]). See Lemm's subtle distinction between Nietzsche's 'great politics' and 'small politics', with the former as the unifying concern—'perspective of the whole'—affirming 'the eternity of the moment' and exposing the 'idea of historical change as merely an illusion' (Lemm 2013:180–182). See also Drochon on 'petty' and 'great' politics, 2016:156–167.
[665] See Nietzsche's discussion of 'when the Germans began to be interesting to the other nations of Europe' (D: §190). See Ruehl's engaging discussion of Nietzsche and Germany's cultural rebirth, 2015:14–16.

tems of valuations and ideologies become hostages of 'kleine Politik', they can and frequently do take the *form* of physical wars between countries and cultures.⁶⁶⁶

In order to develop a fuller appreciation of the complex causality of geopolitical cataclysms, Nietzsche invites us to follow him as he maps the psychology of *slave morality* on to the geopolitical map of the *world of his time*, as well as of the world he saw as coming. Critically, he regards the United States and the British Empire (or England) as the two geopolitical mainstays of *slave morality*, the former in ascendancy and the latter in secular decline (NF-1887:37[9]), but maintaining a united front and resolved to preserve and extend their 'dominion over the earth' (NF-1884:25[112]; BGE: §228).⁶⁶⁷ Nietzsche sees the main geopolitical faultline, along which the major conflicts of modernity would unfold, in the growing antagonism between the Anglo-Saxons, as the custodians of slave morality and the purveyors of 'economic optimism' (Klossowski 1997:152), and the Slavs—the antithesis of 'petty statehood and nervousness' (TI: *Skirmishes*, §39), in whom he intuits:

> [The] kind of will, instinct, or imperative, which is anti-liberal to the point of malice: the will to tradition, to authority, to *responsibility for centuries to come*, to the solidarity of chains of generations, forward and backward ad infinitum (TI: *Skirmishes*, §39; my emphasis)

Geopolitical rivalry between the Anglo-Saxons and the Slavs—i.e., the 'English, Americans and Russians'—creates, on Nietzsche's view, an unequivocal demand on Europe to come together as 'One'.⁶⁶⁸ Although he undoubtedly sees the economic pressures working towards the unified Europe, with 'money alone' able to compel it to 'eventually coalesce into one power' (NF-1885:37[9]), Nietzsche does not relinquish the hope that Europe could remain the world's 'centre of culture' and 'retain its intellectual influence'.⁶⁶⁹ Against this backdrop Nietzsche reflects on Germany's role in unifying Europe and inaugurating its cultural rebirth.⁶⁷⁰ In order to become commensurate with achieving such mighty objectives—i.e., 'the direction and supervision of the total culture of the earth' (HH: II, *WS*, §87)—Germany's role cannot, for any length of time, be restricted to simply that of 'a mediator and broker' in the geopolitical stand-off between the Anglo-Saxons and the Slavs.⁶⁷¹

Nietzsche contends that *outside of the realm of petty politics*, this role entails a difficult choice—i.e., whether to join on the side of the forces of slave morality, or as opposing them. He argues that Germany cannot afford to remain on the sidelines of geo-

---

666 See D: §189; HH: I, *State*, §481; and NF-1888:25[19].
667 In relation to *England/British Empire*, see NF-1884:26[335]; NF-1887:37[9]; and TI: *Skirmishes*, §5. In relation to *America*, see NF-1872:19[21]; GS: §329; and EH: *UM*, §2. See also Nietzsche's discussion in NF-1884:26[335]; BGE: §44; §228; NF-1887:11[234]; TI: *Skirmishes*, §39; NF-1888:18[9]; and EH: *UM*, §2, as well as Shaw 2014:363.
668 See NF-1880:7[205] and NF-1884:25[112] and [137].
669 NF-1884:25[112]. See Drochon's enlightening discussion, 2016:20, 160–162 and 183.
670 See Voegelin 1944; Löwith 1991; Holub 1998; Conway 2013; Dombowsky 2014; and Drochon 2016.
671 NF-1885:37[9]. See Drochon 2016:20 and 155. See also Salter's insightful account, 1917a:364–365.

political rivalry any longer than it can remain on the cross-roads 'between Mephistopheles and Wagner' (HH: I, §408) without succumbing to the 'palpable stagnation of the spirit', which could take the form of either the *paralysis agitans* of "modern ideas"' (GM: III, §26; see BGE: §208 and TI: *Germans*, §4) or, more calamitously, of wondering down the 'secret paths to chaos' (BGE: §244).[672]

The risk Nietzsche sees with regard to Germany's failure to make the choice 'for' or 'against' slave morality—opting, instead, to remain 'indeterminate' and a 'contradiction in terms'—is that it could become an instrument of geopolitics in the Anglo-Saxon—Slav jostling for the 'mastery of the world'.[673] In other words, the 'undecided' Germany could find itself thrust from the sidelines of history into the eye of the geopolitical storm not of its making and with an air of inevitability resembling the tragic accident described by Bulgakov in 'Master and Margarita' (1940), where Berlioz—irredeemably torn between the studious protocol and the predilection for dissentient opinions—slipped on the sunflower oil 'accidentally' spilt by Annuska and got decapitated by the oncoming tram.[674]

Historical readings of Nietzsche's politics, which emphasise Germany's role as a mediator between England's and Russia's geopolitical ambitions, exemplified by the 'great game' (Drochon 2016:158–161), tend to overlook an *asymmetry* in the development of Nietzsche's views on Russia and the United States. The main accent appears to be placed on Nietzsche's changing views on Russia (see Drochon 2016:158–161; Voegelin 1944:203–208), while considerably less critical attention is paid to Nietzsche's growing ambivalence towards the United States and his growing reluctance to be limited by 'American perspectives' (NF-1884:26[336]). These equally important facets in shaping Nietzsche's geopolitical outlook are not necessarily or directly linked to specific dates, actors and events taking place.[675] Instead, these changes reflect his continued examination of the valuations which underpin the machinations of the 'petty' political economy of the West.

There appears to be little doubt in Nietzsche's mind that England and America, each designated by him as the 'great danger on earth', represent the leading fortresses of *slave morality* in the modern world, reincarnated in commercial form. He interprets their geopolitical ambition as wishing to devise a system of global political economy based on striving after the ever greater 'material comforts' (BGE: §228). Achieving such a geopol-

---

[672] Nietzsche contends that 'when the German ceases to be Faust there is no greater danger than that he will become a philistine and go to the Devil - heavenly powers alone can save him from it' (UM: III, *SE*, §4). See also Nietzsche's discussion in UM: I, *David Strauss*, §4; HH: II, *WS*, §282; and NF-1874:32[71].
[673] See TI, *Maxims*, §23, and NF-1884:25[112].
[674] See Nietzsche's discussion of the 'German Attitude to Morality' in D: §207.
[675] See GS: §356; NF-1884:25[137]; and Siemens 2013:83–107. In *Nietzsche's Great Politics* (2016), Drochon argues that Nietzsche's re-assessment of the geopolitical threat presented by Russia occurs around the time of *Beyond Good and Evil*, i.e., 1885–1886. However, the quoted passages from *Twilight of the Idols* (*Skirmishes*, §39, §45), one of Nietzsche's final works, are dated 1888. Nietzsche's consistent sentiment can be also discerned from the late *Nachlass* notes, e.g., NF-1888:18[9].

itical end entails, with the use of slave morality, sculpting the world in their 'own image' under the aegis of the concepts of 'the general utility' and 'the happiness of the greatest number' (BGE: §228). This would ensure that their *own interests* would be 'best served', while the world acquiesces to the view that 'all virtue there has ever been on earth has consisted in just such a striving' (BGE: §228; see NF-1888:14[109]). Nietzsche reminds us, however, that 'for moral values to gain dominion they must be assisted by many immoral forces and affects', and that the individual members of the global political economy, shaped by slave morality, are of 'great value' *only and only if* 'they constitute a community with a uniform feeling and a uniform conscience' (NF-1886:7[6]). Any deviation from this 'uniform conscience' is designated as a threat which is not to be tolerated and must be extinguished, no matter the cost. In Nietzsche's reckoning, capitalism—comprised of democracy and the money-economy—does not represent a sublimation of the Christian doctrine [of Discovery], but its continuation by other means.[676] Just as he detects the bloodthirsty imperialistic kernels at the heart of the doctrine that preaches love, peace and forgiveness, Nietzsche contends that the [democratic] money-economy engenders the propensity to slide into tyranny and war when the 'the age of harmless false-coinage draws to an end' (D: §551).

Since Nietzsche sees the British Empire as gradually entering its twilight years, this becomes particularly relevant in relation to America—the more virulent, 'power-hungry' and 'ferocious' strain of *slave morality* cultivated for many a century on English soil. It is not coincidental, on Nietzsche's view, that the worst excesses of barbaric slavery should have developed precisely there and, in a feat of history's backdraft, were now 'beginning to infect old Europe and ... spreading a lack of spirituality like a blanket'.[677] In contrast, Russia, according to Nietzsche, remained free of the spirit of *ressentiment* (EH: Wise, §6) and was still *uncertain* in terms of the direction in which to discharge its 'will to power'—affirmatively or negatively:[678]

> Russia, the only power today which has endurance, which can wait, which can still promise something—Russia, the concept that suggests the opposite of the wretched European nervousness and petty statehood ... The *whole of the West* no longer possesses the instincts out of which institutions grow, out of which a future grows: perhaps nothing antagonizes its 'modern spirit' so much. (TI: Skirmishes, §39; my emphasis)

---

676 See 1 Corinthians 15: 24-25 for an illustration of the ethos that informed the fifteenth century Papal 'Bulls of Discovery': Romanus Pontifex (1455), issued by Pope Nicholas V and Inter Caetera (1493) issued by Pope Alexander VI, together—the ignominious 'Doctrine of Discovery'.
677 See HAH: I, Tokens, §285; D: §271; GS: §329, §356; NF-1887:11[234]; TI: *Skirmishes*, §5; and EH: UM, §2. See also Drochon's illuminating discussion of Nietzsche's 'entirely negative view of England', 2016:159.
678 For illustrations of Nietzsche's evolving attitude to Russia, see NF-1876:17[53]; NF-1880:7[205]; NF-1884:28[32]; BGE: §13, §251; NF-18887:10[50]; TI: Skirmishes, §45; NF-1888:24[1]]; EH: Wise, §6; and BVN-1888:1134 (Letter to Georg Brandes, dated October 20, 1888)—where Nietzsche speaks of the Russian 'fatalism' that is free from *ressentiment* and 'pessimism of the strong', of Russia as a kind of empire that 'has time and is not of yesterday', and of Russia as a place where one may yet 'live once again'.

When Nietzsche references 'the whole of the West', it is difficult to argue that he does not include the United States under that heading. He certainly does so when discussing the spread of 'modern restlessness' and 'agitatedness' in Human, All Too Human (HH: I, Tokens, §285).[679] Echoing Hobbes and Locke, Nietzsche initially views America as the original 'state of nature', a clean slate and an opportunity to do things differently—a place where 'one can still see and seek out the inaugural and normal motions of the body politic' (HH: II, WS, §287). His assessment undergoes a significant change in his later writings, or, to be more accurate—it reverts to his original misgivings concerning 'the American type of political wheeling and dealing', which he designates as a 'great danger'—i.e., a sign that the logic of the money-economy is imprinting on the character of America's political activity (NF-187219[21]).[680] In line with his assessment of England as having succumbed to the valuations of slave morality to the extent that one had to 'be a soldier ... in order not to lose his credit as a merchant' (NF-1885:37[9]), Nietzsche develops a similar concern about America, which leads him to question America's ability to rise as a *genuine* 'world power' (NF-1884:26[247]). He sees America's political economy getting increasingly afflicted with the valuations of slave morality just as it becomes the 'home of money aristocracy', where the commerce-driven state policies debase the political sphere that they come to dominate (Salter 1917a:357).

Nietzsche's views in relation to the future geopolitical direction of Germany first appear to crystalise in 1884 with a call for the 'unconditional union with Russia', and the urgent need to prevent the Anglo-Saxon agents of slave morality from gaining political influence there (NF-1884:26[336]).[681] Russia's possible pivot towards the 'extended jaws of Asia' (HH: II, WS, §230) would represent an additional peril for Europe and pose a serious challenge to Germany were it to spearhead 'the unification of Europe as a counterweight to Russia and England' (Drochon 2016:20). Nietzsche further contemplates an alliance of 'the German and the Slavic races' with the most gifted financiers, Jews, as a *countermovement* to the spread of slave morality (NF-1884:26[335]). At the same time, Nietzsche entertains a decisive break with the 'English principle of representation of people' in favour of 'representation of great interests', as well

---

[679] Nietzsche maintains that 'modern agitatedness grows greater the *farther west we go, so that to the Americans the inhabitants of Europe* seem one and all ease-loving and epicurean creatures, though in fact they are swarming among one another like bees and wasps' (HH: I, Tokens, §285).
[680] See Hobbes 1991:89 and 232 as well as Locke 1888:296–297.
[681] Earlier in 1881, Nietzsche briefly entertains the notion of the 'Slavic-Germanic-Nordic culture' as 'the smaller one but stronger and harder working (NF-1881:11[273]). In relation to limiting the Anglo-Saxon influence, Russia's more recent experience, as a once nascent market economy and an aspiring democracy, aiming to join the global political economy after the demise of the Soviet Union in 1990s, is instructive. See, in particular, the concept of the 'Grand Bargain', developed by Harvard's Graham Allison and Robert Blackwill in 1991, which emphasised the 'speed of the journey' in advancing democratic and market reforms in Russia by means of supplying debt through the 'international lending institutions' precisely at the time when Russia found 'itself on the political sickbed' (HH: I, State, §472) and the advocacy of 'shock therapy' where Russia would undertake to transform into a market economy and a full democracy as *quickly as possible*' (West 2012:92; Sachs 1995:57–80; my emphasis).

as issuing a resolute 'No to American future' (NF-1884:26[336]). These Nietzsche's geopolitical sentiments survived to the end of his writing years, when he was still willing to 'trade the happiness of the *whole West* for the Russian way of being sad' (NF-1888:18[9]; my emphasis), and considered himself in a 'deeper conflict with the *whole* European and American species of "libres penseurs"' than with 'any of their opponents' (EH: *UM*, §2; my emphasis).

Nietzsche's view on the geopolitical landscape of his time cuts across another persistent liberal myth which pits Russia and Germany against one another as though they were sworn perennial enemies—an enmity engineered by 'kleine Politik', which would plague the 20th century (see Löwith 1991:262). Nietzsche's unorthodox take on the geopolitical entanglements of his time may well remain *sui generis*. His juxtaposition of 'große Politik', as a conceptual medium of valuations, to the 'kleine Politik' of his time, which he regarded as becoming more menacing and more of a threat, yields a different perspective. His approach, which is not strictly historical, draws attention to the importance of valuations which drive history and yet often vanish from view in the bedlam of 'kleine Politik'. Predominantly historical interpretations of Nietzsche's politics miss an important aspect of his philosophical enterprise by situating him exclusively in the historical context of his time. Nietzsche's message to us remains that by undertaking the values-informed conceptual analysis of geopolitics, not as a substitute to historical contextualisation but in addition to it and as an extension of it, shines a different critical light on the play of conflicting forces. This helps to build a better informed perspective on the causality of the crises of modern political economy. It may even help in averting some of them by necessitating the revaluation of values.

Precarious Traverse to a Less Industrious World

Nietzsche's multipronged intellectual challenge to debt economy of the 'industrial world' (HH: I, *State*, §440, and D: §175), developed largely as a reflection on the aftermath of the Long Depression, retains pertinency in light of the experience of the Great Recession of 2008. Contrary to the prevailing interpretations[682] that associate Nietzsche's metaphors—of a man as 'a monster of energy', who 'demands a monster of a task' (NF-1884:26[409]) in the world, which is itself 'a monster of energy' (NF-1995:38[12])[683]—with the advocacy of unbridled economic growth, wonton accumulation of riches and the spirited defence of capitalism, what emerges from Nietzsche's critique is the notion of a considerably less industrious and less economic world (TI: *Errors*, §2).

The contours of such a world become clearer on account of Nietzsche's unequivocal insistence on moderation in relation to possessions (HH: II, *WS*, §285) and the 'max-

---

682 See Benjamin 1996, Sedgwick 2007, Landa 2007, Holub 2005 and 2018, and Graeber 2011.
683 In both cases, 'Ungeheuer von Kraft' makes better sense as 'tremendous force'.

imum economy of consumption' (see NF-1888:14[81]; NF-1879:40[3]), as well as in relation to economic expenditure and accumulation of energy (NF-1884:26[409]). His arguments in favour of the long-term investment horizons (FEI: I, 18–19; GS: §356), required for building a stronger future, rather than living at its expense in the debt-fuelled and increasingly nihilistic present, and his sustained objection to the folly of economic growth (D: §206)—further add to this picture.[684] These views reflect Nietzsche's understanding of economic growth as being subject to the laws of thermodynamics, ultimately finite, and inconsistent with the notion of 'raising humanity higher'.[685] Expressed in the vernacular of political economy, Nietzsche's concern resonates, among others, in the following summation by Georgescu-Roegen in *Energy and Economic Myths* (1976):

> Economic development through industrial abundance may be a blessing for us now and for those who will be able to enjoy it in the near future, but it is definitely against the interest of the human species as a whole, if its interest is to have a lifespan as long as is compatible with its dowry of low entropy. In this paradox of economic development we can see the price man has to pay for the unique privilege of being able to go beyond the biological limits in his struggle for life. (Georgescu-Roegen 1976:58–59)

Nietzsche polemic calls for the de-prioritisation and deleveraging of economic growth until the functioning of economy can become commensurate with the challenges and objectives of supporting humankind's broader-based development conceived within the multigenerational framework, i.e., when 'its pace is slower, but the beat itself is much richer and health increases' (NF-1886:7[8 A]). In this respect, this inquiry shares Shapiro's hypothesis that one of the intentions of Nietzsche's *Umwertung aller Werthe* is to 'suggest the possibility of economies that may not be completely recuperable within the thinking we have practiced for so long, and which so far has had a claim (although only a claim) to be considered as "thinking as such"' (Shapiro 1994:374). Nietzsche urges us to think 'beyond the price' and in terms of sensibility, which reflects 'sacrifice' and is capable of 'cyclopean building' (HH: II, WS, §275, §283).

His approach, consistent with preserving and growing the inter-generational capital, would amount to a considerably lower growth, or even a steady state, political economy that operates at negative rates of return—i.e., it embraces some features of the gift-based, or philanthropic, investment approaches and restricts lending to creditors' risk. In part, this would derive from re-focusing money creation away from the greed of the private banks in the blind chase after profit to serving the needs of economic communalities. Considerably slower, or absent, economic growth would avail the possibility of a frank discussion about the role of debt in the structuring and directing the future of human affairs:

---

[684] See UM: III, SE, §4; HH: II, WS, §286; and GM: *Preface*, §6.
[685] See GS: §318; BGE: §44, §257; and AC: §7.

> If we are in community with our children and grandchildren we have no right to bequeath to them a heavy burden that will be more difficult for them to handle than for us. This will require sacrifice ... due ... to the profligate borrowing and spending these past years (Daly and Cobb 1994:258, 326)

The inference from Nietzsche's polemic on debt is that the absence of economic growth, which shrouds debt's inexorably rising skyscrapers in its histrionics, would have the effect of an ebbing tide which exposes in its wake debt's lifeless dystopian silhouettes towering over the barren seabed of the exhausted economy of life. The absence of growth would not by itself cure the problem of debt but, Nietzsche argues that, if 'the wheel of the world were to stand still', even for a moment, it would yield a dual benefit (HH: I, *HMS*, §106). First, it would help to expose important misconceptions that keep the wheel spinning. Second, it would enable us to see more clearly the consequences of 'the track along which this wheel had yet to roll' (HH: I, *HMS*, §106), and in so doing—present an opportunity to take appropriate corrective action. The absence of growth would remove one of debt's key legitimising narratives and enable the conversation about the possibilities of transforming debt into the capital for supporting development, rather than feeding fictitious growth. Nietzsche's argument, which is well worth reflecting on in this context, raises the difficult but plausible concern. It is whether the modern industrial society, built on [the foundations of] debt economy and governed by democratic politics, can *honestly afford itself* while guided by the worldview which inevitably desires and demands more than is deliverable from society's own inner strength and available resources (i.e., without debt and without encumbering the future), as a result of which it has to resort to the means of maintaining itself, which are in fundamental contradiction with its core values and which, in practice, amount to the actions of a 'subtler version of brigand and extortioner' who can proudly 'display the noble aspect of a great landed proprietor' only after having 'emerged out of plundering and confusion' (HH: II, *AOM*, §343; *WS*, §22, §25)? Put slightly differently, Nietzsche problematises the industrial society, built by the combination of the money-economy and democratic politics, as inappropriate for and incommensurate with the challenges of navigating humankind's development within the constraints of the entropic physical environment.

The logic of Nietzsche's critique suggests that beneath the appearance of conjuring, compelling, or assisting economic growth, debt primarily compels its own growth. This accords with his conjecture about the predominantly *political nature of secular debt*, and raises the question of whether the role of debt within the social architecture of industrial culture could be shifting away from supporting economic growth to fashioning a particular form of social contract (i.e., democracy-in-debt)? [686] If increasing amounts of debt should be required in order to maintain a particular form of social

---

[686] Tooze makes the point that 'the foundations of the modern monetary system are irreducibly political' (Tooze 2018:10) and that debt and money-economy become entrenched and grow politically: 'money and credit and the structure of finance piled on them are constituted by political power, social convention and law' (Tooze 2018:10).

cohesion, particularly in the absence of economic growth, it would become of utmost importance which forces—active or reactive—wield debt's power. This is so because 'those transfixed by hope of eternal salvation would seldom respond with agonistic respect to those who invest themselves entirely in this world ... to do so might place their investments in eternal salvation too much at risk' (Connolly 2008:138):

> Though it is hardly a secret that we inhabit a world dominated by business oligopolies, during the crisis and its aftermath this reality and its implications for the priorities of government stood nakedly exposed. It is an unpalatable and explosive truth that democratic politics on both sides of the Atlantic has choked on. (Tooze 2018:13)

In this way, the questions of agency and governance over the political economy, as well as of its structure and modalities of subordination, are some of the paramount concerns highlighted by Nietzsche's critique. In *The Antichrist*, in order to show just how deep the inertia of valuations runs through the succession of the social orders to the present day, Nietzsche problematises the ubiquitous power of 'the lie of "the moral world order"' that would also do all it can to stymie any attempt at the revaluation of values (AC: §26):

> We know, today our conscience knows, what these uncanny inventions ... are really worth, what ends they served in reducing mankind to such a state of self-violation that its sight can arouse nausea ... these systems of cruelty by ... virtue of which [the priest] became master and remained master ... everybody knows this, and yet *everything continues as before*. (AC: §38; my emphasis)

Almost bizarrely, a view that 'the lifetime of the human race on this planet could come to a shocking end in a few decades if nothing changes in the boardrooms and legislative bodies of the world' (Ayres 2016:485) is growing in acceptance without prompting commensurate action. Notwithstanding the increasing urgency of the calls for the wholesale revaluation of values, doubts have been raised concerning the will of humankind to 'pay the price of its [own] survival' (Heilbroner 1991:183) and—oblivious to the harrowing lessons of the previous great crises of political economy—to resist 'the growing threat of repressive social control systems', emerging from the shadows of the 2008 crisis (Robinson 2014:1; Tooze 2018:472).[687] The realisation that the crises of political economy and repressive control go hand in hand is not simply lacking but is purposefully

---

[687] See John Avery in *Values For The Future* (2016): 'western society urgently needs to find new values to replace our worship of power, our restless chase after excitement, and our admiration of excessive consumption' (Avery 2016:63). See also William Robinson in *Global Capitalism and The Crisis of Humanity* (2014): 'Our world is burning. We face a global crisis that is unprecedented in terms of its magnitude, its global reach, the extent of ecological degradation and social deterioration, and the scale of the means of violence. ... Certainly, the stakes bound up in the raging conflicts of our day are too high for the usual academic complacency' (Robinson 2014:1). Furthermore, see Kümmel 2011:272; Avery 2016:63; Sedlacek 2013:326–327; and Robinson 2014:1.

obstructed by the very same forces that profit from the rising real price of 'buying time'.

Nietzsche posits as the 'greater danger' (UM: III, *SE*, §4) any complacency of expectation that the revaluation of values—as though 'recovering somehow' and 'calming down somewhere' (NF-1887:11[99])—would naturally, unproblematically and without great effort, grow out of the existing values, which have led modernity to its present predicament. The 'prevalent worldview' (NF-1873:27[44]), widely suspected of misleading humankind's development, remains as though dissolved in the background of the world of 'facts' and, increasingly 'alternative facts', delivered by the thoroughly mendacious political rhetoric (NF-1888:23[5]). It is as though, the 'fog of habits and opinions lives and grows almost independently of the people it envelops' (D: §105) in the same manner that 'a post-truth approach to public discourse is simply what the governance of capitalism currently demands' (Tooze 2018:25).

Any crisis, on Nietzsche's view, presents a wide spectrum of possible outcomes (GM: III, §27). The challenge is to identify the 'hopeful' scenarios before it is too late. This, Nietzsche argues, can only be achieved through the 'war of the spirits' (EH: *Destiny*, §1), where the petty power politics of modernity (HH: I, *State*, §481), which has 'driven it into a dead-end street' (TCW: §3), must be overcome (EH: *Destiny*, §1). Nietzsche problematises growth as represented development conceptualised in economic terms, as continually pulling further away from the wholesome concept of humankind's development: 'we are no longer accumulating, we are squandering the capital of our forebears, even in our way of knowing' (NF-1888:14[226]).

Ultimately, reflecting on growth forms part of Nietzsche's attempt to intuit such conditions of existence according to which growth or, more precisely development, would not be a zero-sum game. Nietzsche's thinking on reinvigorating humankind's development concerns the sphere (material or spiritual-intellectual) it should prioritise, the means (debt or capital) it should employ, and the ends (preservation or enhancement) for which it should strive. With this, Nietzsche's 'thinking outside of social orders' (NF-1886:5[71]) may be said to point in the direction of an *aesthetic political economy*, although altering the underlying conditions of humankind's existence would be impossible to conceive of, let alone to implement, absent a wholesale revaluation of values, in the way of which the question of debt, as the unifying concern of modern political economy, stands as the most considerable nemesis, not least in view of the reactive valuations of *slave morality* which it represents and defends to the last.

8 Closing Reflections on NPE: In Search of Direction

Assessing the Findings

This inquiry started by posing questions of whether political economy could be regarded as one of Nietzsche's central concerns and whether his reflections on the political economy's thorny issues of his time has retained pertinence in the context of the present day. Placing Nietzsche into a 'Socratic dialogue' with Smith and Marx, respectively, helps highlight the underexplored aspects of Nietzsche's writings, which illustrate his extensive critical engagement across a wide range of issues examined also by the two towering historical figures of political economy. Exploration of the three chosen themes—slavery, debt, and the division of labour—deemed central to Nietzsche's thought and to the broader conversation on political economy further helps to elucidate the connection between his *oeuvre* and the field of political economy. Joining together the wide-ranging elements of Nietzsche's political-economic thought is his critique of slave morality, the valuations of which he holds responsible for the nihilistic character of modern political economy.

In Nietzsche's time, slave morality's profound effect on the social fabric of modern society was exposed by the crises of its political economy which started with the Panics of 1873. Situating his writings against the backdrop of 'Gründerkrach' and the Long Depression, which ensued from it, amplifies Nietzsche's critique of slave morality's elaborate workings and allows us to draw appropriate and relevant parallels to the financial crisis of 2008 and its aftermath. Contextualising Nietzsche's revaluational project within the protracted crisis of the political economy of his time also allows to approach the question of Nietzsche's relevance from an angle that remains largely untapped by the current scholarship.

The question of the contemporary relevance of Nietzsche's political economy—gauging the value of his own philosophical and economic coinage—requires consideration on at least two levels. The first is to ascertain whether Nietzsche's work retains pertinence as a relentless critique, irrespective of whether he advances a credible alternative to modern industrial culture. The second is to evaluate whether Nietzsche's overall project entails valuable components, even if it did not amount to a comprehensive 'positive project'. In its capacity as a critique, Nietzsche's work should be capable of throwing a probing critical light on the issues of concern in the present day context and as such, act as a directional guide for further critical analyses, as well as being a 'hygienic procedure for consciousness'.[689] Nietzsche's critique mounts an effective intellectual challenge to the prevailing conceptions of mainstream political economy in a way which is otherwise absent from the conversation about the three interlinked *aporias* of industrial culture—debt, slavery and the division of labour. Nietzsche's find-

---

689 Amin and Palan 2001:563.

ings are challenging and revealing in equal measure. All three phenomena, according to him, once existed in a pre-moralised form and meant something entirely different to our current understanding. All three contained vital clues to understanding the organic structure of existence in a way that enabled life's affirmation. These clues have been irretrievably lost as debt, slavery and the division of labour have been fundamentally distorted by the reactive valuations of slave morality which has inverted their original designations. Having been reconfigured by slave morality, debt, slavery, and the division of labour have become tools of reactive power which is turning increasingly oppressive in view of its growing inability to endow either of these phenomena with meaning beyond the senseless and greedy exploitation that sustains modern, highly entropic materialistic existence conceived in economic terms. Nietzsche's political economy problematises slave morality as an expression of the governing worldview which, in his assessment, is driving humankind and our planet towards certain ruin.

By shifting the focus of his critique to the genealogical examination of the values that underpin these key narratives of modern political economy, and painstakingly tracing the historical and ideological 'metempsychosis' of these values (BT: §10), Nietzsche extends the critical reach of his examination beyond the limits of the prevailing discourses in a way that resonates with 'astonishing accuracy' (Stegmaier 2016:390) within the present day context.[690] As Sleinis notes, what differentiates Nietzsche's inquiry and grants it pertinence is that it takes 'to its logical conclusion the critical scrutiny' of modernity's foundational beliefs and values (Sleinis 1994:xvi). In this respect, Nietzsche's 'Socratic dialogues' with Smith and Marx reinforce not only his interest in the matters of political economy but also his earnest intellectual effort to extend the line of inquiry into its pivotal issues beyond the conventional boundaries. Nietzsche does enough to render political economy's old questions 'unfinished' and in need of being 'raised anew' (NF-1887:9[185]). He accomplishes this in a troubling manner which highlights the arduous effort required in order to re-awaken our capacity for change through the revaluation of values, since only 'around the inventors of new values the world revolves' (Z: I, *Flies*).[691] Viewed in this light, Nietzsche's political economy as a critique of values of slave morality, underpinning the socio-economic edifice of modernity, constitutes a necessary, if not sufficient element of its overcoming.

Slavery

Slavery—unlike debt and the division of labour—is ordinarily treated as though it were a solved problem. Nietzsche disagrees and probes the reasons why the slavery's abolition did not and could not amount to its overcoming. His critique of industrial culture and the money-economy, in particular, targets not only their presently functioning var-

---

690 See Klossowski on Nietzsche and metempsychosis, 1997:55.
691 See Salter 1917:372–373.

iants but also their predecessors, 'whose wealth is the guilty return on a homicidal trade in slaves, piously sanctioned by church and state' (Robinson, Carlstroem 2011:122). One of the challenging questions Nietzsche explores is how a society, a culture, a people, a civilisation can own up to a legacy and a history, which is predominantly based on a lie, stolen and built on the blood and the barbarism of slavery (NF-1883:7[167]). Can such a past be overcome in a manner that might grant the present a measure of respite from it and, in so doing, promise a future?

Nietzsche argues that when a future strong enough to redeem the pain, crimes, mistakes and sacrifices of the past is built, the bearers of its memory become less wary of the past. Having paid the highest price for it with the present, built on its foundations, they choose to remember the past, for it no longer haunts, rather than constantly trying to rewrite it. When, however, the present and the future are narrated by the forces of 'descending life' eager to conceal the 'squandering of ancestral capital', the past hangs over them as an unpaid and mounting debt. No matter what attempts are undertaken by the reactive and self-serving forces to beautify, disown, rewrite, or omit the painful chapters and to deny responsibility for the past—the unrequited debt would only continue to plague society's conscience, compelling the unresolved conflicts and traumas of the past to continue resurfacing, playing themselves out in the present and casting a dark shadow over the future.[692] The future is not guaranteed by the past alone but remains destined to repeat it unless the present re-values its cumulative re-relationship with history by birthing an alternative vision and setting the distinctive trajectory for moving forward deriving from the new, revalued and more robust ideals.

Debt

Nietzsche's analysis of debt problematises it as a highly synthetic phenomenon. Irrespective of whether it comes dressed as a theological matter, a moral issue or a financial consideration, *debt is a lie* of the dishonest kind. Debt is capital turned reactive; it is inverted capital. For this reason, it is seized upon by the power-seeking reactive elements, who weaponise it to compensate the intrinsic lack of vitality and authority. These agents use debt as a power tool to subjugate others to their own—ultimately physiological, on Nietzsche's view—deficit. Nietzsche positions debt as the normative lynchpin of the thoroughly nihilistic political economy of industrial culture, which needs the illusion of growth, supplied by debt, to mask its inadequacies and outrun the consequences of the damage it inflicts on the planet and its inhabitants in the process. The unifying concern of Nietzsche's multifaceted critique of debt is the relationship between debt, agency and governance: who governs by debt, to what ends and with

---

[692] It is worth pondering the possible connection between the American slavery, allegedly successfully abolished between 1780 (Pennsylvania) and 1865 (the 13th Amendment), and the disproportionate incidence of black deaths in the coronavirus pandemic in the US in 2020 and the wave of the Black Lives Matter movement across the US as well as in the UK.

what consequences. His critique links debt with the *overall regressive movement* of humankind, which occurs in some proportion to the degree to which humankind comes to rely on debt in its efforts to attain 'progress' measured in terms of material welfare at the expense of spiritual wellbeing.

Debt, as an abstract concept, helps to attain greater material comforts whose very attainment places an intangible but nonetheless painfully real cap on the spiritual development of individuals and communities. Ultimately, for Nietzsche, debt is a detractor. Unlike capital, which can either be squandered or accumulated, debt has to be repaid. The benefits debt confers are ephemeral. By creating an illusion of being able to enjoy benefits of the future in the present debt undermines the strength required to build the future which images it helps to conjure up. Operating in this manner debt ends up concealing the present's true cost so that it would be only felt in the future, when it becomes the present burden of the future generations. As the cardinal value of the money-economy, debt reconfigures the nature of the relationship between the material welfare and the spiritual wellbeing from agonistic into antagonistic. It pits the present against the past and devalues the future: while promising its splendour, debt is painstakingly creating the wasteland.

Within this critical framework, Nietzsche explores the workings of the modern money-economy, laying bare its foundational premises. Most importantly, this includes an interdependence between debt and democratic politics, which creates structural preconditions and multiple venues for the growth of debt. Although it is generally accepted that debt is one of the central features of the capitalist economy, it is not conventional to think of it as the backbone of democratic society. Nietzsche's argument problematises the shared origins of debt and democracy. This genealogy allows him to extend his appreciation of debt to encompass its meanings as an instrument for moulding subjectivity, a mechanism of democratic governance, a key tool of economic policy and a central normative precept of the political economy grounded in the preponderance of the creditor. Consequently, the latter is shielded in times of crises irrespective of their contribution to it. Nietzsche's emphasis on the intrinsically political modalities of debt creation in modern society adds an angle largely missing from today's conversation on political economy. This normative-punitive aspect of debt, highlighted by Nietzsche, leads into the discussion of debt as a complex mechanism and a pervasive set of power relations that sustain the money-economy increasingly by means of debt, the more the ability to do so by other means wanes.

In this context, Nietzsche's critique places agency, conceptualised through the 'degeneration of the rulers and of the ruling classes', at the centre of the debt problem (see NF-1884:25[345], [349]). States, cultures, societies, and social orders are not thwarted by the sheer magnitude of the crises they experience, or by the challenges they face. Rather, the choices made, means employed and institutional levers engaged in dealing with them prove more critical to the outcomes. These, in turn, depend on the quality of the decision-making, which derives from the quality of the decision-makers, understood both institutionally and individually. This, Nietzsche tells us, is where one ought to look for the real causes of problems and origins of the crises. The crises of political economy reveal the governing values of a particular social setting, precisely because these values are being protected first and foremost. Doing so, however, also makes their consequences more visible and those who protect them become exposed. In his final work, *Ecce Homo*, Nietzsche insists that 'a degenerate kind of man ascends to the highest rank among the human species' by sparing no expense in empowering 'falsehood to claim the word "truth" for its own particular standpoint' (EH: *Destiny*, §5).

One challenge Nietzsche would likely pose to democracies today is whether they are capable of producing leaders who would be commensurate with the challenge of reducing debt. It is likely, following Nietzsche's logic, that tackling the problem of debt would be incompatible with the democratic governance of society, while continuing with both—i.e., democracy and growing debt—would represent a progressively more perilous path.

Increasing reliance on debt is customarily associated with stimulating economic growth, particularly in the aftermath of a serious economic slump.[693] Nietzsche's analysis of the physiology and psychology of debt in the context of a creditor-biased system of political economy suggests something altogether different. Juxtaposed with intergenerational capital, as symbolising collective and individual health, strength and moderation, debt is problematised as stifling the development of humankind to a far greater degree than it is able to promote it. The logic of Nietzsche's argument identifies the growth of debt as a symptom of an acute crisis of industrial culture which, having exhausted and squandered other resources in serving the 'greed of the moneymakers', is experiencing a wide-ranging deficit of legitimacy (NF-1884:25[343]). In this context, economic growth, conjured up by debt, does not represent progress but only its appearance, while the reverse is the case in substance. Systemic intolerance to debt forgiveness is an important litmus test of the health and vitality of the creditor-biased system. The narrative of growth becomes more indispensable the more detrimental the impact of debt—both visible and invisible—becomes. The resulting effect is a temporary 'damming up of degeneration', which by the same token 'gathers it and makes it more vehement and sudden' (TI: *Skirmishes*, §43).

In this respect, Nietzsche's analysis of the role of debt in moulding subjectivity raises deeper questions concerning our underlying attitude to development. Nietzsche problematises the prevailing connotations of 'progress' as attained at the price of 'dwarfing' (NF-1887:9[17]) those who are presumed to be progressing, and in the environment where 'making small' (TI: *Skirmishes*, §38) is no longer 'temporary' (NF-1887:9[174]) but symptomatic of protracted 'aimlessness' (NF-1884:[345]). As Salter surmises, this is akin to being 'thrown utterly to the void' (Salter 1917:439) albeit to the soothing utterances of 'sweet melancholy' (Z: II, *Priests*).[694] Such an attitude, for

---

[693] Or, as we saw with the Covid pandemic, as a means of combatting a health emergency, allegedly to protect human life.
[694] Nietzsche objects to the pointless exploitation of any individual member of society. His intention is made clear in NF-1883:9[47]; NF-1887:9[17], [174]; and NF-1888:14[123]. See Salter's nuanced discussion of this in Salter 1917:438–440.

Nietzsche, is emblematic of the broken intergenerational continuity and of a state of affairs where the intergenerational capital has become debt: an instrument of reactive and increasingly repressive petty politics that—although it may remain entirely legal—lacks more fundamental legitimacy (see GS: §356; TI: *Skirmishes*, §39). Nietzsche's stark warning, therefore, is that governing by debt jeopardises human development and makes the relapse back into barbarism far more likely (see HH: I, §251; NF-1881:11[331]).

The Division of Labour

Unlike the undisputed 'evil' of slavery and the 'evil' propensities of debt left to its own devices, the division of labour—from the time of Adam Smith—is ordinarily endowed with the connotations of 'good' (i.e., progress, productivity, growth, civilisation, etc). Nietzsche's views on the division of labour, analysed against the backdrop of Adam Smith's influential polemic, challenge the foundational assertion of political economy that humankind's *overall progress* is achieved by prioritising economic growth. The division of labour, on Nietzsche's view, is a [reactive] modality of the appropriation of the world. Nietzsche argues that the prevailing model for the division of labour in the industrial society, informed by the valuations of slave morality, is dangerously skewed towards the economic appropriation of the world at the expense of the aesthetic engagement with it.

The difference between Nietzsche's and Smith's views on the subject problematises a fundamental normative proposition, which 'organizes modern Western communities on virtually every level': namely, whether the 'the social whole is best served when individuals are allowed to pursue their own interests' (Mieszkowski 2006:113). For Nietzsche, the interest of society is not a simple arithmetic of individual interests, as the value of these interests is very different. Even less so is it a result of the sum made greater with the help of any 'invisible hand', whether providential or market-based. Nietzsche argues that the individuals, released from the constraints of hierarchy, do not naturally emerge as sovereign, ethical, as well as self-directing economic, agents. The formalistic release from the bonds of a paternalistic society, or from slavery, makes them more rather than less vulnerable to the levelling and atomising impact of exploitation experienced within the precepts of industrial society. As such, the release of individual egoisms, on an 'as though equal' basis, into the secular money-economy and their subsequent re-incorporation into the social fabric of industrial society through the division of labour, represents, for Nietzsche, an unforgivable squandering of tremendous energy and resources. Nietzsche's critique of the division of labour identifies the risks associated with turning labour into a commodity as the logical consequence of the money-economy, ruled by the insatiable, yet meaningless greed of the money-makers. Nietzsche's critical point is that 'the goal ... to create as many current human beings as possible' (UM: III, *SE*, §6) in a world of finite natural resources, would inevitably lead to the surplus human beings becoming that very [abundant and renewable] resource, which at some point would end up being used 'as material for heating the great machines' of the money-economy (HH: I, §585).

As such, his discussion, with its emphasis on the deleterious effects of the industrial division of labour, is particularly pertinent in exposing the ideological and ultimately metaphysical underpinnings of the discourse on political economy, in no small measure inaugurated by Adam Smith, who viewed the division of labour as holding the key to the progress of humankind towards the 'civilized society' of 'universal opulence' that would 'extend itself to the lowest ranks of the people' (WN1: 40). Notwithstanding that Smith shared a number of Nietzsche's misgivings concerning the harmful effects of the mechanistic division of labour, including a greater propensity for the exploitation of the 'dividuums' created by the division of labour, Smith did not see striving for material comfort as incompatible with ethical progress of society. Quite the contrary, Smith argued that individuals' moral instincts would act as effective breaks on the tendency of economic self-interest to [generate] excess. Nietzsche remained firmly of the view that prioritising material prosperity would inevitably result in unprecedented 'spiritual slavery' (NF-1881:11[294]) and a dehumanised condition of the humankind manifested in ubiquitous social entropy.

The mechanistic division of labour, within the precepts of industrial culture, does not end with instrumentalising human beings and 'turning them into sand' (D: §174). Nietzsche argues that an individual is only *incidental* to the logic and process of commerce, industry, and exchange (D: §175). As such, he can be instrumentalised only as long as he continues to have 'utility' in relation to this inglorious trio bolstered by the division of labour. As soon as 'making profitable' no longer depends on 'the words 'factory', 'labour market', 'supply'—the 'egoism' of the labour-dividing money-maker will move on with the new 'auxiliary verbs', forsaking the atomised, costly, and inefficient individual (UM, II, UDHL, §7) in every capacity, except as an obsequious consumer (D: §175). This highlights a vital aspect of Nietzsche's critique and a fundamental economic insight. The inevitable consequence of striving to maximise profit is the objective requirement to minimise costs, including the human cost. This means, for Nietzsche, making *cheap humans* and making them on the cheap—i.e., producing atomistic individuals (i.e., 'private persons') with minimum investment into their development and producing as many of these cheap replicas as possible (UM: III, SE, §6). Such 'private persons' or 'dividuums', who were known in Aristotle's day simply as 'idiots', are [easily enough] indoctrinated by the mendacious political narratives and persevere in advancing the economic machine beyond the point where they become superfluous to its requirements and, more importantly, incidental to their own lives. In short, transformed by their own efforts into a myriad of disconnected mechanical and wholly meaningless existences.[695]

---

[695] See Aristotle (1996): *The Politics and The Constitution of Athens*, Cambridge University Press, 1253[a]. See also Nietzsche HH: I, *HMS*, §57; II, *WS*, §33; and A: §16.

Nietzsche problematises the long-term consequences of 'machine culture' and the division of labour associated with it, which 'makes men active and uniform' but provides 'no instigation to enhancement' and through this engenders, in the long run, 'a counter-effect, a despairing boredom of soul, which teaches … to long for idleness in all its varieties' (HH: II, *WS*, §218, §220). Although Nietzsche largely concurs with the logic of Marx's critique of the division of labour, he would heavily qualify Marx's conclusion that 'all free time is time for free development' (CW 29:22). Nietzsche would contend that far not everyone can and would use free time for development even if afforded such opportunity. The echoes of Nietzsche's concerns can today be clearly heard in the on-going debates about the rising tide of the global mental health crisis, as well as in the discussions and experiments with a *Universal Basic Income* ('*UBI*') and the advent of artificial intelligence ('*AI*'). In *Beyond Good and Evil* (1887), Nietzsche forewarns:

> [E]verywhere people are now raving, even under scientific disguises, about coming conditions of society in which 'the exploitative aspect' will be removed—which sounds to me as if they promised to invent a way of life that would dispense with all organic functions (BGE: §259)

Arguably, the meeting point of AI and UBI could be seen as an advent of such 'conditions of society'. Contemporary research estimates suggest that, over the next two to three decades, in excess of 40% of currently manned jobs could be automated affecting tens of millions of people across the globe.[696] Quite possibly, for the first time in history, there appears a genuine prospect of a human no longer needing to exploit another human in a manner, which Nietzsche characterises as 'disgraceful' and 'shameful' (GSt: 165). Yet a remaining question looms large over this prospect: what would become of the displaced? Free from having to work in order to live, would they become creators and explorers of the previously undiscovered spiritual depths in search of new meaning? Following Weber's logic, this should be possible. Throwing off the shackles of the capitalistic obsession with intensifying 'the productivity of human labour' should be liberating of creative energies:

> A man does not 'by nature' wish to earn more and more money, but simply to live as he is accustomed to live and to earn as much as is necessary for that purpose. (Weber 2005:24)

Alternatively, however, could UBI be more accurately viewed as a contrivance for alleviating the 'moral debt'—in effect, paying off the many—so that 'the increasingly wealthy can feel less guilt as they gain more wealth' because they know there is a floor for

---

[696] Nedelkoska and Quintini (2018): 'Automation, Skills Use and Training'; *OECD Social, Employment and Migration Working Papers* 202; Paris: OECD Publishing; https://doi.org/10.1787/2e2f4eea-en, last accessed Feb. 27, 2023. See also Carl Benedikt Frey and Michael A. Osborne, 'The Future of Employment: How Susceptible are Jobs to Computerisation?', last accessed Feb. 27, 2023.

everyone'?[697] In the face of existing and still evolving evidence, based in part on the examples of generations 'addicted to welfare', the promise that the '*AI*-UBI revolution' would bring about emancipation in the sense of spiritual fulfilment appears [at best] uncertain.[698] Furthermore, recent empirical studies consistently warn of 'the mounting evidence of substantial mental health harms related to universal credit'.[699] In this context, Nietzsche's warning to consider carefully the price paid for 'the alleviation of work' (HH: II, *WS*, §288), retains considerable weight, as well as a sense of foreboding:

> Mankind mercilessly employs every individual as material for heating its great machines: but what then is the purpose of the machines if all individuals (that is to say mankind) are of no other use than as material for maintaining them? Machines that are an end in themselves—is that the *umana commedia?* (HH: I, §585)

Does the UBI-AI revolution—the latest conjuration of the division of labour by those who profit from it—simply represent another formalistic and substantively hollow 'abolition of slavery', and how can we make sure that it does not? It is possible here to discern clear echoes of Nietzsche's discussion on the *aporias of industrial culture* resonating through the present-day discourse on the future of humankind. Nietzsche argues that humankind will never dispense with either of debt, slavery or the division of labour and that hitherto, under the guidance of false values promoted by the deficient and mendacious leaders, humankind has grossly mismanaged these phenomena and their interactions in a way that has placed humankind's future in great peril. As a result, Nietzsche's plea is for the urgent re-examination of these phenomena to prevent them from further becoming the forms of modern barbarism. Such re-examination, however, cannot and will not happen, until we achieve a revaluation of the values that continue to underpin them. Precipitating the revaluation is the change in the '*perceived* conditions of existence' (NF-1884:26[45]) which—in the cauldron of the crisis of modern political economy—Nietzsche links inextricably with the question of agency.

---

[697] For an informed discussion UBI, see Heller's 'Who Really Stands to Win from Universal Basic Income' (2018): https://www.newyorker.com/magazine/2018/07/09/who-really-stands-to-win-from-universal-basic-income, last accessed Feb. 27, 2023.

[698] See Gordon Dahl, Andreas Kostøl, and Magne Mogstad (2014): 'Family Welfare Cultures', *The Quarterly Journal of Economics*, 129, No. 4, 1711–1752: https://doi.org/10.1093/qje/qju019, last accessed Feb. 27, 2023. See also Manasi Deshpande (University of Chicago), 'Does Welfare Inhibit Success?': https://microeconomicinsights.org/welfare-inhibit-success-long-term-effects-removing-low-income-youth-disability-rolls/, last accessed Feb. 27, 2023. Finally, see David Daniel's 'Is Our Society Addicted To Welfare (2014): https://thesystemsthinker.com/is-our-society-addicted-to-welfare/, last accessed Feb. 27, 2023.

[699] Sophie Wickham, Le Bentley, Tanith Rose, Margaret Whitehead, David Taylor-Robinson, and Ben Barr (2020): 'Effects on Mental Health of a UK Welfare Reform, Universal Credit: A Longitudinal Controlled Study', Lancet Public Health 5: e157–e164.

The Question of Agency

The three *aporias* of industrial culture examined in this book illuminate the contours of the profound crisis of the ruling ideas (NF-1884:25[211]) of modern political economy:

> False values and delusive words: these are the worst monsters for mortals; long does calamity sleep and wait in them. But eventually it comes and wakes and eats and devours what built huts upon it. (Z: II, *Priests*)

Jointly, these *aporias* should be understood in the context of Nietzsche's undertaking to overcome the onset of social entropy, before the desire 'to obliterate and to extinguish the natural character of a thing, a state, a time, a person' by abolishing difference (NF-1887:10[111]) triumphs and 'mediocratization becomes irreversible' (NF-1885:2[13]).

Nietzsche's argument concerning the *critical role of agency* in political economy is as simple as it is salient (and dangerous to some). His insight, which echoes Aristotle and Plato, is that money should be a consequence of the social relations rather than being their source and that the value of money should reflect these social relations rather than artificially engineering them.[700] He suggests that if we were to honestly contemplate the questions of moderating debt, money in private hands and the vast array of money's and debt's functions in modern political economy that reach over and above simply facilitating exchange, we would reasonably quickly arrive at a realisation that *all of them* run into the same question. This question is that of 'agency' which, on Nietzsche's view, is the unequivocal source of values. No revaluation of values is possible without agency commensurate to such a task since values are its function and, as Nietzsche convincingly demonstrates, agency has been systematically disfigured under the precepts of slave morality.

Nietzsche suggests that the crisis of the ruling ideas has entered its second century (GM: III, §27). It is now harvesting the political (an increasingly, geo-political), economic and social consequences of the previous age, which only 'inquired after supply and demand' in order to determine the value of everything (D: §175). Our present is a more acute phase of the same crisis that Nietzsche detected and scrutinised in his own present. One of its key characteristics, in Nietzsche's assessment, is that the calibre of the leaders—in both politics and business—as well as of the institutions through which they govern, becomes increasingly incommensurate with the magnitude of the challenges facing humankind (NF-1884:25[349]). Nietzsche's critique is not intended to incriminate individual figures, past or present. He views individual actors as manifestations and representatives of particular types of energy, representing active of reactive forces, to which they lend their voice, the valuations of which they help to articulate and the consequences of which they try to implement.

As such, Nietzsche's critique challenges the entire *structures of governance* that, profoundly corrupted by slave morality, have become inept and only capable of bring-

---

[700] See Dodd's insightful discussion of these issues in *The Social Life of Money*, 2014:7–10.

ing to positions of power individuals wanting in terms of their fitness to govern. This aspect, in particular, makes Nietzsche's critique as applicable today as it was during his own time. Today, when humankind urgently needs different rather than simply 'new' ideas, it lacks the leaders capable of generating, let alone implementing, such ideas. Desperately clinging to the values that have long exhausted themselves, the thoroughly dwarfed individuals—'actors and pompous jesters' (Z: I, Flies)—who today pose as leaders, are, in actual fact, only *administrators of slave morality*, incapable of birthing any new, let alone different vision of the future.

Nietzsche considers it crucial that 'the dwarfed' and 'the mediocre' (NF-1884:25[349])—unfit for the challenges of the 'great politics', involving the 'world government' (NF-1884:25[523]) and concerned with the 'common economic management of the earth' (NF-1887:10[17])—do not become the 'guarantors and the bearers of the future', around whom the development of humankind consolidates, as such a future would inevitably succumb to their 'morbid valuations' (NF-1888:14[182]). He identifies one of the 'great risks' of modern times as 'the danger that the world government falls into the hands of the mediocre' (NF-1884:25[523]). It is well possible to argue that we are already past that point and that the dangers are heightened further. Nietzsche warns that when ordinary people start to 'have doubts as to whether there are higher people, the danger is truly great' (NF-1884:25[344]). As though confirming Nietzsche's misgivings:

> *The Journal of Democracy* surveys show that 'Citizens in a number of supposedly consolidated democracies in North America and Western Europe have not only grown more critical of their political leaders, they have also become more cynical about the value of democracy as a political system, less hopeful that anything they do might influence public policy and more willing to express support for authoritarian alternatives'. (Roche McKee, Kennedy 2016:4)[701]

The nihilistic phases of modern social life, problematised by Nietzsche, are by no means innocuous. Nor does the nihilistic uniformity represent a benign political state. Nihilistic society, on Nietzsche's view, is not a serene agglomeration of the disaffected individuals who have everything, aimlessly wondering around and feeling sadness for their lack of purpose and meaning. Rather, a nihilistic society, composed of the 'grains of sand', unavoidably slides towards a *repressive form of political organisation which tyrannises exceptions*' (NF-1887:9[44]). Nihilism is slave morality turning against itself: it emerges when 'all value judgments have turned against themselves' (GM: III, §10; NF-1886:5[71]). The 'grains of sand', increasingly seized by the rising calamity inside, come to resemble the particles that make up gunpowder and the rising discontent threatens to conjure up the proportions of the elements that could well make this social

---

[701] For an in-depth empirical study of the growing global dissatisfaction with democracy and its leaders, see Roberto Foa, Andrew Klassen, Michael Slade, Alex Rand, and Rosie Collins, (2020), 'The Global Satisfaction With Democracy Report 2020', Bennett Institute for Public Policy, University of Cambridge: https://www.bennettinstitute.cam.ac.uk/media/uploads/files/DemocracyReport2020.pdf, last accessed Feb. 27, 2023.

mixture explosive (UM: III, *SE*, §4). Nietzsche's warning, in this respect, concerns the *approaching tyranny* rather than simply bemoaning a coming age of heartless abundance.

Nietzsche's 'Positive Project'

In view of Nietzsche's contention that the crisis of modern political economy is likely to get progressively worse, our continued investigation into Nietzsche's pertinence should focus on the issue of whether he proposes a solution or a way out from the crisis, as the 'necessary counterpart to the Silenean declaration' (Leonard 2015:18–19). What could be seen as constituting Nietzsche's 'great gift' to humankind (EH: *Preface*, §4)? Does he offer a positive project and a credible alternative to modern industrial culture? Or a method for thinking towards a stronger future? After all, he claims that 'the most valuable insights' are discovered last and they 'are the methods' (AC: §13). Could it be both at once, perhaps, one followed by the other? Or is his *gift* something altogether different: a hammer, perhaps?

This study contends that Nietzsche's primary offer is that of a method. Applying the method Nietzsche develops to changing the [perceived] conditions of existence may one day make it possible to appreciate his vision of the future, which today cannot be fully comprehended, let alone endorsed. Nietzsche tells us, that the 'whole phenomenon mankind [still] lies at an incalculable distance beneath' Zarathustra's teachings (EH: *Preface*, §4). It is as if reaching it would require drilling down through the multiple layers of slave-like valuations (NF-1884:25[211]) which cloud humankind's intellectual horizons. It may be, therefore, that one needs a method before one can have a vision.

A notable focus of recent efforts in Nietzsche scholarship has been on excavating a positive project from within Nietzsche's corpus. Inquiries into Nietzsche's thought appear more worthwhile if they claim that a positive project within his *oeuvre* can be identified. Nietzsche is more agreeable if we can see his 'positive, reconstructive face' (Magnus 1986:39), if it can be demonstrated that he pursues 'positive goals' (Schrift 2013:114) and comes up with a 'positive vision of reality' (Rosenow 1986:128) that articulates 'positive alternatives' for the future of humankind (Solomon 1986:82), including 'positive views about value and normativity' (Janaway, Robertson 2012:5) that would amount to a 'positive and comprehensive philosophy' (Golomb 1986:160).

At the same time, Nietzsche who does not present us with a 'positive doctrine' and does not bequeath to us 'a positive body of knowledge', concerning how to build a stronger and loftier future, is regarded as somehow unfulfilled, a failure and, for that reason, less useful and unwelcome (see Sigad 1983:110). Such 'gloomy' Nietzsche is likened to a pendulum, doomed to oscillate 'between his positive doctrine and his skeptic-perspectivist epistemology' without ever arriving at the point of rest (Golomb 1986:168). This habit of differentiating between the 'positive' and the 'negative' Nietzsche is also discernible in the developing literature concerning his politics and economy. Shaw maintains that Nietzsche's scepticism gets in the way of his ability to articulate 'a positive, normative political theory' (Shaw 2007:2, 145). Even Drochon's pathbreaking inquiry into Nietzsche's *Great Politics* is not entirely free of the search for Nietzsche's 'positive vision of what politics might become' and what the 'great politics should be about' (Drochon 2016:14, 160). The impression is created that our search for a positive Nietzsche is somehow interminable as well as, perhaps, self-inflicted. Our perspectives remain informed by the [slavish] sensibility Nietzsche urges us to overcome.

The notion of a 'positive project' is often left undefined—it persists as a silent and unexamined assumption, as if it were something we could all pre-agree on. The meaning of the adjective 'positive', in particular, is not actively explored by the authors and critics who look for the positive interpretations of Nietzsche's undertaking. There is no easy answer to the question of what 'positive' might mean in relation to Nietzsche. Would it simply be the exact opposite of his political scepticism reflected in the scathing critiques of modernity, inclusive of its political economy? Answering this question connects to ascertaining the connotations of 'positive' in the minds of those who look for it in Nietzsche. If there were no 'positive project' to be found in his work, would it invalidate Nietzsche or merely the efforts of those who seek it? The reading of the various conceptions of Nietzsche's 'positive project' suggests that 'positive' retains an unarticulated connotation of 'good', in the sense of a final destination, offering, at least, a durable resolution. It encapsulates anxiety and longs for a sigh of relief to enunciate the moment 'the fear of nihilism—of complete disorientation—will pass' (Stegmaier 2016:393).

As this inquiry attempts to demonstrate by exploring Nietzsche's views on the *aporias of industrial culture*, the main source of his infectious angst is the uncertainty associated with the transition from the current crisis of modern values towards any future constellation of the social and towards the political economy of the future. As such, whether the 'mediocre politics of his day ... is creating circumstances conducive' to cultural rebirth (Abbey, Appel 1998:113) is not a settled matter in Nietzsche's mind. In this respect, Nietzsche is not entirely unlike Marx, who 'had no definite conception of what future society ought to be like, except by contrast with what he saw in the present capitalist society' (Wood 2014:7; see 262–265). Marx made clear his opposition to anyone engaged in 'writing the recipes for the cook-shops of the future' (Marx 1990:99).

Beyond the generic opaqueness of the future that, akin to Hegel's owl of Minerva 'begins its flight only at dusk' (Hegel 1991:23), Marx recognised another important limiting factor, which Nietzsche would be sympathetic towards. The existing political and economic conditions, Marx notes, limit one's horizons for conceiving valuations that do not correspond to these prevailing conditions, just as they limit the emergence of those who would be capable of forging new values. Only in resisting and overcoming these 'perceived' conditions do the outlines of new valuations become possible (NF-1884:26[45]). Therefore, the outlines of communism, let alone of a society based on its principles, could be seen no more clearly than those of a 'movement which abolishes the present state of things' (CW 5:49).

In a similar fashion, and despite acutely recognising the need for the revaluation of values, Nietzsche does not and cannot tell us what these re-valued values would be beyond the notion that they should represent a counterpoint to the values [of slave morality] that have guided humankind's development thus far. Furthermore, Nietzsche highlights the critical importance of agency in birthing these values. The present study contends that the value of what can be learned from Nietzsche, including his views on political economy, is not contingent on identifying a 'positive project' within his work. The value of his experimental philosophy is better gauged by travelling the intellectual journey with him as far as one is able, realising at the same time that even 'a great educator, powerful enough to draw long chains of generations from a lonely height down to himself' can only take his students so far down the path of intellectual and spiritual discovery (see NF-1885:37[7]). Provided one walks this path earnestly, regardless of whether one ends up agreeing with Nietzsche or not, one is reconfigured by this experience and acquires a different pair of eyes—firmly fixed on this world and with the added awareness concerning the direction of its travel.

In the Direction of an Aesthetic Political Economy

Not unlike Marx, who points in the direction of communism as a higher station of human life without speculating on the definitive features it might entail, Nietzsche does not leave behind detailed outlines for what his revaluation would comprise and what values could sustain humankind's stronger and healthier future. Both thinkers, however, left behind a number of clues from which it is possible to discern the direction of their thought. Nietzsche, in particular, commences and concludes his philosophical journey with the *aesthetic justification of the world*.[702] It is customary to associate Nietzsche's forays into aesthetics with his early period works. However, Nietzsche's reflections on aesthetics and his search for the aesthetic political economy were reinforced by his experience of the economic crises of industrial culture rather than being disabled by it. As a result, a significant part of Nietzsche's thinking on this subject is to be found in his late writings, contained mostly in the unpublished *Nachlass*. In these private notes, Nietzsche explores the value-generating capacity of aesthetic sensibility and looks for ways to bridge the divide between aesthetics and science, as well as overcoming the chasm between agency and nature created by the valuations of slave morality (NF-1887:10[167]).

Although Nietzsche concedes that 'it is not possible to *prove* ... the aesthetic significance of existence' (NF-1872:19[123]), there can be little doubt concerning the importance he attaches to the suggestion, which exhibits a distinctly *cultural connotation*. The potential analytical repercussions of this pivot in his political and economic thought are considerable. To begin with, Nietzsche suggests that neither the world

---

[702] See *BT* (§5, §15, §24); NF-1885:2[106] and [110]; NF-1887:11[138]; NF-1888:14[119]; and NF-1888:16[75].

nor existence on the whole can be *justified* as either an economic phenomenon or a political one. In other words, neither of the two principal meaning and value-making domains of modernity are sufficient for this purpose. Nietzsche is unequivocal in his insistence that authentic values have always been created and can only be gleaned far 'away from the market place', and that the 'inventors of new values' have never dwelled near it (Z: I, Flies). His hypothesis, however, reaches further still. What he suggests is that it is *not possible* to accurately know, understand or anticipate the world either politically or economically. It is only possible to create another abstract 'world' using these analytical categories and then to impose such abstract construction upon the real world, necessarily distorting and abusing the latter in all the places where it does not fit neatly enough into the theoretical formulations of how it 'should be'.

The *aesthetic*, for Nietzsche, denotes an important interface missing from the discourse on political economy. Nietzsche envisages a sensibility which could increase our understanding of the world we inhabit and allow our assimilation in it in a way that would be commensurate with the world as it exists, rather than using instrumental reason and moralised value judgements to subjugate the world to our imperfect knowledge, using politics and economics as the tools of reactive and oppressive power with which we impose ourselves on the world and seek to appropriate it. More than simply thinking of 'political action in aesthetic terms' (Abbey, Appel 1998:89), Nietzsche forces us to confront the 'enervating chimeras in the modern age' by continually juxtaposing 'the insipid masks of an ascetic "slave morality"' to 'that Person and *polis* in which "strength and beauty are inseparable from the good"' (Osborn 2010:298–305). This also helps to avoid the common and confusing use of the term 'aesthetic' to denote at least three overlapping concerns—'beauty', 'art' and a mode of cognition and perception of the world, which involves the senses. Nietzsche's meaning of the 'aesthetic' is primarily that of a *sensibility* that we desperately need to re-discover and develop to make our life in the world not only bearable but worthwhile.

Contrary to what has been suggested by some Nietzsche's critics, he does not flee to aesthetics in desperation and contriving a 'rhetorical exit' from his failure to resolve the contradictions of his philosophy, which he inadvertently misconstrues as the social problems of modernity (Shaw 2007:35–45).[703] Neither does he seek to simply become a 'comedian of the ideal' (see Nehamas 1985:133–136; Conway 1997:107), who reduces everything to 'aesthetic artefacts' (Eagleton 1990:257), since 'maintaining the greatest variety of human conditions of existence' is Nietzsche's unabating focus (see NF-

---

[703] See discussion in Kaufmann 2013:323–325; Cutrofello 2005:24–25, Steinbuch 1994:32–35, and Volker 1998:86–90 on whether Nietzsche's aesthetic turn represents a welcome '*uscita grazioso*' from the contradictions of his philosophy in the direction of the 'metaphysics of art'. More recently, Shaw (2007) suggests that Nietzsche's aesthetics is a distinct modality of the 'quest for the post-Christian faith', characteristic of the 19th century in general (Shaw 2007:39).

1880:1[67]; HH: II, *AOM*, §186).[704] For Nietzsche, aesthetics represents a unifying concern, which extends beyond the boundaries of a strictly 'individual self-realisation' (Abbey, Appel 1998:92). His objective in this respect is more accurately understood as a call for the 'reduction of morals to aesthetics' in order to break down the dictate of 'absolute truth' and to enable perspectival re-thinking:

> As soon as we deny the absolute truth, we have to give up all absolute demands and retreat to aesthetic judgments. This is the task—to create an abundance of aesthetically equal valuations: each for an individual, the final fact and the measure of things. (NF-1881:11[79])

Nietzsche's preference for aesthetics is predicated on his firmly held view that it is the only form of human sensibility which is not susceptible to the corruptive influence of the valuations of *slave morality*, which it successfully repels (see NF-1886:7[3]). Aesthetic sensibility represents an effective antidote to slave morality. On closer examination, Nietzsche's formula reveals a considerably deeper concern than a mere proposition that without art life is not worth living.[705] In considering Nietzsche's justification of the world as 'a self-birthing work of art' (NF-1885:2[114]), it is important to place it in the context of his enduring search for the conditions of existence (NF-1884:25[75],§1) —'*Existenzbedingungen*'—which gains prominence in his writings from about 1880. In the *Nachlass* notes from this period, Nietzsche intimates that 'we have not yet found our conditions of existence and are still looking for them' (NF-1880:4[101]). Elsewhere, he asserts that 'we know the conditions of existence of man very inaccurately' (NF-1880:6[421]). Formulated more precisely, Nietzsche attempts to identify such conditions of existence as would not simply enable the preservation ('*Erhaltung*') of life but would prioritise its enhancement ('*Steigerung*'/'*Erhöhung*'): 'life does not want to be just preserved, it wants to grow' (NF-1885:2[179]). As such, the on-going scholarly debate on the possible meaning of Nietzsche's 'aesthetic justification of existence' would benefit from focusing on the practical readings and implication of Nietzsche's endeavours (Church 2015b:289). The present inquiry contends that Nietzsche's undertaking extends considerably further than simply envisaging 'the exemplary individuals' (Church 2015b:290, 304), who would speak to the bigger picture of existence working well.[706]

---

[704] See the excellent discussion connecting Nietzsche's aesthetics and political action in Abbey and Appel 1998:92–93.

[705] See Jameson 1994:35.

[706] As argued earlier, in *Nietzsche on Slavery*, the *oikonomic* architecture entails a 'reciprocity catch': all of its parts—the *oikos*, the slaves, the *oikodespotes*, the order of rank—constitute certain conditions of existence. The latter enable the *Oikodespotes*, themselves the 'luxurious surplus' (NF-1887:10[17]), to produce the *aesthetic surplus of meaning and justification* for the entirety of *Oikos*' existence. At the same time, however, these conditions of existence must be such as to enable rearing the *Oikodespotes* fit for the task of producing such justificatory surplus. These conditions of existence, therefore, circle back to an enormous weight of their personal responsibility and the psychic cost, which far not everyone is cut out to handle (AC: §57). It is that synthesis which forms the basis of Nietzsche's aesthetic justification, which conveys an outward projection of the spirit of *Oikonomia* (EN: *TLEMS*, §2).

Nietzsche's understanding of the physical world, which influences his thinking on the questions of political economy, is profoundly affected by his extensive intellectual engagement with the contemporaneous advances of natural sciences.[707] It is particularly shaped by the laws of thermodynamics, which become an important influence connecting Nietzsche's thinking on the eternal return with his consideration of *aesthetic sensibility*, as a method for addressing the entropic propensities of the material world without condemning it as inferior or worthless.[708] The law of entropy brings to the forefront the question of how human development can be structured to generate an increase in the overall strength through the interactions of the different parts of the social whole rather than squandering life's energy:

> The will to accumulate strength is specific to the phenomenon of life ... not merely the conservation of energy ('Constanz der Energie'): but *the maximum economy of consumption:* so that getting stronger from every centre of force would be the only reality, not self-preservation, but ... becoming more, becoming stronger. (NF-1888:14[81])

Viewed through the lens of entropy, Nietzsche's argument concerning the preservation and enhancement of life suggests that its enhancement is only possible in spheres, which are not directly, or extensively, subjected to the law of entropy (NF-1881:11[165]).[709] As Stiegler aptly surmises, Nietzsche's project of revaluation envisages a 'leap into an economy founded on valuing and promoting negentropy and conceived as a reformulation of 'the great health' required [...] beyond what Nietzsche called active nihilism' (Stiegler 2019:39). Phrased slightly differently, the leitmotif of Nietzsche's thinking on political economy can be understood in terms of conceiving such conditions of existence that would allow humankind to get the most out of the entropic constraints within which humankind exists and develops without denying or neglecting these constraints. The material domain, concerned with life's preservation—the economy—is directly subject to the law of entropy, whereas enhancement of life relates pri-

---

[707] See Babich 1994:65; Rayman 2018:167; Acampora 2004:171, 174 in Brobjer-Moore 2004; Large 1999:151–152; and Safronov 2021:3–24.

[708] Mayer's articulation of the principle of conservation of energy is important to the development of Nietzsche's thought (Small 2017:139–142 and 2010:55–78). Nietzsche's notes from 1881–1882 confirm that he reads Mayer's work on kinetic theory ('*Die kinetische Theorie*') closely (BVN-1882:213) and the first law of thermodynamics becomes a cardinal input to his doctrine of eternal recurrence, with the crucial insistence that 'the law of the conservation of energy demands eternal recurrence' (NF-1886:5[54]). See NF-1881:11[24–25], [201–202], [213], and [292]. Brobjer also presents evidence of Nietzsche's reading of one of Mayer's later manuscripts on the *Mechanics of Heat* ('*Mechanik der Wärme*'), published in 1867 (Brobjer-Moore 2004:38). Nietzsche's critical discussion of the law of entropy can be traced back to his notes drafted mostly in the 1881 *M III, 1 Notebook* (NF-1881:11[148], [150], [197],[245], [265], and [306]) and all the way through to the late *Nachlass* (NF-1887:9[144]; NF-1888:24[1]; and NF-1888:14[188/4]), culminating in the refutation of the *Thom[p]son hypothesis* concerning the effects of the law of entropy (NF-1888:14[188]; last accessed March 12, 2023).

[709] See Del Caro's helpful discussion of Nietzsche's views on the management of the finite, 2004:352–353.

marily to its spiritual dimension—the realm of aesthetics and culture (NF-1887:10[167]). Politics—'only a particular characteristic of all organic existence'—grows out of the agonistic tension between the preservation and enhancement of life—at the juncture of the aesthetic and economic, and as the connection between these two fundamental existential concerns that, 'either allow life to grow and expand, or conversely to wither and dissipate' (Biswas Mellamphy 2008:746). Nietzsche's early hypothesis is the philosopher, who 'stands alongside the man of science and the artist' (NF-1872:19[72]), just as his conception of politics inevitably entails implications of 'an aesthetic activity' (see Franco 2014:465; Abbey and Appel 1998:89).[710]

The critical choice and the balance with regards to the conditions of existence, according to Nietzsche, lies between prioritising the *enhancement* of that which is preserved and merely *improving the modalities of preservation* of that which exists. Assuming, together with Nietzsche, that the law of the conservation of energy holds—if the total energy remains unchanged, then the only thing that matters is the use to which this energy is directed:

> [R]egarded *mechanistically* the total energy of becoming remains constant; from an *economic point of view*, it rises to a climax and sinks down again in an eternal circle; this 'will to power' expresses itself in the interpretation, *in the manner of the expenditure of energy*—transformation of energy into life and life of highest potency, therefore, appears as the aim. (NF-1887:10[138]; my emphasis)[711]

Industrial culture falls desperately short of delivering on that aim because its terms of reference translate into a wasteful 'expenditure of energy', which becomes progressively directed towards 'enhancing' the modalities of our preservation in the short term and neglecting to promote the enhancement of that, which is preserved over the long-term horizon (HH: II, *WS*, §280 and §282). Nietzsche problematises this propensity of industrial culture, expressed in the ascetic ideal, as representing a self-destructive developmental trajectory (see GM: III, §11–13, §18, and §28) on account of the end ('enhancement') and the means ('preservation') having become irreversibly inverted and 're-baptised'.[712]

This illustrates the kind of conflict which is created by the interplay between the non-material and the material, between the infinite and the finite as between consciousness ('nomos') and the physical world ('phusis'). When the material domain's pri-

---

710 Contrary to Williams' suggestion in *Shame and Necessity* (1993) that Nietzsche moved 'beyond the conception of the world as aesthetic phenomenon' but failed to offer 'a coherent politics' (Williams 1993:10), Nietzsche never abandons the aesthetic justification of the world and existence, which is the kernel of his political economy and philosophy more generally.

711 The idea of the cyclical nature of history, reflected as much in the cycles of economy, can already be found in Nietzsche's early notes from the *Nachlass*: 'The peaks of humanity are, more accurately, the centres of the semi-circle. For there is an ascending and a descending line. World history is no uniform process. *Its goal is continually reached*' (NF-1871:7[145]).

712 See Nietzsche's discussion in NF-1881:11[156] and NF-1888:14[182]). See also Mieszkowski 2006:185, fn. 57, and Voegelin 1944:195.

mary concern with preservation of life becomes represented with the help of abstract categories—as though it too were infinite—'infinity becomes a kind of drunkenness', which, unleashed onto the physical world, undermines the subtlety of assessment and produces a 'chaos of contradicting valuations' (NF-1885:44[5]). The material world becomes vulnerable to misconstruals and subject to misuse and manipulation by the reactive forces, which grow from within this chasm, exploiting it as a power relation in the game of 'one-sided preferences' (see HH: II, *AOM*, §186, and NF-1872:19[69]).

Nietzsche associates this kind of ideological portrayal of the world with the abdication of responsibility for it and its future, which becomes sacrificed to the squandersome and 'frivolous deification of the present' (BT: §24).[713] It is secondary whether such ideological misrepresentations are achieved with the help of metaphysical, moral, or secular political and economic categories, such as progress, debt, and economic growth. Living in the world of inexorably rising material entropy, by committing the error of 'making a standard of life out of a means of life' (NF-1888:14[158]), we lose sight of this fundamental constitutive property of the world and in so doing amplify entropic tendencies.

Nietzsche's insistence that representation has to retain commensurability with that which is being represented leads him to contend that any representation has to be 'judged by its consequences on life' (NF-1888:15[42]). In relation to the role of economy this means that where needs are concerned, 'e.g., with regard to food, clothing, housing, heating, climate, etc', we 'must all make sure that we become experts', who seek to 'build life on as many or as few foundations as can be adequately judged' (NF-1879:40[3]). One of Nietzsche's less used images in this context is that of the 'over-climatic man of art, who knows how to compensate for the disadvantages of any climate' (NF-1881:11[274]). When we do not wish to become experts in relation to a particular need, 'we have to deny that need to ourselves' (NF-1881:11[247]). Nietzsche's prescription of 'restricting our needs', while it may have an ascetic ring to it, is a highly pragmatic consideration. It is fully consistent with his stated preference for moderation in relation to economic matters (HH: II, *WS*, §285), which should assist in the accumulation of life's capital (NF-1880:6[183]).

Moderation, for Nietzsche, is always a testament to 'the fullness of power' and the highest form of self-affirmation (NF-1888:14[14]). Moderation is also subject to constant attack from *slave morality* which wishes to thwart aesthetic sensibility and to substitute it for the indiscriminate urges of mediocrity:

> Moderation itself was represented as a matter of severity, self-conquest, asceticism, as a fight with the devil, etc. The natural *delight of aesthetic natures in measure*, the enjoyment of the beauty of measure, was overlooked or denied, because one desired an anti-eudaemonistic morality. The faith in the pleasure of moderation—that pleasure of the rider on a fiery steed!—has been lacking hitherto. —The mediocrity of weaker natures has been confused with the moderation of the strong! (NF-1884:25[348]; my emphasis)

---

[713] See Nietzsche's discussion in UM: III, *SE*, §§4–6, HH: I, §33, GS: §356, and EH: *Destiny*, §§4–8.

The particular resonance of this direct juxtaposition of *capital* [as moderation] to *debt* [as excess], of the aesthetic political economy to that of industrial culture—as modalities of our engagement with the world—is twofold. Firstly, in relation to our use of natural resources and our dealings with the environment, and, secondly, in relation to the development of humankind (NF-1888:14[132]) in terms of 'translating man back into nature' (BGE: §230). Pointing out that 'any analysis of the aesthetic outlook is still lacking' (NF-1886:7[3]), a strong inference we can draw from Nietzsche's analysis is that until and unless we painstakingly develop sufficient understanding of the overall impact of such activities as fracking, bitcoin mining, or AI, for example, in order to be able to gauge their cumulative value, we should not proceed with these. Neither of these phenomena can be effectively contained post-factum, as a diligent afterthought that follows the inadvertent lifting of the lid of Pandora's box of their potential consequences we did not labour hard enough to understand in the first instance. We should particularly resist the urge to give into any 'new need' where it is promoted by the logic of money and profit-seeking (i.e., debt) because this logic invariably rests on the inadequate and frequently on the wilfully distorted representation of life's essential properties. Proceeding in this manner, by restricting the perceived need until sound understanding of its externality is developed, would force us to 'acquire knowledge concerning our needs' in a very different manner (NF-1879:40[3]). It would also tell us that regulating these types of developments (AI included) can only front them to be effective, rather than playing catch up. For this reason Nietzsche urges that scientific endeavour be freed from the intrusions of *slave morality*, deeming it necessary to expel the 'seductions and uncleanliness' from scientific pursuit so that it can become commensurate with the task of producing 'intellectual rectitude' (see NF-1880:4[295]; NF-1888:14[132]). Nietzsche's notion of the 'tragic artist's' approach is poignant in this context:

> The profundity of the tragic artist lies in this, that his aesthetic instinct surveys the more remote consequences, that he does not halt short sightedly at what is closest at hand, that he affirms the large-scale economy which justifies the terrifying, the evil, the questionable—and more than merely justifies them. (NF-1887:10[168])

The wider problem Nietzsche encounters concerns the adequate frame of reference for conceptualising and overseeing the development of humankind in a manner which is commensurate with both 'the existing world' (NF-1884:25[438]) and the objective of humankind's enhancement.[714] Nietzsche claims that it starts with 'how we organize our sensible apprehension of the world'—with aesthetics (Sjoholm 2015:75). In order to better gauge the value of existence, which Nietzsche regards as a 'problem of economy' (*'das Problem der Oekonomie'*), he considers it vital to find a frame of refence within which life could 'carry on as it is' (NF-1888:14[182]), rather than as it does now (NF-1887:9[153])—in other words, un-abridged, un-fragmented and un-subjugated to any

---

714 See GS: §318; BGE: §44, §257; and AC: §7.

single dominant agenda. In this regard, the aesthetic sensibility, as a nucleus of culture, presents itself as an alternative frame of reference and a criterion of judgement (Thiele 1990:913, 923). From some of his earlier writings to some of the latest, Nietzsche maintains that only culture 'knows how to accord to the material, humble, base, misunderstood ... imperfect, one-sided, incomplete ... a proper degree of understanding', and to 'admit all that is necessary for the harmonious endurance of all that is human' (HH: II, *AOM*, §186).[715]

The aesthetic orientation of Nietzsche's thought is significant in that it suggests that the economic ownership and appropriation of the world represent pervasive modalities of its gruesome misappropriation. Economic and financial seizure of the world —both physical and human—is a form of embezzlement which curtails the possibility of our aesthetic engagement with nature, necessary for the unfolding and flourishing of human potential. Humankind, conceptualised and implemented economically, is the humankind deprived of cultural becoming and consigned, instead, to economic being imbued with profound nihilism from which it may not be able to find an exit. Nietzsche contends that where the economic modality of humankind's existence divides and alienates, the aesthetic sensibility incorporates and unites.

Nietzsche clearly suggests that it is a function of aesthetics (as it could be of politics were it not money's obsequious servant) to anticipate future social and economic developments (HH: II, *AOM*, §99). Aesthetic sensibility, he argues, possesses uncanny ability to mediate between the present and the future states of society. In contrast, the realm of economy, composed largely of abstract economic categories, is incapable of pointing beyond itself and outside the range of its self-prescribed theoretical concerns. Neither money nor profit point beyond themselves; they cannot not indicate a future direction that would involve other than creating more of themselves by depleting all available resources, physical and spiritual, at the disposal of humankind. Debt itself is a form of existential dread before the [uncertainty of the] future, which it can only process by straight-jacketing this future with the precepts of *slave morality* (e.g., instrumental reason), thus preemptively undermining its vitality (i.e., castrating it). Therefore, and notwithstanding the predictable objections from economic forecasters, economics does not and cannot fullfil the function of a substantive mediation between the present and the future states of society, in part due to its obliviousness of the past. Its well-documented inability to accurately predict the coming economic crises is but one clear indication of this. Furthermore, economic forecasting invariably relies on considerable doses of 'blue-skies' thinking, which is a euphemism for 'utopian politics (or utopian social philosophy), disguised as political economy' (Meszaros 1970:128). It would be, therefore, a futile undertaking to envisage overcoming the predicament of the industrial culture, let alone overseeing humankind's genuine ascendance to a high-

---

[715] See also Nietzsche's discussion in NF-1872:19[64], where he argues that progress in culture is a critical existential condition for a sentient being, who requires illusion in order to live, and that culture provides an appropriate connection between the finite and the infinite.

er level of development in predominantly economic terms, as was once attempted by Smith. This is why Nietzsche steadfastly refuses to join the collective of professional economists, whom he likens to a 'thief' that, having stolen from the future, continues 'working away at his money-chest, while knowing full well that the chest is empty' (HH: I, §209) and, for that reason, unable to produce anything other than the endless iterations of excusing and justifying the present for the injustices it continues to perpetrate against humankind's future—our future (UM: IV, RWB, §6). Their fundamental differences notwithstanding, Nietzsche's combative thinking in this regard is considerably closer aligned to that of Marx.[716]

Within the range of concerns captured by Nietzsche, we invariably find one of the pivotal issues of political economy: namely, nature, meaning and management of the *surplus* produced by humankind's collective endeavour and held up as the symbol of its wealth and evidence of progress. The on-going debate between liberal and Marxist economic theories focuses predominantly on the economic meaning of wealth and, in consequence, concerns the administration of this 'economic' surplus (a contradiction in terms). Nietzsche's critique suggests that contesting whether such surplus should be managed individually, in favour of the ruling classes (liberals) or collectively (Marxists), not only buries any theoretical possibility of an *egalitarian society* but, more precariously, it overlooks the basic point arising from our dwelling in the world of increasing material entropy: namely, that wealth and surplus denoting humankind's progress as a species are not and cannot be material.

Economic overage should be only an input into the collective effort to generate the spiritual and cultural growth. The latter alone, according to Nietzsche, circumvents all known dilemmas of distribution and bestows the 'highest dignity' on human beings by helping the individual to 'attain universality' by overcoming 'the curse of individuation' (BT: §5–9). Furthermore, in Nietzsche's understanding, only the *aesthetic states* can truly subdue the 'order of rank' (NF-1886:7[3]) by allowing human beings to 'express their membership of a higher, more ideal community' where 'all the caste-like divisions which necessity and arbitrary power have established between men disappear', where 'the slave is a free-man' and 'the aristocrat and the man of lowly birth come together' (DWV: §1).

Nietzsche argues that the inclusive properties of culture are rooted in the aesthetic sensibility, which is more commensurate with processing and incorporating unabridged reality, as well as assimilating to it. It calls for the appreciation of the world as 'fuller, rounder, *more perfect*' (NF-1887:11[138]), revealing in the process a different image of the human being:

> The *artistic force of nature*, not that of an individual artist, reveals itself here; a nobler clay, a more precious marble is kneaded and chiselled here: the human being. (DWV: §1; my emphasis)

---

[716] See Meszaros 1970:124–130 for an enlightening elaboration of Marx's position. See also Vasquez 1973:46–52.

This is the reason for Nietzsche's insistence that the 'tremendous task facing the great spirits of the coming century' is to help humankind to develop an 'altogether unprecedented knowledge of the *preconditions of culture* as a scientific standard for ecumenical goals' (HH: I, *FLT*, §25). Nietzsche's discussion in the late *Nachlass* clearly identifies the need to find the possible ways of transforming 'the weary, exhausted and dried up' world of simulacra with the help of aesthetic sensibility which, as 'the *primum mobile*', is able to 'infuse a transfiguration and fullness into things' (NF-1887:9[102]; see also NF-1887:10[167]). Nietzsche associates the aesthetic sensibility with a *force* that entails the ingredients necessary for forming judgement (WP: §846), making it capable of 'imposing laws and giving a conscience' (NF-1888:16[29]). He argues that, without aesthetics in the picture, the discourse on political economy concerning the development and the future of humanity lacks authenticity and intellectual honesty because it supresses the 'genuine conflict over "principles"' (NF-1888:16[29]). In addition, Nietzsche suggests that unlike the economistic and political modes of thinking, prone to short-termism and expediency which obscure and misjudge the real objectives of society's development, the properly deployed 'aesthetic instinct' 'surveys the more remote consequences'; it does not halt myopically at 'what is closest at hand', and in so doing, it 'affirms the large-scale economy' (NF-1887:10[168]).

Nietzsche is calling for an altogether different modality of knowing to govern our interactions with the world we inhabit, one that connects mythical traditions with empirical ones and culture with science. Viewed in this light, aesthetics is neither a passive interface, nor a reactive process by means of which we receive the world (Belfrage, Gammon 2017:223). Instead, it is an active modality of perspectival knowing, which allows one not only to deal with the 'infinite interpretability of the world' but to also to differentiate between interpretations on the basis of whether they represent 'a symptom of growth or decline' (NF-1885:2[117]):

> The aesthetic state has an abundance of remedies, at the same time with an extreme sensitivity to stimuli and signs. It is the *pinnacle of communicability* and transferability between living beings— it is the source of languages. (NF-1888:14[119]; my emphasis)

Nietzsche contends that using aesthetic approach would enable us to overcome the misleading dichotomy between the 'only apparent moral values' and physiological ones, as well as making it possible to envisage 'a truly scientific order of values' for measuring the 'scale of force', where 'ascent on this scale represents every rise in value; the descent—diminution in value' (NF-1888:14[105]). In this sense, the aesthetic sensibility is an interactive medium, which is as much about the 'formation of the objects that constitute our social milieu', as it is about 'how we constitute ourselves as objects in relation to the world' (Belfrage, Gammon 2017:223). In order to achieve a balanced perspective for the formulation and satisfaction of human needs, it is important, for Nietzsche, to have the rational man, who is 'fearful of intuition' and knows how to meet 'the greatest needs with the foresight, prudence and regularity', standing side by side with the intuitive man, who is 'scornful of abstraction' and regards 'life as real only when it is disguised as make-believe and beauty' (EN: *TLEMS*, §2).

The aesthetic sensibility becomes Nietzsche's preferred mode of proactive acumen, as *'Erkenntnis'*, that informs the meaning of being human in the world of becoming.[717] Nietzsche argues that by furthering and multiplying our taste in existence, aesthetics also 'becomes the basic condition of all the passion of knowledge' (NF-1881:11[162]), just as science 'constantly pushed to its limits must turn into art' (NF-1883:7[7]). Nietzsche's intriguing conjecture is that science and aesthetics only seem opposed to one another where *slave morality* infiltrates the 'scientific view of the world' and subverts it by directing it to 'only value, what can be counted and calculated' (NF-1886:7[3]). In this regard, building on some of his earliest insights concerning the 'two brain ventricles—one for the perceptions of science, the other for those of non-science' (HH: I, §251)—Nietzsche remains committed until the very end to finding the synthesis of 'aesthetic judgements ... put on a scientific basis' (NF-1888:11[88]). The aesthetic sensibility, on his view, invariably possesses value-generating capacity:

> Regarding all *aesthetic values* I now avail myself of this main distinction: I ask in every instance, is it hunger or superabundance that has here become creative? At first glance. Another distinction may seem preferable—it is far more obvious—namely the question whether the desire to fix, to immortalize, the desire for being prompted creation, or the desire for destruction, for change, for future, for becoming. [...] The desire for destruction, change, and becoming can be an expression of an overflowing energy that is pregnant with future (my term for this is, as is known, 'Dionysian'); but it can also be the hatred of the ill-constituted, disinherited, and underprivileged, who destroy, must destroy, because what exists, indeed all existence, all being, outrages and provokes them. (GS: §370; my emphasis)

Already in the *Genealogy*, Nietzsche indicates his intention to tackle the delicate problems concerning the hitherto untouched and unexplored *physiology of aesthetics*' (GM: III, §8). Some of his final *Nachlass* notes reinforce his call to dispell the myth of moral values, which are 'only apparent values compared with physiological ones' (NF-1888:14 [10]. He posits the 'foundation of all aesthetics', as resting 'upon biological values', and 'the aesthetic well-being', as representing first and foremost 'a biological well-being' (NF-1888:16[75]). Although Nietzsche was unable to expand more in this direction, there can be little doubt of the epistemological significance he attributes to this possible connection within the context of his undertaking to 'translate man back into nature', achieved through 'the dehumanization of nature and then the naturalization of man after he has reinstated the purity of the term "nature"' (NF-1881:11[211]; see BGE: §230).

The un-moralised scientific basis of aesthetic judgements is important, on Nietzsche's view, to prevent aesthetics from being turned into a yet another ideology. This is key if the aesthetic sensibility is to retain its regenerative will to seek and its ability to create new meanings (NF-1881:11[165]). Instead of positing aesthetics as a per-

---

717 See Wydra's illuminating discussion of the distinctive properties of *Erkenntnis*, 2015:1–2, 233.

manent cure, it references a particular process in which the creative energy of the world is continually transformed (NF-1885:2[106]; WP: §846). Engaged in this manner, the aesthetic paradigm of political economy also informs the production of meaning, which is seen as the unceasing labour of a perspectival community, of the knowing rather than the moral mankind (HH: I, *HMS*, §107).

Parting Thoughts

What are the implications of Nietzsche's aesthetic perspective on political economy that would be worth exploring further? Adopting an aesthetic approach would have a considerable expository effect in terms of bringing the total cost perspective onto 'the balance sheet of life' (NF-1875:5[188]) by highlighting those aspects of it which are obscured from view by the governing forms of representation.[718] The aesthetic perspective, instead of maintaining the intellectual stance of an, as though 'impartial observer', proceeds by 'assuming that there is always a gap between a form of representation and what is represented therewith' (Bleiker 2001:503). This is a fundamental feature of Nietzsche's conception of political economy. The combative and expository properties of the aesthetic require that 'the full register of human intelligence' be brought to bear in dealing with the stark problems and 'dilemmas that currently haunt world politics' (Bleiker 2001:519). The aesthetic viewpoint equally challenges the manner in which reactive forces justify and reproduce particular politico-economic norms and narratives 'for the purposes of sustaining their own power' (Shaw 2007:13). Nietzsche's critique of values allows us to formulate a number of questions that would be pertinent in today's context, and which—dy design—remain withoout answers in the conventional discourse.

What would be the final consequences and the total cost of the 'one-sided preference' for economic well-being, manifest in the narratives of economic growth, pursuit of material wealth and valorisation of profit-seeking? Why is the *will* lacking to bring the 'invisible costs' fully onto the balance sheet of life, if there is nothing untoward to them? If the unprecedented build-up of debt, mounting environmental problems, and the escalating global mental health crisis are *not hazardous* to humankind's development, why not place them squarely and transparently within the conversation on progress? Why not create a truer version of inflation, by including clean air and unpolluted water into the calculation basket with significant weightings? Why not tax the inflation of financial assets, which is better known to us as the [unequivocally good] growth of the market? Why continue to treat interest on debt as tax deductible when equity dividends are not? Why allow the continued depletion of the non-renewable natural resources—a clear symptom of the unsustainable economic trajectory—to feature as rev-

---

[718] See the discussion by Bourdieu of the total costs of 'economic decisions and economic calculations' in *Acts of Resistance*, 1998:39.

enue and not as depreciation, i.e., as a cost in the corporate and national accounts (see Erikson 2022)? Why allow the profit maximising private equity firms to run the social and healthcare system, if the objective is to have an effective public good commensurate with the dignity allegedly ascribed to human life? Why educate the young in a manner that leaves them in debt and vulnerable to mental health problems if it is to them that our hopes for a healthier and loftier future should be hoisted?

Maybe one does not need Nietzsche to have these thoughts, but Nietzsche can certainly help explain why we should have precisely these critical thoughts by guiding us through the myriad of conventional considerations to expose the valuations at play behind the aforementioned phenomena. As such, these questions offer but a glimpse into how Nietzsche's 'philosophical genealogy' (NF-1884:26[432]), based on disentangling the modern slogans and battle cries from the underlying reality they misrepresent and conceal, translates into a powerful call for the fundamental repositioning and re-prioritisation of the key issues within the conceptual architecture of political economy. Such a revaluation would be assisted by engaging with the aesthetic perspectival method of evaluating. In the end, whether the attraction to Nietzsche's thought is a function of the method he makes available or whether it derives from the attempts to discern the contours of a future society Nietzsche might have envisaged, as though by the will of the circle, his critical analysis keeps returning his readers to the world we presently inhabit. It forcibly places them in front of the mirror into which we ordinarily prefer not to look. Following Nietzsche's method and adopting the aesthetic total cost approach instead of the fictitious and/or incomplete economic 'externality' procedure, informed by the valuaitons of *slave morality*, we inevitably arrive at the necessity of changing our governing values in order to enable change in our world. Reflecting on Nietzsche's blueprint for a possible future from the standpoint of revalued values, which shift the focus from 'the benefits to the society that is currently in existence' to 'the most possible benefits of the future' (NF-1887:9[153]), we are driven to the realisation that the revalued values, enabling such a future society, are unlikely to come to pass until the manner in which the world is managed is changed fundamentally from how it is run today.

Nietzsche's critical insight, which deftly challenges the most fundamental tenet of modern economics and finance, is that in order to build a stronger and intrinsically more valuable future *in lieu* of simply speculating on it, as though the 'bright future' of the liberal Promised Land could, at some indeterminate point in time, descend upon us like the manna from heaven at the wave of an *invisible hand* [of the market], it is necessary, Nietzsche tells us, to walk from the future we dare to envisage resolutely back to the present we inhabit in order to determine what demands achieving such a vision would impose upon us, instead of frivolously embellishing the 'here and now' by cynically discounting the future to the [net] value of the present—i.e., devaluing the future *vis-à-vis* the present—while disparaging, disowning and rewriting the past to unburden ourselves of its troubling legacy as we continue to squander its capital.

NPE urges us to distinguish between discounting <u>from</u> the future we strive for to the present we currently occupy in order to ascertain the magnitude of investment such a feat would require, and discounting of the future which 'the sirens in the marketplace sing to us about' (GS: §377) to the net value of the present which lives by sapping the vitality of the future, as representing two fundamentally different approaches to valuing life and the world we live in. Hitherto, in Nietzsche's assessment, modernity's political economy [of debt] has been unequivocally based on devaluing humankind's prospects and the planet's future vis-à-vis the increasingly enfeebled present, where there is profit to be made and the life-negating forces run the show. The enabling mechanism for changing our valuing perspectives, Nietzsche tells us, lies dormant in us and it must be unlocked before it is too late.

Resonating through both scenarios is the question of 'whether we still want to live: and how' (NF-1881:11[141]). This, in turn, invites perhaps the most important question Nietzsche's philosophy raises: how to become new, how to infuse new meaning into the old and exhausted structures, not as a breath of 'eternal life' to bring them back, but in the form of a spiritual flame, so that something new can grow from of their ashes.[719] He associates such regenerative qualities with aesthetics:

> I myself attempted an aesthetic justification: how is the ugliness of the world possible?—I took the will to beauty, to enduring in the unchanged forms, as a means of *temporary preservation* and a remedy: fundamentally, however, it appeared to me that the eternally-creating, just as the eternally-destroying is of necessity bound to pain. In this light, the ugly becomes the manner of contemplation of things by the will seeking for meaning, seeking to *introduce a new meaning into what has become meaningless:* the accumulated force, which compels the creator to regard what has come hitherto as untenable, misconceived, worthy of negation—ugly. (NF-1885:2[106]; my emphasis)

At this point, Nietzsche hands his project over to us, who have not yet been through the formative experiences that would mould us into the sovereign agents we need to become to answer the call of revaluation that would be capable of altering the course of humankind's history towards a stronger future.

There is no answering the question concerning Nietzsche's pertinence in general terms. His philosophy and his political economy are as much a call to arms as they are a paralysing sense of foreboding and crisis. What it becomes, however, as much as what it *can* become, can only be answered individually, as the first step. Whether this is to our satisfaction or otherwise, from this point onwards, the journey translates into the question of agency: individual at first, and collective later. It becomes a question of what one is and what one is destined to become (BGE: §24, §41). As Staten aptly surmised, 'the only power in Nietzsche's writing is whatever power is felt as power by some actual audience at some moment in history' (Staten 1989:84). Those 'monsters of courage and curiosity' (EH: *Books*, §4), however, who accept Nietzsche's challenge, must, in equal measure, be prepared to consider *all* of Nietzsche's conjectures 'without melancholy' (NF-1871:10[1]), including 'not only understanding the previously negated

---

[719] See Voegelin 1944:195.

aspects of existence' but also engaging in 'a voluntary search for the cursed and wicked sides of existence' (NF-1888:16[32]).

Nietzsche leaves behind the weighty hammer of his experimental philosophy (see NF-1884:26[298], 27[80]) 'for overpowering people' (NF-1883:21[3]), until someone strong enough to wield it comes along. Whether or not 'the most sublime sculpture' sleeps hidden in the rock, which we are, cannot be known until then.[720] It would, however, be a catastrophic mistake to pretend that Nietzsche addresses anyone other than ourselves, or that the burden of proof rests on someone else's shoulders. The one illusion to which —having delved into Nietzsche—we are no longer entitled, is the thought that giving political effectiveness to Nietzsche's philosophical insight has nothing to do with us (NF-1885:35[47]). Nietzsche tells us that the future possesses no lesser power to shape the present and to determine its course than does the past: 'the future that we want affects our now' (NF-1883:7[6]) and what we 'abstain from also weaves at the web of all human future' (Z: III, *Virtue*, §3). In order to overcome the gravity of the past, no less than a 'tremendous self-examination' is required. Only undertaking such an excruciating transformation would enable us to 'become conscious of ourselves not as individuals but as humanity' (NF-1887:9[60]). Nietzsche's name for it is the revaluation of all values.

---

[720] See NF-1883:9[34], 13[3]. Michelangelo's sculptures 'I Prigioni' supply ample meaning to Nietzsche's image of a 'sublime sculpture' hidden within the rock.

Bibliography

Primary Sources

Aristotle ('P'; 1996): *The Politics and the Constitution of Athens.*[724] Stephen Everson (Ed.): Cambridge: Cambridge University Press.
Aristotle ('NE'; 1999): *Nicomachean Ethics.* Terence Irwin (Trans.). Cambridge: Hackett Publishing.
Aristotle (2015): *De Anima.* Robert D. Hicks (Trans.). Cambridge: Cambridge University Press.
Bagehot, Walter (1915): *The Works and Life of Walter Bagehot.* Vol. VIII. Mrs. Russell Barrington (Ed.). London: Longmans, Green, and Co.
Bagehot, Walter (2010): *Physics and Politics.* New York: Cambridge University Press.
Carlyle, Thomas (1843): *Past and Present.* In: Carlyle, Thomas: *Thomas Carlyle's Collected Works.* Vol. XIII, Books III and IV, London: Chapman and Hall, 171–341.
Engels, Friedrich (1970): *Socialism: Utopian and Scientific.* Moscow: Progress Publishers.
Epictetus (1865): *The Works of Epictetus.* Elisabeth Carter and Thomas W. Higginson (Trans.). Boston: Little, Brown and Company.
Freud, Sigmund (1933): *New Introductory Lectures on Psycho-Analysis.* New York: Carlton House.
Hall, Charles (1850): *The Effects of Civilisation on the People in European States.* London: Charles Gilpin.
Hegel, Georg W. F. (1991): *Elements of the Philosophy of Right.* Allen W. Wood (Ed.). Hugh B. Nisbet (Trans.). Cambridge: Cambridge University Press.
Hesiod (2006): *Theogony, Works and Days, Testimonia.* Glenn W. West (Ed. and Trans.). Cambridge and London: Harvard University Press.
Hobbes, Thomas (1991): *Leviathan.* Cambridge: Cambridge University Press.
Josephus, Flavius (1956): The Jewish War. Books I–III. Henry St. John Thackeray (Trans.). London and Cambridge: William Heinemann and Harvard University Press.
Lange, Friedrich Albert (1877): *History of Materialism and Criticism of Its Present Importance.* Boston: James R. Osgood and Company.
Locke, John (1988): *Two Treatises of Government.* Cambridge: Cambridge University Press.
Marx, Karl and Engels, Frederick ('CW'; 1980): *Marx & Engels Collected Works.* London: Lawrence & Wishart.[725]
Mill, John Stuart (1963–1991): *Collected Works of John Stuart Mill.* John M. Robson (Ed.). Toronto: University of Toronto Press.
Mill, John Stuart (1965): *Principles of Political Economy. Collected Works*, Volume II, Books I–II. John M. Robson (Ed.). Toronto: University of Toronto Press.
Mill, John Stuart (1967): *Essays on Economics and Society, 1824–1845.* Collected Works, Volume IV. John M. Robson (Ed.). Toronto: University of Toronto Press.
Newton, Isaac (1999): *The Principia: Mathematical Principles Of Natural Philosophy.* I. Bernard Cohen and Anne Whitman (Trans.). Berkeley: University of California Press.
Nietzsche, Friedrich (1844–1900):[726]
Nietzsche, Friedrich ('EN'; 1867–1879): *Writings from Early Notebooks.* 3rd edition. Raymond Geuss and Alexander Nehamas (Eds.). Ladislaus Löb (Trans.). Cambridge: Cambridge University Press. 2015.

---

[724] Abbreviation of the titles of key texts as used in the body of the text, e.g., Aristotle's Politics ('P') and Plato's Republic ('R').
[725] Cited as 'CW' followed by volume and page, e.g., 'CW 6:57'.
[726] Translations of Nietzsche's texts are arranged in chronological order (title abbreviation and year of completion are placed next to the title in brackets). Year of publication, which is used for the purpose of citing Nietzsche's works, is listed at the end of each reference.

Nietzsche, Friedrich ('GSt', 1872): *The Greek State.* In: Nietzsche, Friedrich: *On The Genealogy Of Morality* ('GM'). Keith Ansell-Pearson (Ed.). Carol Diethe (Trans.). Cambridge: Cambridge University Press, 176–187. 1994.

Nietzsche, Friedrich ('HC', 1872): *Homer on Competition.* In: Nietzsche, Friedrich: *On The Genealogy Of Morality* ('GM'). Keith Ansell-Pearson (Ed.). Carol Diethe (Trans.). Cambridge: Cambridge University Press, 187–195. 1994.

Nietzsche, Friedrich ('FEI', 1872): *On The Future of Our Educational Institutions.* John MacFarland Kennedy (Trans.). In: Nietzsche, Friedrich: *The Complete Works of Friedrich Nietzsche.* Vol. III. Oscar Levy (Ed.). Edinburgh and London: T.N. Foulis, 13 & 15 Frederick Street. 1910.

Nietzsche, Friedrich ('PT', 1872): *On the Pathos of Truth.* In: Nietzsche, Friedrich: *Writings from Early Notebooks* ('EN'). 3rd ed. Raymond Geuss and Alexander Nehamas (Eds.). Ladislaus Löb (Trans.). Cambridge: Cambridge University Press, 248–253. 2015.

Nietzsche, Friedrich ('BT', 1872): *The Birth of Tragedy.* Walter Kauffmann (Trans.). New York: Vintage Books. 1967.

Nietzsche, Friedrich ('BTOW', 1872): *The Birth of Tragedy and Other Writings.* Raymond Geuss and Ronald Speirs (Eds.). Ronald Speirs (Trans.). Cambridge: Cambridge University Press. 1999.

Nietzsche, Friedrich ('PTAG', 1873): *Philosophy in the Tragic Age of the Greeks.* Marianne Cowan (Ed.). Washington, DC: Regency Publishing. 1998.

Nietzsche, Friedrich ('TLEMS', 1873): *On Truth and Lies in an Extra-Moral Sense.* In: Nietzsche, Friedrich: *Writings from Early Notebooks* ('EN'). 3rd ed. Raymond Geuss and Alexander Nehamas (Eds.). Ladislaus Löb (Trans.). Cambridge: Cambridge University Press. 2015.

Nietzsche, Friedrich ('UM', 1873–1876): *Untimely Meditations.* Daniel Breazeale (Ed.). Reginald J. Hollingdale (Trans.). Cambridge: Cambridge University Press. 1997.

Nietzsche, Friedrich: *Unpublished Writings from the Period of Unfashionable Observations.* Richard T. Gray (Trans.). Stanford: Stanford University Press. 1995.

Nietzsche, Friedrich ('HAH', 1878–1880): *Human, All-Too Human: A Book for Free Spirits.* Richard Schacht (Ed.). Reginald J. Hollingdale (Trans.). Cambridge: Cambridge University Press. 1996.

Nietzsche, Friedrich ('D', 1881): *Daybreak: Thoughts on the Prejudices of Morality.* Maudemarie Clark and Brian Leiter (Eds.). Reginald J. Hollingdale (Trans.). Cambridge: Cambridge University Press. 1997.

Nietzsche, Friedrich ('GS', 1882): *The Gay Science.* Walter Kaufmann (Trans.). New York: Vintage Books. 1974.

Nietzsche, Friedrich ('Z', 1883–1885): *Thus Spoke Zarathustra.* Walter Kaufmann (Trans.). New York: Random House. 1954.

Nietzsche, Friedrich ('BGE', 1886): *Beyond Good and Evil.* In: Nietzsche, Friedrich: *Basic Writings of Nietzsche.* Walter Kaufmann (Ed. and Trans.). New York: Modern Library. 2000.

Nietzsche, Friedrich ('GM', 1887): *On the Genealogy of Morality.* Keith Ansell-Pearson (Ed.). Carol Diethe (Trans.). Cambridge: Cambridge University Press. 1994.

Nietzsche, Friedrich ('TCW', 1888): *The Case of Wagner: A Musician's Problem.* In: Nietzsche, Friedrich: *The Anti-Christ, Ecce Homo, Twilight Of The Idols and Other Writings.* Aaron Ridley and Judith Norman (Eds.). Judith Norman (Trans.). Cambridge: Cambridge University Press. 2005.

Nietzsche, Friedrich ('TI', 1888): *Twilight of the Idols, or How to Philosophise with a Hammer.* In: *The Portable Nietzsche.* Walter Kaufmann (Ed. and Trans.). New York: Penguin Classics. 1994.

Nietzsche, Friedrich ('AC', 1888): *The Antichrist: A Curse on Christianity.* In: Nietzsche, Friedrich: *The Portable Nietzsche.* Walter Kaufmann (Ed. and Trans.). New York: Penguin Classics. 1994.

Nietzsche, Friedrich ('NCW', 1888): *Nietzsche Contra Wagner: From the Files of a Psychologist.* In: Nietzsche, Friedrich: *The Portable Nietzsche.* Walter Kaufmann (Ed. and Trans.). New York: Penguin Classics. 1994.

Nietzsche, Friedrich ('EH', 1888): *Ecce Homo: How to Become What You Are.* In: Nietzsche, Friedrich: *Basic Writings Of Nietzsche.* Walter Kaufmann (Ed. and Trans.). New York: Modern Library. 2000.

Nietzsche, Friedrich ('LN', 1885–1888): *Writings from the Late Notebooks.* Rüdiger Bittner (Ed.). Kate Sturge (Trans.). Cambridge: Cambridge University Press. 2003.

Nietzsche, Friedrich ('WP', 1901): *The Will to Power.* Walter Kaufmann (Ed.). Walter Kaufmann and Reginald J. Hollingdale (Trans.). New York: Random House. 1968

Philo (1993): *The Works of Philo.* Charles D. Younge (Trans.). Peabody: Hendrickson Publishers.

Plato ('R'; 1905): *The Republic.* Henry Desmond Pritchard Lee (Trans.). Harmondsworth: Penguin Books Ltd.

Plato ('S'; 1921): *Statesman.* In: Plato: *Plato in Twelve Volumes.* Vol. XIII. Harold N. Fowler (Trans.). London: William Heinemann Ltd., 4–164.

Polybius (2010): *The Histories.* Robin Waterfield (Trans.). Oxford: Oxford University Press.

Pomeroy, Sarah B. (1994): *Xenophon Oeconomicus: A Social and Historical Commentary.* New York: Oxford University Press.

Rabelais, François (1892): *Five Books of the Lives, Heroic Deeds and Sayings of Gargantua and His Son Pantagruel.* Sir Thomas Urquhart of Cromarty and Peter Antony Motteux (Trans.). London: Lawrence & Bullen.

Roscher, William (1878): *Principles of Political Economy.* Vols. I–II. John J. Lalor (Trans.). New York: Henry Holt & Co.

Simmel, Georg (1978): *The Philosophy of Money.* Abingdon: Routledge and Kegan Paul Ltd.

Simmel, Georg (1991): *Schopenhauer and Nietzsche.* Urbana: University of Illinois Press.

Smith, Adam ('LJ'; 1896): *Lectures on Justice, Police, Revenue and Arms.* Edwin Cannan (Ed.). Oxford: Clarendon Press.[727]

Smith, Adam ('WN 1 and 2'; 1904): *An Inquiry into the Nature and Causes of the Wealth of Nations.* Edwin Cannan (Ed.). London: Methuen.

Smith, Adam (1976): *An Inquiry into the Nature and Causes of the Wealth Of Nations.* Roy H. Campbell and Andrew S. Skinner (Eds.). Oxford: Oxford University Press.

Smith, Adam ('TMS'; 1976): *The Theory of Moral Sentiments.* David D. Raphael and Alexander L. Macfie (Eds.). Oxford: Oxford University Press.

Smith, Adam ('EPS'; 1980) *Essays on Philosophical Subjects with Dugald Stewart's Account of Adam Smith. The Glasgow Edition of the Works and Correspondence of Adam Smith.* Vol. III. William P. D. Wightman, John C. Bryce, and Ian S. Ross (Eds.). Oxford: Oxford University Press.

Smith, Adam ('HA'; 1980a): *The Principles Which Lead and Direct Philosophical Enquiries; Illustrated by the History of Astronomy.* Oxford: Oxford University Press.

Smith, Adam ('LRBL'; 1983): *Lectures on Rhetoric and Belles Lettres.* John C. Bryce (Ed.). Oxford: Oxford University Press.

Smith, Adam (1987): *Correspondence of Adam Smith. The Glasgow Edition of the Works and Correspondence of Adam Smith.* Vol. VI. Ernest C. Mossner and Ian S. Ross (Eds.). Indianapolis: Liberty Fund.

Spencer, Herbert (1851): *Social Statics: Or, The Conditions Essential to Happiness Specified, and the First of Them Developed.* London: John Chapman.

Spencer, Herbert (1873): *The Study of Sociology.* London: Henry S. King.

Thomson, William (Lord Kelvin) (1911): *Mathematical and Physical Papers.* Vol. V. Cambridge: Cambridge University Press.

Thomson, William (Lord Kelvin) (2018): 'On the Origin of Life'. In: Thomson, William (Lord Kelvin): *Kelvin's Popular Lectures and Addresses.* Vol. II. London: Macmillan and Company, 132–205.

---

727 Smith's works are referenced by abbreviated titles. 'WN' stands for *The Wealth of Nations* (1776); 'WN1' stands for Volume I, and 'WN2' stands for Volume II. The *Theory of Moral Sentiments* (1759) is referenced as 'TMS'. *Lectures on Justice* (1763) is referenced as 'LJ'. *History of Astronomy* (1795) is referred to as 'HA'. *Lectures on Rhetoric* (1762) is abbreviated as 'LRBL'. *Essays on Philosophical Subjects* (1795) is referenced as *'EPS'*.

Thucydides (1881): *History of the Peloponnesian War.* Benjamin Jowett (Ed. and Trans.). Oxford: Clarendon Press.
Tocqueville, Alexis de (1966 and 1988): *Democracy in America.* J.P. Mayer (Ed.). George Lawrence (Trans.). New York: Harper & Row and Harper Perennial.
Weber, Max (1946): *From Max Weber: Essays in Sociology.* Hans H. Gerth and Charles Wright Mills (Eds. and Trans.). New York: Oxford University Press.
Weber, Max (1978): *Economy and Society. An Outline of Interpretive Sociology.* Guenther Roth and Claus Wittich (Eds.). Berkeley: University of California Press.
Weber, Max (1994): *Sociological Writings.* Wolf Heydebrand (Ed.). New York: Bloomsbury Publishing.
Weber, Max (2005): *The Protestant Ethic and the Spirit of Capitalism.* Talcott Parsons (Trans.). London: Routledge Classics.

Secondary Sources

Abbey, Ruth (2000): *Nietzsche's Middle Period.* Oxford: Oxford University Press.
Abbey, Ruth and Appel, Fredrick (1998): 'Nietzsche and the Will to Politics'. In: *The Review of Politics* 60. No. 1, 83–114.
Abbey, Ruth and Appel, Fredrick (1999): 'Domesticating Nietzsche: A Response to Mark Warren'. In: *Political Theory* 27. No. 1, 121–125.
Acampora, Christa Davis (2004): 'Between Mechanism and Teleology: Will to Power and Nietzsche's "Gay" Science'. In: Moore, David and Brobjer, Thomas (Eds.): *Nietzsche and Science.* Surrey: Ashgate Publishing, 171–189.
Acampora, Christa Davis (2013): *Contesting Nietzsche.* Chicago: University of Chicago Press.
Adair-Toteff, Christopher (2021): *Max Weber and the Path from Political Economy to Economic Sociology.* New York: Routledge.
Adorno, Theodor W. (1976): 'Sociology and Empirical Research'. In: Adorno, Theodor W.: *The Positivist Dispute in German Sociology.* Glyn Adey and David Frisby (Trans.). London: Heinemann, 68–87.
Adorno, Theodor W. (1991): *The Culture Industry: Selected Essays on Mass Culture.* Jay M. Bernstein (Ed.). London and New York: Routledge.
Adorno, Theodor W. (2000): *Problems of Moral Philosophy.* Thomas Schröder (Ed.). Rodney Livingstone (Trans.). Stanford: Stanford University Press.
Adorno, Theodor W. (2003): *Can One Live after Auschwitz?* Rolf Tiedemann (Ed.). Rodney Livingstone (Trans.). Stanford: Stanford University Press.
Adorno, Theodor W. (2005): *Minima Moralia: Reflections on a Damaged Life.* Edmund F. N. Jephcott. London and New York: Verso.
Adorno, Theodor W. (2005a): *Resignation.* In: Adorno, Theodor W.: *The Culture Industry: Selected Essays on Mass Culture.* London: Routledge.
Adorno, Theodor W. (2006): *History and Freedom: Lectures, 1964–1965.* Rodney Livingstone (Trans.). Cambridge: Polity Press.
Adorno, Theodor W. (2007): *Negative Dialectics.* New York: Continuum.
Adorno, Theodor W. (2016): *Philosophische Terminologie I und II.* Berlin: Suhrkamp.
Adorno, Theodor W. (2019): '27. On the Classicism of Goethe's Iphigenie'. In: Adorno, Theodor W.: *Notes to Literature.* Shierry Weber Nicholsen (Trans.). New York and Chichester: Columbia University Press, 415–430.

Note: For ease of use, unless the source is referenced directly in the body of the text, secondary literature is arranged alphabetically. Book titles are *italicised*. The titles of academic journals' articles, individual book chapters, newspaper articles, and policy papers appear in single quotation marks ('...').

Adorno, Theodor W. and Horkheimer, Max (2002): *Dialectic of Enlightenment*. Edmund F. N. Jephcott. Stanford: Stanford University Press.
Allison, Graham T. (1991): *Window of Opportunity: The Grand Bargain for Democracy in the Soviet Union*. New York: Pantheon Books.
Almeida, Rogério Miranda de (2007): *Nietzsche and Paradox*. Albany: SUNY Press.
Althusser, Louis (1971): *Lenin and Philosophy and Other Essays*. New York: Monthly Review Press.
Althusser, Louis (2015): *Reading Capital, The Complete Edition*. Ben Brewster and David Fernbach (Trans.). London and New York: Verso.
Amin, Ash and Palan, Ronen (2001): 'Towards a Non-Rationalist International Political Economy'. In: *Review of International Political Economy* 8. No. 4, 559–577.
Anas Karzai (2019): *Nietzsche and Sociology: Prophet Of Affirmation*. Washington, DC: Rowman & Littlefield.
Anderson, Lanier R. (2021): 'Nietzschean Autonomy and the Meaning of the "Sovereign Individual"'. In: *Philosophy and Phenomenological Research*, 105. No. 2, 362–384.
Anderson, Ralph V. and Robert E. Gallman (1977): 'Slaves as Fixed Capital: Slave Labor and Southern Economic Development'. In: *The Journal of American History* 64. No. 1, 24–46.
Andrew, Edward G. (1995): *The Genealogy of Values: Aesthetic Economy of Nietzsche and Proust*. Washington, DC: Rowman & Littlefield.
Andrew, Edward G. (1999): 'The Cost of Nietzschean Values'. In: *New Nietzsche Studies* 3. No. 3–4: 63–76.
Anker, Christien van den (Ed.) (2004): *The Political Economy of New Slavery*. London: Palgrave Macmillan.
Anomaly, Johnny (2005): 'Nietzsche's Critique of Utilitarianism'. In: *Journal of Nietzsche Studies* 29: 1–15.
Ansell-Pearson, Keith (Ed.) (1991): *Nietzsche and Modern German Thought*. London: Routledge.
Ansell-Pearson, Keith (1994): *An Introduction to Nietzsche as Political Thinker*. Cambridge: Cambridge University Press.
Ansell-Pearson, Keith (2005): 'The Eternal Return of the Overhuman'. In: *The Journal of Nietzsche Studies*. 30. No. 1, 1–21.
Ansell-Pearson, Keith (2011): *Nietzsche Contra Rousseau*. Cambridge: Cambridge University Press.
Ansell-Pearson, Keith, (Ed.) (2013): *Nietzsche and Political Thought*. London: Bloomsbury.
Ansell-Pearson, Keith (2016): 'Naturalism as a Joyful Science: Nietzsche, Deleuze, and the Art of Life'. In: *Journal of Nietzsche Studies* 47. No. 1: 119–140.
Ansell-Pearson, Keith and Bamford, Rebecca (2020): *Nietzsche's Dawn: Philosophy, Ethics and the Passion of Knowledge*. London: Wiley-Blackwell.
Antonio, Robert J. (1981): 'Immanent Critique as the Core of Critical Theory: Its Origins and Developments in Hegel, Marx and Contemporary Thought'. In: *The British Journal of Sociology* 32. No. 3, 330–345.
Appel, Frederick (1999): *Nietzsche Contra Democracy*. Ithaca: Cornell University Press.
Arendt, Hannah (1994): *Critical Essays*. Lewis P. Hinchman and Sandra K. Hinchman (Eds.). Albany: SUNY Press.
Arendt, Hannah (1998): *The Human Condition*. Chicago: University of Chicago Press.
Arrow, Kenneth J. and Hahn, Frank H. (1971): *General Competitive Analysis*. Amsterdam: North-Holland Publishing Company.
Asmis, Elisabeth (2020): 'A Tribute to a Hero: Marx's Interpretation of Epicurus in his Dissertation'. In O'Rourke, Donncha (Ed.): *Approaches to Lucretius: Traditions and Innovations in Reading the De Rerum Natura*. Cambridge: Cambridge University Press, 241–258.
Aspromourgos, Tony (2013): 'Adam Smith on Labour and Capital'. In: Berry, Christopher J., Paganelli, Maria Pia, and Smith, Craig (Eds.): *The Oxford Handbook of Adam Smith*. Oxford: Oxford University Press, 267–290.
Avery, John Scales (2016): *Collected Essays*. Vol. I. Sparsnäs: Irene Publishing.
Avineri, Shlomo (1968): *The Social and Political Thought of Karl Marx*. Cambridge, UK: Cambridge University Press.
Aydinonat, N. Emrah (2008): *The Invisible Hand in Economics: How Economists Explain Unintended Social Consequences*. Abingdon: Routledge.

Ayres, Robert (2016): *Energy, Complexity and Wealth Maximization*. Vienna: Springer International.

Azzam, Abed (2015): *Nietzsche Versus Paul*. New York: Columbia University Press.

Backhaus, Jürgen G. (2006): 'The Word Of Honour'. In: Backhaus, Jürgen Georg and Drechsler, Wolfgang (Eds.): *Friedrich Nietzsche (1844–1900): Economy and Society*. New York: Springer Science+Business Media, 87–111.

Babich, E. Babette (1994): *Nietzsche's Philosophy of Science: Reflecting Science on the Ground of Art and Life*. Albany: SUNY Press.

Babich, E. Babette (Ed.) (1999): *Nietzsche, Epistemology and Philosophy of Science II*. Dordrecht: Springer Science+Business Media.

Babich, E. Babette (2016): 'Towards Nietzsche's 'Critical' Theory—Science, Art, Life and Creative Economics'. In: Heit, Helmut and Thorgeirsdottir, Sigga (Eds.): *Nietzscheforschung*. Berlin: De Gruyter, 112–133.

Babich, E. Babette (2018): 'Querying Nietzsche's Influence and Meaning Today'. In: Polyakova, Ekaterina and Sineokaya, Yulia (Eds.): Фридрих Ницше: Наследие и Проект, Москва: Культурная революция, / *Friedrich Nietzsche: Heritage and Prospects*. Moscow: Cultural Revolution, 391–406.

Babich, E. Babette (2020): 'Between Nietzsche and Marx: "Great Politics and What They Cost"'. In: Payne, Christine and Roberts, Michael (Eds.): *Nietzsche and Critical Social Theory: Affirmation, Animosity, and Ambiguity*. Leiden and Boston: Brill, 226–279.

Backhaus, Jürgen Georg and Drechsler, Wolfgang (Eds.) (2006): *Friedrich Nietzsche (1844–1900): Economy and Society*. New York: Springer Science+Business Media.

Backhaus, Jürgen Georg and Stephen, Frank H. (Eds.) (2008): *Political Economy, Linguistics and Culture: Crossing Bridges*. New York: Springer Science+Business Media.

Balaban, Oden (1990): 'Praxis and Poesis In Aristotle's Practical Philosophy'. In: *The Journal of Value Inquiry* 24, 185–198.

Bamford, Rebecca (2014): 'The Liberatory Limits of Nietzsche's Colonial Imagination in Dawn §206'. In: Stocker, Barry and Knoll, Manuel (Eds.): *Nietzsche's Political Philosophy*. Berlin: De Gruyter, 59–76.

Baptist, Edward E. (2014): *The Half Has Never Been Told*. New York: Basic Books.

Barkai, Haim (1996): 'The Methodenstreit and the Emergence of Mathematical Economics'. In: *Eastern Economic Journal* 22. No. 1, 1–19.

Barreyre, Nicolas (2011): 'The Politics of Economic Crises: The Panic of 1873, the End of Reconstruction, and the Realignment of American Politics'. In: *The Journal of the Gilded Age and Progressive Era* 10. No. 4, 403–423.

Bataille, Georges (1967): *The Accursed Share: An Essay on General Economy*. Vol. I (Consumption). New York: Zone Books.

Bauer, K. (1999): *Adorno's Nietzschean Narratives: Critiques of Ideology, Readings of Wagner*. Albany: SUNY Press.

Baumbach, Günther (1989): 'The Sadducees in Josephus'. In: Feldman, Louis H. and Hata, Gohei (Eds.) (1989): *Josephus, the Bible and History*. Detroit: Wayne State University Press, 173–196.

Baumgarten, Eduard (Ed.) (1964): *Max Weber: Werk und Person*. 1ˢᵗ ed. Tübingen, Germany: J. C. B. Mohr.

Beaud, Michel (1981): 'From the Great Depression to the Great War (1873–1914)'. In: Beaud, Michel: *A History of Capitalism 1500–1980*. Tom Dickman and Anny Lefebvre (Trans.). London: Palgrave Macmillan, 117–144.

Becker, James F. (1961): 'Adam Smith's Theory of Social Science'. In: *Southern Economic Journal* 28. No. 1, 13–21.

Beckert, Sven and Rockman, Seth (Eds.) (2016): *Slavery's Capitalism: A New History of American Economic Development*. Philadelphia: University of Pennsylvania Press.

Belfrage, Claes and Gammon, Earl (2017): 'Aesthetic International Political Economy'. In: *Journal of International Studies* 45. No. 2, 223–232.

Benjamin, Walter (1996): 'Capitalism as Religion'. In: Benjamin, Walter: *Walter Benjamin: Selected Writings*. Vol. I: 1913–1926. Marcus Bullock and Michael W. Jennings (Eds.). Cambridge: Harvard University Press, 288–292.

Berg, Maxine (1990): 'Progress and Providence in Early Nineteenth-Century Political Economy'. In: *Social History* 15. No. 3, 365–375.

Bernstein, Richard J. (2017): 'Nietzsche or Aristotle? Reflections on Alasdair MacIntyre's *After Virtue*'. In: *Soundings: An Interdisciplinary Journal* 100. No. 4, 293–317.

Berry, Christopher J. (2018): *Adam Smith*. Oxford: Oxford University Press.

Berry, Jessica N. (2019): 'Nietzsche's Attack on Belief: Doxastic Scepticism in The Antichrist'. In: *Journal of Nietzsche Studies* 50. No. 2, 187–209.

Biddy, Martin (1991): *Women and Modernity: The (Life)Styles of Lou Andreas-Salome*. Ithaca: Cornell University Press.

Binns, David (1977): 'Max Weber and the Legacy of Political Economy'. In: *Beyond the Sociology of Conflict*. London: Palgrave Macmillan.

Binswanger, Hans Christoph (2016): *Money and Magic: A Critique of the Modern Economy in the Light of Goethe's Faust*. Chicago: University of Chicago Press.

Bishop, Paul (Ed.) (2004): *Nietzsche and Antiquity: His Reaction and Response to the Classical Tradition*. Martlesham: Boydell & Brewer.

Bishop, Paul (2006): 'Nietzsche and Science'. In: *Journal Of European Studies* 36. No. 3, 340–341.

Bishop, Paul (Ed.) (2012): *A Companion to Friedrich Nietzsche: Life and Works*. New York: Camden House.

Biswas Mellamphy, Nandita (2008): 'Corporealizing Thought: Translating the Eternal Return Back into Politics'. In: Siemens, Herman W. and Roodt, Vasti (Eds.): *Nietzsche, Power and Politics: Rethinking Nietzsche's Legacy for Political Thought*. Berlin and New York: De Gruyter, 741–767.

Blackbourn, David (1984): 'Peasants and Politics in Germany, 1871–1914'. In: *European History Quarterly* 14. No. 1, 47–75.

Blackburn, Robin (1976): 'Marxism: Theory of Proletarian Revolution'. In: *New Left Review* 97: 3–35.

Blackwell, Christopher W. (2003): 'The Development of Athenian Democracy'. In: Lanni, Adriaan (Ed.): *Athenian Law in Its Democratic Context*. Center for Hellenic Studies Online Discussion Series. Republished in Blackwell Christopher W. (Ed.) (2003): *Dēmos: Classical Athenian Democracy*. A. Mahoney and R. Scaife (Eds.): The Stoa: A Consortium for Electronic Publication in the Humanities. www.stoa.org, last accessed March 8, 2023.

Blanchette, Olivia (1983): 'The Idea of History in Karl Marx'. In: *Studies in Soviet Thought* 26. No. 2, 89–122.

Blaug, Mark (2008): 'Invisible Hand' in *New Palgrave Dictionary Of Economics*. Steven Durlaf and Lawrence Blume (Eds.). New York: Palgrave Macmillan.

Bleiker, Roland (2001): 'The Aesthetic Turn in International Political Theory'. In: *Journal of International Studies* 30. No. 3, 509–33.

Bobka, Nico and Braunstein, Dirk (2022): 'Adorno and the critique of political economy'. In: Bonefeld, Werner and O'Kane, Chris: *Adorno and Marx*. London and New York: Bloomsbury Academic, 35–55.

Bonefeld, Werner (2011): 'Primitive Accumulation and Capitalist Accumulation: Notes on Social Constitution and Expropriation'. In: *Science & Society* 75. No. 3, 379–399.

Bonefeld, Werner (2014): *Critical Theory and the Critique of Political Economy: On Subversion and Negative Reason*. London: Bloomsbury Publishing.

Bonefeld, Werner (2016): 'Negative dialectics and the critique of economic objectivity'. In: *History of Human Sciences* 29. No. 2, 60–76.

Bonefeld, Werner (2022): 'Conceptuality and social practice'. In: Bonefeld, Werner and O'Kane, Chris (Eds.): *Adorno and Marx*. London and New York: Bloomsbury Academic, 185–205.

Bonefeld, Werner (2022a): 'Cracking economic abstractions: Bringing critical theory back-in'. In: Bonefeld, Werner and O'Kane, Chris (Eds.): *Adorno and Marx*. London and New York: Bloomsbury Academic, 15–35.

Bonefeld, Werner (2022b): 'Economic objectivity and negative dialectics: On class and struggle'. In: Bonefeld, Werner and O'Kane, Chris (Eds.): *Adorno and Marx*. London and New York: Bloomsbury Academic, 99–121.

Bonefeld, Werner and O'Kane, Chris (Eds.) (2022): *Adorno and Marx: Negative Dialectics and the Critique of Political Economy*. London and New York: Bloomsbury Academic.

Booth, William James (1993): *Households: On the Moral Architecture of the Economy*. Ithaca: Cornell University Press.

Bornedal, Peter (2010): *The Surface and The Abyss: Nietzsche as Philosopher of Mind and Knowledge*. Berlin: De Gruyter.

Bottomore, Thomas B. (Ed.) (1963), *Karl Marx: Early Writings*. Thomas B. Bottomore (Trans.). London: C. A. Watts.

Bourdieu, Pierre (1998): *Acts of Resistance: Against the Tyranny of the Market*. Richard Nice (Trans.). New York: The New Press and Polity Press.

Bowles, Paul (1986): 'Adam Smith and the "Natural Progress of Opulence"'. In: *Economica: New Series* 53. No. 209: 109–118.

Bradley, Keith and Cartledge, Paul (Eds.) (2011): *The Cambridge World History of Slavery: The Ancient Mediterranean World*. Vol. I. Cambridge: Cambridge University Press.

Braunstein, Dirk (2022): *Adorno's Critique of Political Economy*. Leiden and Boston: Brill.

Brewer, Anthony (2009): 'On the Other (Invisible) Hand'. In: *History of Political Economy* 41. No. 3, 519–554.

Brobjer, Thomas H. (1998): 'The Absence of Political Ideals in Nietzsche's Writings: The Case of the Laws of Manu and the Associated Caste-Society'. In: *Nietzsche-Studien* 27: 300–318.

Brobjer, Thomas H. (1999): 'Nietzsche's Knowledge, Reading, and Critique of Political Economy'. In: *The Journal of Nietzsche Studies* 18: 56–70.

Brobjer, Thomas H. (2002): 'Nietzsche's Knowledge of Marx and Marxism'. In: *Nietzsche-Studien* 31. No. 1, 298–320.

Brobjer, Thomas H. (2003): 'Nietzsche's Knowledge of Kierkegaard'. In: *Journal of the History of Philosophy* 41. No. 2, 251–263.

Brobjer, Thomas H. (2004): 'Nietzsche's Wrestling with Plato and Platonism'. In: Bishop, Paul (Ed.): *Nietzsche and Antiquity*. Rochester: Camden House, 241–260.

Brobjer, Thomas H. (2006): 'Nietzsche's Magnum Opus'. In: *History of European Ideas* 32. No. 3, 278–294.

Brobjer, Thomas H. (2007): *Nietzsche and the 'English': A Study of Nietzsche's Knowledge of and Relation to British and American Thinking*. In: Amherst: Prometheus Books.

Brobjer, Thomas H. (2014): 'Nietzsche and Economics'. In: Heit, Helmut and Heller, Lisa (Eds.): *Handbuch Nietzsche und die Wissenschaften*. Berlin and Boston: De Gruyter, 307–322.

Brobjer, Thomas H. (2021): 'Sources of Nietzsche's Knowledge and Critique of Anarchism'. In: *Nietzsche-Studien* 50. No. 1, 300–310.

Brooks, Thom (2006): 'Knowledge and Power in Plato's Political Thought'. In: *International Journal of Philosophical Studies* 14. No. 1, 51–77.

Brown, Ellen Hodgson (2007): *The Shocking Truth About Our Money System and How We Can Break Free*. Baton Rouge: Third Millennium Press.

Brown, Norman O. (1959): *Life Against Death: The Psychoanalytical Meaning of History*. New York: Vintage Books.

Brown, Wendy (2000): 'Nietzsche for Politics'. In: Schrift, Alan D.: *Why Nietzsche Still?* Berkeley: University of California Press, 205–224.

Brustein, William (2003): *Roots of Hate: Anti-Semitism in Europe Before the Holocaust*. Cambridge: Cambridge University Press.

Buchwalter, Andrew (2016): *Hegel and Capitalism*. Albany: SUNY Press.

Bunge, Mario (1945): 'Nietzsche and Science'. In: *Nature (London)* 156. No. 3957: 263–267.

Bunyan, John (1910): *The Pilgrim's Progress*. London: T. C. & E. C. Jack.

Burghardt Du Bois, William E. (1920): *Darkwater: The Twentieth Century Completion of Uncle Tom's Cabin.* Washington, DC: Austin Jenkins Co. and Harcourt, Brace & Howe.
Burghardt Du Bois, William E. (2007): *The World and Africa and Color and Democracy.* Oxford: Oxford University Press.
Burkett, Paul (1999): *Marx and Nature.* New York: St. Martin's Press.
Burkett, Paul (2014): *Marx and Nature: A Red and Green Perspective.* Chicago: Haymarket Books.
Burley, Justine and Colman, Alan (2002): 'Science and Philosophy: Bridging the Two Cultures'. In: *Journal of Molecular Biology* 319: 907–915.
Burley, Peter and Foster, John (Eds.) (1994): *Economics and Thermodynamics: New Perspectives on Economic Analysis.* New York: Springer Science + Business Media.
Cameron, Frank and Dombowsky, Don (2008): *Political Writings of Friedrich Nietzsche: An Edited Anthology.* New York: Palgrave Macmillan.
Carson, Ronald A. (1971): 'Nietzsche's Jesus'. In: *CrossCurrents* 21. No. 1, 39–52.
Cherniss, Joshua L. (2021): 'Between Tragedy and Utopia: Weber and Lukács on Ethics and Politics'. In: *Liberalism in Dark Times: The Liberal Ethos in the Twentieth Century.* Princeton: Princeton University Press, 40–67.
Chomsky, Avram Noam (1998): *The Common Good.* Monroe: Odonian Press.
Chomsky, Avram Noam (2003): *Chomsky on Democracy and Education.* Carlos-Peregrín Otero (Ed.). New York and London: Routledge Falmer.
Church, Jeffrey (2015): 'Nietzsche's Early Perfectionism: A Cultural Reading Of "The Greek State"'. In: *Journal of Nietzsche Studies* 46. No. 2, 248–260.
Church, Jeffrey (2015a): *Nietzsche's Culture Of Humanity: Beyond Aristocracy and Democracy in The Early Period.* Cambridge: Cambridge University Press.
Church, Jeffrey (2015b): 'The Aesthetic Justification of Existence: Nietzsche on the Beauty of Exemplary Lives'. In: *Journal of Nietzsche Studies* 46. No. 3, 289–307.
Clark, Charles M. A. (1989): 'Equilibrium for What? Reflections on Social Order in Economics'. In: *Journal of Economic Issues* 23. No. 2, 597–606.
Clark, Charles M. A. (2010): 'Practical Wisdom and Understanding the Economy'. In: *Journal of Management Development* 29. No. 7–8, 678–685.
Clark, Maudemarie (1990): *Nietzsche on Truth and Philosophy.* New York: Cambridge University Press.
Clark, Maudemarie and Wonderly, Monique (2015): 'The Good of Community. In: Young, Julian (Ed.): *Individual and Community in Nietzsche's Philosophy.* Cambridge: Cambridge University Press, 118–141.
Clarke, Simon (1991): *Marx, Marginalism and Modern Sociology: From Adam Smith to Max Weber.* Basingstoke: Macmillan.
Coase, Ronald H. (1976): 'Adam Smith's View of Man'. In: *The Journal of Law & Economics* 19. No. 3, 529–546.
Cohen, Gerald A. (2000): *Karl Marx's Theory of History—A Defence.* Princeton: Princeton University Press.
Colli, Giorgio (1980): *Nach Nietzsche.* Frankfurt am Main: Europäische Verlagsanstalt.
Connolly, William E. (1988): *Political Theory and Modernity.* Oxford: Basil Blackwell.
Connolly, William E. (1991): *Identity\Difference.* Ithaca: Cornell University Press.
Connolly, William E. (2008): *Christianity and Capitalism, American Style.* Durham: Duke University Press.
Conrad, Alfred H. and Meyer, John R. (1958): 'The Economics of Slavery in The Ante Bellum South'. In: *The Journal of Political Economy* 66. No. 2, 95–130.
Conway, Daniel W. (1997): *Nietzsche and the Political.* London: Routledge.
Conway, Daniel W. (2002): *Nietzsche's Dangerous Game: Philosophy in The Twilight of the Idols.* Revised Edition. Cambridge: Cambridge University Press.
Conway, Daniel W. (2013): 'Nietzsche's Immoralism and the Advent of 'Great Politics''. In: Ansell-Pearson, Keith (Ed.): *Nietzsche and Political Thought.* London: Bloomsbury Academic, 197–217.
Conway, Daniel W. and Goff, Peter S. (Eds.) (1998): *Nietzsche: Critical Assessments.* Vol. III. London and New York: Routledge.

Cook, Karen S. and Whitmeyer, Joseph M. (1992): 'Two Approaches to Social Structure: Exchange Theory and Network Analysis'. In: *Annual Review of Sociology* 18: 109–127.

Cook, Deborah (Ed.) (2014): *Theodor Adorno: Key Concepts*. London and New York: Routledge.

Cooper, Ian (2008): 'Nietzsche, Money and Bildung'. In: Siemens, Herman W. and Roodt, Vasti (Eds.): *Nietzsche, Power and Politics*. Berlin and New York: De Gruyter, 605–629.

Cooper, John M. (1985): 'Aristotle on the Goods of Fortune'. In: *The Philosophical Review* 94. No. 2, 173–196.

Copelovitch, Mark and Singer, David A. (2020): *Banks on the Brink*. Cambridge: Cambridge University Press.

Cottarelli, Carlo (2017): *What We Owe: Truths, Myths, and Lies About Public Debt*. Washington DC: Brookings Institution Press.

Crick, Bernard (2002): *Democracy: A Very Short Introduction*. Oxford: Oxford University Press.

Cristaudo, Wayne (2017): *Religion, Redemption and Revolution: The New Speech Thinking Revolution of Franz Rozenzweig and Eugen Rosenstock-Huessy*. Toronto: University of Toronto Press.

Cristi, Renato (2014): 'Nietzsche, Theognis and Aristocratic Radicalism'. In: Knoll, Manuel and Stocker, Barry (Eds.): *Nietzsche as Political Philosopher*. Berlin: De Gruyter, 173–194.

Curtis, Neal (2006): *War and Social Theory: World, Value and Identity*. New York: Palgrave MacMillan.

D'Alisa, Giacomo, Demaria, Federico and Kallis, Giorgos (Eds.) (2015): *Degrowth: A Vocabulary for a New Era*. Abingdon: Routledge.

Daly, Herman E. and Cobb, Jr., John B. (1994): *For the Common Good: Redirecting the Economy Toward Community, the Environment, and a Sustainable Future*. Boston: Beacon Press.

Danford, John W. (1980): 'Adam Smith, Equality, and the Wealth of Sympathy'. In: *American Journal of Political Science* 24. No. 4, 674–695.

Dasgupta, Ajit K. (1993): *A History of Indian Economic Thought*. London and New York: Routledge.

Davies, Hannah Catherine (2018): *Transatlantic Speculations: Globalization and the Panics of 1873*. New York Chichester, West Sussex: Columbia University Press.

Davies, Hannah Catherine (2020): '"Mingled in an almost inextricable confusion": The panics of 1873 and the experience of globalization'. In: *Journal of Global History* 15. No. 2, 291–309.

Davies, Matt (2012): 'The Aesthetics Of The Financial Crisis'. In: *Alternatives* 37. No. 4, 317–330.

Debord, Guy (2005): *The Society of the Spectacle*. Ken Knabb (Trans.). London: Rebel Press.

Debord, Guy (2007): *A Sick Planet*. Donald Nicolson-Smith (Trans.). London, New York, and Calcutta: Seagull Books.

Deflem, Mathieu (2008): 'Max Weber on the Rationalization of Law". In: Deflem, Mathieu: *Sociology of Law: Visions of a Scholarly Tradition*. Cambridge: Cambridge University Press, 37–55.

Del Caro, Adrian (1993): 'The hermeneutics of idealism: Nietzsche versus the French Revolution'. In: *Nietzsche-Studien* 22. No. 1, 158–164.

Del Caro, Adrian (2004): *Grounding the Nietzsche Rhetoric of Earth*. Berlin and New York: De Gruyter.

Deleuze, Gilles (1973): 'Penseé nomade'. In: Gandillac, Maurice de and Pautrat, Bernard (Eds.): *Nietzsche aujourd'hui?* Vol. I. Paris: Union générale d'éditions, 159–174.

Deleuze, Gilles (1983): *Nietzsche and Philosophy*. Hugh Tomlinson (Trans.). New York: Columbia University Press.

Deleuze, Gilles (1995): *Negotiations, 1972–1990*. Joughin, Martin (Trans.). New York: Columbia University Press.

Deleuze, Gilles and Guattari, Félix (1975): 'Psychoanalysis and Ethnology'. In: *SubStance* 4 No. 11–12, 170–197.

Deleuze, Gilles and Guattari, Félix (2003): *A Thousand Plateaus: Capitalism and Schizophrenia*. London and New York: Continuum.

Deleuze, Gilles and Guattari, Félix (2013): *Anti-Oedipus: Capitalism and Schizophrenia*, London: Bloomsbury.

Derrida, Jacques (1991): *Given Time: I. Counterfeit Money*. Chicago: University of Chicago Press.

Derrida, Jacques (1994): *Specters of Marx*. New York: Routledge.

Detwiler, Bruce (1990): *Nietzsche and the Politics of Aristocratic Radicalism.* Chicago: University of Chicago Press.
Diemer, Arnaud, and Guillemin, Hervé (2011): 'L'économie politique au miroir de la physique: Adam Smith et Isaac Newton'. In: *Revue d'histoire des sciences* 1. No. 64: 5–26.
Dodd, Nigel (2012): 'Nietzsche's Money'. In: *Journal of Classical Sociology* 13. No. 1, 47–68.
Dodd, Nigel (2014): *The Social Life of Money.* Princeton and Oxford: Princeton University Press.
Domar, Evsey (1970): 'The Causes of Slavery or Serfdom: A Hypothesis'. In: *Journal of Economic History* 30. No. 1, 18–32.
Dombowsky, Don (2004): *Nietzsche's Machiavellian Politics.* New York: Palgrave Macmillan.
Dombowsky, Don (2014): 'Aristocratic Radicalism as a Species of Bonapartism: Preliminary Elements'. In: Knoll, Manuel and Stocker, Barry (Eds.): *Nietzsche as Political Philosopher.* Berlin and Boston: De Gruyter, 195–211.
Douglas, Alexander X. (2016): *The Philosophy of Debt.* Abingdon and New York: Routledge.
Dover, Kenneth J. (1974): *Greek Popular Morality in the Time of Plato and Aristotle.* Oxford: Basil Blackwell.
Dowd, Douglas (2000): *Capitalism and Its Economics: A Critical History.* London and Ann Arbor: Pluto Press.
Drechsler, Wolfgang (2006): 'Friedrich Nietzsche and Economics: Research Problems'. In: Backhaus, Jürgen Georg and Drechsler, Wolfgang: *Friedrich Nietzsche (1844–1900): Economy and Society.* New York: Springer Science and Business Media, 1–9.
Drochon, Hugo (2010): 'The Time Is Coming When We Will Relearn Politics'. In: *The Journal of Nietzsche Studies* 39: 66–85.
Drochon, Hugo (2016): *Nietzsche's Great Politics.* Princeton: Princeton University Press, 2016
Drochon, Hugo (2016a): 'An Old Carriage with New Horses': Nietzsche's Critique of Democracy'. In: *History of European Ideas* 42. No. 8, 1055–1068.
Drochon, Hugo (2017): 'Nietzsche Theorist of the State?' In: *History of Political Thought* 38. No. 2, 323–344.
Drochon, Hugo (2018): 'Nietzsche Between History, Economics and Politics'. In: *Politics, Religion & Ideology* 19. No. 2, 246–249.
Drolet, Jean-François (2013): 'Nietzsche, Kant, the democratic state and war'. In: *Review of International Studies* 39. No. 1, 25–47.
Drolet, Jean-François (2021): *Beyond Tragedy and Eternal Peace: Politics and International Relations in the Thought of Friedrich Nietzsche.* Montreal and Kingston: McGill-Queen's University Press.
Duncan, Ian (2006): 'David Hume and The Scottish Enlightenment'. In: *Edinburgh History of Scottish Literature: Enlightenment, Britain and Empire (1707–1918).* Ian Brown (Ed.). Edinburgh: Edinburgh University Press, 71–80.
Durkheim, Emile (1984): *The Division of Labour in Society.* William D. Halls (Trans.). London and New York: Palgrave Macmillan.
Dyson, Kenneth (2014): *States, Debt and Power: Saints and Sinners in European History and Integration.* Oxford: Oxford University Press.
Eagleton, Terry (1990): *The Ideology of the Aesthetic.* Oxford: Basil Blackwell.
Eagleton, Terry (2011): *Why Marx Was Right.* New Haven: Yale University Press.
Easton, Susan M. (1977): 'Facts, Values and Marxism'. In: *Studies in Soviet Thought* 17. No. 2, 117–134.
Eichengreen, Barry (1996): *Globalizing Capital: A History of the International Monetary System.* Princeton: Princeton University Press.
Eichengreen, Barry (2008): *Globalizing Capital,* Princeton and Oxford: Princeton University Press.
Eichengreen, Barry (2015): *Hall of Mirrors: The Great Depression, the Great Recession, and the Uses—and Misuses—of History.* Oxford: Oxford University Press.
Eichengreen, Barry (2018): *The Populist Temptation.* Oxford: Oxford University Press.
Einstein, Albert and Infeld, Leopold (1938): *The Evolution of Physics: The Growth of Ideas from Early Concepts to Relativity and Quanta.* Cambridge: Cambridge University Press.

Elliott, Graham and Timmermann, Allan (2008): 'Economic Forecasting'. In: *Journal of Economic Literature* 46. No. 1, 3–56.

Elst, Koenraad (2008): 'Manu as a Weapon Against Egalitarianism: Nietzsche and Hindu Political Philosophy'. In: Siemens, Herman W. and Roodt, Vasti (Eds.): *Nietzsche, Power and Politics.* Berlin and New York: De Gruyter, 543–583.

Elveton, R. (2004): 'Nietzsche's Stoicism: The Depths Are Inside'. In: Bishop, Paul (Ed.): *Nietzsche and Antiquity: His Reaction and Response to the Classical Tradition.* London: Boydell & Brewer, 192–203.

Emden, Christian J. (2005): *Nietzsche on Language, Consciousness, and the Body.* Chicago: University of Illinois Press.

Emden, Christian J. (2006): *Walter Benjamins Archäologie der Moderne: Kulturwissenschaft um 1930.* Munich: Wilhelm Fink.

Emden Christian J. (2008): *Friedrich Nietzsche and the Politics of History.* Cambridge: Cambridge University Press.

Emden, Christian J. (2008a): 'Theorizing the Political in Germany, 1890–1945: Max Weber, Carl Schmitt, Franz Neumann'. In: *European History Quarterly* 38. No. 4, 608–625.

Emden, Christian J. (2014): *Nietzsche's Naturalism: Philosophy and the Life Sciences in the Nineteenth Century.* Cambridge: Cambridge University Press.

Emlyn-Jones, Chris (1987): *Plato: Early Socratic Dialogues.* London: Penguin Books.

Engberg-Pedersen, Troels (1983): *Aristotle's Theory of Moral Insight.* Oxford: Oxford University Press.

England, Christopher M. (2019): *The Existential Foundations of Political Economy: Process and Predicament.* Newcastle: Cambridge Scholars Publishing.

Erikson, Jon D. (2022): *The Progress Illusion: Reclaiming Our Future from the Fairytale of Economics.* Washington, DC: Island Press.

Evensky, Jerry (2005): 'Adam Smith's "Theory of Moral Sentiments": On Morals and Why They Matter to a Liberal Society of Free People and Free Markets'. In: *The Journal of Economic Perspectives* 19. No. 3, 109–130.

Evensky, Jerry (2005a): *Adam Smith's Moral Philosophy: A Historical and Contemporary Perspective on Markets, Law, Ethics, and Culture.* Cambridge: Cambridge University Press.

Feldman, Louis H. and Hata, Gohei (Eds.) (1989): *Josephus, the Bible and History.* Detroit: Wayne State University Press.

Fenves, Peter (1986): 'Marx's Doctoral Thesis on Two Greek Atomists and the Post-Kantian Interpretations'. In: *Journal of the History of Ideas* 47. No. 3, 433–452.

Fiebig, Nils (2019): *Nietzsche und das Geld: Die Banalität des Alltäglichen.* Würzburg: Königshausen & Neumann.

Fitzpatrick, Matthew P. (2008): *Liberal Imperialism in Germany: Expansionism and Nationalism, 1848–1884.* New York and Oxford: Berghahn Books, 59–61.

Fitzsimons, Peter (2007): *Nietzsche, Ethics and Education: An Account of Difference.* Rotterdam: Sense Publishers (Springer).

Foa, Roberto S., Klassen, Andrew, Slade, Michael, Rand, Alex, and Collins, Rosie (2020): 'The Global Satisfaction with Democracy Report 2020'. Cambridge: Centre for the Future of Democracy.

Fogel, Roger W. & Engerman, Stanley L. (1974): *Time on the Cross: The Economics of American Negro Slavery.* New York: W. W. Norton & Co.

Fohlin, Caroline (2007): *Finance Capitalism and Germany's Rise to Industrial Power.* Cambridge: Cambridge University Press.

Foner, Eric (2012): *The Fiery Trial: Abraham Lincoln and American Slavery.* New York: W. W. Norton & Co.

Foot, Philippa (2002): *Virtues and Vices and Other Essays in Moral Philosophy.* Oxford: Clarendon Press.

Ford, Henry (1922): *My Life and Work.* New York: Garden City Publishing.

Forster, Michael (1993): 'Hegel's Dialectical Method'. In: Beiser, Frederick C. (Ed.): *The Cambridge Companion to Hegel.* Cambridge: Cambridge University Press, 130–170.

Foster, John Bellamy (2000): *Marx's Ecology: Materialism and Nature.* New York: Monthly Review Press.

Foster, John Bellamy and Burkett, Paul (2016): *Marx and the Earth: An Anti-Critique*. Leiden and Boston: Brill.
Foster, John Bellamy, Clark, Brett, and York, Richard (2010): *The Ecological Rift: Capitalism's War on the Earth*. New York: Monthly Review Press.
Foucault, Michel (1977): 'Nietzsche, Genealogy, History'. In: Foucault, Michel: *Michel Foucault: Language, Counter-Memory, Practice*. Donald F. Bouchard and Sherry Simon (Trans.). Ithaca: Cornell University Press, 139–165.
Foucault, Michel (1980): *Power/Knowledge*. Colin Gordon (Ed. and Trans.). Harlow: Pearson Education.
Foucault, Michel (1980a): 'Prison Talk'. In: Foucault, Michel: *Foucault: Power/Knowledge: Selected Interviews and Other Writings 1972–1977*. Colin Gordon (Ed. and Trans.). Hemel Hempstead: Harvester Wheatsheaf, 37–54.
Foucault, Michel (1982): 'The Subject and Power'. In: *Critical Inquiry* 8. No. 4, 777–795.
Foucault, Michel (1989): *Foucault Live: Collected Interviews, 1961–1984*. Sylvère Lotringer (Ed.). John Johnston (Trans.). Cambridge: MIT Press and Semiotext(e).
Franco, Paul (2011): *Nietzsche's Enlightenment: The Free-Spirit Trilogy of the Middle Period*. Chicago: University of Chicago Press.
Franco, Paul (2014): 'Tocqueville and Nietzsche on the Problem of Human Greatness in Democracy'. In: *The Review of Politics* 76, 439–467.
Froese, Katrin (2001): *Rousseau and Nietzsche: Toward an Aesthetic Morality*. New York and Oxford: Lexington Books.
Fromm, Erich (2004): *Marx's Concept of Man*. London and New York: Continuum.
Fukuyama, Francis (1992): *The End of History and the Last Man*. New York: The Free Press.
Furman, Jason and Summers, Lawrence (2020): 'A Reconsideration of Fiscal Policy in the Era of Low Interest Rates'. https://www.brookings.edu/wp-content/uploads/2020/11/furman-summers-fiscal-reconsideration-discussion-draft.pdf, last accessed Feb. 27, 2023.
Gadamer, Has-Georg (2000): *Nietzsche l'antipode Le Drame de Zarathoustra; Suivi de Nietzsche et nous: Entretien entre Theodor W. Adorno, Max Horkheimer & Hans-Georg Gadamer*. Paris: Editions Allia.
Galbraith, John Kenneth (1998): *The Affluent Society*. New York: Houghton Mifflin.
Galbraith, John Kenneth (1999): *Free Market Fraud*. Madison: The Progressive Magazine.
Galbraith, John Kenneth (2004): *The Economics of Innocent Fraud*. London: Penguin Books.
Galbraith, John Kenneth (2009): *The Great Crash of 1929*. London: Penguin Books.
Gamble, Andrew (2009): *The Spectre at the Feast: Capitalist Crisis and the Politics of Recession*. London: Palgrave Macmillan.
Gamble, Andrew (2014): *Crisis Without End?—The Unravelling of Western Prosperity*. London: Red Globe Press.
Gat, Azar (2017): *The Causes of War and the Spread of Peace: Will War Rebound?* Oxford: Oxford University Press.
Gemes, Ken (2006): 'We Remain of Necessity Strangers to Ourselves: The Key Message of Nietzsche's Genealogy'. In: Acampora, Christa Davis (Ed.): *Nietzsche's On the Genealogy of Morals: Critical Essays*. Lanham: Rowman & Littlefield, 191–208.
Gemes, Ken and Janaway, Christopher (2006): 'Nietzsche on Free Will, Autonomy and the Sovereign Individual'. In: *Proceedings of The Aristotelian Society*, Supplementary Volumes, 80. No. 1, 321–357.
Gemes, Ken and May, Simon (Eds.) (2009): *Nietzsche on Freedom and Autonomy*. Oxford: Oxford University Press.
Genovese, Eugene D. (1976): *Roll, Jordan, Roll: The World the Slaves Made*. New York: Random House.
Georgescu-Roegen, Nicolas (1971): *The Entropy Law and the Economic Process*. Cambridge: Harvard University Press.
Georgescu-Roegen, Nicolas (1976): *Energy and Economic Myths*, Oxford: Pergamon Press
Geuss, Raymond (1981): *The Idea of a Critical Theory*. Cambridge: Cambridge University Press.
Geuss, Raymond (1994): 'Nietzsche and Genealogy'. In: *European Journal of Philosophy* 2. No. 3, 274–292.

Geuss, Raymond (1999): *Morality, Culture, and History: Essays on German Philosophy.* Cambridge: Cambridge University Press.
Geuss, Raymond (1999a): 'Nietzsche and Genealogy'. In: Geuss, Raymond: *Morality, Culture, and History: Essays on German Philosophy.* Cambridge: Cambridge University Press, 1–28.
Geuss, Raymond (2009): *Politics and the Imagination.* Princeton: Princeton University Press.
Geuss, Raymond (2009a): 'Goals, Origins, Disciplines'. In: *Arion: A Journal of Humanities and the Classics* 17. No. 2, 1–24.
Geuss, Raymond (2014): *A World Without Why.* Princeton: Princeton University Press.
Geuss, Raymond (2017): *Changing The Subject: Philosophy from Socrates to Adorno.* Cambridge: Harvard University Press.
Geuss, Raymond (2020): *Who Needs A World View?* Cambridge: Harvard University Press.
Giouras, Thanasis (1995): 'Wilhelm Roscher: The "historical method" in the social sciences: Critical observations for a contemporary evaluation'. In: *Journal of Economic Studies* 22. No. 3, 106–126.
Glasner, David and Cooley, Thomas F. (Eds.) (1997): 'Crisis of 1873'. In: Glasner, David (Ed.): *Business Cycles and Depressions: An Encyclopedia*, London & New York: Routledge.
Glassman, Ronald M. (2021): 'The Economic Transition to High Technology Industrial Capitalism'. In: Glassman, Ronald M.: *Can Democracy Survive in the 21st Century?* Cham: Springer, 8–26.
Golomb, Jacob (1986): 'Nietzsche's Enticing Psychology of Power'. In: Yovel, Yirmiyahu (Ed.): *Nietzsche as Affirmative Thinker.* Dordrecht: Martinus Nijhoff Publishers, 160–182.
Goodchild, Philip (2009): *Theology of Money.* Durham & London: Duke University Press.
Goodchild, Philip (2017): 'On the Origins of Modern Debt and Value: Revisiting Friedrich Nietzsche and William Petty'. In: *Continental Thought & Theory: A Journal of Intellectual Freedom* 1. No. 2, 306–332.
Goodchild, Philip (2020): *Economic Theology: Credit and Faith II.* Lanham: Rowman & Littlefield.
Goodhart, Charles A. and Hudson, Michael (2018): 'Could/Should Jubilee Debt Cancellations Be Reintroduced Today?'. CEPR Discussion Paper 12605.
Govan, Thomas P. (1942): 'Was Plantation Slavery Profitable?'. In: *The Journal of Southern History* 8. No. 4, 513–535.
Graeber, David (2011): *Debt: The First 5,000 Years.* New York: Melville House Publishing.
Graeber, David (2014): 'The Truth Is Out: Money Is Just an IOU, and the Banks Are Rolling In It'. In: *The Guardian* (March 18th, 2014).
Gramsci, Antonio (2005): *Selections from the Prison Notebooks.* London: Lawrence and Wishart.
Gray, J. Glenn (1953): 'Heidegger "Evaluates" Nietzsche'. In: *Journal of the History of Ideas* 14. No. 2, 304–309.
Greene, Collis Alison (2016): *No Depression in Heaven: The Great Depression, the New Deal and the Transformation of Religion in the Delta.* New York: Oxford University Press.
Grenke, Michael W., Davis, Matthew K., and van Boxel, Lise (2005): *Friedrich Nietzsche: Prefaces to Unwritten Works.* South Bend: St. Augustine's Press.
Grimmer-Solem, Eric (2003): *The Rise of Historical Economics and Social Reform in Germany 1864–1894.* Oxford: Oxford University Press.
Griswold, Charles L. (1999): *Adam Smith and the Virtues of Enlightenment.* Cambridge: Cambridge University Press.
Guettel, Jens-Uwe (2012): *German Expansionism, Imperial Liberalism, and the United States, 1776–1945.* Cambridge: Cambridge University Press.
Haakonssen, Knud (1981): *The Science of a Legislator: The Natural Jurisprudence of David Hume and Adam Smith.* Cambridge: Cambridge University Press.
Haase, Ullrich Michael (1999): 'Nietzsche's Critique of Technology: A Defence of Phenomenology Against Modern Machinery'. In: Babich, Babette E. (Ed.): *Nietzsche, Epistemology, and Philosophy of Science. Boston Studies in the Philosophy of Science.* Vol. CCIV. Dordrecht: Springer, 331–339.
Habermas, Jürgen (1990): *The Philosophical Discourse of Modernity.* Lecture V. Cambridge, MA: MIT Press.
Hahn, Frank H. (1972): *On the Notion of Equilibrium in Economics.* Cambridge: Cambridge University Press.

Hammond, Mark (2004): 'Nietzsche's Remarks on the Classical Tradition: A Prognosis for Western Democracy in the Twenty-First Century'. In: Bishop, Paul (Ed.): *Nietzsche and Antiquity: His Reaction and Response to the Classical Tradition*. Martlesham: Boydell & Brewer, 361–372.
Hanley, Ryan P. (2006): 'Adam Smith, Aristotle and Virtue Ethics'. In: Montes, Leonidas and Schliesser, Eric (Eds.): *New Voices on Adam Smith*. London and New York: Routledge, 17–39.
Hanley, Ryan P. (2008): 'Commerce and Corruption: Rousseau's Diagnosis and Adam Smith's Cure'. In: *European Journal of Political Theory* 7. No. 2, 137–158.
Hanley, Ryan P. (2009): *Adam Smith and the Character of Virtue*. Cambridge: Cambridge University Press.
Hannesson, Rögnvaldur (2015): *Debt, Democracy and the Welfare State: Are Modern Democracies Living on Borrowed Time and Money?* Basingstoke: Palgrave Macmillan.
Hansen, Niles M. (1966): 'Saint-Simon's Industrial Society in Modern Perspective'. In: *The Southwestern Social Science Quarterly* 47. No. 3, 253–262.
Harald Wydra (2015): *Politics and the Sacred*. Cambridge: Cambridge University Press.
Harjuniemi, Timo (2019): 'Reason over Politics'. In: *Journalism Studies* 20. No. 6, 804–822.
Härmänmaa, Marja and Nissen, Christopher (Eds.) (2014): *Decadence, Degeneration, and the End Studies in the European Fin de Siècle*. New York: Palgrave Macmillan.
Harper, Robert Francis (1904): *The Code of Hammurabi King of Babylon about 2250 B.C.* Chicago: University of Chicago Press.
Harris, Edward M. (2002): 'Did Solon Abolish Debt-Bondage?' In: *The Classical Quarterly* 52. No. 2, 415–430.
Harris, Stephen L., and Platzner, Gloria (1995): *Classical Mythology: Images and Insights*. Sacramento: California State University.
Harrison, Peter (2011): 'Adam Smith and the History of the Invisible Hand'. In: *Journal of the History of Ideas* 72. No. 1, 29–49.
Hatab, Lawrence J. (1987): 'Nietzsche, Nihilism and Meaning'. In: *The Personalist Forum* 3. No. 2, 91–111.
Hatab, Lawrence J. (1995): *A Nietzschean Defence of Democracy*. Chicago and La Salle: Open Court.
Hayek, Friedrich A. (1988): *The Fatal Conceit: The Errors of Socialism*. Chicago: University of Chicago Press.
Heidegger, Martin (1977): 'The Question Concerning Technology'. In: Heidegger, Martin: *The Question Concerning Technology and Other Essays*. William Lovitt (Trans.). New York: Garland Publishing.
Heilbroner, Robert L. (1979): 'Modern Economics as a Chapter in the History of Economic Thought'. In: *History of Political Economy* 11. No. 2, 192–198.
Heilbroner, Robert L. (1990): 'Economics as Ideology'. In: Samuels, Warren J. (Ed.): *Economics as Discourse*. New York: Springer Science+Business Media, 101–117.
Heilbroner, Robert L. (1991): *An Inquiry into the Human Prospect: Looked at Again for the 1990s*. New York: W. W. Norton & Co.
Heilbroner, Robert L. (1999): *The Worldly Philosophers*. New York: Simon and Schuster.
Heit, Helmut and Heller, Lisa (2014): *Handbuch Nietzsche und die Wissenschaften*. Berlin and Boston: De Gruyter.
Heit, Helmut und Thorgeirsdottir, Sigridur (Eds.) (2016): *Nietzsche als Kritiker und Denker der Transformation*. Berlin and Boston: De Gruyter.
Henderson, Errol (2002): *Democracy and War, the End of an Illusion?* Boulder: Lynne Reiner.
Henderson, William Otto (1975): *The Rise of German Industrial Power, 1834–1914*. Berkeley: University of California Press.
Hensel, Paul R., Goertz, Gary, and Diehl, Paul F. (2000): 'The Democratic Peace and Rivalries'. In: *Journal of Politics* 64. No. 4, 1173–1188.
Hertz, Noreena (2001): *The Silent Takeover: Global Capitalism and the Death Of Democracy*. New York: Free Press.
Hetherington, Norriss S. (1983): 'Isaac Newton's Influence on Adam Smith's Natural Laws in Economics'. In: *Journal of the History of Ideas* 44. No. 3, 497–505.
Hill, John E. (2018): *Adam Smith's Equality and the Pursuit of Happiness*. New York: Palgrave Macmillan.

Hill, Lisa E. (2007): 'Adam Smith, Adam Ferguson and Karl Marx on the Division of Labour'. In: *Journal of Classical Sociology* 7. No. 3, 339–366.
Hill, Lisa E. (2020): *Adam Smith's Pragmatic Liberalism: The Science of Welfare:* Cham: Palgrave Macmillan.
Hillard, Derek (2002): 'History as a Dual Process'. In: *Nietzsche-Studien* 31. No. 1, 40–56.
Hix, Harvey Lee (1995): *Ghosts Hovering over the Ashes.* Albany: SUNY Press.
Hobbes, Thomas (1990): *Behemoth or The Long Parliament.* Chicago and London: University of Chicago Press.
Hodgson, Geoffrey M. (2015): *Conceptualising Capitalism.* Chicago: University of Chicago Press.
Hofstede, Geert H. (2001): *Culture's Consequences.* Thousand Oaks: SAGE Publications.
Holtfrerich, Carl-Ludwig (2013): 'Government Debt in Economic Thought of the Long 19th Century'. School of Business & Economics Discussion Paper. https://papers.ssrn.com/sol3/papers.cfm?abstract_id=2255977, last accessed Feb. 27, 2023.
Holton, Gerald (1998): 'Einstein and the Cultural Roots of Modern Science'. In: *Daedalus* 127. No. 1, 1–44.
Holub, Robert C. (1998): 'Nietzsche's Colonialist Imagination: Nueva Germania, Good Europeanism, and Great Politics'. In: Lennox, Sara, and Zantop, Susanne (Eds.): *The Imperialist Imagination: German Colonialism and Its Legacy.* Ann Arbor: The University of Michigan Press, 33–49.
Holub, Robert C. (2005): 'Nietzsche Socialist, Anarchist, Feminist, An Essay'. In: Tatlock, Lynne, and Erlin, Matt (Eds.): *German Culture in Nineteenth Century America: Reception, Adaptation, Transformation.* Rochester NY: Camden House, 129–149.
Holub, Robert C. (2016): *Nietzsche's Jewish Problem: Between Anti-Semitism and Anti-Judaism.* Princeton: Princeton University Press.
Holub, Robert C. (2018): *Nietzsche in the Nineteenth Century: Social Questions and Philosophical Interventions.* Philadelphia: University of Pennsylvania Press.
Hont, Istvan (2010): *Jealousy of Trade.* Cambridge: Harvard University Press.
Hont, Istvan (2015): *Politics in Commercial Society: Jean-Jacques Rousseau and Adam Smith.* Béla Kapossy and Michael Sonenscher (Eds.). Cambridge: Harvard University Press.
Hont, Istvan and Ignatieff, Michael (Eds.) (1983): *Wealth and Virtue: The Shaping of Political Economy in the Scottish Enlightenment.* Cambridge: Cambridge University Press.
Hook, Sidney (1973): 'Myth and Fact in the Marxist Theory of Revolution and Violence'. In: *Journal of the History of Ideas* 34. No. 2, 271–280.
Horkheimer, Max (1993): 'Egoism and the freedom movement'. In: Horkheimer, Max: *Between Philosophy and Social Science.* Cambridge: MIT Press, 49–111.
Horkheimer, Max (2013): *Eclipse of Reason.* Mansfield Centre: Martino Publishing.
Horkheimer, Max and Adorno, Theodor (2004): '6. The Illusory Dialectic: From Enlightenment to Totalitarianism'. In: Horkheimer, Max and Adorno, Theodor: *Reclaiming the Enlightenment: Toward a Politics of Radical Engagement.* New York and Chichester: Columbia University Press, 95–114.
Hornblower, Simon (1992): 'The Religious Dimension to the Peloponnesian War, or, What Thucydides Does Not Tell Us'. In: *Harvard Studies in Classical Philology* 94:169–197.
Huddleston, Andrew (2012): *Nietzsche on the Decadence and the Flourishing Culture.* Princeton: Princeton University. Doctoral Dissertation. Copyright Andrew Huddleston.
Huddleston Andrew (2014): '"Consecration" to High Culture: Nietzsche on Slavery and Human Dignity'. In: *Journal of the History of Philosophy* 52. No. 1, 135–160.
Hudson, Michael (2012): *The Bubble and Beyond.* Dresden: ISLET.
Hudson, Michael (2018): *… And Forgive Them Their Debts: Lending, Foreclosure and Redemption from Bronze Age Finance to the Jubilee Year.* Dresden: ISLET.
Hunt, Lester H. (1985): 'Politics and Anti-Politics: Nietzsche's View of the State'. In: *History of Philosophy Quarterly* 2. No. 4, 453–468.
Hunt, Peter (2017): *Ancient Greek and Roman Slavery.* Hoboken: Wiley-Blackwell.
Hurtado, Jimena (2016): 'Adam Smith's Impartial Spectator: Autonomy and Extended Selves'. In: *Econ Journal Watch* 13. No. 2, 298–305.

Hutter, Horst (2005): *Shaping the Future: Nietzsche's New Regime of the Soul and Its Ascetic Practices.* New York and Oxford: Lexington Books.

Hyndman, Henry M. (1902): *Commercial Crises of the Nineteenth Century.* London and New York: Swan Sonnenschein & Co. and Charles Scribner's Sons.

Iliffe, Robert (2016): 'Saint Isaac: Newtonian Hagiography and the Creation of Genius'. In: Beretta, Marco, Conforti, Maria; and Mazzarello, Paolo (Eds.): *Savant Relics: Brains and Remains of Scientists.* Cambridge: Cambridge University Press, 93–131.

Ioan, Razvan (2014): 'The Politics of Physiology'. In: Knoll, Manuel and Stocker, Barry (Eds.): *Nietzsche as Political Philosopher.* Berlin and Boston: De Gruyter, 383–405.

Jackson, Myles W. (1994): 'A Spectrum of Belief: Goethe's "Republic" versus Newtonian "Despotism"'. In: *Social Studies of Sciences, SAGE* 24: 673–701.

Jackson, Tim (2010): *Prosperity without Growth: Foundations for the Economy of Tomorrow.* London: Earthscan Publications.

Jal, Murzban (2010): 'The Irresistible Science of Karl Marx'. In: *Social Scientist* 38. No. 5-6, 22–34.

Jameson, Frederic (1994): *The Seeds of Time.* New York: Columbia University Press.

Janaway, Christopher (2007): *Beyond Selflessness: Reading Nietzsche's Genealogy.* Oxford: Oxford University Press.

Janaway, Christopher and Robertson, Simon (Eds.) (2012): *Nietzsche, Naturalism, and Normativity.* Oxford: Oxford University Press.

Jarvis, Simon (1998): *Adorno: A Critical Introduction.* New York: Routledge.

Jaspers, Karl (1997): *Nietzsche: An Introduction to Understanding His Philosophical Activity.* Charles F. Wallraff and Frederick J. Schmitz (Trans.). Baltimore: The John Hopkins University Press.

Jensen Anthony K. and Heit, Helmut (Eds.) (2014): *Nietzsche as a Scholar of Antiquity.* London: Bloomsbury.

Jensen, Hans E. (2001): 'John Stuart Mill's Theories of Wealth and Income Distribution'. In: *Review of Social Economy* 59. No. 4, 491–507.

Joas, Hans and Knöbl, Wolfgang (2013): *War in Social Thought: Hobbes to the Present.* Princeton: Princeton University Press.

Josefson, Jim (2019): *Hannah Arendt's Aesthetic Politics: Freedom and the Beautiful.* Cham: Palgrave Macmillan.

Jurist, Elliot L. (2000): *Beyond Hegel and Nietzsche: Philosophy, Culture and Agency.* Cambridge: MIT Press.

Kail, Peter J. E. (2011): '"Genealogy" and the Genealogy'. In: May, Simon (Ed.): *Nietzsche's On the Genealogy of Morality: A Critical Guide.* Cambridge: Cambridge University Press, 214–234.

Kaiser, Otto (2006): 'Democracy and Aristocracy in Nietzsche's Late Writings'. In: Backhaus, Jürgen Georg and Drechsler, Wolfgang: *Friedrich Nietzsche (1844–1900): Economy and Society.* New York: Springer Science and Business Media, 229–253.

Katsafanas, Paul (2016): *The Nietzschean Self: Moral Psychology, Agency, and the Unconscious.* Oxford: Oxford University Press.

Kattel, Rainer (2006): 'Justice and Economy from Human, All Too Human to Thus Spoke Zarathustra'. In: Backhaus, Jürgen Georg and Drechsler, Wolfgang: *Nietzsche (1844–1900): Economy and Society.* New York: Springer Science and Business Media, 209–229.

Kaufmann, Chaim (2004): 'Threat Inflation and the Failure of the Marketplace of Ideas: The Selling of the Iraq War'. In: *International Security* 29. No. 1, 5–48.

Kaufmann, Walter (Ed.) (1994): *The Portable Nietzsche.* New York: Penguin Classics.

Kaufmann, Walter (2013): *Nietzsche as Philosopher, Psychologist, Antichrist.* Princeton: Princeton University Press.

Keen, Steve (2022): *The New Economics: A Manifesto.* Cambridge: Polity Press.

Kellner, Douglas (1998): 'Modernity and Its Discontents: Nietzsche's Critique'. https://pages.gseis.ucla.edu/faculty/kellner/papers/FNmod.htm, last accessed Feb. 27, 2023.

Kennedy, Gavin (2009): 'Adam Smith and the Invisible Hand: From Metaphor to Myth'. In: *Econ Journal Watch* 6. No. 2, 239–263.

Keynes, John Maynard (1930): 'Economic Possibilities for Our Grandchildren'. In: Keynes, John Maynard: *J.M. Keynes: Essays In Persuasion*. New York: W. W. Norton & Co., 358–373.

Keynes, John Maynard (1933): 'National Self-Sufficiency'. http://jmaynardkeynes.ucc.ie/national-self-sufficiency.html, last accessed Feb. 27, 2023.

Kim, Hyung Min and Rousseau, David L. (2005): 'The Classical Liberals Were Half Right (or Half Wrong): New Tests of the "Liberal Peace", 1960–88'. In: *Journal of Peace Research* 42. No. 5, 523–543.

Kindleberger, Charles P. (1990): *Historical Economics: Art or Science?* Berkeley and Oxford: University of California Press.

King, Ian T. (1991): 'Political Economy and the "Laws of Beauty": Aesthetics, Economics, and Materialism in Marx'. In: *Science & Society* 55. No. 3, 323–335.

Kitchen, Martin (1978): *Political Economy of Germany, 1815–1914*. London: Croom Helm.

Klapsis, Antonis (2014): 'Economic Crisis and Political Extremism in Europe: From the 1930s to the Present'. In: *European View* 13. No. 2, 189–198.

Klein, Daniel B. (2009): 'In Adam Smith's Invisible Hands: Comment on Gavin Kennedy'. In: *Econ Journal Watch* 6. No. 2, 264–279.

Klein, Daniel B. and Lucas, Brandon (2011): 'In a Word or Two, Placed in the Middle: The Invisible Hand in Smith's Tomes'. In: *Economic Affairs* 31. No. 1, 43–52.

Klein, Martin J. (1969): 'Gibbs on Clausius'. In: *Historical Studies in the Physical Sciences* 1. No. 2, 127–149.

Kline, George L. (1969): '"Nietzschean Marxism" in Russia'. In: Adelmann, Frederick J. (Ed.): *Demythologizing Marxism: A Series of Studies on Marxism*. Chesnut Hill: Boston College, 166–183

Klossowski, Pierre (1997): *Nietzsche and the Vicious Circle*. Daniel W. Smith (Trans.). Chicago: University of Chicago Press.

Knoll, Manuel and Stocker, Barry (Eds.) (2014): *Nietzsche as Political Philosopher*. Berlin and Boston: De Gruyter.

Kojève, Alexandre (1980), *Introduction to the Reading of Hegel*, ed. Alan Bloom, trans. James H. Nichols, Ithaca, NY: Cornell University Press.

Korsch, Karl (1938, 2016): 'The Ultimate Aims of Marx's Critique of Political Economy'. In: Korsch, Karl: *Karl Marx*. Leiden: Koninklijke Brill NV, 112–118.

Kragh, Helge S. (2016): *Entropic Creation: Religious Contexts of Thermodynamics and Cosmology*. Abingdon: Routledge.

Kraut, Richard (2015): 'Aristotle on well-being'. In: *The Routledge Handbook of Philosophy of Well-Being*. London: Routledge.

Kreissig, Heinz (1989): 'A Marxist View of Josephus' Account of the Jewish War'. In: Feldman, Louis H. and Hata, Gohei (Eds.) (1989): *Josephus, The Bible and History*. Detroit: Wayne State University Press, 265–278.

Krugman, Paul (2008): *The Return of Depression Economics and the Crisis of 2008*. New York: W. W. Norton & Co.

Kuehne, Tobias (2018): 'Nietzsche's Ethics of Danger'. In: *Journal of Nietzsche Studies* 49. No. 1, 78–101.

Kümmel, Reiner (2011): *The Second Law of Economics: Energy, Entropy and the Origin of Wealth*. New York: Springer Science+Business Media.

Kurian, Mathew K. (1974): 'Marxism and Christianity'. In: *Social Scientist* 2. No. 8, 3–21.

Laibman, David (2019): 'Acceptance Speech for the World Marxian Economics Award (II): Marxism, Science and Economics'. In: *World Review of Political Economy* 10. No. 4, 531–543.

Lampert, Laurence (1974): 'Heidegger's Nietzsche interpretation'. In: *Man and World* 7. No. 4, 353–378.

Lampert, Laurence (2001): *Nietzsche's Task: An Interpretation of Beyond Good and Evil*. New Haven: Yale University Press.

Lampert, Laurence (2004): 'Nietzsche and Plato'. In: Bishop, Paul: *Nietzsche and Antiquity*. Rochester: Camden House, 205–220.

Land, Stephen K. (1977): 'Adam Smith's "Considerations Concerning the First Formation of Languages"'. In: *Journal of the History of Ideas* 38. No. 4, 677–690.

Landa, Ishay (1999): 'Nietzsche, the Chinese Worker's Friend'. In: *New Left Review* I-236, 3–23.
Landa Ishay (2007): *The Overman in the Marketplace: Nietzschean Heroism in Popular Culture*. Lanham: Lexington Books.
Landa, Ishay (2016): 'The Social Individual and the Last Human: Marx and Nietzsche Agree to Disagree'. In: *Critical Sociology* 45. No. 2, 253–265.
Landa, Ishay (2020): 'Marx, Nietzsche, and the Contradictions Of Capitalism'. In: *Nietzsche and Critical Social Theory*. Christine Payne and Michael Roberts (Eds.). Leiden and Boston: Brill, 147–172.
Langholm, Odd Inge (1984): *The Aristotelian Analysis of Usury*. Bergen: Universitetsforlaget.
Large, Duncan (1999): 'Hermes Contra Dionysus: Michel Serres's Critique of Nietzsche'. In: Babich, Babette E. (Ed.): *Nietzsche, Epistemology and Philosophy of Science II*. Dordrecht: Springer Science +Business Media, 151–161.
Large, Duncan (2000): '"Our Greatest Teacher": Nietzsche, Burckhardt, and the Concept of Culture'. In: *International Studies in Philosophy* 32. No. 3, 3–23.
Large, Duncan (2001): 'Nietzsche's Use of Biblical Language'. In: *Journal of Nietzsche Studies* 22, 88–115.
Latour, Bruno and Antonin Upinay, Vincent (2009): *The Science of Passionate Interests: An Introduction to Gabriel Tarde's Economic Anthropology*. Chicago: Prickly Paradigm Press.
Lazzarato, Maurizio (2012): *The Making of the Indebted Man: An Essay on the Neoliberal Condition*. Joshua D. Jordan (Trans.). Cambridge: MIT Press and Semiotext(e).
Lazzarato, Maurizio (2015): *Governing by Debt*. Joshua D. Jordan (Trans.). Cambridge: MIT Press and Semiotext(e).
Lee, Donald C. (1975): 'The Concept of "Necessity": Marx and Marcuse'. In: *The Southwestern Journal of Philosophy* 6. No. 1, 47–53.
Lefèbvre, Henri (1972): *The Sociology of Marx*. London: Penguin.
Lefebvre, Henri (2020): *Hegel, Marx, Nietzsche: Or the Realm of Shadows*. London: Verso.
Leiter, Brian (2011): 'Who is the "sovereign individual"? Nietzsche on freedom'. In: May, Simon (Ed.): *Nietzsche's On the Genealogy of Morality: A Critical Guide*. Cambridge: Cambridge University Press, 101–119.
Leiter, Brian (2015): *Nietzsche on Morality*. London: Routledge.
Leiter, Brian and Sinhababu, Neil (Eds.): (2007): *Nietzsche and Morality*. Oxford: Oxford University Press.
Lenin, Vladimir I. ('LCW'; 1974): *Lenin's Collected Works*. Julius Katzer (Trans.). Moscow: Progress Publishers.
Lemm, Vanessa (2009): *Nietzsche's Animal Philosophy: Culture, Politics, and the Animality of the Human Being*. New York: Fordham University Press.
Lemm, Vanessa (2013): 'Nietzsche's Great Politics of the Event'. In: Ansell-Pearson, Keith (Ed.): *Nietzsche and Political Thought*. London: Bloomsbury Academic, 179–197.
Lemm, Vanessa (2015): 'Nietzsche's Agon for Politics?' In: *Contemporary Political Theory* 14. No. 1, e12–e17.
Lemm, Vanessa (2020): *Homo Natura*. Edinburgh: Edinburgh University Press.
Leonard, Miriam (2012): *Socrates and the Jews: Hellenism and Hebraism from Moses Mendelssohn to Sigmund Freud*. Chicago: University of Chicago Press.
Leonard, Miriam (2015): *Tragic Modernities*. Cambridge: Harvard University Press.
Leshem, Dotan (2013): 'Oikonomia Redefined'. In: *Journal of The History of Economic Thought* 35. No. 1, 43–61
Leshem, Dotan (2016): 'What Did the Ancient Greeks Mean by Oikonomia'. In: *Journal of Economic Perspectives* 30. No. 1, 225–231.
Leshem, Dotan (2016a): *The Origins of Neoliberalism: Modelling the Economy from Jesus To Foucault*. New York: Columbia University Press.
Levine, Norman (1987): 'The German Historical School of Law and the Origins of Historical Materialism'. In: *Journal of the History of Ideas* 48. No. 3, 431–451.
Levitsky, Steven and Ziblatt, Daniel (2018): *How Democracies Die: What History Tells Us about Our Future*. London: Penguin Random House UK.

Linarelli, John (2008): 'Did Nietzsche Say Anything to Economists, or about Economics'. In: Samuels, Warren J., Biddle, Jeff E., and Emmett, Ross B. (Eds.): *Research in the History of Economic Thought and Methodology: A Research Annual* (26-A). Bingley: Emerald Group Publishing, 117–139.

Linstromberg, Ronald C. (1969): 'The Philosophy of Science'. In: *Journal of Economic Issues* 3. No. 2, 177–191.

Losurdo, Domenico (2019): *Nietzsche, The Aristocratic Rebel: Intellectual Biography and Critical Balance-Sheet. Historical Materialism Book Series*, Vol. CC. Gregor Benton (Trans.). Leiden and Boston: Brill.

Love, John (1986a): 'Max Weber and the Theory of Ancient Capitalism'. In: *History and Theory* 25. No. 2, 152–172.

Love, Nancy S. (1986): *Marx, Nietzsche, Modernity.* New York: Columbia University Press.

Love, Nancy S. (1987): 'Epistemology and Exchange: Marx, Nietzsche, and Critical Theory'. In: *New German Critique* 41, 71–94.

Lowe, Adolph (1975): *Adam Smith's System of Equilibrium Growth.* Oxford: Oxford University Press.

Löwith, Karl (1945): 'Nietzsche's Doctrine of Eternal Recurrence'. In: *Journal of the History of Ideas* 6, 273–284.

Löwith, Karl (1954): 'Man's Self-Alienation in the Early Writings of Marx'. In: *Social Research* 21. No. 2, 204–230.

Löwith, Karl (1991): *From Hegel to Nietzsche: The Revolution in Nineteenth-Century Philosophy.* David E. Green (Trans.). New York: Columbia University Press.

Löwith, Karl (1993): *Max Weber and Karl Marx.* London and New York: Routledge.

Löwith, Karl (1997): *Nietzsche's Philosophy of the Eternal Recurrence of the Same.* Berkeley: University of California Press.

Löwy, Michael (1979): *Georg Lukács: From Romanticism to Bolshevism.* Patrick Camiller (Trans.). Paris: Presses Universitaires de France.

Luchte, James (2010): *The Peacock and the Buffalo: The Poetry of Nietzsche.* James Luchte (Trans.). London and New York: Continuum.

Lukács Georg (1980): *Destruction of Reason.* Peter R. Palmer (Trans.). London: Merlin Press.

Luna, Francesco (1996): 'From the History of Astronomy to the Wealth of Nations: Wonderful Wheels and Invisible Hands in Adam Smith's Major Works'. In: Vaz, Daniel and Velupillai, Kumaraswamy (Eds.): *Inflation, Institutions and Information: Essays in Honour of Axel Leijonhufvud.* London: Palgrave Macmillan UK, 131–157.

Lynn, Matthew (2011): *The Long Depression: The Slump of 2008 to 2031.* London: Endeavour Press.

Mabille, Louise (2009): *Nietzsche and the Anglo-Saxon Tradition.* London and New York: Continuum.

Macfie, Alec (1971): 'The Invisible Hand of Jupiter'. In: *Journal of the History of Ideas* 32. No. 4, 595–599.

Magnus, Bernd B. (1986): 'Nietzsche and the Project of Bringing Philosophy to an End'. In: Yovel, Yirmiyahu (Ed.): *Nietzsche as Affirmative Thinker.* Vol. XIII. Dordrecht: Martinus Nijhoff Philosophy Library and Springer, 39–58.

Mann, Michael (2012): *The Sources of Social Power.* Vol. II. Cambridge: Cambridge University Press.

Mann, Thomas (1987): *Reflections of a Nonpolitical Man.* New York: Ungar.

Mansfield, Edward D. and Snyder, Jack (2005): *Electing to Fight: Why Emerging Democracies Go to War.* Boston: MIT Press.

Mara, Gerald M. and Dovi, Suzanne L. (1995): 'Mill, Nietzsche, and the Identity of Postmodern Liberalism'. In: *The Journal of Politics* 57. No. 1, 1–23.

Marcuse, Herbert (1960): *Reason and Revolution.* Boston: Beacon Publishers.

Marcuse, Herbert (1972): *Counter-Revolution and Revolt.* Boston: Beacon Publishers.

Marcuse, Herbert (1988): *Negations.* Jeremy J. Shapiro (Trans.). London: Free Association Press.

Martin, Bonnie (2016): 'Neighbor-to-Neighbor Capitalism'. In: Beckert, Sven and Rockman, Seth (Eds.): *Slavery's Capitalism*, Philadelphia: University of Pennsylvania Press, 107–122.

Martin, David A. (1990): 'Economics as Ideology: On Making "The Invisible Hand" Invisible'. In: *Review of Social Economy* 48. No. 3, 272–287.

Mathäs, Alexander (2020): *Beyond Posthumanism: The German Humanist Tradition and the Future of the Humanities.* New York and Oxford: Berghahn Books.
May, Simon (Ed.) (2011): *Nietzsche's On the Genealogy of Morality: A Critical Guide.* Cambridge: Cambridge University Press.
Mayer, Karl (1975): 'Max Weber's Interpretation of Karl Marx'. In: *Social Research* 42. No. 4, 701–719.
McCarthy, Brian (1984): 'The Biblical Tradition, the Church, and Marx's Critique of Religion'. In: *CrossCurrents* 34. No. 1, 43–64.
McCarthy, George E. (1994): *Dialectics and Decadence: Echoes of Antiquity in Marx and Nietzsche.* Lanham: Rowman & Littlefield.
McClelland, John S. (1996): *A History of Western Political Thought.* Abingdon: Routledge.
McCloskey, Deirdre N. (2006): *The Bourgeois Virtues: Ethics for an Age of Commerce.* Chicago: University of Chicago Press.
McCloskey, Deirdre N. (2010): *Bourgeois Dignity: Why Economics Can't Explain The Modern World.* Chicago: Chicago University Press.
McCloskey, Deirdre N. (2016): *Bourgeois Equality: How Ideas, Not Capital or Institutions, Enriched the World.* Chicago: University of Chicago Press.
McDaniel, Iain (2018): 'The Politics of Historical Economics: Wilhelm Roscher on Democracy, Socialism and Caesarism'. In: *Modern Intellectual History* 15. No. 1, 93–122.
McLuhan, Marshall (1964): *Understanding Media: The Extensions of Man.* Cambridge: MIT Press.
Meadows, Donella, Randers, Jorgen, and Meadows, Dennis (2004): *Limits to Growth: The Thirty Years Update.* London: Chelsea Green Publishing Company.
Meek, Ronald L. and Skinner, Andrew (1973): 'The Development of Adam Smith's Ideas on the Division of Labour'. In: *The Economic Journal* 83. No. 332, 1094–1116.
Meeks, Wayne A. (1983): *The First Urban Christians: The Social World of the Apostle Paul.* New Haven: Yale University Press.
Meerhaeghe, Marcel A. G. (2006): 'Nietzsche and Business Ethics'. In: Backhaus, Jürgen Georg and Drechsler, Wolfgang (Eds.): *Nietzsche (1844–1900): Economy and Society.* New York: Springer Science and Business Media, 137–145.
Megill, Allan (1985): *Prophets of Extremity.* Berkeley: University of California Press.
Megill, Kenneth A. (1970): 'The Community in Marx's Philosophy'. In: *Philosophy and Phenomenological Research* 30. No. 3, 382–393.
Meikle, Scott (1997): *Aristotle's Economic Thought.* Oxford: Oxford University Press.
Merrick, Allison (2020): 'Nietzsche's Economy: Revisiting the Slave Revolt in Morals'. In: Payne, Christine A. and Roberts, Michael J.: *Nietzsche and Critical Social Theory: Affirmation, Animosity, and Ambiguity.* Leiden and Boston: Brill, 135–146.
Meszaros, Istvan (1970): *Marx's Theory of Alienation.* London: Merlin Press.
Meyer, Matthew (2014): *Reading Nietzsche through the Ancients: An Analysis of Becoming, Perspectivism, and the Principle of Non-Contradiction.* Berlin and Boston: De Gruyter.
Michel, Cécile (2013): 'Economic and Social Aspects of the Old Assyrian Loan Contracts'. In: *La Sapienza Orientale* 9, 41–56 (HAL ID: halshs-01426527).
Mieszkowski, Jan (2006): *Labors of Imagination: Aesthetics and Political Economy From Kant to Althusser.* New York: Fordham University Press.
Mikics, David (2003): *The Romance of Individualism in Emerson and Nietzsche.* Athens: Ohio University Press.
Millbank, John (2006): *Theology and Social Theory: Beyond Secular Reason.* Malden: Blackwell Publishing.
Miller, Stephen (1980): 'Adam Smith and the commercial republic'. In: *The Public Interest* 61, 106–122.
Mills, Charles W. (1999): 'European Spectres'. In: *The Journal of Ethics* 3. No. 2, 133–155.
Milne, Seumas (2012): *The Revenge of History.* London: Verso Books.
Milton, Myers (1976): 'Adam Smith's Concept of Equilibrium'. In: *Journal of Economic Issues* 10. No. 3, 560–575.

Minister, Stephen (2006): 'In Praise of Wanderers and Insomniacs: Economy, Excess, and Self-Overcoming in Nietzsche and Lévinas'. In: *Journal of the British Society for Phenomenology* 37. No. 3, 269–285.
Minowitz, Peter (2004): 'Adam Smith's Invisible Hands'. In: *Econ Journal Watch* 1. No. 3, 381–412.
Mintz, Alex and Geva, Nehemia (1993): 'Why Don't Democracies Fight Each Other? An Experimental Study'. In: *The Journal of Conflict Resolution* 37. No. 3, 484–503.
Misrahi, Robert (1972): *Marx et la question juive.* Paris: Gallimard.
Mixon, Scott (2008): 'The Crisis of 1873: Perspectives from Multiple Asset Classes'. In: *The Journal of Economic History* 68. No. 3, 722–757.
Mokyr, Joel (2017): *A Culture Of Growth: The Origins of the Modern Economy.* Princeton: Princeton University Press.
Mokyr, Joel (2018): 'Building Taller Ladders'. In: *Finance & Development* 55. No. 2, 32–35.
Mommsen, Wolfgang J. (1977): 'Max Weber as a Critic of Marxism'. In: *The Canadian Journal of Sociology* 2. No. 4, 373–398.
Montes, Leonidas (2003): 'Smith and Newton: Some Methodological Issues Concerning General Economic Equilibrium Theory'. In: *Cambridge Journal of Economics* 27. No. 5, 723–747.
Montes, Leonidas (2003a): 'Das Adam Smith Problem: Its Origins, the Stages of the Current Debate, and One Implication for Our Understanding of Sympathy'. In: *Journal of the History of Economic Thought* 25. No. 1, 63–90.
Montinari, Mazzino and Large, Duncan (1997): 'Enlightenment and Revolution: Nietzsche and Late Goethe'. In: *Journal of Nietzsche Studies* 13, 23–29.
Montinari, Mazzino and Large, Duncan (1997): 'Enlightenment and Revolution'. In: *Journal of Nietzsche Studies* 13, 23–29.
Moore, Gregory (2002): *Nietzsche, Biology and Metaphor.* Cambridge: Cambridge University Press.
Moore, Gregory and Brobjer, Thomas H. (Eds.) (2004): *Nietzsche and Science.* Surrey: Ashgate Publishing.
Morrisson, Iain (2018): 'Nietzsche on Guilt: Dependency, Debt, and Imperfection'. In: *European Journal of Philosophy* 26. No. 3, 974–990.
Mosini, Valeria (Ed.) (2009): *Equilibrium in Economics: Scope and Limits.* London: Routledge.
Mosini, Valeria (2011): *Reassessing the Paradigm of Economics: Bringing Positive Economics Back into the Normative Framework.* London: Routledge.
Mousseau, Michael (2000): 'Market Prosperity, Democratic Consolidation, and Democratic Peace'. In: *Journal of Conflict Resolution* 44. No. 4, 472–507.
Mousseau, Michael, Hegre, Håvard and O'Neal, John R. (2003): 'How the Wealth of Nations Conditions the Liberal Peace'. In: *European Journal of International Relations* 9. No. 4, 277–314.
Muldrew, Craig (1998): *The Economy of Obligation: The Culture of Credit and Social Relations in Early Modern England.* Basingstoke: Palgrave Macmillan.
Muller, Jerry Z. (2003): *The Mind and the Market: Capitalism in Western Thought.* New York: Anchor Books.
Müller-Lauter, Wolfgang (1999): *Nietzsche: His Philosophy of Contradictions and the Contradictions of His Philosophy.* Champaign: University of Illinois Press.
Myers, Milton L. (1967): 'Division of Labour as a Principle of Social Cohesion'. In: *The Canadian Journal of Economics and Political Science* 33. No. 3, 432–440.
Nehamas, Alexander (1983): 'How One Becomes What One Is'. In: *The Philosophical Review* 92. No. 3, 385–417.
Nehamas, Alexander (1985): *Nietzsche: Life as Literature.* Cambridge: Harvard University Press.
Nieboer, Herman Jeremias (2010): *Slavery As An Industrial System: Ethnological Researches.* Cambridge: Cambridge University Press.
Nippel, Wilfried (2005): 'Marx, Weber, and Classical Slavery'. In: *Classics Ireland* 12, 31–49.
Nisbet, Robert (1994): *The History of the Idea of Progress.* Abingdon: Routledge.
Nitzan, Jonathan and Bichler, Shimshon (2009): *Capital as Power: A Study of Order and Creorder.* London and New York: Routledge.

Noble, David F. (2006): *Beyond the Promised Land: The Movement and the Myth*. Toronto: Between the Lines.

O'Boyle, Brian and McDonough, Terrence (2017): 'Bourgeois Ideology and Mathematical Economics: A Reply to Tony Lawson*'. In: *Economic Thought* 6. No. 1, 16–34.

Oger, Eric (1997): 'The Eternal Return as Crucial Test'. In: *The Journal of Nietzsche Studies* 14, 1–18.

Ormerod, Paul (1998): *Butterfly Economics*. London: Faber & Faber.

Ortmann, Andreas, Baranowski, David, and Walraevens, Benoit (2019): 'Schumpeter's Assessment of Adam Smith and 'The Wealth of Nations': Why He Got It Wrong'. In: *Journal of the History of Economic Thought* 41. No. 4, 531–551.

Orwell, George (2004): *Nineteen Eighty-Four*. London: Penguin Classics.

Osborn, Ronald E. (2010): 'Nihilism's Conscience: On Nietzsche's Politics of Aristocratic Radicalism'. In: *Modern Age* 52. No. 4, 292–307.

Osborn, Ronald E. (2017): *Humanism and the Death Of God: Searching for the Good after Darwin, Marx, and Nietzsche*. Oxford: Oxford University Press.

Oslington, Paul (2012): 'God and the Market: Adam Smith's Invisible Hand'. In: *Journal of Business Ethics* 108. No. 4, 429–438.

Otteson, James R. (2000): 'The Recurring "Adam Smith Problem"'. In: *History of Philosophy Quarterly* 17. No. 1, 51–74.

Otteson James (2002): *Adam Smith's Marketplace of Life*. Cambridge: Cambridge University Press.

Owen, David (1994): *Maturity and Modernity: Nietzsche, Weber, Foucault, and the Ambivalence of Reason*. London: Routledge.

Owen, David (2009): 'Autonomy, Self-Respect and Self-Love'. In: Gemes, Ken and May, Simon (Eds.): *Nietzsche on Freedom and Autonomy*. Oxford: Oxford University Press, 197–223.

Pack, Spencer J. (2010): *Aristotle, Adam Smith and Karl Marx*. Cheltenham: Edward Elgar Publishing.

Parkes, Graham (2013): 'Zhuangzi and Nietzsche on the Human and Nature'. In: *Environmental Philosophy* 10. No. 1, 1–24.

Patton, Paul (2014): 'Nietzsche on Power and Democracy circa 1876–1881'. In: Knoll, Manuel and Stocker, Barry (Eds.): *Nietzsche as Political Philosopher*. Berlin and Boston: De Gruyter, 93–111.

Payne, Christine A. and Roberts, Michael J. (2020): *Nietzsche and Critical Social Theory: Affirmation, Animosity, and Ambiguity*. Leiden and Boston: Brill.

Perelman, Michael (2000): *The Invention of Capitalism*. Durham: Duke University Press.

Petrucciani, Stefano (2015): 'Adorno's Criticism of Marx's Social Theory'. In: *Critical Theory and the Challenge of Praxis*. Stefano Giacchetti Ludovisi (Ed.). London: Ashgate, 19–33.

Pfau, Thomas (2013): *Minding the Modern: Human Agency, Intellectual Traditions, and Responsible Knowledge*. Notre Dame: University of Notre Dame Press.

Pickett, Kate and Wilkinson, Richard (2010): *The Spirit Level: Why Equality Is Better for Everyone*. New York: Bloomsbury Publishing.

Piketty, Thomas (2014): *Capital in the Twenty First Century*. Arthur Goldhammer (Trans.). Cambridge: Harvard University Press.

Piketty, Thomas (2015): *The Economics of Inequality*. Arthur Goldhammer (Trans.). Cambridge: Harvard University Press.

Piketty, Thomas (2020): *Capital and Ideology*. Arthur Goldhammer (Trans.). Cambridge: Harvard University Press.

Piedra, Alberto M. (2004): *Natural Law: The Foundation of an Orderly Economic System*. New York and Oxford: Lexington Books.

Pilling, David (2018): *The Growth Delusion: The Wealth and Wellbeing of Nations*. London: Bloomsbury.

Pippin, Robert (2009): 'How to Overcome Oneself'. In: Gemes, Ken and May, Simon (Eds.): *Nietzsche on Freedom and Autonomy*. Oxford: Oxford University Press, 69–89.

Poellner, Peter (2009): 'Nietzschean Freedom'. In: Gemes, Ken and May, Simon (Eds.): *Nietzsche on Freedom and Autonomy*. Oxford: Oxford University Press, 151–181.

Pomeroy, Sarah B. (2004): *A Brief History of Ancient Greece: Politics, Society, and Culture.* Oxford: Oxford University Press.
Ponzi, Mauro (2017): *Nietzsche's Nihilism in Walter Benjamin.* Basingstoke: Palgrave Macmillan.
Posner, Eric A. and Weyl, E. Glen (2018): *Radical Markets: Uprooting Capitalism and Democracy for a Just Society.* Princeton: Princeton University Press.
Postone, Moishe (1994): *Time, Labour and Social Domination.* Cambridge: Cambridge University Press.
Potier, Jean-Pierre (2011): 'The Socialism of Léon Walras'. In: *L'Économie politique* 51. No. 3, 33–49.
Prusik, Charles Andrew (2022): 'Society as real abstraction: Adorno's critique of economic nature'. In: Bonefeld, Werner and O'Kane, Chris (Eds.): *Adorno and Marx.* London and New York: Bloomsbury Academic, 141–161.
Rampley, Matthew (2000): *Nietzsche, Aesthetics and Modernity.* Cambridge: Cambridge University Press.
Rasmussen, Dennis C. (2008): *The Problems and Promise of Commercial Society: Adam Smith's Response to Rousseau.* University Park: Penn State University Press.
Ratner-Rosenhagen, Jennifer (2012): *American Nietzsche: A History of an Icon and His Ideas.* Chicago: University of Chicago Press.
Rayman, Joshua (2018): 'Representationalism in Nietzsche's Early Physics: Cosmology and Sensation in the Zeitatomenlehre'. In: *Nietzsche-Studien* 47. No. 1, 167–194.
Reader, Soran (Ed.) (2006): *The Philosophy of Need.* Cambridge: Cambridge University Press.
Redhead, Mark (1997): 'Nietzsche and Liberal Democracy: A Relationship of Antagonistic Indebtedness?' In: *The Journal of Political Philosophy* 5. No. 2, 183–193.
Reginster, Bernard (2011): 'The Genealogy Of Guilt'. In: May, Simon (Ed.): *Nietzsche's On the Genealogy of Morality: A Critical Guide.* Cambridge: Cambridge University Press, 56–78.
Reinert, Hugo and Reinert, Erik S. (2006): 'Creative Destruction in Economics: Nietzsche, Sombart, Schumpeter'. In: Backhaus, Jürgen Georg and Drechsler, Wolfgang (Eds.): *Friedrich Nietzsche (1844–1900): Economy and Society.* New York: Springer Science and Business Media, 55–87.
Reinert, Sophus A. and Reinert, Erik S. (2006): 'An 'All Too Human' Question: Nietzsche, Die Soziale Frage, and the German Historical School of Economics'. In: Backhaus, Jürgen Georg and Drechsler, Wolfgang (Eds.): *Friedrich Nietzsche (1844–1900): Economy and Society.* New York: Springer Science and Business Media, 111–137.
Reisman, David A. (1998): 'Adam Smith on Market and State'. In: *Journal of Institutional and Theoretical Economics* 154. No. 2, 357–383.
Renton, David (Ed.) (2001): *Marx on Globalisation.* London: Lawrence and Wishart Limited.
Rifkin, Jeremy and Howard, Ted (2012*): The Emerging Order: God in an Age of Scarcity.* New York: G. P. Putnam's Sons.
Ritter, Heinrich (1846): *The History of Ancient Philosophy.* Vol. IV. Alexander J. W. Morrison (Trans.). London: Henry G. Bohn.
Roberts, Michael (2016): *The Long Depression.* London: Haymarket Books.
Roberts, William Clare (2017): *Marx's Inferno: The Political Theory of Capital.* Princeton and Oxford: Princeton University Press.
Robinson, Forrest G., Brahm, Jr., Gabriel Noah, and Carlstroem, Catherine (2011): *The Jester and the Sages: Mark Twain in Conversation with Nietzsche, Freud, and Marx.* Columbia: University of Missouri Press.
Robinson, Randall (2000): *The Debt: What America Owes to Blacks.* Boston: E. P. Dutton.
Robinson, William L. (2014): *Global Capitalism and the Crisis of Humanity.* Cambridge: Cambridge University Press.
Roche, David and McKee, Bob (2012): *DemoCrisis: Democracy Caused the Debt Crisis. Will it survive it?* London: Independent Strategy Research Publication.
Roche, David and McKee, Bob (2016): *Democrisis Re-Examined.* London: Independent Strategy Research Publication.
Rockoff, Hugh (2009): 'Upon Daedalian Wings of Paper Money: Adam Smith and the Crisis of 1772'. NBER Working Paper No. 15594, JEL No. N1.

Rodrik, Dani (2011): *The Globalisation Paradox: Why Global Markets, States and Democracy Can't Coexist.* Oxford: Oxford University Press.
Rogan, Tim (2017): *The Moral Economists: R. H. Tawney, Karl Polanyi, E. P. Thompson and the Critique of Capitalism.* Princeton: Princeton University Press.
Roitman, Janet (2005): *Fiscal Disobedience.* Princeton: Princeton University Press.
Rose, Kevin (2014): *Young Money.* New York: Grand Central Publishing.
Rosenberg, Hans (1943): 'Political and Social Consequences of the Great Depression of 1873–1896 in Central Europe'. In: *The Economic History Review* 13. No. 1–2, 58–73.
Rosenberg, Hans (2011): 'Anti-Semitism and the "Great Depression", 1873–1896'. In: Strauss, Herbert A. and Bergman, Werner (Eds.): *Hostages of Modernisation.* Berlin and Boston: De Gruyter, 19–28.
Rosenberg, Nathan (1965): 'Adam Smith on the Division of Labour: Two Views or One?' In: *Economica (New Series)* 32. No. 126, 127–139.
Rosenow, Eliyahu (1986): 'Nietzsche's Concept of Education'. In: Yovel, Yirmiyahu (Ed.): *Nietzsche as Affirmative Thinker.* Vol. XIII. Dordrecht: Martinus Nijhoff Philosophy Library and Springer, 119–131.
Rosenthal, Bernice Glatzer (2001): *New Myth, New World: From Nietzsche to Stalinism.* Philadelphia: Pennsylvania University Press.
Rosenthal, Bernice Glatzer, (Ed.) (2010): *Nietzsche and Soviet Culture: Ally and Adversary.* Cambridge: Cambridge University Press.
Rostow, Walt W. (1992): *Theorists of Economic Growth from David Hume to the Present with a Perspective on the Next Century.* Oxford: Oxford University Press.
Rothbart, Ron (1981): 'Science and Practice in Marx's Political Economy'. In: *Berkeley Journal of Sociology* 26: 41–55.
Rothermund, Dietmar (2014): 'War-Depression-War: The Fatal Sequence in a Global Perspective'. In: *Diplomatic History* 38. No. 4, 840–851.
Ruehl, Martin A. (2003): 'Politeia 1871: Nietzsche "Contra" Wagner on the Greek State'. In: *Bulletin of the Institute of Classical Studies*, Supplement No. 79, *Out of Arcadia: Classics and Politics in Germany in the Age of Burckhardt, Nietzsche and Wilamowitz.* Oxford: Oxford University Press, 61–86.
Ruehl, Martin A. (2004): 'Politeia 1871: Young Nietzsche on the Greek State'. In: Bishop, Paul: *Nietzsche and Antiquity: His Reaction and Response to the Classical Tradition.* Martlesham: Boydell & Brewer, 79–98.
Ruehl, Martin A. (2015): *The Italian Renaissance in the German Historical Imagination, 1860–1930.* Cambridge: Cambridge University Press
Ruehl, Martin A. (2018): 'In Defence of Slavery: Nietzsche's Dangerous Thinking'. In: *The Independent* (January 12th, 2018). https://www.independent.co.uk/a8138396.html, last accessed Feb. 27, 2023.
Ruskin, John (1928): *Time and Tide and Munera Pulveris.* London: Macmillan.
Ruskin John (1997): *Unto this Last and Other Writings.* Harmondsworth: Penguin.
Russell, Bertrand (1946): *History of Western Philosophy.* London: George Allen & Unwin.
Rutherford, Donald (2011): 'Freedom as a Philosophical Ideal: Nietzsche and His Antecedents'. In: *Inquiry* 54. No. 5, 512–540.
Sachs, Jeffrey D. (1995): 'Russia's Struggle with Stabilisation: Conceptual Issues and Evidence'. In: *The World Bank Economic Review* 8. No. 1, 57–80.
Safronov, Dmitri G. (2022): 'Nietzsche, Plato and Aristotle on Priests and Moneymakers'. In: *Nietzsche-Studien* 51. No. 1, 1–32. https://doi.org/10.1515/nietzstu-2021-0025, published online April 12, 2022; last accessed Feb. 27, 2023.
Salomon, Robert C. (1986): 'A More Severe Morality: Nietzsche's Affirmative Ethics'. In: Yovel, Yirmiyahu (Ed.): *Nietzsche as Affirmative Thinker.* Dordrecht: Martinus Nijhoff Publishers, 69–89.
Salter, William Mackintire (1917): *Nietzsche the Thinker: A Study.* London: Cecil Palmer & Hayward Oakley House.
Salter, William Mackintire (1917a): 'Nietzsche and the War'. In: *International Journal of Ethics* 27. No. 3, 357–379.

Sambursky, Shmuel (1956): *The Physical World of the Greeks*. London: Routledge and Keegan Paul.
Samuels, Warren J. (1977): 'The Political Economy of Adam Smith'. In: *Ethics* 87. No. 3, 189–207.
Samuels, Warren J. (2011): *Erasing the Invisible Hand: Essays on an Elusive and Misused Concept in Economics*. Cambridge: Cambridge University Press.
Sanchez-Vasquez, Adolfo (1973): *Art and Society: Essays in Marxist Aesthetics*. New York: Monthly Review Press.
Sarthou-Lajus, Nathalie (1997): *L'éthique de la Dette*. Paris: Presses Universitaires de France.
Scaff, Lawrence (1991): *Fleeing the Iron Cage: Culture, Politics and Modernity in the Thought of Max Weber*. Berkeley: University of California Press.
Schacht, Richard (1991): 'Hegel, Marx, Nietzsche, and the Future of Self-Alienation'. In: *American Philosophical Quarterly* 28. No. 2, 125–135.
Schacht, Richard (Ed.). (1994): *Nietzsche, Genealogy, Morality: Essays on Nietzsche's Genealogy of Morals*. Berkeley: University of California Press.
Schaff, Adam (1973): 'Marxist Theory on Revolution and Violence'. In: *Journal of the History of Ideas* 34. No. 2, 263–270.
Scheidel, Walter (2017): *The Great Leveller*. Princeton: Princeton University Press.
Schiff, Peter D. (2012): *The Real Crash*. New York: St. Martin's Press.
Schmeder, Geneviève and Boyer, Robert (1990): 'Division du Travail, Changement Technique et Croissance un Retour à Adam Smith'. In: *Revue française d'économie* 1, 125–194.
Schofield, Malcolm (2006): *Plato: Political Philosophy*. Oxford: Oxford University Press.
Schotten, C. Heike (2009): *Nietzsche's Revolution: Décadence, Politics, and Sexuality*. New York: Palgrave Macmillan.
Schragger, Richard C. (2012): 'Debt and Democracy'. In: *The Yale Law Journal* 121. No. 4, 860–886.
Schrift, Alan D. (1991): *Nietzsche and the Question of Interpretation*. New York: Routledge.
Schrift, Alan D. (1995): *Nietzsche's French Legacy: A Genealogy of Poststructuralism*. New York: Routledge.
Schrift, Alan D. (1996): 'Rethinking Exchange: Logics of the Gift in Cixous and Nietzsche'. In: *Philosophy Today* 40. No. 1, 197–205.
Schrift, Alan D. (Ed.) (1997): *The Logic of the Gift: Toward an Ethic of Generosity*. New York: Routledge.
Schrift, Alan D. (Ed.) (2000): *Why Nietzsche Still?* Berkeley: University of California Press.
Schrift, Alan D. (2013): 'Spinoza vs. Kant: Have I Been Understood?' In: Ansell-Pearson, Keith (Ed.): *Nietzsche and Political Thought*. London: Bloomsbury, 107–123.
Schumpeter, Joseph A. (1955): *Imperialism and Social Classes*. Heinz Norden (Trans.). Cleveland: The World Publishing Company.
Schumpeter, Joseph A. (1982): *The Theory of Economic Development*. Piscataway: Transaction Publishers.
Schumpeter, Joseph A. (2006): *History of Economic Analysis*. New York: Routledge.
Schumpeter, Joseph A. (2012): *Capitalism, Socialism and Democracy*. 2nd edition. Floyd: Wilder Publications.
Schumpeter, Joseph A. (2017): *Business Cycles: A Theoretical, Historical, and Statistical Analysis of the Capitalist Process*. Vols. I–II. Eastford: Martino Fine Books.
Seaford, Richard (2009): *Money and the Early Greek Mind*. Cambridge: Cambridge University Press.
Sedgwick, Peter R. (2005): 'Violence, Economy and Temporality: Plotting the Political Terrain of On the Genealogy of Morality'. In: *Nietzsche-Studien* 34, 163–185.
Sedgwick, Peter R. (2007): *Nietzsche's Economy*. Basingstoke: Palgrave Macmillan.
Sedgwick, Peter R. (2013): *Nietzsche's Justice*. Montreal-Kingston: McGill-Queen's University Press.
Sedlacek, Tomas (2013): *Economics of Good and Evil*. New York: Oxford University Press.
Sergi, Bruno S. (2011): *Misinterpreting Modern Russia: Western Views of Putin and His Presidency*. London: Bloomsbury Publishing.
Shapiro, Gary (1991): *Alcyone: Nietzsche on Gifts, Noise, and Women*. Albany: SUNY Press.
Shapiro, Gary (1994): 'Debts Due and Overdue: Beginnings of Philosophy in Nietzsche, Heidegger, and Anaximander'. In: Schacht, Richard (Ed.): *Nietzsche, Genealogy, Morality*. Berkeley: University of California Press, 358–375.

Shapiro, Gary (1997): 'The Metaphysics of Presents Nietzsche's Gift, the Debt to Emmerson, Heidegger's Values'. https://issuu.com/urscholarship/docs/the_metaphysics_of_presents-_nietzs, last accessed Feb. 27, 2023.
Shapiro, Gary (2016): *Nietzsche's Earth: Great Events, Great Politics*. Chicago: University of Chicago Press.
Sharlin, Harold Issadore (1979): *Lord Kelvin: The Dynamic Victorian*. Pennsylvania: Pennsylvania State University Press.
Sharma, Soumitra (2020): 'The Death of Political Economy: A Retrospective Overview of Economic Thought'. In: *Economic Research—Ekonomska Istraživanja*, 33. No. 1, 1750–1766.
Shaw, Tamsin (2007): *Nietzsche's Political Skepticism*. Princeton: Princeton University Press.
Shaw, Tamsin (2014): 'The "Last Man" Problem: Nietzsche and Weber on Political Attitudes to Suffering'. In: Knoll, Manuel and Stocker, Barry (Eds.): *Nietzsche as Political Philosopher*. Berlin and Boston: De Gruyter, 345–380.
Sher, Richard B. (1989): 'Adam Ferguson, Adam Smith, and the Problem of National Defense'. In: *The Journal of Modern History* 61. No. 2, 240–268.
Siemens, Herman W. (2009): 'Nietzsche's Critique of Democracy (1870–1886)'. In: *The Journal of Nietzsche Studies* 38: 20–37.
Siemens, Herman W. (2013): 'Reassessing Radical Democratic Theory in the Light of Nietzsche's Ontology of Conflict'. In: Ansell-Pearson, Keith (Ed.): *Nietzsche and Political Thought*. London: Bloomsbury Academic, 83–107.
Siemens, Herman W. and Roodt, Vasti (Eds.) (2008): *Nietzsche, Power and Politics: Rethinking Nietzsche's Legacy for Political Thought*. Berlin and Boston: De Gruyter.
Sigad, Ran (1986): 'The Socratic Nietzsche'. In: Yovel, Yirmiyahu (Ed.): *Nietzsche as Affirmative Thinker*. Dordrecht: Martinus Nijhoff Publishers, 109–118.
Simpson, Sid (2021): 'Nietzsche, irrationalism, and the cruel irony of Adorno and Horkheimer's political quietude'. In: *Contemporary Political Theory* 20, 481–501.
Singh, Rustam (1989): 'Status of Violence in Marx's Theory of Revolution'. In: *Economic and Political Weekly* 24. No. 4, PE9–PE20.
Sjöholm, Cecilia (2015): *Doing Aesthetics with Arendt: How to See Things*. New York: Columbia University Press.
Skidelsky, Robert (2000): 'What's Left of Marx?' In: *The New York Review of Books* 16, 1–11.
Sleinis, Edgar E. (1994): *Nietzsche's Revaluation of Values: A Study in Strategies*. Champaign: University of Illinois Press.
Sloterdijk, Peter (1987): *Critique of Cynical Reason*. Michael Eldred (Trans.). Minneapolis and London: University of Minnesota Press.
Sloterdijk, Peter (1989): *Thinker on Stage: Nietzsche's Materialism*. Jamie Owen Daniel (Trans.). Minneapolis: University of Minnesota Press.
Sloterdijk, Peter (2013): *Nietzsche Apostle*. Steven Corcoran (Trans.). Los Angeles: Semiotext(e).
Sloterdijk, Peter (2013a): *In the World Interior of Capital*. Cambridge: Polity Press.
Small, Robin (2003): *Paul Rée: Basic Writings*. Champaign: University of Illinois Press.
Small, Robin (2006): 'Nietzsche and Cosmology'. In: Ansell-Pearson, Keith and Small, Robin (Eds.): *A Companion To Nietzsche*. Oxford: Wiley-Blackwell, 189–208.
Small, Robin (2007): *Nietzsche and Rée: A Star Friendship*. Oxford: Oxford University Press.
Small, Robin (2010): *Time and Becoming in Nietzsche's Thought*. London and New York: Continuum.
Small, Robin (2017): *Nietzsche in Context*. London: Routledge.
Smith, Craig (2020): *Adam Smith*. Cambridge and Medford: Polity Press.
Smith, David (2004): 'Nietzsche's Hinduism, Nietzsche's India: Another Look'. In: *The Journal of Nietzsche Studies* 28: 37–56.
Smith, Woodruff D. (1991): *Politics and the Sciences of Culture in Germany, 1840–1920*. New York and Oxford: Oxford University Press.

Soddy, Frederick (1926): *Wealth, Virtual Wealth and Debt: The Solution of the Economic Paradox.* London: George Allen & Unwin.

Solms-Laubach, Franz zu (2012): *Nietzsche and Early German and Austrian Sociology.* Berlin and Boston: De Gruyter.

Spengler, Oswald (1918): *The Decline of the West: Form and Actuality.* Vol. I. Charles Francis Atkinson (Trans.). London: George Allen & Unwin.

Springborg, Patricia (1984): 'Aristotle and the Problem of Needs'. In: History of Political Thought 5. No. 3, 393–424.

Stack, George J. (1983): *Lange and Nietzsche.* New York: De Gruyter.

Stack, George J. (2005): *Nietzsche's Anthropic Circle: Man, Science, and Myth.* Rochester: University of Rochester.

Stanley, John L. (1997, 1998): 'Marx's Critique of Hegel's Philosophy of Nature'. In: *Science & Society* 61. No. 4, 449–473.

Staten, Henry (1989): 'The Problem of Nietzsche's Economy'. In: *Representations* 27: 66–91.

Staten, Henry (1990): *Nietzsche's Voice.* Ithaca: Cornell University Press.

Stedman-Jones, Gareth (2018): 'Karl Marx's changing picture of the end of capitalism'. In: *Journal of the British Academy* 6, 187–206.

Stegmaier, Werner (2016): 'Nietzsche's Orientation toward the Future'. Reinhard Müller (Trans.). In: *Journal of Nietzsche Studies* 47. No. 3, 384–401.

Steinbuch, Thomas (1994): *A Commentary on Nietzsche's Ecce Homo.* Lanham: University Press of America.

Stern, Fritz (1970): 'Money, Morals, and the Pillars of Bismarck's Society'. In: *Central European History* 3: 49–72.

Stern, Fritz (1972, 1977): *Gold and Iron: Bismarck, Bleichröder, and the Building of the German Empire.* New York: Alfred A. Knopf.

Stewart, Dugald (1980): 'Account of the Life and Writings of Adam Smith'. Ian S. Ross (Ed.). In: Wightman, William P. D. and Bryce, John C. (Eds.): *Adam Smith, Essays on Philosophical Subjects.* Oxford: Oxford University Press, 266–332.

Stewart, Herbert Leslie (1915): *Nietzsche and the Ideals of Modern Germany.* London: Edward Arnold.

Stiegler, Bernard (2011): *The Decadence of Industrial Democracies: Disbelief and Discredit.* Vol. I. Daniel Ross and Suzanne Arnold (Trans.). Cambridge and Malden: Polity Press.

Stiegler, Bernard (2019): *The Age of Disruption.* Daniel Ross (Trans.). Cambridge: Polity Press.

Stocker, Barry (1997): 'Liberalism after Nietzsche and Weber'. In: *Journal of the Theoretical Humanities* 2. No. 2, 129–140.

Strauss, Leo (1998): *Xenophon's Socratic Discourse: An Interpretation of the Oeconomicus.* South Bend: St. Augustine's Press.

Streeck, Wolfgang (2009): *Re-forming Capitalism: Institutional Change in the German Political Economy.* Oxford: Oxford University Press.

Streeck, Wolfgang (2014): *Buying Time: The Delayed Crisis of Democratic Capitalism.* Patrick Camiller and David Fernbach (Trans.). London and New York: Verso Books.

Streeck, Wolfgang (2016): *How Will Capitalism End?* New York: Verso Books.

Strong, Tracy B. (1992): *Friedrich Nietzsche and the Politics of Transfiguration.* Berkeley: University of California Press.

Strong, Tracy B. (2008): *Nietzsche and Politics.* Surrey: Ashgate.

Strong Tracy B. (Ed.). (2009): *Friedrich Nietzsche.* Surrey: Ashgate.

Sutherland, Thomas (2014): '"The Monument to a Crisis": Nietzsche and the Industrialization of Creativity'. In: *Third Text* 28. No. 6, 545–554.

Tabak, Mehmet (2012): *Dialectics of Human Nature in Marx's Philosophy.* New York: Palgrave Macmillan.

Talay, Zeynep (2011): 'A Dialogue with Nietzsche: Blumenberg and Löwith on History and Progress'. In: *History of European Ideas* 37, 376–381.

Tassone, Giuseppe (2002): *A Study on the Idea of Progress in Nietzsche, Heidegger, and Critical Theory*. Lampeter: Edwin Mellon Press.
Tattersall, Mason (2014): 'Thermal Degeneration: Thermodynamics and the Heat-Death of the Universe in Victorian Science, Philosophy, and Culture'. In: Härmänmaa, Marja and Nissen, Christopher (Eds.): *Decadence, Degeneration, and the End: Studies in the European Fin de Siècle*. New York: Palgrave Macmillan, 17–35.
Taylor, Overton H. (1929): 'Economics and the Idea of Natural Laws'. In: *The Quarterly Journal of Economics* 44. No. 1, 1–39.
Terpstra, Marin (2000): 'Social Gifts and the Gift of Sociality: Some Thoughts on Mauss' Gift and Hobbes' Leviathan'. In: Vandevelde, Antoon (Ed.): *Gifts and Interests*. Leuven: Peeters.
Thiele, Leslie Paul (1990): 'The Agony of Politics: The Nietzschean Roots of Foucault's Thought'. In: *American Political Science Review* 84. No. 3, 907–925.
Thorgeirsdottir, Sigridur (2016): 'Nietzsche's philosophy of guilt/s as a transforming critique of Debt economy of the present'. In: Heit, Helmut and Thorgeirsdottir, Sigridur (Eds.): *Nietzsche als Kritiker und Denker der Transformation*. Berlin and Boston: De Gruyter, 189–206.
Titchener, Edward B. (1914): 'A Note on Sensation and Sentiment'. In: *The American Journal of Psychology* 25. No. 2, 301–307.
Tomich, Dale W. (Ed.) (2016): *New Frontiers of Slavery*. Albany: SUNY Press.
Tooze, Adam (2006): *The Wages of Destruction*. London: Penguin Books.
Tooze, Adam (2014): *The Deluge: The Great War and the Remaking of Global Order 1916–1931*. New York: Viking.
Tooze, Adam (2018): *Crashed: How a Decade of Financial Crises Changed the World*. New York: Viking.
Trever, Albert Augustus (1916): *A History of Greek Economic Thought*. Chicago: University of Chicago Press.
Tribe, Keith (2008): '"Das Adam Smith Problem" and the Origins of Modern Smith Scholarship'. In: *History of European Ideas* 34. No. 4, 514–525.
Tribe, Keith (2015): *The Economy of the Word: Language, History, and Economics*. Oxford: Oxford University Press.
Tucker, Robert C. (Ed.) (1978): *The Marx-Engels Reader*. New York: Norton.
Tuncel, Yunus (2013): *Agon in Nietzsche*. Ashland: Marquette University Press.
Vaihinger, Hans (1922): *Die Philosophie des Als Ob*. Leipzig: Felix Meiner.
Varoufakis, Yanis (2013): *Talking to My Daughter About the Economy: A Brief History of Capitalism*. London: The Bodley Head.
Varoufakis, Yanis (2017): *Adults in the Room*. London: Vintage.
Vattimo, Gianni (2003): *Nihilism and Emancipation*. New York: Columbia University Press.
Victor, Peter A. (2019): *Managing without Growth—Slower by Design, Not Disaster*. 2nd ed. Cheltenham: Edward Elgar.
Vincent-Lancrin, Stéphan (2003): 'Adam Smith and the Division of Labour: Is There a Difference between Organisation and Market?' In: *Cambridge Journal of Economics* 27. No. 2, 209–224.
Viner, Jacob (1972): *The Role of Providence in the Social Order: An Essay in Intellectual History*. Princeton: Princeton University Press.
Voegelin, Eric (1944): 'Nietzsche, the Crisis and the War'. In: *The Journal of Politics* 6. No. 2, 177–212.
Volker, Gerhard (1998): 'Experimental Philosophy: An Attempt at a Reconstruction'. In: Conway, Daniel W. and Goff, Peter S. (Eds.): *Nietzsche: Critical Assessments*. Vol. III. London: Routledge.
Wacholder, Ben Zion (1989): 'Josephus and Nicolaus of Damascus'. In: Feldman, Louis H. and Hata, Gohei (Eds.) (1989): *Josephus, the Bible and History*. Detroit: Wayne State University Press, 147–173.
Waite, Geoff (1996): *Nietzsche's Corps/e: Aesthetics, Politics, Prophecy, or, The Spectacular Technoculture of Everyday Life*. Durham and London: Duke University Press.
Wallace, R. Jay (2007): 'Ressentiment, Value and Vindication: Making Sense of Nietzsche's Slave Revolt'. In: Leiter, Brian and Sinhababu, Neil (Eds.): *Nietzsche and Morality*. Oxford: Oxford University Press, 110–138.

Wallat, Hendrik (2009): *Das Bewusstsein der Krise*. Bielefeld: Transcript.
Walraevens, Benoît (2010): 'Adam Smith's Economics and the "Lectures on Rhetoric and Belles Lettres": The Language of Commerce'. In: *History of Economic Ideas* 18. No. 1, 11–32.
Warren, Mark (1988): *Nietzsche and Political Thought*. Cambridge: MIT Press.
Weber, Marianne (1988): *Max Weber: A Biography*. Harry Zohn (Trans.). Piscataway: Transaction.
Weil, Simone (1958): *Oppression And Liberty*. Arthur Wills and John Petrie (Trans.). Abingdon: Routledge & Keegan Paul.
Weingast, Barry R. and Wittman, Donald A. (2006): *The Oxford Handbook of Political Economy*. Oxford: Oxford University Press.
Wells, Thomas and Graafland, Johan (2012): 'Adam Smith's Bourgeois Virtues in Competition'. In: *Business Ethics Quarterly* 22. No. 2, 319–350.
Werhane, Patricia H. (2000): 'Business Ethics and the Origins of Contemporary Capitalism: Economics and Ethics in the Work of Adam Smith and Herbert Spencer'. In: *Journal of Business Ethics* 24. No. 3, 185–198.
Werner, Richard A. (2014): 'Can Banks Individually Create Money out of Nothing? The Theories and the Empirical Evidence'. In: *International Review of Financial Analysis* 36: 1–19.
Werner, Richard (2014a): 'How Do Banks Create Money, and Why Can Other Firms Not Do the Same? An Explanation for the Coexistence of Lending and Deposit-taking'. In: *International Review of Financial Analysis* 36, 71–77.
Werner Richard (2016): 'A Lost Century in Economics: Three Theories of Banking and the Conclusive Evidence'. In: *International Review of Financial Analysis* 46: 361–379.
Westfall, Joseph (2018): 'Foucault, Nietzsche, and the Promise-Threat of Philology'. In: *Philosophy and Social Criticism* 44. No. 1, 24–40.
Westfall, Richard S. (1971): *Force in Newton's Physics*. London: Macdonald.
Westfall, Richard S. (1980): *Never at Rest: A Biography of Isaac Newton*. Cambridge: Cambridge University Press.
White, Daniel R. and Hellerich, Gert (1999): 'The Liberty Bell: Nietzsche's Philosophy of Culture'. In: *The Journal of Nietzsche Studies* 18: 1–54.
White, Richard (1998): 'The Return of the Master: An Interpretation of Nietzsche's "Genealogy of Morals"'. In: *Philosophy and Phenomenological Research* 48. No. 4, 683–696.
Whitrow, Gerald J. (1971): 'The Laws of Motion'. In: *The British Journal for the History of Science* 5. No. 19, 217–234.
Wickham, Sophie, Bentley, Lee, Rose, Tanith, Whitehead, Margaret, Taylor-Robinson, David, and Barr, Ben (2020): 'Effects on Mental Health of a UK Welfare Reform, Universal Credit: A Longitudinal Controlled Study'. In: *Lancet Public Health*, 5. No. 3, e157–e164.
Wiedemann, Thomas (1980): *Greek and Roman Slavery: A Sourcebook*. London: Routledge.
Wilkerson, Dale (2006): *Nietzsche and the Greeks*. London and New York: Continuum.
Williams, Bernard (1993): *Shame and Necessity*. Berkeley: University of California Press.
Williams, Eric Eustace (1944): *Capitalism and Slavery*. Chapel Hill: The University of North Carolina Press.
Williams, Robert R. (2012): *Tragedy, Recognition and the Death of God*. Oxford: Oxford University Press.
Williams, William D. (1952): *Nietzsche and the French: A Study of the Influence of Nietzsche's French Reading on His Thought and Writing*. Oxford: Basil Blackwell.
Williamson, George S. (2004): *The Longing for Myth in Germany: Religion and Aesthetic Culture from Romanticism to Nietzsche*. Chicago: University of Chicago Press.
Wilson, Charles H. (1966): 'Thucydides, Isocrates, and the Athenian Empire'. In: *Greece & Rome* 13. No. 1, 54–63.
Wilson, David and Dixon, William (2006): '"Das Adam Smith Problem"—A Critical Realist Perspective'. In: *Journal of Critical Realism* 5. No. 2, 251–272.
Wilson, David and Dixon, William (2009): '"Sympathy", "Character" and Economic Equilibrium'. In: Mosini, Valeria (Ed.): *Equilibrium in Economics*. London: Routledge.

Wilson, David and Dixon, William (2014): 'Political Economy and the Social Disciplines: The Modern Life of "Das Adam Smith Problem"'. In: *Cambridge Journal of Economics* 38. No. 3, 623–641.
Winkler, Rafael (2007): 'I Owe You: Nietzsche, Mauss'. In: *Journal of the British Society for Phenomenology* 38. No. 1, 90–108.
Wittgenstein, Ludwig (1978): *Culture and Value.* Peter Winch (Trans.). Oxford: Wiley-Blackwell.
Wolowski, L. (1878): 'Preliminary Essay on the Application of the Historical Method to the Study of Political Economy'. In: Roscher, William: *Principles of Political Economy.* Vol. I. John J. Lalor (Trans.). New York: Henry Holt & Co., 1–48.
Wood, Allen W. (2014): *The Free Development of Each: Studies on Freedom, Right and Ethics in Classical German Philosophy.* Oxford: Oxford University Press.
Worland, Stephen T. (1976): 'Mechanistic Analogy and Smith On Exchange'. In: *Review of Social Economy* 34. No. 3, 245–257.
Worth, Sarah (2000): 'Aristotle, Thought, and Mimesis: Our Responses to Fiction'. In: *The Journal of Aesthetics and Art Criticism* 58. No. 4, 333–339.
Wright, David P. (2009): *Inventing God's Law.* Oxford: Oxford University Press.
Yack, Bernard (1986): *The Longing for Total Revolution: Philosophic Sources of Social Discontent from Rousseau to Marx and Nietzsche.* Princeton: Princeton University Press.
Yamamori, Toru (2017): 'The Concept of Need in Adam Smith'. In: *Cambridge Journal of Economics* 41, 327–347.
Young, Julian (2010): *Friedrich Nietzsche: A Philosophical Biography.* Cambridge: Cambridge University Press.
Young, Julian (Ed.) (2015): *Individual and Community in Nietzsche's Philosophy.* New York: Cambridge University Press.
Yovel, Yirmiyahu (Ed.) (1986): *Nietzsche as Affirmative Thinker.* Dordrecht: Martinus Nijhoff Publishers.
Zimmermann, Rolf (2014): 'The "Will to Power": Towards a Nietzschean Systematics of Moral-Political Divergence in History in Light of the 20th Century'. In: Knoll, Manuel and Stocker, Barry (Eds.): *Nietzsche as Political Philosopher.* Berlin and Boston: De Gruyter, 39–59.
Zucker, Stanley (1975): *Ludwig Bamberger: German Liberal Politician and Social Critic, 1823–1899.* Pittsburgh: University of Pittsburgh Press.
Zuckert, Catherine (1996): *Postmodern Platos: Nietzsche, Heidegger, Gadamer, Strauss, Derrida.* Chicago: University of Chicago Press.
Zumbrunnen, John (2002): Democratic Politics and the 'Character' of the City in Thucydides'. In: *History of Political Thought* 23. No. 4, 565–589.

Index

Abolition 7, 110, 114, 129, 133 f., 136 f., 142, 150, 154, 173 – 179, 186, 272, 279
Aesthetic sensibility 284, 286 f., 289, 291 – 294
Agency 6, 28, 32, 48, 51, 61, 80 f., 91, 95, 105, 111, 121 – 123, 133, 136 f., 167, 199, 226, 229, 242, 247, 259, 261, 269, 274, 279 f., 284, 297
Agon(ism) 24, 46, 121, 150, 229, 242
Alienation 108 f., 111, 114, 128 f., 132 f., 135
America (United States of America) 57, 175, 177 – 179, 186, 200, 207, 215, 224, 233, 238, 243, 262 – 266, 273, 281
Aptitude 44, 66 f., 86 – 88, 165, 188, 260
Archimedes 124
Aristotle 1, 4, 27, 29, 66, 75, 86, 95, 106, 123 f., 154, 158 – 160, 163 f., 193 – 196, 204, 236, 277 f., 280
Artificial Intelligence ('AI') 278
Ascetic priest 46, 108, 117, 145, 170 – 172, 245

Bagehot, Walter 57, 158
Banking 224, 230, 239, 242 – 244, 246 – 248
Bauer, Bruno 117 – 119
Britain (British Empire, England) 57, 70, 179
Bulgakov, Mikhail 172, 263

Capital 2, 25, 52, 76, 90, 100 f., 107 – 109, 111 f., 115, 124, 126 f., 129 f., 132 f., 139, 141, 150 f., 179 f., 185, 190 – 192, 202, 204, 207 – 209, 213, 218, 220, 223, 235, 243, 251, 256, 267 f., 270, 273 – 276, 289 f., 296
Capitalism 1, 3, 6, 16, 21, 23 – 26, 29, 40, 48 – 50, 89 f., 99 – 102, 104, 107 f., 110 – 115, 117, 121 f., 125, 127 f., 130, 132, 134, 136 – 138, 144, 146 – 148, 150 f., 154 f., 163, 177 – 180, 182, 186 f., 206, 221, 224 f., 229, 231, 233, 244, 248, 264, 266, 269 f.
Carlyle, Thomas 102, 182 f., 232
Catastrophe 35, 51, 227
Christianity 18, 36 f., 44, 53, 73, 82 f., 103, 118, 121 f., 125, 130, 142 f., 150 f., 157, 163, 174 f., 210, 212, 231 – 233, 237, 239 f.
Clausius, Rudolf 80
Commodity 48, 84, 94, 100, 114, 132, 139, 141, 150, 182, 277
Conflict 7, 35, 51, 62, 113, 128, 141, 195, 228, 254, 260 – 262, 266, 269, 273, 288, 293
Conservation of energy 8, 52, 81, 287 f.
Corruption 39, 45, 59, 226 – 228, 237 f., 249

Crisis, of: 1 f., 4, 7, 19, 21, 25 f., 33, 35, 39, 51 – 54, 98, 100 f., 181, 183, 193 f., 207, 209, 213 f., 221 – 230, 237, 239, 244, 249, 255, 259 f., 269 – 271, 275, 278 – 280, 282 f., 295, 297
– 2008 1, 19 – 21, 33, 50, 60 f., 111, 117, 146, 190 f., 206 f., 209 f., 213, 220 f., 224 f., 230, 233, 236 – 238, 242 – 245, 248 f., 255 – 257, 259 f., 266, 269, 271, 288
– Financial 19, 22, 25, 30, 33, 37, 48, 100, 160, 165, 179, 183, 186 – 188, 191 f., 202, 206 f., 211 – 217, 221 f., 225 f., 229 f., 234, 237, 243 – 246, 248, 259, 271, 273, 291, 295
– Industrial culture 2, 5, 18, 21 f., 29, 39, 48, 51 – 53, 143, 153 f., 165, 177, 180 – 182, 185 f., 192, 194, 199 f., 209, 217, 231, 247 f., 256, 260, 268, 271 – 273, 275, 277, 279 f., 282 – 284, 288, 290 f.
– Modernity 2 – 5, 7, 18 f., 22, 25, 27, 29 f., 33, 36, 38 – 40, 42, 47 f., 50 – 53, 59, 65, 75, 81, 84, 99, 101, 104, 106 – 108, 112, 115, 117, 124, 132, 143 – 146, 148, 150, 154, 163, 170, 175 f., 178, 180 f., 183, 186, 190 – 192, 194, 196, 209, 213, 220, 225, 230, 238, 244, 248, 254, 259, 261 f., 270, 272, 283, 285, 297
– Political economy 1 – 5, 7, 9 – 16, 19 f., 23 – 33, 35 – 38, 40, 42, 44, 48, 50, 52 f., 55 – 58, 60, 62 f., 65, 69, 71 – 76, 78 – 81, 83, 88, 95, 97 – 99, 101 f., 104, 106 – 110, 112 – 118, 120, 122 – 124, 127 f., 131 – 133, 136 f., 141 – 143, 145 f., 148 – 150, 153, 157, 160, 162, 170 f., 173, 176, 178, 185, 189 f., 192 – 194, 196, 207, 209 f., 213, 217 – 220, 222 – 226, 229 – 231, 233, 244, 246, 248, 254, 257, 259 – 261, 263 – 267, 269 – 277, 279 f., 282 – 285, 287 f., 290 – 293, 295 – 297
– Values 1 – 3, 5, 7 f., 11, 17 – 19, 25, 32, 37, 39 – 42, 44 f., 47, 50 – 53, 65, 69, 71 f., 75, 82 f., 88, 93, 102, 104, 111 – 113, 115 f., 122 – 124, 129 f., 135 – 139, 144, 146 – 149, 151, 161, 163 – 165, 167 – 171, 174, 184, 187 f., 191 f., 194 f., 197 f., 200, 206, 209, 229, 231, 233 – 235, 246, 248, 254, 257 – 260, 264, 266, 268 – 270, 272 f., 275, 279 – 281, 283 – 285, 293 – 296, 298
Culture: 162
– Commercial 5 f., 18, 23, 29, 59 – 61, 64 – 66, 70 – 73, 78, 82 – 86, 90, 92 f., 95 f., 108, 139, 161, 166, 170, 173, 182, 184, 192, 195, 226, 228, 232 f., 238, 250, 261, 263

– Industrial 1, 18, 21f., 25, 35, 48, 60, 64f., 67f., 71, 81, 101, 107, 126, 173, 180f., 190–194, 213, 221, 224f., 231, 238, 243, 248, 252–254, 259f., 266–268, 276f.

Death of God 35f., 111, 144, 156, 174, 213
Debt 2–4, 14, 18f., 21f., 25f., 33, 40, 43, 46, 57, 78, 100, 108, 110–112, 141, 147, 151, 154, 156, 170, 181f., 186f., 190–193, 195–215, 217–222, 224f., 230–249, 251, 254–258, 265–268, 270–276, 279f., 289–291, 295–297
Democracy 6, 21, 23, 31, 48, 54, 110, 143f., 155, 182, 192, 194, 196, 230–242, 260, 264f., 268, 274f., 281
Development 2f., 5, 12, 14, 16, 19, 28, 30, 34, 38f., 44, 54, 58, 60, 64f., 70, 78, 84f., 89f., 96, 102, 106, 108–110, 113, 116, 123, 127, 132, 134, 139, 141, 144–147, 153f., 156–161, 163, 170, 178–180, 186, 188, 190, 196, 199, 203–205, 208–210, 213, 215, 218, 224, 227, 232, 237, 240–242, 247–250, 252–254, 258, 260, 263, 267f., 270, 274–278, 281, 284, 287, 290–293, 295
Division of labour 2–4, 14, 18f., 22, 33, 40, 56–73, 77–79, 81–94, 96, 109f., 126f., 133, 148, 153, 156, 271f., 276–279
Dostoyevsky, Fyodor 213f., 220
Drochon, Hugo 1, 15f., 20, 25, 27, 50f., 54, 66, 94f., 153, 160, 188f., 194, 199, 231f., 261–265, 283

Economics 12, 18, 20, 22, 25, 27–29, 33, 35f., 38, 73f., 76f., 96, 105, 155, 158, 161, 191, 221, 225, 248, 279, 285, 291, 296
Emancipation 26, 109f., 115, 118, 124f., 132, 135, 143, 146, 150–152, 173, 177, 187f., 279
Enhancement 12, 19, 22f., 59, 73, 86, 93, 95, 97, 134, 154, 158f., 184, 188, 240, 253, 270, 278, 286–288, 290
Enlightenment 18, 69, 123, 178, 227, 251
Entropy 8, 49, 52, 80–82, 257f., 267, 277, 280, 287, 289, 292
Environment 42, 45, 192, 198, 249, 268, 275, 290
Epictetus 136, 162f., 169f., 183, 212
Equality 3, 6, 25, 32, 48f., 64, 68f., 78–80, 83–85, 100, 109, 112, 114, 119, 121, 130, 133, 138, 142–146, 149–151, 166, 168, 177, 180, 187, 194, 217, 231–233, 236, 240
Equilibrium 9, 76, 79f., 82, 85
Essenes 86, 117–121, 131, 133, 136, 141, 150, 152
Eternal return (recurrence) 5, 25, 72, 287

Excess 28, 67, 85, 96, 100, 136f., 191, 194f., 199, 205–207, 211, 229, 240, 242–246, 250, 256, 264, 277f., 290
Exchange 22, 48, 62, 66–69, 77, 83–85, 88f., 100, 107f., 111f., 116f., 119, 126, 132f., 138–142, 147, 150, 161, 170, 178, 196, 200, 204, 206, 210, 216, 223f., 226, 233, 243f., 246, 277, 280
Exploitation 20, 24, 43, 49, 89f., 100f., 107, 115f., 125, 128, 146, 153–155, 159, 161f., 166, 170, 177f., 181, 184, 186–189, 199, 216f., 228f., 247, 258, 272, 276f.

Faust 243, 263
Fellowship 90, 131, 165
Five Grades 164
France 224, 243
Franco-Prussian war 226
Freud, Sigmund 43

Geisterkrieg 6–8
Genealogy of values 22, 73, 150
Geopolitics 259, 263, 266
Germany 26, 29, 104, 183, 222, 224–227, 243f., 246, 249, 261–263, 265f.
Goethe, Johann Wolfgang von 103, 130, 243f.
Great Depression, 1929 224f.
Great Recession, 2008 1, 225, 237, 249, 266
Great War 1, 259
Growth (economic) 5, 19, 38, 49, 59f., 65, 67f., 70, 77, 84f., 89–91, 93f., 96, 101, 129, 136, 160, 172, 192f., 195f., 204, 208–210, 221, 224, 230f., 235, 243, 245, 248–258, 266–270, 273–276, 289, 292f., 295
Gründerkrach, 1873 2, 26, 136, 223f., 227f., 238, 249, 261, 271

Hegel, Georg Wilhelm 51, 105, 114, 163, 173f., 283
Heraclitus 124f.
Hesiod 7, 46f., 81f.
Hierarchy 4, 43, 46, 67, 119, 121, 125, 131, 136, 153, 158, 163f., 185, 197, 204, 250, 276
Hobbes, Thomas 49, 265
Homer 32, 193
Hume, David 67, 123, 177

Ideology 36, 39, 58, 107f., 123, 126–128, 132f., 135, 178, 221, 238, 294
Industriousness 25, 64f., 109, 156f., 181, 192, 247f., 260

Inequality 19, 24, 28, 83, 99, 125, 131, 133, 138 – 143, 149 f., 153, 160, 165 f., 187 f.
Inertia 31, 66, 84, 135, 269
Inflation 100, 212, 295
Instrumental (rationality, reason) 70, 108, 128, 147 f., 152, 191, 285, 291
Inversion 3, 14, 46 f., 58, 69, 97, 111, 126, 128 f., 134 f., 140, 151, 174 f., 194
Iron cage 122, 148, 152

Jew (Jews, Jewish) 151, 211, 246, 265
Josephus, Flavius 86, 118 – 120, 131
Judeo-Christianity 18, 170, 173 f., 190, 235

Kelvin, Lord 80

Lange, Friedrich 36, 57, 75 f.
Last man/men 8 – 9, 51 f., 54, 94, 148, 172, 184 – 85
Leadership 1, 19, 153, 159, 171, 183, 193, 242
Lemm, Vanessa 18, 90, 162, 203, 261
Lenin, Vladimir 103, 139, 144 f.
Liberalism 21, 23, 28, 36, 105, 134 f., 182, 227, 229 f., 232, 238, 260
Locke, John 265
Long Depression 1 f., 25, 35, 222 – 225, 231, 237, 249, 260, 266, 271
Löwith, Karl 17, 20, 37, 60, 67, 103, 108, 112 – 114, 117 f., 124, 128, 132, 148, 156, 173, 262, 266

Marx, Karl 2, 6, 23, 26, 28 – 30, 33, 35, 37, 48, 58, 62, 67, 89, 99 – 135, 137 – 152, 156, 160, 170, 173 f., 180, 182 f., 192, 202, 211, 216, 221 f., 234, 238, 244, 256, 271 f., 278, 283 f., 292
Materialism 28 f., 57, 76, 85, 110, 131, 133
Mathematics 28, 33 f., 36, 255
Mental health 43, 154, 157, 181, 192, 278 f., 295 f.
Methodenstreit 28
Mill, John Stuart 57, 96, 106 f., 185
Moderation 160, 195, 208 f., 225, 248, 266, 275, 289 f.
Modernity 2 – 5, 7, 18 f., 22, 25, 27, 29 f., 33, 36, 38 – 40, 42, 47 f., 50 – 53, 59, 65, 75, 81, 84, 99, 101, 104, 106 – 108, 112, 115, 117, 124, 132, 143 – 146, 148, 150, 154, 163, 170, 175 f., 178, 180 f., 183, 186, 190 – 192, 194, 196, 209, 213, 220, 225, 230, 238, 244, 248, 254, 259, 261 f., 270, 272, 283, 285, 297
Moneymakers 193 f., 210, 229, 237, 275

Moneymaking 190, 247
Myth 81, 238, 257, 266 f., 294

Nature 8, 11, 14 – 16, 22, 24 f., 28, 36 f., 44 f., 47, 49, 51, 56 f., 59 – 68, 70, 74 – 77, 83, 87, 94, 99, 101, 105, 107 – 109, 114, 122 f., 125, 127 f., 130, 132 – 135, 141 f., 146, 153, 158, 160 f., 164 – 166, 168 f., 175 – 177, 183, 186 f., 189, 191 f., 196, 198, 202, 204, 208, 213, 220, 222, 228, 231, 234, 239, 242, 251, 257, 259, 265, 268, 274, 278, 284, 288 – 292, 294
Newton, Isaac 74, 77, 103
Nihilism 9, 32, 51 – 53, 65, 73, 101, 108, 111, 148, 176, 187, 219, 260, 281, 283, 287, 291

Oikonomia 29, 157 f., 253, 286
Oikos 68, 119 f., 141, 157 – 161, 170, 286
Order of rank 88, 119, 121, 125, 160, 163, 212, 227, 250 f., 286, 292
Ouroboros(ic) 7, 8, 38, 185
Overman (Übermensch) 23, 54

Pathos of distance 39, 46, 163, 199
Philo 86, 118 f., 124 f., 131, 133
Physics 63, 74, 77, 158, 203, 255
Physiology 7, 40, 44, 62, 83, 87, 110, 142, 166 f., 169, 249 f., 275, 294
Plato 1, 4, 12, 14, 27, 29, 42 f., 66, 68, 75, 95, 123, 136, 154, 159, 193 – 196, 236, 238, 242, 244, 280
Polis 4, 12, 67, 120, 194 f., 285
Praxis 9, 75, 86, 101 f., 105 f., 114, 124, 221
Prometheus 81, 198
Promised Land 82, 84, 94, 254, 258, 296
Property 20, 25, 100 f., 106 f., 110, 112 – 114, 116, 119 – 122, 124, 126 f., 129 – 137, 141 – 143, 146, 149 – 151, 154, 173 f., 190, 218, 220, 236, 238, 251, 253, 289
Psyche 31, 34, 43, 65, 83, 112, 117, 132, 149, 167, 174, 212, 218, 227

Railroads (railways) 223, 243, 249
Religion 14, 33, 63, 92 f., 102, 108, 112, 114, 121 f., 125 – 127, 129, 142 – 144, 147, 155, 157, 167, 188, 212, 216, 228, 232, 245, 258
Responsibility 21, 32, 67, 69, 86, 89, 95, 110, 159, 161, 164 f., 210, 213 – 215, 221, 226, 229, 247, 257, 262, 273, 286, 289
Ressentiment 37, 43, 49, 97, 136, 145, 151, 168, 171, 211, 230, 264

Revaluation (of values) 2, 7f., 17, 19, 32, 39, 44, 46f., 50, 52f., 82, 93, 98, 112f., 115, 137, 148, 151, 184, 188, 197, 246, 248, 259, 266, 269f., 272, 279f., 284, 287, 296–298
Revolution 19, 24, 35, 68, 110, 112–117, 124–126, 129–131, 133–135, 142–146, 148, 150f., 174, 186, 239, 279
Riccardo, David 123, 134
Roscher, William 28f., 57, 101, 138, 160f., 170, 173, 177
Ruehl, Martin 16, 153, 261
Russia 38, 104, 174, 263–266

Schopenhauer 42, 62, 105, 172, 220
Sciences 16, 76, 161, 287
Secularisation 143, 148, 190, 214, 233
Simmel, Georg 17, 20, 25
Slave (herd) morality 4–9, 11, 16, 18, 25, 27, 30, 35–51, 53–55, 57, 59f., 64, 69, 71–73, 85, 92, 97f., 102, 108, 112f., 116f., 119, 122f., 129f., 134, 137, 140–142, 144f., 148–152, 154–159, 161–185, 188, 190–192, 195–199, 202, 206, 208–210, 212, 217f., 220, 223, 229, 231f., 235–237, 242, 245–247, 251, 257, 259–265, 270–273, 276, 280–282, 284–286, 289–292, 294, 296
Slavery 2–4, 6f., 14, 18f., 33, 40, 48–50, 96, 100f., 109, 119–121, 153–158, 160–162, 165–167, 171–189, 253, 264, 271–273, 276f., 279, 286
– Ancient 17, 27, 37, 42, 44f., 68, 88, 112f., 120f., 124, 134, 146f., 154f., 157f., 160f., 164, 168, 175, 193f., 201, 215, 227
– Modern 2–4, 6, 16, 18–21, 25–27, 30–35, 37–39, 48f., 51–55, 59, 62, 64f., 68f., 74, 76f., 86, 92–94, 96, 98–100, 102, 104, 106–110, 112, 114, 121, 124f., 140, 142, 146–150, 153–158, 161, 163, 165f., 172f., 176–187, 190–193, 195–197, 199f., 207, 209, 213–220, 222f., 230, 232, 234–238, 240, 244–248, 252–254, 256f., 259f., 263–266, 268, 270–272, 274, 276, 279–283, 285, 296
– Psychological 6, 16, 25, 34, 43, 46, 49, 63, 65, 72, 88, 96, 101, 104, 116, 153f., 156, 160, 165–168, 170–172, 175f., 180, 182, 189, 197, 200f., 203, 206, 208–210, 212–214, 219, 223, 227, 233, 237, 254
Socrates 39, 42, 69, 75, 180, 191, 254
Spencer, Herbert 18, 57, 62, 182, 257
Spiritual rebirth 148
Subjectivity 25, 128, 180, 192–194, 203, 214, 218, 222, 239–241, 274f.
Surplus (value) 20, 48f., 71, 87, 111, 115, 126f., 134, 138, 160, 216, 250, 277, 286, 292

Tax 140, 295
Theology 38, 141
Thermodynamics 49, 53, 80, 208, 255, 257, 267, 287
Thomson, William 80f.
Tocqueville, Alexis 155, 231f.
Topology 14, 17–19
Triangulation 14, 19
Tripartite soul 42f.

Umwerthung aller Werthe (see revaluation of values 50
Universal Basic Income ('UBI') 278f.
Upside-down world 102, 104, 151

War 6f., 12, 27, 33, 35, 39, 43, 50f., 73, 105, 107, 118, 150, 182, 188, 195, 216, 224–226, 228, 230, 233, 243, 254, 256, 259–262, 264, 270, 279
Weber, Max 99, 101, 104, 122, 137f., 140f., 146–148, 278
Will to power (power will) 17, 34, 144, 199, 209, 241, 256, 264, 288

Xenophon 66, 154, 158–160

Zarathustra 5, 51, 74, 87, 166, 172, 179, 183f., 186, 190, 214, 223, 229, 282

www.ingramcontent.com/pod-product-compliance
Lightning Source LLC
Chambersburg PA
CBHW080910170426
43201CB00017B/2281